SO-BSQ-572

$ 9.50-1

EDUCATION 85/86

Editor

Fred Schultz

The University of Akron

Fred Schultz, professor of education at The University of Akron, attended Indiana University to earn a B.S. in social science education in 1962, an M.S. in the history and philosophy of education in 1966, and a Ph.D. in the history and philosophy of education and American studies in 1969. His B.A. in Spanish will be conferred from the University of Akron in May 1985. He is actively involved in researching the development and history of American education.

Cover illustration by Mike Eagle

The Dushkin Publishing Group, Inc.
Sluice Dock, Guilford, Connecticut 06437

The Annual Editions Series

Annual Editions is a series of over thirty-five volumes designed to provide the reader with convenient, low-cost access to a wide range of current, carefully selected articles from some of the most important magazines, newspapers, and journals published today. Annual Editions are updated on an annual basis through a continuous monitoring of over 200 periodical sources. All Annual Editions have a number of features designed to make them particularly useful, including topic guides, annotated tables of contents, unit overviews, and indexes. For the teacher using Annual Editions in the classroom, an Instructor's Guide with test questions is available for each volume.

PUBLISHED

Africa
Aging
American Government
American History, Pre-Civil War
American History, Post-Civil War
Anthropology
Biology
Business
China
Comparative Politics
Computers in Education
Criminal Justice
Early Childhood Education
Economics
Educating Exceptional Children
Education
Educational Psychology
Environment
Global Issues
Health
Human Development
Human Sexuality
Latin America
Macroeconomics
Marketing
Marriage and Family
Personal Growth and Behavior
Psychology
Social Problems
Social Psychology
Sociology
State and Local Government
Urban Society
Western Civilization, Pre-Reformation
Western Civilization, Post-Reformation
World Politics

FUTURE VOLUMES

Abnormal Psychology
Death and Dying
Drugs, Society and Behavior
Computers in Business
Computers in Society
Congress
Energy
Ethnic Studies
Foreign Policy
Geography
Judiciary
Middle East and the Islamic World
Nutrition
Parenting
Philosophy
Political Science
Presidency
Religion
South Asia
Soviet Union and Eastern Europe
Twentieth Century American History
Western Europe
Women's Studies
World History

Library of Congress Cataloging in Publication Data
Main entry under title: Annual editions: Education.
1. Education—Addresses, essays, lectures. I. Title: Education.
LB41.A673 370'.5 73-78580
ISBN 0-87967-584-5

©1985 by The Dushkin Publishing Group, Inc. Annual Editions is a Trade Mark of The Dushkin Publishing Group, Inc.

Copyright ©1985 by The Dushkin Publishing Group, Inc., Guilford, Connecticut 06437

All rights reserved. No part of this book may be reproduced, stored, or transmitted by any means—mechanical, electronic, or otherwise—without written permission from the publisher.

Twelfth Edition

Manufactured by The Banta Company, Menasha, Wisconsin 54952

Editors/ Advisory Board

Members of the Advisory Board are instrumental in the final selection of articles for each edition of Annual Editions. Their review of articles for content, level, currency, and appropriateness provides critical direction to the editor and staff. We think you'll find their careful consideration well reflected in this volume.

EDITOR

Fred Schultz
University of Akron

ADVISORY BOARD

L. Ross Blythe
Purdue University, North Central

Walter Cast
Southeastern Massachusetts University

Anthony DeFalco
C.W. Post Center, Long Island University

Lloyd Duck
George Mason University

Charles W. Funkhouser
University of Texas, Arlington

Joe Kelly
University of Idaho

Joe L. Kincheloe
Louisiana State University, Shreveport

Walter H. Klar
Framingham State College

Lawrence Klein
Central Connecticut State University

Gertrude Langsam
Adelphi University

Margaret A. Laughlin
University of Wisconsin, Green Bay

John McDermott
Moravian College

David Melendez
Northern Arizona University

Susan Mumford
Mercy College

Joseph Newman
University of South Alabama

James Wm. Noll
University of Maryland, College Park

Joseph Peyser
Indiana University, South Bend

Joseph F. Rousseau
Keene State College

Tom Yonker
Linfield College

STAFF

Rick Connelly, Publisher
Ian A. Nielsen, Program Manager
Celeste Borg, Editor
Addie Kawula, Acquisitions Editor
Brenda S. Filley, Production Manager
Cheryl Kinne, Permissions/Photo Coordinator
Charles Vitelli, Designer
Jean Bailey, Graphics Coordinator
Libra A. Cusack, Typesetting Coordinator

To The Reader

In publishing ANNUAL EDITIONS we recognize the enormous role played by the magazines, newspapers, and journals of the *public press* in providing current, first-rate educational information in a broad spectrum of interest areas. Within the articles, the best scientists, practitioners, researchers, and commentators draw issues into new perspective as accepted theories and viewpoints are called into account by new events, recent discoveries change old facts, and fresh debate breaks out over important controversies.

Many of the articles resulting from this enormous editorial effort are appropriate for students, researchers, and professionals seeking accurate, current material to help bridge the gap between principles and theories and the real world. These articles, however, become more useful for study when those of lasting value are carefully *collected, organized, indexed,* and *reproduced* in a *low-cost format,* which provides easy and permanent access when the material is needed. That is the role played by *Annual Editions.* Under the direction of each volume's *Editor*, who is an expert in the subject area, and with the guidance of an *Advisory Board,* we seek each year to provide in each *ANNUAL EDITION* a current, well-balanced, carefully selected collection of the best of the public press for your study and enjoyment. We think you'll find this volume useful, and we hope you'll take a moment to let us know what you think.

Annual Editions: Education 85/86 reflects major shifts in thought concerning the state of education in the United States. It keeps abreast of public and professional points of view regarding trends and developments that affect students and educators. The volume is unique in that it is the only volume published in the field of education that is revised annually. Readers of the volume are easily made aware of changing opinions and perspectives of students, educators, parents, and taxpayers concerning educational issues.

The critical historical assessments of the American educational experience in the 1960s and 1970s, and the moderate revisionist critiques and syntheses of that experience have led to a more mature and balanced perspective through which to examine education's past and present. The continuing reinterpretation of the American educational past and present has provided a broader and more accurate perspective on which to base judgments of theory and practice in the field of education.

Hard economic times and the continuing pressures for greater emphasis in improving the quality of educational achievement in the nation have had a significant effect in the shaping of current thought about American education. The contents of this volume reflect these current themes.

Many criteria govern the selection of articles for inclusion in the anthology. A most important one is that the articles must address current issues which represent dialogue and concern in the field of education. The volume must represent the general tenor or spirit of debate and discussion regarding matters of widespread concern. Articles, therefore, are often selected which comment on such debate and discussion and which thus represent thoughtful overviews of the topics they seek to address.

The anthology is divided into nine tightly structured units of articles which address the most important educational concerns today. The units in this twelfth edition are concerned with professional and public perceptions of educational systems, alternatives in education, the struggle for excellence in education, the controversies surrounding the various national commission reports, morality in the schools, discipline problems, equality of opportunity, special educational needs, the profession of teaching today, and the future of education.

Throughout each year, the Annual Editions' editor and staff collect articles related to current interests in education. Members of the Advisory Board also submit recommendations for new articles and react to each volume when it is published. Through this process we amass a wide range of articles on a variety of topics relevant to educational development in the United States. The articles are then carefully examined for their relevance to the topic or themes dominating current public and professional concerns. Your reactions to the book are also appreciated. Please let us know what you think. We will do our best to see that the next year's edition reflects your concerns.

Fred Schultz

Fred Schultz

Editor

Contents

Unit 1

Perceptions of Education in America

Six articles consider the present state of education in America. Several national commission reports, educational movements, and the latest Gallup poll of the public's opinion of public schools are examined.

Unit 2

Continuity and Change in American Education

Six selections examine the impact of equality of opportunity, vocational education, computers, bilingual education, and home schooling on current American education.

The concepts in italics are developed in the article. For further expansion please refer to the Topic Guide and the Index.

Unit 3

The Struggle for Excellence: Striving for Higher Achievement

Eight articles discuss the current struggle for excellence in American education. Such topics as approaches to curriculum and instruction, SAT test score controversies, and teacher education are considered.

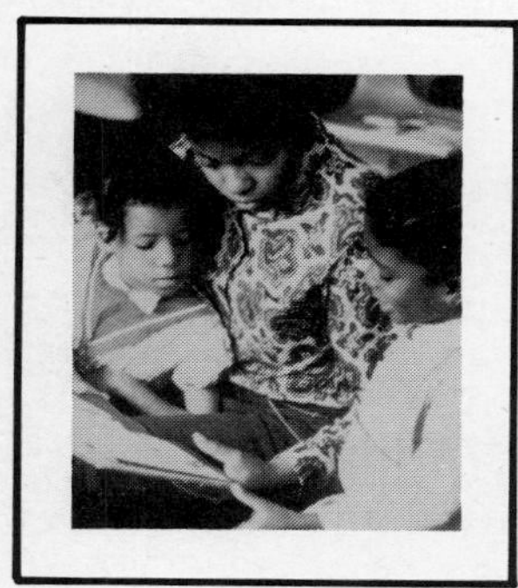

Unit 4

Morality and Values in Education

Four articles examine the role of American schools in teaching about morality and social values.

Unit 5

Discipline Problems in the Schools

Five selections consider the necessity of judicious and effective discipline in American schools today.

Unit 6

Equality of Opportunity and American Education

Five articles discuss the current state of equality of opportunity in the American educational system. The effect of desegregation, the concept of "magnet schools," and the controversy of tuition tax credits are some of the topics considered.

Unit 7

Serving Special Needs and Individualizing Instruction

Six selections examine some of the important aspects of mainstreaming and individualized instruction faced by teachers in America today.

Unit 8

The Profession of Teaching Today

Five articles assess the current state of teaching in American schools. Topics include teacher's responsibility, teacher failure, merit pay, and teacher burnout.

A Look to the Future

Three articles look at the future of education in American schools. Establishing a new ethos for education, a curriculum for the future, and enrollment projections are considered.

The concepts in italics are developed in the article. For further expansion please refer to the Topic Guide and the Index.

Topic Guide

This topic guide suggests how the selections in this book relate to topics of traditional concern to education students and profe sionals. It is very useful in locating articles which relate to each other for reading and research. The guide is arranged alphabetical according to topic. Articles may, of course, treat topics that do not appear in the topic guide. In turn, entries in the topic guide d not necessarily constitute a comprehensive listing of all the contents of each selection.

TOPIC AREA	TREATED AS AN ISSUE IN:
Academic Remodeling	1. Is This Any Way to Build a Better School?
Academic Standards	13. The Continuing Crisis 16. Improving Educational Standards
Alternatives in Education	8. Vocational Education That Works 10. Computers and a New World Order 11. Bilingual/Bicultural Education 12. The New Pioneers of the Home School Movement
Back to Basics Movement	4. The Educational Pendulum
Behavioral Management	25. Good, Old-Fashioned Discipline 26. Disciplinary Strategies 28. Coercion in the Classroom 29. There's Only One True Technique for Good Discipline
Bilingual/Bicultural Education	11. Bilingual/Bicultural Education
Civic Education	22. The Obligations of American Citizenship 23. The Effect Upon Minorities of the Civic Education of Teachers
Civil Rights	27. Class Struggle
Commission and Task Force Reports	1. Is This Any Way to Build a Better School? 2. Education Moves to Center Stage 13. The Continuing Crisis 14. A Nation at Risk 15. A Nation at Risk: How's That Again? 16. Improving Educational Standards 18. Just Among Us Teachers 19. Making Schools Work Again 20. Latest Educational "Reforms"
Computers	10. Computers and a New World Order
Conservative Educational Thought	33. From Equity to Excellence
Continuity and Change	1. Is This Any Way to Build a Better School? 2. Education Moves to Center Stage 7. Who Are These Educational "Experts"? 8. Vocational Education That Works 9. Education and the Sony War 10. Computers and a New World Order 11. Bilingual/Bicultural Education 12. The New Pioneers of the Home Schooling Movement
Curriculum and Instruction	16. Improving Educational Standards 47. Curriculum in the Year 2000
Democratic Values	23. The Effect Upon Minorities of the Civic Education of Teachers 24. Schools and Democratic Values
Desegregation of Schools	30. Achieving Quality Integrated Education 31. Magnet Schools 32. The State of Education for Black Americans 33. From Equity to Excellence
Discipline	25. Good, Old-Fashioned Discipline 26. Disciplinary Strategies 27. Class Struggle 28. Coercion in the Classroom 29. There's Only One True Technique for Good Discipline
Educational Change	13. The Continuing Crisis 46. Forging a New Ethos for Education in America 47. Curriculum in the Year 2000
Educational Goals and Priorities	3. The Good News About American Education
Enrollment Projections	48. The Coming Enrollment Crisis
Equal Opportunity	2. Education Moves to Center Stage 7. Who Are These Educational "Experts"? 30. Achieving Quality Integrated Education 31. Magnet Schools 32. The State of Education for Black Americans 33. From Equity to Excellence 34. Tuition Tax Credits
Excellence	1. Is This Any Way to Build a Better School? 2. Education Moves to Center Stage 3. The Good News About American Education 4. The Educational Pendulum 5. How to Save the Public Schools 13. The Continuing Crisis 14. A Nation at Risk 15. A Nation at Risk: How's That Again? 16. Improving Educational Standards in American Schools 17. What Do the SATs Mean? 18. Just Among Us Teachers 19. Making Schools Work Again 20. Latest Educational "Reforms" 30. Achieving Quality Integrated Education 33. From Equity to Excellence 46. Forging a New Ethos for Education in America
Exceptional Children	35. Mainstreaming: Expectations and Realities 36. A Holistic View of Mainstreaming 37. Mainstreaming 38. A Comparison of Soviet and American Approaches to Special Education 39. Child Sexual Abuse 40. You Can Help a Sexually Abused Child

TOPIC AREA	TREATED AS AN ISSUE IN:
Future of American Education	46. Forging a New Ethos for Education in America 47. Curriculum in the Year 2000 48. The Coming Enrollment Crisis
History of Education	4. The Educational Pendulum 9. Education and the Sony War 13. The Continuing Crisis 20. Latest Educational "Reforms" 21. Ethics Without Virtue 22. The Obligations of American Citizenship 23. The Effect Upon Minorities of the Civic Education of Teachers 24. Schools and Democratic Values 42. Scapegoating the Teachers
Home Schooling	12. The New Pioneers of the Home Schooling Movement
Individualization	26. Disciplinary Strategies 29. There's Only One True Technique for Good Discipline 35. Mainstreaming: Expectations and Realities 36. A Holistic View of Mainstreaming 37. Mainstreaming
Magnet Schools	31. Magnet Schools Used as Tool for Equality
Mainstreaming	35. Mainstreaming: Expectations and Realities 36. A Holistic View of Mainstreaming 37. Mainstreaming
Merit Pay	43. Merit Pay
Moral Education	21. Ethics Without Virtue 22. The Obligations of American Citizenship 23. The Effect Upon Minorities of the Civic Education of Teachers 24. Schools and Democratic Values 46. Forging a New Ethos for Education in America 47. Curriculum in the Year 2000
National Assessment of Educational Progress	3. The Good News About American Education
Public Schools	1. Is This Any Way to Build a Better School? 4. The Educational Pendulum 5. How to Save the Public Schools 7. Who Are These Educational "Experts"? 9. Education and the Sony War 12. The New Pioneers of the Home Schooling Movement 18. Just Among Us Teachers 19. Making Schools Work Again 20. Latest Educational "Reforms" 21. Ethics Without Virtue 22. The Obligations of American Citizenship 33. From Equity to Excellence

TOPIC AREA	TREATED AS AN ISSUE IN:
Private Schools	5. How to Save the Public Schools 34. Tuition Tax Credits
Punishment	25. Good, Old-Fashioned Discipline
Quality of Education	5. How to Save the Public Schools 14. A Nation at Risk 15. A Nation at Risk: How's That Again? 19. Making Schools Work Again 32. The State of Education for Black Americans
Reform of Education	1. Is This Any Way to Build a Better School? 7. Who Are These Educational "Experts"? 13. The Continuing Crisis 16. Improving Educational Standards 20. Latest Educational "Reforms"
SAT Scores	17. What Do the SATs Mean?
Secondary Education	17. What Do the SATs Mean?
Sexual Abuse of Children	39. Child Sexual Abuse 40. You Can Help a Sexually Abused Child
Special Education	35. Mainstreaming: Expectations and Realities 36. A Holistic View of Mainstreaming 37. Mainstreaming 38. A Comparison of Soviet and American Approaches to Special Education
Teacher Burnout	45. Teacher Burnout
Teacher Failure	44. Why Teachers Fail
Teachers and Teaching	1. Is This Any Way to Build a Better School? 18. Just Among Us Teachers 19. Making Schools Work Again 41. The Art of Teaching 42. Scapegoating the Teachers 43. Merit Pay 44. Why Teachers Fail 45. Teacher Burnout
Technology	9. Education and the Sony War 10. Computers and a New World Order
Tuition Tax Credits	34. Tuition Tax Credits
Values Clarification	21. Ethics Without Virtue 23. The Effect Upon Minorities of the Civic Education of Teachers 24. Schools and Democratic Values 46. Forging a New Ethos for Education in America
Vocational Education	8. Vocational Education That Works

Perceptions of Education in America

What citizens *think* is the state of education in the country has day-to-day practical effects on political and educational leaders. How people perceive educational institutions, students, and educators is important because all citizens have some stake—direct or indirect—in what happens in the educational programs of the nation. Never has this been more true than now in the midst of major economical and technological changes of great importance. The perceptions of educators and students are sometimes very different from those of persons in business or politics. There are distinct sets of interests in society when it comes to assessing either public or private educational systems. This unit presents a broad sample of some points of view regarding "the state of the art" in American education.

Although overall public opinion of American public schools is somewhat improved over 1983, the national commission reports and individual critiques of the state of education reflect an intensified criticism of educational institutions and of educators in general. This is not a new attitude in the United States. Yet much of this criticism does reflect the opinion of very powerful economic and political interests in the country. As was reported in the previous edition, the level and intensity of conservative criticisms of the public schools has not been as intense since the post *Sputnik* years between late 1957 and the summer of 1965. There are major perceptual changes developing on the part of conservatives as to what needs to happen in public and private schools. Conservative challenges are shaping up, and a critical dialogue of historic dimensions on these issues is in formation.

It is important to realize that within the incumbency of the national educational system, educators in private schools, their students, and those who support them view the public schools very differently and far more critically than do those who work in public schools. This is not new either, but it is an important factor in current dialogue regarding the purposes of education. Alternative sets of educational aims are becoming more and more clearly articulated as a revitalized and perceptive new era of historical inquiry into the roots of our educational present continues to unfold.

The articles in this unit reflect this dialogue and present a broad view of the current situation in education. The following units contain articles which will focus on the state of affairs described above.

"Is This Any Way to Build a Better School?" presents a thoughtful and insightful point of view on the new wave of criticisms of public education in the United States. Ohanian summarizes the rhetoric in *A Nation at Risk,* the President's Commission Report, and others. She says the "blue-ribbon commissions" make abstract recommendations while not having to confront the day-to-day social and educational realities of life as either a teacher or student in the nation's elementary or secondary schools. She also notes that one of the reasons schools cannot devote all of their time to intellectual achievement is because the teachers and the school systems in general have been forced to take on many nontraditional tasks. This has occurred because of the perception of some that the nation's schools can solve social problems which government and the general public have failed to solve. Ohanian argues that many of the reports of the national commissions are shallow, and further asserts that earlier reports on the state of the schools in the 1950s and 1960s offered similar criticisms to those found in the commission reports of the early 1980s.

Harold Howe II shares his views of the reasons for the recent wave of commission reports on the state of the nation's schools, and notes many additional reports are in the making. He comments on some of the studies of the schools by prominent individual scholars as well. While Ohanian critiqued the efforts at academic remodeling of the nation's schools, Howe synthesizes the basic recommendations which seem to run through all of them. He also discusses those major and still unresolved issues in education to which the reports published in 1983 had not directed adequate attention, such as equality of opportunity. He argues for specific increases in federal support for educational development in school systems and in teacher education.

Archie E. Lapointe's essay describes how the data from the National Assessment of Educational Progress (NAEP) may help in providing a data base for achievable new national educational goals. The essay by Diane Ravitch, a historian of American education, establishes an informative historical perspective on the current debate concerning historical standards. Phil Keisling's essay reflects many concerns stated in the recent critical studies of the public schools. He echoes the current national concern for the quality of education. His prescription for excellence in education suggests many of the same concerns that other recent reports have expressed. Finally, "The 16th Annual Gallup Poll of the Public's Attitudes Toward the Public Schools" reflects a very interesting sample of public opinion which usually generates considerable dialogue.

Unit 1

All of these essays relate to discussions of the purposes of priorities of teacher education and the general aims of education as well. Taken together, they represent a synthesis of public and professional concerns about the quality of education. The current public concern for excellence in schooling is so pervasive in the trade and professional press that it will be reflected in the discourse on the topics of other units in this volume.

Looking Ahead: Challenge Questions

Give your reaction to Ohanion's critique of the recent commission reports on the state of American education. What reasons do you have for your position on her assessment?

Describe some "academic remodeling" being proposed for American schools.

Is there a constructive role for the data being collected in the ongoing National Assessment of Educational Progress (NAEP)? If so, what is the role? If not, why not?

What are some of the things that the more conservative commission reports on the state of American schools are recommending?

What issues raised in the articles relate directly to the education of teachers? What is your position on each of these issues?

Does "The 16th Annual Gallup Poll of the Public's Attitudes Toward the Public Schools" indicate, overall, the same concerns for the quality of public education as many of the national commission reports have expressed?

What is the function or effect of public opinion on national educational policy development?

IS THIS ANY WAY TO BUILD A BETTER SCHOOL?

The academic remodeling recommended by politicians and business leaders may merely alter the facade of an institution in need of fundamental change within.

SUSAN OHANIAN

Susan Ohanian is a staff writer for Learning.

Beautifully printed on rich, glossy paper with potent passages set off in snazzy red type, *Action for Excellence: A Comprehensive Plan To Improve Our Nation's Schools* comes from the Task Force on Education for Economic Growth (June 1983). It is so elegant in execution that I expect to turn a page and find an ad for Blackglama or Steuben glass. Like many of the other recent reports from prominent education task forces, this one is "put forth with an unusual sense of urgency." It calls for "a new ethic of excellence in public education" and "a partnership of government, business, labor and education leaders." Included among its authors are 13 state governors, 3 state legislators, 13 business leaders, 1 labor leader, 1 principal, 1 state commissioner of education, 1 superintendent of schools, 1 education specialist and, oh yes, 1 junior high school teacher. We might well wonder how a true partnership can exist between more than 30 politicians and business leaders and a lone teacher.

Most teachers will welcome "a new ethic of excellence" in our schools. We'd like that ethic in the rest of our lives, too, and can only hope it might rub off on our new partners, those fellows who gave us Agent Orange, asbestos, cars unsafe at any speed, the DC 10, Three Mile Island, red dye number 2, collapsing banks, price fixing and other complications of our modern, quality-controlled, limited-warranty technology. We teachers are publicly exhorted to plan ahead, although our partners in Detroit have not been noted for such planning. As our advisers for excellence gather on the schoolhouse steps to pass out their platitudes (there is no evidence that any of the panel members not actually employed by schools entered a classroom or spoke with teachers), we teachers might be tempted to say, "Business partner, heal thyself."

Several of the reports are organized around the premise that educational productivity determines economic productivity, a rather dubious supposition at best. Schools are being blamed for the fact that the Japanese make automobiles more efficiently than Americans and that the South Koreans have built the world's most efficient steel mill. For sheer effrontery, the task force's pronouncement on remedial classes is hard to beat. We should end remedial classes, they advise us, by doing our work "effectively the first time." I would like to radically transform remedial classes, if not end them altogether, but to claim they exist merely because we didn't do our job right the first time around is to ignore the complexity of the issue. The folk who make the cars that are recalled before they can be paid for are good at glossing over complex problems.

I admit that the multitudinous reports from the blue-ribbon commissions have left me prickly. I can sling bombastic rhetoric as well as the next person, but it ill behooves the captains of industry to imply that the schoolteachers have put this nation at risk. *A Nation at Risk,* with its gut-wrenching title, is getting the most media attention, not because it is the most thoughtful of the commission reports, but because it has those phrases that stick in your mind: "History is not kind to idlers"; "a dimming of expectations"; "weakness of purpose."

Yale University President A. Bartlett Giamatti's observation (*Harper's,* 1980) that teachers "have never been cherished" in this country seems as much an understatement as a shaggy dog punchline. If the Russians beat us into outer space, if the Japanese undercut the car industry, if juvenile crime is on the rise—why, then, write a report blaming the schools for these ills.

What we have before us is not so much an evaluation of pedagogical practices as a zeitgeist of the '80s. We all feel vaguely discontented with the quality of our lives; troubled by violence, skewed values, bad manners, loss of purchasing power. The good life is crumbling around us, and the school seems to be the one last place where we can take a stand. After all, you can't fight Tammany Hall or General Motors. The schools have always been an ideological battleground in this country. It is entirely fitting that Diane Ravitch would title her chronicle of American education *The Troubled Crusade*. Ravitch shows clearly how the schoolhouse is used as a place to fulfill the American dream. As the dream shifts, so, too, do certain priorities in the schools. Schools have been exhorted to affirm the melting pot, to preserve ethnicity, to end poverty, to train a scientific elite, to end segregation, to integrate handicapped people and so on. As even *Life* magazine put it (Feb. 2, 1948): "Education alone cannot heal

Reprinted by special permission of *LEARNING*, The Magazine for Creative Teaching, February 1984, pp. 58-60, 63. ©1984 by Pitman Learning Inc., 19 Davis Drive, Belmont, CA 94002.

the world's wounds. But it can help."

More Recommendations, But Few Solutions

The schools, of course, did not end poverty or create equal opportunity any more than they are going to be able to bring the country into the forefront of high technology. But the accusations and exhortations of national commissions are not easily ignored; they insinuate themselves in subtle ways. Three times the primary teachers in my district voted that we did not want the school board to buy classroom sets of a standard grammar book. We agreed that a resource packet for the teacher would be more beneficial, that a student learns to write by writing, not by studying discrete grammar rules. Then the administrator insisted that "the public needs to know we are accountable." On the fourth vote, the grammar book was approved. Apparently it will be proof positive that we teachers are serious about our craft. Now there is talk of a citywide exam in social studies and science (the students already take annual standardized tests in reading and math). I assume that the purpose of such a test would be to prove that the third grade teachers actually taught the difference between bedrock and loam and that the students actually learned it.

The blue-ribbon commissions make abstract recommendations; they never have to face concrete realities. Doing a job is more difficult than telling someone else how the job ought to be done. They recommend more and more: more hours in school, more math, more chemistry. (There is something quintessentially American about associating "more" with "better.") But we need to look at what goes on in schools right now before we make the day longer. Some task forces hinted at this need but focused on the problem of efficiency, not content. They exhorted us to manage our time better, be more streamlined, cram more information into the day, speed up the skill acquisition of students. Task force members need to understand that what works for the assembly line at General Motors does not necessarily work for the schools.

We have too much crammed into our school day already. In my third grade classroom, 2½ to 3 hours per day are devoted to reading and writing. I would gladly increase that amount of time, but we have to squeeze in gym, study of the solar system, the history of ancient Rome, practice in long division, work with probability and the proper brushing of teeth. We get a 30-minute break for lunch, and by the end of the day we are all exhausted. The students have homework in a minimum of two subjects and I have mounds of their papers to pore over. None of us feels like an "idler."

One of the experts quoted in the National Commission on Excellence in Education report was Paul Copperman. As far as I can determine, Copperman has little, if any, experience in public schools. He did, however, write a book attacking John Holt, Herbert Kohl, the National Council of Teachers of English, Charles Silberman, busing, free health clinics and so on. In his book, Copperman claimed that a "tenet of modern education policy holds that demanding work from students is an old-fashioned and outmoded way to educate children."

The blue-ribbon commissions make abstract recommendations; they never have to face concrete realities.

Copperman states that until now "each generation of Americans has outstripped its parents in education, in literacy and in economic attainment. For the first time in the history of our country, the educational skills of one generation will not surpass, will not equal, will not even approach those of their parents." Copperman treats educational skills like figures to be computed for the Dow Jones average. Our children face a barrage of facts their parents and grandparents never dreamed of. I suspect one major problem of the schools is that we expect children to process too much information; we'd do better to concentrate on a few core skills. (And I don't mean universal enrollment in chemistry.) Copperman's accusation is a cheap shot and must be viewed in light of our attempts in recent years to educate everybody. In 1950, about 50 percent of the white student population and about 25 percent of the black were graduated from high school; in 1979, the numbers were 85 percent of whites and 75 percent of blacks.

Another problem of the schools is that we have taken on the task of educating everybody for just about everything. Send us your smart, your slow, your handicapped, your non-English-speaking, your truant, your violent, and we will try to educate them. Copperman recommends getting rid of those students with "poor authority relations." American schools, for good or bad, find it very hard to eliminate anybody. If a student is reluctant, hostile, even abusive, we try to adapt a program to his needs. Certainly this approach is inefficient, but I find it admirable that our schools are loath to give up on any child, no matter what the quality of his "authority relations" is.

The various commissions for improving our schools have lists of new requirements: four years of English, three years of science and so on. I have no real quarrel with these lists (although I do wish we could drop that old potato "scientific method" once and for all), but I'm bothered by the shallowness that pervades the recommendations. I think the problems of our educational system are much deeper than the particular courses we teach or the length of our school day. I am bemused by the fact that the guys who chide us for the need for remedial courses want every child to take physics and French. Let's hope that our industry mentors who come into the schools to teach physics will get it right the first time. Most of the curricular recommendations are leftovers from earlier reports—spiced up, perhaps, but warmed over nonetheless. Some of us remember when the report makers told us that schools don't make a difference. Now, almost 20 years later, we're expected to assume responsibility for a nation at risk.

A Basic Naiveté

The Task Force on Education for Economic Growth recommends "contracts" between parents, students and schools to "improve student performance." They also want "objective" measurements of "the effectiveness of teachers." I take this to mean no anecdotes, please; but anecdotes are all I really have to offer. Few things in teaching are objective or pure. Anecdotes at least have the virtue of being real.

When Chuck was mainstreamed into my math class, I felt he could become a "regular" member of our group and not just a social experiment (the category to which so many mainstreamed children are relegated) if he could just develop a few good habits—like bringing a pencil to class, staying awake and doing his homework. Chuck and I figured out a number of schemes to improve his performance: he left his pencil in my desk so he could never be "unprepared" when class started; he sat in the front of the class; he chose a buddy to copy assignments for him when he was absent. But Chuck couldn't seem to remember homework. Although he could readily grasp math concepts, Chuck was behind the class in basic math operations. I prepared some work to help him catch up and told him he must practice ten minutes every night; I felt the symbolic value of the homework was even more important than its skill content. I tried to enlist the aid of Chuck's mother by asking if she could see that he did ten minutes of homework each night.

She shrugged. "If he's around. He isn't home much." I suggested that maybe Chuck could do the homework in the kitchen while she fixed dinner. She informed me Chuck seldom showed up for dinner. Was I too subtle? Should I have produced a legal contract for her to sign? Chuck is eight years old. I want to continue fighting for his life in the mainstream, but I have to wonder if his score on some standardized test will mess up my own effectiveness quotient on the "objective" career ladder.

Missing the Picture

The national commissions seem unconcerned with the quality of involvement between the teacher and the student, the student and the text. Everett Reimer asserts in *School Is Dead* that "unless people enjoy, in the main, good human relationships, they can neither be educated nor educate themselves."

Daniel Fader, chairman of the English Composition Board at the University of Michigan, speaks poignantly and powerfully on how student themes of the 1950s compare with those of today. Fader emphasizes that changes in conventions (commas, apostrophes, etc.) are not the most significant ones that have taken place in the last 25 years. What is missing in the work of our present-day student writers is metaphor. Picture language does not exist, and as Fader reminds us, "We can't give them pictures." Fader links the absence of metaphor to the fact that the television set has usurped the kitchen table as family center. Preschool kids spend more time watching TV than doing anything else except sleeping. Kids have no literacy models. No one talks to them. They don't know they have a voice worth listening to when they come to write. Our students are not attended to and they do not attend. We, as teachers, must bring them attention.

I don't know which annoys me more about these reports—the meat or the metaphor. Education commission language is bad enough all by itself, (it ranges from Spongy Bureaucratise to Born Again Baroque), but it bespeaks an underlying arrogance and presumption that contradicts the very nature of learning: "The student will master six irregular verb forms." Anybody who knows anything about kids knows that maybe the student will and maybe he won't. And even if he doesn't, blue-ribbon commission report writers should not take this as proof positive that he or his teacher is an idler.

> The national commissions seem unconcerned with the quality of involvement between the teacher and the student, the student and the text.

A basic naiveté about the nature of schools pervades the reports. I don't think the subtlety of the art of teaching can be reduced to pious epigrams exhorting teachers to be better prepared, better motivated, more dedicated. Pointing to the existence of unfit teachers in the land, report writers pronounce, "Persons preparing to teach should be required . . . to demonstrate an aptitude for teaching." That seems laudable enough, but how does it translate into practice? Would the psychoanalytic profiles of 10,000 good teachers (assuming, of course, we could reach some accord on the nature of goodness) reveal common traits? Would the blood chemistries? I doubt that one can know ahead of time what constitutes a good teacher. I think of Sylvia Ashton-Warner's forthright admission, "I hated teaching on sight" (*I Passed This Way*, 1979). Of course, one must read this statement in the context of her lifelong struggle to provide a meaningful curriculum for her students. Nonetheless, I suspect Ashton-Warner would not have advanced very far on the proposed career ladder.

"Career ladder" is this year's educational buzzword, destined to rise above the ashes of these reports. Differential staffing is a complicated issue, and I doubt that the marginal good of naming some people "masters" will outweigh the harm to teaching in general. For sheer self-serving crassness, surely professor of education John Goodlad's proposal deserves the electroplated piece of chalk. Goodlad recommends creating a new teaching position: head teacher. To qualify for this position it is not enough for a teacher to be "excellent"; she must also have a Ph.D. in—you guessed it—education. As Goodlad points out, the means already exist "for providing a continuing supply" of such persons. Not incidentally, preparing the prerequisite courses for the career ladder options will give the good professors at the schools of education something to do.

I think of my own first year in the public school classroom: I went home every night and cried over the disaster that beset me each day. I think I might have gone back for a second year but was very relieved when I found a college teaching job. When circumstances forced me to apply for another public school job, I cried at the prospect. Acquiring the appropriate attitude was not instantaneous. We should realize that people become teachers—and bankers and plumbers and corporation vice-presidents — for a variety of reasons, not the least of which is economic. Becoming a schoolteacher, as I did, to finance curtain rods may not seem like a noble expression of an aptitude for teaching, but for people like me, aptitude develops over time. I've had 18 years to work at it.

Frances Hawkins rightly insists that it takes five to ten years to learn to teach, and Herbert Kohl reminds us that even after one does learn to teach well, one never learns once and for all. Teaching is a skill requiring constant practice and revitalization. And stamina. How can a selection committee know in advance if a candidate has the toughness to survive and prevail? What's called for is an inner core of steadfast principle overlaid by the flexibility to adjust to any crazy situation, the ability to bounce back from defeat and try again, the conviction that the child's well-being counts more than the rhetoric of blue-ribbon report writers.

Education Moves to Center Stage: An Overview Of Recent Studies

Harold Howe II

HAROLD HOWE II, U.S. commissioner of education from December 1965 through December 1968, is a senior lecturer in the Harvard Graduate School of Education, Cambridge, Mass.

The newfound enthusiasm for "doing something" about education is at once exhilarating and intimidating to educators. Mr. Howe, a former U.S. commissioner of education, examines the "major gaps and unattended issues" left in the wake of the plethora of studies of schooling in America.

A WAVE OF reports and studies of American schools has inundated educators and policy makers in 1983. Although these documents, which have attempted to define the educational problems of the nation and suggest solutions, were expected, their arrival has resulted in a totally new environment for thinking about educational issues in the U.S. Suddenly corporate barons, Presidential candidates, university presidents, governors, and legislative leaders in the Congress and state capitols have mounted a crusade to improve the schools. This newfound enthusiasm for doing something about education is heady wine for most educators, who became accustomed in the Seventies to an atmosphere characterized by reduced funds for schools and media attention focused on their shortcomings, without much commitment to their improvement.

The reasons that national leaders are interested in the schools are numerous and complex. A few of them will have to suffice for the purpose of this discussion.

Photo by Steve Thompson/Corn's Photo Service

From *Phi Delta Kappan*, November 1983, pp. 167-172. Reprinted by permission of the author and Phi Delta Kappan.

A confused public may grow impatient with all the talk and countertalk and tune out.

• Frustration over the diminishing capacity of the U.S. to compete in worldwide markets has awakened new interest in the old idea that the quality of human resources is a key element in the efficiency of the nation's economy. Better schools that produce better-educated workers are thought to be the way to outsell the Japanese and the Germans.

• Another version of the same idea applies to our defense establishment and national security. How can we keep ahead of the Soviets if their youths are better educated than ours? This view is a replay of the Sputnik scenario of the late Fifties. In its more extreme form it has distinctly chauvinistic overtones.

• Dissatisfaction with American education has coalesced because of disillusionment with the resolution of civil rights issues in the schools and because of widespread concern about declining test scores. Today a typically pragmatic American reaction seems to have distilled from these negative views: let's stop complaining about our education problems and do something about them. The reports and studies of recent months have been instrumental in emphasizing this theme.

Despite the widespread knowledge of these national studies of education, it may be useful to make a few general observations about them.

• Little attention has been paid to the valuable efforts of individual scholars. At least two such works (being published this fall by Basic Books) carry powerful insights that augment the more visible national reports. One is Diane Ravitch's history of American education from 1945 to 1980, *The Troubled Crusade*; it offers a perspective on educational issues in the U.S. that transcends any analysis that has appeared in the major reports. A second book, by Sara Lawrence Lightfoot, is titled *The Good High School: Portraits of Character and Culture*. This work is a marvelous analysis of the actual operation of selected schools in all their human complexity. In discussing curriculum, organization, and other structural elements, it takes the *people* in schools into account, a factor that is almost completely ignored by most of the national studies. Reading these two books adds important background information to the reports that have appeared to date.

• Many additional reports are yet to come. The National Science Board's Commission on Precollege Education in Mathematics, Science, and Technology has already issued an "Interim Report to the National Science Board" (January 1983) and will have published its final report before this article appears in print. The Committee on Economic Development, an organization that represents business interests, has appointed a special Subcommittee on Business/Education Relationships, together with a staff and a group of advisors, to prepare a report that will reflect business interests in education. The report will focus on the cost of educational failure and on the needs of business. At its initial meeting, the subcommittee decided to take a careful look at strategies for improving teacher supply and teaching quality. The final report may not be published for two years, but the group intends to publish interim findings. In addition, many states have launched their own studies of education that will augment the national reports. Governors, state departments of education, and legislators have all taken a renewed interest in education.

• Various national education organizations, such as the American Association of School Administrators and the National Association of Secondary School Principals, are issuing interpretive materials about some of the national studies. Critiques of the studies have already appeared in newspaper articles and magazines. It may take a year or two before anyone completes a comprehensive study of the studies, however.

• One example of the recent criticism of the studies can be found in the *New York Times* (Connecticut edition) of June 5, in which Charles Fowler, superintendent of schools in Fairfield, Connecticut, analyzes *A Nation at Risk*, the report of the National Commission on Excellence in Education, and finds it "mediocre." And Fred Hechinger, writing in the August 2 *New York Times*, observes: "This outpouring of concern is a welcome sign of public awareness after years of indifference. But the mass of proposals and the contradictory remedies could well neutralize each other. A confused public may grow impatient with all the talk and countertalk and tune out again."

Amid this plethora of moral urging, analysis, and free advice, educators and policy makers seem to be giving priority to three strategies: 1) seeking ways to keep alive this renewed interest in education, 2) trying to sort out who should do what in response to the countless suggestions, and 3) attempting to deal with the major gaps and unattended issues left on their agendas in the wake of the reports and studies. The remainder of this article will address these three overlapping areas, giving major emphasis to the third point and only brief attention to the first two.

Maintaining the Momentum

Most of us are acutely aware of the fickle ebb and flow of the tides of enthusiasm for education. After World War II a powerful wave of national interest in educational quality began to emerge as a result of criticism of the schools by university professors in the 1950s. This interest was augmented by the launching of Sputnik I; the result was the National Defense Education Act of 1958, with its emphasis on an improved curriculum and better-trained teachers. This wave of constructive change continued to grow throughout the early 1960s, with many beneficial effects on schools at all levels, but by the 1970s it was losing momentum. Some residual effects of those years of reform can still be identified, particularly in the presence of some teachers who were stimulated by the heady experiences with innovative programs and in the continued use of certain curricular materials.

A different, but complementary, type of national interest in education emerged in the mid-Sixties. Energized by the civil rights movement, it carried the banner of equal opportunity. Its centerpiece was the Elementary and Secondary Education Act (ESEA) of 1965, which encouraged more attention by educators to the problems of children from poor families; at the same time, many other federal, state, and local efforts aimed to provide better education for a larger proportion of the U.S. population. This movement viewed education as a major element in addressing our social ills, and it produced some very positive changes in American education. But this wave of interest also lost momentum — partly through controversies surrounding civil rights issues, partly because promised changes were slow in coming, partly because some initiatives simply didn't work, and partly because it became caught up in both scholarly and political crossfire.

Now a new wave of reform appears to have been launched, and American educators must reflect on what they have learned from the past. The main lesson has been that change in educational institutions comes slowly and with great difficulty. Another lesson is that the dedication of federal, state, and local governments to the reform of education is difficult to maintain, because other unforeseen issues arise to alter the agenda. In the Sixties and Seventies, the environment, the decline of older cities, and other press-

New directions suggested by the many studies of U.S. education cannot be accomplished quickly.

ing domestic issues certainly competed for national attention in ways that slowed the momentum of educational reform. Still a third lesson to be drawn from history is that premature scholarly analyses and evaluations can be damaging to programs that are attempting the difficult task of institutional change.

Realistic leaders in education know that new directions suggested by the many studies of U.S. education cannot be accomplished in a year or two; they will require a decade or more. After all, it took almost 15 years to accumulate any solid evidence that Title I of the ESEA was indeed helping to improve learning among disadvantaged children in elementary schools. Will the governors, the corporate leaders, and the others who are now fanning the fires of educational reform be willing to stay with that important task over time? On this point there are some positive early signals.

- The National Commission on Excellence in Education — after the release of *A Nation at Risk* — continued to hold regional meetings around the country in an effort to interpret its thinking and implant its views.
- The Task Force on Education for Economic Growth plans to stay active and to "establish a clearinghouse of information and ideas for states and communities" as a follow-up to its report, *Action for Excellence.*
- The Carnegie Foundation for the Advancement of Teaching plans a program of grants to encourage action on its recommendations.
- An informal Group of Fifty, chaired by David Hamburg, president of the Carnegie Corporation, and Gov. James Hunt of North Carolina, is considering the development of a continuing means of monitoring and publicizing progress and problems.
- State and local leaders are already responding to the new reform agenda; one example among many is the recent action by the New York State Board of Regents to extend the school year and to define a new common core of requirements for high schools.

But we must keep one important fact in mind: the timetable of political leadership is tuned to two- and four-year intervals, while the timetable of educational change operates in longer cycles. We have not yet found a way of dealing with this disparity at the state and national levels of decision making; even at the local level and within the individual school, long-term changes are difficult. And the kinds of changes now being recommended — e.g., improving teacher supply and quality and reducing the smorgasbord nature of the high school curriculum — will not come easily or quickly, because they challenge vested interests.

Educators are generally aware that the kinds of recommendations that have been proposed by the major study groups and the kinds of restructuring proposed by Theodore Sizer, John Goodlad, and Ernest Boyer constitute a long-term agenda for American schools, particularly high schools. But it is essential that the interest of groups outside education be sustained and particularly that business leadership remain supportive, since it is sure to become increasingly clear that one necessity for educational improvement is more tax money to support that improvement.

Priorities and Responsibilities

Even an incomplete listing of the major recommendations that have been made for improving American education boggles the mind and probably leaves the average school board member bewildered and discouraged. I recently saw a list of 20 major recommendations that are found in the reports and studies, and I arbitrarily reduced the list to 10.

1. Achieve greater consensus on the goals of education and the priorities of those goals, as opposed to the present tendency to "do everything for everybody."
2. Focus on a "common core" of learning for all Americans, particularly in high schools.
3. Stiffen both subject-matter and skills requirements for high school graduation and college admission (with little or no comment on how to serve students rejected by this new rigor).
4. Emphasize the attracting, training, and retaining of more able people for the teaching profession, using merit pay as one strategy and providing higher pay generally, along with more subject-matter emphasis in teacher preparation and enhanced use of testing in selecting teachers (all of this with almost no analysis of costs and how to pay them).
5. Renew the focus on basic skills, higher-order skills, and homework, and spend more time in school in order to achieve results.
6. Find ways around teacher certification to meet short-term but critical teacher shortages in mathematics, science, and computers.
7. Emphasize the selection, training, and retraining of school principals (as well as changing their role from school management to instructional and curricular leadership), and restructure the internal workings of schools to provide improved pedagogy, fewer interruptions of learning activities, more efficient use of time, and imaginative ways to enlist students in helping others to learn.
8. Define a strong federal role in education, with emphasis on such issues as math/science/computers, as well as on the primacy of the state and local roles.
9. Seek partnerships with business and higher education in working to improve the schools.
10. Emphasize a balance between quality and equality, with minimal mention of school desegregation, problems of discrimination faced by ethnic minorities and women, or the 20% of students who drop out before completing high school (40% to 45% in the inner cities).

The American nonsystem of education, with its diverse, decentralized, multiple authorities, is not prepared to deal in orderly fashion with recommendations such as these. I am not suggesting, of course, that we adopt centralized control and planning. But we must recognize the difficulties inherent in making changes that will require coordination among individual classrooms and schools, local school districts, and local, state, and federal levels of government. Take the current interest in math/science/computers, for example. For states, localities, and individual schools to start moving on this front without knowing what the federal government (not to mention colleges and universities) will do could result in duplication of efforts and wasted resources. On the other hand, it is certainly better that they *start* moving than that they only play out some grand after-you-Alphonse charade. We must accept the inefficiencies built into our disorderly educational system, in order to gain the freedom and capacity for inventiveness that our diversity provides.

It is important to add, however, that we must settle one issue soon: the role of the federal government in education. The recent studies and reports, including that of the National Commission on Excellence in Education, generally agree that the federal government should play a strong role in identifying national priorities in education, in doing something about them through legislation and appropriations, in supporting research on education, and, particularly, in dealing with issues of equity and equal opportunity. Right now we face a major political division on these matters. Both houses of Congress lean in the direction that the reports suggest, but the President tilts in the other direction, advocating a reduction in federal initiatives and abolition of the Cabinet-level Department of Education. President Reagan's basic program is for prayer in the schools, vouchers for the children of poor parents, and tax credits for parents of private-school students (although he has shifted his ground a bit, under political pressure, to include small-scale activities in science and computer learning). None of these Presidential priorities is recommended in any of the reports and studies. Maybe the 1984 elections will help to overcome this division. Until such time, progress will be difficult.

My own prescription for additions to the federal role in educational renewal is as follows.

• Congress should pass new legislation in the areas of math/science/computer learning to support state, local, and private initiatives with funds for equipment and curricular materials. Such legislation is already in the hopper, but it needs more funding than its sponsors have proposed.

• A new section should augment the old Title I of the ESEA, to help local school districts enrich the education of children from poor families. This legislation should focus on urban secondary schools, which are the disaster areas of education. More than 80% of ESEA funds over the last 18 years have gone to elementary schools. Now it is the high schools' turn.

• Congress should pass a new, comprehensive piece of legislation dealing with the preparation and inservice training of all categories of certified personnel (teachers, principals, and specialists of all kinds), and with the institutions that offer professional training to school personnel. This legislation should include special authorizations in the fields of mathematics, science, and computers, but it should encompass all major disciplines, particularly English, and it should foster the preparation of teachers who are competent to develop the "higher-order learning skills" emphasized so frequently in recent reports and studies. Once there was federal legislation of this kind (the Education Professions Development Act of 1967), but it was allowed to lapse during the Nixon Administration. If we still had it, we'd have something to build on.

The state-level responsibilities for action on the new agenda are clearer than the federal ones. The central role of the states falls into two broad categories: 1) rethinking requirements imposed by states on local school districts with regard to teacher certification, required courses of study, and a host of other matters in which states have ultimate authority; and 2) taking the lead in planning with local school districts to provide the vast increases in funding for education that will be necessary if the new agenda for schools is to have any hope of success. *This last issue will determine whether the new wave of interest in education moves forward or declines.*

There is plenty of room on the new agenda to promote local school board action as well as endeavors within individual schools. Schools and school systems can begin to respond to the many recommendations for change by asking themselves what they want to do and why. Then they can select those areas of action for which they can muster local resources. Including local community leadership and nearby colleges and universities in the development of these plans will enhance their potential for success.

One issue that will surface as local school systems address the confusing and sometimes contradictory agenda emerging from national studies is the extent to which individual schools should have the freedom to be different from other schools in the same system. This issue deserves a separate article; I will note only two brief generalizations here. Obviously, some tension exists between the desire of a school board and a superintendent to impose common requirements and standards on all students and teachers in a district and the desire of principals, teachers, parents, and students in an individual school to work out ways to make their particular building more effective. My first generalization is that schools are more likely to change for the better if central office and school board directives allow individual schools to seek their own definitions of excellence. My second generalization is that individual school initiatives can be strongly encouraged by providing each school with some funds and allowing the staff to decide how this money will be spent. Nothing awakens the energy and imagination of people in schools as much as some extra money to spend on what they think is important. It happens so seldom.

If my suggestions are followed, there will be a few failures and some small amounts of wasted money; there will also be some large gains and less waste than now exists. Moreover, this attention to the prerogatives of individual schools provides the only way to respond to some of the more important and more subtle suggestions found in the in-depth studies of schools by Goodlad and Sizer.

Unattended Issues

1. *The costs of improving education.* The most glaring omission from the new studies of the shortcomings of education and recommendations for reform is any detailed estimate of attendant costs and how they are to be met. The single largest area of additional cost will certainly be the compensation of teachers. The studies all recognize the recent substantial decline in teaching salaries relative to other fields of work; less often do they recognize the subsidy provided U.S. schools for many years by able women who worked at low pay because women were not accepted in other professions. This subsidy has been slowly withdrawn in the last 15 years, as the women's movement has moved toward equity in employment for females. Add to this the calls for extending the school day and year, for attracting more able people to the teaching profession, and for creating merit pay arrangements, and a very rough estimate suggests that at least $20 billion to $30 billion *a year* in new funds will be needed to put the schools on an upward course. There will be a multitude of additional costs, of course, for science equipment, computers, and a variety of other purposes.

The most glaring omission from the studies is an accounting of costs and how to meet them.

The division of the new costs of excellence among federal, state, and local funding sources remains largely unexplored, although the last 15 years have brought major change and progress in our thinking about educational finance. Funding the costs of excellence will remain the most difficult of all the issues raised by the wave of recommendations regarding the reform of schooling. My observations on this vital matter are as follows.

• It seems unlikely that the federal government will assume the costs of paying teachers, even though it might help substantially with their training and retraining and with equipping schools. State and local governments will have to carry the financial load of teachers' salaries and share this load in a fashion that is both politically viable and fair to taxpayers. If the federal government were to become involved, it would have to take into account the relative fiscal capacity of the states to improve teacher compensation.

• The self-interest of business in improving education has led to vigorous participation by corporate leadership in helping the schools; however, business leaders have not yet issued any clear call to the business community to support increased taxes at state and local levels. Most businesses still regard taxes for schools as a cost of doing business that can affect their competitive position — not as an investment in the future. A few corporate leaders have a more enlightened attitude toward cost and tax issues, but whether they can succeed in bringing a strong response from businesses generally is still an open question.

• The current antipathy in the U.S. toward any form of added taxation is so strong that it bodes ill for the political success of extra funding for educational reform. State governors appear most likely to provide strong leadership that can change this attitude. Such leadership has already emerged in Mississippi, North Carolina, and several other states. But it is not yet clear whether governors can actually interest Americans in paying higher taxes.

• New technology may be able to cut the costs of education and make it more efficient. This is no certainty, of course; many problems and even dangers attend the pursuit of these goals. But the combination of computers with sound and video in increasingly flexible and inexpensive formats to provide effective learning is worth serious trial and exploration. Technology *could* result in making education a less labor-intensive enterprise and so reduce costs. We can expect no short-term solutions to cost problems through technology, however; time and substantial investments will first be required.

2. *A narrow focus on the high school and on cognitive elements in education.* It could be argued that the best national investment in improved education would be the establishment of a *universal* system of preschools and kindergartens by every state and school district in the U.S., but this argument is not strongly presented in the recent studies. Instead, the studies focus primarily on the shortcomings of secondary schools — and of high schools more than of junior high schools. In my opinion, the increases in both single-parent families and full-time working mothers indicate the need for more emphasis on early childhood services for children.

Thoughtful educators have long claimed that early adolescents have been badly served by the junior high schools. But the national studies that have emerged so far are more concerned with the curriculum and the teaching in grades 9 through 12. School districts using the reports and studies as an exploratory agenda for action would be wise to assess their sixth-, seventh-, and eighth-grade practices.

I do not mean to say that high schools don't need attention. They do, particularly in the cities. I have already mentioned the high dropout rates characteristic of inner-city schools, but they have numerous other problems — some of which are identified in the various studies — that suggest changes in course requirements, teaching practices, use of time, and the like to repair weaknesses in cognitive learning. These studies pay very little attention, however, to the noncognitive elements of schooling — those practices that build student morale and motivation and that ultimately make possible more demanding cognitive work.

Many of the recent reports (Goodlad, Sizer, and Boyer excepted) give one the feeling that children and youths in schools are mere receptacles into which information and skills can be dumped, so that the graduates of our system will be useful to society. Indeed, the psychological assumption that seems to underlie many recommendations is that the mind is like a muscle that can be improved by strenuous exercise. This view of learning has long been discredited, and it won't do any good to revive it in the name of rigor or economic productivity or national security. A school in all of its human complexity is, next to the home, the most important institution in a young person's life. If a youngster sees school as an unfriendly place that provides the protection of anonymity but offers little in the way of personal attention and recognition, no amount of added emphasis on new curricula will succeed.

In the early 1970s several national commissions examined the problems of adolescents in America and tried to promote understanding of some of the dilemmas they faced. Surprisingly, today's studies make no reference to the important findings of these groups.* The reports of the Seventies, with their attention to the meaning and value of life in the teenage years, would add an important dimension to today's narrow focus on the cognitive. Schools are legitimately concerned with developing positive student attitudes and behaviors, and the atmosphere and human relations of a school — in class and out — relate strongly to this important objective.

3. *The unfinished equity agenda.* All the recent reports and studies recognize in general terms that disadvantaged and minority students have special needs, but they all stop with such generalities. *A Nation at Risk* urges the federal government to do something about these needs, but it doesn't say what. *Action for Excellence* gives this subject only the most general treatment, grouping women and minorities in one sentence of its recommendations for action. The reports fail to mention school desegregation, and they give precious little attention to the demographic facts that are all too clear: the proportion of Hispanics, Asians, and blacks in U.S. schools will increase rapidly in the next 15 years, and most of these groups will concentrate in the cities. These omissions gave rise to my earlier recommendation for a new section of Title I devoted to high schools. Naturally, existing funding for elementary schools from that program should not be reduced.

San Francisco, St. Louis, and Chicago recently made imaginative moves to reduce racial isolation in their schools — all without the necessity for lengthy, disruptive trials and court orders. Instead, consent decrees were the basis for the settlement of suits. One would think that these events, which occurred while the major study groups were conducting their reviews, might have attracted attention as positive moves that recall the principles of the *Brown* decision. But that landmark of American freedom isn't mentioned, either. Clearly there is little remaining commitment to the idea that separate and unequal schools are unacceptable and not enough commitment to equal opportunity to elicit clear and specific recommendations on how these crucial goals are to be pursued.

One of the dangers inherent in all the recommendations for more demanding courses and higher standards is that these more rigorous requirements will be insensitively applied and will force more young people out of school altogether. There is no adequate safety net today for a boy or girl who does not finish high school, and those who are recommending tougher standards for a high school diploma have not suggested one. Yet the first hurdle for any job applicant is still, "Do you have a high school diploma?" It is possible to raise academic standards in high schools without rejecting large numbers of young people, but the difficulties of doing so are insufficiently recognized in many of the new reports.

4. *Neglect of vocational education.* Vocational education is given almost no attention in the new studies, which is surprising in view of the fact that the studies focus primarily on the secondary school years, where most vocational offerings concentrate. Does this omission imply that all is well with vocational education and that it should keep on doing what it has been doing? Or does it perhaps suggest that there just isn't much interest in vocational education, because it is not seen as very significant? I don't know the answers to these questions, but one possible implication may be that the business

---

*See in particular James S. Coleman et al., *Youth, Transition to Adulthood: Report of the Panel on Youth of the President's Science Advisory Committee* (Chicago: University of Chicago Press, 1974).

It may be ungracious to question the motives of education's new friends in high places.

world is more interested in having job applicants with well-developed learning skills and responsible work habits than prospective employees with technical training for particular jobs that may no longer exist. If this is so, then many vocational programs will be challenged by the new emphasis on higher-order learning skills.

5. *Is there a tendency to cheapen educational goals?* Business and political leaders (and some educators) justify their desires for major changes and higher investments in American education by maintaining that these changes are needed to compete with the Japanese and to hold off the Soviets. Surely a better-educated populace will help with both of these problems, and surely these problems are important, say our leaders. So why not let them dominate our motives for improving schools?

However, a careful reading of the various reports reveals that their authors conceived of broader and more timeless goals for the schools. *A Nation at Risk* mentions "civility" and "prosperity and security" in its opening paragraphs; it speaks of "intellectual, moral, and spiritual strengths," and it advocates a "learning society . . . that affords all members the opportunity to stretch their minds to full capacity. . . ."

But I still have a nagging concern about the emphasis of the reports on materialistic motives as a basic platform for educational reform. At the very least, we must remain alert to the danger that such goals can push aside other important educational issues. How do we bring up a generation that will truly make peace with our enemies, identify and change the unfairness in our economic system, and be willing to see other societies as more than just competitors?

In *Action for Excellence*, the Task Force on Economic Growth gives absolute primacy to making our economic system more competitive and then, near the end, states:

> We know that education has deeper purposes than merely to prepare people for jobs. We are aware that to define the mission of the schools along narrowly utilitarian lines would be to misperceive the purposes of schooling. But if preparation for work is not the only aim of education, it is nonetheless a very important aim. And surely education for economic growth is a worthwhile goal around which to organize our efforts to rally the American people in the cause of improving the nation's schools.

I'd find this statement more palatable if its first sentence were at the beginning of the report and if its last sentence were qualified in some fashion. But perhaps I am merely quibbling; it may be ungracious to question the motives of education's new friends in high places. Most educators probably feel that the best strategy is to ride the new wave of interest in education without questioning its values and motives. Nonetheless, my vague worries persist. They have been expressed better than I can word them by Meg Greenfield in her *Newsweek* column of 16 May 1983. I close this article with selected paragraphs from her essay.

> My complaint is that the values we bring to the effort to right the situation are precisely the ones that got us in trouble in the first place and are only likely to perpetuate our grief.
>
> Education as an "investment," education as a way to beat the Russians and best the Japanese, education as a way to get ahead of the fellow down the street — it is true that generations of Americans have been brought together culturally by the great force of our public schools and that millions of them have rightly seen their schooling as a one-way ticket out of economic and social privation. But you really do not generate the educational values that count when you stress only these external, comparative advantages. People do not become educated or liberated so much as they become opportunistic in relation to such schooling. And anyway, on the great national-security issues, when was the last time you heard of a youngster doing his homework because he wanted to be better than the Russians in geometry?
>
> You give a child nothing, I think, when you give him this joyless, driven concept of the meaning of learning. But alas, there are plenty among us who think this is just fine. Following the great cackles of the political antipermissiveness crowd when this report was released, I was struck again by how much such people, who claim to be champions of education, implicitly view education as a disagreeable thing. It is invariably discussed by them — and with relish — as something between a medicine and a punishment that must be administered to its unwilling little subjects for their own good no matter how they howl. It is not supposed to be fun, they admonish, and children cannot be expected to like it — whatever happened to our moral fiber, and so forth.
>
> Schooling needs to be saved from these "friends" — the punishers, the opportunists, and the exploiters who profess an undying devotion to the old-fashioned virtues and the life of the mind. But it will of course not be saved by the purveyors of "fun," whose idea of making education enjoyable is to gut it and teach things not worth knowing. There is a difference — night and day — between this kind of "fun" and the joy of learning, and everyone who has ever had one great teacher of a serious subject knows what it is. So do those kids in a handful of slum schools notoriously programmed to fail who instead thrive because they are in the care of people who know what teaching is about. If we could acquire, come to honor, this great value, if we could truly aspire to become a "learning society," the rest — the competitive and material benefits — would follow. But we keep trying to do it the other way around.

THE GOOD NEWS ABOUT AMERICAN EDUCATION

Here's the good news: if we can agree on what's important and then focus on those objectives, we can achieve results. The head of the National Assessment of Educational Progress provides statistics to back up this assertion.

rchie E. Lapointe

rchie E. LaPointe is executive director of he Center for the Assessment of Educa- ional Progress, Princeton, N.J.

Thoughtful reflection on the quality of J.S. education and careful examination of ome of the facts confirm the observation hat all is not well. But some of the findings re also encouraging. Moreover, this good ews is robust and consistent: if, as a socie- y, we can agree on what is important and hen focus on those objectives for a decent eriod of time, we seem to know how to chieve results.

Data to support this conclusion can be ound in the research literature, in the esults of nationally standardized tests and f state testing programs, and in the ac- umulated statistics of the National Assess- ent of Educational Progress (NAEP), a ongressionally mandated project that is nded by the National Institute of Educa- on. As the nation's report card, the NAEP charged with determining what American oungsters know and can do and with onitoring their performance over time to etect growth, stability, or decline. To ac- omplish these goals, the NAEP has rveyed the performance of 9-, 13-, and 7-year-olds in a variety of content areas nce 1969.

The NAEP survey data cannot be used establish cause-and-effect relationships, ut they can be used for relational analyses. ıst as the grades on an individual's report rd describe only part of that student's performance, so do the NAEP data provide only part of the picture of U.S. education. When juxtaposed with other kinds of data, however, the NAEP findings help complete a complex picture.

For example, the NAEP has much to say about the impact of federal policy and funding decisions on education. President Reagan recently noted that, during the last 20 years, federal expenditures on education have increased 600%, while Scholastic Aptitude Test (SAT) scores have declined. But it is reasonable to assume that few of those federal dollars were spent on programs designed to help the students who typically take the SAT. Moreover, we know that several federal projects during the past 20 years were specifically designed to help minority and disadvantaged students improve their mastery of the basic skills.

And indeed, the NAEP data collected between 1970 and 1982 reveal that performance *improved* in curriculum areas targeted for funding, among those groups of students and in those schools targeted for funding, and at the levels of schooling and in the regions of the U.S. that were targeted for funding. By the same token, the NAEP data show that performance *remained stable or declined*:

- in curriculum areas *not* targeted for funding,
- among groups of students (e.g., whites, older youngsters) *not* targeted for funding,
- in schools *not* singled out for federally funded projects,
- at the levels of schooling that received *no* federal support, and
- in regions of the U.S. that received *less* federal funding than others.

Although this litany sounds convincing, it is important to remember that the evidence is not overpowering and that the NAEP is not structured to develop and substantiate cause-and-effect relationships. But the litany has a consistency that suggests that something more than coincidence is at work.

To be fair, I must also note that public interest, concern, and determination may be as effective as money in bringing about positive change. We are all witnessing right now an impressive renewal of public interest in education — but this interest is accompanied by very few federal dollars. Yet the current focus on educational excellence, organized and orchestrated by the respected and tireless Terrel Bell, may stimulate activities in schools that will yield dramatically positive learning outcomes. And 10 years from now, data will

From *Phi Delta Kappan*, June 1984, pp. 663-667. Reprinted by permission of the author and Phi Delta Kappan.

again be available from the NAEP to document these changes.

WITH THESE caveats in mind, let's take a closer look at some specific findings from the NAEP.

Reading. Between 60% and 70% of all Elementary and Secondary Education Act (ESEA) funds were invested in reading projects of one kind or another at the elementary school level. Ten percent of ESEA funds went for mathematics projects; 4% or less went for science. Meanwhile, the NAEP data for the period from 1970 to 1982 indicate more impressive growth in reading than in mathematics and actual declines in science achievement. Nine-year-olds made statistically significant gains in reading (Figure 1).

Mathematics. As I have already noted, only 10% of the ESEA funds were spent on mathematics projects during this period. Meanwhile, the NAEP data show declines in mathematics achievement for 9- and 17-year-olds and statistically significant growth for 13-year-olds (Figure 2). The 13-year-olds may have benefited from a movement between 1970 and 1982 toward hiring specialists to teach math in the middle and junior high schools.

Science. About 4% of the ESEA resources were spent on science projects. Funds from the National Defense Education Act (for foreign languages, mathematics, and science) were exhausted by the early Seventies. The NAEP found statistically significant declines in science achievement for all three age groups between 1969-70 and 1972-73 (Figure 3). The achievement of 9- and 13-year-olds continued to decline – though less precipitously – between 1972-73 and 1976-77; during that same interval, the achievement of 17-year-olds took another statistically significant slide.

Writing. Composition skills, a reflection of language and reasoning abilities, did not change significantly for the general populations assessed by the NAEP between 1970 and 1980. The gains that occurred seemed to reflect the special attention paid to certain population subgroups. For example, the writing performance of black teenagers improved.

High and Low Achievers. The emphases of the Seventies were on minimum competencies and on improving opportunities for the disadvantaged. And the NAEP data suggest that we achieved some successes (Figure 4). Low achievers among the 9- and 13-year-olds made impressive gains. However, we paid little attention to the high achievers, expecting them to succeed no matter what, and the performance of these youngsters improved less than that of their not-so-able peers. Indeed, the performance of high achievers in science declined dramatically.

Race. In addition to the dollars that the federal government targeted for helping minority youngsters, the courts and a sensitized society supplied motivation to improve the educational opportunities available to black children. The NAEP results – at least with regard to the reading skills of 9- and 13-year-old black students – suggest that these factors have made a difference. Between 1971 and 1980 the reading skills of black 9-year-olds improved by 10 percentage points (moving from 50 to 60), while their white counterparts gained only three percentage points (moving from 66 to 69). During that sa interval, the reading skills of bla 13-year-olds improved by five percenta points (moving from 45 to 50), but t achievement of white 13-year-olds mained unchanged at 63. The achie ment of 17-year-olds of both races also mained constant between 1971 and 19 at 71 for whites and at 52 for blacks.

Type of school. Schools classified disadvantaged urban or as rural were eli ble for greater amounts of available fe eral funds. It is instructive to break c the NAEP findings on students in th buildings and to compare them to t NAEP data on children attending adva taged urban schools. With regard to rea ing, 9- and 13-year-olds attending scho eligible for extra funding improved faster rates than those attending the mo affluent schools. Between 1971 and 19 9-year-olds in disadvantaged urb schools improved their average readi score by five percentage points, while t achievement of their counterparts in t more affluent schools improved by on one percentage point. During that sa interval, 13-year-olds in disadvantaged ban schools improved their average rea ing score by three percentage points, wh their counterparts in the more afflue schools recorded a gain of one percenta point. The reading performance 17-year-olds in both types of scho declined by two percentage points b tween 1971 and 1980 – from 61 to 59 f youngsters in disadvantaged urb schools and from 76 to 74 for those in a vantaged urban schools.

Regions. During the past decade, ce tain states received larger proportions available federal funds than other state When we break the NAEP findings

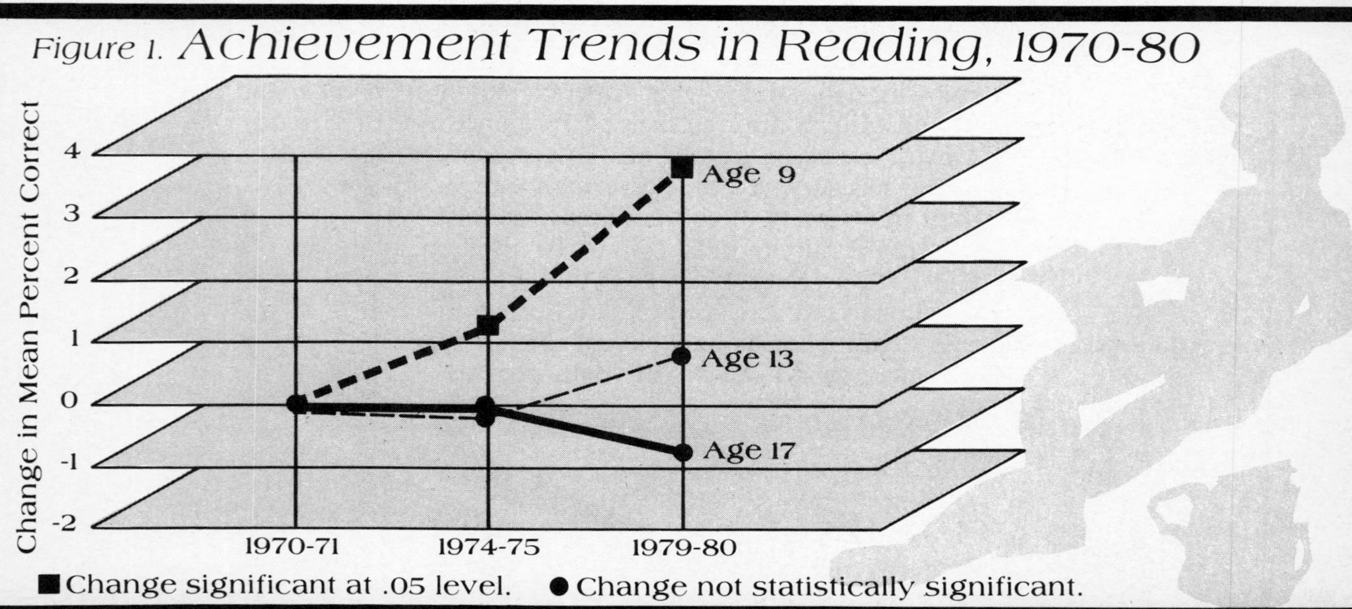

Figure 1. Achievement Trends in Reading, 1970-80

chievement into four regions, we find that the Southeast — which includes a number of the better-funded states — achieved the greatest gains in reading. The reading achievement scores of 9-year-olds in the Southeast rose by eight percentage points between 1971 and 1980. This is double the growth in achievement of 9-year-olds in the Northeast and in the West — and four times the growth in achievement of 9-year-olds in the central states. The reading performance of 13-year-olds and of 17-year-olds living in the Southeast also improved at a faster rate than that of their counterparts in other regions of the U.S., but these improvements were far less dramatic than those registered by the 9-year-olds.

The interest of high school students in science is on the decline, as is their optimism that science can solve problems.

IF IT IS true that we can decide our own fate, what aspects of the educational enterprise currently merit our attention? What's the bad news? In answering these questions, the NAEP findings once again prove helpful.

As we have already seen, the last decade brought dramatic improvements in basic skills among black students, among some disadvantaged groups, and among low achievers. But the largest *declines* in achievement occurred among high achiev-

Figure 2. Achievement Trends in Mathematics, 1972-82

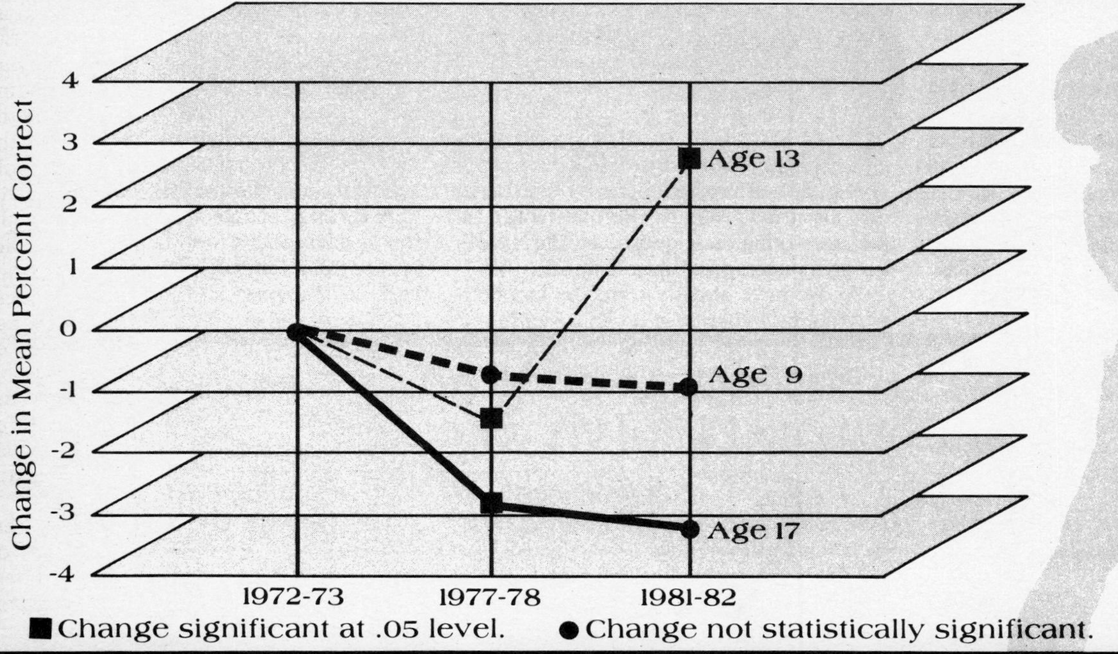

Figure 3. Achievement Trends in Science, 1969-77

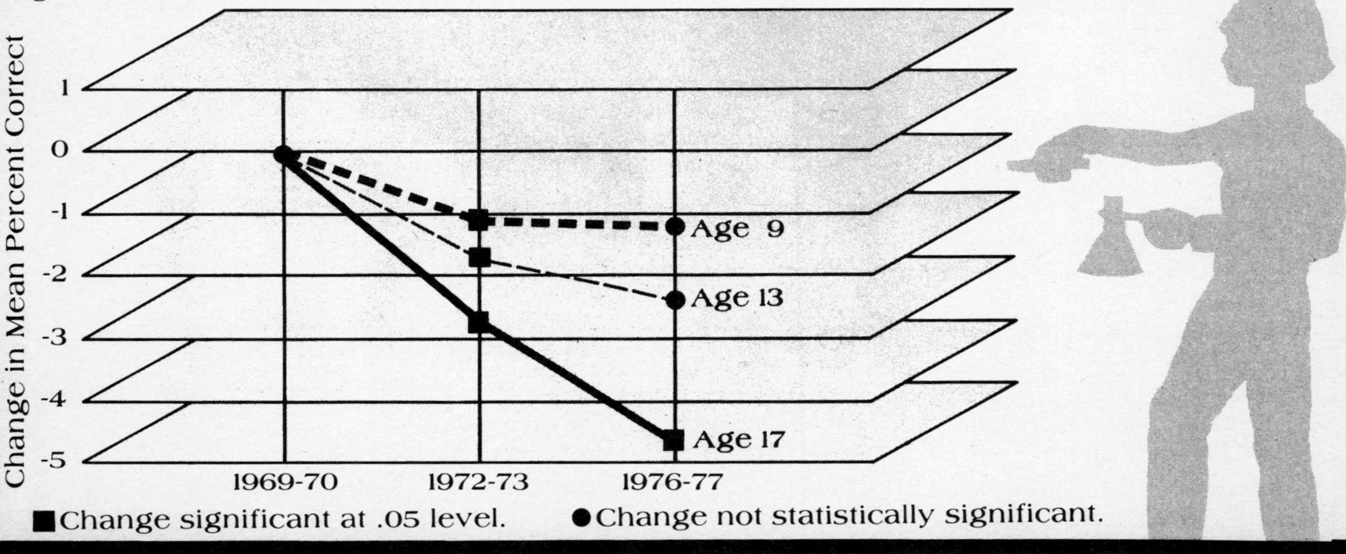

ers — the best students. These findings were consistent and recurring. For example, the NAEP found gains in the mathematics performance of low-ability black students at each age level (9, 13, and 17) and simultaneous declines in the mathematics performance of high-ability white students at each age level.

Closer examination of the data reveals that poorly developed problem-solving skills hinder students' performance in mathematics. Indeed, weaknesses exist in the so-called higher-order skills in general. Most students do well with literal comprehension but lack the skills of inference, analysis, and interpretation. Today's definition of functional literacy calls for these higher-order skills more than ever before, even as students' mastery of them is seemingly on the decline. Clearly, a renewed focus on these skills is needed.

A second trouble spot in U.S. education is identifiable not from the NAEP data on achievement, but from the NAEP data on students' attitudes. The NAEP sample is representative of the total population of 9-, 13-, and 17-year-olds in the U.S. In addition to responding to cognitive items, these young people are asked their opinions on a variety of curriculum-

Our achievements, to which the NAEP findings attest, should give us confidence that we can meet any objective that we set.

related matters. From this part of the NAEP study, we have learned that the interest of high school students in science is on the decline, as is their optimism that science can successfully solve such problems as energy shortages and environmental pollution. Given the reliance of our technological society on well-trained scientists and engineers, this may be a finding that merits attention.

Meanwhile, what about the variety of educational problems that students from language-minority groups encounter? For example, children from homes that are both non-English-speaking *and* disadv taged have greater difficulty learning read than do non-English-speaking c dren who are from homes rich in read materials and who attend schools in vantaged neighborhoods. Clearly, must attend to both home and school sources if we are to improve the read performance of non-English-speaking dents.

I have focused here on reading, mat matics, and science. However, the NA data base contains equally important formation about students' performa and attitudes in the areas of art, mu and citizenship. The NAEP is curre assessing reading and writing; in 1985 the NAEP will assess reading again, alc with mathematics, science, and compu competence. A new design for the NA study will also enrich the value of cognitive, demographic, and attitudi data that are collected.

CURRICULUM speciali and experienced educat have been asked to consi the implications of NAEP findings and to s

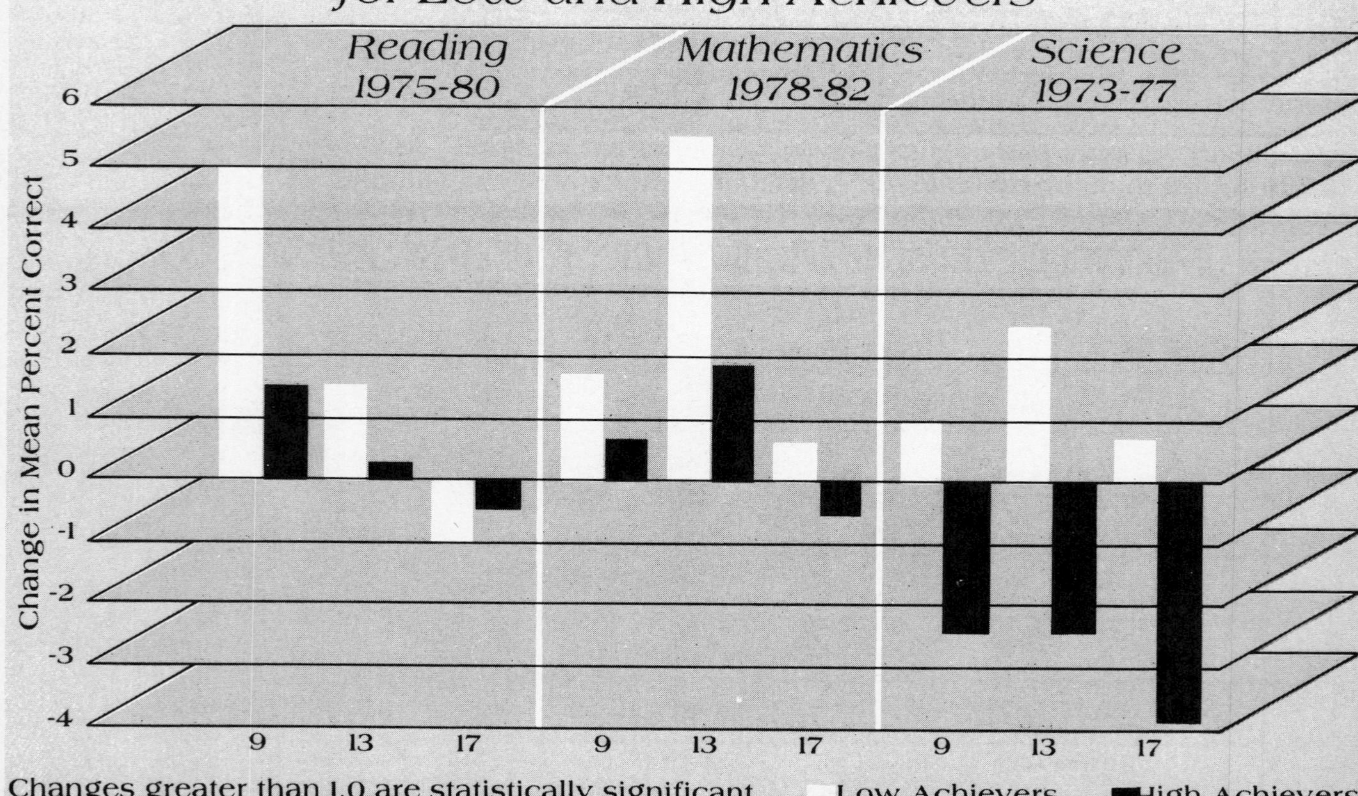

Figure 4. Changes in Reading, Mathematics, and Science for Low and High Achievers

Changes greater than 1.0 are statistically significant.

Photo by Michael Hayman/Corn's Photo Service

gest some possible courses of action. Their recommendations are logical and supported by both the evidence and experience. Their general conclusion is that, if teachers are well-prepared and if students are exposed to certain skills and spend time practicing them, performance improves.

Specifically, these experts suggested that, with regard to reading and the study of literature, educators could:

- teach students inferential as well as literal comprehension skills;
- ask students to read longer passages and books, rather than short paragraphs only;
- ask students to write about their readings;
- encourage students to make careful, thoughtful responses to their readings; and
- ask students to do some hard thinking about issues and opinions.

With regard to writing, the experts suggested that teachers could:

- ask students to write often — and in every content area;
- ask students to write in a variety of modes and for a variety of audiences; and
- ask students to rethink and rewrite papers once they have been critiqued.

With regard to mathematics and science, the experts suggested that teachers could:

- direct students to use calculators to check their work and computers to help them solve problems;
- teach students problem-solving techniques at the same time as they are mastering the basic skills;
- give students more opportunities to interact with one another in the solving of problems; and
- generate excitement among students about mathematics and science by focusing on the contributions that specialists in these fields have made toward helping people and enriching their lives.

These options are for teachers, since they are the ones who can most directly affect students' learning. But educational decisions are made in the U.S. by school boards, by legislators, and by those who mold public opinion. The current debate in this nation about educational excellence has brought all the options, concerns, issues, and dilemmas into the open. There will never be a better time to firmly establish our intermediate and long-range objectives for education. Our recent achievements, to which the NAEP findings attest, should give us confidence that we can meet any objective that we set.

The current debate involves governors, state legislators, state departments of education, the publishers of textbooks and tests, school administrators, teachers, school board members, and parents. The NAEP is making a determined and aggressive effort to provide each of these constituencies with accurate, intelligible information that will be useful in making the difficult choices that lie ahead.

For the reasons cited above, I have made no attempt to draw cause-and-effect conclusions from these data. I offer this information only to help reasonable people evaluate their options. We at the NAEP hope that objective, competent researchers will continue to challenge and explore the significance of these findings. The mission of the NAEP is to provide the highest quality information with which to make decisions about the development of human potential, our most important national resource.

The Educational Pendulum

Diane Ravitch

Diane Ravitch is the author of The Troubled Crusade: American Education, 1945-1980 *(Basic Books) and is an associate professor at Teachers College, Columbia University.*

The schools of America are in crisis—again. In spring, four major commissions declared that the inadequacies of the schools threatened the future of the nation, and this fall several new reports are expected to add to the indictment. Now that the ills of American education are once more a significant public issue, it is a good time to reflect on how we reached this point.

At any given time during most of the past half-century, schools have been the object of well-intended crusades to change or save them. These periodic waves of reform, from one extreme to the other, have led many observers to wonder whether the worst problem of American education is its faddishness. In the 1940s and early 1950s, a "good school" used progressive methods based on student interests and activity projects. After the Soviets put Sputnik into orbit in 1957, a "good school" was defined as one with high academic standards and special programs for gifted students, especially in subjects such as science, foreign languages, and mathematics. By the late 1960s, the once-high standards started to fall, and the "good school" was one where student participation and choice were emphasized. Since the mid-1970s, the educational pendulum has swung back toward "basics," "standards," and a coherent curriculum, and away from the free-wheeling experimentation of the '60s and '70s.

Why so much faddism? Why the constant shift from spontaneity and student interests in one decade to rigor and standards in the next? More than anything else, our educational faddism stems from the deeply ingrained conviction among many Americans that the best way to reform society is to reform the schools. Awareness of a social problem typically leads to the creation of a new school program: To curb the rate of traffic fatalities, a driver-education curriculum is devised; a rise in the divorce rate is followed by new courses on family life; demands for racial integration are met with school busing. Since the needs of society change depending on the social, political, and economic climate, the educational pendulum is pushed first in one direction, then in another.

Through the years, efforts to make the schools relevant to the needs of society have provoked intense struggles over the curriculum between groups with differing views. One source of this tension has been generated within the education profession itself. As the profession emerged and became self-conscious in the early 20th century, it developed a "new class" of policymakers and theorists who were not primarily classroom teachers. As the profession sought to define itself and find its social role, its leaders sought ways in which the profession could make a significant contribution to solving social problems. Unlike the classroom teacher, who had little time or reason to wonder whether the study of history or literature would change society, the growing number of professionals in schools of education, city education departments, state education departments, and professional associations interminably debated how to change the schools in order to serve society better.

While their agreement is widespread that schools exert an important influence on the next generation, a sharp divergence characterizes the question of how schools should meet this responsibility. Historically, the debate on this issue within the education establishment has raged between the progressive educators and the traditionalists. The progressives argue that professional educators must determine how to fit the individual to the society and design their course offerings accordingly; traditionalists, on the other hand, contend that the only way to reform society is by making individuals more intelligent. The zigs and zags in educational development during the past 50 years directly mirror this debate.

The traditionalist idea—that the central purpose of education is to increase students' intellectual powers—dominated American schools until the 1930s. At that time, however, the beliefs of educational philosopher John

> *"The objectives of education are preparation for citizenship; for home and family life; for vocational life; for physical health; for effective personality; for effective use of leisure time; and for development of information, interests, and skills . . . It cannot be expected that the great mass of the populace will spend its leisure time with the classics, the arts, or higher mathematics. Leisure education must then be attuned to the primitive instincts for physical and practical activity, the more familiar pursuits of the masses—the home and its furnishings, nature, sports, games, the radio, and social activities."*
>
> Harl R. Douglass
> Secondary Education for Youth in Modern America, 1937

Reprinted from *Psychology Today* Magazine, Copyright ©October 1983, American Psychological Association.

Growing up to be a good citizen, however, sometimes meant learning how to be a practical consumer.

Dewey and his followers made substantial inroads in schools of education, professional associations, and public-school systems. Because of the Depression, which destroyed the job market for adolescents, many young people who would normally have gone to work stayed in high school. The swelling of the high-school enrollment by non-college-bound students made many educators dissatisfied with the traditional academic curriculum. The progressive philosophy—which argued that in school there should be a society that would define what the larger society should be—encouraged broadening the curriculum for this new brand of student. Under the influence of progressivism, many schools introduced vocational and personal-service courses while reducing academic offerings.

After World War II, this kind of progressivism came to be known as "life-adjustment education" and became a major force in American education. Principals boasted that their programs adjusted students to the demands of real life, freeing them from dry academic studies. The new curriculums centered around vocation, leisure activities, health, personal concerns, and community problems. The schools in Des Moines, Iowa, for example, offered a course called "Developing an Effective Personality," while junior-high-school students in Tulsa learned what shade of nail polish to wear and how to improve their appearance. Some schools had no curriculum at all, while others pointed with pride to new courses in which projects or activities such as running a barbershop or decorating the girls' washroom replaced traditional studies.

Since the public never fully understood why these innovations were introduced, some communities became embroiled in heated political controversies. In Minneapolis, for example, a progressive superintendent merged English and social studies into a new required course called "Common

> *"To what desirable patterns of group behavior does [education] contribute? With any child, the secret for success is being fitted . . . It is vain and wasteful to take a girl who would make a fine homemaker and try to fit her into the patterns of training which make a lawyer, or to take a boy who would be successful in business and try to fit his training to that which produces doctors."*
>
> Paul R. Mort and William S. Vincent
> A Look at Our Schools: A Book for The Thinking Citizen, 1946

Learnings" in which pupils studied their own personal and social problems. A parent group, led by university professors including poet and novelist Robert Penn Warren, persuaded the local school board to permit their children to choose traditional academic subjects instead of "Common Learnings."

By the early 1950s, "life-adjustment education" had been introduced in many school districts across the nation, and it became the target of ridicule by scores of critics, most of whom were concerned laymen, such as Mortimer Smith, who later went on to found the Council for Basic Education, and university professors such as Arthur Bestor, who wrote the controversial book, *Educational Wastelands*. Critics charged not only that life-adjustment education was conformist and anti-intellectual, but that it was undemocratic because it provided academic studies only to college-bound students. Among the most outspoken critics was Robert Hutchins, chancellor of the University of Chicago, who complained that schools were failing to equip youngsters with intellectual power, feeding them instead a poor diet of vocational training and miscellaneous dead facts. By trying to meet all the needs of students, Hutchins charged, the schools were disintegrating their program since students have so many needs. "Perhaps the greatest idea that America has given the world," Hutchins wrote, "is the idea of education for all. The world is entitled to know whether this idea means that everybody can be educated, or only that everybody must go to school."

Although progressive educators defended their programs and charged that the critics were reactionaries, out of touch with the modern world, the launch of Sputnik finished the debate, at least for the moment. Almost overnight, the nation became obsessed with the failure of the schools. School boards hastily installed new programs in mathematics, science, and foreign languages. Admiral Hyman Rickover insisted that the schools had damaged the nation's security by neglecting those with talent. And the federal government, which had refused to approve any general federal aid to education for nearly a century, appropriated nearly $1 billion in the National Defense Education Act, which spurred the teaching of the hard sciences and foreign languages.

The post-Sputnik effect was almost immediate. For the first time in the century, enrollments in foreign-language classes rose. With federal funds, more teachers of science, mathematics, and foreign languages were trained, and schools had money to modernize their laboratories. Through the encouragement of the National Science Foundation, courses in the physical sciences, mathematics, and social science were substantially rewritten by leading scholars to reflect recent advances in knowledge.

By the time the new curriculums were ready for use in the classroom in the mid-1960s, however, the furor over Sputnik had abated. The calls for academic excellence had faded away, drowned out by the rising tide of social conflict in the cities and the disorders on college campuses.

The contemporary climate of social unrest, racial tension, and anti-war protest produced a new wave of critics and reformers, who—in keeping with the American tradition of saving society by changing the schools—pointed the finger of blame at the schools for all that had gone wrong. According to the typical analysis, society was in deep trouble because the schools were too authoritarian in their insistence on standards of academic performance, dress, and behavior and, in addition, were responsible for perpetuating institutional racism.

The federal government responded to the mood of crisis by enacting a major school-aid program whose primary beneficiaries were poor children. Critics contended that this would not alter the fundamental structure of education or society. What was needed, they said, was more freedom and spontaneity, which would surely produce higher motivation and therefore better learning. In the universities, students demanded courses that were relevant to political and social issues of the day.

During the late 1960s and early 1970s, schools again swung towards progressivism. Many elementary schools adopted "open education," which varied from place to place but often meant that the walls between classes were knocked down, and that students could exercise considerable choice about what to do each day. At the high-school level, graduation requirements were lowered, enrollments fell in such "hard" subjects as science, mathematics, and foreign languages, and alternative schools were established for students with special interests. Traditional subjects gave way to independent study, student-designed courses, and topical electives.

The subject areas affected most in the new era of student freedom were English and social studies. Typically, these courses gave way to a plethora of electives. In many schools, English was replaced by courses on the mass media, pop culture, and popular fiction. Writing, once a part of every student's daily regime, became a special course. Social studies, or history, was often splintered into mini-courses on black history, women's history, or "rap" sessions about values.

By the mid-1970s, academic indicators began to reveal a steady, nationwide downturn. For example, the number and proportion of students who received high scores on the SAT dropped dramatically. Not only college entrance examination scores but other tests taken by students in junior and senior high school showed a marked drop. In 1977, a blue-ribbon panel appointed by the College Board identified such in-school phenomena as grade inflation, absenteeism, frivolous courses, the absence of homework, and a striking diminution in reading and writing assignments as reasons for falling test scores. Other studies

> *"Parents are slow in realizing how unimportant the learning side of school is. Children, like adults, learn what they want to learn. All prize-giving and marks and exams sidetrack proper personality development. . . . All that any child needs is the three Rs; the rest should be tools and clay and sports and theater and paint and freedom."*
>
> A.S. Neill
> Summerhill: A Radical Approach to Child Rearing, 1960

> *"There is no inherently indispensable body of knowledge that every single child should know. . . . What children carry in their heads as 'chair' or 'aunt' or 'black' will never be absolutely identical. . . . In open education the teacher is mainly assistant to, not director of, the child's activity."*
>
> Charles Rathbone
>
> Open Education: The Informal Classroom, 1971

consistently found that during the 1970s high-school students took more nonacademic courses and fewer of the advanced courses necessary for college preparation.

As evidence accumulated that the schools were slipping as academic institutions, public confidence plummeted. Parents called for a "back-to-basics" curriculum, demanding the restoration of academic standards and discipline. In every year but one since 1969, the Gallup Poll has reported that the public's greatest educational concern has been the lack of discipline in the schools.

As usual, the schools followed society's shifting mood. One of the first things to go was the "new math," a prominent post-Sputnik curriculum reform, which most students and many teachers and parents found incomprehensible. Many schools that had torn their walls down for open education now replaced them. While alternative schools survived, their numbers shrank and their purpose became more clearly defined. By 1978, nearly 40 states adopted minimum competency tests to ascertain whether students had learned enough to be promoted or to graduate.

The latest swing of the educational pendulum has now taken us back, at least rhetorically, to the post-Sputnik era, when educators, policymakers, and parents feared that America's schools were producing (as one book was titled) "second-rate brains." The fear expressed in the most recent batch of commission reports is that the United States, through the failings of its schools, is losing the international competition for jobs and markets. When Sputnik was first launched by the Soviets, critics worried that the United States was falling behind in the race for space, technological prowess, and military superiority. Today, they worry less about falling behind in the space race, but just as much about the lags in our technological innovation and our place in the world economy.

While it is likely that American education will continue to be responsive to social change, certain facts will moderate future swings of the pendulum. For one thing, the use of polls in sounding school issues will restrain faddism to some extent, because the public has consistently expressed fairly traditional ideas about curriculum and student behavior. For another, the continuing spread of interdependence in the global economy will make it difficult for American schools to neglect the basic subjects.

What has been the effect of this history of educational fads? It is impossible to say how society has been changed as a result. For one thing, no single educational innovation has ever been universally adopted; even when a fad was at its height, many teachers and schools simply ignored the fashion. For another, there is no simple barometer with which to measure social change or with which to tie together causes and effects. What is clearly discernible, however, is the effect of these trends in the schools. When high school graduation requirements fell, enrollment in courses such as science, mathematics, and foreign languages dropped; in some high schools, foreign languages were eliminated, as were advanced courses in numerous hard disciplines.

If the past is any guide, we can expect that the current interest in excellence will last as long as there is a general perception that society's welfare depends on our ability to compete successfully in the international marketplace of goods and ideas. If we experience an internal crisis of confidence comparable to the Depression or to the late 1960s, then we may expect a return to the kind of educational progressivism that stresses self and community rather than competition and achievement.

Whatever the state of politics and society, America's schools need an anchor, an informed constituency of citizens and professional educators who will continue to press for the kind of liberal education that all children should have. Even back in the 1930s, when progressives and traditionalists first began to battle, they all agreed on the importance of literacy. The appeal of educational progressivism to parents lies in its promise to improve children's learning by increasing intrinsic motivation. Traditionalists have insisted that some kinds of extrinsic motivation, some external discipline such as grades and course requirements, are necessary. In either case, it is clear that parents and the public want children to become literate in school.

That is why, today, educators speak not just of reading and writing but of scientific literacy, cultural literacy, and historical literacy. Fads may come and go, but American schools now appear to be aiming at this broadened definition of literacy.

> *"Excellence in education means several related things. At the level of the individual learner, it means performing on the boundary of individual ability in ways that test and push back personal limits, in school and in the workplace. Excellence characterizes a school or college that sets high expectations and goals for all learners, then tries in every possible way to help students reach them. Excellence characterizes a society that has adopted these policies, for it will then be prepared through the education and skill of its people to respond to the challenges of a rapidly changing world."*
>
> A Nation at Risk
>
> The National Commission on Excellence in Education, 1983

How to Save the Public Schools

PHIL KEISLING

Phil Keisling is an editor of *The Washington Monthly*.

In 1960 six-year-old Ruby Bridges braved the taunts of white racists to become the first black to enroll in New Orleans's then-segregated public school system. Two decades later, Bridges took her three children out of that same school system and placed them in a parochial school. "I don't like to put down public schools," she said to a reporter about her son, "but he wasn't really learning the way he should have."

As Bridges painfully learned, integrating the public schools is only half the battle—and probably the easier half. A more insidious evil than segregation is a public school system that's bad and getting worse. The signs of decline—from the nineteen-year stretch of plummeting SAT scores (broken only this year by a minuscule rise) to the three hundred thousand "functional illiterates" who graduate from American high schools each year—are already familiar. Less often considered are the millions of children, many already victimized by racial prejudice and poverty, who will be consigned to lives of failure because their high school diplomas are the educational equivalent of worthless notes from the Weimar Republic.

So Bridges and a growing number of other parents are defecting to private schools, motivated not so much by strong religious convictions or a desire to ensure their children's high social status as by a conviction that the public schools have betrayed them. Some of their children are landing in plummy institutions such as Andover and Phillips Exeter; at this gilded end of the private school spectrum, competition has grown so fierce that kindergartens in Washington, D.C., charging $4,000 a year are now turning away four times as many applicants as they accept. Other children—to the delight of the new right and the outcries of liberals—are turning to fundamentalist Christian schools and white academies.

Nevertheless, the typical private school in America remains the one Bridges chose: a parochial school operated by the Catholic Church. Two-thirds of the nation's five million private school students attend such schools and, contrary to popular misconceptions, they are relatively inexpensive (tuition seldom exceeds $1,000 a year); involve little overt religious instruction (explained partly by the fact that 75 percent of all parochial school teachers are lay instructors); and have relatively unrestrictive admission and retention policies (according to one recent study, 60 percent of these schools don't expel a single student during the school year.) In many inner cities—Chicago, Detroit, Washington, D.C., and New Orleans, to name just a few—the majority of parochial school students are black.

Private schools have co-existed with public ones throughout American history, but until recently they've escaped the scrutiny of the professional sociologist. University of Chicago professor James Coleman, along with associates Thomas Hoffer and Sally Kilgore, has now put an end to that neglect with this path-breaking study. Coleman surveyed 58,000 students in 893 public and 122 private high schools, gathering information that ranged from each school's financial resources to the attitudes of its students. Achievement tests were then given to students in the 10th and 12th grades. After performing the various mysteries of the sociologists' craft—ordinary least squares regression analyses, standard deviations, independent variable weightings—Coleman came to a disturbing conclusion. Students in a typical private school—a parochial school with larger classes, lower paid teachers, and substantially fewer

Reprinted by permission of *THE NEW REPUBLIC*, ©1982, The New Republic, Inc.

resources—achieve more than those in the average public school.

WHEN COLEMAN first announced his results a year ago (this book reprints his study in more detail and includes a rebuttal to some of the major criticisms), many in the educational establishment reacted as if he'd just endorsed public hangings for juvenile delinquents. Fellow sociologists assaulted Coleman for his methodological "sloppiness" and criticized the specific techniques he used to filter out the effects on achievement of family income and race. The criticisms went beyond the normally staid bounds of academic discourse. Professor Arthur S. Goldberger of the University of Wisconsin, for example, claimed the report "reeked of incompetence and irresponsibility." Political liberals were no less upset, particularly when Coleman endorsed tuition tax credits. This last criticism—that Coleman was inappropriately enlisting social science on behalf of a controversial political issue—was somewhat ironic, since many of the same critics had used a previous Coleman study, *Equality of Educational Opportunity* (1966), to justify large-scale busing to promote integration.

It doesn't take a sociologist to detect methodological shortcomings in Coleman's book. For example, Coleman doesn't fully account for the effect on a child's achievement of having parents who care enough about education to begin with that they're willing to pay private school tuition. Likewise, the achievement tests Coleman used partly measure the effects of elementary education, not high school.

Such flaws aren't surprising; after all, the only unimpeachable scientific comparison would require sending a child through a public high school, deprogramming him of everything he learned there, reversing the aging process, and after all that sending him back through a private school. But of far more interest to the general reader is the almost banal simplicity of Coleman's major conclusions. Whoever once dubbed sociology the "quantification of the intuitive and the glorification of the obvious" might have had this study in mind. Despite an occasional surprise—for example, if income and religion are equal, blacks are more likely to send their children to parochial schools than whites—his findings seem obvious. Private schools are more rigorous; their students, for example, are 50 percent more likely to have over an hour's worth of homework every night than students in public schools. Private schools impose stricter disciplinary rules and maintain more order in their classrooms. Most important, private schools put a much greater emphasis on academic subjects. Seventy percent of their students are enrolled in an academic program compared to only 34 percent for public school. Fourteen percent of private school students take a third-year language, compared to just 6 percent in the public schools. For chemistry the comparable figures are 53 percent and 37 percent; for geometry, 84 percent and 53 percent.

In other words, private schools demand more of their students—and they get more. But Coleman doesn't suggest that private schools are automatically better than public ones; in fact, according to his comparison of "high performance" public and private schools, there is little difference between the two in student achievement. Rather, Coleman's important finding is this: the characteristics that result in higher achievement are much more likely to be found in a private school than in a public one.

IT'S A SIMPLE, even obvious, conclusion; what's most interesting are the great number of people who choose to distort or ignore it entirely. Their reaction reveals the paucity of thinking these days about public education, particularly on the left. Among most Democrats, the educational agenda has only two major items: opposition to tuition tax credits and support for increased educational spending. It's a distinctly unimaginative agenda—which perhaps explains why, among those leading Democrats urging the party to formulate new ideas in response to the new right, education is barely on the radar screen. Paul Tsongas's *The Road from Here* doesn't list education among the "eight realities" Democrats need to reconsider. Mark Green's *Winning Back America* and Tom Hayden's manifesto, *The American Future*, are similarly silent.

Tuition tax credits aren't a good idea; they're more an admission of defeat than a sensible way to improve public education. But just as tuition tax credits won't revitalize our public schools, neither will the traditional liberal panacea of simply dipping deeper into the public purse. Is there good reason to believe that higher salaries for public school teachers will automatically make a substantial difference in student achievement when private school teachers work longer hours, have to manage larger classes, and make about $5,000 less per year? Unfortunately, there is no good reason, and those desiring proof need look no further than the experience of the last two decades. During that period expenditures for public elementary and secondary education increased nearly sixfold to almost $120 billion, more than keeping abreast of inflation. Meanwhile, the quality of our schools has plummeted.

ONE CAN POINT accusing fingers at the influence of TV, apathetic parents, and even junk food, but the lion's share of the blame must fall on that segment of the educational system with the most direct influence on children: the nation's 2.2 million teachers. Never particularly high, the quality of the nation's teaching corps today is embarrassingly low, and sinking further. The profession is attracting the nation's least academically gifted and creative students. Just one measure: in 1979-1980 those college students planning to major in general education scored an average of 339 on the verbal portion of the SAT—80 points below the already dismal national average. Those who justifiably might point out the imperfect link between SAT scores and teaching ability should also consider the experience of the Lemon Grove School District in Southern California. There a literacy test scaled to eighth-grade levels was given prospective teachers, all possessed of paper degrees and certificates. Thirty-five percent flunked one or more parts.

The education methodology courses required for a teacher's certificate—usually so stultifyingly dull that most college students avoid them—are partly to blame. As J. Myron Atkin, an education professor at Stanford, has observed, "It is doubtful if as many as two dozen of the 1,300 institutions that prepare teachers are maintaining programs that a bright youngster would find demanding." Another cause is more heartening, but no less reassuring. A quarter-century ago widespread sexism gave intelligent, motivated women access to few professions other than teaching; today, those same women are pursuing careers in law, medicine, and business. Unfortunately, what is long-overdue equity for women is also our children's loss. Indeed, the aversion to the classroom of talented men and women alike provides but a sad commentary on contemporary values. Something is seriously amiss when a society gives more financial reward to those who hunch over a convoluted legal brief, in search of some new obstructionist tactic to use in an obscure contract dispute, than to those who teach a child to appreciate the eloquence of the written word or the elegance of mathematics.

THE NATION'S two major teachers' unions—the American Federation of Teachers and the National Education Association—don't dispute the low quality of teachers so much as enlist this unhappy situation in arguing for higher teachers' salaries. Their argument is simple: when it comes to public schools, Americans are getting what they pay for. And if they want better schools, they'll simply have to pay substantially more for better teachers.

Welcome to the great circular argument of public education. In the abstract, higher teacher salaries are both fair and sensible. Yet in the real world, what would be the result if teachers' salaries were doubled overnight? Very little, except that the incompetent and mediocre teachers now in the classroom would get a lot more money—and would probably be that much less inclined to quit.

That latter point is important because replacing bad teachers with good ones, after all, is the whole raison d'être of raising salaries. But retirement or resignation now are about the only ways to get rid of incompetent teachers; administrators, school board members, and even candid teachers will admit that firing a tenured teacher—and most fall into that category after just three years' experience—is virtually impossible. In the name of the great liberal shibboleth of "due process," such a warren of legal obstacles has been erected that only in the most egregious cases do school districts even bother to initiate dismissal proceedings. In the last six years, for example, Philadelphia has dismissed only 24 of its 13,000 teachers; a typical dismissal takes two years, and involves expensive legal fees.

Short of changing various rules governing tenure and due process, both the AFT and the NEA contend that better teachers can be incorporated into the ranks over a period of years. (To help ensure the quality of these new teachers, the AFT favors some competency testing; the NEA steadfastly opposes any measurement attempts.) But putting aside the question of whether the nation's children should be forced to wait several decades for these better teachers so no one has to be fired, this gradual approach has a graver flaw: it won't work.

Again, it's important to focus on the educational world as it is. The American Federation of Teachers predicts 55,000 existing teachers will be laid off this school year—which hardly leaves much room for those bright, new hirees. (Incidentally, union contracts usually dictate that lay-offs be on the basis of seniority, not competence—yet another way bad teachers are protected while our schools deteriorate). Nor is there much reason to expect such lay-offs will abate, notwithstanding the unions' warnings that a slight rise in student enrollments toward the end of this decade will help spawn a new teacher shortage. Student enrollments peaked twelve years ago, yet in 1981 there were more elementary and secondary teachers than at any other time in the nation's history. The explanation lies in the "shrinking classroom": in 1962 there were 25.6 students per teacher while today there are just 18.9. If the nation were to return to the 1962 ratio, it could lay off almost 500,000 more teachers. That would be unwise, to be sure, but further decreases are hardly unreasonable, especially when one considers that the traditional argument for smaller classes has been improved quality of education. But in light of recent history, that's hardly a compelling argument—which perhaps explains why both the AFT and the NEA are increasingly trying to make classroom size a negotiable item in collective bargaining agreements.

Higher salaries for some teachers may prove necessary to improve our public schools; indeed, the dire shortage of math and science teachers now plaguing most districts can be resolved in the near term only by paying more for these specialities. (Again, the NEA and to a lesser extent the AFT oppose such salary differentials, insisting that salaries for all teachers, even those in oversubscribed fields such as English and social studies, rise together.) But absent other changes in our public schools, spending more money will only produce more dashed expectations.

This is where the Coleman report holds its most important lesson. Rather than glorifying private education, the report suggests that public schools would be wise to emulate the best aspects of private schools—aspects which have little to do with money. One of the most obvious places to begin is with academic requirements. Fewer than half of our public high schools now require more than one year of math and science for graduation; little wonder a recent National Science Foundation report warned that ours is a nation fast approaching "scientific illiteracy." As reflected in the dearth of third-year language students, foreign language requirements are virtually unknown in American schools. Our schools' neglect of both science and foreign languages stands in glaring contrast to the schools of Western Europe and Japan, countries whose economies, not so incidentally, are more robust than our own.

Certainly not all private schools offer adequate academic programs. Some—particularly fundamentalist Christian schools—lose more from narrow-mindedness than they gain in rigor. Even so, as Coleman discovered, parochial schools have proved far less susceptible to the academic relativism in which a course entitled "TV—The Medium is the Message" is put on a par with one teaching the basics of grammar and expository writing.

Another characteristic that Coleman linked to higher achievement is the private school's insistence on a more orderly learning environment. Not only did parochial schools have stricter disciplinary standards, but their students were more likely to feel they were treated "fairly" than their public school counterparts. Perhaps more important, whereas one in ten public school students rated their teachers' interest in them as "excellent," for parochial schools, where the classes were even larger, the figure was one in four. Of course, one cannot expect public schools to duplicate the spiritual mystique of parochial schools, where the implied presence of a higher moral authority suffuses the classrooms. But public schools can and should pay far more attention to fostering a coherent set of shared values and establishing more clear-cut lines of authority—if for no other reason than students themselves seem to prefer it.

As for specific disciplinary measures, the Coleman report suggests that public schools need to reevaluate some dearly held notions. In theory, any child can be transformed into an attentive student with a little understanding and patience. In practice, that noble sentiment is one of the most destructive illusions of modern education. It takes only a few disruptive students to poison the learning atmosphere for everyone. Many of these students should be removed from regular classrooms so that teachers can focus their energies on students who've shown a willingness to learn. This at first may sound harsh and uncompassionate, but it's far less cruel than denying a much greater number of students a decent education. In our insistence on giving as many children as possible the traditional token of success—the high school diploma—we've inadvertently ensured that far too many of them will fail later in life.

PERHAPS the most important lesson of private schools—and one Coleman unfortunately didn't examine—involves teachers. Almost no private schools require teaching certificates; instead, the emphasis is on whether instructors know their subjects and can teach them well. Pay in private schools is substantially lower than in public ones, but outstanding performance is usually rewarded with merit pay. Teachers who prove to be incompetent can be easily fired or simply not re-hired when their contracts come up for renewal.

Compare this with public schools. Only people with proper credentials can teach, even though many without them know their subject far better than those who hold them. Once in the classroom, most of these teachers are paid without regard to ability or the need for their services, but according to seniority and the possession of additional academic degrees. While a beginning math teacher might get $12,000 a year (assuming the school district can find one), an English teacher with 15 years' experience and a master's degree can command twice as much or more—even though he performs far worse than his younger, lesser-paid colleagues. The result is a system that protects incompetent teachers, demoralizes excellent ones, and makes mediocrity the best most of our children can hope for.

The major defenders of this system—the AFT and the NEA—once offered their members badly needed protection from the caprices of administrators and the penury of school boards. But the unions have succeeded all too well, having grown sufficiently powerful to undermine the quality of public education in the name of protecting their members. When a bad teacher is kept in the classroom while a far better candidate waits in the wings for a job opening, the children are the real losers.

SOLVING THIS PROBLEM doesn't require abolishing the unions so much as forcing them to stop having it both ways. On the one hand, the unions demand that their members be treated as "professionals," with commensurate salary and status; on the other, that they should effectively be immune from judgments of quality. As is the case with academic requirements, the relativism behind the credo that "all teachers are equal" allows schools to avoid difficult decisions about the merit of individuals—but in the process undermines excellence. A similar attitude has been all too prevalent on automobile assembly lines, where quality control is ultimately someone else's responsibility. The defective automobile that results can always be recalled; unfortunately, the same is not true for children with defective educations.

Instituting stricter curricular and disciplinary standards will be relatively easy; what will truly test the sincerity of liberals who claim they want to reverse the decline of public education is their treatment of teacher's unions. They are among the nation's most powerful lobbies; the NEA alone provided over 10 percent of the delegates and alternates to the 1980 Democratic National Convention. Their power is even greater on the state level, where they often lead the PACs in spending for legislative races. The bulk of their largesse is lavished on Democrats.

Unfortunately, most liberals aren't showing the stomach for this necessary battle with their traditional allies, preferring instead to tell themselves that the problems with our nation's schools can be solved with a bit more money here, a few more specialized programs there. But such incrementalism is a prescription for the continued deterioration of our public schools, and as they fail the nation loses more than just the well-educated citizenry it needs to compete successfully in an increasingly competitive international economy. The failure of our schools also threatens democracy itself. As more people abandon the public schools to those too poor to escape them, ours becomes a society increasingly stratified, not so much by race as by social class.

Is such a bleak outcome inevitable? Not at all. In fact, for all its criticism of the public schools, Coleman's study is strangely heartening, far more so than his 1966 study mentioned earlier. Fifteen years ago, Coleman concluded that the most important determinant of a child's achievement was his socioeconomic background and that of his peers; little could alter the educational outcome except perhaps trying to mix rich white children with poor black ones—hence the resulting passion for busing.

This latest report suggests an opposite and far more optimistic conclusion: schools *do* make a difference. Though Coleman found that the achievement gap between white and minority students widened between the 10th and 12th grade in public schools, he found it actually narrowed in private ones. Strange as it may sound, that should be comforting news *especially* to liberals, for it suggests that schools really can overcome the debilitating effects of poverty and race.

This is why it's so distressing that, so far, the lessons of the Coleman report have been embraced mainly by conservatives. Indeed, one of the most dismaying failures of American liberalism has been its allowing the right to assume the initiative in calling attention to the deterioration of our public schools. The public understandably has grown impatient with those who make excuses for poor schools or seek refuge in unrealistic—and discredited—solutions such as large, new infusions of public money. Conservative nostrums such as tuition tax credits aren't much better and are probably worse; unfortunately, for many parents concerned about their children's education, they're the only game in town.

Good public schools needn't become an endangered species. But if their ostensible friends continue to ignore danger signs such as the Coleman report, it won't take a sociologist to perform a post-mortem. Parents like Ruby Bridges could just as easily explain what went wrong.

High School Achievement: Public, Catholic, and Private Schools Compared by James S. Coleman, Thomas Hoffer, and Sally Kilgore (Basic Books, 277 pp., $20.75)

The 16th Annual Gallup Poll Of the Public's Attitudes Toward The Public Schools

George H. Gallup

George H. Gallup, creator of scientific polling and one of the most influential men of this century died in Switzerland on July 27, 1984.

Purpose of the Study

THIS SURVEY, which measures the attitudes of Americans toward their public schools, is the 16th annual survey in this series. Funding for this survey was provided by Phi Delta Kappa, Inc. Each year the poll attempts to deal with issues of greatest concern both to educators and to the public. New as well as trend questions are included in this and every survey.

To insure that the survey would embrace the most important issues in the field of education, Phi Delta Kappa organized a meeting of various leaders in the field of education to discuss their ideas, evaluate proposed questions, and suggest new questions for the survey.

We wish to thank all those who contributed their ideas to this survey.

Research Procedure

The Sample. The sample used in this survey embraced a total of 1,515 adults (18 years of age and older). It is described as a modified probability sample of the United States. Personal, in-home interviewing was conducted in all areas of the U.S. and in all types of communities. A description of the sample can be obtained from Phi Delta Kappa.

Time of Interviewing. The fieldwork for this study was carried out during the period of 18-27 May 1984.

The Report. In the tables that follow, the heading "Nonpublic School Parents" includes parents of students who attend parochial schools and parents of students who attend private or independent schools.

Due allowance must be made for statistical variation, especially in the case of findings for small groups in which relatively few respondents were interviewed, e.g., nonpublic school parents.

The findings of this report apply only to the U.S. as a whole and not to individual communities. Local surveys, using the same questions, can be conducted to determine how local areas compare with national norms.

Summary of Findings

Americans are more favorably disposed toward the public schools today than at any time in the last decade. In this year's survey, more Americans (42%) grade their local schools A or B for their performance than at any time since 1976 — with an 11-point increase just since last year. Virtually the same dramatic increase occurs among the parents of public school children — with a 10% rise since last year in the percentage giving the local schools an A or B rating.

Americans have also become significantly more favorably disposed toward public school teachers and administrators. In 1981, 39% gave teachers a grade of A or B, whereas today the figure is 50%. Moreover, the A or B grades given to principals and administrators have risen from 36% to 47% during this same three-year period.

A final indicator that reveals an increase in favorable feelings toward the schools is the public's increased willingness to pay the price for public education. The percentage of Americans who say that they would be willing to pay more taxes for education has risen from 30% to 41%.

Americans continue to feel that public education contributes more to national strength than either industrial might or military power. More than eight in 10 say that developing the best educational system in the world will be "very important" in determining America's future strength, compared to 70% who favor developing the best industrial production system and only 45% who favor developing the strongest military force.

The American public is divided in its support for the various recommendations proposed in the recently published reports concerning U.S. education. The public strongly favors 1) increasing the amount of schoolwork and homework in both elementary and high school, 2) basing all grade promotions on examinations, and 3) employing nationally standardized tests for high school diplomas. Support for each of these proposals has increased in recent years.

Americans also support, by wide margins, the ideas of career ladders for teachers and state board teacher examinations in every subject. To a lesser degree, the public feels that salaries for teachers are too low; Americans support higher pay for teachers where shortages exist, including mathematics, science, technical subjects, vocational training, and other critical areas.

Americans give top priority to the traditional "basics" — math and English — as has been the case since these annual surveys were initiated; there is virtually unanimous agreement that these courses should be required of all high school students — both college-bound and non-college-bound. Several of the so-called "new basics" (i.e., science and computer science) are considered less important, though both have recorded gains since 1981, particularly computer science. Similarly, vocational training as a requirement for non-college-bound students has registered substantial gains. The issue of foreign language as a requirement for college-bound students, however, has made little progress in recent years. The number of Americans who feel that extracurricular activities are very important to a young person's education has dropped from 45% in 1978 to 31% today.

The public appears to be unwilling to make some of the necessary sacrifices or commitments to help implement some of the recommendations of the school reform reports. Americans are opposed to extended school years or longer school days, which would provide the time for additional schooling. (Support for both ideas has increased somewhat in the last few years,

From *Phi Delta Kappan*, September 1984, pp. 23-28. ©1984 Phi Delta Kappan, Inc.

however.) Furthermore, nonparents as well as parents oppose by a 2-1 margin the tougher college admission standards that are the logical extension of stricter standards at the elementary and high school levels.

Although teachers oppose merit pay as a means of rewarding outstanding teaching performance by a margin of roughly 2-1, the public (including parents and nonparents) *favors* the idea by about 3-1. Among the half of the population who are familiar with merit pay, support rises to roughly 4-1.

Approximately seven Americans in 10 favor school prayer — one of the most controversial issues facing the public schools today. At the same time, though the survey question omitted the word *voluntary*, a separate Gallup Poll measuring support for *voluntary* prayer shows some decline in support for the proposal.

Although Americans have tended to favor Ronald Reagan as President over Walter Mondale, they feel that Mondale would be more likely than Reagan — by 42% to 34% — to improve the quality of education. In addition, 66% of Americans say that they would be more likely to vote for a candidate who favored increased federal spending for education; only 22% say that they would be less likely to vote for such a candidate.

The American public continues to regard discipline as the most important problem facing the public schools; about one-fourth of Americans cite discipline as the predominant problem, as they have done for more than a decade. Our analysis indicates that this is probably an outcome of the public's exaggerated perceptions of specific disciplinary problems that occur in the schools — especially when these findings are compared to the testimony of those most likely to know the actual situation, the teachers. Half of the American public feels that drugs are used in the local schools "most of the time" or "fairly often." About one-third of the public feels that theft of money or personal property, drinking of alcoholic beverages, theft of school property, and carrying of knives or other weapons occur "most of the time" or "fairly often."

MONITORING MEASURES

Education in America's Future

The American public is strongly in favor of developing the best educational system in the world. In fact, U.S. citizens believe — as they did in 1982, when this question was first asked — that education will be more important in determining America's place in the world 25 years from now than our industrial system or our military might.

The question:

In determining America's strength in the future — say, 25 years from now — how important do you feel each of the following factors will be — very important, fairly important, not too important, or not at all important?

	Very Important %	Fairly Important %	Not Too Important %	Not At All Important %	Don't Know %
Developing the best educational system in the world	82	13	2	1	2
Developing the most efficient industrial production system in the world	70	23	3	1	3
Building the strongest military force in the world	45	36	13	3	3

Those responding very important	1984 %	1982 %
Developing the best educational system in the world	82	84
Developing the most efficient industrial production system in the world	70	66
Building the strongest military force in the world	45	47

1984 Rating of the Public Schools

The downward trend in the public's rating of the public schools recorded in these surveys during the last decade has ended. This year, 42% of those interviewed gave an A or B rating to the public schools in their communities, up sharply from 31% in 1983. Not since 1976 have these ratings been so high.

The higher rating given the schools this year may have resulted from two developments. First, the reports of the national commissions that have examined schooling in America have caused widespread debate concerning the quality of public education. Citizens have taken a closer look at their own schools and presumably found them better than they had previously believed. Also, many schools have heeded the criticisms made in the reports and have instituted reforms in their educational programs.

It is noteworthy that parents also give their schools a higher rating this year: 52% A or B, as opposed to 42% in 1983.

The question:

Students are often given the grades A,B,C,D, and FAIL to denote the quality of their work. Suppose the *public* schools themselves, in this community, were graded in the same way. What grade would you give the public schools here — A,B,C,D, or FAIL?

	National Totals %	No Children In School %	Public School Parents %	Nonpublic School Parents %
A rating	10	8	15	4
B rating	32	31	37	33
C rating	35	35	32	42
D rating	11	10	12	16
FAIL	4	5	3	4
Don't know	8	11	1	1

Ratings Given The Local Public Schools	National Totals								
	1984 %	1983 %	1982 %	1981 %	1980 %	1979 %	1978 %	1977 %	1976 %
A rating	10	6	8	9	10	8	9	11	13
B rating	32	25	29	27	25	26	27	26	29
C rating	35	32	33	34	29	30	30	28	28
D rating	11	13	14	13	12	11	11	11	10
FAIL	4	7	5	7	6	7	8	5	6
Don't know	8	17	11	10	18	18	15	19	14

Rating of Teachers in the Local Public Schools

The 1984 survey indicates that the public has increasing respect for the teachers in the local schools. Half of all respondents give teachers an A or B rating. This is considerably higher than the rating given to teachers in the 1981 survey.

The highest ratings go to teachers in small communities — those with a population under 2,500. The lowest ratings go to teachers in the central cities, where the teaching problems are greatest.

Respondents living in the Midwest give their

teachers a slightly higher rating than do citizens living in other areas of the U.S.

The question:

Now, what grade would you give the teachers in the public schools in this community?

	National Totals %	No Children In School %	Public School Parents %	Nonpublic School Parents %
A rating	13	13	15	6
B rating	37	35	43	34
C rating	31	31	29	42
D rating	7	6	8	9
FAIL	3	3	3	1
Don't know	9	12	2	8

NATIONAL TOTALS	1984 %	1981 %
A rating	13	11
B rating	37	28
C rating	31	31
D rating	7	9
FAIL	3	6
Don't know	9	15

Tax Increases to Support The Public Schools

Since the spring of 1983, when the National Commission on Excellence in Education presented its report, a slight increase has been registered in the percentage of citizens who favor a tax increase in situations where the schools say that they need much more money.

The percentage of public school parents who favor such a tax increase has risen from 48% in 1983 to 54% today, while the percentage of those opposed has dropped from 45% to 38%.

Those respondents who have attended college are most in favor of tax increases. When sections of the U.S. are compared, residents of the western states are found to be most in favor of raising taxes to help the schools.

The question:

Suppose the local public schools said they needed much more money. As you feel at this time, would you vote to raise taxes for this purpose, or would you vote against raising taxes for this purpose?

	National Totals %	No Children In School %	Public School Parents %	Nonpublic School Parents %
For raise in taxes	41	37	54	42
Against raise in taxes	47	50	38	51
Don't know	12	13	8	7

Increasing the Length of The School Year

Public sentiment in favor of increasing the length of the school year by one month is growing. In the 1982 survey a total of 37% approved of this plan. In 1983 approval reached 40%, and in the present survey the comparable figure is 44%. However, 50% in this year's survey still oppose this plan.

Those who are most in favor of a longer school year are residents of the cities with populations over one million. Most opposed are people living in smaller cities and in towns of 2,500 and under.

Those who have attended college favor a longer school year by a margin of 51% to 45%. Residents of the western states also approve a longer school year by a margin of 59% to 35%.

The question:

In some nations, students attend school as many as 240 days a year as compared to 180 days in the U.S. How do you feel about extending the public school year in this community by 30 days, making the school year about 210 days or 10 months long? Do you favor or oppose this idea?

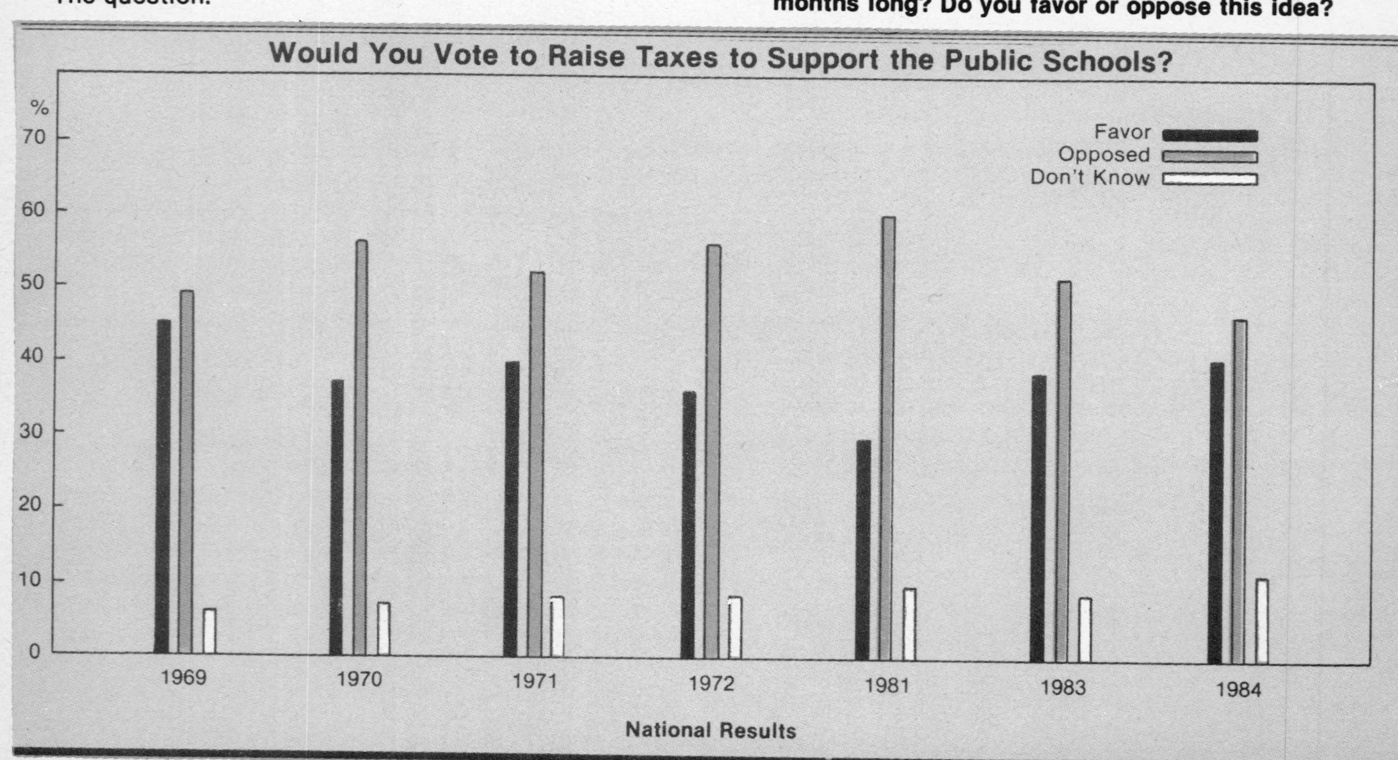

	National Totals %	No Children In School %	Public School Parents %	Nonpublic School Parents %
Favor	44	44	45	46
Oppose	50	49	52	46
No opinion	6	7	3	8

NATIONAL TOTALS	1984 %	1983 %	1982 %
Favor	44	40	37
Oppose	50	49	53
No opinion	6	11	10

Extending the School Day by One Hour

Although this year's survey findings indicate that the public is slightly more in favor of increasing the length of the school day by one hour than in 1982, a majority remain opposed.

Residents of the western states and the largest cities most strongly favor the longer school day. Residents of the Midwest are the most opposed.

The question:

How do you feel about extending the school day in the schools in this community by one hour? Do you favor or oppose this idea?

	National Totals %	No Children In School %	Public School Parents %	Nonpublic School Parents %
Favor	42	42	41	38
Oppose	52	51	56	58
No opinion	6	7	3	4

NATIONAL TOTALS	1984 %	1983 %	1982 %
Favor	42	41	37
Oppose	52	48	55
No opinion	6	11	8

Amount of Schoolwork Required of Elementary and High School Students

All segments of the U.S. population agree that students in elementary schools and high schools are not made to work hard enough in school or on homework. This opinion has remained fairly constant in three surveys, the first in 1975.

Only 5% of those interviewed in this year's survey think that students are made to work too hard in elementary school, and only 4% think students in high school are made to work too hard. By contrast, 59% say that students are not required to work hard enough in elementary school, and 67% say that they are not required to work hard enough in high school.

Perhaps the best judges of whether students are being given enough schoolwork to do in school and at home are the parents of these students. Parents agree that their children are not being required to work hard enough. Only 7% of parents with children now enrolled in the public schools say that children in elementary school are required to work too hard; 54% say that they are not required to work hard enough. In the case of high school students, 5% of parents with children enrolled in public schools say that children are required to work too hard; 62% say that they are not required to work hard enough.

The question:

In general, do you think *elementary* schoolchildren in the public schools here are made to work too hard in school and on homework or not hard enough?

	National Totals %	No Children In School %	Public School Parents %	Nonpublic School Parents %
Too hard	5	5	7	4
Not hard enough	59	60	54	56
About right amount	24	20	34	30
Don't know	12	15	5	10

NATIONAL TOTALS	1984 %	1983 %	1975 %
Too hard	5	4	5
Not hard enough	59	61	49
About right amount	24	19	28
Don't know	12	16	18

The question:

What about students in the public *high schools* here — in general, are they required to work too hard or not hard enough?

	National Totals %	No Children In School %	Public School Parents %	Nonpublic School Parents %
Too hard	4	4	5	–
Not hard enough	67	69	62	69
About right amount	18	15	25	22
Don't know	11	12	8	9

NATIONAL TOTALS	1984 %	1983 %	1975 %
Too hard	4	3	3
Not hard enough	67	65	54
About right amount	18	12	22
Don't know	11	20	21

Subjects the Public Would Require

Mathematics and English head the list of subjects the public would require of high school students who plan to attend college; mathematics was mentioned by 96% of respondents, and English was mentioned by 94%.

In addition, a large majority would require history/U.S. government and science. Slightly fewer, but still a majority, would require courses in business, foreign language, and health education.

For *non*-college-bound students, the public would also require math and English and by virtually the same percentages as for those planning to go to college. Somewhat fewer respondents feel that history and science should be required of non-college-bound students, and far fewer favor a foreign language requirement.

Not surprisingly, a much larger percentage of Americans feel that vocational training should be required for non-college-bound students than for those planning to go to college. Similarly, business as a required course is favored by a slightly larger percentage for non-college-bound students.

Support for computer science as a required course — for both college- and non-college-bound students — has dramatically increased from 43% to 68% in just three years. Although support for a science requirement for non-college-bound students has risen only marginally, support for a science requirement for those planning to go to college has risen from 76% to 84% since 1981. On the other hand, support for a foreign language for college-bound students has made little progress in the past three years.

The questions:

Would you look over this card, which lists high school subjects. If you were the one to decide,

what subjects would you require every public high school student who *plans to go on to college* to take?

What about those public high school students who do *not plan to go to college* when they graduate? Which courses would you require them to take?

	Should Be Required	
	For Those Planning To Go to College	For Those Not Planning to Go To College
	%	%
Mathematics	96	92
English	94	90
History/U.S. government	84	71
Science	84	61
Business	68	76
Foreign language	57	19
Health education	52	50
Physical education	43	44
Vocational training	37	83
Art	24	18
Music	22	18

Special Areas of Instruction That Should Be Required

The public would like the public schools to provide instruction in many aspects of modern life, in addition to the subjects traditionally included in the school curriculum. Heading the list of these special areas of instruction is drug abuse, followed by alcohol abuse. Large majorities of the population would also require instruction in such areas as driver education, computer training, race relations, and the dangers of nuclear waste.

The question:

In addition to regular courses, high schools offer instruction in other areas. As I read off these areas, one at a time, would you tell me whether you feel this instruction should be required or should not be required for all high school students.

	Should Be Required	Should Not Be Required	No Opinion
	%	%	%
Drug abuse	82	15	3
Alcohol abuse	79	18	3
Driver education	73	25	2
Computer training	68	28	4
Race relations	65	29	6
Dangers of nuclear waste	61	34	5
Communism/socialism	57	37	6
Parenting/parent training	55	39	6
Dangers of nuclear war	51	43	6

Importance of Extracurricular Activities

About three-quarters of the U.S. public (77%) feel that extracurricular activities are either "very important" or "fairly important" to a young person's education. At the same time, however, there has been a decline in the percentage of those who say that extracurricular activities are "very important" — from 45% in 1978 to 31% in 1984. During this same period there has been an increase in the percentage of the public who say that extracurricular activities are "not too important" — from 9% to 18%. This decrease in support may reflect, to some extent, the heavy emphasis placed on the academic curriculum by the various national reports on the state of education.

Better-educated Americans are more inclined to feel that extracurricular activities are important. A total of 84% of those who have attended college say that these activities are "very important" or "fairly important," while only 68% of those whose education ended with grade school regard such activities as important.

The question:

I'd like your opinion about extracurricular activities such as the school band, dramatics, sports, and the school paper. How important are these to a young person's education — very important, fairly important, not too important, or not at all important?

	National Totals	No Children In School	Public School Parents	Nonpublic School Parents
	%	%	%	%
Very important	31	31	32	30
Fairly important	46	45	48	52
Not too important	18	18	16	14
Not at all important	4	4	3	3
No opinion	1	2	1	1

National Test for Graduation

The American public shows remarkable unanimity in favoring a standard nationwide test for graduation from high school. Only in communities under 2,500 is sentiment fairly closely divided on this proposal.

This question was first asked of a national cross section of adults in 1958, and the idea was favored at that time by a margin of 50% to 39%. When the same question was asked in 1981, 69% favored the proposal, 26% opposed it, and 5% had no opinion. Roughly the same results were found in this year's survey: 65% in favor, 29% opposed, and 6% with no opinion.

Many nations require students to pass standard examinations for graduation; in the United States, however, because of varying local conditions, such a plan has never been adopted. Nevertheless, the public appears to see merit in such a policy.

The question:

Should all high school students in the United States be required to pass a standard nationwide examination in order to get a high school diploma?

	National Totals	No Children In School	Public School Parents	Nonpublic School Parents
	%	%	%	%
Yes	65	65	65	59
No	29	29	29	35
No opinion	6	6	6	6

Raising College Entrance Requirements

Many educators have argued that raising the entrance requirements of colleges and universities would be an effective way of inducing the public schools to raise their standards. However, this proposal fails to win the approval of the public.

Analysis of the opinions of various groups in the population reveals that all major groups oppose this suggestion, especially those most concerned: parents of children now attending elementary or high school. Even those who have attended college vote against the idea.

The question:

Do you feel that four-year colleges and universities should raise their entrance requirements or not?

	National Totals %	No Children In School %	Public School Parents %	Nonpublic School Parents %
Yes	27	28	24	21
No	59	57	64	61
No opinion	14	15	12	18

State Board Examinations for Teachers

Survey findings reveal widespread agreement that prospective teachers should be required to pass state board examinations to prove their knowledge in the subjects they plan to teach.

More than eight in every 10 respondents have favored this policy in the three surveys in which this same question has been asked: 1979, 1981, and 1984.

The question:

In addition to meeting college requirements for a teacher's certificate, should those who want to become teachers also be required to pass a state board examination to prove their knowledge in the subjects they will teach before they are hired?

	National Totals %	No Children In School %	Public School Parents %	Nonpublic School Parents %
Yes	89	89	89	92
No	7	7	8	7
No opinion	4	4	3	1

NATIONAL TOTALS	1984 %	1981 %	1979 %
Yes	89	84	85
No	7	11	9
No opinion	4	5	6

Career Ladder for Teachers

The proposal to adopt a career ladder for public school teachers that is grounded in classroom effectiveness, with accompanying salary increases, is favored by a substantial majority (75%) of the public. In fact, by approximately the same percentages, all segments of the population agree that this is a good plan.

The question:

It has been suggested that public schools adopt a career ladder for teachers, based primarily upon demonstrated effectiveness in the classroom, with salaries increasing accordingly. Would you approve or disapprove if such a plan were adopted by the public schools in this community?

	National Totals %	No Children In School %	Public School Parents %	Nonpublic School Parents %
Approve	75	74	77	79
Disapprove	16	16	16	16
No opinion	9	10	7	5

Attitudes Toward Merit Pay Programs

Although the issue of merit pay for teachers seems to have provoked a great deal of discussion recently, when this survey was conducted only half of those interviewed said that they had heard or read anything about such programs.

When those who said that they were aware of merit pay proposals were asked whether they generally favored or opposed the idea, three-fourths (76%) said that they approved of it, 19% were opposed, and 5% had no opinion. For the total sample, the percentage who approve of the idea of merit pay is 65%, with 22% opposed and 13% having no opinion.

In 1970 and again in 1983 a merit pay question was asked in this form: "Should each teacher be paid on the basis of the quality of his or her work, or should all teachers be paid on a standard-scale basis?" In 1970, 58% said that teachers should be paid according to "quality of work," 36% on a "standard scale," and 6% said "don't know." Comparable figures for 1983 were 61%, 31%, and 8%.

How do you, yourself, feel about the idea of merit pay for teachers? In general, do you favor or oppose it?

Total Sample	National Totals %	No Children In School %	Public School Parents %	Nonpublic School Parents %
Favor	65	63	69	75
Oppose	22	23	20	14
No opinion	13	14	11	11

Criteria to Be Used in Awarding Merit Pay

One of the greatest hurdles facing merit pay is the difficulty of agreeing on the criteria to be used in deciding which teachers should receive extra pay. A list of possible criteria was compiled. To determine which criteria are most acceptable to the public, respondents were asked in the case of each criterion whether they thought it should or should not be used to decide which teachers should be given additional pay.

Seven criteria are listed below in order of their acceptability to the public. Improvement achieved by students as measured by standardized tests is rated highest. Virtually the same rating is given to the evaluations of administrators. Gaining almost the same high approval is an advanced degree, such as the master's or Ph.D. Evaluation by other teachers, length of teaching experience, students' evaluations, and parents' opinions have support, but not majority support.

The question:

This card lists possible criteria for giving additional pay to teachers for special merit. As I read off each one by letter, please tell me if you think it should or should not be used to determine which teachers should receive merit pay.

	Should Be Criterion %	Should Not Be Criterion %	No Opinion %
Academic achievement or improvement of students (as measured by standardized tests)	68	25	7
Administrators' evaluations	67	26	7
An advanced degree, such as a master's or Ph.D.	66	27	7
Evaluation by other teachers in the system	48	42	10
Length of teaching experience	48	47	5
Students' evaluations	45	47	8
Parents' opinions	36	55	9

Teaching as a Career

Although teaching as a career has lost favor steadily during the last 15 years, the results from this year's survey indicate that the downward trend may have ended. In 1969, 75% of parents said that they would like to see one of their children enter public school teaching as a career. In 1983 only 45% said this.

In the 1984 survey, the question differed from that asked in 1969 and 1983, which dealt with "a child of yours." The question this year asked respondents first if they would like a daughter to take up teaching as a career; the same question was then asked about a son.

Fully 50% of those interviewed said that they would like a daughter of theirs to take up teaching in the public schools as a career. Slightly fewer (46%) said that they would like a son of theirs to make a career of teaching.

The question:

Would you like to have a *daughter* of yours take up teaching in the public schools as a career?

	National Totals %	No Children In School %	Public School Parents %	Nonpublic School Parents %
Yes	50	49	54	46
No	39	40	34	35
No opinion	11	11	12	19

The question:

Would you like to have a *son* of yours take up teaching in the public schools as a career?

	National Totals %	No Children In School %	Public School Parents %	Nonpublic School Parents %
Yes	46	45	51	41
No	42	43	37	40
No opinion	12	12	12	19

	Daughter		Son	
NATIONAL TOTALS	1984 %	1981 %	1984 %	1981 %
Yes	50	46	46	43
No	39	44	42	47
Don't know	11	10	12	10

Prayer in the Public Schools

Prayer in the public schools is an issue that has been hotly debated in recent years. A majority of those interviewed in this year's survey favor a constitutional amendment that would allow school prayer. However, the least support for such an amendment is found among the best-educated citizens and among the youngest adult age group — and these two groups will

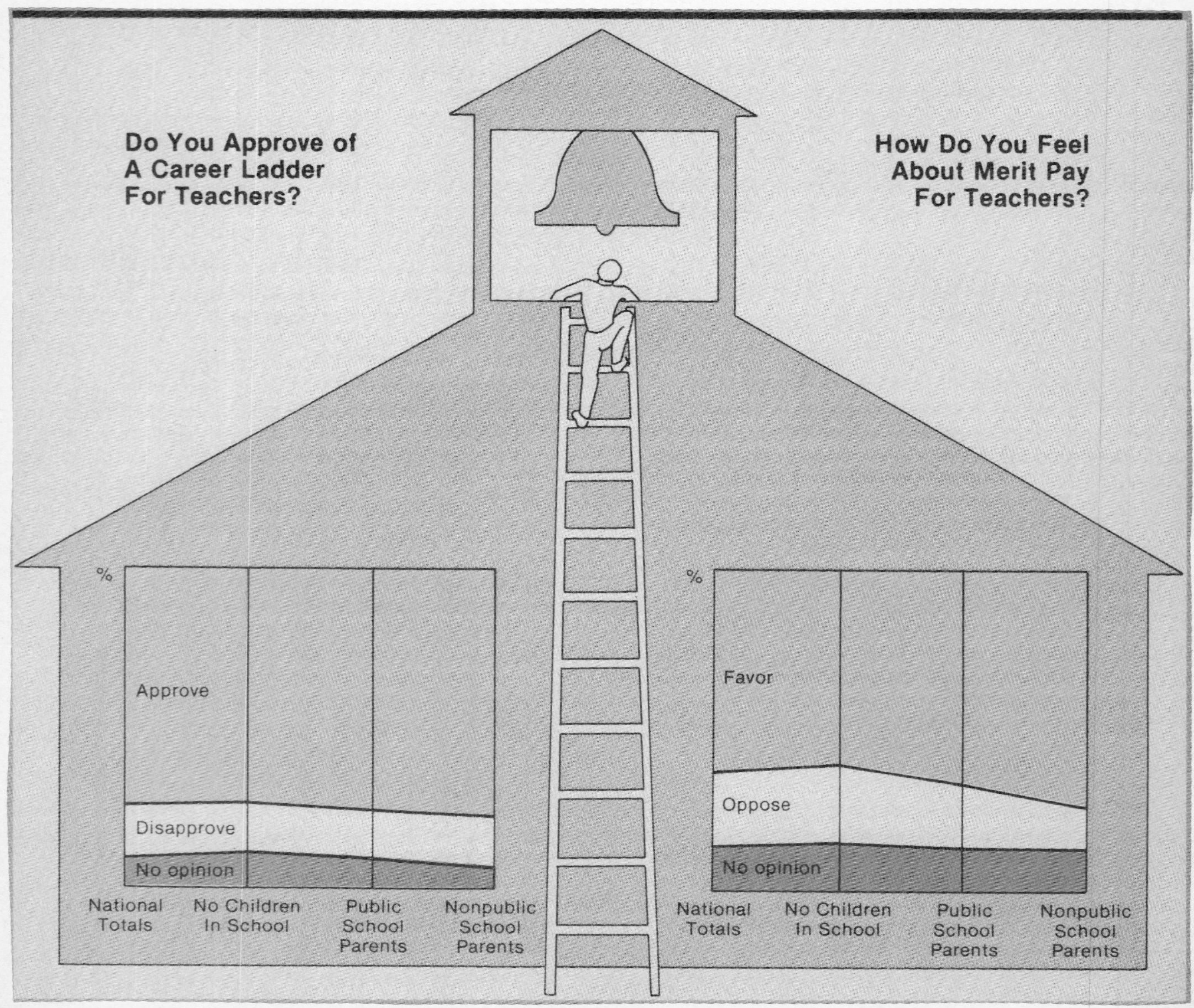

play the greatest role in determining future trends in public attitudes.

The question:

Have you heard or read about a proposed Amendment to the U.S. Constitution that would allow prayer in the public schools?

	National Totals %	No Children In School %	Public School Parents %	Nonpublic School Parents %
Yes	93	93	95	93
No	6	7	4	7
Not sure	1	*	1	-

*Less than one-half of 1%.

The question:

Do you favor or oppose this proposed Amendment?

Those Aware of Amendment	National Totals %	No Children In School %	Public School Parents %	Nonpublic School Parents %
Favor	69	68	73	68
Oppose	24	25	21	21
Don't know	7	7	6	11

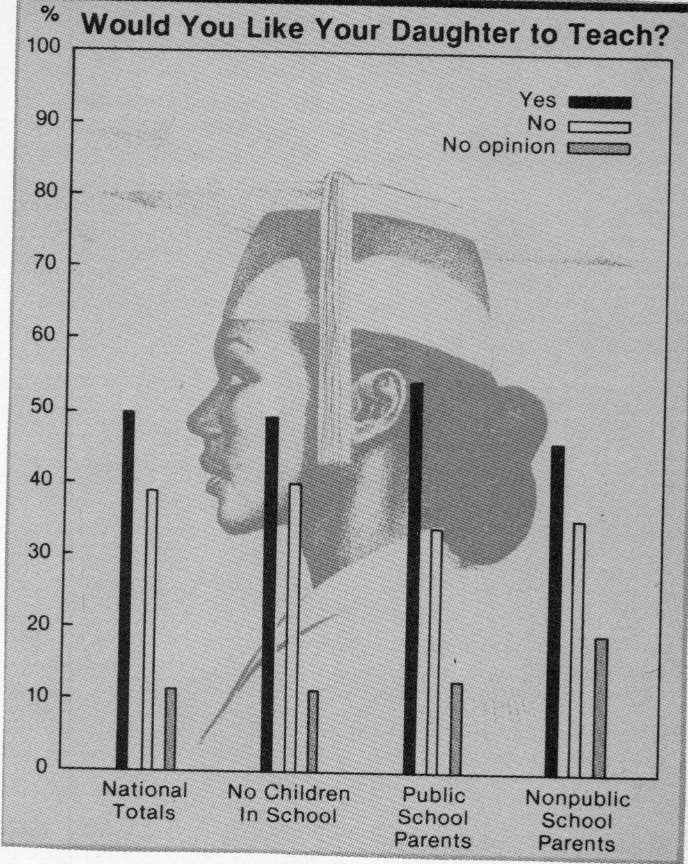

PERENNIAL ISSUES

Major Problems Confronting the Public Schools in 1984

Although discipline continues to be cited most frequently by respondents as the top problem with which their local schools must contend, parents who now have children enrolled in the public schools mention this problem significantly less often than in 1983.

In the 1983 survey, 29% of the parents interviewed named "discipline" as the biggest problem of their schools; 23% mentioned discipline in this year's survey. Since parents of children now in school are likely to be best informed about discipline, their views must be given special credence.

The top five problems found in the 1983 study are also the top five problems cited in 1984. Next to discipline, "use of drugs" and "poor curriculum/poor standards" are mentioned most often. Tied for fourth place are "lack of proper financial support" and "difficulty getting good teachers."

The question:

What do you think are the biggest problems with which the *public* schools in this community must deal?

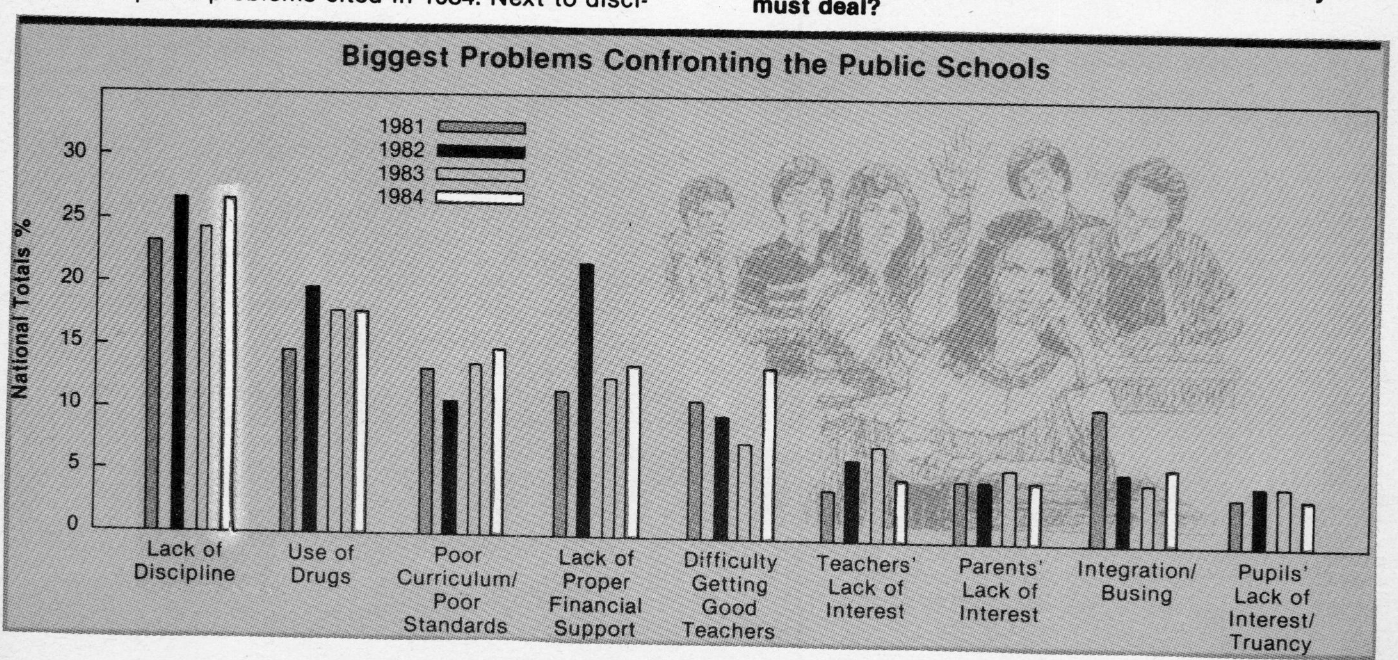

1. PERCEPTIONS OF EDUCATION

	National Totals %	No Children In School %	Public School Parents %	Nonpublic School Parents %
Lack of discipline	27	28	23	36
Use of drugs	18	18	20	10
Poor curriculum/poor standards	15	16	14	18
Lack of proper financial support	14	12	17	13
Difficulty getting good teachers	14	13	15	13
Integration/busing	6	.7	3	4
Teachers' lack of interest	5	4	6	7
Parents' lack of interest	5	5	6	7
Low teacher salaries	4	3	6	5
Pupils' lack of interest/truancy	4	4	4	4
Drinking/alcoholism	4	3	5	5
Large schools/over-crowding	4	3	4	8
Lack of respect for teachers/other students	3	3	4	2
Problems with adminis-tration	3	3	2	4
Crime/vandalism	3	3	2	2
Mismanagement of funds	2	1	2	5
Lack of proper facilities	2	2	1	1
Moral standards	1	1	2	2
Teachers' strikes	1	1	1	2
Communication prob-lems	1	1	2	1
Parental involvement with school activities	1	*	1	1
Lack of needed teachers	1	1	1	–
Fighting	1	*	2	–
Government interference	1	1	1	1
There are no problems	1	1	2	1
Miscellaneous	4	4	5	7
Don't know/no answer	10	12	4	5

(Figures add to more than 100% because of multiple answers.)
*Less than one-half of 1%.

The Public's Perceptions About Discipline

One way to measure attitudes regarding discipline is to ask respondents how serious a problem discipline is in their schools. Not surprisingly, those most closely connected with schools — the parents of students — hold different views from non-parents about discipline and about many other problems with which the local schools must deal. Thus 29% of parents with children enrolled in the public schools say that the discipline problem is "very serious." In answer to the same question, 36% of those who have no children in the public schools say that the discipline problem is "very serious."

The question:

How serious a problem would you say discipline is in the public schools in this community — very serious, fairly serious, not too serious, or not at all serious?

	National Totals %	No Children In School %	Public School Parents %	Nonpublic School Parents %
Very serious	34	36	29	32
Fairly serious	34	34	35	38
Not too serious	22	18	29	25
Not at all serious	4	3	6	3
No opinion	6	9	1	2

As I read off the following problems by letter, would you tell me how often you think each problem occurs in the public schools in this community — just your impression?

NATIONAL TOTALS	Most of the Time or Fairly Often %	Not Very Often or Almost Never/Never %	Don't Know %
Schoolwork and homework assignments not completed	64	23	13
Behavior that disrupts class	60	29	11
Skipping classes	56	31	13
Talking back to/disobeying teachers	56	32	12
Truancy/being absent from school	53	36	11
Use of drugs at school	53	33	14
Selling of drugs at school	47	37	16
Sloppy or inappropriate dress	47	42	11
Cheating on tests	46	38	16
Vandalizing of school property	39	49	12
Stealing money or personal property belonging to other students, teachers, or staff	38	46	16
Drinking alcoholic beverages at school	35	50	15
Theft of school property	34	51	15
Carrying of knives, firearms, or other weapons at school	29	55	16
Sexual activity at school	24	57	19
Racial fights between whites, blacks, Hispanics, or other minorities	22	64	14
Taking money or property by force, using weapons or threats	18	66	16
Physical attacks on teachers or staff	15	71	14

The Goals of Education

The goals of education are difficult to separate from the goals of life. It is equally difficult to separate the responsibility of the schools for reaching these goals from that of other institutions in American life.

Nevertheless, this year's survey attempted to obtain some evidence of how the public rates the importance of many suggested goals. The ratings given to the goals listed reveal a pragmatic people who view education primarily as a means to economic success rather than to intellectual development. Near the bottom of the list is the goal of appreciation of the arts and letters, learning as a lifetime program, and participation in the democratic process.

The goals are listed below on the basis of the number of respondents who gave a "10" (the highest rating) to the goal in question.

The question:

I am going to read a list of possible goals of education. I would like you to rate the importance of each goal on a scale of zero to 10. A zero means a goal is not at all important and should not be part of the public school program. A 10 means a goal is the most important goal — before all others. A rating between zero and 10 means you consider the goal to be somewhere in between in importance.

	Highest Rating			
	National Totals %	No Children In School %	Public School Parents %	Nonpublic School Parents %
To develop the ability to speak and write correctly	68	65	74	71
To develop standards of what is "right" and "wrong"	64	63	68	61

	Highest Rating			
	National Totals %	No Children In School %	Public School Parents %	Nonpublic School Parents %
To develop an understanding about different kinds of jobs and careers, including their requirements and rewards	56	54	60	54
To develop skills needed to get jobs for those not planning to go to college	54	52	59	61
To develop the ability to use mathematics for everyday problems	54	52	56	60
To encourage respect for law and order, for obeying the rules of society	52	52	54	53
To help students make realistic plans for what they will do after high school graduation	52	50	56	43
To develop the ability to live in a complex and changing world	51	50	57	42
To develop the desire to excel	51	49	56	51
To develop the ability to think — creatively, objectively, analytically	51	49	55	58
To help develop good work habits, the ability to organize one's thoughts, the ability to concentrate	48	46	52	42
To prepare for college those who plan to attend college	46	43	53	57
To develop the ability to deal with adult responsibilities and problems, i.e., sex, marriage, parenting, personal finances, alcohol and drug abuse	46	44	49	43
To gain an understanding of science and technology	45	43	50	51
To help students get good/high-paying jobs	45	43	51	43
To help students overcome personal problems	45	42	51	45
To develop the ability to understand and use computers	43	41	47	51
To develop the ability to get along with different kinds of people	42	42	43	40

	Highest Rating			
	National Totals %	No Children In School %	Public School Parents %	Nonpublic School Parents %
To gain knowledge about the world of today and yesterday (history, geography, civics)	42	40	46	39
To encourage the desire to continue learning throughout one's life	41	40	45	39
To develop respect for and understanding of other races, religions, nations, and cultures	39	39	39	39
To develop an appreciation for and participation in the arts, music, literature, theater, etc.	35	33	39	37
To develop an understanding of democracy and to promote participation in the political process	33	32	35	32
To develop an appreciation of the "good" things in life	32	33	32	24
To promote physical development through sports programs	20	19	23	19

Who Should Determine the Curriculum?

If the public were given the right to decide who should have the greatest influence in deciding what is taught in the public schools, the top choices would be the local school board and parents; the public would give the state government and the federal government relatively little say in this matter.

This view is in sharp contrast to the policies followed in most nations, where the national government typically sets the curriculum.

The question:

In your opinion, who should have the *greatest* influence in deciding what is taught in the public schools here — the federal government, the state government, the local school board, local public school teachers, or parents of public school children?

	National Totals %	No Children In School %	Public School Parents %	Nonpublic School Parents %
Local school board	27	29	25	29
Parents	24	22	30	23
State government	17	18	14	16
Teachers	11	11	11	12
Federal government	9	9	9	4
Don't know	12	11	11	16

Continuity and Change in American Education

The qualitative reconstruction of American education has been a recurrent theme since the late nineteenth century. The search for effective alternative educational choices and for changes in the manner of helping students learn is not a new one; it is as intense a search today, late in the twentieth century, as it was in the first two decades of this century. In the late 1960s and early 1970s the search for and development of alternative schools and alternative methods of educating persons dominated the literature in education. Today the striking advances in computer-assisted learning and the continuing search for modes of cooperation between school systems and their respective publics are forging a generation of alternative approaches to learning both in and out of schools.

There is a continuing search for a resolution of the problem of how to preserve the best and noblest of our traditions in education on the one hand, and how to create effective learning alternatives which serve the interests of those who desire or need alternative learning opportunities on the other. The resolution of this problem is complicated by the great diversity of popular needs and interests to be served in the nation's schools. The rate of technological change in society has generated enormous changes in many schools. It is amazing to witness the ever expanding availability of more and more advanced computer software products designed to help people learn everything from the 3Rs to advanced mathematical and statistical problem solving. Technology for learning which was not even imagined by the great educational theorists of the early twentieth century are now available to schools and homes. As in the past it is the poor and disadvantaged who often have the least access to these changes. However, as the nation's public schools expand the availability of advanced learning technology in the schools, it will be possible to expose all children to these new modes of learning.

Another concern among many educators and students of the teaching-learning process involves the legitimacy of the recommendations of "outside experts." Teachers are asked to instruct students at several different ability levels, learn how to use computer software, and create different ways to teach vocational skills in order to "link" schools and the industrial sector of society.

The articles in this section reflect all of the above concerns. Herbert Kohl takes a very skeptical look at the many recent criticisms of the schools and at recent commission reports. He points out that educational reform will ultimately be achieved if the teaching profession is well informed and takes a leadership role in reform efforts.

Gilbert Sewall's essay explores some of the developments in vocational education in recent years. He cites several innovations in educational programs for persons seeking specific vocational skills.

Joel Spring recommends that government stop recommending changes in school curricula simply as an antidote to political and economic needs. He, like Herbert Kohl, raises the issue that many recently recommended curricular changes ignore the agenda for social equity in educational opportunity established in the 1960s and 1970s. Spring believes that business interests exercise too much influence over curricular priorities. Some conservatives might respond by saying that economic needs must be met if social needs are to be met and schooling is a bridge from the dependence of childhood and early adolescence to the independence of adulthood. The schools are the only institutions capable of preparing the masses of American youth for survival in a technologically advanced social order. Soviet schools reflect Soviet economic and political needs as much as American schools reflect America's economic needs.

The essay on the use of computers in enhancing learning opportunities describes how computers can integrate advanced technology with the instructional process.

Finally, the essays on bilingual education and the home schooling movement emphasize the importance of freedom of choice to pursue alternative ways of learning. There are many issues surrounding both these movements. The advocates of bilingual/multicultural

Unit 2

education emphasize the rights of children of linguistic minorities to be able to learn English as well as the language of their parents. The home schooling movement is a continuing alternative effort to focus attention on a major alternative educational model. Proponents seek acceptance of their efforts and cooperation from local and state educational agencies.

The articles in this unit deal with the relationship between political and economic changes in society and change or continuity in schools. There is no consensus on either the aims of education or the issue of change. Education's best traditions are intact. We are now, however, seeking ways to broaden the educational alternatives of persons in a swiftly changing "high tech" society.

Looking Ahead: Challenge Questions

To what extent can schools be restructured to most effectively emphasize academic achievement as well as intangible but important factors such as the development of character?

What do you make of this new generation of educational reformers? What social values or socioeconomic interests do their recommendations reflect? How can academic quality and equality of educational opportunity be best enhanced?

What are the major issues in vocational education today?

Are there more political and economic pressures on educators than they can be reasonably expected to manage? Is this sort of pressure avoidable? If so, how? If not, why not?

What have you learned about the use of computers in shaping educational alternatives?

What social conditions in the United States brought multicultural and bilingual education into the nation's schools?

Should parents have the right to educate their children at home? What are the advantages or disadvantages to having children educated informally in the home and community?

WHO ARE THESE EDUCATIONAL "EXPERTS" . . . AND WHAT ARE THEY REALLY UP TO?

All the munificently funded studies in the world won't change our schools. But change must occur—before the schools fall apart or are torn apart.

HERBERT KOHL

Herbert Kohl is a special assignments editor for Learning, *a teacher and the author of many books about education.*

There was hardly a mention of racism or poverty, or of the unequal treatment of males and females in the schools.

In 1957 James Bryant Conant, former ambassador to Germany and president of Harvard University, received, in Conant's own words, a "generous grant" from the Carnegie Corporation of New York to study the condition of public schooling and teacher training in the United States. The study was initiated partly as a result of the post-Sputnik hysteria about the United States falling behind the USSR in science and technology. No matter that the rhetoric of our being "behind" the Soviets was backed up by no more substantial evidence then than it is now. It was easy to blame the schools for the nation's failure, and in so doing, to mobilize university, foundation and corporate support to make the development of a scientific and technological elite a major priority of public education.

Conant's study, although focused on math and science, did not slight the arts and the value of a broad liberal arts education. His recommendations placed an emphasis on what has come to be called inquiry learning as opposed to rigid drill and practice, showing an understanding that mechanical learning is not conducive to scientific creativity. Conant also called for teacher specialization in the secondary schools, with an integrated curriculum in the primary schools, where thinking skills as well as the so-called basics would be taught. Conant wanted skilled humanitarians in the early grades, and in the secondary schools he wanted specialist teachers who were knowledgeable about technical developments in contemporary science or who were qualified to teach college writing. In 1963, Conant wrote that it would be ideal to end up with high school teachers who taught only their specialties—no generalists. He recommended making the high school a scaled-down version of college.

It's hard to deny the attractiveness of many of Conant's suggestions. And yet, despite the strength of his thoughts on science and math, and his proposals for the development of creative sensitivity, his sentiments overlooked entirely social and economic considerations. There was hardly a mention of racism or poverty, or of the unequal treatment of males and females in the schools. Nor was much regard shown for teachers, nor trust in parents to make decisions for themselves about their children's education. Conant's recommendations emerged not from an understanding of the lives and work of children, parents and teachers, but from professors' rarefied views of what these ought to be.

This elitist view of education, coming, as it did, from outside the elementary and secondary systems, virtually guaranteed that the Carnegie study and its recommendations would receive no support from either teachers or parents. Although for a brief time American schools and the American public did in fact mobilize for educational change, it is clear that the impetus came not from the Carnegie study but from the specter of the Soviets dominating outer space. When the specter faded, so did the zeal for reform.

Educational Psychologists, Not Reformers

In the mid-1960s, John I. Goodlad, one of Conant's collaborators on the Carnegie study, did a follow-up study of the effect of the implementation of Conant's recommendations in the public schools. Goodlad and his colleagues studied 260 kindergarten to third grade classes. They summarized their findings by saying that "on a general and impressionistic level, teachers and students did not appear to be intensely interested in their work." Inquiry learning, creativity in the arts, and an early start on developing thinking skills simply were not happening, Goodlad observed. "As far as our sample of schools is concerned, we are forced to conclude that much of the so-called educational reform movement has been blunted on the classroom door."

But the Carnegie Corporation is tenacious. In the late '60s, it offered a grant to Charles Silberman, a former editor of *Fortune* magazine, to study conditions in the public schools and to make recommendations. Silberman published his findings in the widely read *Crisis in the*

Reprinted by special permission of *LEARNING*, The Magazine for Creative Teaching, January 1984, pp. 26-29. ©1984 by Pitman Learning, Inc., 19 Davis Drive, Belmont, CA 94002.

Classroom (Random House, 1970), in which he talked about the "mindlessness" he saw in teachers and administrators throughout the country, and in which he called for major structural and curricular changes, many of them similar to those suggested by Conant.

It is interesting that all three of these "educational psychologists," as I call them—Conant, Goodlad and Silberman—considered themselves reformers. And yet none of them was part of the open education or the free school movement. They were not concerned with changing the economic or social structure of this society and were not part of the major movements for change of the '60s and '70s. They were in-house reformers, more concerned with keeping up with the Soviets and developing academic and technological elitism than with social and economic justice, which was central to the work of the so-called radical reformers. They were never partisans in the struggle to make education more responsive to the needs of children and to the ideals of democracy.

The people called upon to study the schools and recommend changes came not from within the schools, from across the hall; they were distinctly unlike Herndon, Holt, Dennison, Kozol et al.—those who had considerable school experience and who had not moved to some secure place outside of public education. They came instead from the foundation, university and corporate world and saw their role as making analyses and suggestions based on objective, even scientific, data. It was not part of their role to implement their suggestions. They did not have to, as Goodlad might put it, blunt their ideas on the classroom door. They stayed away from attempting to influence the classroom altogether. If anything blunted their ideas and made their books—despite how widely read they might have been—ineffectual, it was the fact that they had no direct relationship with the people whose lives are most affected by public education: ordinary parents, children and working teachers.

Another Study, Another Dead End

Now, more than 20 years after the Conant report was issued, comes yet another study of the public schools, this one directed by Goodlad and given generous support by a multitude of foundations and government organizations, among them the Ford Foundation, the Rockefeller Foundation and the U.S. Office of Education. To implement it, Goodlad and his collaborators marshaled a professional staff of 30 researchers, 13 research assistants, 12 support people and 7 site coordinators. They commissioned 3 books, 9 data compilations (which, according to Goodlad, are "too massive for general distribution") and 35 technical reports that bear such titles as "The Contextual Correlates of the Relative Expenditures of Classroom Time on Instruction and Behavior" and "An Inter-Observer Reliability Study of the S.R.I. Observation System as Modified for Use in a Study of Schooling."

The results of all this scurrying around and data collecting are summarized in Goodlad's new book, *A Place Called School: Prospects for the Future* (McGraw-Hill, 1983), which also puts forth suggestions drawn from the researchers' observations. Reading through the book was a déjà vu experience for me: I had been there before, had heard about the few good schools and about the boredom, the lack of creativity, the scientific ineptness and the mechanical learning characteristic of most schools. There was nothing new here.

Yet Goodlad's indictment, however worn, is not malicious. His touch is light and kind. He does not call anyone bad or evil, does not reproach any particular aspect of the public school system. No one should be angry; rather, we should all work together to make the schools "better places" and take the well-intentioned and beneficent advice of the academicians and do what is good for us, teachers and parents.

There is no arguing with much of Goodlad's advice, for it is sensible and should be quite familiar to us by now. Schools should be smaller, with 100 to 200 students and a core of teachers. Decisions should be made on a local level, decentralization should be encouraged, and parents' advice sought as much as possible. Junior high schools should be eliminated and the schools divided into four-year clusters, with a primary school, a middle school and an upper school. Curriculum should be integrated in the lower grades, specialized and modernized in the upper grades. Teacher aides and computers should be responsible for most of the mechanical and rote learning and record keeping, freeing teachers to focus on the complex, interactive task of teaching. Thinking and creativity should be emphasized.

All of these changes (the interim ones are spelled out in a chapter called "Improving the Schools We Have," and the larger-scale ones—such as involving the community and businesses in education—are enumerated in the last chapter, "Beyond the Schools We Have") add up to a series of permutations and combinations of educational ideas that have been with us as long as there has been concern about making the schools work in a liberal democracy. They have their antecedents in the work of all those who have believed in quality and equality of educational experiences. In Goodlad's incarnation, however, the ideas are presented without the force of Dewey's early work or the passion of Kozol's current work. Bad schools are not translated into the pain of children who must attend them, or of teachers who feel compelled to teach in them, much less into the despair of parents who see no means of change short of starting all over again with the task of providing quality education for all the children of all the people. When recommendations for change are couched in the terms of overfunded, pseudoscientific data collections, they sound the hollow, sad admission that the academicians cannot change the schools but can only make informed suggestions.

Who *Can* Change the Schools?

After more than 20 years in the business of trying to change the schools, I understand that the barriers to sensible reform are not educational. I also understand that the relationship between data collecting and suggestions for change is tentative at best. In this respect, Goodlad's work is at least instructional. After sorting out thousands of bits of information and performing dozens of multivariant analyses, Goodlad and his colleagues reach the same point of transition between diagnosis and prescription as those of us who have been teaching for some years. Their suggestions, too, come out of their moral, social and political values and from their desire to improve the future lives of children. The data are not the source of their recommendations, for the simple reason that data do not provide answers; they merely justify the ideas people already had when they began data collecting.

The Goodlad report raises several key questions: Why continue to study the schools when there is no reason to believe that the conclusions of such studies will lead to change? What is the point of employing large numbers of people to surround teachers with observation tests and assessments if the teachers themselves are neither fundamentally involved nor interested in creating excellent schools in collaboration with their students and the parents and the members of the community they work in? And finally, why give more credibility to the values of researchers than to those of other people with informed opinions about the schools, such as teachers, students, parents and community members? Academic credentials and statistical studies do not validate beliefs or ideals.

If, as I am suggesting, most questions of educational reform are matters of working to change the current social, political, moral and economic values of the schools, what then is the role of the educational psychologist or the professional analyst of the schools? To provide data, perhaps, but to whom and with whose support? Educational psychologists are like professional pollsters: they are paid to gather information; they are not paid to formulate opinions. But they have confused their role, and because they are not partisans, they make their suggestions, take the money and run.

Should education be sold on the free market or perhaps subcontracted out to the Japanese or others noted for their high-quality products?

Who, then, is in a position to reform the schools, granting that they can be reformed at all? (The questions have been raised: Should we even bother to reform the schools, or should vouchers or other forms of educational choice occupy the efforts of those concerned about a democratic future for children? Should education be sold on the free market or perhaps subcontracted out to the Japanese or other people noted for the high quality of their products? Such questions may sound irrational, but they are not uncommon fantasies among people who have to send their children to public schools or among teachers who try to teach well under repressive administrators.) In fact, we must all become partisans of school reform, whether we come from the world of foundations and corporations, from communities, or from within the teaching profession. And it is not just the schools that are in need of reform, because the very ideas of decency and justice have been undermined in the current social, political and educational climate.

Especially as teachers, we must organize against the complacency and educational conservatism of our current leadership. We must take our case directly to teacher and administrative organizations and make it clear just how close the public schools are to falling apart or being torn apart. When militancy is manifested in striking for higher salaries, rather than in struggling to work harder and better, we lose respect for our profession and end up with organizations that use their strength to bully the public and protect incompetent workers.

The tension that exists between the public and school authorities, and that leads corporations and foundations to study public education in the first place, cannot go unresolved much longer. If public education is to survive, teachers must take a long, hard, critical look at their work and not leave it to educational psychologists or to angry parents to be the vehicles of reform (or perhaps destruction) of the public school system as we now know it.

I've said this many times before, and now I feel a need to shout it: Teachers must become the leaders in making the schools decent, creative, enriching places for children to learn. We should not have to be told how to do our work by academicians or politicians. We have to become the experts, the leaders, the advocates of children, and the respected employees of the communities we serve.

The choice placed before teachers these days seems clear: Teach well or don't teach at all. Put energy, effort and love into the work, or expect to discover one day that there's no job. Teacher power will survive only if we can demonstrate to the community that children are receiving powerful teaching.

VOCATIONAL EDUCATION THAT WORKS

THE IDEA EXERTS talismanic force, reaching deep into national folklore. Vocational education has long pledged to supply a steady stream of trained labor, wake up all those kids dozing off on geography or Chaucer, and even—through courses in cooking and consumer education—create happy homes. These are appealing claims, but are they valid? Many high school auto shops and sewing classes have in fact become crucibles of illiteracy, fake diplomas, and chronic unemployment for their poorly prepared graduates. They are a powerful current in what the National Commission on Excellence in Education called last April "a rising tide of mediocrity" in America's public schools.

GILBERT T. SEWALL

Gilbert T. Sewall taught history and economics at Phillips Academy and was education editor of Newsweek. *His book* Necessary Lessons: Decline and Renewal in American Schools *was published in November, 1984.*

Without ample mental furniture, today's 18-year-olds forfeit their chance for fat paychecks and interesting work. As never before, complex equipment, baffling technical manuals, and work with numbers drive the everyday lives of industrial and office workers. Solid foundations in language, mathematics, and science are basic to getting and holding these jobs.

In a time of swift change and global competition, cerebral skills seem an imperative resource for the country too. "Academic discipline should not be reserved for the privileged few," says Honeywell Chairman Edson W. Spencer, 57, a trustee of the Ford Foundation and former Rhodes Scholar. "We must pay as much attention to education in other countries as to our own." Like other leaders of high-tech companies, he worries that foreign competitors, notably Japan, get some of their edge because their workers are better educated.

Thoughtful critics such as Spencer aren't suggesting that "hands-on" vocational education be abolished. They urge instead drastic reform of the worst of the system—which happens to be most of it—the part of the system found in general-purpose public high schools. Courses bearing titles like "My Future Home" may seem harmless pap for marginal students. But do-nothing courses also attract perfectly bright students low on ambition. They distract both students and faculty from worthwhile pursuits. Good vocational education requires costly equipment, expensive teachers, and rigorous standards. Most public high schools are short on all these qualities, and several recent studies have suggested that they should severely curtail their programs.

The vocational education system comprises a bewildering array of programs and objectives, born and expanded haphazardly over the last 100 years. It reflects a series of state and federal goals: first to stamp out the scourge of child labor and supplant the factory apprentice system, then to fight unemployment and poverty. During the 1960s and 1970s social engineers enlisted vocational education to counteract juvenile alienation, train the disabled, and obliterate sex bias in the classroom and workplace. They

From *Fortune,* September 19, 1983, pp. 68-69, 71, 75, 78. ©1983 Time Inc. All rights reserved.

By training *in Ella T. Grasso-Southeastern's kitchens, students hope to become dietitians, chefs, bakers, butchers, or caterers in the rapidly expanding food-services industry.*

didn't accomplish all these noble aims, of course, though thousands of teenage boys learned to sew while the girls hammered away in shop.

Through the far-flung empire of vocational ed, which costs taxpayers an estimated $6.7 billion a year, glaring contrasts abound. Some 19,300 high schools, career centers, technical institutes, and community colleges of widely differing quality enroll some 17 million students in hundreds of different vocational programs. The courses range from horse production and plumbing to radiology and computer systems repair.

In Bishop, California, a clutch of high school hot-rodders loiters outside auto shop, marking time until the end of the school day. Spending effort that might be put to better use on their families' farms, a horticulture class near Joliet, Illinois, grades a cornfield to make a golf course. From Seattle to Miami, students dutifully pull down their dark Plexiglas hoods and turn on their welding torches—though for all but the most specialized tasks robots are taking over this job in U.S. factories. Welding courses vary so radically in quality, concluded Charles S. Benson and E. Gareth Hoachlander in a 1981 report to the National Institute of Education, that they "share nothing in common except the same six-digit Office of Education code."

The gravest problems lie in the general-purpose high schools that most parents know best. In 1980-81 about 10.5 million of 14 million public secondary students took at least one vocational course—and far too many of the courses were drivel. In Brainerd, Minnesota, for instance, students can choose from dozens of vocational electives that include Advanced Clothing III, Creative Foods, and Car Services/Maintenance—a menu that one state education official terms "typical" of high school offerings.

Even if all-purpose high schools did take job training seriously, they probably could not succeed. Few secondary vocational budgets can stand the expense of high-quality, up-to-date industrial and clerical equipment. As a result, thousands of high school shops, filled with antiquated drill presses and rusting lathes, resemble industrial museums. At a time when word-processing equipment is transforming office work, some 16-year-olds still peck at manual typewriters. Outmoded courses clutter the curriculum. "Trying to get students a job in cabinetmaking after they graduate is nearly impossible," says Roger C. Claar, director of the Wilco Area Career Center near Joliet. "But there is tradition, plus a lot of parents who think their kids need wood shop. So the white elephants remain."

WILCO REPRESENTS the next step up the ladder from the public high schools. It is one of about 1,400 U.S. "career centers," a rage among vocational planners during the 1970s. The idea was that, through a pooling arrangement, several high schools could share equipment and thus offer programs beyond any single school's capacity. Like "magnet schools" offering innovative instruction in academic subjects, the career centers were also supposed to promote racial integration. Wilco opened in 1976, with federal and state money meeting 60% of its $2.5-million construction cost. Each weekday it buses in about 700 students from neighboring high schools in the county, with the school day divided into three shifts. Students split the day between their local school, where they fulfill their academic requirements, and the career center, where they receive vocational training on modern machines.

What the career centers have demonstrated, unfortunately, is the difficulty of reforming a corrupt system more interested in its own survival than in the welfare of its students. In the high schools that were supposed to feed into the career centers, vocational education goes on as before, while some gleaming new shops of the career centers are only partially filled. Why ride a bus to take tough courses when you can coast through with your buddies back home?

BUT IF A TOUR of the world of vocational ed offers many disappointments, it reveals some gratifying success stories as well. Quite surprisingly, a number of old-fashioned trade schools clustered in big cities and northeastern states may turn out to be among the hot alternative schools of the 1980s. These special vocational schools differ from career centers in that students attend them full-time from ninth or tenth grade until graduation. Some, like New York City's Aviation High School, concentrate on one category of jobs. Others offer a wide range of trades. Many have long waiting lists, since they provide educational havens for ambitious kids from poor neighborhoods who don't want to end up washing windows. Academic demands may well exceed those of general high schools. "Our students come, twiddling their thumbs, advanced for doing nothing," says guidance counselor Robert S. Agnese at Ella T. Grasso-Southeastern Vocational Technical School in Groton, Connecticut, the newest of the state's 17 trade schools. "The first year is a shocker, when they realize they can't pull the rabbit out of the hat."

In ninth grade every student begins with a basic program in English, math, science, and history, as well as a required course in blueprints. Last year the school red-flagged 45 of the 230 ninth-graders, warning them to pull up their grades. Toward the end of the year, each pupil takes 13 exploratory one-week shops, such as health services, shipbuilding, and automobile repair. Students without mechanical talent might choose culinary arts, a program that runs the 120-seat Top of Fort Hill restaurant in one wing of the school, open to the public for cheap, tasty lunches. After the students choose a specialty in tenth grade, they alternate three weeks of shop and three weeks of book study. Toward graduation, shop instructors at Ella Grasso act as placement officers, seeking jobs for their graduates at local restaurants, the nearby shipyard where General Dynamics' Electric Boat division makes nuclear subs, or other major employers in the area such as Pfizer. On average, 20% of the graduates go on to college and 80% of the rest land good jobs within a few months in the field for which they trained.

Another bright promise in vocational education is a new generation of technical institutes, which take in students with varied backgrounds: high school juniors and seniors ready to tackle a tough curriculum, high school graduates who choose the institutes instead of a community college, and perhaps most important, people in their 20s who have had a bruising brush with low-paying jobs and come back to school to learn a trade.

Among the best of these schools are the two Hennepin Technical Centers in suburban Minneapolis, where 12,800 students take courses ranging in length from a few weeks to two years. The schools are free for high school students, while others pay a modest tuition of $4.44 a day.

AS VOCATIONAL standbys like agriculture, construction, and machining fade in popularity, technical and clerical programs thrive. Last year the Hennepin centers placed 80% of their 2,600 post-secondary grads in such high-paying fields as medical technology, electronics, diesel mechanics, plastics, and metallurgy, where entry-level salaries

Many vocational educators *seek to expand services to handicapped youth. At one of Minneapolis's Hennepin Technical Centers, a student peruses manuals in a television repair shop. Upon graduation he stands to make an entry-level salary of $1,000 per month.*

averaged $1,200 to $1,400 a month.

At the twin centers, each containing 39 classrooms and 67 shops and laboratories, the equipment alone is worth $18 million. In one shop, a 19-year-old tired of working in a fast-food franchise learns to repair behemoth packaging machines. To do so he should understand electrical circuitry, hydraulics, and microprocessing. In another lab neophyte dental technicians enrolled in a 20-month course carve dentures, crowns, and bridges. Printing is the fifth-largest industry in Minnesota; advanced graphics students spend nine months on subjects such as color theory and laser-based color separation. Programs in electronics and metallurgical technology bluntly advise entrants to come equipped with backgrounds in algebra, physics, and chemistry.

Hennepin's graduates have something extra going for them: the vigorous economy of the Twin Cities region. Along with the area's six community colleges, the schools feed the voracious appetites of such local corporations as Control Data, Honeywell, and Minnesota Mining & Manufacturing. But as other states have learned, technical institutes can be used to get regional development going. As part of an effort to lure industry, create new jobs, and reverse a long-term population decline, Oklahoma has opened 39 of them, expressly designed to act in partnership with new and existing industry. "We are trying to build a corps of workers able to compete with high-precision production in any part of the country," says Oklahoma's vocational education director, Francis Tuttle.

The results include Stillwater's Indian Meridian Area Vocational Technical Center, a $13.5-million complex. The showcase school offers familiar programs like welding and masonry. But its chief interest lies in innovative industrial training, to prepare students who might someday operate flexible manufacturing systems. This fall, for example, Indian Meridian will open a $475,000 computer-aided design and manufacturing lab hooked into its adjacent data-processing center.

Much of the stimulus comes from Mercury Marine, a major local employer. In 1975 the marine-engine manufacturer opened its Stillwater plant, a vertically integrated factory with the complicated task of turning aluminum ingots into 4,600 rpm, 330-hp engines. Indian Meridian's assistant superintendent, Jimmy V. Wilson, 45, and plant manager, R. E. Agner, 47, collaborated. Agner needed 900 workers for casting, machining, and assembling. "We simply couldn't do all the training from scratch, when most of our potential employees were coming from jobs in a grocery store or McDonald's," he says. With Wilson's help, Agner started on-site training programs. For its part, through a $350,000 contribution from Mercury, Indian Meridian designed and installed a $750,000 integrated systems trainer.

Prospective dental technicians *learn their craft at Hennepin. In Minneapolis and other cities, demand for skilled health-care workers of all kinds far exceeds supply.*

Today this training machine acts as the core of a state-of-the-art industrial technology program at the school. The computer-controlled machine spans 160 feet. In a central spot, four pneumatic logic robots load 224-cubic-inch metal blocks from lower to upper carousels. But unlike its brothers in factories, the system is programmed to break down: an instructor can trigger any of 400 possible faults, then ask students to identify, analyze, and fix the glitches.

Such detective work and mechanical ability do not come through intuition. In the labs surrounding the trainer, special stations for electronics, hydraulics, pneumatics, mechanics, fluid transfer, and instrumentation give students the chance to study part of the system before tackling the intricacies of the integrated machine. If this sounds like complex study requiring ability to absorb the arcana of technical manuals and applied physics, it is. Ideally, says Indian Meridian's Wilson, high school graduates entering the industrial technology program should be able to read near college level and understand algebra. Some of them don't and find the course quite a struggle.

THE DEMANDING standards of the best technical schools are worlds removed from the attitudes in Washington and the state capitals, where the semiautonomous establishment that runs vocational education has traditionally been reluctant to push for tough standards. For years these vocational educators have sold hands-on training as a compassionate way to manage the nation's least able students. Says Madeleine B. Hemmings, vice president for policy at the National Alliance of Business, a Washington group concerned with finding jobs for minorities: "They are genuinely convinced that their students can't survive academic courses. This is not a recipe for Nobel Prizes, and it doesn't always produce the technical skills that businesses want and need."

Working up from 282,000 instructors to the powerful American Vocational Association, the vocational education realm constitutes the nation's oldest educational special-interest group. It dates back to 1917, when Washington took its first plunge into local school policy by enticing states through financial incentives to establish vocational courses. Since then the vocational lobby has become well lodged in the halls of government. Kentucky Congressman Carl D. Perkins, chairman of the House Committee on Labor and Education and a champion of vocational education, has long been a devoted, big-spending ally.

The vocational education lobby has reason to be nervous. The $700-million Vocational Education Act, one of the federal government's largest subsidies to secondary education, expires September 30, 1984. And contradicting the blue-sky rhetoric of the past, recent studies commissioned by Congress and private foundations indicate that overall, vocational education fails to make the grade. By common agreement high school courses are scandalously poor; the Vocational Education Act is beset by "ambiguous objectives and ineffective administration," to use the words of analysts Benson and Hoachlander in their report to the National Institute of Education. Congress, which has authorized vocational funds almost automatically for 66 years, could turn as cool as Education Secretary Terrel H. Bell and Budget Director David A. Stockman, who would like to gut the program by cutting appropriations in half.

Young women *learn sophisticated keyboard work and data-processing techniques at Stillwater, Oklahoma's Indian Meridian vocational institute. Of all occupations, the 1980s will provide the largest number of jobs for secretaries and clerical workers.*

VOCATIONAL planners have the chance to get started on some overdue reforms. As some of the schools cited in this article demonstrate, vocational education has merit when solid grounding in language and math is a prelude to hands-on training. Most employers want literate, reliable workers, who come to work ready to profit from rapid on-the-job training. But corporations, not to mention small businesses, don't want to start from scratch. Effective on-the-job training often first requires fairly intimate knowledge of a machine, process, or procedure.

Regular high schools might best serve vocationally oriented students by winnowing nonacademic instruction to a few well-chosen basic courses, such as typing, mechanical drawing, and computer operation. Acknowledging their inability to compete with good technical schools, they might try to cajole students into early mastery of verbal and mathematical fundamentals, and then place them full-time in trade schools or technical institutes.

The promise of vocational education rests primarily in the technical institutes, community colleges, and other schools aimed at high school graduates and older people. Even if they have some catching up to do, students entering these schools are more mature, motivated, and realistic about the workplace than are 16-year-olds. Attending out of choice rather than compulsion, they are often looking for a "second chance"—and are willing to learn the basics the hard way. Specialized programs proceed at a fast clip, on equipment out of the reach of high school shops.

At a time of national concern about the plight of displaced workers, technical institutes are a logical place to situate retraining programs. When the $3.6-billion Job Training Partnership Act goes into effect on October 1, many schools will use the money to offer additional courses to adults—for example, contracting with the local councils that will help administer the program to train 50 data-processors over 60 days to specific performance standards. Even some high school career centers are moving into the kind of adult education that will be paid for by the new program. At Joliet's Wilco, secondary enrollments have been dropping for two years, most rapidly in familiar industrial trades. By contrast, the school is doubling its space to meet new adult demand for clerical instruction, heaviest among women in their 20s trying to cope with word processing and computer-based information systems.

A more orderly vocational house depends, too, on the mood in executive suites. More business leaders should speak out frankly about scholastic shortcomings. In recent years corporate interest in education has rarely gone far beyond tax-deductible donations and easy promises by plant managers to hire more local graduates. C.E.O.s have either supported vocational education reflexively or griped about the schools' failure to deliver trained workers tied with a bow. In coming years, corporate officers would do well to make what goes into the heads of the people they'll hire in five or ten years a top concern. Their firms' future competitiveness may rest on it.

■ Vocational education can make people more employable, but first they need the mental basics and self-discipline to learn skilled trades. The high schools should stick to the job of giving firm foundations in academic subjects, expecting more from all students, not tracking slow or reluctant pupils prematurely into job-training courses. Congress could send a signal by failing to renew the Vocational Education Act. By dropping disadvantaged 16-year-olds into academic black holes, much current vocational education wastes taxpayers' money and helps perpetuate an underclass of ill-educated young people who aren't wanted by the labor market.

Education And the Sony War

Until the federal government and state legislatures stop basing curricular changes on political and economic needs, the public schools will continue to be in a state of chaos, says Mr. Spring. As it is, the schools are captive to the profit motive of U.S. industry.

Joel Spring

JOEL SPRING is a professor in the College of Education, University of Cincinnati.

IN THE EARLY 1960s one would have been quickly branded a radical for arguing that the U.S. educational system was geared to meet the needs of international corporate competition. Times have certainly changed. The recent reports from federal, state, and private groups demanding an increase in academic standards in the public schools, particularly in science and mathematics, are unanimous in the contention that higher standards in the schools will help keep America competitive in foreign markets.[1]

It is important to ask why a ground swell of opinion supporting the idea that the public schools should be geared to meet the needs of high technology is cresting now. What has happened to the U.S. economy to cause educational concerns to shift from the problem of widespread unemployment that dominated the 1970s to a demand for increased academic requirements? The answer lies in the demographic changes of the last two decades and the response of U.S. business to those changes. The connection between changes in educational policy and industrial needs is direct.

The Seventies were years of declining growth in productivity, dwindling capital investment by U.S. industry, and relatively high unemployment, particularly among young workers. But there was no decrease in the demand for workers during this period. Instead, the high unemployment figures during the Seventies were caused by the large numbers of youths — members of the postwar baby boom — entering the labor market.[2] This flooding of the labor market caused wages to decline, particularly for entry-level occupations. In the 1970s and into the early 1980s young people in the U.S. have had a difficult time finding employment at wages comparable to those of the previous decade.[3]

Because of these circumstances, government educational policy in the 1970s concentrated on the problem of youth unemployment. Career education and vocational education became major educational concerns of all levels of government. Federal policy was typified by the Youth Employment Act of 1977, which provided training and employment opportunities.[4] The response of the U.S. business community to a labor surplus and declining wages was to become more labor intensive and to decrease capital outlays.[5] For instance, a company might choose to increase production by adding a second or third shift, rather than by investing in new equipment.

These changes in labor use and capital investment led to the decline in the growth of productivity of U.S. industry. Productivity may be simply defined as the level of output divided by the amount of labor needed to produce it within a certain time. Under this definition, the increased use of labor naturally led to reduced growth in productivity. By 1977 the level of labor productivity in the U.S. was the same as it had been in 1960. On the other hand, Japan increased its labor productivity during the same period by approximately 255%.[6]

THE TRENDS IN the early 1980s have been almost the exact opposite of those of the 1970s. With the passing of the baby boom, fewer youths are now entering the labor market. One set of figures shows that the average number of new workers entering the labor force in the 1970s was approximately 2.5 million per year and that, by the late 1980s, this number will decline to approximately 1.5 million workers per year.[7] Another forecast estimates a 14% decline in the 1980s in the number of persons between 14 and 24 years old and a 20% decline in high

From *Phi Delta Kappan,* April 1984, pp. 534-537. Reprinted by permission of the author and Phi Delta Kappan.

school enrollments and graduates.[8] Col. George Bailey, former director of continuing education for the U.S. Army, argues that "during the next decade, the military, the colleges, and business and industry will all be competing for the same limited supply of people."[9]

The response of business and industry to the end of the baby boom has been twofold. On the one hand, employers are concerned about the decrease in the number of qualified employees for entry-level jobs. This dwindling pool of workers threatens to drive up wages. Thus business has been working with the schools to maximize the size of the labor pool by improving the education of those students who would have been marginally employable in the 1970s. This newfound interest in education is reflected in adopt-a-school programs, Jobs for America's Graduates, and local alliances between businesses and schools. It has also led to increased emphasis on career preparation in the schools themselves. In his study for the Carnegie Corporation, Michael Timpane details the extent of these new cooperative programs and argues that they have sprung up primarily in response to the growing shortage of entry-level workers. "For the first time in a generation," Timpane writes, "there will probably be, in several urban locations, an absolute shortage of labor supply for entry-level positions. Urban employers already report great difficulty in locating qualified employees for entry-level positions."[10]

On the other hand, the U.S. business community finds itself in difficulty because of delayed capital investments and declining productivity. Both business and political leaders have called for greater technological development to meet the growth of international competition. With regard to educational policy, this has meant a call for increased graduation requirements in mathematics, science, and other academic fields. Policy makers hope that these new graduates will lead U.S. industry to victory in the worldwide technological competition.

Both of these trends in educational policy are designed to provide U.S. business with an expanded pool of potential employees — and consequently a decline in wages. This will be particularly true if high unemployment continues to characterize the 1980s. If these two trends are successful, the market will be flooded with high school graduates with good work attitudes and minimum basic skills for entry-level positions and with highly qualified scientists and engineers.

Meeting the short-term needs of U.S. business and industry does not necessarily result in economic benefits either to the economy or to the individual. After all, the decision of business not to invest in new plants and equipment in the 1970s and instead to reap short-term profits is partly responsible for the present technological crisis. *The failure of the public schools did not cause the problem.* Indeed, it is hard to predict the social, political, and economic needs of the world that the first high school graduates to have completed 12 years of schooling under the present educational proposals will face in 1995.

In fact, if the schools continue to be geared to meet the changing needs of U.S. business, we can expect still another change in educational policy in the next decade to meet those changing desires. Thus the public school system becomes a captive of the profit motive of U.S. industry. And, let me emphasize again, this relationship guarantees neither an improved economy nor a higher standard of living for individuals. Indeed, such a close connection between education and industry might lead to *lower* wages, as different segments of the labor market are flooded by workers channeled there by the public school system. In effect, American business would be using the public school system to exploit the American worker.

Meeting the short-term needs of U.S. business and industry does not necessarily result in economic benefits either to the economy or to the individual.

EDUCATORS HAVE been quick to accept the demands that business makes on the schools because of the constant promise of more money for education. Over the last three decades U.S. educators have been willing to accept the extravagant claims that public schooling can win the Cold War, end poverty, and eliminate unemployment. Although all of these claims have been built on shaky premises, educators have seen them as ways of convincing the public of the worth of the schools and of the need for more money. In other words, extravagant claims about the power of public education provide an important means of public relations for public school educators.

The report of the National Commission on Excellence in Education is a case in point. It stresses both the importance of future investment in education and of an educational plan to meet the current needs of industry. The report argues that investment in public education is the key to solving the economic problems of the U.S. "If only to keep and improve on the slim competitive edge we still retain in world markets," the report urges, "we must rededicate ourselves to the reform of our educational system for the benefit of all. . . ." In language designed to frighten readers into shelling out more money for public education, the report states, "If an unfriendly foreign power had attempted to impose on America the mediocre educational performance that exists today, we might well have viewed it as an act o war."[11] The picture painted in *A Nation a Risk* is that of a tired giant losing a globa trade war because of the failure of it public schools. The solution to the prob lems of international trade, according t the report, is the reform of public school ing.

In making these claims, the Nationa Commission offered no evidence that pub lic schooling can solve the problems of in ternational trade and economic develop ment. Indeed, the commissioners seem t have assumed that the economic problem of the U.S. are not being caused by prob lems in the economic system itself but b problems in the development of huma capital. Again, they offered no proof Ample proof is offered of the decline o public schools but not of the relationshi of this decline to economic problems.

All the historical evidence from the las three decades of federal involvement i public schools suggests that public school ing is *not* the answer to social and eco nomic problems. In the 1950s the publi schools were called on to win the Col War against the Soviet Union by provid ing more mathematicians and scientists (The parallels between today's rhetori and that of the 1950s should be noted.) I the 1950s the key to our technological rac with the Soviet Union was believed to b the public schools. The National Defens Education Act was passed in 1958 to pro vide more funding for science, mathema ics, and foreign language instruction. Thi legislation was very similar to several bill now pending in Congress. In addition there was a fivefold increase in funding t the National Science Foundation to devel op new curricula for the schools.[12]

What was the result of this federal in volvement? There is no evidence that won the military/technological war wit the Soviet Union. In fact, all the evidenc marshaled by the National Commissio indicates that the public schools actuall declined shortly after the National De fense Education Act was passed. Thoug it cannot be proved, there may even be causal relationship between federal in volvement and the academic decline of the schools.

In the 1960s Presidents Kennedy and Johnson called on the public schools to end poverty and improve the economic conditions of minority groups. The major piece of federal legislation in this "war on poverty" was the Elementary and Secondary Education Act of 1965. In the 1970s Presidents Nixon and Ford tried to solve the problems of unemployment by expanding career and vocational education programs. Despite all of these efforts to solve social and economic problems through public schooling, the U.S. still faces high unemployment and chronic poverty.

Now we face another demand: change the educational system to fit the national goal of increased technological development for improved international trade. The National Commission recommends that state and local requirements for high schools be changed to include, as a minimum, what the report calls the "five new basics." These new basics include four years of English, three years of mathematics, three years of science, three years of social studies, and one-half year of computer science.

The proposals of the National Commission parallel exactly what is happening as states try to improve their economic conditions by requiring more math and science courses as a means of attracting high-technology industries. As of May 1983 the Oregon state legislature was considering the establishment of a state high school for science and mathematics; Wyoming was considering scholarships for math and science teachers; New York was considering training programs and special scholarships for math and science teachers; and Connecticut was considering some form of loan program for math and science teachers. In all, 30 states were considering some form of special aid for math and science teaching. In addition, Congress was considering a $425 million math and science education bill.[13]

There is a certain irony in the fact that these proposals are designed to correct problems resulting from earlier proposals linking public goals with academic requirements. Most existing state-mandated academic standards are the products of some previous effort to achieve political, economic, or social goals. After its survey of trends in the high school curriculum, the National Commission concluded that "secondary school curricula have been homogenized, diluted, and diffused to the point that they no longer have a central purpose." But because the Commission does not analyze the causes for this diffuse curriculum, it travels down the same path that brought the schools to their present predicament.

Educators have been quick to accept the demands that business makes on the schools because of the constant promise of more money for education.

Through the years the states and the federal government have continually added to and subtracted from the curriculum according to social, political, and economic needs. The public schools have been asked to solve problems ranging from driver safety to fighting communism. As Gene Maeroff writes, "Schools have been viewed by Congress primarily as instruments of social change. It is perhaps flattering to public education that it was awarded so pivotal a role in the perfecting of society, but the responsibility is a burden nonetheless."[14]

WHAT THIS RUSH to save U.S. international trade means is that the public school curriculum is being biased toward yet another goal: namely, technological development. But is this the only problem faced by the United States? One could argue that the economic problems of the U.S. have been primarily political in origin. For instance, U.S. economic problems could be related to the high deficits and runaway inflation caused by the Vietnam war and the federal government's handling of the energy crisis of the 1970s. If this were true, then one might argue for more political education in the schools. But the point is that it is wrong to bias public school curricula in *any* one direction when there is no proof as to what are the most important social, economic, and political problems — much less their solutions.

This issue becomes clearer when one considers possible alternatives to raising academic requirements for secondary schools. Suppose America's problems stemmed from an inability of the population to think through important issues clearly. If this were true, why not have all secondary schools require three years of philosophy? Suppose the problem is the inability of the population to understand and act on political, social, and economic issues. One might then replace the meaningless hodgepodge of social studies courses with a requirement that all secondary students take three years of sociology, three years of economics, and three years of political science. Or suppose society has been ruined by too much technology and not enough appreciation of the arts and humanities. If this were true, why not require three years of music, three years of art, and three years of literature? All of these curricula could be defended in terms of some national need or purpose.

Until the federal government and the state legislatures stop making curriculum changes on the basis of social, political, and economic needs, the curriculum of the public schools will continue to be in a state of flux and chaos. The real question regarding the curriculum is, What knowledge is of most worth? In a democratic society, the answer to that central question should be given by individuals, not by governments. State legislatures must stop establishing academic requirements, and the federal government must stop trying to influence the curriculum to serve national policy objectives.

The recommendations of the National Commission offer no real hope for a reform that will cure the ills of U.S. education. All the problems addressed by the report have their origin in the present structure of public schooling. Merely changing academic requirements to suit the latest whim of the government — to serve some particular policy goal — will do nothing to alter that basic structure.

How long will the American public continue to believe extravagant claims about the value of public schooling? How many more generations will accept the public relations strategy of public school educators, as they offer their product as a panacea for practically every social, political, or economic ill? How many more years will Congress and the state legislatures go along with the grandiose claims of the lobbyists for public education? Perhaps society will see through the current fog of rhetoric that envelops the recommendations of these new commissions; perhaps this time the public will realize that the public schools cannot solve such problems as the weakened position of the U.S. in international trade or the failure of the domestic economy. Indeed, we might even harbor the hope that someday the public schools will no longer be captives of the profit motive of U.S. industry and that the education of Americans will not be determined by the economic goals of business.

---

1. Three of the major reports are Education Commission of the States, *Action for Excellence: A Comprehensive Plan to Improve Our Nation's Schools* (Denver: ECS, 1983); Twentieth Century Fund Task Force

on Federal Elementary and Secondary Education Policy, *Making the Grade* (New York: Twentieth Century Fund, 1983); and National Commission on Excellence in Education, *A Nation at Risk: The Imperative for Educational Reform* (Washington, D.C.: U.S. Government Printing Office, 1983).

2. See Daniel Quinn Mills, "Decisions About Employment in the 1980s: Overview and Underpinning," and Michael Wachter, "Economic Challenges Posed by Demographic Changes," in Eli Ginzberg et al., eds., *Work Decisions in the 1980s* (Boston: Auburn House, 1982).

3. "For example, while males 20 to 24 years old earned $73 for every $100 by prime-age males in 1955, they earned only $58 for every $100 in 1977," according to Wachter, p. 43.

4. For a discussion of the Youth Employment Act of 1977, see Joel Spring, *American Education*, 2nd ed. (New York: Longman, 1982), pp. 117-21.

5. "In fact, in the mid-1970s American manufacturing firms were cautious about capital investment, but relatively expansive about employment. . . . In the most telling comparison, American manufacturers and manufacturers in France, Japan, and Germany increased output between 1972 and 1978 by somewhat similar amounts. During the same period employment fell in France by 2.2%, in Japan by 4.7%, and in Germany by 12%; but in the United States, manufacturers increased employment by 615%," according to Mills, pp. 8-9.

6. Ibid., p. 5.

7. Wachter, pp. 35-42.

8. Michael Timpane, *Corporations and Public Education*, report distributed by Teachers College, Columbia University (New York: Carnegie Corporation, May 1982), pp. 8-9.

9. Quoted in Anne C. Lewis, "Washington Report: The Military Enters the Competition for Technically Trainable Graduates," *Phi Delta Kappan*, May 1983, p. 603.

10. Timpane, p. 8.

11. *A Nation at Risk*, p. 5.

12. A history of federal involvement in public schools after World War II can be found in Joel Spring, *The Sorting Machine* (New York: Longman, 1976).

13. "State Proposals to Bolster Math and Science Teaching," *Education Week*, 18 May 1983, pp. 14-16.

14. Gene Maeroff, *Don't Blame the Kids: The Trouble with America's Public Schools* (New York: McGraw-Hill, 1982), p. 8.

Computers and a New World Order

James Dray and Joseph A. Menosky

JAMES DRAY is a researcher with the Communications and Information Technology Division of the congressional Office of Technology Assessment. JOSEPH A. MENOSKY is an associate producer of National Public Radio's current-affairs program "NPR Dateline."

AMID the popular utopian visions of the world's computerized future are some troubling questions about who really will benefit. Must the computer revolution widen the gulf between rich and poor? Will it only perpetuate technological elites?

In reaction to such concerns, the French government has established a research group whose goal is to start a revolution of its own. The World Center for Microelectronics and the Human Resource ("Centre Mondial Informatique et Ressource Humaine") in Paris supports a cadre of scientists who are studying—and suggesting ways to change—the computer's impact on people and societies. The scientists ultimately envision the widespread use of computers by ordinary people in all countries, making them an integral part of human culture. In particular, they hope to transfer microcomputers to Third World countries and the poorer regions of industrial countries. They also hope to design computer languages, software, and hardware simple enough to make the machines truly useful to their recipients.

French President François Mitterrand opened the center early in 1982 with a good deal of fanfare and a budget for the year of $20 million. Since then, the budget has been cut by almost half, the staff has undergone a devastating shakeup, and the program itself has provoked considerable controversy. Now its future is uncertain, and the center remains an intriguing mix of science and politics, savvy and naivete, technical solutions and world-class problems.

Among its founders were Jean-Jacques Servan-Schreiber, the French writer, publisher, and politician who is the center's president; Seymour Papert and Nicholas Negroponte, computer scientists from M.I.T. who took leaves of absence from their academic posts to become the center's directors; and a number of other top computer scientists, educators, and socially active intellectuals. From the beginning, then, the center has been driven by the ideas of a disparate group of people—above all by Papert's vision of the computer as an agent of intellectual freedom, and by Servan-Schreiber's ideal of a new world order based on access to information and high technology.

Over the past decade, Papert has guided the development of a sophisticated computer language, called "Logo," for use as a learning tool. (He wrote about the experience in a book for a popular audience, *Mindstorms*, published in 1980.) His studies of children grappling with Logo convinced him of the radical effect computers could have on the way children learn to reason, and on their subsequent ability to deal with novel situations and complex problems.

Papert thinks that even very young children and uneducated adults can master difficult intellectual concepts if a computer is used to convey the ideas to the learners. For example, he recalls that, as a child, he was fascinated by gears. Later, when he was introduced to algebraic equations in school, he was able to understand them by thinking of an equation as a gear. He writes, "By the time I had made a mental gear model of the relation between x and y, figuring out how many teeth each gear needed, the equation had become a comfortable friend." Papert believes that just as the gear acted for him as a "transitional object," a computer can serve the same function. "Because it can take on a thousand forms and can serve a thousand functions, it can appeal to a thousand tastes," he says.

This potential of computers to alter radically the nature of education and work remains unexploited, Papert argues, because "our society consistently casts computers in a framework that favors the maintenance of the status quo." To counteract this emphasis, he would like to see "alternative computer cultures": minority groups, women, or poets, for example, who would adapt microcomputers to their own interests and needs.

Servan-Schreiber took up some of Papert's themes in his book *The World Challenge*, published in 1981. He claims that countries of the Third World will eventually join together to confront the developed world with a demand for high technology. He argues that former colonial powers have a moral obligation to help developing countries take advantage of the microcomputer's social and economic potential, and that failure to do so will worsen North-South tensions and lead to worldwide political upheavals. But with the assistance of the advanced technological powers, Servan-Schreiber says, Third World countries might someday even "jump above industrial society into the new information society."

The transfer of microcomputer technology that Servan-Schreiber proposed was to be implemented along the lines Papert had suggested for alternative computer cultures, but his full vision goes far beyond. First, individuals who have used the Logo system to learn new ways of thinking would band together in local groups to solve common problems. For

Reprinted with permission from TECHNOLOGY REVIEW, copyright 1983.

Seymour Papert thinks even young children and uneducated adults can master difficult concepts via computers. He spent a decade developing a computer language called "Logo" for use as a learning tool. Here he's using it with children in Dakar, Senegal.

example, farmers in a small Third World community could use computers to keep better tabs on the availability and distribution of supplies. Moreover, the very act of "exploring" with the computer could engender a flexibility of thought that would, in turn, allow the farmers to find novel ways of combining the efficiency of modern agricultural practices with their traditional cultures.

The next step is for communities to widen their knowledge and power bases by linking up, via satellite, with similar communities across a wide region. For example, farming communities could pool their experience about the success of new agricultural techniques so that each farmer need not start from scratch. Finally, networks of communities could become a new social force, with political and economic systems changing accordingly. Within a developing country, this might mean that historically disenfranchised groups could gain enough power to demand a more equitable distribution of rights and resources. And in Servan-Schreiber's ultimate vision, the entire Third World would become an electronically linked network of countries ready to cooperate or compete with developed nations.

The Politics of Computer Cultures

The center has so far devoted much of its budget to trying computers at two test sites: the West African city of Dakar, Senegal, and Marseilles, France.

In Dakar, a team from the center is working with government-sponsored educators and computer scientists to adapt microcomputers to many aspects of Senegalese life, including industry, agriculture, and medicine. The team has begun by tackling the educational system, and the first project has elementary school children learning to program computers using a French version of Logo. (French is the European language spoken most widely in Senegal.) The system is also being adapted to the local culture, beginning with the translation of Logo programs into Wolof—one of the major Senegalese national languages—which many children speak at home. Once children have mastered the basics of computers, they can use the computer as what Papert calls "an instrument for learning everything," particularly science, mathematics, and language.

Robert Lawler, an educational expert at the center and longtime colleague of Papert's, demonstrated to one of us how a prototype program in Wolof can help children learn language. First, Lawler typed the Wolof word for "sun," just as the children would do when taught to spell it by their teachers. An image of the sun appeared promptly on the screen. Then he instructed the computer, again in Wolof, to put the sun in the sky, and the image on the screen moved up. With a few more commands, the screen soon showed the sun rising over a man as he walked to his house. The computer adds a visible "reality" to keyed words, and Logo permits even young children to add new words and designs to such "microworlds." It is this simplicity, feedback, and adaptability for the individual that Papert and others believe can change minds in fundamental ways—and that make the Logo language suitable for many cultures that would otherwise be out of reach of computer technology.

In Marseilles, researchers from the center are preparing for the delivery of some 500 microcomputers this year to schools, houses, and social-service agencies in a working-class district with high unemployment. In effect, the project will be a large-scale laboratory experiment in creating a "computer culture." The team will study the impact on the community and work with the residents to help them adapt the computers to their own needs. Project staffers hope residents will "seize" the microcomputers, bringing the machines into their lives "as a tool, as a game, as a companion, as a mirror." For example, Papert says unemployed young people, especially high-school dropouts, could make use of their easy access to computers to learn marketable skills. Another possibility is that self-employed artisans will use the computers to boost their productivity. For instance, carpenters might use computers to estimate more accurately the cost of jobs, control inventory, and even design their products.

The rest of the 75 researchers employed by the center are working on an array of other projects. For example, some are improving laser videodisk memory technology that will enable "interactive" computers to respond even faster than when equipped with standard floppy disks. Some are developing new programming languages to make computer systems more flexible and easier for untrained people to use. Some are designing durable and compact microcomputers suited for use in remote areas. And some are developing portable "expert" medical systems to assist rural health workers in diagnosis and treatment of disease.

All these projects are still in their early stages, and most seem to be loosely organized and minimally defined. In fact, many of the center's teething pains seem to arise from its slippery mandate and shifts in its objectives. The center's priorities already seem to have been diverted from the project in Senegal and others planned for Third World countries to social programs that could relieve unemployment in France, and then to research to make the French telecommunications system stronger. "The center is terribly sensitive to the winds of French politics," Lawler says. "There is no buffer between research and the pressing needs of the French nation."

The center's political volatility contributed to Seymour Papert's resignation, in a flurry of publicity, last December. (Since then, Negroponte has announced that, in August, he too will leave.) Papert charged that Servan-Schreiber was using the center to further his political career and aid the French computer industry at the expense of more humanistic goals. For his part, Servan-Schreiber says that Papert is "a very difficult man . . . interested in only one thing—how to train very young children by computer." But, he adds, "It's not a personal thing for me." Observers say the flap between Papert and Servan-Schreiber turned on personal and philosophical conflicts as well as on their noisier disagreements over how the center ought to be administered.

Technological Colonialism?

Problems deeper than these internal matters, however, may prevent the center from ever making significant contributions. An obvious barrier to the transfer of microcomputers to poor and unskilled people is illiteracy; most computer programs depend on written language. One center project has begun to focus on the issue of literacy, and other alternatives are being examined as well. Edward Ayensu of Ghana, who is the president of the Network of African Scientists and one of the center's founding members, claims that it will soon be possible to develop a computer program that understands spoken Wolof. Another suggestion is to design a computer that can recognize physical gestures, allowing for the transmission of a nonwritten, nonverbal "language." But both ideas are pipe dreams, according to Joseph Weizenbaum, a computer scientist at M.I.T. and longstanding critic of the more extravagent claims current in his field. He describes these language programs as "an artificial-intelligence project of absolutely staggering proportions." Weizenbaum argues, "There's no clue to date as to whether these problems are even attackable by any means that we have now."

Critics have also questioned the center's economic, political, and moral premises. For example, American reviewers greeted *The World Challenge* with almost universal disdain, judging Servan-Schreiber's grasp of global economics—and his notion of the Third World leap-frogging its way into the Information Age—to be naive at best. As George W. Ball, the undersecretary of state in the Kennedy and Johnson administrations, wrote in the *New York Times*, "Yes, Virginia, there is noise out there, but what you are hearing is not the [Third World] hammering on the gates of Europe [for technology]; it is only Servan-Schreiber pounding his typewriter."

Servan-Schreiber's ideas in *The World Challenge* were based on the promise of Third World solidarity, as evidenced by the strength of the OPEC cartel. But OPEC is now troubled and divided, and the "challenge" presented to developed nations by the Third World's demands for high technology seems less likely to materialize than he predicted. Indeed, Servan-Schreiber dropped all references to such demands when he testified before a congressional subcommittee in mid-1982. Instead, he predicted that "an army of 50 million jobless will appear on the horizon and signal a situation of despair," unless the developed nations seek creative methods of adapting to computers.

Perhaps the most damaging question raised about Servan-Schreiber and the center concerns the conviction that helping Third World countries acquire computer technologies would be beneficial. To many critics, such a goal is an artifact of colonialism, imposing Western values and definitions of progress on other cultures for less than altruistic reasons. Some have charged that the center was founded because Mitterrand's government saw the Third World as a vast market for the French microcomputer industry—a market largely untouched by American or Japanese firms. "This reminds me of times long ago when white Europeans decided that African women should wear dresses and men pants," Weizenbaum says. "One wonders which came first: the desire to help the Third World or the desire to open up a gigantic new market for cloth."

Those involved in the center's work reject the charge of colonialism, arguing that they wish only to provide a useful tool with which non-Western cultures can meet their needs as they see fit. "Helping people control the most important technology of our time is not colonialism," Lawler says. Servan-Schreiber bristles at those who speak of colonialism. "It is an insult," he says. "It is the Senegalese themselves who have asked for this."

The leaders of Senegal have indeed asked for the center's help, as have the leaders of many other countries. Concluding that the Senegalese *people* also want microcomputers demands a leap of faith, however. And it remains unclear who will enjoy the benefits and who will bear the costs in Third World countries. The technology may be just as easily—perhaps more easily—used by those in power to increase the distance between rich and poor and to monitor dissidents.

Unlike Servan-Schreiber, Papert has always admitted that life in Third World countries could become harder rather than easier with the introduction of computers. "I don't want to present myself as a computer utopian. The computer in Senegal, or anywhere else, could create a little enclave in which there is very rapid development, ultimately at the expense of everything around. It absolutely could happen," Papert says. But for him, this danger is far outweighed by the possibility for good and the need to prepare for the coming microelectronics revolution.

The Mitterrand government still supports the center, which has a budget of about $13 million this year. The center has restructured its social-sciences staff and has signed an agreement with Carnegie-Mellon University in Pittsburgh to exchange staff and expertise. Raj Reddy of Carnegie-Mellon, a longtime ally of the center, will work part-time in Paris directing its scientific efforts. The center has also inspired other countries—Colombia, Canada, and Japan—to consider establishing similar programs.

Those close to the center are convinced that its efforts will pay off. "Adapting computers to the various cultures of the world is an idea whose time has come," Lawler says. "The center began this effort, and if it doesn't succeed in Paris, it will succeed somewhere else. The idea is too powerful not to work." Indeed, Papert has had some amazing successes with children using Logo, but the demonstrations have occurred in controlled environments under the guidance of talented teachers. Whether his results can be replicated in cruder settings is uncertain.

The center's intention to analyze and possibly predict the computer's social impacts in both developed and undeveloped countries is undeniably noble. And the center's proposed "counter-revolution"—to be born out of locally initiated computer cultures—is tantalizing. Perhaps groups of people outside society's mainstream can indeed find radically different, creative uses for computers. There are modest precedents with other technologies.

The "rap music" now popular is an example. Emerging out of the black communities of New York City, rap music involves a rhythmic, verbal bantering accompanied, in its most elaborate form, by records played on two or more turntables. The "rapper" delivers his or her monologue while a disc jockey manually cuts back and forth between turntables, spinning them backward as well as forward and establishing new beats as the rap proceeds.

This is a radical use of an established sound technology—a significant extension of the limited use for which the stereo turntable was designed. Given that the computer is, in Papert's words, "the Proteus of machines," it is interesting to consider what might result if blacks in Harlem appropriated that technology. But whether this sort of appropriation can be the basis for a new world order is open to serious question.

Bilingual/Bicultural Education: Its Legacy And Its Future

Carlos J. Ovando

CARLOS J. OVANDO (University of Southern California Chapter) is director of the Bilingual/Crosscultural Specialization, School of Education, University of Alaska, Anchorage.

Like the intricate baobab tree of Africa, which is a natural haven for myriad fauna, bilingual/bicultural education has become an educational phenomenon that serves many different groups. Beyond this point, however, the simile takes a different turn. For, unlike the baobab tree, with its largely self-regulating web of life, bilingual/bicultural education has many wardens who monitor its status with a great deal of interest. At one extreme are parents who (understandably) want to know what is going on inside the bilingual or English-as-a-second-language (ESL) classroom in terms of curricular content, first- and second-language development, and cultural emphasis. At the other extreme are politicians and journalists who are eager to extract a great deal of mileage from a topic that has consistently, during the past 15 years, touched some of the most sensitive sociopolitical and pedagogical nerves in U.S. society.

Both participants and observers view bilingual/bicultural education in a variety of ways. Some embrace with zeal the revitalization of languages and cultures through the public schools. They see bilingual education as a natural consequence of the sociocultural realities of a pluralistic society. For them, dual language instruction is a logical vehicle for cognitive and language development for those students with limited proficiency in English — and for those students whose first language is English, as well. They believe that bilingual/bicultural education will be personally satisfying to all students and that it will help them to develop the interpersonal skills and attitudes that are essential to a healthy society. Students with limited proficiency in English, these advocates would argue, are entitled to a fair share of the goods and services of the society, and this includes equal access to high-quality educational opportunities through the use of the language spoken in each student's home.

Those individuals at the other extreme argue that the positive effects of bilingual education on academic achievement, dual language development, cultural affirmation, national integration, and psychological well-being have been exaggerated. Such critics often suggest that support for bilingual education springs from faith, not from empirical evidence. They fear that the institutionalization of bilingual education in the public schools will further fracture social cohesion by encouraging youngsters to depend on languages other than English and to adhere to cultural patterns that may be in conflict with the mainstream U.S. culture. Such results, these critics argue, will only hamper upward mobility for students with limited proficiency in English.

Somewhere between these two extremes are those individuals who concede, on ideological and pedagogical grounds, that students with limited proficiency in English are entitled to schooling in their primary language until such time as they can assume the demands of an all-English curriculum — but the sooner, the better. Where this view of bilingual education is dominant, students with limited proficiency in English are generally removed from the bilingual program — somewhat arbitrarily — after one or two years of instruction. Bilingual education is only a means of pushing and pulling the speaker of limited English as quickly as possible into the mainstream American culture (whatever that is).

Finally, some individuals believe in the importance of nurturing ancestral languages and cultures, but they also believe that such endeavors should take place somewhere other than in the public schools. Consider, for example, the Korean community of about 2,000 in Anchorage, Alaska. Sensitive to the fact that its children were forgetting their mother tongue, becoming alienated from their culture, and having trouble communicating with their parents (who speak limited English), the Korean community, with help from the Korean consulate, started a Saturday school to teach these youngsters the Korean culture and language. The Japanese community in Anchorage also operates such a school, as do many other ethnic groups throughout the U.S.

Although it is useful to isolate and examine the myriad voices competing for attention on the topic of bilingual/bicultural education, the debate is much less clear in reality. The formulation of a national policy on language would compel the articulation and examination of language-related issues. Such a policy could function as a sounding board for debates on the homogenization or the pluralization of U.S. society. To what extent, why, how, and by what means should we move in one direction or the other? A national policy on language would resolve the often conflicting language policies that the U.S. has randomly and almost unconsciously followed to date. The National Defense Education Act (NDEA) of 1957 and the Title VII bilingual education legislation of 1968 epitomize this conflict. The NDEA affirmed the significance of foreign languages as integral components of national security; the bilingual education legislation, by contrast, was designed

This article originally appeared in the *Phi Delta Kappan*, Vol. 64, No. 8 (April 1983). Copyright 1983 by *Phi Delta Kappan*.

to allow the rich linguistic experiences of the immigrant and indigenous minority communities in the U.S. to atrophy.

To establish the need for a national policy on language, we must look back at the pedagogical and the sociopolitical development of bilingual/bicultural education since the late 1960s. By isolating these two closely interrelated strands of development, we can see that both the pedagogy and the sociopolitics of bilingual education have suffered from a general lack of direction. The usual approach has been one of ad hoc experimentation. This is natural in the early stages of developing a new program, but it also demonstrates more clearly the need for a national policy on language.

Bilingual Pedagogy

Pedagogically, bilingual education was based on the assumption that building instruction on what students with limited proficiency in English already knew would result in more learning than would total instruction in a second language. Those who held this view also assumed that cognitive skills acquired in one language can be transferred to other languages and cultures. The general objective of bilingual education was to open up two-way communication between the world of the limited-English-speaking student and the school in subject-area content, in first- and second-language development, and in cultural awareness. The long-term goal was to improve the academic achievement of students with limited proficiency in English.

The partial institutionalization of bilingual education in U.S. public schools was an admission that defects in the regular curriculum accounted, at least in part, for the poor academic showing of limited-English-speaking students. Through bilingual/bicultural education, educators, parents, and policy makers expected to improve the marginal academic achievement and the equally marginal sociocultural status of these students.

But those educators charged with carrying out this dual mission had no reliable research to guide them. In fact, not until federally sponsored bilingual education was 10 years old, in 1978, did the now-defunct Department of Health, Education, and Welfare direct a Title VII committee to monitor a research agenda in the following areas: 1) assessment of national needs for bilingual education, 2) improvement in the effectiveness of services for students, and 3) improvement in Title VII program management and operations.[1] The data from these research efforts were to be ready for the congressional hearings for reauthorization of Title VII in 1983.

Approaches to language delivery illustrate the experimental nature of bilingual education during the Seventies. Teachers who were bilingual themselves often used the concurrent method — switching back and forth between two languages during lessons — for delivery of content and development of students' language. The concurrent method was a commonly prescribed mode of delivery in early Title VII programs. More recently, this approach has come into disrepute, however. Teachers have found it time-consuming, tedious, and — more important — not conducive to the development of a second language. Rather than actively listening to the second language, students learn to wait passively until the teacher returns to their first language. Similarly, teachers tried and then often discarded many varieties of the alternate and preview/review models for delivering language.

As with modes of language delivery, approaches for developing literacy skills in the bilingual classroom have varied tremendously. Some programs have introduced reading skills exclusively through the first language, while English as a second language is developed separately. Other programs have chosen to immerse children in English exclusively. Still others have experimented with introducing reading and writing simultaneously in students' first and second languages.[2]

Two of the most debated issues in bilingual education have concerned *who* should participate and *for how long*. Educators have used a wide variety of instruments to assess the language skills of learners slated for entry into or exit from bilingual or English-as-a-second-language programs. Some educators have been interested in instruments that would identify only those students most in need of bilingual instruction — and that would deem these youngsters ready for exit from such programs as quickly as possible. Others have looked for instruments that would identify many students with diverse language needs and that would demand higher levels of achievement in the areas of language and literacy before returning these youngsters to regular instructional programs. It was not until 1978 that Title VII made provisions to assess all four language skills — listening, speaking, reading, and writing. Even then, a gap existed between this policy and the availability of instruments to carry out these tasks with sufficient validity and reliability.

The policy regarding which youngsters to include in bilingual/bicultural programs has also been subject to change. The major intent of early bilingual legislation, for example, was to address the needs of limited-English speakers, who were frequently children of poverty. But a 1978 amendment to Title VII encouraged the inclusion of other students, provided that they did not exceed 40% of the total classroom population. Thus it was possible to have in one classroom indigenous minority students whose parents wanted them to reclaim their ancestral languages, English-dominant majority students whose parents saw the benefits of acquiring a second language, highly bilingual children whose parents wanted them to develop in both languages, and students with limited proficiency in English. The instructional implications for each of these groups are quite different. For instance, indigenous minority students whose dominant — or only — language is English may have endured negative experiences associated with their linguistic or cultural identities. To focus in the classroom on a language or culture that a student has rejected may be a delicate endeavor. Furthermore, such children — even though their dominant language is English — may in fact speak a nonstandard version of English. Often, their needs are overshadowed by the glaring language deficits of limited-English-speaking students — and thus not given the attention they deserve.

Such instructional problems stem in part from the shortage of classroom-tested research findings to shape and buttress program designs. Bilingual teachers, many of them novices, have been given a complex charge. They must 1) provide literacy instruction in two languages for a variety of students; 2) understand and apply theories of language acquisition; 3) organize their classrooms for the triple goals of language development, cognitive growth, and intercultural awareness; 4) stay abreast of the latest research findings; and 5) keep up to date on the constantly changing federal, state, and school district regulations. Simultaneously, bilingual teachers must manage their classes, which are characterized by linguistic, cultural, and academic diversity.

What have we learned during the past 15 years that can help us realize more fully the promise of bilingual education? To begin with, linguists have made important progress in understanding first- and second-language acquisition. Their research suggests that the developmental process is similar and predictable for both children and adults. Thus the acquisition of a second language requires time and experiences that are tailored to a learner's developmental stage.

One stage is manifested in the informal language that we all use as we deal with our immediate environments. Because the context is clear, this level of language is characterized by incomplete responses, a limited vocabulary, and many nonverbal cues. An average non-English-speaking student learns to communicate at this level after about two years of instruction.

A second developmental level consists of the language used in school and in many facets of adult life. Here the context is less clear; instead, communication depends on a speaker's (or writer's) ability to manipulate the vocabulary and syntax with precision. Students with limited proficiency in English need at least five to seven years of instruction to master this formal language.[3]

The implications for timing the exit of students from bilingual programs into the regular curriculum are clear. In assessing the language proficiency of such students, we must be certain that they can handle this formal (i.e., context-reduced) language. However, assessments during the Seventies of children with limited proficiency in English often measured only context-embedded communication, not the formal language that students need for sustained academic growth.

During the past 15 years we have also learned that certain methods promote natural acquisition of language, while other methods promote only a mechanical ability to manipulate rules of grammar. Moreover, because learners follow a neurologically programmed sequence of stages in acquiring a second language, we now recognize that our expectations for second-language production should follow that sequence. Likewise, the language to which teachers expose learners during language lessons should reflect those stages. To be comprehensible, teachers should begin with concrete objects, firsthand experiences, and visual contexts. In other words, students with limited proficiency in English are likely to make more progress in one hour of carefully designed, *comprehensible* input than in many hours of simply sitting in a regular classroom listening to what, to them, is "noise." In addition, Stephen Krashen has found that students' attitudes toward the second language are as important as their talents for learning languages; the students' ages, their previous exposures to the second language, and their levels of acculturation are also factors that teachers must take into account.[4]

We have also learned that bilingualism and biculturalism are not detrimental to cognitive development, and that cognitive skills are transferable across cultures and languages. In fact, some evidence suggests that bilingualism may encourage the development of divergent thinking and creativity.[5] This new view of bilingualism challenges the view that researchers held from the Thirties through the Fifties: that bilingualism hindered cognitive and linguistic development because the brain could not deal with multiple linguistic tracks.

The evolution of bilingual education has caused us to recognize the fact that social context affects learning outcomes in bilingual settings. For example, programs that immerse youngsters in a second language are successful only when they do not stigmatize the students' primary languages and home cultures. Thus the attitudes of the host society toward groups that speak another language have an enormous impact on minority students' perceptions of themselves and of the school.

Much pedagogical experimentation and learning took place during the Seventies in the areas of language and cognitive development, but not all the findings were pleasant. The most publicized negative findings were those of the report by the American Institutes of Research (AIR),[6] which suggested that students enrolled in Title VII bilingual programs did not achieve at a higher level than counterparts who were not enrolled in such programs. However, Doris Gunderson points out that:

> Although there is insufficient research documenting the effects of bilingual education, there is no research to substantiate the claim that bilingual education and bilingualism are harmful. Moreover, the available research indicates that bilingual education is either beneficial or neutral in terms of scholastic achievement, giving the student the added advantage of exposure to two languages.[7]

A variety of longitudinal studies have also revealed positive academic gains for students who have been enrolled in bilingual programs for at least four years.[8]

To date, many students who would qualify for bilingual or English-as-a-second-language programs have not received such instruction — and, in general, such students are still not achieving on a par with students whose native language is English. There is still much work to be done. As bilingual educators become better acquainted with theories of language acquisition and the methods they imply, with the relationships that research is disclosing between cognition and language, and with the findings related to the optimal organization of classroom programs and resources, bilingual education will become increasingly effective. But better bilingual education also depends on a supportive sociopolitical environment.

The war of words regarding bilingual/bicultural education has centered on three disputed issues: 1) the use of public funds for special educational programs for students with limited proficiency in English, 2) the function of language as a bonding or polarizing force in society, and 3) the extent to which language — and not other socioeconomic and cultural factors — is responsible for academic failure.

Historically, bilingual programs emerged in the U.S. wherever ethnic communities believed that it was in their interest to create such programs. But 1968 marked the beginning of an uneasy relationship between the federal government and such ethnic communities, brought about by the enactment of Title VII of the Elementary and Secondary Education Act. The primary purpose of Title VII was to improve the academic performance of economically deprived children who also had difficulty with English. Congress appropriated the initial funds to teach such students in their home languages, but these students were to transfer into the all-English curriculum as soon as they were able to handle such instruction. Congress did not intend the legislation either to promote minority languages or to pluralize society. Rather, the intention was to use the home languages and firsthand experiences of these students to assimilate them as rapidly as possible into the regular (i.e., English-dominant) school program. Congress supported Title VII on the premise that these low-income youngsters needed all the help they could get to overcome their linguistic, cultural, and environmental handicaps and thus to equalize their opportunities for success in U.S. society.

Title VII recognized the importance of building on what the students already knew. However, this legislation was not intended to maintain the rich linguistic resources that these children represented. Much of the debate about bilingual education during the Seventies focused on this issue. One side favored prolonged attempts by the schools to maintain children's home languages; the other side believed that the period of bilingual instruction should be as short as possible. As the debate on the length of programs grew more heated, participants focused less attention on the quality of bilingual instruction.

From the debate about language maintenance versus rapid transition to English, a second question arose that the public found more worrisome: would bilingual education cause students to develop divided linguistic and cultural loyalties? The federal guidelines for Title VII implied that the schools would encourage a common culture, since they would eventually return bilingual students to regular classes. At the community level, however, ethnic minorities were beginning to see that they could join the societal mainstream politically, educationally, and economically without forgetting their first languages and their cultural traditions.

Should linguistic minority groups have the right to participate fully in American life without being completely assimilated into the mainstream culture? This issue is still not resolved. Court decisions have consistently affirmed the civil rights of all residents without regard to race, language, or national origin.[9] However, many defenders of monolingualism and monoculturalism have argued that, with respect to bilingual education, the courts have limited the rights of local communities to run their schools as they see fit. Therefore, even though the intent of the courts has been to protect the civil rights of all students, many individuals have interpreted these decisions as invidious vehicles for social engineering.

Moreover, bilingual education is intertwined with such sensitive issues as governmental attitudes toward immigrants and indigenous minorities. The U.S. has received in the recent past large numbers of political refugees, economic refugees, and undocumented workers. But consistent policies regarding who can enter the U.S. and on what criteria are nonexistent. Nor do clear policies exist with regard to trade relations with the developing nations or political relations with oppressive regimes. It is hard to examine the pedagogical value of bilingual instruction without becoming entangled in such sensitive political issues as the rights and status of undocumented workers.

Given these tensions and the current trend toward less federal involvement in education, some observers feel that bilingual programs are doomed to extinction. However, the 1982 cutbacks in bilingual education were no more severe than those in other federal programs, and it looks as though Congress will reauthorize funding in 1983. Furthermore, extensive state legislation is now in place to continue the funding of bilingual education. It would be pedagogically unsound and sociopolitically imprudent to return to the sink-or-swim methods of the past. Bilingual education is a reality that even Nathan Glazer, one of its most ardent critics, admits is here to stay.[10]

This does not mean that bilingual education will have smooth sailing. As we reflect on the experiences of the past 15 years and consider the political, demographic, and economic realities of the future, we must recognize the need to define more clearly the mission of bilingual education. This mission is to meet — rationally and realistically — the linguistic and cognitive needs of students with limited proficiency in English. This mission assumes greater importance when we consider that the non-English-speaking population in the U.S. is expected to increase from 30 million in 1980 to about 39.5 million in the year 2000.[11] There will never be a more appropriate time for the U.S. to develop a clear language policy.

An official language policy toward ethnolinguistic minorities would create a better balance between the learning needs of students with limited proficiency in English and the national interest. Such a policy would stress the universal language needs of all learners; it would also consider both the importance of breaking down the social barriers between ethnic groups and the potential for cognitive development of intracultural and cross-cultural affirmation. Likewise, such a policy would recognize the role of language in the promotion of academic excellence, and it would encourage the development of multilingualism in the larger society. In this era of global interdependence, such multilingualism would help to advance U.S. trade and political interests. Although it is difficult to quantify, the humanistic rationale for encouraging individuals to maintain or acquire a second language is also important. Through language, human beings discover one another's worlds.

The public is still somewhat uncertain today about the content and the process of bilingual education, about its posture regarding goals for national unity, and about the balance that bilingual education strikes between benefits and costs. But despite these uncertainties, most Americans seem to agree that language development and cross-cultural studies advance national interests. The final report of the President's Commission on Foreign Language and International Studies, *Strength Through Wisdom: A Critique of U.S. Capability*,[12] confirms this positive attitude. Largely as a result of the commission's recommendations, a consortium of 10 organizations involved in language instruction — called the Joint National Committee for Languages — has begun to assess governmental support for a more coherent national policy on language.

Such a language policy must be responsive to the desires and needs of local communities. As it relates to the education of children with limited proficiency in English, however, this policy could aim to accomplish three general goals: 1) the affirmation of children's right to maintain their home languages, 2) the collection and dissemination of research findings on the role of the home language in cognitive development, and 3) the collection and dissemination of research findings that compare the outcomes of carefully designed bilingual education programs with those of undifferentiated instruction in an all-English environment.

The U.S. should nurture the rich linguistic resources that ethnic minorities provide. A national language policy will increase the likelihood of a flexible support system for children whose home language is other than English. Such a policy will also foster the acquisition of second languages among English-speaking students and can be adjusted to meet the needs of local communities.

---

1. Betty J. Mace-Matluck, *Literacy Instruction in Bilingual Settings: A Synthesis of Current Research* (Los Alamitos, Calif.: National Center for Bilingual Research, 1982), pp. 19-20.
2. Eleanor W. Thonis, "Reading Instruction for Language Minority Students," in *Schooling and Language Minority Students: A Theoretical Framework* (Los Angeles: Evaluation, Dissemination, and Assessment Center, California State University, 1981), pp. 162-67.
3. Jim Cummins, "Four Misconceptions About Language Proficiency in Bilingual Education," *NABE Journal*, Spring 1981, pp. 31-44.
4. Stephen D. Krashen, "Bilingual Education and Second Language Acquisition Theory," in *Schooling and Language Minority Students. . .* , pp. 76-77.
5. Elizabeth Peal and Wallace E. Lambert, "The Relation of Bilingualism to Intelligence," *Psychological Monographs: General and Applied*, no. 76, 1962, pp. 1-23.
6. Malcolm Danoff, *Evaluation of the Impact of ESEA Title VII Spanish/English Bilingual Education Program* (Palo Alto, Calif.: American Institutes for Research, 1978), pp. 1-19.
7. Doris V. Gunderson, "Bilingual Education," in Harold E. Mitzel, ed., *Encyclopedia of Educational Research*, Vol. I, 5th ed. (New York: Free Press, 1982), p. 210.
8. See, for example, Wallace E. Lambert and Richard Tucker, *Bilingual Education of Children: The St. Lambert Experiment* (Rowley, Mass.: Newbury House, 1972); William Mackey and Von Nieda Beebe, *Bilingual Schools for a Bicultural Community: Miami's Adaptation to the Cuban Refugees* (Rowley, Mass.: Newbury House, 1977); and Bernard Spolsky, "Bilingual Education in the United States," in James E. Alatis, ed., *Georgetown University Round Table on Languages and Linguistics: International Dimensions of Bilingual Education* (Washington, D.C.: Georgetown University Press, 1978).
9. See, for example, *Aspira of New York* v. *Board of Education of the City of New York*, 423 F. Supp. 647 (S.D.N.Y. 1967); *Lau* v. *Nichols*, 414 U.S. 563, 566 (1974); and *Castañeda* v. *Pickard*, 648 F. 2d 989 (5th Cir., 1981).
10. Nathan Glazer, "Pluralism and Ethnicity," in Martin Ridge, ed., *The New Bilingualism: An American Dilemma* (Los Angeles: University of Southern California Press, 1982), p. 58.
11. *The Prospects for Bilingual Education in the Nation: Fifth Annual Report of the National Advisory Council for Bilingual Education, 1980-81*, p. xii.
12. President's Commission on Foreign Language and International Studies, *Strength Through Wisdom: A Critique of U.S. Capability* (Washington, D.C.: U.S. Government Printing Office, 1979).

The New Pioneers of the Home-Schooling Movement

Diane Divoky

DIANE DIVOKY covers California education for the Sacramento Bee.

"Parents have a right to educate their children at home, and this right bears constitutional protection."

That credo comes not from a radical educator or libertarian theorist, but from the Rockland (Massachusetts) School Committee, which last August approved a home-schooling policy that gives school officials the right and responsibility to approve home education programs but provides parents with significant control over the *way* their children will be educated at home. For example, the Rockland policy states that, in line with recent state court rulings, the school committee will not pry into parents' reasons for wanting to educate their children at home. Furthermore, the committee will not worry about "the lack of a curriculum identical to that of the public schools" or the lack of group experiences for home-schooled children.

The Rockland policy, developed by parents and school officials, gives those who wish to educate their children at home clear guidelines under which to apply for program approval. Parents are also afforded the right to a hearing to explain and answer questions about their plan; at this hearing, they may be represented by counsel and call witnesses.

"We believe that people can be educated in places other than schools," explains John Rogers, superintendent of the Rockland schools. "I don't think we have a monopoly on education. Who's to say where children can get a proper education?" The Rockland school district is one of a handful that are known to be friendly to home schoolers; as a result, people who want to school their children at home "are moving into town, knowing they won't be hassled," Rogers says. He adds that the district is willing to provide books and programs for home-schooled children; in fact, he plans to start placing such youngsters on the district rolls, in order to collect state funds for them.

The tiny San Juan Ridge Union School District in Nevada City, California, has had home-schooled youngsters on its rolls for several years. When administrator Marilyn DeVore realized that about a dozen children who lived within the district were being schooled at home, she decided to work with their parents rather than to fight them. Under the arrangement she devised, the students are tested by the district, and DeVore herself supervises the courses of study that the parents propose and teach. "The board approves each individual course of study," she says. So far, the children learning at home are performing very well on district tests.

A subversive activity until a very few years ago, home schooling is quickly becoming a national movement with its own gurus, publications, and support networks. Not many school systems are as cooperative with parents who educate their children at home as Rockland or San Juan Ridge. But few superintendents are unaware of the movement and of parents' reasons for choosing this option, according to Kathleen O'Malley, an attorney with a Harrisburg, Pennsylvania, law firm that handles a sizable number of home-schooling cases. "In some cases, the superintendent will still say, 'If I let you do this, everyone will want to do it,' " O'Malley notes, "but usually superintendents can be educated about the legal rationale for home schooling and are willing to negotiate some sort of compromise."

"The New Pioneers of the Home-Schooling Movement," Diane Divoky, *Phi Delta Kappan*, February 1983. Reprinted by permission.

The home schoolers themselves — estimates put the number at about 10,000 nationally — are coming out of the closet. Ten years ago, such parents would have insisted that their children stay inside the house during school hours, for fear that neighbors would report them to the truant officer. Today, home schoolers are more likely to appear on TV talk shows and to grant interviews to reporters about this educational option. For example, Joyce Kinmont of Brigham City, Utah, who schools her seven children at home, publishes books, makes tapes, and speaks frequently before groups about the advantages of home schooling.

In Grants Pass, Oregon, Jane Joyce writes favorably about home schooling for an area newspaper; she charges that the public schools quash creativity and foster dullness. "Why is education compulsory, if it's so good?" she asks. Joyce, who has been willing to submit her home learning program to the local district for approval and to have her children tested, is no longer certain that she wishes to continue accommodating the system to that degree. She contends that it is her right to educate her children in any way she chooses, and she chafes at the idea that "my papers must be in order and approved so that I can do this." Joyce urges other home schoolers in her area to deal more confidently with school officials. "You can't be Little Miss Muffet," she exhorts. "You don't have to be mealymouthed and embarrassed about what you're doing."

Meanwhile, home schoolers in Indiana are going on the legal offensive for the first time. A sudden flurry of prosecutions of home schoolers has arisen in that state, despite a fairly liberal state policy. Parents are responding by joining a suit filed in federal court in February 1982 by a South Bend area family, the Mazanecs, against the North Judson-San Pierre School Corporation. The suit charges that the school district — under cover of the compulsory education laws — has violated the civil rights of the Mazanec family by harassment. The plaintiffs are asking $310,000 in damages for the emotional stress they claim to have suffered because of school officials' actions.

"It's a model case," says Ed Nagel, director of the National Association for the Legal Support of Alternative Schools in Santa Fe, New Mexico, an organization that supports home schoolers. "We're signaling the system that it can't use public money to intimidate parents, to make them live in fear. We're saying to school officials that, if you go after parents, they'll turn around and sue you. It's time the bureaucrats begin to assume responsibility for their vindictive prosecution of parents under vague, ambiguous laws."

Nagel adds that, although parents have a high win rate — somewhere between 90% and 95% — when districts take them to court, "individual wins aren't enough, because in every case parents have to be on the defensive, and it's an expensive and time-consuming business. We're trying to turn that around." He describes home schooling as "a rapidly growing movement that school administrators cannot thwart."

John Holt, best known for his books on education reform and perhaps the preeminent spokesman for home schooling, agrees with Nagel. "These parents are tough, determined, and slippery, with a real pioneer spirit," says Holt, whose bimonthly newsletter, *Growing Without Schooling*, provides support, legal information, ideas, and resources to some 3,600 subscribers.*

"The beauty of the anarchistic structure of the home-schooling movement," according to Holt, "is that it spans quite comfortably a wide range of views," including those of every ideological and political stripe. Both Holt and Nagel come out of the liberal school reform movement; by contrast, Raymond Moore, an educational researcher from Michigan who writes in favor of home schooling and provides expert court testimony for parents, is a conservative — a Seventh-Day Adventist who believes that children should learn religious and moral principles from their parents before being exposed to the secular culture of the schools.

Parents choose home schooling for a number of reasons. For some, the decision springs from personal experiences as teachers or parents who have worked to reform the schools from within. Linda Ashton of Lawton, Oklahoma, says that her years as a third-grade teacher taught her "how much time had to be wasted by virtue of having 30 students" in the classroom. "It was either hurry-up or busywork," Ashton recalls. "I knew that I couldn't give the children the kind of attention they needed. One-on-one makes so much more sense."

An Esparto, California, mother who didn't become involved in home schooling until her youngest child was 12 explains: "Over the years I became more and more disillusioned with the schools. I've raised seven children. I've worked as an aide in the classroom and served on all the committees. I asked questions about accountability and why the schools couldn't teach composition. I watched youngsters pick up more bad habits in school than their parents could counteract. And finally I got wise and realized that the school is not our friend, that those people really don't care about us and our children."

Other home schoolers are simply working for self-sufficiency in a society that they perceive as too technological and too institutionalized. For them, home schooling is an extension of a lifestyle that often includes living on the land and growing their own food. And life in a rural environment — where children necessarily spend more time with their families than with peers — seems unusually compatible with home schooling.

For example, in rural Plumas County, California, the Gorbet children begin the day with three hours of studying under their mother's tutelage; in the afternoon they do outdoor chores around the family ranch and care for their own horses. Accomplished riders, they often win prizes at local and regional horse shows. Similarly, Pat Mattison of Middlebury, Vermont, explains that her home-schooled children are responsible for feeding and watering the family's farm animals. "These are not token chores — but real work that is necessary in order for us to have the life we choose," she points out.

Probably a majority of home schoolers are religious fundamentalists, unhappy with the failure of the public schools to teach religious and spiritual tenets and with what they sometimes describe as the "secular humanism" that these schools allegedly espouse. Gina Gorbet says that the primary reason for schooling her eight children at home is so that "they will absorb the traditional Catholic philosophy," which, she explained, stresses modesty in dress and speech, separation of the sexes, and the importance of proselytizing. Ruth and Peter Nobel of Dorr, Michigan, who gained national publicity in 1980 when a court ruled that they had a constitutional right to educate their children at home, are devout Calvinist Christians who rejected the public schools because of "the immorality, the dress, the attitudes, the speech" that they found there.

Florence Wolf of Brooks, California, who teaches her two children and a nephew at home, complains that in the public schools "there is no right or wrong; values are variable." She also believes that children can pick up dangerous ideas in sex education classes. "As Christians, we're concerned with children's self-worth, their ability — with God's help — to say no when that is required," explains Brit Fillmore of Gridley, California, an Adventist who is schooling her children at home. "Children can be swayed so easily by peer pressure."

In spite of the diverse reasons that draw parents to home schooling, they share a profound belief that the public schools are not providing a healthy environment for their children. They also share a need to have some control over their children's learning and development. And they are all willing to be different, to take a socially unorthodox route to rearing the kind of children they want.

2. CONTINUITY AND CHANGE

On a political level, home schooling is an act both revolutionary and reactionary: revolutionary because it flies in the face of the established social order, reactionary because it means turning one's back on the larger society and on the time-honored assumption that parents and society share in the rearing of the young. On a more practical level, home schooling is a remarkably gutsy effort. Parents must be willing, first of all, to negotiate with, stare down, or hide from school authorities — and to live as outsiders in their own communities. They must also develop enough confidence to be able to ward off doubts about whether they are doing right by their children.

Most difficult of all is the nonstop, year-in, year-out job itself. Even in the rare cases where two parents share the work, it is psychologically and physically demanding. Most often, however, the mother alone becomes the unpaid teacher in uncharted territory. "Home schooling requires enormous personal confidence, enterprise, and tenacity," notes a home schooler in Sacramento, California. "It is not a step taken lightly — or done as a protest or an ego trip." She points out that, if nothing else, most parents are grateful to use the schools as a baby-sitting service. "Because I am both educating and caring for my children, I have no time for myself, no break," she says.

For the majority of families with young children, home schooling is logistically impossible, no matter how attractive the idea seems. The current economy does not allow most parents to remain at home, even when career advancement is not at issue.

Holt likes to think that it is possible to school children at home, even when both parents work. He suggests that children over age 8 "don't need to be baby-sat," that like-minded families can rotate home-schooling responsibilities, that working parents with younger children can send them to homes where older home-schooled children can supervise them, and that older people in the community can be recruited to do the job. These are all interesting ideas — but probably not practical, except in special circumstances.

Nagel suggests that, to avoid the mom-stays-at-home-and-does-it-all routine, an older son or daughter might serve as tutor or a college student might be offered room and board in exchange for tutoring. A number of families might share a tutor, he says, as long as parents keep the arrangement small enough so that it doesn't grow into a school, with all the same problems that the families are trying to avoid.

The hardest part of the job for many home schoolers appears to be getting started, given their preconceived notions about how children learn. Kinmont warns interested parents that they probably won't do a very good job the first year, as they work to overcome their ingrained sense of what school is all about. She advises parents to give themselves at least a year to try out home schooling before abandoning the idea. Angel Eberlein of Brooks, California, says that, when she began schooling her two children at home, she hired a teacher to check on their progress periodically; as she grew more confident, she no longer needed that backup, however. "Common sense and dedication are the main ingredients needed to teach one's own children," according to Eberlein. "When I started out, I didn't have any of the confidence I have now," Gorbet concurs. "But slowly I learned my strengths and where I was weak, where I needed to call for some help."

Many parents said that the shakiness of the first few months was replaced by confidence, as they saw their children thriving. A number, whose children had attended public schools before beginning home schooling, also noted that the youngsters had needed some time to shed bad habits and to regain a sense of self-direction.

"We had a specific curriculum for the first three or four months when we started this," says Francis Turano of Somerset, Massachusetts, whose daughters — now 12 and 14 — have been schooled at home since 1978. "But then we found we didn't need it, so now we just use it as a reference or guide. At first, when we took them out of public school, they seemed to have lost the ability to think and learn on their own — their zest and curiosity. They had lost the natural instinct to learn. Then, after a period of time, it was like: 'Look out, here we come.' They're studying more now, on their own, because they want to. My wife (who was a public school teacher for seven years) and I just oversee their studying now. We assist them, but they're pretty much on their own."

The goal, many veteran home schoolers suggest, is to be able to get out of the way of children's learning, to simply provide an environment that allows youngsters to be self-directed. "We leave Krista pretty much on her own," says Karen Elder of Princeton, New Jersey, of her 7-year-old, who is schooled at home. "We have a lot of books, some textbooks (which are the least used, because they are the least interesting), lots of paper, various machines (typewriter, calculator, TV, tape recorder, stereo, electronic games, and a borrowed minicomputer), sports equipment, small animals, and ourselves and our work."

Holt recommends a free-flow curriculum for home-schooled children, which exposes them to as many community resources as possible. "Let the interests and the inclinations of the children determine what happens, and give children access to as much of the parents' lives and the world around them as possible," he advises, adding that three to five hours of formal instruction per week is "perfectly sufficient."

However, the popularity of such highly structured correspondence courses as the Calvert Home Instruction Courses and the Christian Liberty Academy program suggests that many parents need a crutch for their home schooling. These programs provide for a structured morning or afternoon of study each day. They also give parents some feedback about their children's progress by evaluating their work, scoring their tests, and reporting back with grades.

Many programs — and many experienced home schoolers — urge parents to spend their time working side by side with their children, integrating skill development with such tasks as cooking, shopping, planning menus, gardening, and doing carpentry and repairs. Home schoolers who wish their children to have time to socialize with their peers are also advised to sign them up for such out-of-school activities as Scouts, sports teams, church groups, hobby clubs, and community classes.

In spite of the growth of the home-schooling movement, there is still little consistency among the school districts in a given state — much less from state to state — regarding the acceptability of home schooling. "Often, it's up to the individual superintendent's interpretation of state law, his particular bias," says attorney Kathleen O'Malley. "In Pennsylvania, for example, the state department of education has never decided whether correspondence courses fulfill the compulsory education law. So you have superintendents who are suspicious of home schoolers, and others who will wink at home schooling."

Turano, a police officer, notes that his home state, Massachusetts, "has districts that are both the toughest and the most lenient" with home schoolers. "Each system here has its own idea of how much it can invade the privacy of families," he says.

In general, California is benign in dealing with home schoolers — requiring only that they file an affidavit each fall that registers them as private schools. However, the largest school district, Los Angeles, interprets the law strictly and does not allow home schoolers to register as private schools, even if the parents hold proper credentials for teaching the grades in which their children are enrolled. "We consider any home-teaching situation a tutoring situation; we require that the teacher have the proper credentials — and, in any case, the teacher cannot be the parent," says Kathleen Smith, a district official. To enforce that policy, any school with fewer than six or seven students is investigated, and parents who persist in home teaching are turned over to the city attorney.

At about the same time that the highest court in West Virginia tightened the home-schooling policy in that state, denying that parents have a religious right to teach their children at home without the approval of the local school board, the Arizona legislature passed a law allowing parents to teach their children at home without the permission of the local school board — a major victory for home schoolers in that state.

Amid the patchwork of court decisions and regulations, parents use a number of ploys to avoid legal controversy. Some enroll their children in private schools that are willing to serve as fronts for home-schooling families. Such "shelter schools" often provide materials and lesson guides or testing services for parents; some actually allow home-schooled children to attend one day or so each week. Other parents do what is legally required in a particular district or state to meet compulsory education laws: hire a certified teacher as a tutor, become certified teachers themselves, or write curricula for their children and submit them to the district for approval.

Michelle Carnevale of Grass Valley, California, who is educating her daughter at home, thinks that most problems with school officials can be avoided if children are kept out of school from the beginning, so that their absence is never noticed. Other parents simply tell a district that they are moving elsewhere when they begin home schooling. Even these tactics may not be discreet enough, particularly in urban areas. Raymond Moore maintains that three-fourths of the children who are pursued by school districts come to the attention of school officials because neighbors report them.

Given the diminishing financial resources of the schools, engaging the parents of each home-schooled child in a protracted legal battle seems a ludicrous and ultimately self-defeating task for school districts. By contrast, a cooperative arrangement between a district and home schoolers — one that allows parents to use district resources, while the district continues to receive state funds for each child — may satisfy the needs of both parties. "It's such a sensible arrangement," says Holt. "There's nothing in the laws that says that attendance has to mean that bodies are in certain classrooms all day, that districts should be prevented from collecting aid if students are schooled at home."

"The legal decisions are going against the system anyway," echoes Nagel. "So if districts want to hold on to their average daily attendance, why don't they make materials and resources available to these parents in exchange for enrollment? How much more sense it makes to set up an educational center for the use of home schoolers and others, instead of spending that money fighting them. The superintendents can't stop the movement anyway, so why not work with it?"

The Struggle for Excellence: Striving for Higher Achievement

A controversy has developed over the many commission and individual reports on how to improve the quality of schooling. Professional educators in the nation's educational system are beginning to respond. The political and economic ramifications of the quest for excellence in education are going to be significant. Major revisions in the federal tax structure are already being debated in the national government which will force state legislatures to reconsider how state or provincial tax bases will be affected by changes in federal tax laws.

One of the great and wholly unanswered questions which runs through all of the current debate over excellence in education is: How will national and state governments respond to the recommendations of the various commissions' think tanks and individual studies of how to enhance the quality of education? Most local school districts cannot finance many of the reform measures being proposed, such as a longer school day or year (which means more salary costs), merit pay for teachers, more testing, and improved curricula. A national furor exists over the quest for academic excellence, but little or no agreement has been reached on the means to carry reforms to the implementation stage.

Yet it is not just the political and economic issues which wait to be resolved in the struggle over whose model of excellence will triumph in our nation's schools. There is still the very big matter of the unfinished agenda of equality of opportunity left over from the 1960s and 1970s. There is no doubt that these issues will have to be resolved within

Unit 3

the context of an assertive pursuit of excellence in education, a pursuit shared by minority and majority parents.

The first article in this unit sets the context in which the drive for excellence in education is proceeding. Diane Ravitch raises issues regarding the response of educators to the recent reports, and describes how trends in curriculum development in the past century have contributed to the current state of the schools. Both articles on *A Nation at Risk* give the reader an idea of what educational issues need to be faced when dealing with the struggle for greater excellence in the schools. The article by Daniel and Lauren Resnick summarizes the curricular controversies to be dealt with on this matter. They propose a common national curriculum prior to high school.

One of the really big issues in the drive for improving the quality of schooling centers around how the schools can change to better meet the challenges. Dan Morgan's essay concerning the SAT tests discusses the development and use of SATs and the controversies surrounding the use of these tests. Two very interesting perspectives on how teachers are affected by the current round of criticisms of the quality of schooling are provided by Harry N. Chandler and Robert A. Blume. Finally, C.H. Edson's essay compares current efforts to reform American education to earlier reform efforts in the late nineteenth and early twentieth centuries.

The courses in which this anthology is used relate heavily to the social context of schooling and the issues facing educators. The essays in this unit could relate to those parts of a course dealing with either curriculum issues or the history of education. The articles in this unit can also be discussed with the issues raised in Unit 6 on equality of opportunity, because there are some thorny problems to be faced as the nation strives to optimize attainment of both quality and equality of opportunity in its schools. The broad base of concern underlying the articles in this unit are relevant to all discussions of the social context of education.

Looking Ahead: Challenge Questions

What changes in society and in its schools have created such intensified interest in striving for academic excellence?

What can be learned from the recent reports on the state of American education? What are your views on the recommendations being offered to improve the quality of schooling?

How could school curricula and instructional practices be modified to encourage excellence in teaching and learning?

What minimum academic standards should high school graduates have achieved?

What relevance do SAT scores have? Should their use be continued? What issues are raised by their use?

What are teachers' concerns amidst the rhetoric of the debate over excellence in education?

What can we learn about the struggle for excellence in schooling from a historical perspective on the history of efforts to reform education?

The Continuing Crisis

Fashions in Education

Diane Ravitch

DIANE RAVITCH, adjunct professor of history and education at Teachers College, Columbia University, is the author of The Troubled Crusade: American Education, 1945–1980 *and* The Great School Wars: New York City, 1805–1973.

In the spring of 1983, unsuspecting American citizens woke up one morning to discover in the morning's headlines that we were "a nation at risk"; that other countries were challenging our leadership in "commerce, industry, science, and technological innovation"; and that "a rising tide of mediocrity" was threatening "our very future as a Nation and a people." The National Commission on Excellence in Education warned, in the kind of flashy prose that commands media attention, that "if an unfriendly foreign power had attempted to impose on America the mediocre educational performance that exists today, we might well have viewed it as an act of war. . . . We have, in effect, been committing an act of unthinking, unilateral educational disarmament."

This was strong stuff, but it was only the first in a series of critical reports on the quality of American schooling. Within weeks, several other state-of-education study groups weighed in with dire pronouncements about the need for change, and the fall season opened with a new crop of critical books and studies about the schools. The daily papers and weekly newsmagazines responded to the new issue by expanding their coverage of education, but the only fact of which the media seemed certain was that the schools were in a "crisis." Customarily uninterested in long-term educational trends, the news media offered no explanation for the plethora of critiques: as first one and then another study appeared, each was duly reported, but without reference to any context to explain the tidal wave. Why did so many reports appear simultaneously? What did it mean? No one hazarded a guess.

Since the National Commission on Excellence in Education was appointed by a conservative Republican president, there was a tendency in some quarters to treat its report as a statement of Reaganism. However, this was a superficial and perhaps defensive reaction, for the commission itself did not have a partisan cast. Nor could the conclusions of the other studies and reports be dismissed out of hand as machinations of an administration intent on dismantling the federal role in education and reviving school prayer. (Indeed, one of the best of the recent studies was *High School,* written by Ernest Boyer, the last commissioner of education in the Carter administration.) Political partisanship was not a factor in any of the reports. The president had been saying that the involvement of the federal government had caused the decay of the schools, but none of the reports (including that of his own commission) supported that argument. Another federally funded commission, the National Science Board's Commission on Precollege Education in Mathematics, Science, and Technology, recommended additional federal spending of about $1 billion a year to improve instruction in these areas, even though the president clearly opposed increased federal funding of education.

If there was a single event that precipitated the present enthusiasm for educational reform, it was probably the announcement in 1975 by the College Board that scores on the Scholastic Aptitude Test had fallen steadily since 1963. This college-entry test of verbal and mathematical skills has been in use since the late 1920s, though only since the late 1950s has it been taken by large numbers of high school students. The substantial decline of the national average, especially

Reprinted from THE AMERICAN SCHOLAR, Volume 53, Number 2, Spring, 1983, pp. 183-193. Copyright ©1983 by The United Chapters of Phi Beta Kappa. By permission of the publishers.

on the verbal portion of the test, meant different things to different people. For most people, the falling SAT scores suggested that something was seriously wrong with the schools, and that the freewheeling educational experimentation of the 1960s and 1970s had undermined the teaching of basic skills. The nascent back-to-basics movement gathered momentum, and during the late 1970s nearly forty states passed minimum competency tests for high school students, to assess whether they had mastered the basics. Since minimum competency tests guaranteed only that those at the bottom had attained minimal literacy, the spread of such tests did not allay doubts about the quality of precollegiate education.

Not everyone saw the SAT score decline as a catastrophe. There were those who said that the falling scores meant nothing at all because the drop in the mean was caused by the increased numbers of poor, black, and female students taking the tests. And then there were those like Ralph Nader and his associates who said that the test itself meant nothing at all, so it scarcely mattered whether national scores went up or down.

In search of reasons for the score decline, the College Board created a blue-ribbon panel, headed by former secretary of labor Willard Wirtz. The panel's report was issued in 1977 and concluded that a substantial increase in the proportion of low-scoring test takers had accounted for most of the score decline until 1970. After 1970 the demographic composition of the test takers remained relatively constant, yet test scores continued to fall (the national verbal mean went from 478 in 1963 to 460 in 1970, then dropped even faster to 429 in 1977). The perception that a real erosion of verbal skills had occurred was reinforced by the fact that the number and proportion of students scoring over 700 dropped by 50 percent between 1967 and 1974.

The Wirtz panel held that the score decline "warrants serious attention," but it was notably coy in casting stones at perpetrators. The grand villain was "pervasive change," the rise of great impersonal social forces like television, Vietnam, Watergate, and family dissolution. How these were related to falling scores other than as "distractions" was unclear. What was clear, however, was that much had changed within the school during this critical period. The panel noted, first, an expansion of electives, accompanied by a decline in enrollments in basic academic courses. For example, the number of Massachusetts schools offering courses in filmmaking and mass media had grown, while the number offering junior-year courses in English and world history had declined. Second, standards within the schools had clearly fallen: "Absenteeism formerly considered intolerable is now condoned. An 'A' or 'B' means a good deal less than it used to. Promotion from one grade to another has become almost automatic. Homework has apparently been cut about in half." Third, one of the panel's internal studies concluded that eleventh-grade textbooks were currently written at a ninth-to-tenth-grade reading level, that the portion of the typical text devoted to pictures and graphics had expanded, and that textbook assignments generally asked "only for underlining, circling and filling in of single words." Lastly, the panel concluded that "the critical factors in the relationship between curricular change and the SAT scores are (1) that less thoughtful and critical reading is now being demanded and done, and (2) that careful writing has apparently about gone out of style." The principle of Occam's razor surely should have indicated that such in-school practices were sufficient to explain declining verbal skills of the college bound, even without the social and political calamities beyond the classroom door.

As the Wirtz panel was composing its findings, citizens' groups across the country were vocally criticizing low standards, lax discipline, and social promotion. Legislatures responded to these pressures by ordering tests of students and teachers. Educators and policymakers responded by creating committees. By 1981, when President Reagan appointed the National Commission on Excellence in Education, at least two dozen committees, study groups, and task forces were already considering the condition of the schools, and most of these were specifically studying the high school. There seemed to be a general recognition that the course of study in the elementary years was essentially the same for all students, but that something was amiss in the later years (the junior high years—certainly no less important than the years that preceded or followed them—were conspicuously ignored).

As the reports began to pile up, so did the evidence of poor educational performance. The National Commission on Excellence in Education offered a broad list of particulars:

"About 13 percent of all 17-year-olds in the United States can be considered functionally illiterate"—a figure that was dwarfed by the estimate that "functional illiteracy among minority youth may run as high as 40 percent."

"Average achievement of high school students on most standardized tests is now lower than 26 years ago when Sputnik was launched."

From 1963 to 1980, SAT scores fell by more than fifty points on the verbal section and nearly forty points on the mathematics section.

"There was a steady decline in science achievement scores of U.S. 17-year-olds as measured by national assessments of science in 1969, 1973, and 1977."

"Between 1975 and 1980, remedial mathematics courses in public 4-year colleges increased by 72 percent and now constitute one-quarter of all mathematics courses taught in those institutions."

"Business and military leaders complain that they are required to spend millions of dollars on costly remedial education . . . in such basic skills as reading, writing, spelling, and computation."

3. THE STRUGGLE FOR EXCELLENCE

American high schools are usually divided into academic, vocational, and general tracks, and "the proportion of students taking a general program of study has increased from 12 percent in 1964 to 42 percent in 1979."

What did the "general track" consist of? "Twenty-five percent of the credits earned by general track high school students are in physical and health education, work experience outside the school, remedial English and mathematics, and personal service and development courses, such as training for adulthood and marriage."

Enrollments in traditional academic courses were not reassuring: "We offer intermediate algebra, but only 31 percent of our recent high school graduates complete it; we offer French I, but only 13 percent complete it. . . . Calculus is available in schools enrolling about 60 percent of all students, but only 6 percent of all students complete it."

Students were found to be doing less homework (two-thirds of high school seniors reported less than one hour per night), and "grades have risen as average student achievement has been declining."

"A 1980 State-by-State survey of high school diploma requirements reveals that only eight States require high schools to offer foreign language instruction. Thirty-five states require only 1 year of mathematics, and 36 require only 1 year of science for a diploma."

In response to this curricular vacuity, the national commission urged that state and local graduation requirements be strengthened to include: four years of English, three years of mathematics, three years of science, three years of social studies, and one-half year of computer science; in addition, it proposed that college-bound students study two years of a foreign language. The National Center for Education Statistics, the data-gathering branch of the United States Department of Education, examined transcripts for the high school graduating class of 1982 and concluded that only 2.6 percent actually met the commission's proposed graduation requirements (not including foreign language). Even among those planning to go to a four-year college, only 22.6 percent had taken as much English, mathematics, science, and social studies as the commission recommended.

In the fall of 1983, the National Science Board observed that "students in our Nation's schools are learning less mathematics, science and technology, particularly in the areas of abstract thinking and problem solving. Since the late 1960s, most students have taken fewer mathematics and science courses. Mathematics and science achievement scores of 17-year-olds have dropped steadily and dramatically during the same period." The science board's panel recommended at least sixty minutes per day of mathematics and thirty minutes per day of science in the elementary grades, and a full year of math and science in both seventh and eighth grades. In high school, it called for a requirement of at least three years of mathematics and three years of science and technology for all students.

In California, a group of business executives calling themselves the California Roundtable was several months ahead of the national commission. In the fall of 1982, the roundtable laid out a case for reforming the state's schools. It pointed out that the school day and the school year had grown shorter, and that academic demands had been reduced. High school seniors received academic credit for work experience unrelated to their studies, and less than one-fifth of them reported completing a single homework assignment per week. As school work diminished, remedial work in the state's colleges expanded: "Over half of the students entering the state university and college systems take remedial courses in English, and about half also take remedial math courses, despite having received good grades in the required high school courses in these subjects." The roundtable's study also identified a disturbing decline in academic course enrollments, linked with a marked increase in nonacademic electives. The roundtable recommended the phasing in of higher state graduation requirements: four years of English, three years of mathematics, two years of science, one year of computer studies, three years of social studies, one year of American government, two years of American history, two years of foreign language, and two years of physical education.

In the states, the national commission's report generated a flurry of activity, and new commissions were created by legislatures, state education departments, school boards, interest groups, and governors. Some of this interest predated the commission's report, since the problems that concerned the national commission were also apparent at the local level. By the fall of 1983, many states were considering educational reform, centered largely on such matters as the status and compensation of teachers and on high school graduation requirements. These two reforms are inextricably intertwined, since it will be pointless to raise curricular requirements unless there is an adequate number of skilled teachers available. A number of states have increased their graduation requirements, especially in such subjects as mathematics, science, and foreign languages, but these are areas where there have been severe teacher shortages.

Most of the national commissions and task forces have recommended a basic required curriculum for all students—on grounds that the schools must educate everyone and that a democratic society needs a citizenry in which cultural and scientific literacy is highly developed. The goal of cultural and scientific literacy need not imply a monolithic curriculum, but it does imply a minimum foundation of required studies in the centrally important academic disciplines. Common requirements, however, have long been opposed by a substantial segment of the education profession, which harbors a deeply ingrained hostility toward such words as "standards," "subject matter," and even "excellence" (which is perceived as a code word for academic elitism). Excellence, it turns out, is a threatening concept when it is defined in relation to a required curriculum.

It is instructive to note, for example, the reaction in New York State when the state board of regents proposed new graduation requirements: three years of math, science, and a foreign language, and four years of English and social studies. This proposal, though it was in line with the recommendations of the various national study groups, was soon under attack. Teachers of home economics, vocational education, and others denounced the new requirements for their narrowness (meaning that their own specialties were not among the required subjects); the chancellor of the New York City schools insisted that students in vocational programs and in art and music courses would be unduly burdened by the raising of requirements in science and mathematics; others, claiming to speak for minority youth, charged that the dropout rate would rise along with the new standards.

No one should be surprised by the degree of dissension within the education profession, for it has been virtually a canonical principle of modern pedagogy that not all children can "take" an academic curriculum, which is of value only to the college-bound student. For more than sixty years, the curriculum field has been dominated by a species of social efficiency or functionalism that judges curricular offerings by their utility and that insists on a close fit between what students study and what roles they are likely to assume as adults. Added to this orientation is a set of complementary beliefs such as: the curriculum must be constructed to meet the needs of society and of children; since children differ, the curriculum must vary according to the needs of the children; since society is constantly changing, the curriculum must constantly change to meet society's needs. In theory, any one of these precepts is defensible; children do differ, society does change, and the curriculum of the school must take into account the dynamic quality of the world around it as well as the specific abilities and needs of students. But in practice, these otherwise unassailable precepts have provided justification for educational practices that range from the unwise to the bizarre. Under their banner have marched the advocates of relevance, arguing the case for trendiness in the curriculum, and the advocates of vocational tracking, dividing children into educationally separate tracks in accordance with their presumed fitness for certain educational experiences.

Aside from the pedagogical principles that reside in many textbooks as a ready rationale for a plunge into vocationalism or politicization, Americans have a problem—or, as we would say today, a hang-up—about authority. Education, usually, is by its nature an exercise in authority, since it implies that students are gathered to learn from teachers. The activity of teaching necessarily involves a belief in authority, since the teacher presumably seeks to impart something that the student does not know or cannot do. But many Americans have wished to find ways to avoid this inescapable relationship, and periodically the sentiment is expressed that teachers must learn from their students, that experience is corrupting, that innocence (ignorance) is bliss. Without looking abroad to Rousseau, pedagogues can cite Emerson's opposition to educational uniformity: "I suffer whenever I see that common sight of a parent or senior imposing his opinion and way of thinking and being on a young soul to which they are totally unfit. Cannot we let people be themselves, and enjoy life in their own way?" It was this same spirit of educational laissez-faire that attracted so much admiration to A. S. Neill's Summerhill, where students learned what they wanted, when they wanted, but only if they wanted. Neill's model attracted much attention during the heyday of educational romanticism, appealing to those who longed for the naturalistic style of education on demand. Summerhill went too far for public school educators, since it was not a usable model in communities that prized a semblance of order and such conventional measures of achievement as reading scores. In the late 1960s and early 1970s, though, a variety of less-extreme experiments, like open education, struck a responsive chord by their claim that children learned best in the absence of authority, that their own choices were always better than anything imposed on them by coercion.

Policies were implied in the distaste for authority: the elimination or weakening of requirements for admission to and graduation from college, of requirements for graduation from high school, and of promotional standards from grade to grade. When colleges ceased requiring certain subjects for admission, many high schools could not find a good reason to maintain their requirements for graduation. Nor did it seem right to require all students to study science or mathematics, because some students didn't like those subjects. By the same token, other students didn't see why they should learn to write essays or study history. For those who planned to go to work instead of to college, there were always courses in vocational education or personal service courses, such as training for marriage and adulthood. Pushed by a philosophy of consumerism, the high school curriculum burgeoned with new electives, enrollment in mathematics and science courses diminished, homework and expository writing faded away. The guiding principle, it seemed, was to give students what they wanted; in this way, they would stay in school longer, have higher motivation to learn, and cause less trouble while there, while adults could compliment themselves for having met the needs of their students without using coercion.

It should have been a successful formula, but it was not. Once the principles of utility, relevance, and free choice became the touchstones of the curriculum, the consequences described by the Wirtz panel and the National Commission on Excellence in Education followed. When students were left on their own to decide whether to learn science, mathematics, and foreign language, it could hardly be surprising that enrollments dropped or that the supply of future teachers in these areas diminished accordingly. When student preferences determined course offerings, the explosion of electives became inevitable, particularly in history and English, where teachers were encouraged to split their courses into increasingly specialized and exotic mini-courses to catch the mood of the market. Not even science was immune to the rush to electives. Paul DeHart Hurd of Stanford University, who prepared a paper on science education for the national commission on excellence, showed that more than one hundred new science courses were added to the junior and senior high school curriculum during the late 1960s and 1970s, including such offerings as astronomy, meteorology, oceanography, metric measurement, sex education, and human genetics.

Probably the single most significant result of these trends was the fractionation of the curriculum—not only in content but in student enrollment in courses of vastly different quality. Responding to the new freedom from requirements, students tracked themselves into academic, vocational, and general programs. In high school, subjects like foreign language, mathematics, and science—once required of all students, regardless of their ability—became options. To liken the patterns that developed to a cafeteria—as so many critics have done—is not entirely correct; better to say that there were three different cafeterias, one for the academic track students (about 35 percent of high school students), another for the vocational track (about 25 percent), and the third for the general track (about 40 percent). The three cafeterias, where students could help themselves to the courses they wanted, differed in several ways: by the extent of academic content; by the degree of challenge; and by the intrinsic, long-range value of the offerings. Given the fairly substantial differences among the three cafeterias, it was not surprising that the wide divergence in skills and knowledge between students at the top and those at the bottom was exacerbated by the triple-track curriculum, or that high school graduates could no longer be said to share a common body of knowledge, not to mention a common culture.

The arrangement had certain virtues. For one thing, educators felt satisfied that they were meeting the needs of different children by providing them with specialized offerings; at the same time, they were meeting society's needs by keeping adolescents in school instead of on the street or in the job market where they were not wanted. They often proclaimed as an article of faith that the diversification of the high school curriculum had lowered the dropout rate. It was true that the dropout rate had dropped steadily over the past forty years, but, oddly, it had remained steady at about 25 percent since the mid-1960s. In other words, the dilution and diffusion of the high school curriculum during the past fifteen years did not—contrary to the conventional wisdom—lower the dropout rate. Over the decades, the rise in the proportion of young people who finished high school has apparently been owing to economic and demographic factors, not to changes in the curriculum. Thus, the charge that an increase in requirements and in the assignment of essay writing and homework will cause more students to drop out may or may not be true, but it is not based on evidence.

The current debate has roots that extend over the past century. In the late nineteenth century, educators worried about the seeming disorganization of the high school curriculum and wondered whether there should be differentiation between students bound for college and those bound for work. A prestigious commission was appointed, which included five college presidents (its chairman was President Charles W. Eliot of Harvard). Known as the Committee of Ten, the group, in its report of 1893, proposed that all students be liberally educated, regardless of whether they were college bound or not, and that all should study English, history, foreign language, science, and mathematics. Recognizing that only a small minority of high school graduates went on to college, the committee asserted that "the secondary schools of the United States, taken as a whole, do not exist for the purpose of preparing boys and girls for colleges." Some students might study longer than others in a given subject field, but the committee believed that a common liberal education was the best preparation for the duties of life, whatever the pupils' later destination.

For a time the views of the Committee of Ten were influential in the high schools, but its academic orientation was at odds with the mainstream of the new education profession. As enrollment in the high schools grew, professional educators felt constrained by the weight of academic traditionalism. John Dewey gained a substantial following for the view that the curriculum should be built around the interests of the child and should be better related to the community and to so-called real-life activities. There was a growing sense among education policymakers that the schools would never be able to play a constructive role as a social agency until they broke free of the limitations imposed by traditional academic goals. In 1918, a new group, the Commission on the Reorganization of Secondary Education, issued a statement called the Cardinal Principles of Secondary Education. Unlike the Committee of Ten, the 1918 commission was composed largely of high school principals, professors of education, and educational bureaucrats. Its credo was that "secondary education should be determined by the needs of the society to be served, the character of the individuals to be educated, and the knowledge of educational theory and practice available." On each of these grounds, the commission argued for a fundamental shift in the means and ends of a high school education. The main objectives of education, the commission concluded, were "1. Health. 2. Command of fundamental processes. 3. Worthy home-membership. 4. Vocation. 5. Citizenship. 6. Worthy use of leisure. 7. Ethical character." The only reference to the academic function of the school was "command of fundamental processes."

The cardinal principles statement facilitated the redefinition of the high school curriculum along functional lines and conferred respectability on vocational, technical, socio-personal, and other sorts of new courses—at first in addition to, and later instead of, the academic subjects. The notion that the student should be fitted to the curriculum and vice versa legitimated what we now call tracking. The academic curriculum, no longer considered appropriate for all students, became a special program for those who intended to go to college. Others, who were heading for the workplace, were directed to more practical pursuits better fitted to their later destination. The controlling principles in this readjustment were social utility and efficiency. Every subject was judged by whether it was immediately useful and whether it met the needs of the students. By that test, students who were not going to college had no use and no need for foreign language, or for anything more than a smattering of history, science, literature, and mathematics.

In the nearly seventy years since the publication of the cardinal principles, the debate has continued in a seesaw fashion. The utilitarians dominated the field in the 1940s, then the argument tilted to the champions of liberal education in the period just before and after *Sputnik*. During the past fifteen years, the cardinal principles have again held sway, as schools have tried to adjust the curriculum in order to reflect the changing moods of society and of students. The challenge that has never been met, whichever side was in the ascendancy, was to democratize the academic curriculum—both what was taught and who was taught—without cheapening it or without excluding large numbers of students from its reach.

What the various task forces and national commissions are now saying is that our educational systems must take on the job of making all young people literate, and their definition includes both cultural and scientific literacy. No one knows whether it can be done, because we have never tried to do it on a mass scale. If we make the attempt, it should be done with full knowledge of where we have gone astray in the past. At one extreme, the perfervid traditionalists have been content to educate those at the top without regard to the welfare of the majority of students; at the other, the perfervid progressives have cooperated in dividing and diluting the curriculum, which left the majority with an inadequate education. Most schools and teachers are not at the extremes, but they have little ability to blunt the lure of either progressivism or traditionalism, particularly to an indiscriminate media and to hyperactive policymakers. Pedagogical practice follows educational philosophy, and it is obvious that we do not yet have a philosophical commitment to education that is sound enough and strong enough to withstand the erratic dictates of fashion.

A Nation at Risk: The Report of the National Commission On Excellence in Education

Milton Goldberg and James Harvey

MILTON GOLDBERG, former acting director of the National Institute of Education, is executive director of the National Commission on Excellence in Education. JAMES HARVEY is a senior research associate with the Commission.

TWO HUNDRED leaders of U.S. education, industry, and government gathered in the White House on April 26 to watch the ceremonial presentation to President Reagan of the report of the National Commission on Excellence in Education. Nearly five months later, the tumultuous reception of the report by the press and the public has yet to subside.

Such magazines as *Time, Newsweek*, and *U.S. News & World Report* have provided detailed coverage of the report, which has also been the focus of extensive discussions on several network television programs, among them "The McNeil-Lehrer Report," "Good Morning America," and "Nightline." Prompted by this publicity, the public demand for the Commission's report has been astonishing. The Government Printing Office, besieged by requests for the report, is now into the fourth printing; at least 200,000 copies of the text have been printed separately by various education publications, and an estimated three million readers have had access to shortened versions of the report in such newspapers as the *Portland Oregonian*, the *Washington Post*, and the *New York Times*.

The public's response suggests that Secretary of Education Terrel Bell, who created the Commission in 1981, is correct in hailing the report as a possible "turning point" in an era when U.S. schools face "the challenge of the postindustrial age." Bell also vowed not to allow the report "to be remembered as the warning our Nation failed to heed."

If the public response to the report has been remarkable, so are the activities already under way in response to it. The Pennsylvania State Board of Education recently announced its intention to adopt new high school graduation requirements that will triple the amount of science and mathematics required for graduation and that will add computer science as a diploma requirement. Within weeks of the release of the report, the school board in Ypsilanti, Michigan, announced its intention to lengthen the school day for elementary students and to increase high school graduation requirements. The Tulsa, Oklahoma, superintendent published an extensive "Open Letter to the People of Tulsa," outlining the standing of schools in that city with respect to the National Commission's recommendations.

Not since the heady days following the launching of Sputnik I has U.S. education been accorded so much attention. Although the Commission released its report almost five months ago, major U.S. newspapers and network television programs continue to focus on the problems of education. President Reagan has already discussed the report at several regional forums, with other such forums scheduled for early fall. Individual members of the Commission and of the Commission staff continue to be deluged with requests to address meetings and convocations across the nation. Meanwhile, other prestigious individuals and panels have added their voices to the rising chorus of concern about the quality of U.S. schools; these include the Twentieth Century Fund, the College Board, and the Task Force on Education and Economic Growth (chaired by Gov. James Hunt of North Carolina).

The unprecedented attention now being paid to education is evidence of public concern. But this attention also provides — as the president of the American Federation of Teachers, Albert Shanker, pointed out to his constituents in early July — "unprecedented opportunities" for education in the coming months.

The Imperative for Reform

What has generated all this fuss? The answer is: a deceptively short report to the nation, in which a panel of distinguished Americans warns that the "educational foundations of our society are presently

Reprinted from *Phi Delta Kappan*, September 1983. Copyright ©1983, Phi Delta Kappan, Inc.

being eroded by a rising tide of mediocrity that threatens our very future as a Nation and a people." Titled *A Nation at Risk: The Imperative for Educational Reform*, this report has sparked a national debate on education that could prove to be seminal to the development of an ethic of excellence in education and in American life.

Commission Aims and Process

That debate was quite consciously sought by members of the Commission, under the leadership of David Gardner, then president of the University of Utah, who has recently assumed the presidency of the University of California. It was Gardner's idea that the report be in the form of an open letter that would, in the words of Commission member Gerald Holton, serve as a "clarion call" to the American public. The call was intended to remind Americans of the importance of education as the foundation of U.S. leadership in change and technical invention and as the source of U.S. prosperity, security, and civility.

The National Commission conducted its work and collected its information in an extraordinarily open manner, which also helped to encourage public response to *A Nation at Risk*. Practically everywhere one turned in the last two years, there was evidence of the Commission at work. Six public hearings and three symposia were held across the U.S., so that administrators, teachers, parents, and others could discuss their perceptions of the problems and accomplishments of American education. Forty papers were commissioned from a variety of experts and presented to the full Commission.

In virtually every city in which the Commission held a meeting or a hearing, the Commission members also visited local schools and corporate training facilities. It has been estimated that, during the 18 months between the first Commission meeting and the release of *A Nation at Risk*, Commission members were involved in a public event somewhere in the U.S. every three weeks. All of this highly visible activity created a national audience for the Commission's work; indeed, we knew several months before the report was issued that the response to it was likely to be unprecedented in education.

The Commission also examined the methods that other distinguished national panels had used to generate public and governmental reactions to their findings. The commissioners learned that the effective reports concentrated on essential messages, described them in clear and unmistakable prose, and drew the public's attention to the national consequences of continuing on with business as usual.

Essential Messages

The first essential message from the National Commission on Excellence in Education is found in the title of the report: the nation is at risk. It is at risk because competitors throughout the world are overtaking our once unchallenged lead in commerce, industry, science, and technological innovation. As the Commission observed, the problem has many causes and dimensions; education is only one of them. But education is the primary factor undergirding our "prosperity, security, and civility."

The Commission is not the first national body to draw attention to the central importance of education to our national well-being. Indeed, in 1980 the President's Commission for a National Agenda for the Eighties reported that "the continued failure of the schools to perform their traditional role adequately . . . may have disastrous consequences for this Nation."

Just as assuredly, the Commission is not the last national body to draw attention to the central importance of education. One week after the release of *A Nation at Risk*, the Twentieth Century Fund Task Force called U.S. schools "the Nation's most important institution for the shaping of future citizens" and warned that "threatened disaster can be averted only if there is a national commitment to excellence in our public schools."

But the Commission may be the first national body to insist — as the essential first premise, not simply as an afterthought — that inattention to the schools puts the very well-being of the Nation at risk.

The second essential message from the Commission is that mediocrity, not excellence, is the norm in American education. *A Nation at Risk* paid tribute to "heroic" examples of educational excellence, but it made clear the fact that, on balance, "a rising tide of mediocrity" threatens to overwhelm the educational foundations of American society. And the consequences of that tide are staggering.

- On 19 international assessments of student achievement, U.S. students never ranked first or second; in fact, when compared only with students from other industrialized nations, U.S. students ranked in last place seven times.
- Some 23 million American adults are functionally illiterate.
- About 13% of U.S. teenagers (and up to 40% of minority adolescents) are functionally illiterate.
- From 1963 to 1980 a virtually unbroken decline took place in average scores on the Scholastic Aptitude Test (SAT).
- Similarly, a dramatic decline took place in the number of students who demonstrate superior achievement on the SAT.
- Between 1975 and 1980 the number of remedial mathematics courses offered in four-year public colleges increased by 72%.
- Only about one-fourth of the recent recruits to the Armed Services were able to read at the ninth-grade level, the minimum necessary to follow safety instructions.

The third essential message from the Commission is that we don't have to put up with this situation. We *can* do better, we *should* do better, and we *must* do better.

That message is found most clearly in a section of the report titled "America Can Do It." This section cites the remarkable successes of the American educational system in responding to past challenges as justification for the Commission's optimism that we can meet the current challenges. The past successes of U.S. education have included:

- the research and training provided by land-grant colleges and universities in the 19th century, which helped us develop our natural resources and the rich agricultural bounty of the American farm;
- the educated workforce that U.S. schools provided from the late 1800s through the mid-20th century, which sealed the success of the Industrial Revolution and provided the margin of victory in two world wars; and
- the schools' role to this very day in transforming vast waves of immigrants into productive citizens.

The message that "America Can Do It" also appears in the letter from Gardner that accompanied the formal submission of the Commission report to Bell. Said Gardner: "The Commission deeply believes that the problems we have discerned in American education can be both understood and corrected if the people of our country, together with those who have public responsibility in the matter, care enough and are courageous enough to do what is required."

The message can be found as well in the first paragraph of the report, which notes that Americans can take "justifiable pride in what our schools and colleges have historically accomplished and contributed to the United States and the well-being of its people." But the Commission's optimism is perhaps most apparent in the recommendations it sets forth in *A Nation at Risk*. These recommendations provide more than a prescription for improving American schooling; they also provide a framework within which parents and educators across the U.S. can consider their own unique situations and then determine for themselves how best to proceed. The elements of this framework — the amount of time devoted to learning, the content to which students are exposed, the expectations we hold for ourselves and our children, the teaching, and the leadership – constitute, in the final analysis, the tools that local districts can use to improve the processes of education.

Recommendations

The Commission made five broad recommendations, each with several implementing recommendations.

Content

The recommendations regarding content were grounded in the Commission's conclusion that secondary school curricula have been homogenized, diluted, and diffused to such an extent that they no longer have a central purpose. According to *A Nation at Risk*, today's U.S. high schools offer "a cafeteria-style curriculum in which the appetizers and the desserts can easily be mistaken for the main courses."

The Commission recommended that all students seeking a high school diploma be required to lay a foundation in "five new basics" by taking four years of English, three years of mathematics, three years of science, three years of social studies, and one-half year of computer science. Several implementing recommendations suggested the kinds of skills that high school graduates should possess in each of these areas. The implementing recommendations also stressed the desirability of proficiency in a foreign language and stated that the teaching of foreign languages should begin in the elementary grades. In addition, the Commission recommended that the schools offer rigorous coursework in the fine and performing arts and in vocational education; that the elementary curriculum be improved and upgraded; and that such groups as the American Chemical Society and the Modern Language Association continue their efforts to revise, update, improve, and make available new and more diverse curricular materials.

Standards and Expectations

The Commission concluded that we expect far too little of our students and that we get, by and large, exactly what we expect. Evidence of our low expectations is widespread. For example:

- the schools are requiring less and less homework of students;
- two-thirds of the states require only one year of mathematics and one year of science for a high school diploma;
- one-fifth of the four-year public colleges and universities offer open admissions to all graduates of high schools in the state, regardless of the courses they have taken or the grades they have earned; and
- many U.S. colleges and universities reported lowering their admissions requirements during the 1970s.

The Commission recommended that high schools, colleges, and universities adopt more rigorous and measurable standards and higher expectations, both for academic performance and for student conduct, and that four-year colleges and universities raise their requirements for admission. The implementing recommendations focused on improving the reliability of high school grades as indicators of academic achievement, on raising college and university admissions requirements (including the scores required on standardized achievement tests in the five basics), on establishing a nationwide – but not federal – program of achievement testing for students who are passing from one level of schooling to another, on upgrading textbooks, and on the need for new instructional materials that reflect the most current applications of technology.

Time

The members of the National Commission were struck by the fact that many other industrialized nations have much longer school days and far longer school years than does the United States. Because the level of mastery of curriculum content is directly related to the amount of time that students devote to learning, the Commission made a number of recommendations designed to use available time more effectively and to prompt consideration of extending the amount of time available for learning.

The Commission recommended that significantly more time be devoted to learning the "five new basics." This will require more effective use of the existing school day, a longer school day, or a lengthened school year. The implementing recommendations included more homework, the provision of instruction in study and work skills, consideration of a seven-hour school day and of a 200- to 220-day school year, the reduction of disruption, the improvement of classroom management, and stronger policies on school attendance.

Teaching

The Commission concluded that too few academically able students are attracted to teaching; that teacher preparation programs need substantial improvement; that the professional working life of teachers is, on the whole, unacceptable; and that a serious shortage of teachers exists in key fields. The recommendation on teaching has seven parts, quoted here in full:

1. Persons preparing to teach should be required to meet high educational standards, to demonstrate an aptitude for teaching, and to demonstrate competence in an academic discipline. Colleges and universities offering teacher preparation programs should be judged by how well their graduates meet these criteria.
2. Salaries for the teaching profession should be increased and should be professionally competitive, market-sensitive, and performance-based. Salary, promotion, tenure, and retention decisions should be tied to an effective evaluation system that includes peer review so that superior teachers can be rewarded, average ones encouraged, and poor ones either improved or terminated.
3. School boards should adopt an 11-month contract for teachers. This would ensure time for curriculum and professional development, programs for students with special needs, and a more adequate level of teacher compensation.
4. School boards, administrators, and teachers should cooperate to develop career ladders for teachers that distinguish among the beginning instructor, the experienced teacher, and the master teacher.
5. Substantial nonschool personnel resources should be employed to help solve the immediate problem of the shortage of mathematics and science teachers. Qualified individuals, including recent graduates with mathematics and science degrees, graduate students, and industrial and retired scientists, could, with appropriate preparation, immediately begin teaching in these fields. A number of our leading science centers have the capacity to begin educating and retraining teachers immediately. Other areas of critical teacher need, such as English, must also be addressed.
6. Incentives, such as grants and loans, should be made available to attract outstanding students to the teaching profession, particularly in those areas of critical shortage.
7. Master teachers should be involved in designing teacher preparation programs and in supervising teachers during their probationary years.

Leadership and Fiscal Support

Finally, the Commission recommended that citizens across the U.S. hold educators and elected officials responsible for providing the leadership necessary to achieve these reforms – and that citizens provide the fiscal support and stability required to bring about the reforms. The implementing recommendations in this area concentrated on the leadership roles of principals and superintendents; on the roles of local, state, and federal governments; and on the need for educators, parents, and public officials to assist in implementing the reforms proposed by the Commission. This section of *A Nation at Risk* concluded with these words: "Excellence costs. But in the long run mediocrity costs far more."

Other Issues

Although the overall response to the Commission's report is gratifying, several of us associated with the report have been disappointed at the scant attention paid to several major themes.

Learning Society

For example, the press has frequently misinterpreted *A Nation at Risk* as an attack on education and educators. Far from it. The report stands instead as an eloquent reaffirmation of education as a key element undergirding our society. Indeed, in light of new developments in computers, miniaturization, robotics, lasers, and other technologies, the report calls for the development of a learning society. The Commission states that:

> At the heart of such a society is the commitment to a set of values and to a system of education that affords all members the opportunity to stretch their minds to full capacity, from early childhood through adulthood, learning more as the world itself changes. . . . In our view, formal schooling in youth is the essential foundation for learning throughout one's life. But without lifelong learning, one's skills will become rapidly dated.

Excellence

In similar fashion, little comment has been forthcoming about the Commission's careful definition of "excellence" in education, particularly the Commission's view of excellent individual performance. For the individual, the Commission defined excellence as performing on the boundary of individual ability in ways that test and stretch personal limits, both in school and in the workplace.

Implicit in this definition is the notion that each of us can attain individual excellence — although the boundaries that each of us tests and extends will clearly differ. This concept of excellence prompted the Commission to state that "our goal must be to develop the talents of all to their fullest." It also led the Commission to insist that the pursuit of excellence and the pursuit of equity are not incompatible educational goals and that we cannot permit one to yield to the other "either in principle or in practice."

Public Commitment

There has also been little attention given to the Commission's stand that, of all the tools at hand for improving education, "the public's support . . . is the most powerful." On the contrary, when informed of the report's findings and its recommendations, many educators and legislators have asked how these suggested reforms can possibly be funded. In the eyes of many of the commissioners, this response puts the cart before the horse. As one of them said, "If education demonstrates that it is willing to put its house in order, then the public will respond with increased support." As justification for this belief, the Commission cites results of national polls that indicate the public's steadfast regard for education as a major foundation of the nation's strength, the public's conviction that education is important to individual success, and the public's support for rigorous curricular offerings.

But it was toward another facet of the public's support for education that the Commission turned in seeking constructive reform:

> The best term to characterize [this facet] may simply be the honorable word "patriotism." Citizens know intuitively what some of the best economists have shown in their research: that education is one of the chief engines of a society's material well-being. They know, too, that education is the common bond of a pluralistic society and helps tie us to other cultures around the globe. Citizens also know in their bones that the safety of the United States depends principally on the wit, skill, and spirit of a self-confident people, today and tomorrow. . . .
>
> And perhaps more important, citizens know and believe that the meaning of America to the rest of the world must be something better than it seems to many today. Americans like to think of this Nation as the preeminent country for generating the great ideas and material benefits for all mankind. The citizen is dismayed at a steady 15-year decline in industrial productivity, as one great American industry after another falls to world competition. The citizen wants the country to act on the belief, expressed in our hearings and by a large majority in the Gallup Poll, that education should be at the top of the Nation's agenda.

Parents and Students

Finally, although our correspondence provides ample evidence that educators understand the importance of the Commission's message to parents and students, the message has received too little attention. Because the roles of parents and students in the improvement of educational quality are even more important than the responsibilities of teachers, administrators, or legislators, the Commission took the unusual step of addressing these groups directly in its report.

A Nation at Risk bluntly reminds parents of their responsibility to launch their children into the world with the soundest possible education, coupled with respect for first-rate work. It also reminds them of their right to demand the best that our schools and colleges can provide and of their obligation to serve as living examples of the kind of excellence the U.S. requires.

Students receive equally forthright advice: "You forfeit your chance for life at its fullest when you withhold your best effort in learning. When you give only the minimum to learning, you receive only the minimum in return. . . . [I]n the end it is *your* work that determines how much and how well you learn."

From Risk to Confidence

Americans have not only lived with change in the past but also welcomed and encouraged it. Faced with the dangers of an uncharted continent, they spanned and mastered it; awed by the vastness of space, they investigated and explored it; perplexed by the mystery of the atom, they plumbed and solved it. Now a new challenge beckons: how to use our enormous educational system to turn to advantage the current risk to our values, our standard of living, and our international security.

The evidence that we can do so successfully is all around us. It can be found in the past successes of American education, from the development of the one-room schoolhouse to the development of our great research universities. It can be found in the attention paid to the Commission's report by the President and the secretary of education, as well as in the high visibility of education as a major issue on the national agenda. It can be found in the spirited debate we are witnessing on the issue of merit pay for teachers, for this issue touches on many of the elements we must address in seeking excellence — merit, reward for performance, evaluation, and the role and status of teaching.

The evidence can be found in the letters that the National Commission has received from students. Predictably, some students have complained about increased homework or a longer school day. One letter writer suggested that President Reagan contact his junior high school and cancel the book reports that teachers had assigned for the summer vacation. Other letters have been less amusing.

3. THE STRUGGLE FOR EXCELLENCE

One seventh-grader wrote a six-page letter of despair. Teaching study skills during study hall would be fine, she wrote, "if there was anything to study, and if anybody did any studying. There isn't and they don't." She said she would opt instead for six demanding hours of history, math, composition, foreign languages, geography, literature, and science. "Then my school days would be worth getting up for. To lengthen our existing days would be merely to extend the monotony, boredom, frustration, and agony. . . ."

The evidence that we are up to the challenge is perhaps most apparent in the many schools, districts, and states that have already responded to the Commission's report or have appointed task forces and commissions of their own to chart their next steps. But it is also apparent in corporate and foundation boardrooms, in legislative cloakrooms, in meetings of the Cabinet, and in meetings of learned societies, where discussions of the report, of its implications for the nation, and of what the discussants should do about it are the order of the day.

All of this is as it should be, for it was precisely this kind of discussion, debate, and excitement about education that the Commission set out to provoke. If the level of interest remains high and leads to the kind of positive responses anticipated by the Commission, then we may eventually look back on the release of *A Nation at Risk* as a turning point in American education.

Clearly, the Commission's report has touched that chord in the American consciousness which governs the hopes, aspirations, and apprehensions of Americans about the future well-being of their children, their schools, and their society. The task for all of us now is to take this renewed commitment and dedicate it to the creation of a learning society. That responsibility does not belong solely to any one group. As *A Nation at Risk* concludes:

> It is . . . the America of all of us that is at risk; it is to each of us that this imperative is addressed. It is by our willingness to take up the challenge, and our resolve to see it through, that America's place in the world will be either secured or forfeited. Americans have succeeded before, and so we shall again.

A Nation at Risk: How's that again?

Remember how we promised (*Embrace excellence; tinkerers be damned,* July) we wouldn't mislead you about the report of the National Commission on Excellence in Education? Not so others in high places. Seems misrepresentations of that august body's findings have been insinuating themselves into the record, and now the commissioners themselves (or at least some of them) are trying to tell us what they *really* meant to say.

The problem started almost before the ink was dry on *A Nation at Risk.* On April 28—just two days after the report was unveiled to a fanfare of slightly off-key White House trumpets—the *Washington Post* reported "confusion" over the commission's recommendations. As news buffs no doubt will recall, President Reagan used the occasion of the report's release as a convenient soapbox for reiterating his support of tuition tax credits, education vouchers, and school prayer—issues never mentioned in the report itself.

As if that weren't enough, the President went on to call the report "consistent with our task of redefining the federal role in education"—a task his Administration has openly avowed to be more a matter of reduction than of redefinition. Commission member Gerald Holton, a Harvard physics professor, found Mr. Reagan's interpretation of the report startling, to say the least. "Contrary to Reagan," Holton told the *Post*, "we made a clarion call for the federal government to identify the national need and finance what's necessary. . . . If the states cannot afford it, and it's a national emergency, then the money must come from the only source that has it—the federal government."

Since that April day, President Reagan has wasted no opportunity to make political hay of the commission's report. But what were the commissioners really asking for—a New Federalism for education, or a continued, even strengthened, federal role? Late this summer, Representative Carl Perkins (D-Ky.), chairman of the House subcommittee on elementary, secondary, and vocational education (and no friend to the President's education policies), decided the time had come to set the record straight. His tactic: to survey the 18 commission appointees for their "individual views" on such questions as these: (1) Does the report conclude that additional federal funds should be provided for education? (2) What about state and local funds? (3) Are tuition tax credits, education vouchers, and school prayer "discussed, suggested, or endorsed" in the report?

Now, anyone who has had even a remedial course in reading comprehension can take a stab at answering those questions simply by scanning the pages of *A Nation at Risk.* But what Representative Perkins was looking for—and what he says he got—was a horse's-mouth refutation of the President's reading of the commission's handiwork.

Take federal support for public education, for example. Eight out of the ten commissioners who responded to Perkins's survey agreed the report assumed more, not less, of it. The key word here is *assumed.* Yale president and commission member A. Bartlett Giamatti explains: "The report clearly envisions a partnership among local, state, and federal entities in order to meet the needs of the 40 million-plus students in our public schools. Yes, I believe the report foresees federal money joining state and local money. No, I do not believe this is a 'conclusion' of the report; I believe it is an assumption. Clearly, the commission was not of one mind about federal aid."

The commission, it seems, had agreed to come up with a unanimous report, one that would not in any way be qualified or diminished by dissenting opinions. "But one price to be paid for [that unanimity]," Gerald Holton observed, "was that some issues were not spelled out in detail—and above all the question of 'additional federal funds,' a prospect which was ideologically . . . unacceptable from the beginning to at least two or three of the 18 appointees." Holton went on to say that he, and "probably the majority" of the commission members, would favor increased federal aid to public schools.

Among the respondents to Perkins's survey, only commissioners Annette Kirk (of Kirk Associates, a communications consulting firm in Michigan) and New Rochelle high school teacher Jay Sommer were opposed on this point.

As for tuition tax credits, education vouchers, and school prayer—reform notions on which the current Administration has pinned some hope for educational excellence—nine out of ten respondents agreed these proposals were not treated by the commission in its deliberations nor included in its report. The lone holdout was Annette Kirk, who said, "While such proposals are not endorsed as such in the report, it would be possible to extract from the document support for them."

But remember: Only ten of the 18 commission members responded to the survey, and at press time, Perkins's office told the JOURNAL that replies from the remaining members still had not been received. If you've kept careful count you'll realize, then, that on the crucial issue of education funding, only 8 of 18 commissioners *actually* say Mr. Reagan has read them wrong—a not-so-resounding 44 percent, in other words. (On tuition tax credits and the like, the percentage edges up to 50.)

We're not gifted in telepathy, so we don't presume to speak for the silent commissioners. Still, we note (as Representative Perkins undoubtedly has) the presumably unanimous paragraphs in *A Nation at Risk* in which the commission spells out the federal government's role in public education: "The federal government has *the primary responsibility* [the commission's emphasis] to identify the national interest in education. It should also help fund and support efforts to protect and promote that interest."

That language provides plenty of latitude, and although we might not agree with Representative Perkins's claim that his survey adds up to "an emphatic No" to funding cuts, we quietly applaud his statement to the House that cutbacks in federal funding for education "are hardly responsible when the need for educational improvement is imperative."

Reprinted, with permission, from *The American School Board Journal*, October 1983. Copyright 1983, the National School Boards Association. All rights reserved.

Improving Educational Standards in American Schools

Daniel P. Resnick and Lauren B. Resnick

DANIEL P. RESNICK is a professor of history at Carnegie-Mellon University. LAUREN B. RESNICK is a professor of psychology and co-director of the Learning Research and Development Center at the University of Pittsburgh. *An earlier version of this article served as the executive summary of a commissioned report to the National Commission on Excellence in Education. Major segments of the research on which this article is based were supported by a grant from the Carnegie Corporation of New York. The Ford Foundation supported comparative studies in Europe.*

The authors discuss curriculum, testing, and tracking — three factors that they view as at the center of efforts to improve learning in U.S. schools.

SHOULD WE BE optimistic or pessimistic about the state of American education? Both moods mark the report of the National Commission on Excellence in Education. Never has so large a portion of the population of any nation had an opportunity for so extended a period of schooling. Yet U.S. educational standards have been falling while competitor nations have been trying harder and doing better. Why is this so, and what can be done about it?

Educational standards are a function of the demands placed on students and of the opportunities they are given to learn in the classroom. We believe that U.S. educators can take effective steps to increase these demands and opportunities in three key areas, which we will discuss here. We shared our views formally and at much greater length in hearings before the Commission.

Three major elements affect U.S. educational standards. They are: 1) what is taught (the curriculum), 2) how learning is assessed (tests and examinations), and 3) how students are grouped (tracking). Our analysis focuses on these three factors because they are likely to remain at the center of efforts to improve learning in U.S. schools.

Curriculum

What is taught is a major determinant of what is learned in schools. For this reason, our assessment of educational standards begins with an examination of the school curriculum. Both the content of instruction and the extent to which all students should study the same material have been continuing sources of debate and disagreement over the past century.

In practice, neither an absolutely common course nor a completely differentiated program has prevailed.

The increasing variety of students in attendance has tended to press secondary schools toward differentiated curricula as a way of capturing students' interest and holding them in school. Although differentiation has sometimes meant some form of vocational preparation, it has more often meant a less demanding version of the college preparatory curriculum or a series of poorly coordinated elective courses.

Weighed against the pressures toward differentiation, which stem from a desire to attract and accommodate increasing numbers and varieties of students, has been a continuing set of beliefs favoring a common course of studies. These beliefs are rooted in the nation's democratic and egalitarian traditions, which demand that there be a common core of shared knowledge and assumptions among U.S. citizens and that there be maximum opportunity for social mobility, particularly into the more powerful and privileged sectors of society.

In practice, neither an absolutely common course nor a completely differentiated program has prevailed. High schools compromise by requiring a minimum amount of work in the basic disciplines and then permitting students to choose electives — including vocational courses — to fill in the rest of their programs. The requirements, often quite minimal, can sometimes be met by such a variety of courses that the seeming commonalities in the program are actually nonexistent. Furthermore, the content of courses in the traditional disciplines has been affected by the demand for a practical orientation. As a result, such courses often include the study of applications and topical concerns, all at the expense of the more traditional content.

One result of our tendency to resolve the tension between common and differentiated curricula by ad hoc compromise is that we have (but often fail to admit that we have) several different curriculum standards in operation simultaneously in our schools. Under these conditions, the ques-

From *Phi Delta Kappan,* November 1983, pp. 178-180. Reprinted by permission of the authors and Phi Delta Kappan.

tion of educational standards must be addressed separately for different programs and different groups of students.

For the college preparatory student, the picture is varied. On the one hand, there are some very demanding and carefully organized courses, particularly at the advanced high school levels. These courses came out of the curriculum reform efforts and accompanying examination programs that followed Sputnik. They are available only in some high schools, however, and a minority of college-bound students enroll in them. Meanwhile, the basic academic courses are usually less demanding, and the lack of a strong set of required course sequences further weakens the high school program for the college bound. The decline in Scholastic Aptitude Test (SAT) scores, even among the most able students, reflects a secondary school curriculum that requires a minimum of language study (including both English and foreign languages) and, in some cases, only a course or two in mathematics and science.

Vocational education is also in difficulty. It is not at all clear that the schools are better able than employers themselves to teach students those skills that are specifically related to the workplace. Moreover, the changing nature of jobs is causing general competence in language and computation to take precedence over specific "vocational" skills. This means that those students who end their education with high school need — yet generally fail to receive within vocational programs — the same kind of general academic program as college-bound students. Movement toward this goal would require a reaffirmation of the central place of such subjects as mathematics, language, science, history, and the social sciences in the educational programs of all students.

Having argued the existence of a generally undemanding curriculum in U.S. high schools, it is appropriate that we now consider the mechanisms for curriculum improvement that are available to an educational system committed to decentralized control. One such mechanism is course requirements. Although states have the constitutional authority to maintain standards through required courses and course sequences, most have been reluctant to do so. When certain states have required specific courses other than U.S. history and civics, most often these courses have been in such nonacademic areas as health and physical education. Only a few states have used their power to establish academic course requirements. This is an area in which states could act quickly to improve educational standards. Indeed, some state legislatures are now taking steps to stiffen course requirements.

An important step toward raising standards is to raise the level of instruction in the middle school.

Despite the absence of centrally imposed curriculum requirements, one powerful force presses U.S. schools toward considerable similarity in curriculum. This force is the textbook. In each school subject, a few textbooks dominate the field. Moreover, an inspection of the major textbook series makes it clear that variations in content and format are not so great as to expose users of different series to anything even approaching truly different curricula or widely varying standards. Since the economic survival of a given textbook depends on sales to large school districts and to states that engage in statewide textbook adoption, editors try to anticipate and provide the kind of content that is likely to appeal to adoption committees. In response to the demand for textbooks suitable for increasingly heterogeneous student bodies, publishers have tended to reduce reading levels, the complexity of content, and other intellectually demanding features. But the sensitivity of publishers to the marketplace could work in the other direction as well, if textbook adoption committees were to begin to call for changes in the direction of more demanding content and higher reading levels.

A third mechanism for raising curricular standards has been the reform efforts of national panels and commissions. Over the past century, the recommendations of several study commissions have influenced the shape of the U.S. school curriculum. In the aftermath of Sputnik, which focused concern on the low quality of preparation in mathematics and science, extensive resources went into the development of new and updated curricula and into the provision of training workshops for teachers. These programs have influenced the high school curriculum — but not as deeply as their developers hoped, perhaps because they have been perceived as suited primarily to the most academically talented students. A new round of public investment in curriculum reform, aimed at the full spectrum of the school population, is needed. By involving states, school districts, and textbook publishers in the process, a variety of high-quality curricular options can become available to U.S. schools.

Tests and Examinations

Tests and examinations have traditionally served as major means of setting and maintaining educational standards. They do this in two ways: by monitoring the performance of educational institutions and by controlling individual students' access to programs and diplomas. Although recent critiques of testing have focused public attention on the role of tests in the selection and placement of individual students, the U.S. as a whole has tended more often to use educational testing to serve the purposes of accountability to the public, program evaluation, and institutional comparison. The standardized testing movement developed in a period when booming school enrollments, large building programs in local school districts, and a cult of efficiency in industry combined to encourage the schools to justify their performance in quantitative ways. Even today, the publication of district test scores serves more often to compare the performance of individual schools than to affect the course of education for individual students.

An important characteristic of U.S. tests is that they are typically divorced from the curriculum. This is true even of tests that are used to make important educational decisions for individual students, such as the SAT and the American College Testing (ACT) Program entrance examinations. As a result, U.S. tests are not well-suited to serve as incentives or guidelines for higher educational standards. Because they are useful as indicators, able to signal rises or declines in the performance of the schools, they can monitor educational standards. But they cannot effectively shape them.

A consideration of the testing and examination systems used in other countries reveals an interesting set of alternatives. Of greatest relevance to the U.S. are the mechanisms of assessment used in England, a nation that shares our deep commitment to local control over education. In that country, a complex system of several national examinations, among which schools can choose and for which school courses prepare students, serves as an effective instrument for the maintenance of educational standards. In America the Advanced Placement tests of the College Board and some minimum competency testing programs function as examination programs capable of directly influencing educational standards, but these affect only a minority of students. The development and wider use of examinations tied to course syllabi — perhaps under the auspices of the states, as has been the case with the New York State Regents Examination — offers an opportunity for improving educational standards that is entirely in keeping with the American tradition of local control.

Minimum competency tests can be viewed as an effort to proffer educational enfranchisement to the least able students by allowing them to earn credentials based on a known standard of performance. By focusing on minimal performance, however, the competency testing movement severely limits its potential for upgrading educational standards. In fact, available evidence suggests that minimum competency examinations tend to restrict the range of what is taught and thus to *lower* the standard of education for all but the weakest students. Competency tests could become a much more powerful tool for improving standards across a wide range of the school population, if they regularly tested a broad range of objectives (going beyond the minimum standard for an age or grade level) and offered certification that recognized different levels of performance within the passing range.

Current practice fails to use the full potential of standardized tests for improving achievement.

Tracking

The question of the relationship between educational standards and tracking is a troublesome one, both because reliable evidence on the relationship is difficult to gather and because decisions about tracking involve deep-seated social and political beliefs. Tracking systems that assign students to classes according to academic performance permit the establishment of a very demanding curriculum and high standards of performance for the top groups. Since the public image of a school system that engages in tracking tends to rest on the performance of the top track, such a school system is likely to enjoy a reputation for having high standards in its schools. However, this may be at the cost of lower standards for the middle and lower tracks.

Our nation's greatest difficulty with the issue of tracking is our failure to make a clear choice. We maintain a generally undemanding common curriculum in the middle schools, in the hope of reaping social benefits from a school system that does not sort children according to academic performance. Then we track within the comprehensive high school — but on the basis of a middle school preparation that is often too weak to permit really high-level study, even for the most able students. Thus, an important first step toward raising educational standards is to raise the level of instruction and performance in the middle school.

There are two ways to impose higher curriculum standards in the middle school (and hence in the high school). The easy way is to begin tracking earlier; this would allow us to reap the benefits of a longer period of intensive study for the more able students. But earlier tracking would be unlikely to improve the performance of other students. The harder but preferable path is a nontracked middle school curriculum that sets high intellectual standards in a core program required of *all* students — even those who have effectively been denied, up to now, the stimuli of high expectations and challenging programs.

Although this alternative has been proposed several times during the past century, it has never been tried. But the current growth in demand for technical skills and the decline in the number of traditional manufacturing jobs are creating a bigger demand than ever for the kinds of intellectual abilities that the schools are best able to develop. As young people and their families come to recognize these structural changes in the nature of work, it is reasonable to expect a revaluation of schooling to occur. If this revaluation were to be coupled with an educational program that expected serious intellectual performance from all segments of the school population, we might discover that an academically oriented common program can succeed to an extent not previously thought possible.

WE HAVE outlined three areas in which action to improve American schools is both necessary and possible. First, we suggest that the curriculum in U.S. high schools must be made more demanding and more focused. Our suggestion that course requirements be tightened — both by state and local authorities and by colleges and universities, whose admissions requirements strongly affect the high school curriculum — echoes the recommendation of the National Commissi[on] on Excellence in Education. So, too, d[oes] our suggestion that those in charge [of] textbook adoption use their positions [to] influence the quality of the textbooks t[hat] publishers make available. Finally, [we] propose that the U.S. can ill afford to [ig]nore the potential for upgrading c[ur]riculum that is inherent in curricul[um] development projects of the kind that [oc]curred in the period immediately follo[w]ing Sputnik. On this politically sensiti[ve] matter, the Commission was less dir[ect] than we (as private citizens concern[ed] with the state of American education) c[an] afford to be. The important point, [we] think, is that conflict does not necessa[ri]ly exist between large-scale curricul[um] development projects and state and lo[cal] control of education, if the curricul[um] development projects are properly co[n]ceived.

The second major domain in which [we] suggest action is that of tests and examin[a]tions. We believe that, despite the [na]tional taste for standardized tests, curre[nt] practice in the U.S. fails to use the f[ull] potential of such tests for improvi[ng] school achievement and learning. We se[c]ond the Commission's call for judicio[us] use of achievement tests at key transiti[on] points throughout the educational syste[m]. However, we caution that adoption of t[he] kind of standardized achievement te[sts] now commonly used in U.S. schools w[ill] fail to serve one of the most importa[nt] functions of tests and examinations: [fo]cusing teaching and learning activiti[es]. For this purpose, we need examinati[on] systems that are tied to the curriculu[m] for which teachers can legitimately p[re]pare students, and for which students c[an] study. We agree with the Commission th[at] such systems cannot be limited to mi[ni]mum competencies without having t[he] effect of restricting learning opportunit[ies] for average and, especially, for hig[h-]ability students. Developing such exar[mi]nation systems, in forms consonant w[ith] decentralized responsibility for setti[ng] curriculum requirements, will require [in]genuity. But the existence of statewi[de] and districtwide testing programs sho[ws] that this task is not impossible.

On the final area for action, tracki[ng] and differentiated curricula, the Comm[is]sion report is silent. It says strikingly lit[tle] about the relationship of the "standar[ds] problem" to decisions over the decades [to] adapt the high school curriculum to t[he] perceived capabilities and interests of [an] expanding school population. By cho[os]ing not to address this issue, the Comm[is]sion insured that its analysis and reco[m]mendations would be acceptable to bro[ad] segments of the American public. Ho[w]ever, those who must act to improve U.[S.] schools will not be able to remain silent questions related to tracking and differentiated curricula. They will have difficult choices to make. We propose that U.S. educators focus on an intellectually demanding common curriculum in the years prior to high school, coupled with competitive-entry tracking, beginning at about age 15. More important than our specific recommendation on this matter, however, is our counsel to those responsible for action in the schools that they squarely address and openly debate the question of tracking and differentiated curricula as they develop their programs.

Who are those responsible for action? They are the same broad public addressed by the Commission in its report — legislators, parents, teachers, and school administrators. Each of these groups has a role to play in shaping the expectations and opportunities for learning in U.S. schools. The American educational system allows a great deal of individual initiative at a variety of institutional levels. An effective response to *A Nation at Risk* will depend on the willingness of local school superintendents to make individual schools — and perhaps school districts — examples of how performance can be improved by changes in curriculum, testing, and other practices. Meanwhile, states can respond by reassessing their graduation requirements and, perhaps, by developing statewide examination systems. Researchers can work with educators at all levels to develop the courses and the evaluation techniques necessary to sustain these reform efforts. Such actions — open to and requiring participation from all individuals who are concerned with educational quality — are feasible and timely ways to revitalize American schools.

WHAT DO THE SATs MEAN?

SATs ARE GETTING IN THE WAY OF EDUCATION

DAN MORGAN

Mr. Morgan is editor of The Washington Post Outlook.

Question: The Scholastic Aptitude Test (SAT) is:

☐ A clever device used by the educational establishment to avoid its responsibilities.

☐ A hurdle of much-exaggerated importance for high school seniors trying to get into college.

☐ One symbol of what's wrong with high school education in America.

The SAT itself does not allow an answer of "all of the above," but in this case, that is the correct answer. The declining status and significance of this test is one sign that the hidebound American secondary education system is at last undergoing some significant changes.

Old institutions die slowly, and the SAT still has a powerful mystique. It remains a tense rite of passage for nearly half of all high school seniors. Yesterday, some 267,000 filed nervously into classrooms and auditoriums around the country to agonize over its multiple choice questions about vocabulary, grammar and math.

IS THE TEST OUTMODED?

Yet there is a growing belief among educators that the SAT is an outmoded educational instrument that is sending the wrong message, or at least an incomplete one, to the nation's high schools. In the 58 years of its existence, its creators have yet to define satisfactorily what, exactly, the SAT *tests*. It comes too late in high school careers to be much use in spotting areas where students need more help. And it does not examine how well kids have actually mastered high school subjects such as chemistry, Spanish, American history or geography.

One sign of changing times was a little-noticed report from Harvard College this winter. Harvard confirmed that it was considering allowing future candidates for admission to skip the SAT altogether. Instead, applicants would have the option of submitting the results of tests that evaluate their mastery, or "achievement," in five high school academic subjects.

The new thinking about testing is part of a fundamental reevaluation of what is needed to improve the quality of American secondary education, a reevaluation that marks a clear (and controversial) break with the recent past.

Educational reformers have been urging schools to radically revamp their curriculums, to eliminate the junk courses that have accumulated in them over the past two decades, and to require all students, not just college-bound ones, to master academic subjects such as world history and science.

For that, the nation clearly will need an overhauled testing system that helps students identify their strengths and weaknesses early in the game, instead of one that sorts out the gifted (or the good test-takers) from the not-so-gifted at the end of the academic process.

The United States, alone of all major industrial countries, relies primarily on a vague concept called "aptitude" to evaluate secondary school students.

This year 1.5 million seniors will take the SAT, the nation's leading aptitude test. Defenders of the exam say it tests a student's ability to think and reason. Many of the questions certainly do that; they are abstract puzzles requiring skills that some feel are beyond the schools' ability to teach. The defenders also say the SAT does test a certain kind of verbal and mathematical achievement. But the SAT does not test knowledge of high school courses.

That is not the main purpose, either, of the American College Testing Program exam (the ACT), which 900,000 students, most of them in the Midwest, will take this year.

ACT does ask some questions about social studies and natural science, but it is similar to the SAT.

ONLY A MINORITY OF TAKERS

Remarkable as it may seem, only a small minority of U.S. high school students presently take standardized, national tests that evaluate what they have actually learned in high school academic courses. In recent years, many states have adopted "minimum competency" requirements for high school diplomas,

From *Current,* May 1984, pp. 9-13. Originally appeared in *The Washington Post Outlook,* January 29, 1984, pp. D1-D2. ©The Washington Post.

but the requirements have been set so low that almost all can pass.

There is nothing in this country comparable to the British O (for Ordinary) Level tests—the stringent three-hour, written examinations that all English 16-year-olds take in up to 10 different subjects. The O Levels, instituted in the 1950s, replaced the old elitist system of British academic selection.

Last year, only 280,000 high school seniors out of 3 million (less than 10 percent) took the achievement tests offered in 13 subjects by the Educational Testing Service in Princeton, the same company that produces the SAT. Most of those who did were candidates for elite colleges and universities that often require them. Only 86,000 (3 percent) took the ETS's achievement test in writing, which consists of a 20-minute essay. (The achievement tests are one-hour multiple-choice exams that examine knowledge of foreign language, history, English, science and math. The questions are made up after extensive consultation with high school teachers and college professors all over the country.)

It is easy to see why the U.S. educational establishment has been loath to test what high school students have learned.

As several major reports issued in the last few months state, high school curriculums in America are a "smorgasbord." The National Commission on Excellence in Education has reported that high schools have a "cafeteria-style curriculum in which the appetizers and desserts can easily be mistaken for the main course." Only 31 percent of high school graduates complete intermediate algebra and only 16 percent finish a geography course.

ELECTIVE COURSES

In an Illinois sample, it turned out that more than 2,100 different subjects were taught in the state's high schools, and a large portion of them were non-academic. That was in 1977. Since then, economic cuts and state-ordered reforms have sharply reduced electives, but curriculums everywhere are still bloated with such courses. Large high schools typically offer 150 or more courses, including subjects such as driving, speed-reading, gourmet cuisine, bowling, office management, food services, medical careers, "tots and toddlers" (baby care), women in society, wilderness survival and whale watching.

The available evidence is not reassuring about what high school students actually do learn. In 1976, one out of seven 17-year-olds thought the president did not have to obey the law and only 12 percent were aware that plastics are petroleum products.

International comparisons are risky, given the uniquely broad base of U.S. public education, but results of such comparisons have not been flattering to the United States. In one, done between 1973 and 1977, American 13-to-18-year-olds tested near the bottom of industrial countries in civics, mathematics and reading comprehension.

AVOIDING THE QUESTION OF QUALITY

Why has a schoolroom "smorgasbord," and its shoddy results, been tolerated for so long in a country that constantly boasts of its commitment to education? The answer is that the nation's educational leaders—its college deans, teachers' organizations, testing companies, high school principals and state and local authorities—have found convenient excuses to avoid taking action. They have persistently claimed that they can't agree among themselves on what students *should* know. And they have fallen back on an almost religious-sounding incantation: local authorities, not outsiders, should decide what is taught in local schools.

The SAT, with its alleged objectivity and its claim to be "curriculum free," has helped educators avoid the real issues of educational quality. For years, it provided admissions offices at elite colleges and universities with a convenient way to finesse the problem of identifying students' accomplishments, while still funneling gifted applicants to them.

Because it almost defied definition, the SAT enabled educators to duck the charge that they were dictating what schools should teach.

What makes recent proposals for educational reform so intriguing is that the proposals take a first stab at identifying the knowledge and skills that American students should acquire in high school. Several of the proposals call in so many words for something this country has never had: a high school curriculum, rooted in academic subjects and specific academic skills, that is generally accepted nationwide.

DEFINABLE GOALS

Last year, the College Board, a non-profit organization of 2,500 colleges, schools and school systems, issued a 36-page booklet identifying "what [college] students need to know and be able to do." It listed six academic subjects (English, the arts, mathematics, science, social studies and foreign language), and six academic "competencies" (reading, writing, speaking and listening, mathematics, reasoning, and studying). The booklet was general enough to avoid charges that the College Board was "dictating" to the schools, but it went much further than ever before in saying that there are a set of definable goals for all schools. In some areas it got specific. Under world history, it said students should not only know about the Renaissance and the Industrial Revolution, but also "the spread of Islam."

The booklet was followed last summer by the release of two major reports that questioned current high school curriculums.

One, the report of the National Commission on Excellence in Education, recommended that state and local authorities require all students seeking a diploma to take four years of English, three years of mathematics, three years of science, three years of social studies and one-half year of computer science.

The other was former U.S. Commissioner of Education Ernest L. Boyer's book, "High School," written for the Carnegie Foundation for the Advancement of Teaching. Boyer called for schools to establish a "core of common learning," with required courses in literature, the arts, foreign language, history, civics, sciences, mathematics, technology and health. Boyer called for an end to the tracking of students into "academic" and "general" programs. Under his plan all students would take a solid group of academic subjects.

Boyer's ideas have been attacked on grounds that they could lead to a "homogenous" system that would keep schools from tailoring curriculums to local needs. Doesn't a school in an Iowa farm community have different educational priorities and values than one serving ethnic neighborhoods in Chicago, they asked? Boyer contends that question dodges the real issue.

"If a school district is incapable of naming the things it wants high school graduates to know, if a community is unable to define the culture it wants high school graduates to inherit, if education cannot help students see relationships beyond their own personal ones, then each new generation will remain dangerously ignorant, and its capacity to live confidently and responsibly will be diminished," wrote Boyer.

For better or worse, the testing system is sure to have a major impact on whether these curriculum reform proposals get off the ground.

The SAT became a mass, nationwide test after World War II, when higher education was expanding rapidly and colleges and universities needed some uniform indicators. Initially, SAT scores were thought to be an excellent predictor of college performance. When subsequent studies questioned that assumption, the rationale for the SAT changed.

The current, more modest view of the College Board, which sponsors the test, is that it is "one helpful piece of information."

Spokesmen for some college admissions offices say SAT scores help students evaluate their own scholastic strengths, so that they can "self-select" colleges that fit those abilities. It identifies "gifted" (if high scores automatically warrant that adjective) students who otherwise might get lost in the admissions shuffle because they attend an undistinguished high school. And it provides a check on whether grades on high school transcripts accurately reflect a student's ability.

EDUCATIONAL REFORM

But Boyer and others suggest that the most important use of the SAT today is one for which it was never intended: as a report card on schools, not students. The decline in average SAT scores starting in 1964 has been a prime mover in calls for educational reform. And rightly or wrongly, communities often judge the quality of individual schools on how well students score on the test.

THE SAT IN COLLEGE ADMISSIONS

Most colleges, and ETS itself, have come to recognize the limitations of the SAT. Nevertheless, it is still associated with academic "merit," through the Preliminary SAT (PSAT), the exam in junior year which is used to select semi-finalists for National Merit Scholarships. If anything, students, parents and schools seem more obsessed than ever with SAT results, and a whole industry has grown up around coaching students to raise their scores.

This is ironic in view of considerable evidence that SAT scores will have little bearing on whether the vast majority of high school students enter the college of their choice.

SELECTIVITY

"Most private colleges in America today, including some with rather prestigious names, are *not* highly selective," writes Richard Moll in "Playing the College Admissions Game," a handbook for parents and students. "High price, a declining number of college-age Americans, apprehension regarding the worth of a bachelor's degree in the job market and the growth and strength of the state university system nationwide have created this phenomenon. . . . Unfortunately, many colleges pose as being more selective than they really are."

According to Moll, not more than 40 private colleges (and far fewer public ones) "enjoy the luxury of admitting one out of two of their candidates, and not more than half a dozen private colleges admit [as few as] one out of five."

Most colleges still require SAT scores, but less than 2 percent use them as the single most important criterion for admission.

"After you get beyond the first 50 or 75 most selective colleges, the problem is who *not* to admit," says Alexander Astin, director of the Higher Education Research Institute at the University of California in Los Angeles. For them, the SAT is useful mainly in weeding out the very worst students (or worst test takers)—not in selecting the brightest.

To students in the Washington area who have their hopes set on highly selective, prestige colleges such as Swarthmore, Yale or the University of Virginia, SATs are still important. But such students are in a minority nationwide.

Of this year's 1,750,000 college-bound

seniors, nearly 700,000 will enter two-year colleges that, for the most part, have open enrollments. Another 400,000 will enter state universities, most of which—the Big Ten schools in the Midwest, for example—accept all applicants from their states. (The University of Wisconsin stopped requiring the test entirely in 1972.)

Another 650,000 go on to four-year colleges. Many of these do use tests and are selective; but they are not nearly as selective as many students believe.

In all, probably no more than 80,000 of next year's freshman places will be in the 100 or so institutions where the combined math and verbal scores of entering freshmen average 1,100 or better out of a possible 1,600, according to UCLA's Astin. In other words, a score of 650 on the verbals and 450 on the math would still be high enough to give a student a reasonable chance at a selective college. A combined score of 1,200 is high enough to get a student into 90 percent of the 50 most selective schools, Astin estimates.

IS A NEW TEST NEEDED?

One concern of educators such as George Hanford, president of the College Board, is that the message of Boyer and other reformers may be misinterpreted as a call for a return to a rigid curriculum emphasizing rote and fact learning. In emphasizing achievement and mastery, he warns, we could sacrifice thinking and reasoning. And in a rapidly changing world, those two qualities will be more important than acquiring knowledge.

In Hanford's view, the SAT is a good test of those important qualities. "I worry about too much emphasis on achievement," he says.

But even if the SAT does serve some useful purposes, it seems urgently in need of major modification.

For one thing, it ignores the needs of hundreds of thousands of students who are not going on to college, but who still need guidance in planning their futures. Boyer proposes replacing the SAT with a Student Achievement and Advisement Test (SAAT), which all students would take. It would evaluate their academic achievement (not aptitude), linking it to a "core" academic curriculum. An accompanying questionnaire could collect information about their interests, goals, job history and experiences. That information could then be used to help them choose suitable academic or employment opportunities.

ETS has already begun work on a new series of diagnostic tests that teachers could use in classrooms to pinpoint students' strengths and weaknesses all through the academic year.

"We need better testing at the school level for purposes of instruction and learning," says ETS president Gregory Anrig. "Our present tests don't answer the question, 'How am I doing in progressing toward my goals?' We don't have tests that are helpful teaching tools."

A revamped testing system would create a new set of standards for schools and students. One obvious possibility would be combining achievements and SATs, to get a more complete picture of a student's ability to reason *and* master academic subjects. Such a test could do a better job of recognizing personal qualities such as hard work, determination, curiosity and love of learning—all indispensable for doing well in academic subjects, but not necessarily for scoring high on aptitude tests.

Changes of this magnitude would face bureaucratic resistance. If implemented, there would be less need for teachers of "electives," but more demand for teachers who are really competent in their academic fields, as European and Japanese secondary school teachers tend to be.

Such reforms are bound to run into criticism that they favor students from affluent school systems blessed with gifted teachers. There is concern that raising academic standards too high might force kids out of school, especially minorities. That would defeat the purpose of U.S. public education, which has always strived to be open rather than exclusive. But it is hard to see how that could happen. It is the lack of higher education facilities, not the tests, that make European education selective. There are only 40 academic colleges in all of England, while nearly two out of three U.S. high school students go on to one of the nation's 3,000 colleges and universities.

The pressing issue for the United States is not wider access to higher education. It is the disappointing level of knowledge, academic skills and motivation of young people who feel, unjustifiably, that they have had a good education in high school.

Just Among Us Teachers

***Teachers will try to change in response to the mood of the nation, says Mr. Chandler, himself a teacher. But he cries out against the shortcomings of* A Nation at Risk.**

Harry N. Chandler

HARRY N. CHANDLER (Yamhill County Oregon Chapter) is a secondary school resource room teacher in McMinnville, Ore., and education editor of the Journal of Learning Disabilities.

MY FIRST impressions and reactions to the report of the National Commission on Excellence in Education, *A Nation at Risk: The Imperative for Educational Reform*, have been altered by the unexpected response it has generated. Politicians at all levels have expressed alarm about the findings of the report; syndicated columnists, from Mike Royko to James Kilpatrick, have written about it; and the report has received the "five-minute, in-depth" treatment on television news broadcasts, as well as generating discussion on the public radio program, "All Things Considered." Educational organizations, from the American Association of School Administrators to the National Education Association and the American Federation of Teachers, have issued position papers on the report; meanwhile, civic organizations ranging from chambers of commerce to church groups have sought speakers who can explain its implications for business, religion, and the larger society.

The Commission's report has something for everybody. Perhaps that's why it didn't just fade away, as did the comments of the Twentieth Century Fund Task Force and those of the National Task Force on Education for Economic Growth. Even John Goodlad's recently released study has been seen as a footnote to the Commission's statement that U.S. schools are generally worthless. *A Nation at Risk* briefly and condescendingly states that some schools and teachers do well. The report also insists that schools should be locally financed and controlled. Then it states that the federal government should spend money on special programs for special students. The reader can almost hear Commission members compromising frantically to include everyone's viewpoint. *U.S. News & World Report* has listed education as one of the five major domestic issues in the 1984 election campaign.[1] The National Commission's report supplies ammunition for all politicians, regardless of their leanings.

As a teacher I'm pleased that education is receiving national attention. I would be more pleased if the attention and attendant debate centered on a more respectable, data-based document. That *A Nation at Risk* is a mass of opinion pretending to be fact is not surprising; after all, the Commission members were not, for the most part, public school educators, nor was the report meant to be of value to educators. It is a political document.

Among the 18 Commission members, there was only one public school teacher. There were also two principals and a lone superintendent — who was included, I hope, for his educational background and not just for his Hispanic surname. The other Commission members came from business and from that part of educational management which is hardly distinguishable from industry.

By contrast, when the "Grace Commission" (President Reagan's private-sector survey on cost control) was formed to study how the federal government did business, the 1,300 members of that group came "mostly from business."[2] Apparently U.S. business can be trusted to study the way the federal government conducts its own business and the way it regulates the very businesses whose representatives are studying this issue — but U.S. education cannot be trusted to see itself clearly.

NOW THE organizations of educators are warning their members not to respond defensively by pointing out the many ambiguities and errors in *A Nation at Risk*. These organizations are right, of course. After all the publicity about terrible teachers in second-rate schools, who would believe us anyway? But since this article is just among us teachers, I will dwell on some of the weaknesses in the Commission's report. Readers will be able to spot many others on which I will not waste space (among them, accepting out-of-date Scholastic Aptitude Test scores as valid indicators of educational quality and comparing U.S. schools to those of other cultures).

The Commission assumes that a monolith called "U.S. education" exists, that it is mediocre throughout, and that all regions of the nation need, desire, and can pay for the same type of schooling. The Commission pays lip service to local control, but it recommends an educational program for the nation that does not take regional differences into account. Perhaps led by futurists among its members, the Commission makes a further assumption: that the states are united, not just in a political union but in a common acceptance of technology and its applications to daily life. However, it is not necessarily true that what the Commission sees as proper education for the year 2000 will also be perceived as proper by the citizens of Manhattan, of Yamhill County, of Minneapolis, and of Plaquemines Parish.

In one of its many inconsistencies, the report says that schools are "routinely called on to provide solutions to personal, social, and political problems" that other institutions cannot resolve — and then blames schools and teachers for America's economic problems and charges them with solving those problems. Here we can detect the Commission's view of the purpose of schooling: schools must become instruments of national policy. Although this view is never stated, it dominates *A Nation at Risk*, which clearly emphasizes throughout the notion that effective schools turn out well-trained, highly competitive workers for business and industry.

The Commission asserts that its formula for reforming the schools is appropriate for all students, yet what it has recommended is really a college-preparatory curriculum. I don't disagree with emphasizing the "five new basics" (English, mathematics, science, social studies, and computer science), but I wouldn't place money on the idea that all students (and their parents) want that many academic courses in that much depth. The "diluted" curriculum of today — if it exists at all — is more the product of legislative mandates than of educational theory. And legislative mandates in a democracy presumably reflect the public will.

I am sure that at least 80% of all students can learn what the Commission wants them to learn, if teachers know how to teach this content well and if the necessary support services and materials are supplied. But I also know that, by the time they reach high school, many students are taking full responsibility for all decisions related to their schooling. One such decision might be to drop out if the

From *Phi Delta Kappan*, November 1983, pp. 181-182. Reprinted by permission of the author and Phi Delta Kappan.

school offers too few alternatives. It is true that many students are already deciding to do "the minimum work necessary for the moment, then coast through life." I deplore this decision, but I would not outlaw it as a possible democratic choice, especially in a society in which many teenage (and adult) idols — with the help of the business community — preach via records, television programs, and movies the quick and easy pursuit of happiness.

A Nation at Risk not only emphasizes academic excellence as the road to higher education and thus to commercial or scientific success, but the report also implicitly denigrates those youths and adults who do not — or *cannot* — choose that road. The curriculum that the Commission recommends would be of value to anyone. But some students — perhaps a majority of them — also want to spend some time studying such things as art, auto repair, metal working, music, or food preparation.

It is useless to counter that parents should teach these skills, that they should be covered in private lessons after school, that they should be studied in technical schools after graduation from high school, or that the public schools cannot teach these skills well. If students are not at least exposed to these skills in school, they may lack both the motivation and the opportunity to learn them elsewhere. Moreover, if the schools can teach academics well, they can also teach — or learn to teach — the vocational and artistic basics effectively. The Commission's stand on this matter does great damage to that most democratic of U.S. institutions, the comprehensive high school.

Another problem with *A Nation at Risk* is that it terms the eight years before high school "crucial," but it devotes only one paragraph to schooling during the elementary and middle years. Schools serving these age groups are seen as prologues to high school, not as enterprises important in themselves and just as deserving of support as their secondary counterparts. The Commission report does not even mention kindergarten, preschool, or such early childhood compensatory programs as Head Start. Some of the recommendations in the report do apply to grades 1 through 8, but the Commission clearly regards older students — the ones preparing for college — as the most important age group. This attitude reflects the general stance of our supposedly child-centered society: those individuals who hold political or economic power tend to value children only when they are old enough to function as independent consumers and workers. Clearly, politicians appoint commissions to validate preconceived ideas.

Another preconceived idea that runs throughout *A Nation at Risk* is the notion

By robbing Peter to pay *all* we will end up weakening education in other disciplines or at other grade levels.

that professional teachers are of little value. The Commission advocates the use of "nonschool personnel" from industry and higher education to teach science and mathematics, and it suggests that methods courses in teacher training institutions should be replaced by "subject-matter" courses. (What are the appropriate subject-matter courses for a primary teacher?)

Indeed, the Commission seldom misses an opportunity to take a shot at teachers, and this shotgun approach works; it attracts attention and does not require a scholarly consideration of actual school conditions. Firing into a group of terrorists and their hostages will kill some of the guilty, if you don't care about the innocent. In fact, the Commission's blasts *have* hit some of the guilty. There *are* poor teachers who, through administrative incompetence or union strength, remain in classrooms. There *are* some education courses that benefit only the instructor (who is paid to teach them). One reason it is difficult to argue publicly with the Commission's report is that parts of it are at least partly true.

However, even those parts have a "yes, but" attached to them:

- Teacher salaries are too low. Yes, but where do we get the money to improve them?
- We need more direct teaching time in the classroom. Yes, but is increasing the length of the school day and school year the most effective way to resolve this problem?
- School board members should be more interested in education, instead of functioning solely as fiscal watchdogs. Yes, but they ran for election on the promise of cutting school budgets.
- Parents should play a more active role in their children's education. Yes, but that is difficult to do in this era of high unemployment and divorce rates, when so many families are under stress.
- Teachers need more than just intrinsic rewards for doing an effective job. Yes, but how can we determine fairly which teachers should receive merit pay or promotions?
- Students should take education more seriously. Yes, but educators have been trying to get them to do that for years. Any practical suggestions?

Meanwhile, the Commission's recommendations are going to cost money — and the Commission says that these extra funds should come from local governments, which are already facing tax revolts. Thus many of the Commission's suggestions can only be implemented in communities with heavy concentrations of upwardly mobile, middle-class citizens who think as the Commission members do. This is because the Commission report is much like a brainstorming session, where one comes up with as many solutions to a problem as possible without examining the problem (to see if it is real) or the solutions (to see if they are practical).

THE COMMISSION chooses to ignore one fact that teachers cannot forget: we are members of a larger society, and, although we like to think that we have great influence on our students — and, through them, on U.S. culture — we face stiff competition for children's time and attention. But we teachers will try to implement as many of the Commission's recommendations as we can, since *A Nation at Risk* reflects the mood of the country and we teachers are experts at responding to the country's mood. Indeed, we teachers will *have* to change, because educational philosophy in the U.S. (what little we know of it) is so fragmented that we have no shared professional ideal with which to stave off even the most idiotic suggestions for reform; because educational psychology (what little we understand of it) is so at odds in its findings that we have no proven methodology to fall back on in the face of attacks; and because our own craft (carried out independently in isolated cubicles) has given us few strong bonds beyond our unions, which are too absorbed in internecine warfare to defend us.

Therefore, we will try to change, even though by robbing Peter to pay *all* we will end up weakening education in other disciplines or at other grade levels. We will once again rush headlong into ill-conceived but widely advertised innovations that will hang like millstones from the curriculum long after the Commission and its report have been forgotten. Because we are teachers and we really do want to teach well, we will also spend long hours in stuffy rooms with stuffy committees, trying to decide whether we have done what is best.

---

1. "Tomorrow," *U.S. News & World Report*, 8 August 1983, p. 11.
2. " 'Nobody Has Any Guts' in Washington," *U.S. News & World Report*, 25 July 1983, pp. 53-56.

Making Schools Work Again

As teaching again becomes a strong and honored profession, the quality of the student will improve immeasurably.

Robert A. Blume

Robert A. Blume is professor of education at the University of Florida, Gainesville, and president of the Association for Humanistic Education. He is active in the movement to replace corporal punishment in schools with more humane forms of discipline.

Many people are saying that the schools are not working any more. This complaint is not entirely new, but the number of people who agree with it is even greater than during the post-Sputnik era, when schools were blamed for our failure to beat the Russians in the space race.

Educators themselves are getting a lot of bad press these days, especially public school teachers. The mood of America has grown angry about the schools' failures, and everyone points to a scapegoat on which to blame the sorry state of affairs. Teachers are the most obvious culprits, and teacher educators, school administrators, and "lazy" children come in for their share of criticism, too.

THE PROBLEM

The National Commission on Excellence in Education reported this past May that we are "a nation at risk." There seems to be little doubt that a serious problem exists in education today. "The problem," in summary, is that: (1) *some* children do not acquire basic skills by grade twelve; (2) *many* children do not acquire thinking skills by grade twelve; (3) *many* children do not feel motivated to learn in school; (4) *many* children do not learn to behave responsibly by grade twelve; (5) *many* children think less of themselves by grade twelve (their self-concepts decline each year).

It is only fair to add as perspective that there has never been a time in our history when *all* children did learn these things. We tend to glorify the past and compare today's children unfairly to an idealized and mythical time when everything worked as it should. It is important to be clear on this point and not harbor illusions that make the situation more depressing than it is in reality. Our system of schooling has always been far from perfect, and that is certainly true today. The sad fact, however, is that schools overall have not improved since World War II, and in some respects—as the "Nation at Risk" report points out—they have become somewhat less productive over the past two or three decades.

We educators might deflect some of the criticism by pointing out that we are dealing with a culture in upheaval. A series of wars, and a continuing cold war, have kept our government preoccupied with military defense. A situation in which the Constitu-

This article first appeared in THE HUMANIST issue of January/February 1984, pp. 9-12, 32, and is reprinted by permission.

tion says one thing while legislative bodies frequently behave in opposition to the Constitution, especially in regard to the treatment of minorities and women, has created a number of rifts or divisions in our society. We are also trying to educate *all children* today, something we did not do in the past. In 1950, approximately 40 percent of the student population dropped out before graduation. Today it is closer to 10 percent, so we cannot compare test scores of today's graduates with the 1950 graduates.

It is not the purpose of this article to deflect criticism from educators; it is to suggest a new direction for public policy and some steps that need to be taken to improve American education.

> The mood of America has grown angry about the schools' failures, and everyone points to a scapegoat on which to blame the sorry state of affairs. Teachers are the most obvious culprits.

EDUCATING TEACHERS

Rather than make excuses for what is wrong with the schools, we should focus on the problem itself and propose a way out of the morass. When I graduated from college, I did not feel adequately *educated* to be a teacher, nor did I feel adequately *trained* to be a teacher when I entered my first classroom as a fully certified teacher.

To compound the problem, I received precious little help from the school administration during my first year of teaching. The most valuable help I did receive came from a veteran teacher down the hall who was willing to spend time with me discussing problems and answering questions. Not every first-year teacher is as lucky as I was in finding a well-qualified mentor who is so willing to assist a neophyte.

Today, thirty-three years later, we still turn out teachers in about the same way, and they still teach themselves to teach, with a little help from their friends. So the process of induction into the profession looks like this:

- An inadequate liberal arts education *and* inadequate professional preparation squeezed into a four-year program
- New teachers having a total-immersion experience on the first day of school, with only a few months of student teaching and other field experiences to prepare them for that day
- Almost no help from the school administration; but, of course, many demands for paperwork and record keeping, as well as a crowded classroom and parents who are increasingly critical of teachers
- New teachers who invent their own teaching methods or borrow them from colleagues, in effect teaching themselves to be teachers

This is not an adequate preparation for professionals who must do work that is infinitely complex and demanding and who have a profound effect on the next generation of adults in a democracy.

Because teacher education is inadequate, it is not respected by teachers themselves and certainly not by members of other professions. New teachers are often told by gray-haired colleagues to "forget all that stuff they told you in the college of education; it won't work out here in the real world."

Education professors, stung by such criticism, have over the years attempted to make their courses more "practical." In the process, they have reduced the amount of theory presented to students of education. This trend has alarmed many people involved in the education of teachers, and a reversal of this process is now underway. Without theory, there can be no profession.

There is further evidence of a push away from professionalism:

- Teachers have no control over who or how many people enter teaching each year, as members of some other professions do.
- Teachers have no control over the tools of their craft—textbooks and other curriculum materials.
- The teaching profession has no body of knowledge which its members alone possess—as do other professions.

The process of teacher recruitment must be changed to encourage more young people to aspire to become teachers. As it is today, our society recognizes that teachers receive low pay, and to most people that means low quality (an unfair assumption, but one often made). Fewer and fewer students enter teacher education, and most of those who do graduate with teaching certificates. Most of these graduates are hired, and most teachers are retained even if their performance has been mediocre.

Suppose this process were altered by a series of significant pay increases for teachers, equal to three or four times the annual inflation rate each year. Teacher recruitment might then look like this:

- People would realize that teachers have been getting big raises (accompanied by the assumption that teachers are "getting better")
- Many more young people would aspire to become teachers
- Not all who aspire to become teachers would be admitted to teacher education programs

(which in itself would make teaching more attractive)

- Teacher education standards would become stiffer as more applicants would be turned away
- There would be more graduates of higher quality, but not all would be hired
- Because a good supply of high-quality applicants would be available, not all teachers would be re-hired

As a result of this process, a measure of selectivity would exist which is lacking today. During the 1970s, when the school system was shrinking, this process began to work in part; but the school-age population is now growing again. Teacher shortages will mean a lowering of entry standards and a reluctance to let people go when it is uncertain who will be available to take their places.

The politicians are proposing "merit pay" as the cure for the problem of low-paid teachers. Nothing could be further from a cure, because the various schemes that have been tried over the past half-century, as well as those being proposed today, all have one thing in common: they propose to give higher pay to a few teachers, while keeping the salaries of the vast majority at the lowest possible level. The net effect is to spend about the same amount of money on teachers' salaries after the initial jump for the meritorious teachers has been paid. Such plans will not change perceptions of teachers' salaries generally, and that is what must happen if more of our talented youth are to be attracted to the field of teaching.

PROFESSIONAL DECISION-MAKING

Significant increases in salaries would definitely improve the teaching profession, but much more than that is needed. Schools need a *strong* profession of teaching, one which has the authority and the power to make certain that professional decisions are made by the professionals who work directly with the clients. As it is now, many professional decisions are made by administrators, by school boards, or by governmental bodies at the state or national level.

> It is likely that a well-trained teacher will find many ways to use computers that no one has dreamed of as yet. But the key is *the teacher*, and the computer is but another tool to be used *by the teacher.*

Politicians are experts at feeling the pulse of the body politic, but they are not experts at educating children. They have a penchant for spending huge sums of money on hardware instead of on people. Following Sputnik (1957), it was believed by many people that television was the key to better education. Enormous sums were spent on television sets and tapes of "excellent teachers" to be watched by thousands of children with upturned faces.

We are now seeing schools, which cannot pay decent salaries to teachers, buying computers by the dozens in the hope that they will be the salvation of education. Today's computers alone will no more save education than yesterday's televisions.

This is not to say that computers are worthless in schools or that teachers cannot make good use of them. On the contrary, it is likely that a well-trained teacher who is skilled in the use of computers will find many ways to use them that no one has dreamed of as yet. But the key is *the teacher*, and the computer is but another tool to be used *by the teacher*.

Politicians are making another grotesque error by foisting on the schools the massive testing programs which some states have recently implemented. The hope seems to be that, if we can first find out where the low scores are, then it will be obvious where the bad teaching is occurring. These low scores can be publicized, and the pressure will be on the teachers to work harder to raise the scores. One of the first states to initiate a large (and very expensive) testing program has now instituted a new plan: divide the state into regions and have them compete against each other for high test scores. The commissioner of education, a former businessman, said that he got the idea from business, where it is a common practice to establish sales regions and give prizes to the regions that sell the most or make the most improvements.

Diverting money to a new expensive venture, such as testing, starves existing programs that are already malnourished. Something else pernicious happens in the case of teaching: *teachers teach for the test*. This is not meant as a criticism of teachers who do so; it is simply a statement of fact. Teachers have no choice but to teach for the test, because test scores are assumed to be the indication of quality.

The proponents of testing say, "At least the kids will learn that way." However, that is not necessarily true. By focusing on a single test which is well known, the teacher tries to make certain that the children know the answers to the specific questions to be asked; but, in order to do that, nearly everything else is ignored. The focus becomes very narrow, and the mode of learning becomes memorization, which rules out thinking. Without thinking, most educators would agree, children have not really learned anything of value. They may have acquired the ability to answer a series of memory questions, but they lack the ability to use those bits of information to solve a problem or as a tool to help them learn other information.

Very little time in many elementary schools is devoted to social studies, in the mistaken belief that until children can read "on grade level" there is no possibility of their learning about society, history, geography, or people. Again, the opportunity for *thinking* is passed over in favor of more time spent in the memorization of small bits of information.

The neglect of both writing and science in the curriculum can also be laid at the door of the "reading is the only important thing" mentality that has come out of the back-to-basics movement. If the massive, machine-scored test is to be the ultimate measure of success in education, how do we include the ability to write in that test? If we cannot test it, maybe it is not really important. Such is the logic of accountability.

> If the machine-scored test is to be the ultimate measure of success, how do we include the ability to write in that test? The logic seems to be, if we cannot test it, maybe it is not really important.

DISCREDITING PUBLIC SCHOOLS

Besides the real deficiencies of the schools, there are some phony problems. In fact, there is a nationwide smear campaign underway now to discredit public schools. The purpose of this campaign is to urge people to transfer their children to private schools, thus lowering the enrollment and costs of the public school system. This will, it is hoped, reduce taxes and let parents assume more of the costs of education, thus reducing costs for corporations and taxpayers in high tax brackets.

A parallel movement would have the government pick up some of those private school costs through income tax credits (for those whose incomes are high enough to be reduced by such credits) or through tuition vouchers. Such vouchers would be more democratic than tax credits but still would help the rich more than the poor. Saving money is the main purpose of both the smear campaign and the tax-credit or voucher movement.

How will the voucher system save the taxpayers money? How will it help the rich more than the poor? Consider the fact that high-quality private schools are run as profit-making ventures and serve the interests of those who pay the tuition. The patrons of such schools tend to be upper and upper-middle-class parents, and, even if tuition vouchers were available to rich and poor alike, the children of the poor would not be admitted to the better schools. For one thing, there will be a transportation problem. Parents would have to take their children to a private school because public school buses would not be available. And then there would be the extra expenses not included in the tuition paid by vouchers; such things as uniforms and special clothing, class trips, and special equipment and supplies needed by the individual student will have to be paid for by the parents. Because of these added expenses, most poor families will probably send their children to the nearest public school or to a church-related private school close to home—in both cases schools which would be highly segregated.

Once the middle- and upper-middle-class children are removed from the tax-supported schools, public interest in these schools will wane. We spend little energy or time thinking about institutions which we believe do not affect us. The public schools probably will enjoy as much public interest and support as public housing or welfare. It will be an institution maintained for the poor, the handicapped, and the retarded, while mainstream America will use tuition vouchers to buy their children's education in mostly segregated private schools.

When the public cost of this system is added up, education will take fewer dollars from the public treasury than is currently the case. This saving is the main purpose of the push for vouchers. Providing education for white children in a middle-class atmosphere, with very few middle-class minority children, is another big motive. The appeal of both is strong in middle America today. Many people would be willing to pay a little more for a few years for their child's education in a private school if they could be spared the high cost of educating other people's children in what seem to be very expensive public schools.

Getting the government to pay for Christian religious education is another motive behind the voucher movement, and the heavy hand of the right wing can be seen clearly here. Those who believe that children should have their religious ideas shaped by school know that they are up against the U.S. Constitution when it comes to introducing religion into the public schools, but they now want to have their religious schools funded by tax money—one way or another.

The smear campaign accuses teachers of being atheists who dispense immorality along with their pedagogy. School texts are being effectively censored on the grounds that they are "immoral" or "un-American" or "anti-family" or "anti-God."

The outpouring of criticism through the media has people in general believing that public schools are hopelessly inadequate. This is not true, of course, and there is no evidence that private schools in general are better than public schools in general. The Excellence in Education Study made no distinction between the two in its criticisms.

The public schools cannot be killed by this movement, but they can be crippled. If a mass exodus of white, middle-class children occurs, the public schools will exist only for the minorities and the handicapped. Such an unfortunate development would serve the interests of those who want to *re-segregate education* in America, as well as those who want to *Christianize education* and take the tax load off big taxpayers.

Here are three specific suggestions that might help to improve the situation.

First, as a society we need to rethink what we want out of education. What is its purpose, and what are we willing to pay for it? As a part of this re-thinking, we should think the unthinkable: maybe we cannot afford thirteen years of free public education. Maybe we should reduce that to ten. For example, we might start educating children at three and teach them until they are thirteen. We should face up to the fact that, as a society, we have so far not been willing to pay the true cost of high-quality schools, kindergarten through grade twelve, and we have been asking teachers to subsidize it by accepting low salaries.

Second, we must stop blaming teachers for not being masters of all subject areas. When a physical education teacher with a math minor is drafted to teach math full time, he or she is pilloried in the press as an inadequate teacher. Here is a person who wants to coach basketball but is willing to help out as a math teacher, and people are critical of him or her. It isn't the coach's fault that he or she is being asked to teach math. Why can't schools pay as much for a math major to teach as industry does to have the same person analyze sales figures? Teaching math, or any other subject, is simply not valued highly enough in our society.

Third, we must build a strong teaching *profession*. It must be responsible for setting standards of excellence for new members; for setting standards for teacher education; for resisting educational decision-making by slogans; and for using its power to influence legislation concerning licensing, funding, and any other matters that have to do with the educational welfare of children. Only teachers themselves can build such a profession, but they must have the support of the people in order to do it. Teachers, administrators, and teacher educators must be controlled by their professional knowledge and research—not by political forces in our society.

There is no easy cure for these problems, but the direction in which we should move is very clear: we, as a society, must insist on and pay for high-quality schools, even if the amount of education must be reduced in order to do that.

We must stop blaming teachers for deficiencies that they had no part in creating. We must support teachers in their efforts to build a strong profession of teaching, turn over the job to the teachers, and hold them accountable for doing it well.

Latest Educational 'Reforms' Ring A 19th Century Bell

C. H. Edson

C. H. Edson is an associate professor of education at the University of Oregon. This essay is a shortened version of an article published in the national journal, "Issues in Education."

Charles W. Eliot, President of Harvard University from 1869 to 1909, and one of the preeminent advocates of educational reform during the four decades surrounding the turn of the last century, would find much of the current debate about excellence in education familiar. Indeed, many of the recent national reports advocating educational reform appear to echo Eliot's calls for excellence in education proposed nearly a century ago. A comparison of Eliot's nineteenth-century pronouncements with those made by the National Commission on Excellence in Education in their 1983 report, "A Nation at Risk; The Imperative for Educational Reform," underlines important similarities and differences between then and now.

In 1892, the National Education Association called upon Eliot to chair The Committee of Ten on Secondary School Studies. The Committee's findings and recommendations were written by Eliot and published in 1893. The Committee of Ten report, one of the landmark statements about American high schools, became a reform agenda for secondary education in the United States for the next quarter century. By examining the pronouncements of Eliot and the Committee of Ten and comparing their findings with those of the National Commission, we may broaden our understanding about the findings and assumptions of the Nation at Risk report.

First, the two reports make strikingly similar recommendations about secondary school curricula. Emphasizing enrichment, uniformity, and a return to the basics, both the Committee of Ten report and the Nation at Risk report advocate that all students take four years of English, three years of history or social studies, three years of science, and three years of mathematics.

Although the two sets of recommendations differ in the areas of foreign languages and computer science, they remain similarly focused on an academic core. The Committee of Ten called for four years of foreign language while the National Commission recommends two years for the college-bound. In addition, the National Commission advocates one-half year of computer science, the only new subject to appear in the National Commission's "Five New Basics." Indeed, the "Five New Basics" of today look suspiciously like the "old basics" of nine decades ago.

Second, to achieve equality of educational opportunity, both the Committee of Ten and the National Commission argue that the same basic curriculum should be taken by all students. Eliot vehemently urged educators not to differentiate between pupils who were college-bound and those who were not. Following Eliot's recommendations, the Committee of Ten unanimously declared, "every subject which is taught... should be taught in the same way and to the same extent to every pupil so long as he pursues it, no matter what the probable destination of the pupil may be, or at what point his equation is to cease." The Nation at Risk report differs slightly from the Committee of Ten report in recognizing that different textbooks will be necessary for "disadvantaged students, the learning disabled and the gifted and talented," however, it is in agreement with the 1893 report that all students seeking a diploma be required to take the same basic curriculum. Both groups, therefore, seek to achieve equal educational opportunity by providing the same curriculum for all students.

Third, in addition to similar curricular recommendations and similar

From *The Register-Guard,* Friday, July 6, 1984, p. 14A. Reprinted by permission.

definitions of equal educational opportunity, both the Committee of Ten and the National Commission direct their reform proposals primarily to an elite, college-bound audience. Although the 1893 Committee of Ten report stated that "secondary schools of the United States taken as a whole, do not exist for the purpose of preparing boys and girls for colleges," it recognized that most parents at that time could not afford to keep their children in school until they reached 18 years of age. The goal of secondary education in 1893, according to the Committee of Ten report, was "to prepare for the duties of life that small proportion of all the children in the country—a proportion small in number, but very important to the welfare of the nation—who show themselves able to profit by an education prolonged to the eighteenth year, and whose parents are able to support them while they remain so long at school."

By recommending a return to an academic core, the National Commission appears to echo Eliot's belief that secondary school reform should be tailored to college-bound youth. What we need to appreciate, however, is that since the 1890s a fundamental and far-reaching revolution has taken place in the structure and functions of secondary education in this country. We must remember that in the late nineteenth century public high schools were distinctly minority institutions. In 1890, only 6.7 percent of the 14–17 year olds were enrolled in high schools. Thus school reform at that time was being directed toward the few. Today, well over 90 percent of the 14–17 year olds are enrolled in secondary education, a group of some 13.5 million youth.

It appears paradoxical, therefore, that the National Commission calls for greater uniformity and standardization based on a prescribed academic curriculum at a time when high schools are being asked to serve a culturally and academically heterogeneous group of over 13 million students. We may expand our understanding of the apparent inconsistency between an elite school curriculum and a heterogeneous student population by questioning whether we, like Eliot, are employing a 19th century philosophy of social Darwinism to guide our search for solutions to educational problems.

In the late 19th century, an ideology of survival—social Darwinism—helped Americans to understand and respond to cataclysmic changes taking place in society. The architects of social Darwinism, among them Herbert Spencer and William Graham Summer, reasoned that life was a competitive struggle and that the strongest only—those who had the necessary resources to sustain themselves—could survive. In turn, the pressures of survival stimulated the strongest to develop adaptive skills that would benefit human evolution. Inequality, therefore, was both natural and beneficial for society, as species-survival depended upon those individuals capable of adapting. Governmental intervention to alleviate social or economic inequities, conversely, was perceived as unnatural and anti-evolutionary for it would interfere with the process of natural selection.

Charles Eliot's prescriptions for school reform reflected an acceptance of social Darwinism. Eliot's belief that the purpose of secondary education was "to prepare for the duties of life that small proportion of all children in the country" assumes—at least implicitly—that all children were not capable of further study and that social institutions should not contravene evolutionary forces by attempting to make universal that which is naturally attainable only by the few. In advocating a more rigorous curriculum, Eliot further reflected the ideology of survival. The more difficult and the more competitive the struggle, the stronger and more skilled the survivors and the society would be. Thus, Eliot's call for a uniform rather than differentiated curriculum, insured that a single measure of excellence would be employed to clear the way for natural selection.

In similar fashion, a prevailing ethos of a new social Darwinism appears to rationalize the National Commission's apparent inconsistency in recommending an elite curriculum for a heterogeneous audience. Like the Committee of Ten, an ideology of survival permeates The Nation at Risk report. In the words of the Commission, "Our Nation is at risk... the educational foundations of our society are presently being eroded by a rising tide of mediocrity that threatens our very future as a Nation and a people." In a contemporary reflection of the 19th century philosophy of survival of the fittest, the National Commission suggests that our educational system has grown soft and only by returning to the basics can we restore it—and the nation as well—to its former position of strength. By recommending that all students take the "Five New Basics," the National Commission hopes to eliminate what they label a "curricular smorgasbord." Translated into 19th century social Darwinistic terms, this soft and diffuse curriculum coddles those least able for competitive survival and thus interferes with natural selection.

Reflecting the belief that competition stimulates the strongest to develop adaptive skills that benefit human evolution, the National Commission advocates that rigorous and measurable standards be adopted and that students be required to take nationwide achievement tests at major transition points in their school careers. Likewise, they propose that competition should be restored to the teaching profession through more effective teacher evaluations and performance-based salaries. Again in 19th century terms, uniform salary scales for teachers are anti-evolutionary as they artificially support weak teachers and fail to promote competition that would stimulate individual improvement.

Given these selective historical comparisons, what observations can we make concerning the educational reforms advocated by the National Commission in their Nation at Risk report?

• First, the elite nature of the reform proposals made by both the Committee of Ten in 1893 and the National Commission in 1983 appear to reflect the interests of their elite memberships. College presidents and professors dominate both committees: six of the ten members of the Committee of Ten and seven of the eighteen members of the National Commission were drawn from institutions of higher education. We might question why school teachers and administrators—those most directly involved with the daily operations of the schools and those most familiar with the heterogeneous students they serve—are so consistently underrepresented on these "blue ribbon" panels.

• Second, one corollary of the elite, academic curriculum advocated by Eliot was an increase in school elimination and grade retardation. Despite growing secondary school enrollments early in the century, most children dropped out prior to completing high school, and more students were being held back to repeat grades. In 1909, Leonard Ayres, in a book entitled "Laggards In Our Schools," estimated that Americans were then wasting 27 million dollars a year on grade repeaters in city school systems alone. As the National Commission today advocates a uniform academic curriculum, longer school years, greater amounts of homework, and more rigorous testing, we should expect greater and greater numbers of high school drop-outs and grade repeaters. It is an issue that we cannot afford to ignore in a period of declining school resources, and especially at a time when few permanent employment opportunities exist for youth not attending school.

• Third, although the educational reforms advocated by Eliot did not have much impact on youthful unemployment, as most youths already worked by age 13 or 14, the reforms advocated by the National Commission have important opportunity costs for many American youth. In recommending longer school days, longer school years, and increased homework assignments, the National Commission may effectively—whether intentionally or unintentionally—remove a mass of part-time teenage workers from the job market.

• Fourth, unlike Eliot's time, when assimilation, Americanization, and the "Melting Pot" were held to be desirable social goals, we publicly respect immigrant cultures and acknowledge how cultural diversity enriches our society by supporting bilingual and bicultural classrooms. In this context, the recommendations of the National Commission, calling for greater uniformity and standardization based on a prescribed academic curriculum, appear to reverse the direction of recognizing and promoting cultural diversity in the American public schools and in society at large.

• Fifth, and finally, we need to question whether we are unwittingly employing a philosophy of social Darwinism to guide our search for solutions to educational and social problems. It is as though after 90 years we have come around again to a position that once pervaded American social thought and policy, namely to survive we must promote competitive struggle, we must accept the existence of social and economic inequality, and we must recognize that governmental intervention is antithetical to natural selection. To the extent that we have revived a biological explanation for social and individual development, we must ask whether an ideology of survival provides an adequate philosophical blueprint for educational reform.

It would seem an appropriate task therefore, to undertake a thorough analysis of differing conceptions of excellence in education before we attempt to institutionalize any one particular interpretation. Charles W. Eliot and the National Commission on excellence in Education have provided us with elite conceptions of educational reform and similar guidelines for institutionalizing these conceptions of American schools. We must extend our understanding of educational reform beyond the limits they have outlined to insure that American secondary education will serve the interests of all its students.

Morality and Values in Education

While there continues to be widespread public interest in the subject of moral education, there is also a division of opinion regarding how the schools should deal with this issue. The whole area of morality and the process of educating persons in methods of personal moral decision making is of great importance to all citizens. Since Socrates (and before), schools have been encouraged to teach certain "civic values" related to responsible life in society. That has been taken to mean different things, however, in terms of political, economic, and cultural traditions. What is meant by moral education? What ethical principles should students learn? Readers of this unit will notice the intensity of the controversy surrounding moral education.

Various religious groups would like to see their cherished core values taught in the schools, but moral education involves much more than the issue of religion in tax-supported schools. It involves the education of persons in what constitutes the "good life" or "just citizen" from the perspectives of several conflicting systems of ethics. There is no moral consensus in North America. There is, however, a consensus of cherished civic values which the majority of citizens in the United States and Canada share, such as the belief in equality before the law, respect for life, the right to safety, the right to one's own convictions, the value of participation as equals in the life of the nation, etc.

Since the eighteenth century, schools in the United States and Canada have been teaching certain standards of justice and civic morality as well as cherished national traditions. Educators are confronted with social studies curricula and norms of student conduct which clearly reflect specific standards of value. But the matter goes beyond social studies and standards of student conduct. The current debate over moral education centers around several key issues. First, how can methods of ethical decision making be taught in such a way as to also encourage specific commitment to conceptions of what it means to be a virtuous and just person? Second, how can this be done in pluralistic nations such as the United States and Canada in a manner in which students will retain their freedom to choose substantive standards of value?

On the one hand, educators should not merely teach superficial methods of choosing in the absence of any instruction as to what specific standards of virtue and moral behavior are available to students. On the other hand, educators should not impose their own values on students.

The articles in this unit address these concerns. Christina Hoff Sommers reviews past and current emphasis on moral education in the United States. She critiques some of the approaches to moral education and values clarification used in the schools in recent years, and summarizes the whole spectrum of controversy regarding approaches to ethical decision making and conceptions of virtuous and just behavior. The articles by Paul L. Murphy, Faustine C. Jones-Wilson, and Sanford A. Lakoff focus on the role of educators in developing responsible civic attitudes in students and in the teaching of democratic theories of value. They emphasize the important role of the schools in encouraging students to develop just and tolerant personal ethical standards.

The articles in this unit can be related to either the historical or the philosophical foundations of education, as well as to issues such as public pressures on schools, the rights of minorities, the social responsibilities of schools, ethics in teaching, the teacher as role model, and societal expectations of the schools.

Looking Ahead: Challenge Questions

What is moral education? Why do many people today wish to see some form of moral education in the schools?

What are some of the problems with the manner in which ethics and ethical decision making skills have been taught in the schools? For what reasons is there continuing controversy regarding this topic?

What is civic education? How do states encourage the teaching of civic education in the schools?

Should schools be involved in helping people learn how to reason about moral questions? Why or why not? If not, who should do it? Why?

What ethical principles should prevail in teaching about morals and ethics in schools?

What is the difference between indoctrination and instruction?

Is there a national consensus concerning what specific form moral education should take in the schools? If not, is such a consensus likely in the near future?

What attitudes and skills are most appropriate for learning responsible approaches to moral decision making?

Unit 4

Ethics Without Virtue

Moral Education in America

CHRISTINA HOFF SOMMERS

Christina Hoff Sommers, assistant professor of philosophy at Clark University, is the editor of an anthology, Vice and Virtue in Everyday Life *(Harcourt Brace Jovanovich).*

What do students in our nation's schools do all day? Most of them are clearly not spending their time reading the classics, learning math, or studying the physical sciences. It is likely that, along with photography workshops, keeping journals, and perhaps learning about computers, students spend part of their day in moral education classes. But these classes are not, as one might expect, designed to acquaint students with the Western moral tradition. Professional theorists in schools of education have found that tradition wanting and have devised an alternative, one they have marketed in public schools with notable success.

A reform of moral education is not a task to be undertaken lightly. The sincerity and personal integrity of the theorist-reformers is not at issue, but their qualifications as moral educators is a legitimate subject of concern. The leaders of reform do not worry about credentials. They are convinced that traditional middle-class morality is at best useless and at worst pernicious, and they have confidence in the new morality that is to replace the old and in the novel techniques to be applied to this end. In 1970 Theodore Sizer, then dean of the Harvard School of Education, co-edited with his wife Nancy a book entitled *Moral Education*. The preface set the tone by condemning the morality of "the Christian gentleman," "the American prairie," the McGuffey *Reader*, and the hypocrisy of teachers who tolerate a grading system that is "the terror of the young." According to the Sizers, all of the authors in the anthology agree that "the 'old morality' can and should be scrapped."

The movement to reform moral education has its seat in the most prestigious institutions of education. Its theories are seldom contested, and its practice is spreading. Students who have received the new moral instruction have been turning up in freshman college classes in increasing numbers. While giving college ethics courses during the past six years, I have become convinced that the need for a critical appraisal of the claims and assumptions of the movement is urgent. My experience is that the students who received the new teaching have been ill served by their mentors.

One gains some idea of the new moral educators from the terminology they use. Courses in ethics are called "values clarification" or "cognitive moral development"; teachers are "values processors," "values facilitators," or "reflective-active listeners"; lessons in moral reasoning are "sensitivity modules"; volunteer work in the community is an "action module"; and teachers "dialogue" with students to help them discover their own systems of values. In these dialogues the teacher avoids discussing "old bags of virtues," such as wisdom, courage, compassion, and "proper" behavior, because any attempt to instill these would be to indoctrinate the student. Some leaders of the new reform movement advise teachers that effective moral education cannot take place in the "authoritarian" atmosphere of the average American high school. The teacher ought to democratize the classroom, turning it into a "just community" where the student and teacher have an equal say. Furthermore, the student who takes a normative ethics course in college will likely encounter a professor who also has a principled aversion to the inculcation of moral precepts and who will confine classroom discussion to such issues of social concern as the Karen Ann Quinlan case, recombinant DNA research, or the moral responsibilities of corporations.

Reprinted from THE AMERICAN SCHOLAR, Volume 53, Number 3, Summer, 1984. Copyright ©1984 by The United Chapters of Phi Beta Kappa. By permission of the publishers.

The result is a system of moral education that is silent about virtue.

The teaching of virtue is not viewed as a legitimate aim of a moral curriculum, but there is no dearth of alternative approaches. From the time the values education movement began in the late nineteen sixties, its theorists have produced an enormous number of articles, books, films, manuals, and doctoral dissertations; there are now journals, advanced degree programs, and entire institutes dedicated exclusively to moral pedagogy; and for the past several years, teachers, counselors, and education specialists have been attending conferences, seminars, workshops, and retreats to improve their skills in values-processing. At present, two opposing ideologies dominate moral education: the values clarification movement, whose best-known proponent is Sidney Simon of the University of Massachusetts School of Education; and the cognitive moral development movement, whose chief spokesman is Lawrence Kohlberg, a professor of psychology and education, and director of the Center for Moral Education at Harvard.

Values clarification, according to Sidney Simon, is "based on the premise that none of us has the 'right' set of values to pass on to other people's children." Its methods are meant to help students to get at "their own feelings, their own ideas, their own beliefs, so that the choices and decisions they make are conscious and deliberate, based on their own value system." The success of the values clarification movement has been phenomenal. In 1975 a study from the Hoover Institute referred to "hundreds perhaps thousands of school programs that employ the clarification methodology" and reported that ten states have officially adopted values clarification as a model for their moral education programs. Proponents of values clarification consider it inappropriate for a teacher to encourage students, however subtly or indirectly, to adopt the values of the teacher or the community. In their book, *Readings in Values Clarification*, Simon and his colleague Howard Kirschenbaum write:

> We call this approach "moralizing," although it has also been known as inculcation, imposition, indoctrination, and in its most extreme form brainwashing. Moralizing is the direct or indirect transfer of a set of values from one person or group to another person or group.

The student of values clarification is taught awareness of his preferences and his right to their satisfaction in a democratic society. To help students discover what it is that they genuinely value, they are asked to respond to questionnaires called "strategies." Some typical questions are: Which animal would you rather be: an ant, a beaver, or a donkey? Which season do you like best? Do you prefer hiking, swimming, or watching television? In one strategy called "Values Geography," the student is helped to discover his geographical preferences; other lessons solicit his reaction to seat belts, messy handwriting, hiking, wall-to-wall carpeting, cheating, abortion, hit-and-run drivers, and a mother who severely beats a two-year-old child.

Western literature and history are two traditional alienating influences that the values clarification movement is on guard against. Simon has written that he has ceased to find meaning "in the history of war or the structure of a sonnet, and more meaning in the search to find value in life." He and his colleagues believe that exposure to one's cultural heritage is not likely to be morally beneficial to the "average student."

> Because values are complex and because man's thoughts and accomplishments are both abundant and complicated, it is difficult to recommend that the average student rely on this approach. It takes substantial mental stamina and ability and much time and energy to travel this road. While the study of our cultural heritage can be defended on other grounds, we would not expect it to be sufficient for value education.

The values clarification theorist does not believe that moral sensibility and social conscience are, in significant measure, learned by reading and discussing the classics. Instead Simon speaks of the precious legacy we can leave to "generations of young people if we teach them to set their priorities and rank order the marvelous items in life's cafeteria."

As a college teacher coping with the motley ideologies of high school graduates, I find this alarming. Young people today, many of whom are in a complete moral stupor, need to be shown that there is an important distinction between moral and nonmoral decisions. Values clarification blurs the distinction. Children are queried about their views on homemade Christmas gifts, people who wear wigs, and whether or not they approve of abortion or would turn in a hit-and-run driver as if no significant differences existed among these issues.

It is not surprising that teachers trained in neutrality and the principled avoidance of "moralizing" sometimes find themselves in bizarre classroom situations. In a junior high school in Newton, Massachusetts, a teacher put on the blackboard a poster of a Hell's Angel wearing a swastika. The students were asked to react. "He's honest, anyway. He's living out his own feelings," answered one. "He's not fooling," said another. When the students seemed to react favorably to the Hell's Angel, the teacher ventured to suggest that "an alienated person might not be happy."

The following conversation took place between a values clarification teacher and her students:

STUDENT: Does this mean that we can decide for ourselves whether to be honest on tests here?

TEACHER: No, that means that you can decide on the value. I personally value honesty; and although you may choose to be dishonest, I shall insist that we be honest in our tests. In other areas of your life, you may have more freedom to be dishonest.

AND ANOTHER TEACHER: My class deals with morality and right and wrong quite a bit. I don't expect them all to agree with me; each has to satisfy himself according to his own conviction, as long as he is sincere, and thinks he is pursuing what is right. I often discuss cheating this way, but I always get defeated because they will argue that cheating is all right. After you accept the idea that kids have the right to build a position with logical arguments, you have to accept what they come up with.

The student has values; the values clarification teacher is merely "facilitating" the student's access to them. Thus, no values are taught. The emphasis is on *learning how*, not on *learning that*. The student does not learn *that* acts of stealing are wrong; he learns how to respond to such acts.

The values clarification course is, in this sense, contentless. As if to make up for this, it is methodologically rich. It is to be expected that an advocate of values clarification emphasizes method over content in other areas of education, and indeed he does. Many handbooks, strategies, board games, and kits have been developed to help teachers adapt the methods of values clarification to such subjects as English, history, science, math, and even home economics and Spanish. Values clarification guides for girl scout troops and Sunday school classes are also available, as well as manuals to assist parents in clarifying values at the dinner table.

Simon and his colleagues explain that it is useless and anachronistic to teach the student at a "facts level." In a history lesson on the Constitution, for example, the teacher is advised not to waste too much time on such questions as where and when the Constitution was drawn up. Undue attention should also not be given to the "concepts level," where, for example, the teacher discusses the moral origins of the Bill of Rights. When the learning of subject matter is unavoidable, Simon and his colleagues recommend that it be lifted to a higher and more urgent level where students are asked "you-centered" questions, such as, "What rights do you have in your family?" Or, "Many student governments are really token governments controlled by the 'mother country,' i.e., the administration. Is this true in your school? What can you do about it?" And, "When was the last time you signed a petition?"

The classical moral tradition will not be revived by the practitioners of values clarification. Indeed, it is, in their eyes, an alien tradition that is insensitive to the needs and rights of the contemporary student.

II

Lawrence Kohlberg, the leader of the second major movement in moral education, shares with values clarification educators a low opinion of traditional morality. In his contribution to Theodore and Nancy Sizer's anthology, *Moral Education*, he writes, "Far from knowing whether it can be taught, I have no idea what virtue really is." Kohlberg's disclaimer is not a Socratic confession of ignorance; he considers the teaching of traditional virtues to be at best a waste of time and at worst coercive. Like Sidney Simon, he, too, uses the language of conspiracy to characterize the American educational system. He refers often to the "hidden curriculum" and insists that the teacher must not be "an agent of the state, the church, or the social system, [but] rather . . . a free moral agent dealing with children who are free moral agents." Kohlberg cites as an example of covert indoctrination a teacher who yelled at some boys for not returning their books to the proper place. "The teacher would have been surprised to know that her concerns with classroom management defined for her children what she and her school thought were basic values, or that she was engaged in indoctrination." Kohlberg and his disciples are currently busy transforming some of the best school systems in the country into "just communities" where no such indoctrination takes place.

Kohlberg's authority derives from his cognitive developmental approach to moral education. Following John Dewey, Kohlberg distinguishes three main stages of moral development (each of which is partitioned into a higher and lower stage, making six in all). The first stage is called the premoral or preconventional reward/punishment level. In the second stage morals are conventional but unreflective. In the third stage moral principles are autonomously chosen on rational grounds. Kohlberg's research applies Piaget's idea that the child possesses certain cognitive structures that come successively into play as the child develops. According to Kohlberg, the latent structures are a cross-cultural fact of cognitive psychology. Kohlberg's more specific thesis on the unfolding of the child's innate moral propensities has received a great deal of deserved attention. The literature on Kohlberg is controversial, and it is far too early to say whether his ideas are sound enough for eventual use in the classroom. Kohlberg himself has urged and already put into practice pedagogical applications of his ideas.

From the assumption of innateness, it is but a short step to the belief that the appropriate external circumstances will promote the full moral development of the child. It then becomes the job of the educator to provide those circumstances "facilitating" the child to his moral maturity. The innate structures are essentially contentless, and Kohlberg and his followers do not think it is the job of the moral educator to develop a virtuous person by supplying the content—that is, the traditional virtues. To do that would be, in Kohlberg's contemptuous phrase, to impose on the child an "old bag of virtues." Kohlberg and his associate Moshe Blatt remark in the *Journal of Moral Education*:

> Moral education is best conceived as a natural process of dialogue among peers, rather than as a process of didactic instruction or preaching. The teacher and the curriculum are best conceived as facilitators of this dialogue.

If moral education is to be a dialogue among peers, the relation between teacher and student must be radically transformed. Fully prepared to accept these consequences, Kohlberg, in 1974, founded the Cluster School in Cambridge, Massachusetts. It consisted of thirty students, six teachers, dozens of consultants, and Kohlberg—all of whom had an equal voice in running the school. According to Kohlberg, "The only way school can help graduating students become persons who can make society a just community is to let them try experimentally to make the school themselves." As he soon learned, these student-citizens were forever stealing from one another and using drugs during school hours. These transgressions provoked a long series of democratically conducted "town meetings" that to an outsider look very much like EST encounter groups. The students were frequently taken on retreats (Kohlberg and his associates share with the values clarification people a penchant for retreats), where many of them broke the rules against sex and drugs. This provoked more democratic confrontations where, Kohlberg was proud to report, it was usually decided that for the sake of the group the students would police one another on subsequent retreats and turn in the names of the transgressors. Commenting on the rash of thefts at the Cluster School, Kohlberg said, "At the moment there is clearly a norm in the Cluster School of maintaining trust around property issues. But there is uncertainty about whether the norm has [fully] developed." Since the Cluster School lasted only five years, this uncertainty will never be resolved.

In turning to the just communities, Kohlberg has consciously abandoned his earlier goal of developing individual students to the highest stages of moral development. The most he now hopes for is development to stage four, where students learn to respect the new just social order. His reasons are revealing. In 1980 in an anthology edited by Ralph Mosher, *Moral Education: A First Generation of Research and Development*, Kohlberg writes, "Perhaps all stage six persons of the 1960's had been wiped out, perhaps they had regressed, or maybe it was all my imagination in the first place."

The Cluster School has been the subject of a great many articles and doctoral theses. Careers have been advanced just by praising it. In Mosher's anthology one critic writes about the school:

> Cluster School . . . in my judgment, is a unique secondary school environment, characterized by a respect and caring for persons and a determination to make the governance structure one in which students can experience the roles necessary for full participation in democracy.

From these remarks—and similar ones by others who visited Cluster School—you would never guess that the school was in shambles and just about to close. The school was racially divided; drugs, sex, and theft were rampant; and Kohlberg was fighting bitterly with the teachers. Here was a school —with thirty students and six exceptionally trained and dedicated teachers—that by any objective standard must be counted a failure. Yet in American professional education nothing succeeds like failure. Having scored their failure at the Cluster School, the Kohlbergians have put their ideas to work in more established schools. (For example, they now exercise a significant influence in such diverse public school systems as Pittsburgh, Pennsylvania; Salt Lake City, Utah; Scarsdale, New York; and Brookline, Massachusetts.)

Brookline High School in Massachusetts

provides a particularly sad example of the way the new ideologies can penetrate a fine high school. The school administration has been taken over by Kohlbergians who, with the help of federal funds, are trying to turn it into a "just community." To this end the governance of the school has been given over to the entire school community—students, teachers, administrators, secretaries, and janitorial staff. To make the process work smoothly, not all students are invited to the weekly "town meetings," just their representatives. But, because many of the two thousand or so students are indifferent, many student representatives are self-appointed. And a big problem is that most of the teachers do not attend (nor, of course, do tired secretaries and maintenance workers).

I attended one meeting with thirty students, five teachers, two student visitors from Scarsdale who are working with Kohlberg and studying the Brookline program in hopes of using it in New York, and two observers from the Carnegie-Mellon Foundation, who were there to investigate the possibility of making a film about the Brookline experiment for public television. The kids who participated in the meeting were charming and articulate, and the Carnegie-Mellon people were clearly pleased, and they will make their film. Like many educational experts who admire the Brookline town meetings, these observers are probably unaware that many of the teachers feel harassed and manipulated by the Kohlberg administration. So far, the participants in the town meetings—who are mostly teenagers exercising more power than they will ever be granted in college or graduate school—have voted to rescind a rule against Walkman radios on campus, to prohibit homework assignments for vacation periods, to disallow surprise quizzes, and they have instituted a procedure for bringing teachers who give tests or assignments that are too demanding before a "Fairness Committee." One teacher told me that the students had never asked for the powers they now enjoy. According to the teacher, the school authorities handed these powers over to students "for their own good." Just communities are Kohlberg's answer to the oppression exercised by established authority. Evidently, Kohlberg sees no need to question his assumption that established authority is intrinsically suspect. In any event, it is ironic that now, when teachers with authority are so rare, educational theorists like Kohlberg are proposing that authority itself is the evil to be combated.

Ralph Mosher, a Harvard-trained Kohlbergian, is the chief educational consultant to the Brookline High School. In his anthology he writes the following about the standards that had been in place:

> Moral education, all the more powerful because it is "hidden," is embedded in the tacit values of the curriculum and the school. For example, the most worthy/valued student in Brookline High School is the one who achieves early admission to Harvard on a full scholarship. How few can accomplish this is obvious. Yet teachers, counselors, and parents put great, albeit subtle, pressure on the many to do likewise. . . . What the research [in moral education] has attempted to do is to make some schooling more just.

Mosher's attitude is instructive. Ideals, it seems, are not goals to aim for. They must be attainable by the majority of students. If any goals are set up, they must be ones to which most students can realistically aspire. For Mosher, vigilance against superimposing a hidden agenda with elitist bias is the order of the day.

Kohlberg's ideas have taken hold in the better schools, where one can still find a fair number of parents who can afford to hold attitudes against elitism. Should the public schools of Brookline, Cambridge, or Scarsdale fail to provide the education necessary for admission to the best colleges, those parents have recourse to some fine private schools in the neighborhood. In the meantime they can indulge the unexceptionable concept of a just community, whose egalitarian character is welcomed by those who find themselves uncomfortably well-fixed, particularly after the radical views they held in the halcyon sixties.

The values clarification and cognitive development reformers are well aware that they are riding a wave of public concern about the need for an effective system of moral education. Thus Mosher writes:

> [A] high proportion of Americans (four of five in recent Gallup Polls) support moral education in the public schools. What the respondents mean by moral education is, of course, moot. Probably the teaching of virtues such as honesty, respect for adults, moderation in the use of alcohol/drugs, sexual restraint and so on. . . . Educators would have to exceed Caesar's wife not to capitalize on an idea whose time appeared to have come.

This last remark about capitalizing on the parent's desire for higher moral standards is disarmingly cynical. Naturally the public wants its "old bag of virtues," but educational theorists such as Mosher are convinced that giving the public what it wants is ineffective and unjust. The traditional moralists have failed (witness Watergate), so now it's their turn. Mosher's attitude to the benighted parents is condescending. No doubt for Mosher and Kohlberg, the morally confident leaders of the reform movement, theirs is the right kind of elitism.

The deprecation of moralizing common to values clarification and cognitive development theory has been effective even in those schools where the reforms have not yet penetrated. Increasingly nowadays, few teachers have the temerity to praise any middle-class virtues. The exception is the virtue of tolerance. But, when tolerance is the sole virtue, students' capacity for moral indignation, so important for moral development, is severely inhibited. The result is moral passivity and confusion and a shift of moral focus from the individual to society.

III

The student entering college today shows the effects of an educational system that has kept its distance from the traditional virtues. Unencumbered by the "old bag of virtues," the student arrives toting a ragbag of another stripe whose contents may be roughly itemized as follows: psychological egoism (the belief that the primary motive for action is selfishness), moral relativism (the doctrine that what is praiseworthy or contemptible is a matter of cultural conditioning), and radical tolerance (the doctrine that to be culturally and socially aware is to understand and excuse the putative wrongdoer). Another item in the bag is the conviction that the seat of moral responsibility is found in society and its institutions, not in individuals.

The half-baked relativism of the college student tends to undermine his common sense. In a term paper that is far from atypical, one of my students wrote that Jonathan Swift's "modest proposal" for solving the problem of hunger in Ireland by harvesting Irish babies for food was "good for Swift's society, but not for ours." All too often one comes up against a grotesquely distorted perspective that common sense has little power to set right. In one discussion in my introductory philosophy class, several students were convinced that the death of one person and the death of ten thousand is equally bad. When a sophomore was asked whether she saw Nagasaki as the moral equivalent of a traffic accident, she replied, "From a moral point of view, yes." Teachers of moral philosophy who are not themselves moral agnostics trade such stories for dark amusement. But it appears that teachers in other disciplines are also struck by the moral perversity of their students. Richard M. Hunt, a professor of government at Harvard University, gave a course on the Holocaust to one hundred Harvard undergraduates. In the course he was disturbed to find that a majority of students adopted the view that the rise of Hitler and the Nazis was inevitable, that no one could have resisted it, and that in the end no one was responsible for what happened. Hunt's teaching assistant remarked to him, "You know, I think if some of our students were sitting as judges at the Nuremberg trials, they would probably acquit—or at least pardon—most of the Nazi defendants." Professor Hunt has dubbed his students' forgiving attitude toward the past "no-fault history."

It is fair to say that many college students are thoroughly confused about morality. What they sorely need are some straightforward courses in moral philosophy and a sound and unabashed introduction to the Western moral tradition—something they may never have had before. But few teachers will use that tradition as a source of moral instruction: the fear of indoctrination is even stronger in the colleges than it is at primary and secondary schools. In a recent study of the teaching of ethics prepared by the Hastings Center, a well-respected institute for the study of ethical questions, the authors write:

> A major concern about the teaching of ethics has been whether and to what extent it is appropriate to teach courses on ethics in a pluralistic society, and whether it is possible to teach such courses without engaging in unacceptable indoctrination.

And elsewhere in the same report:

> No teacher of ethics can assume that he or she has a solid grasp on the nature of morality as to pretend to know what finally counts as good moral conduct. No society can assume that it has any better grasp of what so counts as to empower teachers to propagate it in colleges and universities. Perhaps most importantly, the premise of higher education is that students are at an age where they have to begin coming to their own conclusions and shaping their own view of the world.

It would, however, be altogether incorrect to say that the colleges are ignoring moral instruction. The spread of moral agnosticism has been accompanied by an extraordinary increase in courses of applied ethics. Philosophy departments, isolated and marginal for many years, are now attracting unprecedented numbers of students to their courses in medical ethics, business ethics, ethics for everyday life, ethics for engineers, nurses, social workers, and lawyers. Today there are dozens of journals and conferences, hundreds of books and articles, and—according to the Hastings Center—eleven thousand college courses in applied ethics.

The new interest in applied ethics is itself a

phenomenon to be welcomed. Public discussions of controversial issues will surely benefit from the contributions of philosophers, and the literature of applied ethics should be read by anyone who seeks a responsible understanding of topical issues. In reading the anthologies of applied ethics, a student encounters arguments of philosophers who take strong stands on important social questions. These arguments often shake a student's confidence in moral relativism. Nevertheless, the literature of applied ethics, like the literature of values clarification and cognitive moral development, has little or nothing to say about matters of individual virtue. The resurgence of moral education in the college thus reinforces the shift away from personal morals to an almost exclusive preoccupation with the morality of institutional policies. After all, most students are not likely to be involved personally in administering the death penalty or selecting candidates for kidney dialysis; and, since most will never do recombinant DNA research, or even have abortions, the purpose of the courses in applied ethics is to teach students how to form responsible opinions on questions of social policy. A strong ethical curriculum is a good thing, but a curriculum of ethics without virtue is a cause for concern.

The applied ethics movement in the universities started in the late nineteen sixties when philosophers became interested once again in normative ethics. Between 1940 and 1968 ethics had been theoretical and methodologically self-conscious, to the relative neglect of practical ethics. A large number of philosophers emerged from the sixties eager to contribute to national moral debates. But like Simon, Kohlberg, and their followers, these philosophers were suspicious and distrustful of moralizing and deeply averse to indoctrination. It is no small feat to launch a powerful and influential movement in normative ethics without recourse to the language of vice and virtue and a strong notion of personal responsibility, but that is exactly what is being attempted. The new university moralists, uncomfortable and ideologically at odds with the discredited middle-class ethic, are making their reform movement succeed by addressing themselves, not to the vices and virtues of individuals, but to the moral character of our nation's institutions. Take a look at almost any text used today in college ethics courses—for example, *Ethics for Modern Life*, edited by R. Abelson and M. Friquegnon, *Today's Moral Problems*, edited by R. Wasserstrom, or *Moral Problems* by J. Rachels—and you will find that almost all of the articles consist of philosophical evaluations of the conduct and policies of schools, hospitals, courts, corporations, and the United States government.

Inevitably the student forms the idea that applying ethics to modern life is mainly a question of learning how to be for or against social and institutional policies. Appropriately enough, many of the articles sound like briefs written for a judge or legislator. In that sort of ethical climate, a student soon loses sight of himself as a moral agent and begins to see himself as a moral spectator or a protojurist. This is not to deny that many of the issues have an immediate personal dimension. They do, but the primary emphasis is not on what one is to do as a person but on what one is to believe as a member of society—in other words, on ideology and doctrine rather than on personal responsibility and practical decency.

The move to issue-oriented courses is hailed as a move back to the days when moral instruction played a significant role in education. Nothing could be further from the truth. Where Aristotle, Aquinas, Mill, and Kant are telling us how to behave, the contemporary university moralist is concerned with what we are to advocate, vote for, protest against, and endorse. Michael Walzer has compared the applied ethics movement to the scholarly activities of the Greek Academicians, the Talmudists, and the medieval Casuists. The comparison is inept, for those earlier moralists were working in a tradition in which it was assumed that the practical end of all moral theory was the virtuous individual. The ancient sophist, with his expertise in rhetoric and politics, is a more convincing analogue to the teachers of issue-oriented ethics, who find little time for the history of ethical theory with its traditional emphasis on the good and virtuous life. One may therefore be wary of the widespread enthusiasm for the "exciting new developments" in the teaching of ethics. Especially misleading is the frequent observation that the revival of interest in practical ethics is a great advance over the earlier preoccupation with evaluative language (meta-ethics). Admittedly the preoccupation with meta-ethics that characterized the teaching of ethics a decade ago left the student undernourished by neglecting normative ethics. But, in all fairness, neither students nor teachers were under any illusion that meta-ethics was the whole of ethics. Today the student is learning that normative ethics is primarily social policy. This being so, moral action should be politically directed; the individual's task is to bring the right civic institutions (the true moral agents) into place. The student tacitly assumes that ethics is not a daily affair, that it is a matter for specialists, and that its practical benefits are deferred until the time of institutional reform.

The result of identifying normative ethics with public policy is justification for and reinforcement of moral passivity in the student. Even problems that call for large-scale political solutions have their immediate private dimension, but a student trained in a practical ethics that has avoided or de-emphasized individual responsibility is simply unprepared for any demand that is not politically or ideologically formulated. The student is placed in the undemanding role of the indignant moral spectator who needs not face the comparatively minor corruptions in his own life.

How, finally, is one to account for the ethics-without-virtue phenomenon? A fully adequate answer is beyond me, but clearly there is a great deal more to the story than the national disenchantment with a system of education that "failed to prevent" moral lapses such as Watergate. A historian of ideas would probably take us back to romantics like Rousseau and to realists like Marx. George Steiner has written of this theme in Rousseau:

> In the Rousseauist mythology of conduct, a man could commit a crime either because his education had not taught him how to distinguish good and evil, or because he had been corrupted by society. Responsibility lay with his school or environment for evil cannot be native to the soul. And because the individual is not wholly responsible he cannot be wholly damned.

The values clarification theorists can find little to disagree with in this description.

For social-minded reformers, justice is the principal virtue, and social policy is where ethics is really "at." The assumption is that there is an implicit conflict between the just society and the repressive morality of its undemocratic predecessors. An extreme version of this theme is presented in a little book edited by Trotsky, *Their Morals and Ours,* with it searing attack on the "conservative banalities of bourgeois morality." For Trotsky, of course, social reform requires revolution, but his indictment of the hypocrisies and "brutalities" of "their morals" must sound familiar to the Kohlbergians. The fate of those societies that have actually succeeded in replacing personal morality with social policy is the going price for ignoring the admonition of Max Weber: "He who seeks salvation of the soul—of his own and others—should not seek it along the avenue of politics."

An essay on contemporary trends in moral education would be incomplete without mention of the Moral Majority. I have refrained from discussing this movement partly because it receives a great deal of public attention compared to the relative neglect of the movements inspired by the New England professors of education. But I suspect another reason for my silence is my own dismay that at this moment the Moral Majority constitutes the only vocal and self-confident alternative to the ethics-without-virtue movement.

The Obligations of American Citizenship: A Historical Perspective

Paul L. Murphy

Murphy is a Professor of American Constitutional History and American Studies at the University of Minnesota.

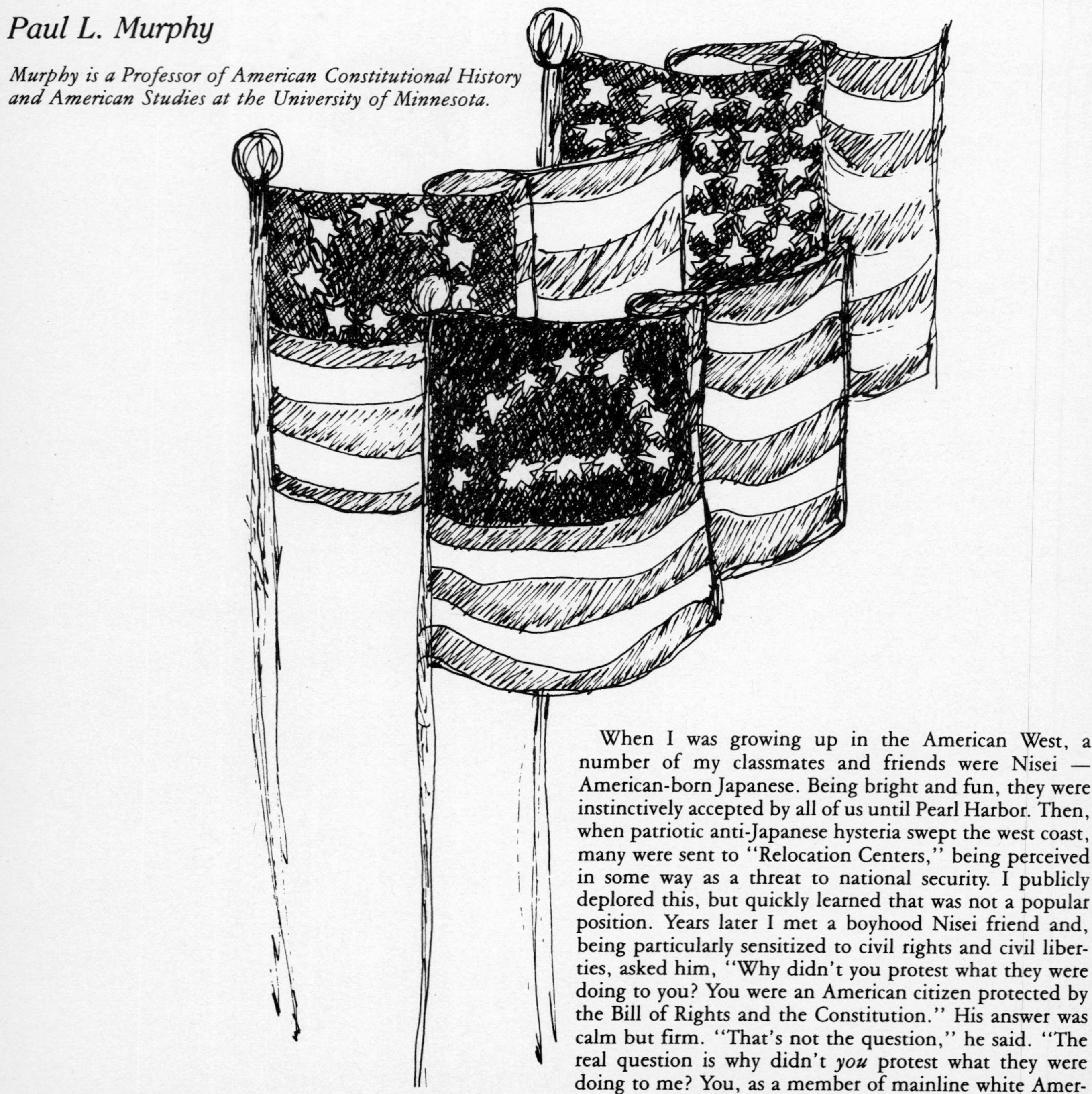

When I was growing up in the American West, a number of my classmates and friends were Nisei — American-born Japanese. Being bright and fun, they were instinctively accepted by all of us until Pearl Harbor. Then, when patriotic anti-Japanese hysteria swept the west coast, many were sent to "Relocation Centers," being perceived in some way as a threat to national security. I publicly deplored this, but quickly learned that was not a popular position. Years later I met a boyhood Nisei friend and, being particularly sensitized to civil rights and civil liberties, asked him, "Why didn't you protest what they were doing to you? You were an American citizen protected by the Bill of Rights and the Constitution." His answer was calm but firm. "That's not the question," he said. "The real question is why didn't *you* protest what they were doing to me? You, as a member of mainline white Amer-

Reprinted with permission from the *Journal of Teacher Education*, November/December 1983, pp. 6-10.

ica, whose rights were safe, would have had far more influence than I could at that time."

I have thought about the implications of that conversation many times. Being a responsible citizen takes not only knowledge of the constitutional system and of the guarantees of American freedom, but the courage to stand up and fight when those guarantees are threatened. The latter is largely personal, and how we do this most effectively is varied. But the former is the responsibility of those charged with civic education in this country.

Idealists among us like to think that an earlier generation understood those values almost instinctively. One case is worth mentioning. During the Watergate days of the early 1970s, Archibald Cox, who had been appointed Special Prosecutor and then was fired in what came to be known as the Saturday Night Massacre, expressed a certain wonderment about American citizenship. Cox had been gravely apprehensive as to whether then President Nixon would stick with his claims of executive privilege to the point of denying a court order requiring him to comply with a judicial decree. To Cox's relief, Nixon did comply and a new Special Prosecutor was appointed and the independence of the Watergate Special Prosecution Force was restored.

Being a responsible citizen takes not only knowledge of the constitutional system and of the guarantees of American freedom, but the courage to stand up and fight when those guarantees are threatened.

What to Cox was remarkable was not the compliance, but the outrage of the American people that the President would even think twice about complying with his obligation under law. As Cox (1976) wrote a few years later, "That principle, that even the President is subject to the rule of law, is not a principle you will find in the Constitution, however carefully you read it. But it is sufficiently central to the belief system of the American people that even a Nixon was reluctant to defy it" (pp. 8-9). He then mused openly on the sources and limits of the American people's attachment to constitutionalism — an attachment so strong that it forced a popularly elected President to reverse his field and comply with the order of even an inferior court.

The Bicentennials of the Constitution in 1987 and the Bill of Rights in 1991 are coming up. This is a good time to explore the American people's commitment to constitutionalism with an eye toward stimulating their obligation to support and protect it. But first they must understand it. Hopefully, the Bicentennials will afford an opportunity to enhance that understanding.

The idea of constitutionalism and public responsibility for its protection comes from our founding fathers. To them constitutionalism meant limited government and the rule of law. That is to say, that governments only exist to serve specified ends and function according to specified rules. They drew heavily in their thinking upon theorists and spokesmen, going back into classical antiquity.

A constitution has always been a standard of legitimacy embodying the defining character of civil society. Classically the concept had to do with constituents of a society — the term constituent and constitution coming from the same root. Civil institutions were to function in accordance with the constitutional ordering of society, an ordering in which the constituents were to play a significant role. But since, when people think about the kind of government they want for themselves, they think in terms of how it will affect them, and also how it will affect other people — both deserving and undeserving. Constitutionalism has always been thought of in terms of human nature. This is because a constitution can never be divorced from human capacities and needs, and above all, human deficiencies. The classical solution to seeing that constitutionalism was adhered to was through the active and expansive participation of "naturally free men." Somehow, if these citizens, which excluded "natural slaves," took part in politics or elected representatives to speak for them, as in the Roman Senate, this would insure that the requirements of the constitution were met.

The Greeks saw constitutions as the proper basis for assertions against the designs of institutionally independent and despotic rulers. But there were problems here which became sufficiently serious to undermine the concept. The Greeks were great believers in rationality. They rejected the absolute, the higher truth, which man not being able to understand should dutifully accept. Submission to a higher authority imposed by a ruler on his own terms was an unwarranted response, since it was an irrational response. Man was the maker. Man could and should create his own political institutions. If men knew themselves (and the first point of wisdom was "know thyself"), they could create a rational state in which justice, virtue, and civility could and would prevail.

In improving and knowing themselves and human nature, the Greeks came also to know that people have their irrational sides. This is why in Greek drama the furies are always lurking on the side ready to stir up and push the masses of the people to accept the security of the charismatic despot who will solve people's problems and relieve them of the burden of their civil responsibilities. These furies were always there to play on people's emotions, prejudices, biases, and insecurities and were one of the greatest threats to constitutionalism. If they prevailed, and people turned to a rule of men, and not of law, limited government and government which did proceed by specified rules would end as well. But there was an answer to this. Rational man not only had the right to resist tyranny, and expose governmental deceit and the abuse of power and the rights of the citizen, he had the duty to overthrow tyranny, and restore constitutionalism if things did go so far as to see it temporarily violated or eliminated.

Such a theory of constitutionalism has serious deficiences, deficiencies which John Locke, 16 or 17 centuries later, also found nettlesome. It is all well and good to say that there is a right of revolution, or that the standard means of defending the constitution was to eliminate the tyrant, but these are last ditch remedies, and often happen after the tyranny has been occurring for sometime. The question (which the Greeks never solved and the American colonists came to realize they had not solved, when the British began tightening the screws following 1763) was

Modern constitutionalism then infers: free individuals; people with rights of their own; people with freedom of conscience and the right of open inquiry without fear as to the consequences of that inquiry; and people who realize the need to establish a government — a government to which they accede voluntarily, (government by consent), and which they manage and control.

that of institutional arrangements to limit government before the tyranny succeeds, before man's irrational nature leads him to fritter away his birthright. What structural and substantive frameworks can and should rational man erect to maintain the principle of constitutionalism on a continuing, steady, regular and predictable basis? How shall he manage them? Here we must acknowledge and make clear that ancient, medieval, and modern constitutionalism do have sharp and important differences.

Ancient constitutionalism, particularly in its Roman form, had conceived of the all-encompassing rational law of nature as the eternal framework to which constitutions, laws, and policies ought to conform. The law of nature was the constitution of the universe. But Rome fell, feudalism followed, national states eventually reappeared, and with that development came the blending of national and religious authority; Christianity endowing the Romans' universal constitution with a clearly monarchical cast. The Christian God was the ruler of the universe. His laws were passed down to men from above and were to be obeyed. Christians were under an obligation to try to constitute their earthy cities on the model of the City of God, though in their ignorance and sinfulness they would never be able totally to succeed.

Thus came the blending of national religious authority with the ruler's sanction frequently underwritten by the church. Medieval constitutions were considered legitimate because they were believed to be ordained by God. Confirmation by officers of the Christian church was regarded as a prerequisite for the legitimacy of secular rulers. Defiance of such authority was defiance not solely of secular power, but of divinely ordained rules. Rules which came not from man's rational inquiry or scientific probings but from Genesis *et al.* Rational inquiry was a form of defiance of divine authority. Thus, although Galileo persisted in his investigation of natural laws and laid the basis for modern experimental science his pursuit of scientific truth led to his being subjected to the Inquisition. The state had a duty to quash those who would defy God's wisdom. Its leaders, religious and civil, were prepared to use political instrumentalities to do so.

Further, secular authorities tended to underwrite such a role giving it a more secular justification. Thomas Hobbes was prepared to think in terms of government by contract, but he also assumed that only man would violate the contract. Therefore the sovereign head had to have massive power and authority to maintain law and order, and was free to use the army, aristocracies or the centralized church to save self-seeking, brutish man from himself and others. The idea that the sovereign head could be tyrannical was inconceivable. If he became arbitrary, it was obviously justified. The idea that some body of limiting civil law applied also to the ruler was ridiculous.

In the years following the Reformation, on through the days of the Enlightenment, the secular state began to take shape. With this, and especially with the rejection by the people of divine rights, of religious sanctions, and the growing call for separation of church and state, came a new desire and willingness to limit power in that state. This meant limiting its stricture on people's freedom and creativity. By the end of the eighteenth century popular sovereignty had begun to supplant absolutism, carrying with it the notion that the state *was* the consciously contrived creature of the people. It was further felt that government entailed a Lockean social contract between governed and their governors — a compact with mutual rights and obligations — above all a contract which placed limits on power and designated processes to assure those confines. Hence the hallmark of modern constitutionalism was its reliance on formal limitations — limitations which were in turn tied directly to popular sovereignty — the concepts that the authority for government came from the people.

Maybe it is time to back to an Aristotelian view that the proper end of the state was the attainment of the very highest good, and to use the state to enhance the moral development of the citizen.

All of this meant that modern constitutionalism involved a redefinition of the term. A society's constitution was secular and separate from the church. Its role was primarily to define that society's political institutions and processes, and establish standards for their evaluation and readaptation. This was expected to reflect the popular will and in this way, something of the force of tradition and shared experience was captured. At the same time current challenges could be dealt with through an adaptable and appropriate rule of law. Modern constitutionalism then infers: free individuals; people with rights of their own; people with freedom of conscience and the right of open inquiry without fear as to the consequences of that inquiry; and people who realize the need to establish a government — a government to which they accede voluntarily, (government by consent), and which they manage and control. There is a further inference here. Good citizens must be prepared to devote some time to the political process. It means manifesting civic virtue which can be

Students must be again exposed to the constitutional basics of why we retain a two hundred year old document, the principles and values it incorporates, where it has worked and when and how it has failed.

simply defined as the willingness to subordinate private self-interest to the public-interest or the general welfare. This concept of citizen participation then becomes central if modern constitutionalism is to work and to prevail.

American constitutionalism is a unique form of modern constitutionalism since it grows out of the experience of a people who had dealt with the ambivalence of a combination of initially loose and finally coercive centralized colonial rule, and a high degree of "local option" regarding the application and enforcement of that rule. It starts with one premise which was a dramatic rejection of prior British citizenship. In Britain, the assumptions were and to some degree remain that one man may be over another, and that government comes from some sources outside the indigenous culture, or if not from outside, set apart from its day to day functioning. Americans from the beginning of their national self-consciousness insisted that rulers were not to be so much over the ruled or apart from them as proceeding from them and responsive to them. Further, this perception emerged from a sort of Rousseauian "general will" or to use John Rawls' (1971) modern construct, from a consensual "original position," to which there was sufficient mutual agreement in advance to make it logical and acceptable (p. 17). The corollary was that any mechanisms which were evolved to advance this proposition had to work, not only for governors, but for the constituency which they were designed to serve.

This is implicit in the uniquely American structure and in the political institutions and processes which the founding fathers came ultimately (after one false start in the Articles of Confederation) to erect. To take one simple but vital example, America's brief written constitution provided a standard by which the legitimacy of governmental actions was to be judged. Thus the particularly American practice of judicial review is the practice of imposing constitutionalism on the legislative and executive branches. In the abstract sense it is even more than that. It is an endeavor to judge positive law in the light of ultimate values, checking the acts of administrative and legislative officials against the higher principles incorporated in our governmental structure. This is what Archibald Cox is talking about when he refers to an "attachment" to constitutionalism.

But how do we bring home and revitalize the people's obligation to support such vital abstractions? How does one reactivate what John Adams once called "the voluntary good sense and restraint of the people?" This dilemma plagued the American revolutionary generation and continues to challenge our own. Does civic virtue result from the instillation of proper public values by governmental stimulation, exhortation, legislation, or prescriptive adjudication? Or is government's role to control public vice and the human frailties through limitations and checks and restrictions? If the latter approach is more plausible, is it really adequate? Is the application of formal mechanisms a positive device for creating civic value? Or as modern critics charge, do such mechanisms simply constitute negative devices to prevent people from abusing power, abusing one another and taking advantage of the situation? Maybe it is time to back to an Aristotelian view that the proper end of the state was the attainment of the very highest good, and to use the state to enhance the moral development of the citizen. Although to many, this has overtones of returning to a medieval constitutionalism. We seem more comfortable with a government which acts as a restraint on misbehavior, rather than one committed to prescriptive and uniform morality.

But if government's moral role is principally to be the nightwatchman, who is responsible for inducing specific kinds of formal good and constructive behavior — the public schools, private voluntary organizations, religious groups, civic bodies, self-appointed single issue groups, the family, the community? Are these the bodies to get young people to accept some level of public responsibility — to see pay-offs for themselves in being constructive citizens — to conceptualize in terms of government as not they, but we; as not them, but us?

The Founding Fathers were centrally concerned with this very problem. As a generation that had made remarkable personal sacrifices in an active and ongoing participation in public life, they did not want to see their own commitments and the fruit of those commitments — a new American constitutionalism — erode for want of public support. They knew they could not continue to assume full responsibility for making the Republic experiment work. People had to be made to feel that responsibility, but the process was one about which they worried constantly.

But rather than stating how these people thought and felt, let them in these Bicentennial times, tell you themselves:

JOHN ADAMS: All things must give way to the public.

SAMUEL ADAMS: A citizen owes everything to the commonwealth.

BENJAMIN RUSH: Every man in a Republic is public property. His time, his talents — his youth — his manhood — his age — nay more, his life, all belong to his country.

THE REVEREND PHILLIPS PAYSON: (In an election day sermon in 1778.) The slavery of a people is generally founded in ignorance of some kind or another, and facts are abundant which prove the human mind may be sunk and debased, through ignorance, and its natural effects, as even to adore and kiss the chains. Hence knowledge, and learning may well be considered as most essentially requisite to a free righteous government.

JOHN JAY: Let virtue, honor, the love of liberty, and science, be and remain the soul of this constitution, and it will become the source of great and extensive happiness to this and future generations. Vice, ignorance, and want of vigilance will be the only enemy able to destroy it. Against these provide, and of these, be forever jealous. Every member of the state ought diligently to read and study the constitution of his country, and teach the rising generation to be free. By knowing their rights, they will sooner perceive when they are violated, and be the better prepared to defend and assert them.

THE MASSACHUSETTS CONSTITUTION OF 1780: Wisdom and knowledge, as well as virtue, diffused generally among the body of the people, being necessary for the preservation of their rights and liberties, it is imperative that the government spread the opportunities and advantages of education in the various parts of the country and among the different orders of the people.

4. MORALITY AND VALUES

> THOMAS JEFFERSON: In every government on earth is some trace of human weakness, some germ of corruption and degeneracy, which cunning will discover, and wickedness insensibly open, cultivate and improve. Every government degenerates when trusted to the rulers alone. The people themselves therefore are its only safe depositories. And to render even them safe, their minds must be improved to a certain degree. An amendment of our constitution must here come in aid of the public education. The influence over government must be shared among all the people. If every individual . . . participates of the ultimate authority, the government will be safe.

And particularly, the Father of our Constitution:

> JAMES MADISON: A popular government without popular information, or the means of acquiring it, is but a prologue to a farce or a tragedy; and a people who mean to be their own governors must arm themselves with the power which knowledge gives.

> Again MADISON: Learned institutions ought to be favored objects with every free people. They throw that light over the public mind which is the best security over crafty and dangerous encroachments on the public liberty. They are the nurseries of skillful teachers for the schools, distributed throughout the country. They are themselves schools for the particular talents required for some of the public trusts, on the able execution of which the welfare of the people depends. They multiply the educated individuals, from among whom the public may elect a due portion of their public agents of every description.

> And finally, again from MADISON, late in his life: My lengthened observation, making me more and more sensible of the essential connection between a diffusion of knowledge and the success of Republican institutions, I derive pleasure from every example which enhances the vital chemistry of that process.

The Bicentennial era is an especially good time to enhance the vital chemistry of that process. Students must be again exposed to the constitutional basics of why we retain a two hundred year old document, the principles and values it incorporates, where it has worked and when and how it has failed. Above all they should understand what they can do generally and concretely to see that it continues to function to restrain human frailty and channel human creativity toward the positive ends of a society dedicated to "liberty and justice for all."

References

Cox, A. (1976). *The role of the Supreme Court in American government.* Cambridge, MS: Harvard University Press.

Rawls, J. (1971). *A theory of justice.* Cambridge, MS: Harvard University Press.

The Effect Upon Minorities of the Civic Education of Teachers

Faustine C. Jones-Wilson

Jones-Wilson is a Professor of Education at Howard University, Washington, D.C.

United States citizens who are also members of racial minority groups have a special interest in the philosophies, methods, and curricula of teacher preparation programs in this society. Thus the revival of civic learning as a teacher education plan attracts our attention in terms of its potential effects upon minorities. The heart of such a plan is that

> . . . the fundamental ideas and values upon which our constitutional order is built should be the [common] core of sustained and explicit study, based upon realistic and scholarly knowledge and searching criticism, carried on throughout the school years from kindergarten through high school. Thus all teachers should be prepared for this task in their liberal and professional teacher education . . . the educational profession, especially in schools and departments of education, should be trying much more rigorously and vigorously to become knowledgeable and explicit about the substantive concepts and ideas that form the common core of American citizenship. Serious and sustained work on such ideas and concepts could well be the heart of . . . joint enterprise . . . for . . . faculties of education, social science, and the humanities. (Butts, 1982b, p. 14)

Because so much of the ethics and morality transmitted to the young come through the education process, it is extremely important that the teachers who are responsible are themselves systematically taught the values and ideals of this society, including the primary purpose of maintaining a system of schooling at public expense. That purpose is to prepare children and youth to become citizens who know and understand the principles, concepts, and precepts of democracy, and who are fully committed attitudinally and emotionally to use that knowledge through their participation in the society as informed, rational, humane adults.

I agree with James A. Joseph (1982) that "no educational system has the luxury of turning out graduates who do not understand how our political and economic system works and who benefits from it" (p. 325). Thus minorities care a great deal about how *all* prospective teachers and administrators are educated, especially those of majority group membership, since the largest numbers of educators, administrators, planners, and policymakers will come from that group.

Minorities are necessarily ever-conscious that schools do play a strong social role in shaping the young. The eternal question is in which direction they will be molded. In this era where there is a resurgence of right-wing activity in the U.S., what will youth be taught about the place of such

In this era where there is a resurgence of right-wing activity in the U.S., what will youth be taught about the place of such organizations as the Ku Klux Klan, the Neo-Nazi Party, even the Moral Majority, within the American constitutional system?

organizations as the Ku Klux Klan, the Neo-Nazi Party, even the Moral Majority, within the American constitutional system? How will they be taught to evaluate a March on Washington in 1963 for the passage of civil rights legislation designed to enforce constitutional guarantees that were then almost a hundred years old? What does it mean to march on Washington again 20 years later, 1983, for jobs, peace, and freedom? The civic education of America's teachers is one way to insure that informed and responsible instruction about such issues will be possible in

Reprinted with permission from the *Journal of Teacher Education,* November/December 1983, pp. 11-13.

the schools in which these educators are, or will be, employed.

If we look at the field of education we see that the dominant theme among educators relative to the education of minorities (who are almost always discussed as disadvantaged) is that of discovering the reasons for their relatively lower academic performance and devising means to remedy it. Nowhere in the entire educational enterprise is there anything like equal time and attention given to the root problem, prejudice within the majority group — the dominant group — that maintains institutional structures and fosters attitudes designed to keep minority persons in

Nowhere in the entire educational enterprise is there anything like equal time and attention given to the root problem, prejudice within the majority group — the dominant group — that maintains institutional structures and fosters attitudes designed to keep minority persons in positions of inferiority.

positions of inferiority. Civic education can direct more of the energies of society to the changes required in the dominant group, so that at least the problems of minorities are seen as something more than deducing corrective measures to get Black children to perform at certain levels in school (West, 1972, pp. 1-3).

Turning from the majority group to minorities, it is clear that minority teachers have a vested interest in participating in plans for social, educational, political and economic reconstruction within the framework of America's constitutional system. They must be taught how to use the system to effect social change that will correct the serious imperfections in American life. Minority citizens have demonstrated that change can be initiated within the established framework of their social system by concerted action grounded in knowledge and commitment to basic democratic values. For example, the black civil rights movement gave form, shape, and substance to domestic politics during the 1960s. This movement was followed by similar efforts on the part of Native American Indians, Chicanos, women, the elderly, gays, and other citizens.

The enormous efforts of these "minorities" to achieve equal citizenship rights continue into the 1980s. The education profession, including its minority teachers, has a responsibility to take a leadership role in understanding and explaining the forces and conditions responsible for these and other social movements. The goal is not to teach people how to be American, but to raise the consciousness of people as to what the American Creed really says, and what it means. The discrepancies between the American Creed's lofty moral values and the realities of everyday living are very vivid to minorities and women.

Minorities and women have, throughout this century, used education as a tool to attain personal, occupational, economic, political, and group goals. Among the minority groups of this country, Black Americans, in particular, have placed great value upon the teaching profession. It was an irony of the formally segregated system that some of the best Black minds were channeled into public school teaching, and into the faculties of Black colleges where more teachers were being produced. Although today enrollment in teacher education programs in Black colleges is declining, minority teachers still are being prepared in these schools. They must be educated to understand the common heritage that we share as citizens, but also the exigencies of the contemporary world and its problems (West, 1981).

Minority teachers have a special obligation in preparing youth to read, write, compute, and think but also to make informed choices regarding options that will contribute to the preservation of democracy in the U.S. The survival of minorities is tied to that concept and its effective implementation. Minority teachers also are obliged to teach youth so that they will not fall into the man-made traps that would reduce democracy — simply because they are ill-educated. In these changing times, social responsibility cannot be taken for granted. Teachers must instruct in ways that promote it. They are role models for the young.

To attain these desired ends, what knowledge and values do teachers and administrators need in their liberal and professional training in order to fit them to prepare their students to become effective and responsible citizens in a democratic republic? Included in teacher education programs must be a core curriculum that will provide them with normative, interpretive, and critical knowledge about the American political democracy. R. Freeman Butts has spelled out the nature of what that prescribed curriculum ought to include (1982a, pp. 391-398). It is essentially a liberal education plan designed to impart knowledge about ten concepts that ought to be used as a common civic core. These are: justice, freedom, equality, diversity,

Minority citizens have demonstrated that change can be initiated within the established framework of their social system by concerted action grounded in knowledge and commitment to basic democratic values.

authority, privacy, due process, participation, personal obligation for the public good, and international human rights.

These concepts and their supportive materials are to be taught and used in such a way as to balance, honor, and promote the desirable pluralistic and individualistic elements in our society. This curriculum aims at "combining the values of a stable pluralism with the values of a cosmopolitan civism," toward the goal of making the many diverse elements of our society into a oneness — a unity — that would endure and prosper despite the continuing strains of rapid and pervasive change. Butts is aware that no universal agreement exists as to what these key values and concepts mean, but the effort to reach consensus is in itself educative.

Butt's proposal for the civic education of teachers is consistent with the views of Boyer and Kaplan in *Educating for Survival* (1977). They argue for a core curriculum that would expose our people educationally to their common bonds, and express the belief that the social survival of the American experiment might well depend on educational leaders returning to a core of learning.

Thirty years ago William O. Stanley (1953) argued that reestablishing a common perception of the purposes and principles constituting the public welfare was the central pedagogical problem of our time. His arguments deserve another hearing in this decade of dissonance where there is an eroding commitment to equality and justice for minorities, women, and the poor. Stanley opted for the democratic tradition as the foundation of social integration, and argued that the welfare of a society depends on acceptance by the majority of a common system of basic values and beliefs. United social action is possible only to the extent that a substantial majority of the nation possesses common convictions about the ends and purposes of society, common standards of the public's welfare, and a common faith in an authoritative method by which conflicting interests and opinions may be adjudicated peacefully. He felt that our democracy must reestablish fundamental social consensus by rational and peaceful methods. In this sense Stanley follows in the tradition of John Dewey (1945), who much earlier had held that "the very heart of political democracy is adjudication of social differences by discussion and exchange of views."

In *An American Dilemma* Gunnar Myrdal placed great value on education as a genuine social force for positive change (1962). C. Wright Mills (1961) was another theorist who proposed that schooling for adolescents provide a climate of free and open inquiry hospitable to deep and wide political debate. Schools should be a place where these students will be led by the teachers to acquire rational insights into their personal troubles and to connect those with larger issues. It is expected that discussants would emerge from such instruction and participation knowing more about themselves, their communities, their social institutions, and their society. This problem-centered methodology would focus its content on what Mills called "iron problem-areas," the real troubles faced by people trying to live fully in this chaotic, twentieth-century, urban, industrial, internationalized society. These real problems are "iron" because they are difficult, complex, and often defy individual or personal solution (pp. 139-142).

From training and experience the minority teacher can be an excellent person to fill this role of preparing the young not only in values and skills, but also in what Mills called "sensibilities." These are cultural, social, political, and technical "awarenesses" emerging from the process of self-development. Effectively developed sensibilities produce "genuine members of a genuinely liberal public."

Boyer and Kaplan argue for a core curriculum that would expose our people educationally to their common bonds, and express the belief that the social survival of the American experiment might well depend on educational leaders returning to a core of learning.

Today's civic education efforts may be reminiscent of similar efforts recommended in the crisis years of the Great Depression of the 1930s when the nation was similarly traumatized by seemingly intractable, insoluble problems. Civic education now has the possibility of emphasizing the development of individual attitudes, individual feelings of responsibility, and individual commitments within the framework of American political democracy.

There may be a danger that civic education will be reduced primarily to cognitive outcomes. But to make the ideal of social democracy concrete, cognitive outcomes are insufficient to address the problems of prejudice and discrimination which we all recognize to be deeply imbedded in our society. We, as teachers, must instill the values that are to be dominant in American society, and affect the attitudes, beliefs, sensibilities, and commitments of individuals and groups so as to give direction to the course of change toward the goal of the preservation and progress of our democratic government and way of life.

References

Boyer, E. L., & Kaplan, M. (1977). *Education for survival.* New Rochelle, NY: Change Magazine Press.

Butts, R. F., and others. (1983). *Civic learning in teacher education.* Minneapolis: Society of Professors of Education, 1983.

Butts, R. F. (1982). The revival of civic learning requires a prescribed curriculum. *Liberal Education, 58,* 377-401.

Butts, R. F. (1982, February). *Teacher education and the revival of civic learning.* 7th Annual DeGarmo Lecture, presented at the meeting of Society of Professors of Education, Houston.

Dewey, J. (1945, January). Challenge to liberal thought. In *Fortune* (Reprinted from *Time).*

Joseph, J. A. (1982). Education for citizenship: Excellence, equity, and employment. *Liberal Education, 68,* 323-328.

Mills, C. W. (1961). *The sociological imagination.* New York: Grove Press, Inc., Evergreen Edition.

Myrdal, G. (1962). *An American dilemma* (rev. ed.). New York: Harper.

Stanley, W. O. (1953). *Education and social integration.* New York: Teachers College, Columbia University.

West, E. H. (1972). The little end of the tap root. *The Journal of Negro Education, 41,* 1-3.

West, E. H. (1981). Wanted: Teachers. *The Journal of Negro Education, 50,* 367-369.

SCHOOLS AND DEMOCRATIC VALUES

SANFORD A. LAKOFF

Sanford A. Lakoff is a fellow at the National Humanities Center at Research Triangle Park, North Carolina, and professor of political science at the University of California/San Diego.

THOSE WHO care deeply about democracy have always been concerned about the role of education in preparing the young to assume their responsibilities as citizens. Jeane J. Kirkpatrick, now our representative to the United Nations, addressed this concern thoughtfully, from a modern perspective, in the pages of this magazine two years ago ("The Teaching of Democratic Values," *American Educator*, Spring 1979). In an eloquent essay, she rejected the vogue for "value-neutral" education and pointed out that "democracy makes unusually difficult demands on both rulers and citizens." No other government, she says, "requires so much voluntary participation in power and poses so many limits on its exercise." For just this reason, she concluded, "If democratic government is to survive, schools should teach democratic values."

And so they should—provided there is a clear understanding of the all-important difference between education and indoctrination.

In urging that the schools teach democratic values, Ambassador Kirkpatrick is in good, even venerable, company; the Founding Fathers of this republic shared exactly the same view. They, too, recognized that because it required restraint in the exercise of power, as well as a high degree of citizen participation, a democratic system of government could not be maintained unless loyalty to its ideals could be instilled at an early age.

As usual, it was Thomas Jefferson who put the common conviction most incisively. In drafting a report proposing the establishment of a university in Virginia, he distinguished between the role of the university and that of what he called "primary" education. The university, Jefferson held, should concentrate on developing the talents of those who had shown themselves to be especially gifted and virtuous—the "natural aristocracy" that would provide the country's leadership. Primary education should be universal and should be designed to give each individual not only "the information he needs for the transaction of his own business" but also the moral and civic instruction "to understand his duty to his neighbors and country" and "to know his rights; to exercise with order and justice those he retains; to choose with discretion the fiduciary of those he delegates; and to notice their conduct with diligence, with candor, and judgment."

In prescribing these goals, Jefferson took full account of the need for young people to acquire specific skills and substantive knowledge, but it was not enough, he thought, for schools simply to train people to fend for themselves. Above all else, the aim of schooling in a democracy must be to develop moral and responsible citizens, "to instruct the mass of our citizens in these their rights, interests, and duties as men and citizens."

What beliefs constitute the core values of democracy that schools should aim to inculcate? Ambassador Kirkpatrick admits that no single checklist can be drawn up that can be said to have authoritative standing, but she contends that there must be widespread consensus on certain basic items, amounting to a democratic creed: "A belief in political equality for all citizens; a belief that rulers should be chosen by competitive, periodic elections (and not by force or heredity); a belief that rulers and ruled alike are bound by the ordinary laws of the land and entitled to due process; a belief that all persons have certain rights—including those of life, liberty, and

This article first appeared in the Summer 1981 issue of *AMERICAN EDUCATOR*, the quarterly journal of the American Federation of Teachers.

property—that may not be legitimately abrogated by government."

Here, too, she is on firm ground. Studies of the political theory of American democracy and of the fundamental beliefs held by the overwhelming majority of Americans show that there is a strong consensus over these ultimate values. Americans differ in the emphasis and interpretations they put on the particulars and the means most appropriate for realizing them. There are real and significant differences of opinion between contemporary liberals and conservatives, as there were earlier between Federalists and anti-Federalists, Whigs and Jacksonian Democrats. Nevertheless, compared to the ideological discord that often separates people in other countries into warring camps, controversies among Americans tend to be contained within a more encompassing and unifying commitment to the democratic process.

In fact, the consensus over fundamental values has been so pervasive that it can easily go unrecognized. As the political scientist Robert Dahl explains in a textbook intended for introductory courses in American politics, "Americans are a highly ideological people. It is only that one does not ordinarily notice their ideology because they have, to an astounding extent, all agreed on the same ideology."

GIVEN THIS general agreement on fundamental principles, why should it now be necessary to urge that a deliberate effort be made in the schools to inculcate democratic values? One reason is that a good deal of confusion has grown up in recent years about the nature of these ideals. As Frances Fitzgerald has shown in her recent book *America Revised*, the textbooks used to teach American history have traditionally mirrored (though imperfectly) the general consensus as it changes from decade to decade. Lately, however, they have been tailored to suit a variety of "markets," defined by age, as well as by social class and region. As a result, she points out, with the textbooks of the 1970s in mind, "The messages that children must receive are rather confusing: love everyone in the elementary grades, fight communism in junior high, and face endless intractable problems in high school."

This confusion is compounded by a growing ignorance of the way the political system actually works. As Fitzgerald also points out, a recent survey found that 47 percent of the nation's seventeen-year-olds did not even know that each state is represented by two senators.

Confusion over values and political ignorance go hand in hand. Young people who might otherwise become responsible and active citizens acquire what Thorstein Veblen called a "trained incapacity" for political life because they never really learn what it means to live in a democracy. This, of course, is not just a result of the instruction they receive or do not receive in school. The schools must compete against powerful outside influences, not the least of which is the pervasive output of the media of mass communication. Studies of the political socialization of American school children have turned up dramatic evidence of the growing influence of the mass media. Since the turn of the century, when the media began to acquire its present enormous influence, surveys of children's heroic role models have shown a steady trend toward the replacement of political and patriotic figures by popular idols in the various fields of entertainment and athletics.

Other evidence suggests that in recent years the adults from whom children take their political cues have experienced a loss of confidence in the legitimacy of this country's political institutions. The contributing causes are well known; they include such wrenching social experiences as the controversy over the Vietnam war, the rash of political assassinations, and the Watergate scandal. Now, traditional pride in American ideals is being tested anew by the spread of incivility, drug addiction, crime, and almost casual violence in our major cities and, increasingly, in the suburbs and rural areas.

Ambassador Kirkpatrick lays some of the blame for the deterioration of civic and moral standards on the belief held by too many educators that, for various reasons, it is wrong to impose values in the classroom. She indicts a series of modern ideas, including moral relativism, the notion that objectivity requires moral neutrality, the belief that in a pluralistic society moral values should be left to subcultures, and the objection that to transmit social norms is merely to promote acquiescence to the status quo.

In responding to these attitudes, she points out that some questions, such as genocide and racial discrimination, do not admit relativistic answers. In the daily life of the classroom and playground, moral questions arise that demand to be resolved in accordance with such ethical principles as honesty and fairness. When they teach literature, history, and social studies, teachers inevitably "communicate and inculcate moral principles." Pluralism, she argues, does not require that *all* values be left to subgroups to teach their adherents, but only those, such as religious beliefs, that are not essential to the democratic creed. The rise of totalitarianism in this century, not only in Germany and Eastern Europe but even in "Jonestown," shows all too clearly that democratic values will not be acquired automatically: "The notion of the 'natural' moral man turns out to be no more tenable than the notion that children learn best when left alone to motivate themselves, discipline themselves, teach themselves."

AS COMPELLING as this argument is, especially in comparison with some of the woollier theories of open-ended, "de-schooled," wall-less, and mindless pedagogy that have been advanced in recent years, the conclusions that seem to follow may raise troubling problems unless a clear distinction is drawn between education and indoctrination. If teachers are told nothing more than that they should not be value-neutral and scrupulously objective, what is to inhibit some of them from using their classrooms to subject the young to propaganda on behalf of whatever one-sided version of American democracy they choose to inflict? Some would surely try to promote an uncritical allegiance to some glossily unrealistic, rose-tinted vision of the American Way of Life, as it appears to the most myopic super patriots, while others would use their new license to paint America in more lurid colors—as the home of racism, imperialism, sexism, and assorted other evils.

If the schools are to catechize students in the democratic creed, why not in the religious values of the various communities they serve? What could be said to those who now claim that teachers of biology should not be free to teach Darwin's theory of evolution because it contravenes religious teachings or that they should be allowed to do so only on condition that they give equal attention to "creationism"? Those who take this position are also arguing that education cannot and should not be value-neutral, but the conclusion they draw is that the schools should indoctrinate the young with Christian values, as understood by fundamentalists and evangelicals, even at the expense of scientific education.

There is also good reason to fear that if the schools are made instruments of indoctrination they will become, more than ever, the object of attention not only by self-appointed guardians of public morality but also by the agencies of government. If the Arkansas legislature can mandate the teaching of creationism, what is to prevent any legislature from prescribing the orthodox standard interpretation of American history and government? If a federal investigator can sit in on a class (as one did recently at the Berkeley law school) to investigate the charge that a particular professor was making comments derogatory to women, what is to stop an army of government auditors from being dispatched into every classroom in the country once it becomes the law of the land that schools must indoctrinate students with some prescribed national creed?

Even if the legislatures and courts can be trusted to deny themselves such an exercise of their power (which in view of recent experience, is most unlikely), the idea that society should rely on its teachers to implant approved values is not necessarily any more appealing. There would remain the problem so wonderfully portrayed in Muriel Spark's novel *The Prime of Miss Jean Brodie* and in its memorable film version. As those who know it will recall, the fictional Miss Brodie thought it her mission in life to transform her impressionable charges from mere girls to votaries of the higher morality as understood by the avant-garde. The version of bohemianism then current involved a mixture of aesthetic and political romanticism, including the adoration of Mussolini and his Blackshirts. As a result of her proselytizing, one of her pupils becomes entangled in the Spanish Civil War and comes to a tragic end; another, recognizing that she was being induced into entering a liaison with an older, married art instructor, turns upon Miss Brodie and instigates a review of her conduct that leads to her dismissal. On at least one level of analysis, the moral of this story is that there is a serious distinction between dedicated teaching and the seduction of the innocent.

DOES THIS mean that dedicated teachers must ignore questions of morality and citizenship, that Ambassador Kirkpatrick and Jefferson before her have been wrong in urging that the young be prepared to become loyal and active citizens by an education in the values of democracy? No, far from it. Perhaps an example from my own experience will indicate how the sort of education that is appropriate and necessary can be distinguished from mere indoctrination.

It was my good fortune to be the pupil of an extraordinary teacher in the public high school that I attended. In the classroom, she opened our minds to the work of great writers and essayists. She taught us all how to use our native intelligence to reach out beyond our own limited experience, to see our cultural values with a measure of detachment, and to learn to appreciate, even if we could not accept, the arguments that might be made intelligently from perspectives other than our own. So devoted was she to our education that she also taught a special seminar for the best students in the class (Jefferson's natural aristocracy?) one evening each week. We began by reading the *Iliad* and went on to Plato's *Republic,* more or less in keeping with the "Great Books" approach that was then popular. In retrospect, I wonder whether, had it been up to some committee of public safety, she would have been allowed to introduce us to the *Republic* in view of its scathing attack on Athenian democracy. It was, for me, an especially provocative work not just because it struck a responsive chord in my youthful idealism but was also quite hostile to what seemed to be ideals of my own society. Then and since, I have wrestled with this paradox and reflected on it with my own students. And that, of course, was exactly what my teacher wanted to happen. She wanted to stimulate us to think about our personal values and about what it meant to live in a democracy.

While she was doing such a splendid job of teaching us literature and introducing us to challenging ideas, she also set an example outside class of what it means in practical terms to be a citizen of a democracy, for she was one of the leading spokespersons of the local teachers organization. I remember vividly what happened when the board of education decided to retaliate against the teachers by "exiling" their leaders to grammar schools where they were required to serve as substitute teachers, even though they were not actually needed. My teacher used her first day's free time to sit in the teacher's room and write an essay on the relevance of Machiavelli's *The Prince* to local politics. The piece so delighted the editor of our daily newspaper that he printed it on the front page. Meanwhile, we students circulated a petition demanding that the teachers be reinstated; the board of education, reconsidering its decision, did so. It had been quite a little lesson in the rights and duties of democratic citizenship.

THE LARGER lesson to be drawn from such personal experience as this is that good teaching must begin with the same deeply felt vocation that led Socrates to seek to open the minds of the young to a richer reality than they could possibly appreciate from their own experience. It must proceed with respect for their independence of mind, however immature or premature that independence. It must aim to give them the tools for reading and expression with which they can appease their curiosity and deepen their understanding long after they have completed their schooling. It must introduce them to the most serious moral issues by explaining what is meant by such values as integrity, courage, responsibility, and compassion, and by such democratic beliefs as those guaranteeing individual rights, self-government, and due process of law.

Unlike mere indoctrination, a true education must challenge the young to weigh these values against the alternatives, to test them not only against their own experience of life but also against that of people in other societies and at other times. This sort of education must make it clear how comparatively rare and fragile democracy is and how rampant are dictatorship and terror; it must treat the problems of democracy in our own society but also consider the far worse problems facing those elsewhere who yearn to be free but must struggle against thought control, secret police, and the threat of imprisonment and exile.

Such an education, finally, should aim to help young people recognize that because the highest aim of a democratic society is to promote the liberty of the individual, the fate of that society rests with each of them—with what they make of their talents and with the ways they resolve the ethical and practical choices that will confront them separately and collectively. This is a kind of education that is best conveyed by example, as well as by precept. It is as far from indoctrination as legal tender is from counterfeit—as sound as the other is base, as individual as the other is repetitive, as valuable as the other is worthless. When it comes to the role of the schools in inculcating democratic values, the standard is the same as in all other aspects of academic instruction: education, yes; indoctrination, no!

Discipline Problems in the Schools

Unit 5

The behavior of students in schools has always been matter of concern to educators. There are many moral ıd legal questions involved in discussions of "school scipline." It is a highly value-laden topic on which there great diversity of opinion, at least in the United States. ıere are many professional issues related to this topic oncerning different professional perspectives on which chniques of behavior management are more or less effective and which ones are more or less desirable. This ıit seeks to explore the various dimensions of how achers can best manage student behavior in an instruconal setting.

In the interest of creating genuine and humane condions for learning in schools, educators are taking seriously forts to improve student behavior. The dimensions and cope of this problem cross socioeconomic boundaries. erious discipline problems exist in middle income suburan schools as well as in urban school districts. Teachers re demanding the respect to which all working people re entitled. They want safety, peace, security, and the opportunity to practice their art in environments where that ffort is sincerely appreciated.

The National Education Association (NEA) and the merican Federation of Teachers (AFT) each have taken trong stands for the respect of teachers from the merican adult public and children. If the quality of both eaching and learning in this nation is to improve, the peole of this nation and their government will not scapegoat eachers. Instead they will support them. If this concern genuine it will be reflected in public support of efforts make those schools experiencing severe discipline roblems into places where learning can proceed in peace r both students and teachers. The nation wants and eeds good teachers and excellent schools. In order to ttract talented people into the profession of teaching, the nvironments in which they teach must be ones in which ıeir dignity and worth as working people are respected.

The articles in this unit broaden our understanding of ıe nature of school discipline problems and present some nportant insight into what can be done about them. The uthors of the lead article take a look at "good, oldashioned discipline" and point out the problems ssociated with it. They try to show that there are some serious problems with "good-old-days" stereotypes of what are asserted to be optimum learning conditions in classrooms. Talent and Busch discuss specific strategies of behavior management that can help teachers in their work. The article follows with an essay on problems involving the searching of students. It touches on issues relating to the rights of students, teachers, and administrators. Benjamin Spock's article considers the emotional well-being of students and humane means of controlling student behavior. He argues that harsh and coercive teacher behavior sometimes creates discipline problems rather than solves them. Spock reviews medical and psychological studies which can be related to teacher leadership skills in the classroom. In conclusion, Susan Ohanion's essay on managing classroom discipline places emphasis on individualized strategies for solving student behavior problems.

The articles in this unit can be used in several sectors of basic foundations courses. They can be related to issues involving classroom management, teacher leadership skills, and rights of students and teachers. That the unit falls between the units on moral education and equality of opportunity is relevant since it can be directly related to either or both of them. The selections could also be related to issues involving curriculum and instruction or individualized approaches to teaching.

Looking Ahead: Challenge Questions

What is behavior management?

What are some of the best techniques for helping someone learn self-control?

Should there be a place for corporal punishment in disciplining students? What reasons can be given for or against it?

What civil rights do students have? Do public schools have fewer rights to control student behavior problems than private schools? Why or why not?

Are there any coercive approaches to behavioral management in schools which work better than noncoercive ones?

What responsibilities do teachers have to the emotional well-being of their students?

What are the rights of teachers in managing students?

Good, Old-Fashioned Discipline: The Politics Of Punitiveness

Illustration by Mark Braught

Irwin A. Hyma
and John D'Alessandr

IRWIN A. HYMAN (Temple Universi Chapter) is director of the National Center f the Study of Corporal Punishment and Alte natives in the Schools and a professor of scho psychology at Temple University, Philade phia, where JOHN D'ALESSANDRO is a do toral student in school psychology. This artic is based in part on Congressional testimo given by the authors.

Millions of schoolchildren each year ar subjected to physical punishment, suspension, and expulsion. The authors call for an end to outmoded notions of the desirability of corporal punishment as a primary pedagogical strategy.

IN THE ANNUAL Gallup Poll of th Public's Attitudes Toward the Publi Schools, respondents consistentl rank discipline as the major problen plaguing U.S. education. The attentio given by the mass media to this finding each year is a mixed blessing, illuminatin

From *Phi Delta Kappan*, September 1984, pp. 39-45. Reprinted by permission of the authors and Phi Delta Kappan.

national concern but also engendering a ırmful overreaction. Politicians, the edia, and special interest groups — all of ıom benefit from the myth that U.S. hools are in chaos — foster a "get ugh" response. Thus encouraged, the ıblic calls on school leaders and legistors to resolve the discipline problem th a haste that precludes careful planng, execution, and evaluation of potenıl solutions. Indeed, as Robert Rubel ıs noted, "school systems across the untry find themselves attempting to reond in rational ways to irrational ımuli."[1]

Violence and lack of discipline are ɔth historical and contemporary realities the schools. But the sensational treatent of these problems in the media today ıcourages continual political warfare tween liberals and conservatives over sues of freedom and control. In other ords, the political struggles over school scipline spring from ideological differences (which, in turn, tend to foster incurate assessments of the nature and extent of the problem).

The Reagan Administration has estabshed school discipline as a major camaign issue. In March 1984 the Adminisation also established (through a nonɔmpetitive grant) a National School afety Center, designed to orchestrate and romote an avowedly right-wing aproach to school discipline. We intend in ıis article to critically analyze the Admintration's policies with regard to discipline in the schools. We will attempt to resent a rational, data-based view of this ighly politicized issue, but in some inances we will have to fight fire with fire nd engage in political rhetoric.

HE BAUER REPORT

The current focus on discipline in the chools began on 8 December 1983 when 'resident Reagan, speaking in Indianapos, suggested that we solve the problems f U.S. education, without spending more ıoney, simply by a return to "good, oldashioned discipline." His comment, and barrage of later press releases and peeches, took their substance from a eport issued by the Working Group on chool Violence/Discipline of Reagan's Cabinet Council on Human Resources. 'he report originally bore the title, Chaos in the Classroom: Enemy of American Education," an indication of its eneral tenor. The unsigned report is genrally credited to Gary Bauer, deputy unersecretary of education, who has been ts chief spokesperson.

The Bauer Report suggests that probems of discipline really began when stuents gained the protection of due process gainst arbitrary actions by school oficials. The report asserts that the extension of constitutional rights to students has tied the hands of school administrators who must deal with troublemakers — and has thereby increased substantially the number of episodes of classroom disruption and violence. To rectify the current imbalance in power between school officials and students, the report proposes that the Department of Justice file friend-of-the-court briefs to increase the authority of administrators and teachers and to discourage the filing of suits related to discipline.

> **A realistic assessment of available data indicates that the hands of school administrators are not tied by due process.**

However, a realistic assessment of available data indicates that the hands of school administrators are *not* tied by due process or by other constitutional considerations. Indeed, it is difficult to reconcile the image of powerless school administrators that the Bauer Report projects with the number of suspensions, expulsions, and pushouts that take place in U.S. schools each year. Education Department figures show that only 72.8% of all students who started high school with the class of 1982 actually graduated; by contrast, 77.2% of the class of 1972 received diplomas. In inner-city high schools, the figures are more dramatic. For example, most inner-city high schools in New Jersey lose more than half of each class prior to graduation.

Meanwhile, the Bauer Report attempts to elicit support for its position from minority groups by pointing out that minority students are most often the victims of school violence. Although this is true, minority students are also punished by school officials more frequently and more severely than white students. In a study of 56 schools, for example, Gary Gottfredson found that 31% of black males had been suspended at least once during the term just past — a rate double that of white males. Black males also received corporal punishment far more often than their white counterparts.[2]

The Bauer Report is a series of disjointed statements, skewed statistics, and questionable assumptions that clearly reflect right-wing ideology. The conclusions of the document mislead the uninformed reader, who could hardly be expected to guess the next step in the Administration's hidden agenda: the establishment of a national center. Before exploring the real purpose of the Bauer Report, however, let us turn to the statistics around which the ideological battle lines are drawn.

THE DATA ON SCHOOL CRIME

Valid interpretation of the data on school crime is difficult. All crime is underreported for a variety of reasons, which range from lack of faith in the system to fear of spiraling insurance premiums. Hence, any change in the procedures for reporting a crime will be accompanied by a corresponding change — which may be more apparent than real — in the number of reported offenses. Thus an increase in school crime can be validly inferred only if the reporting procedures have been held constant.

The Bauer Report fails to take methodological changes into account. For example, the report cites a National Education Association (NEA) poll that shows a 53% increase in the number of incidents of school violence directed at teachers between 1977 and 1983. But the NEA revised its poll questions twice during that interval to make them more inclusive. These revisions make it impossible to determine whether violence directed against teachers actually increased — or perhaps even decreased — between 1977 and 1983.

The establishment of security offices in many schools, a movement that began in earnest during the late Sixties, may likewise have stepped up the reporting of school crimes. There are two reasons for this. First, heavy-handed security measures tend to provoke, rather than to deter, certain kinds of crimes.[3] Second, security officers have a vested interest in reporting crimes, the raison d'être for their jobs. By contrast, school principals, who had typically been responsible for the reporting of school crimes prior to the creation of the security offices, have a vested interest in drawing attention away from the extent of such problems in their buildings.

Valid comparisons of school violence from one year to another are further hampered by the vagaries of classifying offenses. In preparation for testifying before Congress, we examined the records of 40 reported assaults on teachers in an urban school district. These incidents, considered the 40 most serious by district officials, ranged from throwing candy at a teacher to a bona fide physical attack. The difficulty of extracting valid meaning from such data highlights our concern about the Bauer Report, which draws conclusions regarding crime rates over time. In actuality, crime rates may vary in a district simply because of a change in a school's chief disciplinarian; differing definitions of offenses can also cause crime rates to fluctuate across districts.

Interpreting the data on school crime is also hampered by other problems. It is incorrect to assume, for example, that offenders and victims form mutually exclusive groups. Nor can school crime be understood in isolation from the neighborhoods in which it occurs.[4] *The Safe School Study* stressed that a community's crime rate — which correlates strongly with its rates of unemployment, family disruption, and poverty — best predicts the level of school violence in that community. Secretary of Education Terrel Bell supports this position, although Undersecretary Bauer has contradicted it, claiming that poverty is no excuse for misbehavior.

Conventional wisdom holds that students commit most of the violent acts in the schools, but one study challenges even that basic assumption. Using data from the 1974-75 National Crime Survey, Jackson Toby found that most violent crimes in the schools had been committed by intruders. For example, he estimated that 100% of teacher rapes and 94% of student rapes in the 26 cities included in that survey were committed by "stranger intruders."[5] A return to "good, old-fashioned discipline" would do little to reduce the problem of intruders in the schools.

Given the complexity of the problem of school crime and the difficulties of interpreting the data, what can be validly deduced? From an analysis of the research on school crime, Oliver Moles, a staff member with the National Institute of Education, concluded that the data contradict the popular notion that school crime is progressively increasing.[6] Most other researchers who have studied school crime have echoed his opinion.[7]

Meanwhile, how has the Reagan Administration recommended that we solve the complex problem of school crime? Through "good, old-fashioned discipline." This remedy evokes an earlier time when schools were invariably peaceful and children unquestioningly obeyed teachers and other authorities — a utopia that never existed.

GOOD, OLD-FASHIONED DISCIPLINE

An extensive review of U.S. history shows colonial schools to have been coercive and repressive. Children were taught by repetitive drill, and corporal punishment was the primary method of discipline. Nor were the students alone in finding their schools oppressive; newspapers carried numerous advertisements between 1750 and 1770 that offered rewards for the location and return of runaway teachers.[8] The literature of this period contains few allusions to serious violence by students — perhaps because so many youngsters were excluded from schooling altogether.

"Good, old-fashioned discipline" was bad for both teachers and students in the good old days, and it remains so today.

As education became more widespread in the 19th century, so did school violence. The schools of that time were still woefully inadequate with regard to physical facilities, teaching methods, and disciplinary practices. Rote drill continued to be the most common teaching method; the schools were also characterized by strict adherence to rigid rules and by training for reflexive obedience through the pervasive use of corporal punishment.

"Good, old-fashioned discipline" was bad for both teachers and students in the good old days, and it remains so today. Moreover, despite President Reagan's contentions to the contrary, "good, old-fashioned discipline" is alive and well in contemporary American classrooms. Millions of schoolchildren each year are subjected to physical punishment, suspension, or expulsion.

An ongoing series of studies by the National Center for the Study of Corporal Punishment and Alternatives in the Schools (NCSCPAS) reveals that large numbers of American students are regularly paddled — especially in the Southeast, where corporal punishment is strongly defended.[9] The national press has covered incidents in which students have been struck with such items as doubled-over belts, lacrosse sticks, jai alai sticks, baseball bats, arrows, electrical cords, bamboo rods, rubber hoses, hammers, and wooden drawer dividers. Some teachers have used cattle prods and similar devices to administer electric shocks to children. Other youngsters have been kicked, choked, or punched — forced to eat cigarettes or to have their faces smeared with hot sauce. One Chicago principal used a pocketknife to drill a hole in a pupil's fingernail.

Such extreme incidents are rare, but they reveal this society's acceptance of pain as a legitimate pedagogical te nique. Indeed, teachers and admin trators have frequently been exonera of abusive actions toward schoolchild that would have been judged illegal h these educators used the same approac to discipline their own children. Me while, research has shown that oppress responses to students' disruptive haviors scarcely ever yield effective so tions.[10] Yet the Reagan Administrati seems resolutely committed to a philo phy of punitiveness.

The President himself commended J seph Clark, a New Jersey high sch principal who expelled 10% of his st dents during his first week on the jc Other politicians and reporters for t media quickly joined Reagan in maki Clark a folk hero. Yet Clark's tenure principal has been marked by a strict a proach to discipline that has yielded 50% dropout/pushout rate. On "The P Donahue Show," Clark credited his tec niques with doubling the minimum co petency test scores of his 3,000 students just six months. He also asserted th schools are no places for thugs, punk and hooligans.

Clark's public utterances strike responsive chord with the American pu lic. But what happens to the 50% Clark's students who have dropped out been pushed out of school between grad 8 and 12 in an urban community with hi youth unemployment? Has his repressi approach to discipline solved the proble or merely made it worse? We deplore t endorsement of this kind of solution.

DISCIPLINE IN A DEMOCRACY

Americans tend to turn reflexively punishment as a solution for behavior problems. Indeed, most Americans vie *punishment* and *discipline* as synon mous.

But discipline in a democracy shoul spring from internal controls, not fro fear of punishment. Effective disciplina techniques in a democracy also incorp rate respect for the rights of individuals. schools that use such disciplinary tec niques, the students perceive their teac ers and administrators as fair and jus Successful approaches to discipline in th schools enhance individuals' self-estee and encourage cooperation. Althoug necessary at times, punishment in suc schools is used rationally — not merely humiliate and alienate students. To esta lish an effective disciplinary progran school officials must first understand th motives for student misbehavior.

Our statements above suggest that su cessful disciplinary programs bring th *process* of democracy into the schools nfortunately, however, too many people onfuse democracy in education with permissiveness. This misunderstanding gives itics an easy label with which to attack ose who propose such an approach to scipline.

Neither educators nor the lay public n examine the issues of discipline and inishment objectively. Discipline is mething we have all experienced from rth. It comes from parents, religious aders, teachers, employers, and, increasgly, from community and governmental encies. No wonder we have difficulty beg objective. Yet recent research reveals at our own disciplinary practices depend ore on the manner in which we ourselves ere disciplined as children than on any her consideration.[11]

In addition, disciplinary practices are ow to change because of ignorance of e causes of student misbehavior. Disciinary problems in a school can be used by many things, among them: 1) adequate parenting, 2) ineffective teach- training, 3) poor school organization, inadequate administrative leadership, inappropriate curricula, 6) the overuse suspensions and other punishments, 7) born traits of individual students (such neurological impairments) that may inract with certain environments to cause vere behavioral or learning disorders, 8) oor self-esteem and frustration with arning, 9) overexposure to violence rough television and the other mass edia, 10) racism, 11) lack of employent opportunities, 12) peer pressures, 3) overcrowding, and 14) specific social, olitical, and bureaucratic factors that igore the needs of the young.

ROMOTING EFFECTIVE DISCIPLINE

There are many remedies to disciinary problems, and no single approach ill be universally successful. But our andling of disciplinary problems in the hools can be improved in many ways. s we proceed with this effort, here are a w things that we ought to consider.

Improving the data base. To make the search on discipline more useful, we ust establish clear descriptions of misbeavior and of punishment. For example, CSCPAS staff members are currently eveloping a school-based, computerized, niform reporting system,[12] from which lministrators and teachers can retrieve ata on given children, teachers, types of ffenses, and so on. This system, which ovides important feedback, can be used monitor and redirect efforts aimed at e prevention of disciplinary problems.

Improving schools. The best way to nprove school discipline is to improve hool climate. However, many facets of hool climate are easily measured but hard to change. To be effective, improvement efforts require the support, understanding, and commitment of the school board, the district administrators, the building administrators, the teaching staff, and the support staff.

Research shows that school vandalism is dramatically reduced when students view their schools positively as places of learning.

Improving school staffs. Few U.S. educators have received formal training in the theory, research, and practice of school discipline. The vast majority of U.S. educators will require inservice training to help them link theory and practice effectively.

Our approach to such training assumes that teachers have differing predispositions toward discipline and that, for many reasons, children respond differently to any given disciplinary technique.[13] This training approach also assumes that teachers will change when they discern a discrepancy between how they believe they should handle discipline and how they actually do handle it. To make participating teachers aware of such discrepancies, outside observers pay a series of visits to their classrooms. The teachers also complete questionnaires and consent to have videotapes made of their teaching. Group work with other teachers, consultations with school psychologists, self-exploration activities, and the reading of selected resource materials also encourage teacher participants to change their disciplinary methods.

Systemwide change is difficult, but individual principals have great latitude. *The Safe School Study* clearly indicates that building administrators set the disciplinary tone for their schools.[14] Moreover, effective administrators do not espouse "good, old-fashioned discipline." Indeed, most data indicate that punitive administrators merely cause students to suppress their anger and hostility until the inevitable moment when it erupts against people and property. Research also shows that school vandalism is dramatically reduced when students view their schools positively as places of learning. By fostering an appropriate climate for learning, each principal has the power to help his or her students view their school in this light.

In recent years, many administrators have turned instead to discipline codes, although there is scanty empirical evidence that such devices are effective over time. Dolores Lally, in what appears to be the first data-based study of discipline codes, found that disciplinarians most frequently evaluated their schools' codes as effective if they had played a major role in developing them.[15] Although discipline codes may be helpful, they are not panaceas. Too often administrators use them rigidly, without regard for extenuating circumstances. We need more research to identify the strengths and weaknesses of such codes.

We do know that most of the principals who seek consultations on discipline are individuals who are willing to experiment with new ideas. Unfortunately, it is much harder to convince many other principals and teachers of the need for positive approaches to discipline.

Improving teacher training. Staff members at the NCSCPAS have conducted exhaustive studies of programs for training teachers to discipline their students effectively.[16] The approaches they have examined have included behavior modification, transactional analysis, reality therapy, teacher effectiveness training, social literacy, Adlerian approaches, and training in human relations. In addition to analyzing each program separately, the NCSCPAS staff members looked for common features.

Their analyses showed that most of the training programs focus on seven general techniques with which teachers can motivate students and deal with disciplinary problems: 1) providing feedback to students about their behaviors, feelings, and ideas; 2) using diagnostic strategies to better understand students and student/teacher interactions; 3) modifying the classroom climate; 4) applying techniques of behavior modification; 5) using democratic procedures for solving classroom problems; 6) expressing emotions appropriately; and 7) using therapeutic approaches to behavioral problems. Other research by NCSCPAS suggests a need for more individualization in the training of teachers.

Other considerations. In addition to the general remedies we have just discussed, educators can employ a number of specific measures to improve school discipline. Prevention is a prime example. At first glance, prevention seems expensive and difficult to implement, but it is cost-effective in the long run. For example, potential delinquents who are identified early and whose families receive appropriate counseling cost society less than their counterparts who actually become delinquents.

Other effective strategies to promote

good discipline include well-planned alternative school programs, in-school suspensions (though inadequate funding often makes this tactic more punishing for teachers than for students), and automatic calling machines that relay recorded messages to parents of truant children. Time-out is a helpful punishment technique, if it is not overused. In cases of theft or vandalism, schools have used restitution programs successfully. Peer and cross-age counseling have proven helpful to youngsters with behavioral problems. Special after-school programs have benefited latchkey children. (Indeed, after-school recreation programs and other youth activities are simple but effective ways to structure the leisure time of *all* children.) Some schools have found that they need well-trained security personnel and judicious safety measures. Last but not least, caring, enthusiastic, and masterful teachers go a long way toward preventing serious discipline problems from arising in the first place.

There are many models of effective school discipline from which schools can choose; they should be matched to the needs of schools.

THE POINTS we have made above, and other research data as well, have been systematically distorted, inadequately presented, or totally ignored by the Reagan Administration. The Bauer Report and the call for "good, old-fashioned discipline" appear to have been intended solely to woo votes from alarmed citizens, to curry favor with teachers and administrators who favor a get-tough stance, and to set the scene for the establishment of the National School Safety Center.

Despite President Reagan's rhetoric against the use of federal funds to improve discipline in U.S. schools, his Administration awarded a noncompetitive grant of $4.5 million to Pepperdine University in March 1984 to create the National School Safety Center. The Democrats were quick to attack this move. The 23 May 1984 issue of *Education Week* listed some of the concerns of Democratic members of the House and Senate subcommittees. These included: 1) suspicions of political patronage, because of the long and friendly association of Edwin Meese III and George Nicholson, director of the Center, with Pepperdine University; 2) the lack of consultation with recognized experts on school discipline; 3) the political (rather than educational or scientific) orientation of the Center staff; and 4) the possible use of the Center to undermine Section 1983 of the Civil Rights Act of 1964.

The source of funding for the Center is another concern. The funding is part of $15.7 million in noncompetitive grants awarded by Alfred Regnery, director of the Office of Juvenile Justice and Delinquency Prevention (OJJDP). Regnery, son of ultraconservative publisher Henry Regnery and a frequent seminar presenter with Moral Majority leader Jerry Falwell, believes that the OJJDP has focused too much effort on prevention and rehabilitation.[17] His views on this matter are under attack by most professionals in the field.

Meanwhile, the Human Resources Subcommittee of the House Education and Labor Committee has reported the existence of a secret Justice Department memorandum alluding to the Civil Rights Act of 1964. Informed sources report that the memorandum — written by Roger Clegg, assistant attorney general for legal policy — suggests that the emphasis of the Center on safer schools could be used to undermine Section 1983 of the Civil Rights Act, which enables students and parents to sue school officials for civil rights violations. The implications are chilling, since the Civil Rights Act is much broader. Repeal or weakening of this Act would deny the right it provides for *any* citizen to sue *any* public official for a civil rights violation.

From the Bauer Report and from the stance of most of those individuals who have been involved in funding and staffing the Center, it appears that the Center will focus on injecting right-wing ideology into the schools. This would be a clear reversal of the trend in the Seventies to increase the constitutional rights of students, especially the right of due process in cases involving discipline. The following information regarding the establishment of the Center supports this contention.[18]

• Pepperdine University is widely perceived as a conservative liberal arts college with a "Christian" orientation. It offers no programs in juvenile justice and has on its faculty no recognized experts on school discipline or school safety.

• Pepperdine does not usually seek federal funds and has never overseen a federal research project. In fact, Nicholson asked Pepperdine to accept the Center grant so that he could organize the Center
300 miles away, in Sacramento, wh
and many of his staff members live.

• President Reagan and Meese, a
time political ally of Nicholson, ar
annual contributors to the universit
least $1,000.

• Bill Treanor, executive direc
the National Youth Work Alliance,
fied during a Senate hearing in M
1984 that the Justice Department ha
continued the National School Res
Network, an organization serving
tially the same function as the new C
Treanor called the whole affair "a rip

• A. L. Carlisle, who heads th
tional Steering Committee of Stat
venile Justice Advisory Groups, pu
stated that she had never heard of G
Nicholson before his appointme
Center director. She also stated th
National School Safety Center is un
sary and that the money could have
better spent to fully fund the appa
successful projects on the preventi
school violence that were cut off
Regnery became administrator o
OJJDP.

• Many fear that any potential
tributions of the Center will be
promised by the fact that Nicholso
his staff lack background in schoo
cipline. Although unknown natio
Nicholson has had a stormy po
career in California. Law enforce
officials identify him with the ex
right because of his "law-and-order"
nouncements as executive director c
California District Attorneys Ass
tion. He reinforced this image in hi
as deputy district attorney in Ala
County, California, a position previ
held by Meese, who later became his
political ally. An audit of the Calif
District Attorneys Association u
Nicholson's leadership caused a furo
ended in his return of funds tha
claimed to have received through a
puter error and that he had used to
personal expenses. The association
returned a substantial additional su
the state after Nicholson left his pos
as executive director. During his
years with the California Justice De
ment, Nicholson overspent his budg
approximately 100%. When he ra
the post of state attorney general, his
indiscretions were well-publicized. T
included the improper use of official
stationery and facilities to promote
servative political causes. Nichol
flamboyance and zeal earned him
weak support from some elements o
conservative establishment, which p
ably contributed to his election loss.
image was not enhanced when the Ca
nia Bar Association frustrated his bi
a judgeship by rating him unqualifie

THE STRIDENCY of our attack on the Center, its political context, and its director may seem one-sided. However, in our opin-n, the infusion of an extreme political eology into an area of education that orely needs objectivity justifies this kind f response. Educators and educational searchers can choose to ignore a bad sit-ation or to enter the political fray. We elieve that entering the fray is crucial hen educational issues are taken out of e realm of reason.

The awarding of a large, noncompeti-ve grant to fund the Center was clearly a istake. There are many other approaches improving school discipline. For exam-e, the expanding knowledge base re-uires rational examination and transla-on into practice. We already know of any models of effective school discipline om which schools can choose.[19] Op-mally, these models should be matched the needs of specific schools; thus we ould develop guidelines to help individ-al schools evaluate the models and select opropriate ones. Moreover, as commu-ities and schools change, so must our ap-roaches to discipline change.

Meanwhile, we should develop a na-onal pool of experts on discipline, who ill train at least one staff member in each articipating school. For such training, we iggest that the schools choose teams that nclude both a high-level administrator ith organizational clout and a school sychologist, social worker, or counselor ho understands the developmental, ocial, and emotional facets of mis-ehavior.

Most important, we can improve dis-pline in the schools by improving the eneral quality of education. This ap-roach will not be cheap. But we believe at it will prove less expensive than deal-g with citizens who have been pushed ut of an inflexible educational system to ecome unemployable adults.

We exhort the Reagan Administration nd other policy makers to reflect objec-vely on what we already know about dis-ipline. From such reflection will surely ome a disavowal of outmoded notions bout the desirability of punishment as a rimary pedagogical strategy.

We can improve discipline in the schools by improving the general quality of education. This approach will not be cheap.

1. Robert Rubel, *The Unruly School* (Lexington, Mass.: Lexington Books, 1977), p. 10.

2. Gary Gottfredson, "School Discipline," testimony before the Subcommittee on Elementary, Secondary, and Vocational Education of the Committee on Education and Labor, U.S. House of Representatives, 23 January 1984.

3. G. Roy Mayer, Tom Butterworth, Mary Nafpaktitis, and Beth Sulzer-Azaroff, "Preventing School Vandalism and Improving Discipline: A Three-Year Study," *Journal of Applied Behavior Analysis*, Winter 1983, pp. 355-69.

4. Joan McDermott, "Crime in the School and in the Community: Offenders, Victims, and Fearful Youths," *Crime and Delinquency*, April 1983, pp. 270-82.

5. Jackson Toby, "Violence in School," in Michael Tonry and Norval Morris, eds., *Crime and Justice: An Annual Review of Research, Vol. 4* (Chicago: University of Chicago Press, 1983).

6. Oliver Moles, *Trends in Interpersonal Crimes in School* (Washington, D.C.: National Institute of Education, 1983).

7. Irwin Hyman and John D'Alessandro, "School Discipline in America," testimony before the Subcommittee on Elementary, Secondary, and Vocational Education of the Committee on Education and Labor, U.S. House of Representatives, 24 January 1984.

8. Joan Newman and Graeme Newman, "Crime and Punishment in the Schooling Process: A Historical Analysis," in Keith Baker and Robert J. Rubel, eds., *Violence and Crime in the Schools* (Lexington, Mass.: D.C. Heath, 1980). See also Ellwood P. Cubberly, *The History of Education* (Boston: Houghton Mifflin, 1920).

9. Jacqueline Clarke, Rebecca Liberman-Lascoe, and Irwin Hyman, "Corporal Punishment in the Schools as Reported in Nationwide Newspapers," *Children and Youth Services*, vol. 4, 1982, pp. 47-56; Jacqueline Clarke, Richard Erdlen, and Irwin Hyman, "Analysis of Recent Corporal Punishment Cases Reported in National Newspapers," paper presented at the annual convention of the National Association of School Psychologists, Philadelphia, 20 April 1984; and Irwin Hyman and James Wise, *Corporal Punishment in American Education* (Philadelphia: Temple University Press, 1979).

10. Daniel Duke, "The Etiology of Student Misbehavior and the Depersonalization of Blame," *Review of Educational Research*, vol. 48, 1978, pp. 415-37; Irwin Hyman and David Bogacki, "Legal and Ethical Issues in the Discipline of Emotionally Disturbed Children," in Marvin Fine, ed., *Systematic Intervention with Emotionally Disturbed Children* (Jamaica, N.Y.: SP Medical & Scientific Books, 1984); Irwin Hyman, Dennis Flanagan, and Kathleen Smith, "Discipline in the Schools," in Cecil Reynolds and Terry Gutkin, eds., *A Handbook for the Practice of School Psychology* (New York: John Wiley & Sons, 1982); Irwin Hyman, "Corporal Punishment: America's Officially Sanctioned Form of Child Abuse," in Gertrude Williams and John Money, eds., *Traumatic Abuse and Neglect of Children at Home* (Baltimore: Johns Hopkins University Press, 1980); idem, "Democracy, Mental Health, and Achievement: A Modern Educational Mythology," *Annual Yearbook* (n.p.: New Jersey Association of Secondary School Teachers, 1970); and idem, "Some Effects of Teaching Style on Pupil Behavior" (Doctoral dissertation, Rutgers University, 1964).

11. Naomi Lennox, "Teachers' Use of Corporal Punishment as a Function of Modeling" (Doctoral dissertation, Temple University, 1983); and Beth Sofer, "Psychologists' Attitudes Toward Corporal Punishment" (Doctoral dissertation, Temple University, 1983).

12. Gary Berkowitz, Irwin Hyman, and Dolores Lally, "The Development of a Schoolwide Computerized Uniform Reporting System," paper presented at the annual convention of the National Association of School Psychologists, Philadelphia, 20 April 1984.

13. Mariann Pokalo and Irwin Hyman, "The Teacher Improvement Model for Organization Development," paper presented at the annual convention of the National Association of School Psychologists, Detroit, 24 March 1983.

14. National Institute of Education, *Violent Schools, Safe Schools: The Safe School Study Report to the Congress, Vol. 1* (Washington, D.C.: U.S. Department of Health, Education, and Welfare, 1977).

15. Dolores Lally, "Administrators' Perceptions of the Effectiveness of Discipline Codes in New Jersey High Schools" (Doctoral dissertation, Temple University, 1982).

16. Irwin Hyman and Dolores Lally, "The Effectiveness of Staff Development Programs to Improve School Discipline," *Urban Review*, vol. 14, 1982, pp. 181-96.

17. See, for example, Susan Cunningham, "Discretionary Justice: The Furor over Juvenile Research Funds," *American Psychological Association Monitor*, July 1984, pp. 1, 14; and Larry Bush, "Fat Grants and Sleazy Politics: Reagan's Porn Paranoia," *Playboy*, August 1984, pp. 51-52.

18. Information on George Nicholson has been obtained, in large part, from a series of newspaper articles in the *Sacramento Bee*, written primarily by Claire Cooper.

19. Numerous models to prevent school violence are described in documents published by such groups as the National Institute of Education, the Justice Department, the Phi Delta Kappa Commission on Discipline, the Center for Social Organization of Schools at Johns Hopkins University, the National Alliance for Safe Schools, and the National Center for the Study of Corporal Punishment and Alternatives in the Schools.

Disciplinary Strategies

BARBARA K. TALENT
and SUZANNE G. BUSCH

Dr. Talent is an instructor of Psychology in Pediatrics, Washington University Medical School Department of Pediatrics, and assistant director of the Psychology Laboratory, St. Louis (Missouri) Children's Hospital.

Ms. Busch is the educational consultant, Psychology Laboratory, Washington University Medical School, and Department of Pediatrics, St. Louis Children's Hospital.

Innumerable books, articles, and even whole courses have been devoted to the topic of classroom management. Our experience, however, suggests that there is a great difference between understanding the principles of behavior management on a theoretical level and applying those principles in a real classroom setting.

We, therefore, try to make our suggestions as specific and concrete as possible. Feedback from teachers who have actually used our ideas has helped us do this. We have tried to address the day-to-day issues of classroom teaching and take into account the restrictions with which the average teacher must cope: 30 to 40 children in a classroom, a scarcity of support personnel and resources, limitations on preparation time, and little or no cooperation from parents.

While we believe a teacher plagued by these difficulties can successfully apply our techniques for classroom management, we do not mean to imply that it will be simple. Teachers who use our approaches must be active, creative, flexible, and capable of adapting rules to children's particular needs. Even for such teachers, these approaches will not be a panacea for all behavior problems. Applied consistently and thoughtfully, however, they can be invaluable tools for helping children become more successful in the classroom.

Behavior Patterns

In our experience, most children with behavior problems fall into two main groups (although rarely will any one child fit neatly into one group or the other). In one group are youngsters who are actually fairly compliant; they are willing to work, particularly on a one-to-one basis, and do not openly defy their teachers. On the other hand, they are disorganized, work carelessly, and tend not to finish assigned work. They daydream, seem to have a short attention span, and are easily distracted.

In the second group are the more actively disruptive and openly defiant children. These students are easily frustrated and vent their frustrations in temper outbursts. Adults often say they have a chip on their shoulder. Such children will often refuse to begin an assignment. If they do begin, they give up quickly, often angrily tearing up their papers and throwing them on the floor or scribbling over what they have already done.

After describing ways to get started, we will describe general behavior management techniques that we have found useful for children who behave in either of these ways. Then we will give suggestions aimed more specifically at each type.

Starting the Program

Attempting to change too many behaviors at once almost alw
guarantees failure. The first st
therefore, in implementing a
havior management plan is cho
ing the behaviors you most wa
child to change. We suggest
following procedure:

1. Make a list of the chil
behaviors that you find disrupti
Take a good look at what you h
written. A sample list mi
read—

- Taps pencil against desk
- Never finishes assignment
- Talks out instead of raisi
hand
- Tips chair back against wal
- Spends a lot of time d
dling.

2. Decide which behaviors
serve priority. Which one or t
(at most) do you need to deal wi
immediately? On the sample li
"never finishes assignments" f
lowed by "talks out instead of ra
ing hand" would most likely
the ones you would choose.
though the rest are certainly a
noying, you should ignore the
until you have been able to modi
the more serious ones. Again, t
quickest way to ensure failure
your plan is to try to change t
many behaviors at once.

3. Be very clear in your ov
mind what it is you want
change. This usually means
scribing in observable, measural
terms the behavior you will co
centrate on. Thus, "helping Joh
ny learn to *finish what he starts—*
time" is a concrete, measurable b
havior, while "helping Johnny *b*
better student" is too vague. N
that you target not only the beha
ior you want to change (never fi
ishes assignments), but also t
behavior you want to develop (fi
ishes assignments on time).

4. Inform the student of yo

"Disciplinary Strategies," Barbara K. Talent and Suzanne G. Busch, *Today's Education*, February/March 1982. Reprinted by permission.

intention to help him or her behave differently. Pick a time when things have been going fairly well, when the student is fairly calm—*not* a time right after misbehavior. Your explanation should be short, simple, and direct—something like:

> "Janice, you know we've had some trouble getting along in class this school year. I understand that sometimes you feel very angry and that it is hard to control your temper. I have some ideas about what we can do to help you develop more self-control. By self-control, I mean not yelling or hitting or pinching when you are angry and not giving up when you feel the work is hard.
>
> "I know there are times when you are not very pleased with your actions and you would like to make things go more smoothly. I appreciate that, and I know we can make things better. It won't be easy, and it won't happen overnight, but with both of us working together, we can do it."

Make sure that your students understand that you are firmly committed to helping them develop more appropriate behaviors and that you sincerely believe that working together, you will be successful.

5. As far as the rest of your class goes, you will need to be prepared to answer their questions about any special arrangements you make with a particular child (earning special privileges, filling in progress charts, keeping track of certain behaviors). Answer the other students' questions briefly and matter-of-factly: "Janice and I are working together to help her strengthen a weak area. We all have our strengths and weaknesses, and at various times I will most likely have special arrangements with different students in our classroom."

General Techniques

Thoughtfully applied, but liberally meted out, positive reinforcement is one of the most powerful tools you have available for strengthening the behaviors you want children to develop. It is important to be alert for instances of appropriate behavior. Recognize and praise even approximations of the desired behaviors; praise progress and improvement—don't wait until a student has a perfect day.

Shape the target behavior by going over to the student, possibly touching her or him, and honestly praising the behavior: "Janice, I noticed that Steve accidentally bumped your desk, and you looked up, but then kept working. That was really good self-control!" or "Johnny, you are doing a good job of trying hard to solve these math problems, and I know they aren't easy." Praising appropriate behavior shows children when they are acting properly and gives them frequent chances to experience success in their lives.

Positive reinforcement is a tool that is easy to apply to the class as a whole. Let all your students know that you appreciate appropriate behavior. The other behavior management techniques will not be effective unless you regularly use positive reinforcement.

How you praise is an important aspect of shaping behavior. Make sure to praise the behavior you like, not the child. Try to keep praise specific and informative. Thus, "Good job of staying in your seat during math, Johnny," rather than just "Good boy, Johnny," tells Johnny exactly what you liked about what he did and makes very clear what you expect from him in the future.

Again, when trying to help children develop the ability to "keep working even when the work is hard," be sure to reinforce effort rather than just the final product. To feel less frustrated, these children need to learn that trying, even when it's hard, is just as important as "getting it all right."

A second powerful tool for changing behavior is ignoring behavior you want to discourage. Learning to ignore annoying but less severe problem behaviors is quite a challenge. But remember that all attention (both positive and negative) is reinforcing. Stopping a class to correct one student gives that student a powerful dose of attention and actually reinforces the behavior you want to eliminate. A much more effective strategy is to ignore that behavior and attempt to make a model of a child who is behaving in an appropriate manner.

By doing this, you tell students, "Behave appropriately and you will get recognition," not vice versa. If Janice is not working on her assignment, you might walk over to a child near her who is on task and say, "I see you are working hard on your spelling words, Doug. Good job!"

You cannot, of course, ignore all misbehavior. If Johnny gets up and starts to walk around the room, simply say, "During class time, we need to stay in our seats." Then, quickly escort him to his seat with the minimum amount of discussion (attention). Briefly remind him of what he should be doing and then busy yourself with another child who is working. As soon as Johnny picks up his pencil or looks as though he is turning to the assigned page, promptly reinforce this with a remark like, "I like the way you are ready to work. Do you have any questions?"

Developing Better Work Habits

The techniques we have discussed so far should prove helpful regardless of the type of behavior problem you are dealing with. The following suggestions are aimed more specifically at those children who have trouble sticking with tasks they consider difficult or uninteresting.

1. Make sure the child understands the assignment. When you have finished giving the class directions, you might go over and ask the child to explain to you just what he or she is to do.

2. If necessary, break the assignment down into smaller, less overwhelming units. For example, ask the student to start with only one row of math problems or answer only the first three social studies questions, then to raise his or her hand to let you know the work is done. This will allow you to check the student's work and praise effort.

After this bit of encouragement, give the student another short section to do, again briefly checking it when the work is completed. Your goal here is to ensure success, praise effort, and build some independence in work habits. After this student has consistently met with success, you can begin to gradually lengthen the amount of independent work you require.

3. Help the student set realistic short-term goals. Encourage him or her to construct and keep simple progress charts.

For instance, you might make a chart dividing the day into short units (15 to 20 minutes). You and your pupil put checks on the chart for each time period without a temper outburst or without wandering around the room.

When various milestones are reached, a brief note or phone call to the student's home will give parents a chance to congratulate the child for trying hard.

4. Use attainable, enforceable contingencies ("first . . ., then . . ." situations). Make participation in favored activities (e.g., drawing, playing games, time at interest centers) contingent upon "getting your work done first." No exceptions. Verbalize this often.

Phrase the contingencies positively, focusing on the behavior you want, rather than on the undesirable behavior—e.g., "As soon as you finish this assignment, you can draw," not "If you don't finish your work, you can't draw."

If the child you are working with has been particularly good, you might surprise her or him by providing a reward unexpectedly: "You did such a good job of sticking with that assignment that I'd like you to help me put up the bulletin board this afternoon."

5. When a student gets discouraged, provide reminders of other well-handled difficulties: "Remember the division work on Monday? You stuck with it, tried, and did fine."

Disruptive Behavior

What about the child who is behaving in a way that disrupts the whole class? We suggest the use of a time-out place.

The choice of an appropriate time-out place requires careful consideration. A time-out place should be as quiet and unstimulating as possible—a place where the student receives no attention and where there is virtually nothing to do. If you are lucky, a room supervised by an adult might be available. A coatroom is another possibility. If no other room is available, you can set up a corner of your own room as devoid of distracting sights and sounds as possible.

Time out should last for only five to 10 minutes. Time out that lasts longer becomes banishment and is less effective.

Students should know ahead of time that the purpose is to allow them to regain self-control. When you send children to time out, it is very important that (1) you tell them briefly why they are going—e.g., "Janice, you are yelling and disturbing others—time out!" and (2) you do not lecture or scold them. Calmly escort the child to the designated spot, without any arguing or justifying. When the time is up, simply direct the child to rejoin the class.

When disruptive behavior includes angry outbursts of yelling or hitting, the following strategies should be useful:

1. Discuss with the child alternative methods of dealing with anger. Have this discussion when the child is calm, not when he or she is frustrated and angry. The phrase "count to 10" is trite, but still can be an effective reminder to pause for a few seconds instead of giving in to angry feelings.

Let the child know that telling someone how you feel is also a good outlet. Making a real attempt to "ignore little things" is another way the child can try to deal with frustration.

When discussing these strategies, be concrete and specific, and try to give some true-to-life examples: "Suppose Joey walked by and knocked your book off your desk: What could you do?" "What if Ann poked you? What would you do?"

2. Intervene early. If you see a potentially explosive situation, get to the youngster quickly to help him or her regain control. Try using a firm arm around the shoulder and a quiet reminder that there are alternative ways of handling anger.

3. Deal with the child as calmly and matter-of-factly as possible. Help the student gain control through your own relaxed, in-control manner. Try to use your physical presence, too; standing next to the child is far more effective than talking across a room.

A Final Reminder

As we stated earlier, learning to react to children's problem behaviors in a calm, thoughtful, and above all consistent manner is hard work. It is important to remember that you are modifying not only the child's behavior pattern but also your own. This takes time. Behavior change occurs slowly, and progress is marked by many starts and stops.

After a definite improvement has occurred in a child's behavior, some regression is not unusual. If you anticipate this, you won't become disheartened when it occurs. Rather, review the rules with the child and continue your efforts, always remembering to enforce consequences, positive as well as negative. The consistent application of these techniques, coupled with your own knowledge and enthusiasm, will produce improved classroom behavior.

Class Struggle: Should Schools Permit Searching of Students for Weapons, Drugs?

Anne Mackay-Smith

Staff Reporter of The Wall Street Journal

Detroit high-school student Lynn Bittner says she was standing around with three of her friends outside school, waiting for their first class, when a policeman demanded their student ID cards. He herded them into the school security office, and without waiting for a woman security guard, stood them against the wall and frisked them.

"It was incredible. Thrown up against the wall like a criminal, when we hadn't done anything," Miss Bittner, 17 years old, says.

Students like Miss Bittner, who has since transferred to a Catholic school, dislike being subjected to searches. But not all searches are fruitless. Since the beginning of the year, special squads carrying metal detectors have found 59 guns and 69 knives and other weapons on Detroit students. Parents, concerned about their children's safety, generally support such efforts.

The situation in Detroit illustrates a dilemma faced by schools nationwide: how to protect students and the learning atmosphere without infringing on students' rights to be free of unreasonable searches. The issue is emotional. Proponents of the right to search note that when weapons are available, schoolyard scuffles have become matters of life and death.

DIFFERING VIEWS

"What's reasonable for someone standing on Main Street might be different from what's reasonable in school. We are dealing with children, and the state has the responsibility to protect them," says Allan J. Nodes, deputy attorney general in New Jersey.

But Barry S. Goodman says, "The real issue is whether students shed their rights when they enter school." The two are arguing a New Jersey suit now before the U.S. Supreme Court as to whether a staffer's search of a teen-ager's purse constituted illegal search.

Until now, the courts haven't been of much help in resolving the conflicts. Rulings in dozens of cases have been complex and contradictory. Many school officials are hoping that the Supreme Court will lay some ground rules. The court is expected to rule in the New Jersey case before its term ends in July.

The case started when a Piscataway High School teacher found a girl, identified in the suit only as T.L.O., smoking in the bathroom, and an assistant principal demanded a confession. When T.L.O. refused, he checked her purse for cigarettes. He removed the cigarettes and saw rolling papers, then turned the contents of the purse over and found marijuana. The student was convicted of possession of marijuana with an intent to distribute it, and her appeal of that conviction is before the Supreme Court.

ISSUES IN APPEAL

At issue are whether the assistant principal had a right to search the girl's purse and whether the evidence obtained that way should be admissible in court. Mr. Nodes argues that it is, and that there should be a less stringent standard for searches in schools than elsewhere. But Mr. Goodman believes the search violated the most lenient standard for searches because there wasn't any reason for it: Smoking was permissible in some areas of the school, so finding cigarettes wouldn't have proved the girl was smoking in the bathroom. The plain-

Reprinted by permission of *The Wall Street Journal,* May 30, 1984, p. 1, ©Dow Jones & Company, Inc. 1984. All Rights Reserved.

tiff argues that suppression of the evidence would deter such illegal searches in the future.

Increasingly, schools and some courts have tried to carve out a middle ground between giving schools full rights to search and the stricter "probable cause" standard for police officers, requiring that there be strong evidence to believe the person to be searched has committed a crime.

Search conflicts occur across the country. In Bridgeport, Conn., teachers are working to expand their right to search; teacher DeOla Jones Barfield says her interest was spurred by finding a high-school student carrying a gun in a gym bag. Nancy Demartra, a Louisville, Ky., fifth-grade teacher, says that there have been two shootings in city schools this spring and that teachers should have the right to search students and their property at any time.

But in the last two years, strip searches of students to find stolen money have prompted a spate of angry newspaper articles in Rockford, Ill., and two lawsuits in New York. Nationwide, dozens of suits have been filed questioning school searches.

KILLINGS IN BROOKLYN

The debate as to when to search becomes most emotional when violence breaks out. Two students at the Samuel J. Tilden High School in Brooklyn, N.Y., were knifed to death in incidents six weeks apart this spring, the second in full view of students streaming out of the building after classes. Tilden, which prides itself on its academics and its winning football team, exploded with pleas from teachers, parents and more than 100 students that metal detectors be used to search students at the school doors.

Two weeks after the second death, the issue was heatedly debated at a meeting of the Parent-Teachers Association in the school's auditorium. Stephen Dorf, a resources teacher at the school, dismissed the civil-liberties concerns. "The good kids have to suffer with the bad sometimes. Sometimes we have to pick the lesser of two evils," he said.

But others argued that mass searches would erode students' rights. "We will become the school that has our children pass through these portals and be presumed guilty. That is not the principle on which this society is founded," Agnes Green, president of the PTA, said. "I ask you to reconsider."

Mrs. Green says it took some agonizing thought to come to her position. She says she still worries about both physical danger to her 15-year-old son, and the scarring effect of close association with violence. As PTA president, she received early notification of the second stabbing, and she vividly recalls her son's reaction when she told him the victim had died.

"He said, 'You know, I figured as much, because of the way the blood was coming out of her body, and the way she fell to the sidewalk,'" Mrs. Green recounts. "Within a few weeks, my son has seen more death and destruction than I have in my whole life."

Her position against metal detectors seems to have triumphed. While the school has set up a task force to discuss ways to improve school security, metal detectors aren't likely to be one of them, the school's assistant principal says.

Parents of some third graders at P.S. 282 in Brooklyn sued school officials over a strip-search. They charge that the officials, who were looking for about $50 stolen from a substitute teacher's purse, stripped most of the class in spite of the fact that most of the stolen money was found on the first child they examined. Among the charges is that "all students who had been searched . . . were forced to stay outside the search chamber and listen to their classmates crying as they were being searched."

Two of the officials, a school guidance counselor and the district superintendent, filed a response in U.S. District Court in New York denying the allegations. Counsel for the school principal declined to comment on the charges, but said he believed the suit would be settled within a few weeks.

Richard Emery, a lawyer for the New York Civil Liberties Union representing the plaintiffs, says that the effects of such a search are lasting, and that all searches are unsettling. "Very few of us can maintain a feeling of innocence and confidence when official authorities are searching, or even inspecting," he says. "The best people at maintaining a composed demeanor are usually the worst criminals."

J.L. Skelton, a senior at Detroit's Finney High School, has a scar at the side of his nose from a knife thrust during a school argument two years ago. Nevertheless, he agrees that the increased presence of security guards with metal detectors has a chilling effect.

"You could be walking by, and you don't have nothing, but you shut up, boom," he says. "I've seen plenty of students walking by using regular slang language, and they numb up. Go straight as a board."

GUARDS' PROCEDURE

Security guards say they search only when they have "reasonable cause" to believe a student may be carrying a forbidden item. Causes might include smelling marijuana on a passing student, or a report, usually from another student, that someone is carrying a weapon.

But some students say that searches are less reasonable and more random than that implies, and they are aware that some are legally questionable. Suzanne Koten, a teacher at Detroit's Denby High School, says discussion erupted in her class on Basic Law when they began discussing search and seizure practices. "At that time, the police were in the building all the time, and the kids wanted to know why the police could just search them at any time," she recalls. "They feel that it's an infringement on their privacy to just be stopped like that. I do, too."

But students say weapons are common in Detroit schools. Finney senior Skelton says, "I know plenty of girls that have things on them—knives, box cutters, razors, scissors, nail files. As for the guys, some of them could sneak a .22 in here, any type of gun, if they really wanted to. I don't see how they could prevent it, unless you put bars on every door and every window."

Hiram McGee, a security guard in Philip Murray Wright High School, says he found a student making a gun stock for a rifle in woodshop class. He checked his locker and found all the other parts except the firing mechanism ready for assembly.

SELF-DEFENSE ARGUMENT

For students who live in dangerous areas, carrying weapons for self-defense is a way of life. In Detroit, some parents gave their children knives last fall after a number of girls were attacked and raped on their way to school.

Others say weapons are a status symbol, while Taris Jackson, a 17-year-old Denby senior, adds, "The reason some of them bring them is to protect things they've got on. Two-hundred-dollar chains, and $60, $70 track shoes. I said, why would you bring something that people would kill you to get, and they say they got to look sweet."

Lawrence Boyer, sharp-eyed after nine years as a guard in Detroit schools, has taken knives, drugs, and other contraband from dozens of students so far this year. At 10 paces, he spots a three-inch, cylindrical leather case, half-concealed in the hand of one of a stream of passing students. It holds a canister of Mace.

"You know you're not supposed to have this in school?" he asks.

"I need that to get home!" the student exclaims. "There's two German Shepherds on my block. Loose," he emphasizes.

Nevertheless, Mr. Boyer impounds the Mace. In one hour and a half on duty, he tells a dozen students to take off their hats and asks eight others why they are in the hall during a class period. One student, who was trying to sneak back into the building after a trip outside, is taken to the assistant principal's office for a search. He is subsequently suspended for carrying 10 marijuana cigarettes.

Most teachers and principals believe that the threat of violence outweighs erosion of student rights. Arthur Jefferson, Detroit's superintendent of schools, says he believes rights violations are kept to a minimum. But if they do occur, he says, "I'm not apologizing for that." He adds, "The stakes are too high, in our schools and in our community."

Paul Richards agrees. He is principal of Detroit's Philip Murray Wright High School, a normally quiet school that exploded in violence on April 19 that ended in a threat to Mr. Richards's life. It came from two brothers who were fighting with a former student and chased him into the school. There, at least 10 of the former student's friends joined the fray, wielding a hammer, nightsticks and umbrellas. The former student fled, guards captured one of the brothers, and the other was beaten unconscious. "When I got there, he was motionless, lying in a pool of blood," Mr. McGee, the security guard, says.

The violence may continue. "Supposedly, they have a contract out on me. I've been looking over my shoulder for the last few days, because you never know," Mr. Richards says. "I think if they do it, it'll be a shooting. Because there are so many guns around."

Not surprisingly, Mr. Richards is a proponent of strong measures to keep the schools safe. "Until we get serious about a few things, like handgun control, metal detectors don't bother me. If it keeps weapons out of the school, I'm for it," he says. "You have folks saying it's like a prison. But hell, if it saves one life, to me it'd be worth it."

SCHOOL REFORM

COERCION IN THE CLASSROOM WON'T WORK

Learning by doing and sensitivity to feelings are the keys to academic progress

Benjamin Spock, M.D.

Benjamin Spock is a pediatrician, a child psychologist, a medical school teacher, and a political activist. At the present time, he is working on a fourth revision of Baby and Child Care.

THE RECENTLY RELEASED report of the National Commission on Excellence in Education has, to my mind, little to do with excellence. Its recommendations—more homework, and longer school days and longer school years—could better be labeled "A Plea for More Coercion in the Schools." Yet a chief reason why so many schools achieve so little education of value is that they already rely too much on coercion. They ask students to read a text or listen to the teacher and then to regurgitate what they've read or been told, or risk a failing grade.

Attitudes about the rearing and education of children vary between two extremes. One, which might be labeled "authoritarian" or "coercive," rests on an assumption that children are by nature irresponsible and lazy, and will do their schoolwork only if they are penalized for a poor performance.

The opposite view might be labeled "progressive" or "democratic." It rests on the assumption that children who are brought up with love, trust, and clear but kind leadership are eager to grow up and be like their parents, eager to explore, learn, master skills, and take on responsibility; they need guidance but not sternness or punishment.

Teachers and parents who incline toward the authoritarian attitude are scornful of "frills." They consider lecturing, memorization, recitation, and grading to be the basics, as they remember them from their own school days. They believe in withholding promotion from

From *The Atlantic,* April 1984, pp. 28-30, 32, 34-35. Copyright ©1984 Benjamin Spock. Reprinted by permission of Lescher & Lescher, Ltd. New York.

children who have not satisfactorily completed the year's work in all subjects, despite the evidence that when children are made to repeat a grade, they do not do as well in the following years as similar children who were promoted. To authoritarians, education is not a means to help each child to mature but a series of hurdles over which everyone, of no matter what capability, must jump. A policy of withholding promotion means ignoring the fundamental and complex question of why the children failed and what needs to be done to correct that problem.

Children whose measurable intelligence falls moderately below the class average may be unable to keep up with their classmates, though this need not be a problem when a resourceful teacher individualizes work so that the child can be kept productively busy, happy, and learning. Specific learning disabilities, such as the fairly common handicap in visual memory that keeps a child confused between *god* and *dog*, *was* and *saw*, can powerfully discourage *all* schoolwork. These disabilities call for special teaching or tutoring methods.

Many kinds of emotional problems interfere with learning, such as fear of failure, preoccupation with family crises, and neglect by parents. Laziness is often blamed—but I've never seen such a case. Children are born curious and eager to achieve. When these qualities are missing, investigation shows, some hurtful influence destroyed them.

Poor teachers are ready to condemn pupils who don't fall in line, without trying to find motivation in them. Teachers both of Winston Churchill and of Charles Darwin complained to the boys' parents that they were hopelessly poor students and would never amount to anything.

The Commission on Excellence has recommended more homework, though the amount of conventional, repetitive homework has been found to make little difference in pupils' mastery of subjects or in their final grades.

I'd make a sharp distinction between that kind of homework on the one hand and library research or a scientific project that the student selects and carries out on the other. The second kind of work fosters self-reliance in thinking and acting, which in turn becomes part of the student's character. With the right teaching methods, this quality can be developed not only outside the classroom but also in it.

Now for grading. A study that measured the relationship between grades achieved in medical school and the level of competency of general practitioners a dozen years after graduation found, amazingly, no correlation whatever between grades and competency. Those who were practicing superior medicine came equally from the top, middle, and bottom of their medical-school classes. And those practicing poor medicine also came equally from the top, middle, and bottom.

I believe that grading is an abomination. It misdirects the efforts of students into memorizing for recitations and tests. It misleads teachers into thinking that the grades they give represent something gained from the course. What grades do measure, I'd say, is the ability to memorize, freedom from learning disabilities, and conformity in thinking, which is not a valuable trait, to my mind.

The commission has recommended longer school days and years. That might make sense if evidence were available that students felt challenged by their present curricula. But in a majority of schools, particularly high schools, the students are bored because they feel so little connection between their interests and their schoolwork.

If the recommendations of the commission are carried out without spending the vast amount of money and undertaking the vast amount of training necessary to improve the quality of teaching, the only result will be greater boredom and more dropouts.

MEDICAL EDUCATION provides a useful focus for evaluating teaching methods because we can find out whether medical curricula are creating the kinds of physicians that people and hospitals feel they need—in contrast, for example, to liberal-arts programs, whose aims are more difficult to assess.

Competence in medicine cannot be achieved by memorizing lectures or textbooks, though this has a role. Students can learn anatomy in a usable way only by dissecting cadavers. They can learn to diagnose and treat disease only by working with sick patients—fitting together histories, physical examinations, and laboratory tests. Then they must think through the various alternative diagnoses, under the supervision of an instructor. They must do this again and again, in school and during internship and residency training. This is the learning by doing that John Dewey, philosopher, educator, and inspirer of the "progressive-education" movement, advocated as the key element in his conception of usable, lasting education.

In the 1920s, dissatisfaction with physicians was widespread. When asked in public-opinion polls how they rated their doctors, many people gave answers like "He seems to know what he is doing. But I can't talk with him about the things that are really bothering me. He looks embarrassed or he asks me a question about something else."

This discomfort with personal or psychosomatic matters, though these account for more than half the problems for which people consult a physician, was traceable to the rapid development of the basic sciences of medicine—physiology, biochemistry, microbiology, and particularly pathology (the study of diseased tissues)—in the last half of the nineteenth century. The German pathologists, who were leading the crusade for scientific medicine, scorned anything that seemed to them inexact, unprovable, or mushy. Medical schools everywhere fell in line.

In the 1930s, in response to criticism, medical schools had to call on the members of their often meager departments of psychiatry to teach not only about mental and psychosomatic illnesses but also about human relations and the doctor–patient relationship.

But the psychiatrists found it tough going. Students who had spent two years studying only the basic sciences, without ever seeing a patient, and had been taught by instructors who had chosen careers in these impersonal fields of medicine, had become so desensitized that it was difficult to get them to recognize the feelings of their patients—or the feelings in themselves.

The most effective method I saw for preventing this desensitization was at Case Western Reserve Medical School, where I taught for twelve years. Each student was assigned to one family, from the beginning of the first year, to follow a mother during the last trimester of her pregnancy, stay with her throughout her labor and delivery, and then serve primarily as a pediatrician (in training) for the baby. The students' sense of responsibility kept them keenly alert, hastened their learning, and intensified their sensitivities.

SOME ACADEMIC teachers in high school are snobbish about "practical" subjects like driver training, typing, electronics, and human relations. (Universities are even more prejudiced against such practical courses.) This attitude is based on the belief that the head is the only worthy part of the body, that intellectual achievement is the only truly admirable kind, and that practical subjects pollute the academic atmosphere. This view ignores the most important aspects of human existence and the fact that the complexity of technology is rapidly erasing the old distinctions between mental and manual work.

A sad fact is that the liberal-arts departments (literature, history, anthropology, sociology, psychology, economics), which used to dominate the universities, are being undervalued as students demand more and more of the courses that appear promising to them, in technology and in business administration. But, as the working world becomes more complex, more specialized, the need for teaching the humanities increases, chiefly to keep students from losing their awareness that they are flesh and blood and must get along with other similar creatures.

Moreover, the humanities, in the broadest sense, keep students from burrowing prematurely into their future specialties and closing off all other avenues of inquiry, as happens, for example, when admission to medical school is determined primarily on the basis of grades in the pre-medical subjects. The eager beavers take as many of these science courses as the undergraduate college will allow and shun the humanities as a waste of time. Thus, some students enter medicine literal-minded, uninformed about the world, and insensitive.

Excessive, early specialization in one's education may also lead to a dead end. Modern high-technology industries are staffed mainly by engineers. But when higher-level administrative positions have to be filled, those jobs are often offered to candidates with backgrounds in law or finance, because the engineers can't see beyond the engineering.

Breadth in education helps a worker to see the faults and limitations in the way he does things and to conceive of improvements, to see the connections between his particular job and the ones related to it laterally and vertically, to understand the feelings and insecurities of fellow workers and clients—so that in dealing with others he can bring out the best in them.

The present distinctions in education between practical or technical subjects, the sciences, and the humanities are outmoded and should be reduced to the minimum. All high school students—even those firmly intending to study and work at computers or dress design—should be seduced, by inspired teaching methods, into studying the sciences and humanities that have a bearing on their chosen fields. And students who are bound for college—or are already there—should not be dissuaded from taking some courses in practical fields.

All students by the time they leave high school (or technical school) should have learned, I believe, something about the principles of mathematics, physics, and chemistry; the way our bodies work; why we behave as we do in our communities, in our families, and as individuals, and why we need to be ethical; the past, through history and literature; how to express ideas through speech and writing; and the practice of at least one art (such as dramatics, music, painting, sculpture, ceramics), so that they can feel the excitement of creation and gain some respect for the arts in general. In addition, I think schools should be prepared to give training in all technical skills.

Obviously, the depth of the teaching will depend greatly on the capabilities and motivation of the students as well as on the skills of the teachers. But even when courses are relatively brief and simple, they should not be in the traditional survey-lecture form but should involve the students in activities and projects that demand their participation and leave a lasting impression.

As for specific educational methods, John Dewey emphasized learning by doing (rather than by being told and memorizing). He meant that when you are confronted by a new learning situation in which you yourself must find the way to accomplish the task, the learning goes deep because it involves a sense of responsibility, at least a touch of anxiety and perhaps excitement, weighing alternatives, and activity of some kind—going to the library, for example, or interviewing a person, or visiting an industry. You may give or write a report. Each step is engraved on your consciousness; it gives you a sense of accomplishment or frustration. This process of groping and acting is very different from listening—or not listening—to a teacher talk.

Students in an elementary school class can learn arithmetic by acting as salesclerks in the school store. They can focus on some aspect of health by making scrapbooks of clippings from newspapers and magazines. Junior high and high school students can discuss ways in which an actual community problem might be solved, or choose and organize an educational expedition—to an industry, a hospital, a police station, a court, or a convalescent home—talking to the people there, taking notes, discussing and writing up reports. Students can think up and carry out experiments in science. These are examples not only of learning by doing but also of taking the initiative and accepting responsibility for work.

The teacher doesn't sit by but enters the discussion, asks questions that have to be considered, makes suggestions, and acts as the presiding officer, though as far as possible he leaves the initiative and the decisions to the group members—even when they seem to be making mistakes. The teacher must keep order, not by being overbearing but by creating an atmosphere of mutual respect. A productive atmosphere does not require that pupils all sit docilely at their desks. They can be allowed to move about and talk, when necessary for their projects, as long as they don't disturb others.

John Dewey also emphasized the value, in elementary and secondary school, of linking several of the topics to be taught each year to some central project or theme that naturally appeals to children and inspires their learning. A simple example at the third-grade level would be native Americans. A class can use for readers books on native Americans, study nature as they did, discuss in social studies how and where they lived.

They can cooperatively paint a mural or build a model of a native American village. They can select classmates who are more advanced readers to go to the library for more information.

The project method works particularly well to stimulate pupils whose skills or enthusiasm is below average, since it allows the teacher to ask from each child a contribution appropriate to his capability.

Another way to capture the interest of students is to start where their readiness is—rather than where the textbook happens to start. College textbooks on psychology, like the one I had to read, begin with definitions of consciousness, illusions, and hallucination, and go on to the history of the subject, next to a diagram of a neuron, and then to the nervous system of a single-celled paramecium. The human being is at the back end of the book. All this seems logical, even obligatory, to the professor. But to the student it is boring, and it kills interest in the subject. The instructor might start the introductory course with a book (maybe a novel) and classroom discussions focused on the interests, problems, worries, mental diseases, sex life, concepts of marriage, causes of divorce, career motivations, of young women and men. If the students get involved and curious, they may want to get back to definitions, history, and the paramecium.

Elementary school pupils are fascinated with nature, computers, space exploration, the power of the atom, cartoon characters, far more than they are with abstract numbers and the namby-pamby adventures of the children in traditional readers. The smart teacher takes advantage of these preoccupations to motivate reading, writing, math, and social studies. A class of black children, deprived by poverty, were slow to warm up to reading. But they caught fire when the teacher told them—and then encouraged them to read—about heroic slaves who had defied the law in order to become literate.

I remember an imaginative high school teacher whose pupils were from the most deprived, crime-infested part of town. She encouraged them to write themes, a task that is often distasteful or impossible for such students, by telling them they could write about the worst experiences they had ever had or had heard about, and could use the vilest language. Soon all the members were writing sordid stories. The teacher's comments were predominantly positive and focused on originality, ability to portray character, and so forth. Spelling, punctuation, and neatness were not mentioned. After weeks of telling dirty stories, the students began to branch out into other topics, which they found could also be fun to write about. And after a couple of months, the teacher started calling attention to the values of grammar and spelling.

Progressive educators emphasize that children learn by feeling as much as they learn by doing and by thinking. This is clear in the dramatic play of children at home or in a good nursery school. A child will try to overcome the fear she experienced in the doctor's office—and the shame of having been afraid—by pretending to be a doctor to a doll and jabbing it with a needle. She will digest the scoldings she has received from her parents—and will learn to be a parent—by playing "house" and dealing out similar scoldings to a doll or to a smaller child.

All students in professional schools—law, divinity, engineering, education—should study the kinds of interpersonal problems that seem characteristic of their chosen occupations. High school students need to understand better through discussions in class—with the guidance of mature teachers of English, history, sociology, psychology—the tensions they experience, or will experience, with one another, with their parents, with employers. Elementary school pupils can be helped to understand their quarrels. Even the most highly trained experts will prove ineffective if they can't get along with others.

Other permanent qualities of character that schools should try to develop are creativity or originality, so that people can imagine better and more beautiful ways to do things; initiative, so that they can get started on solving problems without waiting to be prodded; responsibility, so that they can be counted on to do the right thing whether or not someone is watching.

These qualities cannot be inculcated by lecturing or preaching or teaching mottoes. (Young children who have been taught to recite the Pledge of Allegiance or the Lord's Prayer every day rarely have the vaguest idea what they mean.) These qualities will be absorbed to a degree through identifying with parents and teachers whom children love and respect. But they can become firm aspects of character only through being deliberately and consistently encouraged (by parents and by teachers), and by being practiced by children—hour by hour, day by day, year by year—not in special exercises but as part of all their activities.

I'd like to summarize an experiment done many years ago that dramatically brings out this point. It was designed to show the difference between imposed, authoritarian discipline and inner discipline fostered by responsibility and democratic leadership.

An after-school activity program for boys ten or twelve years old was set up by psychologists who played the role of the authoritarian or the democratic leader. The authoritarian leader announced that the purpose of the club was for each boy to build a single piece of furniture, such as a chair-side table. He told the boys exactly how to proceed at every step and he kept strict order. The democratic leader explained that the club belonged to the boys, and that they should decide what to make. The boys held lengthy discussions about the possibilities, with the leader helping them to discard totally impractical suggestions (by asking questions), and they reached their own consensus. When they finally decided on building birdhouses, he guided them in answering such questions as what tools would be necessary and how they could be secured, what size and style of birdhouses should be built, how much lumber would be needed, where the lumber could be found and which members of the group were to get it, and what would be the sequence of the steps to be taken.

As you may imagine, building by the democratic method took *much* longer. But when the leader went out of the room, the work went on almost as efficiently as it had gone on when he was there, because the boys felt the project was theirs. They knew the next steps, they had been trusted with responsibility, and they had been shown respect. By contrast, when the authoritarian leader left the room, the boys began to horse around, pick on the timid members, and abuse their projects. Plainly, they did not feel that these were really theirs, and they expressed their pent-up resentment against the bossiness of the leader.

A third style of discipline was also included in the experiment. It was labeled *laissez faire*, let them do what they want. The leader stayed in the room and answered questions but offered no leadership at all. No project was ever developed, no work was done. The more mature members tried every once in a while to get the group to organize, but their leadership was not strong enough to control the anarchy of the least mature ones. The nonleading adult proved to be, if anything, a disturbing factor. Things were a little more calm when he was out of the room than when he was in. The implications seem obvious. Progressive education and learning by experience in the school and wise parenting at home do not require that teachers and parents sit by and leave children leaderless. Good democratic leadership may be less obvious than authoritarian leadership, but it is no less real or constant, and it demands more skill and effort.

True excellence in education has little to do with the quantitative recommendations of the commission. It requires teachers who challenge students of var ious capabilities; it requires stimulating projects, learning by doing, and the con ferral of responsibility; it requires relat ing classroom subjects to the students lives and feelings.

Excellence means selecting matur candidates for teacher training. It mean giving teachers the same respect teach ers should give children.

There's Only One True Technique for Good Discipline

Susan Ohanian

Susan Ohanian, a contributing editor for Learning, *is a language arts teacher at W.K. Doyle Middle School in Troy, N.Y.*

Four years after our middle school opened, teachers were still grumbling about the absence of an official discipline policy. Then, in the fifth year of our discontent, the school board adopted the Discipline Code—a holy writ of conduct distributed to teachers, parents and children. Teachers, of course, quickly discovered that official rules didn't help them achieve Authority in the Classroom, and the code was filed with other bureaucratic memorabilia.

Our discipline code did not leap full-blown out of the head of an administrator. It was developed by a committee of caring, concerned people—members of the school board, administrators, teachers, parents, students. They meant well; they tried hard. Authority, however, cannot come from a committee. A teacher's authority comes from her own savvy; it is a part of her style and cannot be distributed by fiat or handed out like chalk and rubber bands.

Borrowing from sociologist Max Weber's model, I see three kinds of authority operating in schools: traditional, legal and charismatic. Traditional authority relies on sacred custom. The teacher is always right: respect the office, if not the person. I was raised in that mode: "If you get hit at school, you'll get hit twice at home." The crumbling bulwark of most principals, traditional authority is already dead for most educators outside of military academies and some parochial schools. Nowadays parents are more likely to say, "Stop harassing my child!" And if a student is supended, she comes to the hearing with a lawyer.

With the second kind of authority, legal, committees at the local and state levels hold meetings, set policies, write guidelines. They issue documents to establish law and order in the schools. Principals rely heavily on the edicts spewn forth: "It is state mandated" is a response designed to end all discussion.

Loopholes in the blanket of legal authority have attracted some who aren't schoolteachers, but ed-biz whizzes. Flitting around the country offering teachers the holy grail of classroom management, these trend followers provide a psy-fi fix in the form of barter systems, contracts and the M & M exchange. Too often their programs lead to a student extortion racket: give me a verbal massage (or some candy or gold stars), and I won't drive you nuts.

The third kind of classroom authority, charismatic, is more elusive. This personal authority emanates not from a tradition or a legal document or a manipulative barter system, but from individual personality. It can survive change in reading programs, change in dress code standards, change in ethnic makeup of the student body; it can survive amidst chaos.

One does not find charisma in its pure form very often, nor are descriptions of charismatic authority usually very helpful to educational acolytes. The charismatic teacher holds her kids—in the style of the Ancient Mariner—by her glittering eye, not her handfuls of M & M's. The charismatic teacher knows in her bones when she is right. She doesn't have checklists to prove it. She expresses herself in the work she does, not in pretty slogans and colorful charts.

Several years ago, in *Schools Where Children Learn,* Joseph Featherstone told us that "there are no educational 'models' that can be mass produced." He pointed out that the systems approach is generally inappropriate to education, where most of the problems are human, not technical. "Learning is far more complex in its sequences and motives than the simple models constructed by behaviorists, which are drawn from observations of pigeons eating corn friskies . . ." How naive, then, to suppose that a teacher can take a course, learn a set of dialogues, and parrot a sequence of 63 positive statements to get children behaving correctly.

School administrators intone that "in order for learning to take place, there must be order in the classroom." That may be true, but I feel the emphasis is in the wrong place. In order that learning may take place, there should be something worth learning. Sad to say, an orderly classroom is too often considered accomplishment enough for teachers. One need not take home a book, prepare a lesson, or do anything beyond assign daily reading in class; teachers who never file disciplinary referrals make the administrative honor role.

The behaviorist ed-biz whiz gang has moved in and capitalized on this administrative yearning for order. Once the behaviorists had curriculum whipped into shape with their lists of objectives and criterion-referenced tests and brightly colored skill packets, discipline

Reprinted by special permission of LEARNING, The Magazine for Creative Teaching, August 1982. ©1982 by Education Today Company, 530 University Avenue, Palo Alto, California 94301.

became the obvious target. Now they offer their programs as a contract: You do this and the child will do that. Their classroom management schemes—the frozen waffles of junk pedagogy—are packaged in promises and contain few redeeming qualities. I know because I have recently read 15 books on discipline. They have chapter titles like The Ecology of Classroom Discipline, Contingency Contracting, Congruent Communication, Assertive Discipline, Operationally Defined Misbehavior and Minimal Intervention. The self-proclaimed educational experts who write them make a good buck dispensing wisdom and conducting training sessions to show teachers how to organize their classrooms. Training and control are neatly packaged and marketed under the name of "learning." Classroom management and teaching become the same thing in the eyes of the trainers, and, I fear, too often in the eyes of the teachers.

The pseudo-specialized vocabulary of child control adds to the confusion. I am uneasy when I read that a "response cost is defined as the removal of specified amounts of positive reinforcement after (contingent on) a behavior." I read that "punishment is the presentation of an environmental event, contingent on a behavior, which decreases the strength of that behavior," and my brain buzzes. I read of "compliance devices," "token economics," "deceleration targets," "alternate responses," "environmental alterations" and "terminal behavior," and I break out in a rash. I read about the teacher as "operant conditioner," "reinforcer," "facilitator" or "psychodynamicist," and I shout, "NO!" (I must confess, however, to a certain fascination with the expression "terminal behavior." If these guys could guarantee that the next time Selina snaps her gum at me it would be her terminal act, I might sign up for their course.)

The bold assertions amaze me! Without equivocation or hesitation, the behavior mod folks state that the child's "behavior extinguishes since it is no longer successful in obtaining the reinforcement (attention of the teacher) the child desires." Personally, I don't think I've ever extinguished a child's behavior. Furthermore, I agree with James Herndon that all the operant conditioning in the world won't change "simply a mean son-of-a-bitch, no matter how he got that way." Of course, the positive self-image people usually don't talk about the crazies or the 6-foot hoodlum with his fist in your face. Most of their classroom dramatizations deal with children passing notes and speaking without raising their hands.

None of the books I read on classroom management addressed the issue of teacher physical prowess. For inner-city kids at least, body language is more important than sweet words. I am not talking about physical strength or abuse; I have never used physical force on any of my students. I do know, however, that Jack respects me and accepts my authority because one day I put my 103-pound body on the line against him. Jack is a big, angry seventh grader who can't read. He has average intelligence, good auditory memory, and I don't know why he can't associate squiggles on paper with words. I know only that he is in a rage most of the time.

I discovered that mine was one of the few classes in which Jack was disruptive. He was allowed to be absolutely passive in other classes. As long as he didn't cause trouble, no one bothered him. In one class he was given an 80 for "good attitude." He got a 55 in my class because he would not try language experience stories and refused all tests I gave him. One day Jack was leaning back in his chair, needling another boy who was trying to work. The second boy pushed Jack on the chest, causing him to fall over backward onto the rug.

The probability of a blow being struck was about 99 percent. No way could Jack be put down like that in front of his peers without retaliating. I dashed over and shouted, "Jack, you had it coming! You were bothering him!" Jack quickly turned his anger on me. Towering over me, he actually began to huff himself up bigger. I leaned in very close and said, "He was wrong to touch you, but don't make it worse by touching him. You were wrong, too. Calm down."

Jack huffed a couple more times and tried to stare me down. I leaned even closer and stared back. Then he walked out of the room. I followed in a couple of minutes, and he was able to talk to me and eventually to the other boy. They shook hands. I consider this incident one of the most positive things that happened between us in the first five months of school. Jack found out that I wouldn't let him get out of control, that he didn't have to hit me, and that I wouldn't let him hit anyone else. I didn't stop Jack by saying, "You are angry." I stopped him with my voice and my body.

Not long after that confrontation, Jack and I began a different kind of interaction. One day he waited for all the other kids to take their spelling tests, then said, "I'm ready for mine." Five rhyming words. He got 100. He asked me to sign the paper and carried it off. We were in the process of doing winter stories. A bank of marvelous words and phrases—like *icy misery, frozen Arctic regions, shattered water pipes, windy walloper*—stretched the length of the hallway. I told Jack to choose five words, which I'd help him turn into a story. A couple of days later he heard me tell another student to go out in the hallway and find ten good winter words. "You only gave me five," Jack frowned. "I guess I better go get another five."

Jack wrote his stories, read them, typed them, read them again, and hung them in the hallway. To me, this was worth 100,000 gold stars or "I like the way Jack is sitting down" statements. I venture to guess that Jack would rather have those stories than a whole packet of M & M's.

I once heard Jack tell someone, "Ohanian's mean. She don't let you do nothin'." Sometimes in our daily notes he writes to me, "Get off my bak," signs his name and, in tiny letters, adds, "I am jus kidn." Jack's words are high praise. Jack is getting discipline; he is getting a bit of control over his own education; he is learning to do things because he has to.

I tell this long story because I think the teacher who gave Jack an 80 is wrong. He has given up on the kid, but for the sake of peace passes him on.

Only when teachers begin to hate themselves for their toughness are they beginning to grow and to make it as teachers, says Herbert Foster, author of *Ribbin', Jivin', and Playin' the Dozens: The Unrecognized Dilemma of Inner-City Schools*. Foster says that 2 or 3 percent move beyond the "discipline" phase to what he calls humanization. I suspect this latter phase is very similar to what I'm calling charismatic. Students can relax because they know the teacher is in charge physically, spiritually and intellectually. I don't think it is an overdramatization to refer to this physical-spiritual-intellectual power as grace, in Weber's sense of the word. The person who possesses it must constantly revalidate it in action. It is nontransferable: one doesn't get grace in an in-service course.

Most discipline schemes, euphemistically known as classroom management techniques, reek of manipulation. Honest emotion is forsaken in the name of control and quietude. Lee and Marlene Canter, authors of *Assertive Discipline*, would even have teachers plan ahead how ney will praise their students; they ecommend practicing with a col-eague the phrase, "I like the way you lid your work." Where is conscience, esponsibility, passion?

I see no need to become a different erson eight hours a day because I am teacher. I answer students with nyself—with my concern, joy, pleaure, anger—not with the gimmickry f 63 positive responses learned from manual. Because I regard my style as ny essence, I resent it when I tell a ositive reinforcer about a good classoom experience only to have her mile tolerantly and tell me, "That's ne of our techniques," as if what the hildren and I do so well together vere invented by a behavior mod uru and could best be learned hrough a copyrighted publication.

These social hustlers are promoting dangerous panacea. They say, Do it ecause it works. But if the positive troking is an end in itself, students nay never understand the joy that can ome from a job well done. In the vords of educator and author Edgar riedenberg, "Behavior modification s planned to mold desirable behavior lirectly, without rooting it in ethical urposes. It seeks to operate at ohlberg's lowest level of moral judgnent: behavior is good because it is ewarded. This is a serious denial of he humanity of the person subjected o it." Allegedly humanitarian people vho are aghast at the suggestion that lectric cattle prods would very uickly bring order to chaotic hallvays might ask themselves how they an blithely administer their kneeerk jolts of positive reinforcement. The positive approach folks—so lib in their upbeatness—are wrong oo when they insist that a teacher's ulnerability (what educator George Dennison calls the "teacher's moment f doubt and defeat") can be nanipulated or bargained away. My tudents know that they can make me ry. The greatest defense against ulnerability is not a prepackaged, ast-fix management system; it is cometence. Teachers must be intellecually, spiritually and physically ompetent—basically able to deal vith kids. If they aren't, then all the ehavior charts and checklists and nagpie jingles in the world will do ittle good.

My teaching career began in a Queens high school in the middle of a term. To say that my lasses were undisciplined is to put it nildly. LeRoy serenaded the class with trumpet mouthpiece every day. I could never quite catch him with it, and when accused of making disturbing noises, he put on his dramatic "Who, me?" act to further entertain the class. Two of my students were blind. They didn't like each other and did their best to punch each other out. I tried to keep them apart, but if one sensed the other was near, there would be a pitiful flailing of arms and cursing. I dragged myself home every night in utter defeat and tears.

On a most memorable occasion, three quarters of the class got into an ice-cream fight. Kids who couldn't remember to bring a pencil organized themselves to come to class with piles of ice-cream sandwiches, which they promptly spread over one another and the room. Although I knew a teacher was supposed to handle her own dirty linen, I made a desperate call to the department chairman. He gave me some valuable advice. He didn't tell me to punish the kids or to barter with them or to offer them contingency contracts. He told me to become a better teacher. He gave me specific suggestions on how to improve my curriculum. I have never forgotten that discipline "technique." It worked from the very start, and I use the suggestion to this day. When a kid is in trouble in my class, I don't change the way I smile—I alter his curriculum.

That department chairman invested a lot of time in me. He came to my class every Monday and watched how I applied a suggestion for getting across curriculum from the previous Monday's conference. Then he added an item to the list. Slowly, layer upon layer, he helped me to build mastery of the material I was teaching. He borrowed veteran teachers' notes for me, he taught demonstration lessons, he arranged for me to observe other teachers. He was certainly the administrative exception; too often, administrators tell us they have no time to teach demonstration lessons—that it is their job to administer, not to teach. They demand that teacher competence arrive on the first day of school, along with the room keys.

I suspect it is their unwillingness to get involved in teaching that leads administrators to support cosmetic behavior mod schemes so wholeheartedly. Such schemes keep kids out of the office, and that is all that matters. For in their offices, many administrators are busy writing perfect and impossible statements that they expect teachers to enforce. I discovered the truth of that observation—along with other, more heartening, revelations—during my first year of teaching. From on high came a fiat forbidding students to wear denim pants. Right outside the school, kids were fighting a racial gang war. In my classroom, they were threatening to throw one another out the third-story window. And I was supposed to worry about the cotton content of their trousers? You bet I was. From time to time the assistant principal in charge of discipline would stop me and remark that he'd noticed Jerome Wright wearing denim pants and that I hadn't reported it.

The enforcement of strict dress codes has lost some importance in recent years, but every once in a while a principal will come barreling into my room and insist that a kid remove his hat. It seems a terrible waste of administrative energy to me. I'd be more impressed if an administrator came in and asked what I am doing to teach Johnny to read.

I used to think a kid couldn't learn if he was feeling lousy about himself, but now I'm convinced he'll never feel better unless he develops some skills. Control and quiet may be the administrative way of judging teachers, but that does not mean we teachers should settle for such a paltry goal. We are not plumbers; we need to know more than how to locate the on and off spigots of a child's behavior. We need to be more than mere mechanics in the classroom—keepers of compliance devices and counters of environmental events. Educational bureaucrats and their fellow travelers insist that education must be objective and quantifiable. Maybe someday soon, when parents show up at open house, the teacher—or classroom-facilitator—will not need to be present at all. Parents will be able to get all they need to know from a file: Johnny's grade on the CAT, the Stanford, the whatever. They will also see a carefully kept record of how many times Johnny called out without raising his hand and how long it took to "extinguish" this behavior. Let us hope that when this day arrives, someone will have kept in the archives a videotape showing what Maria Montessori called "the first dawning of real discipline." She described this dawning as the moment "a child becomes keenly interested in a piece of work, showing it by the expression in his face, by his intense attention, by his perseverance in the same exercise. The child has set foot upon the road leading to discipline." The teacher doesn't need to say "I like the way Bill has settled down" on such an occasion.

Equality of Opportunity and American Education

We have witnessed one of the greatest struggles for equality before the law in all of human history. That struggle is well known to all those who practice the art of educating. More than thirty years ago, in 1954, the Supreme Court of the United States gave the first of what was to be a long chain of decisions affecting majority-minority relations in American schools. This struggle to achieve the full implementation of the American Constitutional promise to equality of opportunity in the field of education has been a triumphant testimony to the possibility of social justice under law. Future generations of Americans and other free peoples will forever look with awe at the struggle for civil rights in American schools from 1954 to the closing years of the present century. Rarely have free people asserted their rights under law as forcefully and affectively as the American people have on the question of equality of educational opportunity.

Determined to keep our Constitutional promises, and inspired by the knowledge that significant progress has been made on this issue, we face the closing years of this century with renewed hope and confidence. A vast body of legal research and opinion has evolved from the many federal court decisions on this issue since 1954. Furthermore, a large body of social science literature and many studies in social history have been produced regarding this matter. Problems of equity in the schools have been well documented, and the nation is developing increased sophistication and effectiveness in the development of solutions to these problems. The racial desegregation of American schools has been forcefully initiated all over the nation, and progress is continuing in majority-minority relations in the schools. Women's rights issues, affirmative action in employment and admission to professional schools, and student's rights issues are other categories of civil rights issues that have been dramatically advanced in the past several years based on the same Constitutional arguments and precedents established in the major school desegregation cases and the Civil Rights Act of 1964. Likewise, the rights of linguistic minorities to learn the English language in the public schools have been based on these same Constitutional principles. As a result, every American has benefited, either directly or indirectly, from these decisions.

Selections in this unit inform us of major equity issues and document or represent authentic sources of information concerning equality. Willis Hawley's essay on how to achieve quality integrated education deals with some of the major policy issues in implementing school desegregation processes. Gene Maeroff's article on magnet schools describes what has become the most popular alternativ to busing in efforts to achieve school desegregatio Beverly Coles considers the education of minority childre and youth from a black perspective. Fred Pincus discusse the principles of quality and equality, and the tension i volved in trying to implement both of these concepts i the national effort to improve educational developmen He contrasts the "new right" and the "centrist" perspe tives of the 1980s and explains how these perspective have affected the national equity agenda in educatio Finally, Martha McCarthy's essay on tuition tax credits an insightful historical and legal analysis of efforts to pr vide tuition tax credits for parents of children in privat schools. This relates directly to Constitutional questior involving the First Amendment rights of all American Freedom of religion and separation of church and stat freedom of speech and of the press are basic necessitie for any free people. Her analysis is relevant to the ma theme of this unit in that the whole issue of tuition ta credits relates directly to a significant cluster of equi issues in education.

The essays in this unit can be related to many of th major themes in undergraduate courses for preservic teachers. The profession of teaching is subject to signi cant pressures from many different kinds of equity intere groups in the United States. These articles relate not on to the general issue of equality of opportunity in the fiel of education, but to the specific issues of women's right the rights of linguistic minorities to assistance in learnin English, students' rights to due process, and affirmati action in school systems and personnel policies.

Looking Ahead: Challenge Questions

What are the Constitutional issues involved in scho desegregation cases?

What are magnet schools? How are they part of th remedy for racial segregation?

How far has the United States really progressed in th area of equality of opportunity in education?

What does it mean to desegregate a school system

What are the similarities and differences between th "new right" and "centrist" conservatives in educatior How is their national educational agenda different fro the liberal perspective?

What Constitutional issues are raised by proposals f tuition tax credits? How would such tuition tax credits a fect public schools, if at all?

What are fair criteria for protecting the rights of studen and teachers?

Unit 6

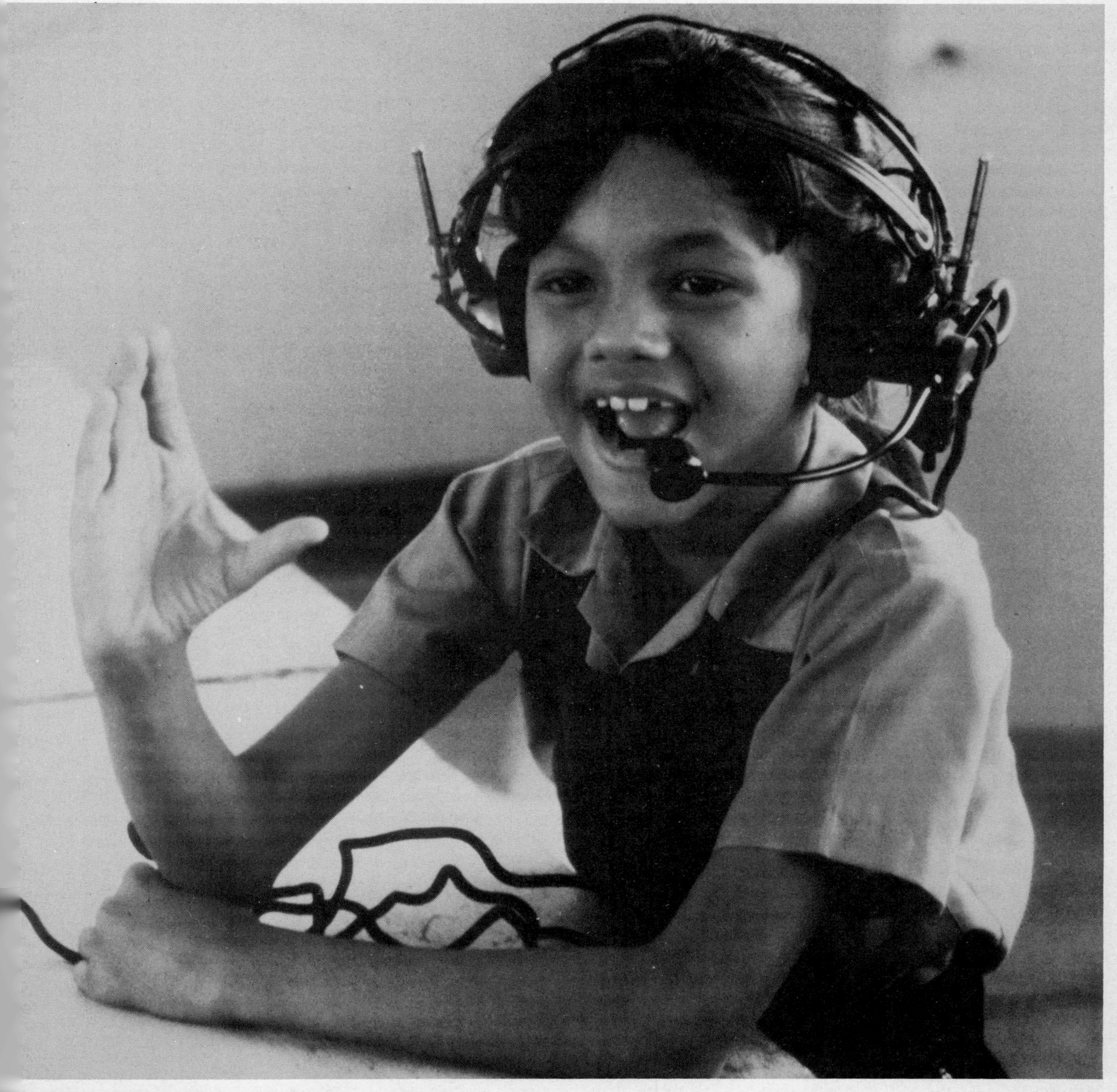

Achieving Quality Integrated Education — With or Without Federal Help

Willis D. Hawley

WILLIS D. HAWLEY is dean of the George Peabody College for Teachers and a professor of education and political science, Vanderbilt University, Nashville, Tenn. This article is a revised and abridged version of "Effective Educational Strategies for Desegregated Schools," which appeared in the Peabody Journal of Education, *July 1982. An earlier version was presented at the annual meeting of the American Educational Research Association, New York City, March 1982.*

Is school desegregation a policy whose time has come and gone? Probably not. Hundreds of school systems, including some of the largest in the U.S., are involved in the desegregation of racial and ethnic groups. This does not seem likely to change dramatically. Although the flow of new cases into the courts has slowed substantially, courts continue to find that districts must desegregate, and most efforts to achieve relief from the jurisdiction of the courts are unsuccessful.

But two important developments in the last two years suggest that desegregation will not be the same issue in the years to come. First, many education policy makers seem to have decided that high-quality education rather than equal educational opportunity should be the primary goal of public education. (I will resist the temptation to argue that other concerns have *always* been more important than equal educational opportunity.) Clearly, the future acceptance of desegregation by both whites and minorities will depend, much more than it has in the past, on the belief that excellence and equity are mutually reinforcing, rather than competing, goals. Second, the Reagan Administration has reduced both the federal pressure to desegregate and the federal support for desegregation efforts. The Administration opposes mandatory desegregation (i.e., busing) and has essentially repealed the Emergency School Aid Act (ESAA), the primary mechanism through which the federal government encouraged voluntary desegregation. ESAA funds also increased the probabilities that academic achievement would be enhanced when schools desegregated.[1]

Given these changes in attitudes and in federal policies, how can desegregation result in quality integrated education and what can the federal government do to promote this outcome? In trying to answer these questions, I will identify several strategies that school systems can use to increase the benefits of desegregation for students. These strategies do not depend on federal support for their efficacy. Then I will explore some low-cost, non-intrusive actions that the federal government can take to improve the quality of education in districts in the process of desegregation.

Overview

Students in desegregated school systems usually exhibit the full range of learning capabilities. Thus effective educational strategies for students in desegregated schools should be a combination of the strategies that are most effective for children who are handicapped, have limited or no English-speaking ability, require compensatory education, are academically gifted, and have no special needs. In other words, most strategies work for different types of children whether their schools are desegregated or not.

In some ways, of course, desegregation makes it more difficult to provide effective education. But before I discuss these problems and their possible solutions, let me call attention to the opportunities that desegregation can create to enhance the education of students. Desegregation can create possibilities for (and sometimes enforce) changes in curricula, classroom structures, instructional practices, and the behavior of teachers and administrators. Moreover, racially integrated schools have one certain advantage over racially isolated schools: They offer opportunities to learn from and about people of different races. In most cases, students in desegre[gated] schools will also have more interac[tion] with persons of different social back[grounds] than will students in school sys[tems] that have not been desegregated.

The evidence on the overall effects o[f] desegregation shows that in desegregate[d] schools the educational achievement o[f] minorities improves and the achievemen[t] of whites is not undermined.[2] More[over], race relations usually improve when schools take appropriate action to achiev[e] this end.[3] There is also evidence that de[segregation] in schools improves student[s'] prospects for future employment and in[creases] their chances of attending a deseg[regated] college.[4] These contributions o[f] desegregation to the education of youn[g] people are surprising, not only becaus[e] they fly in the face of popular notions bu[t] also because they have been achieve[d] amid considerable opposition, half-hear[ted] implementation, and a lack of share[d] knowledge about the process. What fo[l]lows is *not* a full prescription for effectiv[e] education. I intend to suggest some pra[c]tices that appear to be important in dese[g]regated schools *in addition* to those th[at] should provide all children with a hig[h] quality education.

People differ on their definition [of] "quality education." For purposes here, [I] define quality or effectiveness in terms [of] 1) academic achievement in mathemati[cs] and language arts and 2) tolerance an[d] understanding of people of different rac[es] and social backgrounds.

My conclusions are based primarily o[n] the findings of a recent study that r[e]viewed and synthesized 1) the conclusio[ns] of about 1,200 books, articles, papers, r[e]ports, and commentaries on the effects [of] desegregation;[5] 2) surveys of educators[;] and 3) the results of interviews with 1[3] local and national desegregation experts[.] Evidence from more recent research [is] also discussed.

Changes After Desegregation

When school systems desegregate, t[he] relationship of the community to [...]

Reprinted with permission of the author and *Phi Delta Kappan.* Copyright ©1983, Willis D. Hawley.

schools changes. Changes also occur in the context and circumstances in which instruction takes place and educational programs are presented. These alterations in the "conditions of schooling" require special attention if schools are to reap the benefits of otherwise productive educational practices and if the advantages of desegregation are to outweigh its costs. Most of the specific changes in the conditions of schooling that result from desegregation can be grouped into four general categories.

• *Diversity.* Because race is associated with socioeconomic status, interracial schools and classrooms tend to be more heterogeneous academically than their racially segregated counterparts. Traditional instructional strategies are poorly suited to settings in which students have so broad a range of educational needs.[8]

• *Potential conflict.* The possibility of interracial conflict in desegregated schools worries many parents.[9] Moreover, the key challenge of desegregation is to increase student interaction across racial lines so as to enhance race relations in schools and in the larger society.[10]

• *Discontinuity.* Both students and parents feel this change. Parents may feel that desegregated schools are not accessible, because they are far away and unfamiliar. Students may find themselves in environments in which the expectations they experience at home and in their neighborhoods are very different from those they experience in school.[11]

• *Change.* In desegregated schools, teachers, administrators, and students experience substantial change that simultaneously affects the social environment, the nature of instruction and curricula, and personal beliefs. For example, desegregation often requires teachers to take part in a broader range of educational programs, some of which may involve externally imposed requirements and paperwork. Such multidimensional change can greatly increase the workload and sometimes lead to a loss of self-confidence.

Diversity, conflict, discontinuity, and change characterize many schools. But schools that are desegregated by explicit social policy are more likely than others to face these problems and to be forced to resolve them all at once.

These challenges are also opportunities through which more effective education can be achieved. Some school systems have seized these opportunities; others have not. Those that have not seized these opportunities have had their effectiveness reduced and their progress impeded; those that have seized them have often become more effective than they were before desegregation.

Strategies of Response

The challenges posed by the diversity, conflict, discontinuity, and change that often characterize a desegregated school can be met by one or more of a dozen practices.

1. *Desegregate children as early as possible.* Differences in the achievement of students of different races are narrower in early grades, and racial prejudices are not yet ingrained. Thus possibilities for positive, equal interaction among races are greatest at early ages. Such interaction is critical to the mitigation of racial prejudice.[12] In addition, it appears that the positive effects of desegregation on the academic achievement of minorities are greatest in the early grades.[13]

2. *Employ instructional strategies that retain heterogeneous classes and work groups.* Such practices avoid resegregation and encourage teachers to retain high expectations for students of all groups. They also deemphasize competition and encourage student interaction. Examples of such practices are cooperative team learning,[14] the multi-ability classroom,[15] and peer tutoring.[16] Evidence of the effectiveness of such strategies on enhancing achievement and improving race relations is strong.[17] Similarly, there is growing evidence that pull-out strategies are ineffective.[18]

3. *Avoid tracking and other rigid forms of ability grouping.* Tracking usually leads to resegregation within schools and the denial of educational opportunity to low achievers. The increased diversity of students and programs in desegregated schools often leads to a proliferation of pull-out programs and special education assignments. Such assignments may have the effect of tracking and resegregation.[19] Without expertise in classroom management and knowledge of instructional strategies most appropriate for heterogeneous classes, most teachers will be frustrated by extreme student diversity, and the learning needs of students will not be met.[20] Clearly, some students will require special classes if their needs are to be met. But the possible misuse of special programs should be monitored closely.

4. *Retain a critical mass of the minority students in each school and classroom.* When students are in too small a minority, they may be excluded by the majority or withdraw of their own accord. A critical mass of 15% to 20% of students of a given race may help to avoid this problem in desegregated schools.[21] However, in multiracial or multiethnic situations, intergroup conflict tends to be highest when the two groups are about equal in size. Some evidence also suggests that this potential for conflict may be greatest when the students involved are of low socioeconomic status.[22]

5. *Employ minority teachers and counselors.* Minority teachers may act as models for minority children. Some weak but positive evidence exists that minority students do better when they have minority teachers.[23] There is also evidence that minority teachers are less likely to misassign and stereotype students and that they are more likely to relate effectively to minority parents.[24]

6. *Develop a comprehensive approach to human relations that involves substantial interracial contact.* Human relations should be an integral part of the curriculum both in its substance and in the way material is taught. Human relations programs that involve parents are more effective than those that do not,[25] and the most effective human relations programs are those that embody substantial interracial contact.[26] A multiethnic curriculum provides substantive material that may be more meaningful to minority students, and it can provide opportunities for discussing issues that are important to the students' relations with one another. But curricular change alone is not likely to be enough to improve human relations; what teachers do with that curriculum makes all the difference.[27]

7. *Develop interracial extracurricular activities.* Extracurricular activities can offer a chance for success to students whose academic achievement affords them little status within the school. Moreover, extracurricular activities can provide opportunities for interracial contact in cooperative, nonthreatening situations that often require teamwork.[28]

8. *Develop a rigorous but fair disciplinary program.* Developing a well-defined and widely understood code of student conduct and enforcing that code in consistent, firm, and equitable ways are essential elements of an effectively desegregated school. Such a program can help dispel parental anxiety,[29] minimize conflict,[30] and maximize learning.[31]

9. *Create smaller and more supportive learning environments.* Fostering continuity of instruction that avoids anonymity among students and creating a feeling of community that derives from shared values are effective ways to increase order and improve teachers' responses to student needs. Smaller schools and classrooms are not essential to this strategy, but they make it easier to employ flexible instructional strategies and to create manageable environments.[32]

10. *Involve parents directly in the education of their children.* In order to reduce the discontinuity between home and school environments, schools should engage parents directly in the education of their children. Studies on the importance of parental involvement in desegregated schools generally support this conclusion.[33]

11. *Once the desegregation plan is in effect, make an effort to maintain some stability in the educational experiences of*

the child. Such stability helps teachers focus on the educational needs of students, reduces parental anxiety, and gives students a greater sense of security.[34]

12. *Develop a comprehensive program for inservice training.* Staff training is always important, but it becomes even more important when large changes have taken place.[35]

Each of these several strategies responds to at least one of the four conditions of desegregated schooling. Some are positive responses to one or more of the conditions, but they tend to exacerbate one of the others. For example, avoiding tracking and rigid approaches to ability grouping is an appropriate way to respond to student diversity, but it makes it harder for teachers to manage their classrooms.

Implications for Federal Policy

With the demise of the Emergency School Aid Act, the federal government cannot exert the influence it once could on the educational effectiveness of desegregated schools. Through its enforcement powers, the Office for Civil Rights can insist that racial isolation in school systems that have engaged in *intentional* segregation be reduced. Thus it can affect the conditions under which desegregated schools operate. Moreover, housing and employment policies and actions of the Justice Department can affect desegregated schools, but these federal actions do not usually affect the learning process. Assuming that the federal role will no longer involve substantial expenditures or assertive action to require desegregation, let me suggest some general ways that the federal government could enhance the potential educational and social benefits of desegregation for elementary and secondary school students.

Collection and dissemination of information. A fair amount is known about how desegregated schools can become more effective, and many school systems have already implemented successful practices. This information needs to be collected, synthesized, and disseminated. Some steps in systematically collecting information have been taken, but much more needs to be done. The dissemination of research findings has not even reached the federally funded Desegregation Assistance Centers.[36] Among the more than 240 "Ideas That Work" that are publicized by the National Diffusion Network, only *one* deals directly with school desegregation. The National Institute of Education and various federal programs that provide technical assistance and that support professional development could become major vehicles for disseminating information about school desegregation.

Technical assistance and professional development. The largest single federal resource that could influence the instruction students receive in desegregated schools is the set of technical assistance and professional development programs authorized by Title IV of the Civil Rights Act. We now know a good deal more about what works in desegregated schools than we did just a few years ago. But the current "system" that provides assistance is decentralized and uneven in quality. Refocusing these programs — the Desegregation Assistance Centers, the training institutes, state education agencies, and direct discretionary grants to school systems — on improving the education children receive in desegregated schools could make a substantial difference.

Research and development. The federal effort in research and development (especially in the area of desegregation) has been less effective than it might be. Two of the most significant reasons for this failure are the shotgun approach to research funding and the absence of a research and development *system.*

For organizational and political reasons, federal research efforts have distributed available funds widely to address a host of topics. This has meant an inadequate effort in some specific areas, including research on effective desegregated schooling. The justifications for such a shotgun approach to research funding have nothing to do with the development of "usable knowledge." Given limited resources, the federal government should consider focusing attention on a limited number of questions. A good start would be to synthesize what is known and derive from this synthesis a research agenda. Some consensus is required about which issues of high-quality desegregated schooling can be most fruitfully resolved in the near future. Even an imperfect consensus about the issues to be studied would prove more profitable than the scatter-gun approach now in use.

The usual way in which individuals learn can be seen as a cycle that begins in the concrete experiences, dilemmas, or problems that an individual is motivated to consider. These experiential data become the object of reflection and analysis; then concepts and generalizations are derived from them. Next, the implications of these concepts and generalizations are tested in new situations, and the concrete outcomes of these tests provide new data with which to begin the cycle again.[37]

This everyday process is similar to the scientific method used in laboratory research. But the learning cycle for social science inquiry is usually truncated, and responsibility for performing various roles in the development of knowledge is diffused throughout institutions and groups within institutions, often with no explicit connections among them. For example, universities are often organized so that those who perform "basic research" are housed in different places, have different reward systems, and are given higher status than are those who conduct applied research or assist in policy development. The lower rewards for policy-related research and for program evaluation have meant that these functions have been increasingly assumed by contract research firms. These firms, though often technically sophisticated, have no incentives to pursue theory development. Moreover, the cost of field-based research is often so high that resources are unavailable either to test newly developed hypotheses or to replicate studies. Thus, as a society, we learn very slowly and largely without the benefit of well-developed and well-tested theories.

Within its various agencies and programs, the federal government has the elements of a learning cycle. We can think of basic or applied research leading to the development of products or programs that are demonstrated (tested) and then evaluated. The results of the evaluation are then reconsidered in the light of the theory explicit or implicit in the research stage of the process. Unfortunately for the development of knowledge, various stages in the process are the responsibility of agencies whose work is seldom coordinated.

The new Office of Educational Research and Improvement (OERI) in the Education Department (ED) — even after the Education Consolidation and Improvement Act of 1981 — encompasses all the components of the learning cycle (though the evaluation of federal programs rests elsewhere in ED). OERI could structure a research and development process, or, by funding external research consortia, it could link the different stages of the process. Such a strategy, however, would require extraordinary interorganizational cooperation, and the autonomy of some organizations would be reduced. Moreover, both universities and the contract research industry seem likely to resist such efforts.

Parental involvement. Direct involvement of parents in the education of their children seems to be of significant educational benefit. Moreover, parents may increase the sensitivity of educators to discriminatory practices.[38] Most school systems, however, have been ambivalent or even hostile to meaningful parental involvement, though some of the reluctance of educators may be due to a lack of knowledge about ways that parents can be constructively involved.

Federal policies should encourage or require, depending on the program, that districts receiving federal funds actively involve parents. There is no one best way to involve parents, but parent advisory councils at the district level are *not* one of the effective alternatives. Districts should be allowed to construct their own plans to involve parents, and they should be required to make their plans public before they implement them. But parents need to be involved more directly than district-level councils permit. Various technical assistance agencies should know the full range of alternative strategies for involving parents, and the National Institute of Education could publish a handbook on the subject.

Gertrude Stein might have said that a good school is a good school is a good school. But desegregated schools face special challenges in their quest for excellence. With or without federal assistance, desegregated schools can do a great deal to meet those challenges. However, the ability of local school systems to provide high-quality integrated education would surely be enhanced by the relatively inexpensive and non-intrusive federal actions suggested above.

There is no necessary trade-off between equity and high quality. Desegregation creates conditions that require changes in schools, in instruction, and in professional behavior. But the major problems posed by desegregation are not educational; they are political. Most objections that focus on the negative effects of desegregation on students do not hold water. Evidence from research and experience indicates that the difficulties can be overcome and that education in many desegregated districts has improved — especially for minority students.

But the public does not believe the best evidence we have. The reasons for this disbelief raise serious doubt about the possibility of providing high-quality education for all children. Desegregation is more than a challenge to the capacity of schools to provide high-quality education. It is a test of our national commitment to social mobility and to racial equality. So far, we have been doing less well on this test than our schoolchildren have a right to expect. The federal government could help us pass the test by accurately representing the story of the nation's progress to its people.

---

1. John E. Coulson and Anne H. MacQueen, *Emergency School Aid Act (ESAA) Evaluation: Overview of Findings from Supplemental Analyses* (Santa Monica, Calif.: System Development Corp., 1978).
2. Robert L. Crain and Rita E. Mahard, "Some Policy Implications of the Desegregation/Minority Achievement Literature," in Willis D. Hawley, ed., *Assessment of Current Knowledge About the Effectiveness of School Desegregation Strategies, Vol. V* (Nashville, Tenn.: Vanderbilt University, Institute for Public Policy Studies, Center for Education and Human Development Policy, April 1981).
3. Janet W. Schofield, "Desegregation School Practices and Student Race Relations Outcomes," in Hawley, ed., *Assessment of Current Knowledge . . . Vol. V;* and John B. McConahay, "Reducing Racial Prejudice in Desegregated Schools," in Willis D. Hawley, ed., *Effective School Desegregation: Equity, Quality, and Feasibility* (Beverly Hills, Calif.: Sage, 1981).
4. James M. McPartland and Jomills H. Braddock, "Going to College and Getting a Good Job," in Hawley, ed., *Effective School Desegregation. . . .*
5. Willis D. Hawley et al., *Strategies for Effective Desegregation: Lessons from Research* (Lexington, Mass.: Lexington Books, D.C. Heath, 1982).
6. William T. Trent, "Expert Opinion on School Desegregation: Findings from the Interviews," in Hawley, ed., *Assessment of Current Knowledge . . . Vol. V.*
7. Ibid.
8. Valerie Cook, Janet Eyler, and Leslie Ward, *Effective Strategies for Avoiding Within-School Resegregation* (Nashville, Tenn.: Vanderbilt University, Institute for Public Policy Studies, Education Policy Development Center for Desegregation, December 1981).
9. John B. McConahay and Willis D. Hawley, *Reactions to Busing in Louisville: Summary of Adult Opinions in 1976 and 1977* (Durham, N.C.: Duke University, Institute of Policy Sciences and Public Affairs, 1978).
10. McConahay, "Reducing Racial Prejudice. . . ."
11. William J. Tikunoff and José A. Vasquez-Faria, *Effective Instruction for Bilingual Schooling* (San Francisco: Far West Regional Laboratory for Educational Research and Development, 1982), pp. 22-24.
12. Schofield, "Desegregation School Practices. . . ."
13. Crain and Mahard, "Some Policy Implications. . . ."
14. Robert E. Slavin, "Cooperative Learning and Desegregation," in Hawley, ed., *Effective School Desegregation. . . .*
15. Elizabeth G. Cohen, "A Multi-Ability Approach to the Integrated Classroom," paper presented at the annual meeting of the American Psychological Association, Montreal, 1980.
16. Hawley et al., *Strategies for Effective Desegregation. . . .*
17. Robert E. Slavin, "Cooperative Learning in Teams: State of the Art," *Educational Psychologist*, vol. 15, 1980, pp. 93-111; and Shlomo Sharan, "Cooperative Learning in Small Groups: Research Methods and Effects on Achievement, Attitudes, and Ethnic Relations," *Review of Educational Research*, vol. 50, 1980, pp. 241-72.
18. H. Carl Haywood, "Compensatory Education," paper prepared for the National Institute of Education, Vanderbilt University, Peabody College for Teachers, January 1982; and Cook, Eyler, and Ward, *Effective Strategies for Avoiding. . . .*
19. Cook, Eyler, and Ward, *Effective Strategies for Avoiding. . .* ; Roger Mills and Miriam M. Bryan, *Testing . . . Grouping: The New Segregation in Southern Schools* (Atlanta: Southern Regional Council, 1976); and Joyce Epstein, "After the Bus Arrives: Resegregation in Desegregated Schools," paper presented at the annual meeting of the American Educational Research Association, Boston, 1980.
20. Carolyn M. Evertson, Julie P. Sanford, and Edmund T. Emmer, "Effects of Class Heterogeneity in Junior High School," *American Educational Research Journal*, vol. 18, 1981, pp. 219-32.
21. Hawley et al., *Strategies for Effective Desegregation. . . .*
22. Willis D. Hawley, "Effective Educational Strategies for Desegregated Schools," *Peabody Journal of Education*, July 1982, pp. 209-33.
23. Gary Bridge, Charles Judd, and Peter Moock, *The Determinants of Educational Outcomes: The Effects of Families, Peers, Teachers, and Schools* (New York: Teachers College Press, 1979).
24. Epstein, "After the Bus Arrives. . . ."
25. System Development Corporation, *Human Relations Study: Investigations of Effective Human Relations Strategies, Vol. 2* (Santa Monica, Calif.: System Development Corp., June 1980).
26. Schofield, "Desegregation School Practices. . . ."
27. Robert E. Slavin and Nancy Madden, "School Practices That Improve Race Relations," *American Educational Research Journal*, vol. 16, 1979, pp. 169-80.
28. Cook, Eyler, and Ward, *Effective Strategies for Avoiding. . . .*
29. Peter O. Peretti, "Effects of Teachers' Attitudes on Discipline Problems in Schools Recently Desegregated," *Education*, vol. 97, 1976, pp. 136-40.
30. Gary D. Gottfredson and Denise C. Daiger, *Disruption in 600 Schools* (Baltimore: Johns Hopkins University, Center for the Social Organization of Schools, Technical Report No. 289, 1979).
31. Stewart C. Purkey and Marshall S. Smith, "Effective Schools — A Review," *Elementary School Journal*, in press.
32. Hawley, "Effective Educational Strategies. . . ."
33. Coulson and MacQueen, *Emergency School Aid Act (ESAA) Evaluation. . .* ; and Jean B. Wellisch et al., *An In-Depth Study of Emergency School Aid Act (ESAA) Schools: 1974-1975* (Santa Monica, Calif.: System Development Corp., July 1976).
34. Purkey and Smith, "Effective Schools — A Review. . . ."
35. William J. Genova and Herbert J. Walberg, *A Practitioner's Guide for Achieving Student Integration in City High Schools* (Washington, D.C.: National Institute of Education, November 1980); and Mark A. Smylie and Willis D. Hawley, *Increasing the Effectiveness of Inservice Training for Desegregation: A Synthesis of Current Research* (Washington, D.C.: National Education Association, 1982).
36. Willis D. Hawley and Barry Schapira, *The Title IV Race Desegregation Technical Assistance Centers: Some Directions for Change* (Nashville, Tenn.: Vanderbilt University, Institute for Public Policy Studies, Center for Education and Human Development Policy, December 1981).
37. David A. Kolb, Irwin M. Ruben, and James M. McIntyre, *Organizational Psychology: An Experimental Approach* (Englewood Cliffs, N.J.: Prentice-Hall, 1971).
38. Jennifer Hochschild and Valerie Hadrick, *The Character and Effectiveness of Citizen Monitoring Groups in Implementing Civil Rights in Public Schools* (Washington, D.C.: National Institute of Education and the Office for Civil Rights, 1980).

Magnet Schools Used as Tool For Equality

Gene I. Maeroff

Throughout the long and turbulent history of school desegregation, one of the most inflammatory issues has been the requirement that families send their children to schools not of their choosing.

Thus a concept known as the "magnet" school, adopted on a limited scale during the 1970's, has had special appeal because it is based on voluntarism: The family selects the school that it wants. Schools in minority neighborhoods are made to offer some attraction powerful enough to bring about that choice, such as a special emphasis on music or science or basics.

Fresh attention is being focused on this concept because of an agreement by the Federal Government on Wednesday to allow the public school system in Bakersfield, Calif., to use a racial desegregation plan that avoids mandatory busing in favor of an exclusive reliance on the voluntary approach embodied in magnet schools. "This is a blueprint for desegregation," said William Bradford Reynolds, Assistant Attorney General for civil rights.

Can it be that magnet schools are a solution for achieving desegregation without any child being forced to attend a school against his will? Could these schools have avoided the rancor of the past?

There is wide agreement among educators that magnet schools are an effective and academically sound tool for promoting racial desegregation. The main question in light of the Bakersfield situation, though, is whether it is possible to bring about full desegregation—especially by inducing whites to attend schools in minority neighborhoods—using only magnet schools.

It remains to be seen whether there are enough possible different kinds of meaningful programs, especially at the elementary level, to make every school distinctive and attractive.

In Bakersfield, only four of the 32 schools are considered "racially isolated" and so a magnet program alone may desegregate them. But, contrary to Mr. Reynolds's assertion, the only reason some of the other schools meet desegregation guidelines is because of earlier reassignments that compel some junior high school students to leave their neighborhoods.

A report issued last fall by the United States Department of Education concluded that magnet schools have played an important role in desegregating many school districts but have always been part of an overall plan that invariably includes assigning many pupils to schools not necessarily of their choice. "Progress can be made with magnet schools, but the thing is that districts made the most progress using a combination of methods," said Rolf K. Blank, an author of the report.

The potential impact of a magnet school can be seen in the dilapidated Coney Island area at Mark Twain Junior High School, which until 1975 had an enrollment almost entirely of black and Hispanic children and one of the lowest achievement records in New York City. A suit in Federal court led to an order by Judge Jack Weinstein to desegregate the school. Today, it contains gifted and talented youngsters from throughout Community School District 21 in southern Brooklyn. It is 65 percent white; every student is there by choice, and there is not room for all who want to attend.

Mark Twain has had the highest reading score of the city's almost 300 junior high schools for most of the last half-dozen years, persuading such parents as Joseph Manichini Jr. to send his son to Mark Twain by bus even though there is a junior high school a block from their home.

From *The New York Times*, January 31, 1984, pp. C1, C6. Copyright ©1984 by The New York Times Company. Reprinted by permission.

"Our neighborhood school isn't of the quality of Mark Twain," said Mr. Manichini, who lives in the all-white Bensonhurst section, far from Mark Twain.

Just a few blocks from Mark Twain, however, Public School 288 is 1 percent white and Public School 329 is 2 percent white. Both are neighborhood schools with no attraction for outsiders.

In other words, magnet schools alone do not necessarily assure the desegregation of an entire school district.

In Pittsburgh, the school system began desegregating in 1979 using only magnet schools, but the Pennsylvania Human Relations Commission said that the plan did not bring enough desegregation. Pittsburgh has satisfied the commission by redesigning its plan to compel many students to attend schools outside their neighborhood.

Buffalo, too, has been hailed for its use of magnet schools. Even in Buffalo, however, the magnet schools account for only 13,000 of the system's 46,700 students and so mandatory assignments are made for many other pupils. "It's not practical to rely entirely on magnets for desegregation," said Kenneth Echols, an assistant superintendent in Buffalo. "You need a variety of other approaches."

But in recent years the resistance of families to having their children sent long distances to schools not of their choosing has prodded policy makers to reassess whether more of the burden for desegregation can be put on magnet schools.

"It is much more palatable to parents," said Robert Spillane, the school superintendent in Boston, where the desegregation plan that took effect in 1974 depended largely on compulsory reassignment of students, stirring resentments and contributing to white flight.

In keeping with this mood, a new group, the National Association of Magnet School Development, was formed four months ago by David K. Lerch to help school districts make wider use of magnet schools.

"Parents want neighborhood schools until they find a program they support and then they will send a child halfway across the county if the education program is attractive," said Mr. Lerch.

Educators maintain that for a magnet school to succeed it must be considered safe and it must offer an educational program that is perceived as being more desirable than would otherwise be available to the youngster. This has been demonstrated in Community School District 4 in the East Harlem section of Manhattan, which has created one of the country's most extensive networks of magnet schools. There are schools for students interested in performing arts, mathematics, environmental science and sports, as well as for potential dropouts.

"You have to do more than just put a 'magnet' label on a school or else it will be the same old lousy school and parents will recognize that," said Sy Fliegel, the deputy superintendent in District 4. "You have to appoint a creative principal, extra teachers, someone to recruit students and build an educational program based on quality. If the quality isn't any better than the regular schools, you will lose the children."

The State of Education for BLACK AMERICANS

Beverly P. Cole

Dr. Cole is Director of Education Programs, National Association for the Advancement of Colored People, New York City.

THE struggle to obtain equal access to quality education for black Americans has been long and arduous. Before the Civil War, every slave state had laws against blacks being educated. When the education of blacks was finally permitted, it was established on a separate and decidedly unequal basis. Not until 1954 (*Brown v. Board of Education*) did the Supreme Court hand down its historic decision that, in the field of education, the doctrine of separate but equal had no place. The court further declared that "It is doubtful that any child may reasonably be expected to succeed in life if he is denied the opportunity of education. Such an opportunity is a right which must be made available to all on equal turns."

In the 1980's, this right is being greatly undermined at the Federal level by anti-busing legislation, severe budget cuts in education and student assistance, proposals for tuition tax credit, the granting of tax-exempt status to schools that blatantly discriminate, the exemption of certain schools from civil rights regulations, the revision of affirmative action requirements, and the abdication to the states of the Federal government's role of monitoring and enforcing equal access to quality education.

On the local level, the right to a quality education is being denied by indifferent and insensitive teachers and administrators, by the lack of school accountability, low expectations of students' potential, pushing-out due to discriminatory disciplinary practices, inadequate equipment, poor curricular and career counseling, racially isolated schools, labeling, tracking, and discriminatory school financing policies.

In spite of these obstacles, blacks have made some progress educationally. There has been a significant increase in school enrollment, with 51% of blacks aged 25 or older graduating from high school. Today, more blacks stay in school longer and go on to college than they did a quarter of a century ago.

On the other hand, this progress has been inadequate to close the gap between black and white educational attainments and, indeed, is miniscule when compared to the overwhelming educational needs of blacks. In many ways, the progress can be described as one step forward and two steps backwards.

In evaluating the educational attainments of blacks, one must not only look at enrollment rates, but also at completion rates, as well as the quality of the educational experience.

- The dropout rate for blacks in high school is 28%, as compared to 17% for whites. Although blacks comprise 10% of the college population, whites are still twice as likely as blacks to be college graduates. Many attribute these statistics to an unresponsive school system.
- In most inner-city schools, where approximately 75% of black students are in attendance, achievement levels are usually two or more years behind the national norm.
- Studies have shown that black children tend to drop below grade level in elementary school and fall further behind as they get older, until, at age 16, at least 35% are below their modal grade.

Many theories have been offered to explain this disgrace; most built upon the notion of "blaming the victim." "Cultural deprivation," "the culture of poverty," the deficit model, "the disadvantaged"—all explained why the low socioeconomic student could not overcome the problems of poverty and social pathology and be expected to learn.

Nevertheless, the results of the "effective schools" research clearly demonstrate that children can be educated successfully, regardless of their family background. However, one of the main prerequisites is a belief and expectation on the part of the teacher and principal that this feat can be accomplished. Schools must demonstrate respect for the dignity of all students and be committed to the principle that all students are educable, regardless of their race or economic background.

Educators know what practices make schools effective, but in many cases are unwilling to implement them. We must hold schools accountable and stop entertaining excuses. As parents and interested citizens, we must also accept our fair share of the responsibility for motivating

Reprinted from *USA Today*, May 1983. Copyright 1983 by Society for the Advancement of Education.

students, supporting them, and serving as advocates to insure that they receive a quality education.

Improving the quality of education

NAACP branches across the nation are attempting to improve the deteriorating quality of education received by blacks by insisting upon:

- Equal access to quality integrated education at all levels from pre-school to professional schools.
- High expectations on the part of teachers in terms of achievement and behavior.
- Basis academic skills being taught and mastered at an early age (reading, mathematics, written and oral communications).
- A curriculum that develops skills of logic, analysis, problem-solving, and test-taking.
- Multi-cultural textbooks and materials.
- Teachers trained in multi-ethnic education/relations with more inner-city student teaching experiences.
- The utilization of a multi-method approach to evaluation and assessment.
- The elimination of tracking or homogeneous grouping.
- More teacher accountability.
- Counseling programs that encourage and advise students concerning varied career opportunities, the required courses, financial assistance, and other resources needed to pursue post-secondary education or other experiences consistent with their career goals and potential.
- Policies and procedures which insure racial fairness in classrooms and schools such as fair grading and evaluations, fair involvement in student activities, and fair discipline.
- Participation of parents and community leaders in the school process.
- Affirmative action in the hiring and promotion of black teachers and administrators to ensure that black students have appropriate role models.

These goals and objectives were chosen because of various reasons. Black children continue to be confined to separate and unequal schools; over 70% of black students are in predominantly minority schools. When desegregation occurs, research such as the seven-year study on The Effectiveness of School Desegregation produced by Vanderbilt University has shown that the achievement scores of minority students increase significantly and the achievement gains are likely to be maximized when desegregation is begun in the early grades. These findings notwithstanding, "neighborhood school proponents or anti-busing foes are accusing mandatory pupil assignments—for purposes of desegregation—of destroying public education and blighting entire communities across the country with its divisive impact." This is a myth and a gross exaggeration. Approximately 50% of schoolchildren are bused to school and, of this number, only three per cent are bused for purposes of desegregation. It is obvious that busing is not the real issue. The real issue is avoidance of quality integrated education.

Busing is not the goal, but only a means or technique for accomplishing the goal. If the purpose of education were only to teach selected academic subjects, then perhaps there would be no need for the desegregation of schools. All that would be needed is the enhancement of the present racially isolated schools. However, since the education institution is one of society's primary means of socialization, then it needs to teach our children to associate with different races and economic groups in order to exist compatably in this pluralistic country and the world. Integration is an essential component of a quality education for everyone—black, white, brown, yellow, and red. The anti-busing amendment recently passed by the Senate as well as local initiatives are threatening to prevent this ideal from ever becoming a reality.

As was alluded to earlier, teacher expectation is one of the most crucial determinants of student effort, motivation, and achievement. Rosenthal's famous Pygmalion experiment demonstrated how teacher expectation creates the self-fulfilling prophecy. If teachers expect that some children will fail, more than likely the children will fail. This occurs because the varied expectations, based often on race and income, are translated into different behavior. This treatment communicates to the students what behavior and achievement the teacher expects from them and affects their self-concepts, achievement motivation, and levels of aspiration.

The curriculum is another major source of concern. Students must be offered competent instruction in reading, writing, mathematics, and the process of logical thought. Beyond the minimum basic skills, the curriculum should be challenging in order to stimulate students to develop skills of logic, analysis, problem-solving, and test-taking—all of which they will need in this highly technological society. Stressing minimum basic skills is good only if the minimum does not become the maximum offered.

Secondly, our society is a pluralistic one, and the textbooks and materials must reflect this. Black children need to know about the contributions that their race has made to America. They can not learn to be proud of their heritage if all they encounter in school are the achievements of whites. In an effort to enhance the self-image and sense of worth of minority students, as well as to inform white youth, school officials should replace all biased and stereotyped schoolbooks and curriculum aids with materials which accurately reflect in text and illustrations the history and participation of blacks and other minorities.

In order for teachers to be responsive to the needs of minority children, they need more training in multi-cultural/multi-ethnic education and they need more inner-city student teaching experiences. Most teachers have very little knowledge of the poor's urban experiences. For this reason, teachers and administrators should be required to attend in-service training programs geared toward helping them come to terms with their own behavior and attitudes toward students from different cultural, ethnic, racial, and social backgrounds.

In addition, we must press for affirmative action in the hiring of black teachers and administrators to insure that black students have appropriate role models. In order to achieve this, educational systems must set goals and timetables in order to measure the effectiveness of recruitment, retention, and promotion efforts.

In terms of teacher accountability, administrators should expect more and demand more. New procedures need to be instituted for relieving the school system of those teachers who are indifferent, ineffective, and unwilling or unable to improve.

The I.Q. tests, the standardized aptitude tests, and the recent competency tests have been greatly misused in relation to black students and have caused great harm in terms of damaging self-images and life chances. Tests have been used for channeling black students into "slow tracks" and mentally retarded classes and for screening them out of higher education and jobs. For blacks, tests have meant exclusion, rather than inclusion into America's mainstream, and thus have been used to further stratify the society.

It is obvious that some type of assessment is needed, and testing for purposes of evaluation or diagnosis, when used in order to improve skills of the student, is both meaningful and desirable. A good assessment program utilizes a multi-method approach for evaluation. No one sole criterion should be used for such critical determinations as graduation, promotion, certification, college entrance, and hiring. Yet, the reality is that it is much easier to accept a standardized test score than to analyze systematically the strengths and weaknesses of students by multiple means. Therefore, accuracy has been sacrificed for expediency.

Culturally biased I.Q. tests are infamous for causing a disproportionate number of blacks to be placed into "special education" and mentally retarded classes. It would amaze you to know the number of outstanding black professionals who at one time in their early life were labeled in this manner.

Competency testing, which is being used by some 38 states, tends to place the burden of accountability solely on the students. This form of testing should be done at a stage where remedial action can be taken, and teachers as well as students should be held accountable in terms of which skills have been introduced and which skills have been mastered. In those school systems which use competency tests for purposes of promotion, students should be assigned to non-graded classes where they can advance according to their individual achievement and where the stigma of repeating a grade would be avoided.

"Tracking" or homogeneous grouping is synonymous with "trapping" at a very early age. This procedure can cause a child to view himself as being incompetent and consequently establish the self-fulfilling prophecy. Based on test scores, students are often placed into a "slow group" and kept there in the less rigorous dead-end curricula all the way through school, which often creates segregation within a desegregated school. No child is slow in everything. In a heterogeneous environment, there is opportunity for the strong to help and inspire the weak.

Another area that requires careful monitoring is guidance and counseling. The counseling is very limited in inner-city schools; often, a student will not see a counselor unless he is in trouble. It is important that when advice is given it is not based on false assumptions about presumed abilities and aspirations because of the student's racial or class identification. Counseling programs must be provided that will encourage and advise students concerning the required courses and available financial aid to attend college, post-secondary education, or other experiences consistent with their career goals and potential.

In terms of administrative practices, there is a need for the elimination of dehumanizing and exploitative practices for all students. Policies and procedures must be designed to insure racial fairness in classrooms and schools such as fair grading and evaluations, fair involvement in student activities, and fair discipline and suspension. It has been shown that, at the high school level, blacks are suspended three times as often as whites. While minority students are about 25% of the school population, they constitute about 40% of all suspended and expelled students. Furthermore, black students are suspended for longer periods of time. All schools need to examine carefully those conditions at the school which precipitate pushouts and dropouts.

Parental and community involvement are essential ingredients for quality education. Confidence in the school and support for its endeavors occur when parents believe that they have access to school personnel and have some influence over what happens to their children. The family and community must support school efforts and the school must serve the community. Lack of parental involvement in the educational system to a large extent has been primarily because parents feel intimidated and unwelcomed, and lack the skills and information to impact upon the school system. Therefore, many black parents become disenchanted and withdrawn from the educational process. Yet, they still hold high hopes for their children's education, for they know that education is the means to employment, upward social mobility, recognition, and esteem.

Another factor that explains the difference in the scope, content, and quality of the education that blacks receive is the inequitable distribution of revenues and resources to inner-city schools. Despite the overwhelming need, our society spends less money educating inner-city children than children of the suburbs. This is due largely to the declining city tax base and increasing competition from municipal needs (*e.g.*, police, welfare, fire) for the tax dollar. The suburbs, where these demands are less, allocate twice the proportion of their total budgets to education as do the cities. Several judicial decisions have attempted to make school spending independent of property values in order to reduce the gap in per-pupil expenditures between wealthy and low-income school districts.

Researchers have also studied the relationship between students' socioeconomic status and the amount of school resources made available to them and have found that school districts allocate substantially fewer dollars to schools in poor and black neighborhoods. The intra-district disparities are often just as great as the inter-district ones. Other formulas and methods for financing need to be devised.

The budget squeeze

The Reagan Administration has taken steps that will widen the gap between black and white educational attainment. The budget requested for education for 1983 is $10,300,000,000, as compared to $13,000,000,000 proposed to be spent on education in the fiscal year 1982. These proposed budget cuts adversely affect minority education programs the most and represent a big step backward in educational opportunities for the disadvantaged.

The Council of Great City Schools is an organization that represents the nation's 28 largest urban school districts, serving 5,000,000 students, of which 75% are minorities. This council stated that the proposed cuts in education would be especially severe in their areas where 16% of big-city school revenues come from Washington, as compared to the national average of eight per cent.

These school systems estimate a loss of $300,000,000, which will have the cumulative effect of jeopardizing 12,000 jobs and curtailing or eliminating services to about 235,000 inner-city youngsters. The bulk of the cuts would occur in Title I funding, a program designed for low-achieving students in low-income areas. Some 78% of U.S. school districts receive Title I aid and approximately 50% of the children served are from minority groups—29% being black.

Several research studies have shown that the Title I program has been very successful in improving achievement, especially for minority students. The National Assessment of Educational Progress indicated improvement in the relative performance of black youth at ages nine and 13 in five learning areas. It is believed that this may be attributed to Federal programs designed to foster equal educational opportunity, especially Title I.

In spite of Title I's success, the President is proposing to cut its funds by 40% from the 1981-82 funding level. If Congress approves the proposed budget cuts, it would eliminate nearly 2,500,000 children from the program, leaving only 27% of the nation's children who need the services actually receiving them.

Another move which would restrict access to higher education—and consequently to the mainstream of society—is the drastic reduction in student financial assistance. Proposed for 1983 is a 44% reduction in the over-all student assistance program, which will impact approximately 2,000,000 needy students. Since over 80% of all black students enrolled in post-secondary institutions receive some form of Federal assistance either through a loan or a grant or both, black progress in higher education stands to be severely impeded.

The Pell Grant program, the largest of the Education Department's major aid programs for needy students, has been cut by 36% for 1983, requiring parents to contribute more for their children's education. Changes in the eligibility criteria for Pell Grants would eliminate about 1,000,000 students by 1983. Three programs—Supplemental Grants, State Incentive Grants, and National Direct Student Loans—would not receive any funds for 1983. The proposed reduction of college workstudy funding would eliminate 250,000 needy students from the program. The trio program specifically designed for the disadvantaged would be reduced by 47%. The budget would kill three of the five trio programs. The pre-college counseling programs—Talent Search and Equal Opportunity Centers—would vanish under the proposal. Graduate and professional opportunity fellowships as well as assistance to needy students in the law school Cleo program would be eliminated.

Graduate students would be eliminated from the Guaranteed Student Loan program under the new proposal. Six hundred thousand students, more than half the current graduate school enrollment, depend on guaranteed student loans, and the majority of them probably will not be able to stay in school if the Administration's proposal to withdraw graduate aid entirely is approved by Congress. In addition, the Social Security Administration is planning to phase out payments to children of deceased, retired, or disabled parents at the rate of 25% each year until the program ends in 1985—with no checks being issued for the summer months. Any student not enrolled in college full-time by May, 1982, would not be eligible for Social Security aid. It is estimated that over 150,000 high school seniors will become ineligible for Social Security assistance for college.

The cumulative effect of such cuts, at a time of rising college costs (15% to 20%) and reductions in other programs, can tip the balance between the student's looking to education to better his employment possibilities or giving up. For blacks, attrition in higher education to a great extent is affected by financial aid policies. The dropout rate for blacks who do not receive any aid is 46%, as compared to 29% for whites.

Costs to society

The costs to our society of not educating one person in terms of crime, welfare expenditures, and foregone productivity are far higher than the expense of a quality education from birth. When considering the cost effectiveness of programs like Title I, we should remember that it costs $26,000 a year to keep a man in prison.

The black community is quite concerned about Congress placing educational categorical programs such as the Teacher Corps and the Emergency School Aid Act—a program designed to assist school districts struggling with problems of racial isolation and desegregation—into block grants. It is feared that the objectives of these programs will be lost, and that the special needs of the poor and minorities will be left to the discretion of thousands of state and local officials, whose decisions about the allocation of funds will be based upon the political pressure in their jurisdictions. Past experiences have shown that states have not provided sufficient funds for the disadvantaged and minorities, and their funding formulas have been discriminatory.

Increased Federal legislation had to be developed in order to address the needs of the poor and minorities. If more control is relinquished to the local school systems, then the Federal government in turn must ensure that minority and disadvantaged students will receive adequate and appropriate resources.

With the proposed dismantling of the Department of Education and replacing it with the Foundation for Education Assistance, the Administration has decided to redefine the Federal role from one of promoting and ensuring equal access to quality integrated education to one of data collection and analysis, administration of block grants, and student financial assistance. The Foundation's civil rights role is limited to providing counsel, advice, and technical assistance concerning civil rights compliance upon request to recipients of Federal aid. Civil rights enforcement, however, would be turned over to the Justice Department.

Regardless of what happens to the Office of Civil Rights in the Department of Education, the Administration has made it clear that the role of the Federal government is one of advancing civil rights, not enforcing it, using cooperation rather than threatened sanctions to achieve its objectives.

The laws and regulations that took decades to achieve are being dismantled in a matter of months. The new affirmative action regulations would require fewer employees to file affirmative action plans and subject them to fewer reviews. Approximately 80% of the colleges and universities which previously were investigated and ordered to draw up detailed affirmative action plans to hire and promote women and minorities will be exempt. This poses a serious problem not only in terms of employment for minority professionals, but decreases appropriate role models for minority youth as well.

In addition, the Reagan Administration has decided to exempt from anti-discrimination laws those colleges at which guaranteed student loans are the only form of Federal aid. The new rules would significantly limit the number of colleges and universities that must comply with civil rights laws. This shift in policy and reinterpretation of what constitutes Federal assistance is designed to have the same effect as the decision to grant tax-exempt status to schools which racially discriminate.

Finally, the President has introduced tuition tax credit legislation. When you begin to analyze the implications of these actions, you can not help but conclude that access to the mainstream is being deliberately restricted by those who have a stake in their privileged position. When you see being proposed at both the local and national levels legislation that would provide tuition tax credits for parents of children enrolled in private schools, you realize that these tax credits are not designed to provide all parents with a choice concerning the education of their children, for it would not help the 8,600,000 blacks below the poverty level. It was designed to provide relief for the tax-burdened middle class and to encourage escape from the urban public schools with their growing enrollment of poor and minority youngsters. If enacted, these measures would increase social class and racial isolation by establishing a two-tiered educational system in this country—the private schools for the white and middle class and the public schools for the poor and minority. Private education should not be enhanced at the expense of public education, which is the cornerstone of our democracy.

Much remains to be done to finish the uncompleted task of guaranteeing all children in this nation an equal chance at a quality education. The issues of the 1980's are difficult, but not impossible. More concerted effort is needed on the part of all to ensure that black children will receive the kind of training that will equip them to thrive in the pluralistic technological society of which they are a part. We can no longer afford to point the finger and pass the blame. We should all heed the words of Thomas Carlyle: "That there should be one man [to] die ignorant who had the capacity for knowledge, this I call a tragedy."

From Equity to Excellence: The Rebirth of Educational Conservatism

Fred L. Pincus

FRED L. PINCUS is assistant professor of sociology at the University of Maryland Baltimore County.

If the 1960s go down in history as the decade of liberal educational reform, the 1980s will most likely be known as the decade of conservative restoration. Although many reforms were eroding by the late 1970s, they came under direct assault in the 1980s, especially after the election of Ronald Reagan.

A key concern of "liberal consensus" of the 1960s and 1970s was "equity," and the federal government took the lead to end de jure racial segregation in education and to promote increased educational opportunities for minorities, women, and the economically disadvantaged. In addition, the federal government increased its financial support for the production of knowledge in higher education, which enabled both private industry and the defense establishment to grow and prosper. Federal spending for, and regulation of, education at all levels sharply increased between 1960 and 1980.

Of course, the growth of this liberal consensus did not occur in a vacuum. Minority communities were challenging the legitimacy of American institutions during the 1960s, as were the women's movement and the predominantly white student movement. Left-wing scholars began to argue that the schools were being used by the business class to maintain their own power at the expense of working people and minorities. Mainstream scholars and prestigious commissions began to worry that colleges were educating too many students compared to the number of available college-level jobs.

In other words, the liberal consensus was actually an attempt to defend the American capitalist system. Enlightened schools can create avenues of upward mobility and promote social equality, critics and cynics were told. Give the system another chance before turning to revolutionary alternatives, said the liberals.

By 1980, the liberal consensus had begun to unravel, and two different forms of educational conservatism began to gain strength. The New Right conservatives, led by the Heritage Foundation and a small but well-organized group of fundamentalist ministers and political idealogues, called for a return to states' rights in education and increased competition between public and private schools. A larger but more heterogeneous group of educators, politicians, and businessmen, which I will refer to as "centrist conservatives," called for a shift in federal policy from equity to excellence. Although there is some overlap between the New Right and the centrist education policies, there are basic differences with regard to the missions of the schools and the appropriate role of the federal government.

Since the election of Ronald Reagan in 1980, the entire political center of gravity has shifted sharply to the right. In this article, I will try to outline both strands of educational conservatism. Then I will examine the effects that these policies are likely to have on the schools and on the larger society.

NEW RIGHT CONSERVATIVES

The most articulate voice of the New Right conservatives is the Heritage Foundation, the Washington-based think-tank. Eileen Gardner, a Black educator, is the current education policy analyst at Heritage; she replaced Onalee McGraw early in 1983. Other scholars who are close to Heritage include Russell Kirk, E.G. West, David Armor, Thomas Sowell, and George Gilder.

The major New Right spokespersons on educational issues in Congress are Sen. Orrin Hatch (R-Utah) and Sen. Jesse Helms (R-N.C.). Jerry Falwell and Tim LeHay, two fundamentalist ministers, Mel and Norma Gabler, the "textbook analysts," and Arthur Laffer, the supply-side economist, are also important voices in the movement.

All of the problems facing the schools can, according to the New Right, be traced to a single cause—overcentralized decision-making caused by increased federal control. This has allowed the schools to become "monopolized" by powerful "vested interests"—teachers' unions, educational associations, and federal bureaucrats. The Heritage Foundation, for example, states:

> The most damaging blows to science and mathematics education have come from Washington. For the past 20 years, federal mandates have favored "disadvantaged" pupils at the expense of those who have the highest potential to contribute positively to society. . . . By catering to the demands of special-interest groups—racial minorities, the hand-

From *Social Policy,* Winter 1984, pp. 50-56. SOCIAL POLICY published by Social Policy Corporation, New York, New York 10036. Copyright 1984 by Social Policy Corporation.

icapped, women, and non-English-speaking students—America's public schools have successfully competed for government funds, but have done so at the expense of education as a whole.

Rather than stressing educational diversity, goes the argument, the vested interests have forced a unified curriculum based on the principles of secular humanism into most of the nation's schools. This not only prevents students from learning basic skills but also teaches children a set of values that are opposed to the traditional values of most of their families.

The New Right generally talks about the goals of education in the most general of terms. According to Heritage, for example, "The ultimate function of education is to help mankind reach its potential. To attain this, an educational program must provide leadership, emphasize excellence, and profess and pursue the highest of values."

The only people who have a right to make this general principle concrete, they believe, are local parents' groups, working in consultation with local educators and local elected officials. Schools should be diverse enough to provide families with a wide range of choices about their children's education.

The main goal of the New Right is to decentralize education in order to create more diversity and return control to the parents. In order to accomplish this goal, two main policies are seen as necessary.

"The eventual goal should be the complete *elimination of federal funding,*" according to Heritage. As a first step, the Department of Education should be abolished and most of its functions eliminated. Equity, like all other educational matters, should be decided at the local levels.

Second, *tuition tax credits* for the parents of children in private and parochial schools should be adopted by the federal government. "Tax credits should certainly get higher priority than any other education issue, and probably higher than most social issues that, unlike this one, carry political costs with some Reagan-leaning constituencies," says Heritage. This would allow more children to attend private and parochial schools, so the argument goes, especially those from disadvantaged families. As a result, there would be more diversity, which would lead to more competition between schools, which would increase educational standards. The New Right does not consider tuition tax credits to be a form of federal aid to education. Instead, they are viewed as "a financial facility" to give parents more choice in the education of their children.

Until these two policies can be implemented, the New Right calls on the federal government to replace categorical grants with block grants and to cut sharply levels of federal spending. Civil-rights regulations should be sharply downgraded, including the Internal Revenue Service policy of denying tax-exempt status to private schools that discriminate on the basis of race. In addition, the federal government is not supposed to be involved in curriculum development projects, especially those concerned with "values education."

The New Right religious fundamentalists are promoting a constitutional amendment to permit prayer in the public schools. They also favor the teaching of "scientific creationism." In addition, they have been active in trying to remove what they believe to be dirty, antifamily, anti-American books from the shelves of school classrooms and libraries. Finally, the fundamentalists have attacked the cultural relativist approach to values education and any approach to sex education.

Arthur Laffer, the premier supply-side economist, has recently put forward a simple proposal to increase the quality of education: students who score highest on the SATs should be paid bonuses of several thousand dollars. This could then be applied to their college education. It remains to be seen whether other New Right groups will pick up on this unusual idea.

CENTRIST CONSERVATIVES

The centrist conservatives include a diversity of individuals and groups who fall somewhere in between the New Right conservatives and traditional liberals. The intellectual core of the centrists consists of individuals with ties to the American Enterprise Institute, a conservative think-tank, and to *The Public Interest* and *Commentary,* two conservative publications. Usually referred to as neoconservatives, this group includes Nathan Glazer, James Q. Wilson, Chester E. Finn, Daniel P. Moynihan, James Coleman, and Joseph Adelson.

The reports of several study commissions that were issued in the spring of 1983 also fall into the centrist conservative tradition. This includes the National Commission on Excellence in Education (NCEE), the Twentieth Century Fund's Task Force on Federal Elementary and Secondary Education Policy, the National Task Force on Education for Economic Growth, and the Business-Higher Education Forum.

Albert Shanker, president of the American Federation of Teachers, often reflects centrist conservative thinking as does educator Diane Ravitch and syndicated columnist George Will. Although centrist conservatives do not agree on all issues, they do share many criticisms of the educational process.

Centrists argue that there are two basic causes of the educational problems in the 1980s. First, the social experiments of the 1960s and 1970s made too many demands on the schools. According to Adelson, "The story of education in [the post-World War II period] is a story of experiments—an abundance, a cornucopia of reforms and breakthroughs, each introduced breathlessly, each kept afloat by publicity, and each sinking out of sight, soon to be replaced by more publicity and more disappointment."

Second, federal intervention to promote educational equity was excessive. When the three branches of the federal government intervene, says Adelson, "they do so with almost no regard to the financial costs involved. And once they have done so, their decisions, however erroneous or short-sighted these turn out to be in practice, prove nearly impossible to modify or rescind." The federal courts and bureaucracies "know but a single thing, that thing being a distended and distorted idea of equality, distended in that it puts equality above all other values, and distorted because it has transformed the original idea of moral equality . . . to the ideas of numerical equality, that all groups must be represented equally in all statuses."

As a result of the social experiments and excessive federal intervention, continue the centrists, the quality of education began to suffer. In its final report, the NCEE put it this way:

Our once unchallenged preeminence

in commerce, industry, science, and technological innovation is being overtaken by competitors throughout the world . . . . The educational foundations of our society are presently being eroded by a rising tide of mediocrity that threatens our very future as a nation and a people. . . . If an unfriendly foreign power had attempted to impose on America the mediocre educational performance that exists today, we might well have viewed it as an act of war. As it stands, we have allowed this to happen to ourselves. . . . We have, in effect, been committing an act of unthinking, unilateral educational disarmament.

Centrist conservatives argue that there are three general missions for the schools. First, the schools have an important role in *promoting economic growth* for the nation. High school and college graduates must have the technical skills needed by business and industry to compete with Japan and Western Europe. In addition, higher education has the responsibility of producing the needed scientific and technological developments.

Educational institutions cannot adequately perform this mission, they say, unless there is some coordination at the national level. According to the NCEE, for example, "The federal government has the *primary responsibility* to identify the national interest in education. It should also help fund and support efforts to protect and promote that interest."

The centrists argue that both the schools and the federal government have failed in this mission and have allowed Japan and Western Europe to overtake American industry in several key areas.

Second, the schools must help to *preserve a common culture* by teaching students the basic values upon which America capitalism is based. According to Andrew Oldenquist,

> We can use the apparatus of the State to perpetuate an already existing moral consciousness. . . . What this implies is a system of moral education that is conservative in *both* form and content . . . . In our own society, the moral core consists of principles of social mobility such as honesty, fairness, willingness to work, disavowal of criminal violence, respect for the democratic political process, together with personal virtues such as courage, diligence, and self-respect. . . . The inculcation of civilized moral habits . . . is essential to any society even minimally safe and satisfying.

George Will underscores the importance of this mission:

> The fact that American education has always aimed to serve commercial vigor has imposed on education a special duty. It is the duty to strengthen the social bonds that are weakened by the dynamism of a restless society of atomized individuals preoccupied with getting and gaining.

Centrists argue that the schools have been inconsistent in carrying out this mission. They are particularly critical of the "cultural relativist bias" that is found in many courses called "values clarification," since this could "undermine" traditional American values. Courses in minority and women's studies are generally seen as extraneous electives or un-American attacks on American culture.

The third legitimate mission of education is the *promotion of educational equity*. In order to be avenues of upward mobility, the schools should give minorities, women, and the disadvantaged the same opportunities for educational achievement as they give middle-income white males.

The centrists argue that the federal government has an important role to play in this regard. The 1983 Twentieth Century Fund's Task Force report, for example, states: "Certainly, federal intervention was not only appropriate but necessary in bringing about desegregation of the public schools, and in providing needed assistance to poor and handicapped children." According to Chester Finn, because of the federal government, "Millions of individuals have had greater access to more education than otherwise would have."

However, the centrists argue that things have gotten out of hand. According to the task force, the federal government's "emphasis on promoting equality of opportunity has meant a slighting of its commitment to educational quality." A redefinition of the

Centrists argue that all levels of education should have a larger number of required academic courses, more homework, and wider use of "objectives tests" to measure student achievement.

federal role in promoting equity is now needed, they argue.

The centrist conservatives all agree on the need to increase educational standards, redefine but not eliminate the role of the federal government, and increase the possibility of cooperation between business and education. Of course, they are not always in agreement on the concrete measures that are needed to carry out these principles.

On the subject of *quality,* centrists argue that all levels of education should have a larger number of required academic courses, especially in the areas of math, science, and other basic skills. More homework should be assigned and less time should be spent on nonacademic electives. So-called "objectives tests" should be more widely used to measure student achievement, and social promotions should be abolished. High school graduation and college admission requirements should be sharply increased. As a result of these higher expectations, goes the argument, student achievement will increase.

In the area of *discipline,* since orderly classroom environments and regular attendance are necessary factors in student achievement, the schools should have the right to expel disorderly and truant students. Teachers and school administrators should reassert their traditional authority, which has been weakened by a wide range of court decisions pertaining to "student rights."

As for *teacher quality,* two recent trends—lower ability students entering the teaching profession and qualified math and science teachers leaving the schools for private industry—must be reversed, say the centrists. Economic incentives are the main weapon to increase teacher quality. Merit pay will reward good teachers and special bonuses to math and science teachers will help to keep them in the profession. Some centrists also call for better overall pay and working conditions for all teachers. Although Albert Shanker has traditionally opposed merit pay, he seems to be willing to entertain this policy if overall salaries are also increased.

And although centrists agree that the federal government has a role in promoting *equity,* they argue that this role should be redefined and be more limited. Generally, they oppose hiring quotas, court-ordered busing for racial balance, and other ''excessive'' federal intervention.

According to James Q. Wilson, questions of educational equity should be seen as ''claims'' where the government can decide whether or not to allocate resources in a specific way on the basis of usefulness and cost-efficiency. Many women and minorities, however, view equity as a question of ''rights,'' according to Wilson. In this case, an individual or group makes a moral demand of the government. What should be a question of ''claims,'' continues Wilson, has become defined as a question of ''rights'':

> Converting a set of claims into a statement of rights creates problems because a right has the special political quality that no argument of cost or convenience can be allowed to stand against its implementation.

Many centrists argue that the federal government has already taken care of most of the pressing issues regarding educational equity. Nathan Glazer, for example, states:

> I see very little that the federal government can do today to advance racial equality. . . . The legislation of the 1960s and 1970s was directed to problems of access, opportunity, and equality of treatment. But today's problems for Blacks are not problems of access, opportunity, and equality of treatment. I do not think that these are issues now—today, in effect, they have been reduced to nonissues. For example, only about 2 percent of all college teachers are Black. This is a nonissue because there are no federal policies suitable to address it.

Of course, Glazer and other centrists reject the concept of racial hiring quotas and ''goals,'' both of which they characterize as ''reverse discrimination.''

Centrists tend to reject federal policies intended to desegregate public systems of higher education on two grounds. First, this would hurt the quality of the traditionally white schools. Second, they argue, it is inconsistent to preserve the racial atmosphere of traditionally Black institutions and also to increase their quality.

Finally, centrists tend to dismiss the importance of the IRS in denying tax-exempt status to private schools that discriminate. Since these are not high-quality schools, and since Blacks don't want to attend them anyhow, they argue, the action of the IRS and the courts is simply another example of excess federal intervention.

In the area of *federal spending,* centrist conservatives argue that the federal government should be more selective. The 1983 Twentieth Century Task Force report, for example, states: ''Federal education policy must function, moreover, in ways that complement rather than weaken local control. This calls for a change in direction, replacing the current emphasis on regulations and mandates with a new emphasis on incentives.'' The task force goes on to recommend federal spending on a national Master Teacher Program and on a campaign to promote literacy in English. In addition, they recommend that the impact aid program be reformulated to provide funds to areas with large numbers of immigrant students.

Diane Ravitch, a task-force member, also calls on the federal government to provide scholarships and loans to prospective math, science, and foreign-language teachers, and she lauds the National Endowment for the Humanities for their summer seminars for high school teachers in the fields of history, literature, and foreign language. Unfortunately, since most centrists are more concerned with what the federal government should not do than what it should do, their specific suggestions for federal spending are not very concrete.

Finally, as regards *business/education cooperation,* centrists believe that the business community should be more involved in education in a number

The New Right wants to turn the clock back to some mythical time in the nineteenth century when free-market competition, with no government interference, solved the major problems of the day.

of ways. The Business/Education Forum 1983, for example, favors more federal tax credits for donating equipment to colleges and universities and for cooperating in long-term research. At the community college level, customized contract training programs are being developed to prepare students for specific jobs in specific companies, often at the taxpayers' expense. Adopt-a-school programs and the exchange of teaching and industry personnel at the K-12 level are also being encouraged.

In spite of the general agreement among centrist conservatives regarding educational policy, there are also substantial areas of disagreement. One particularly controversial area is the appropriate balance between private and public schools. On the one hand, the Twentieth Century Fund Task Force does not ''recommend a major redefinition of the relationships between public and nonpublic schools.'' They believe that ''provision of free public education must continue to be a public responsibility of high priority, while support of nonpublic education should remain a private obligation.'' AFT President Albert Shanker would agree with this position.

On the other hand, James Coleman and Daniel Moynihan argue that the federal government should act to increase the role of the private schools to enhance educational competition and parental choice. In a controversial report, for example, Coleman said that private and parochial schools are less racially segregated than public schools and are more likely to have atmospheres conducive to learning.

Still others, like Chester Finn and George Will, fall somewhere in between. Although Finn is in favor of more help to private schools, he states:

"The first educational obligation of government is to provide high-quality public schooling."

Among those who favor a greater role for private schools, there is substantial disagreement on how to accomplish this goal. Moynihan favors tuition tax credits for the parents of private and parochial school students. Milton Friedman, whose views are to the right of most centrists, favors a system of unrestricted educational vouchers. John Coons and Stephen Sugarman favor a more restricted set of vouchers where families using them could not add on any of their own money; this is supposed to help ensure educational equality.

There is also substantial disagreement on the role of teachers' unions. Most centrists would like to see less influential unions so curriculum changes could be more easily made, and teachers who are seen as incompetent could be more easily fired. Not surprisingly, Albert Shanker argues for stronger unions, while other centrists fall somewhere in between.

Finally, although most centrists argue that traditional values should be taught, they are more concerned with criticizing the cultural relativists than in making concrete suggestions for change.

CONTRADICTIONS BETWEEN CONSERVATIVES

The New Right and centrist conservatives have vastly different political analyses of the educational system. The New Right favors open competition in the so-called free market and argues that the federal government has no role to play in educational policy. The centrists, on the other hand, believe that the federal government has to be involved so that the schools can carry out their social missions. The problem, according to centrists, is that the federal government has exceeded its proper role.

Although the two conservative trends overlap on some important issues, their positions are not identical. Both tend strongly to oppose hiring quotas and court-ordered busing for racial balance, for example. The centrists object because they see this as an attempt to redistribute resources through reverse discrimination; they tend to support policies that simply prevent overt discrimination. The New Right, on the other hand, thinks all of these matters are state and local issues—the federal government should not be involved.

Both trends also tend to favor an increased role for the private schools. The New Right, however, tends to be opposed to public education, while it actively promotes private and religious education through tuition tax credits. The centrists tend to see a permanent role for the public schools and disagree on the extent to which private schools should be encouraged and on the means to accomplish this.

The cultural-relativist approach to teaching values is also strongly criticized by both conservative trends, but the proposed alternatives differ. The New Right wants to reinstate the teaching of simplistic fundamentalist values—including school prayer, creationism, and knee-jerk patriotism—wherever possible. Their concept of diversity would permit different schools to teach different values. The centrists, on the other hand, want all of the schools to teach a common set of values that are relevant to late twentieth-century capitalism. This would not include prayer and creationism. Both conservative trends, of course, would balk at any fundamental criticism of capitalism.

The centrists also seem to be somewhat more concerned with the Constitution and Bill of Rights than the New Rightists. The New Right strongly supports such things as an amendment permitting school prayer and a law limiting the power of the federal courts to order busing to achieve racial balance in the schools. The centrists are not interested in school prayer, and, while they are opposed to court-ordered busing, they have not resorted to such blatantly unconstitutional measures to achieve their goal.

In other words, while there is ample space for coalitions between the centrists and New Right conservatives, there are also many contradictions between them. It is well-known that representatives of both conservative trends are present in the Reagan Administration and are struggling for power. During its first year in office, the Administration closely followed the recommendation of the Heritage Foundation and received the appropriate praise from the New Right. During the second year, on the other hand, the Administration began to stray towar the centrist position and was severel criticized by the Foundation.

Secretary of Education Terrel Bell i generally regarded as a centrist. In th struggle over the future of his depart ment, Bell's proposal for a Foundatio for Educational Assistance gave th federal government a limited role much to the dismay of those to his right He seemed uncomfortable with th extent of budget cuts in his departmen and acknowledged that some of the pro grams to aid the disadvantaged wer successful. Although the enforcemen of civil-rights legislation was severel curtailed, he retained a formal commit ment to oppose explicit discrimination His support of the NCEE report (" haven't read a sentence in the repor with which I disagree") and his suppor of tuition tax credits is also consisten with the centrist position. It is signifi cant that most New Right spokeperson have called for Bell's resignation.

President Reagan, on the other hand is more difficult to characterize. Afte the release of the NCEE in the spring he seized on the theme of educationa excellence in a series of speeche around the country. However, h insisted that education was a state an local matter and refused to commi additional federal resources other tha calling for school prayer and tuition ta credits. The New Right is losing faith i the President, charging him with giving verbal support to these issues but no trying to push them through Congress It is likely that the Administration wil continue to try to appease both conser vative camps.

Congress, on the other hand, ha tended to reflect the centrist educa tional philosophy, especially wit regard to advocating a clear federa presence. Spending cuts have bee more modest than the Presiden requested, and most members of Con gress have insisted on at least a forma commitment to civil rights. Many Republicans were actually upset abou the Administration's position on the tax-exempt racism issue. It is doubtfu that Congress will pass an amendmen permitting school prayer, if only because it is so clearly unconstitu tional.

It is also doubtful that Congress wil act on the question of tuition tax cred its, although this proposal is pushed by both the New Right and some centrists

Some are concerned with this proposal's questionable constitutionality, while others are more concerned with the cost to the public schools and the negative effect it would have on them.

Although the educational conservatives have put liberals in Congress and throughout the country on the defensive, there is an important larger question: Will either conservative policy actually solve the educational, political, and economic problems faced by the United States in the 1980s? Although gazing into a crystal ball is always dangerous for social scientists, some tentative answers are fairly clear.

The New Right conservative policy would be an unmitigated disaster from the standpoint of both the business community and the majority of the population. The New Right wants to turn the clock back to some mythical time in the nineteenth century when free-market competition, with no government interference, solved the major problems of the day. History tells us, however, that the federal government, with the support of the business community, began to get involved in education over 100 years ago to solve some of the political and economic problems that were caused by competitive capitalism. This role became even more important during the post-World War II period, especially since 1960.

Removing the federal government from involvement in educational policy would cause political and economic chaos, and this would be strongly opposed by most of the business community. A curriculum based on simplistic Christian fundamentalism is not what the business community needs to boost their sagging profits.

The centrist conservatives understand this and want the federal government to help overhaul the schools in their own image. Increased standards and discipline, along with a more modest civil-rights policy and more business-education cooperation is supposed to help raise the levels of student achievement and make the United States more competitive with its capitalist rivals. While this vision, which is taking the country by storm, is closer to the views of the business community, it is also filled with contradictions and unanswered questions.

First, will the imposition of higher standards and more required courses actually boost the level of student achievement? Many liberals and radicals have emphasized the importance of higher expectations on the part of teachers, especially regarding minority and disadvantaged students; children tend to do better when their teachers have faith in them. But this is quite different from putting a set of hurdles in front of students in the form of more required courses, minimum competency tests to graduate, and higher grade-point averages and SAT scores to enter college. The centrists' move to increase standards will probably have a polarizing effect, motivating some of the better students while making it even more difficult for some of the slower students.

Only 350,000 new computer programmers and systems analysts will be needed by 1990. On the other hand, 600,000 new janitors and 800,000 new fast-food workers and kitchen helpers will have to be employed.

If the level of student achievement does increase, a second question arises: Will students be able to utilize these skills in the labor market of the 1980s? Since the early 1970s, there has been general agreement that the level of educational achievement has been growing faster than the increase in the skill requirements of the available jobs. It is highly likely that this trend toward "overeducation," especially with regard to the number of college graduates, will continue for the immediate future.

In spite of all the talk about high technology as the wave of the future, even *Business Week* agrees that its effect on employment has been exaggerated. Less than 4 percent of the labor force will be employed in high-tech industries by 1990, says the influential business magazine, and most of these jobs will involve relatively low levels of skill and salary. Levin and Rumberger studied the number of new jobs that will be created between 1978 and 1990 and found that only 350,000 new computer programmers and systems analysts will be needed. On the other hand, 600,000 new janitors and 800,000 new fast-food workers and kitchen helpers will have to be employed by 1990.

There is a great disjuncture between the centrists' call to upgrade standards to produce more skilled people for the labor market and the skill-level of the jobs that will actually be available in 1990. If students believe that higher test scores will lead to better jobs, they may be in for a big shock. If they don't believe in the school-job connection, there is little reason for them to respond to the centrists' call for higher achievement.

A third problem with the centrists' position concerns their policy toward civil-rights enforcement: What will happen to minority and disadvantaged students whose expectations were raised by the policies of the 1960s and 1970s? The more liberal policies of the past two decades were, in part, a response to growing anger and militance in minority communities. The education gap between whites and minorities diminished, somewhat, but it became clear to many that simply opposing explicit discrimination was not enough. Affirmative-action policies were necessary for progress to continue.

Now, the centrists are telling minorities, as well as women and the disadvantaged, that they have gone far enough, perhaps even too far. Strict color-blind policies are all that can be expected in the near future. It is doubtful that minorities will look to the centrist conservatives for support, and the level of anger, and possibly militance, will increase in the coming years.

A fourth issue, the centrists' view of discipline, also has severe limitations. Student drinking, drug use, and violence is simplistically seen as a form of social pathology that is primarily caused by the diminished authority of school personnel who have been shackled by liberal court decisions. Their solution is an educational version of law and order—expel unruly students.

Although discipline is a problem in many schools, law and order is not the solution. While student alienation from the schools and the larger society was expressed as political activism in the late 1960s, it is expressed through "acting out" behavior like drugs and alcohol in the 1980s. Increasing unemployment and economic insecurity only make matters worse. Just as the death penalty does not get to the root cause of crime, massive student expulsion won't get to the root cause of alienation and "acting out" behavior.

Finally, it is doubtful that the centrists' educational policies will help the United States be more competitive with its capitalist rivals. The automobile industry is in trouble because the Big Three companies wanted to make more profits building big gas-guzzling cars rather than small fuel-efficient cars. The steel industry is in trouble because it refused to invest in advanced technology, preferring to wring as much as it could out of antiquated plants. Neither of these problems has anything to do with the falling SAT scores or supposedly excessive civil-rights legislation.

Neither conservative approach to education will solve the problems faced by the schools in the 1980s. Like the more humane liberal policies of the 1960s and 1970s, both the centrist and the New Right educational policies have their own contradictions. In a society characterized by racism, class conflict, and economic stagnation, there is little that the schools can do to help create a better society. Liberal policies can make things less bad and create limited avenues of upward mobility for a few individuals. Conservative policies will simply lead to the reproduction of a blatantly inequitable social system.

REFERENCES

Adelson, Joseph. "What Happened to the Schools?" *Commentary* (March, 1981), pp. 36–41.

Bell, T.H. "The Federal Role in Education." *Harvard Educational Review* (November, 1982), pp. 375–380.

Business-Higher Education Forum. "America's Competitive Challenge." *The Chronicle of Higher Education* (May 18, 1983), pp. 10–13.

"America Rushes to High Tech for Growth." *Business Week* (March 28, 1983), pp. 84–90.

Coleman, James. "Private Schools, Public Schools, and the Public Interest." *The Public Interest #64 (Summer, 1981), pp. 19–30.*

Coons, John E. and Stephen D. Sugarman. *Education by Choice: The Case of Family Control.* Berkeley: University of California Press, 1978.

Finn, Chester E., Jr. "The Future of Education's Liberal Consensus." *Change* (September, 1980), pp. 25–30.

— "Why Public and Private Schools Matter." *Harvard Educational Review* (November, 1981), pp. 510–514.

Friedman, Milton and Rose. *Free to Choose.* New York: Avon, 1979.

Gardner, Eileen. "What's Wrong with Math and Science Teaching in Our Schools?" *Heritage Today* (May/June, 1983), pp. 6–7.

Glazer, Nathan. "Responses." *Harvard Educational Review* (November, 1982), pp. 460–462.

Holwill, Richard N., ed. *The First Year: A Mandate for Leadership Report.* Washington, D.C.: Heritage Foundation, 1982.

— *Agenda '83: A Mandate for Leadership Report.* Washington, D.C.: Heritage Foundation, 1983.

Laffer, Arthur B. "For Better Schools, Pay Achievers." *Education Week* (June 9, 1983), p. 24.

Levin, Henry M. and Russell W. Rumberger. *The Educational Implications of High Technology.* Palo Alto, Calif.: Institute for Research on Educational Finance and Government, Project Report 83–A4, 1983.

McAllister, Eugene J., Ed. *Agenda for Progress: Examining Federal Spending.* Washington, D.C.: Heritage Foundation, 1981.

National Commission on Excellence in Education. "A Nation at Risk: The Imperative for Educational Reform." *Education Week* (April 27, 1983), pp. 12–16.

Oldenquist, Andrew, " 'Indoctrination' and Societal Suicide." *The Public Interest* (Spring, 1981), pp. 81–94.

Pincus, Fred L. "The Heritage Foundation and Federal Educational Policy." *The Radical Teacher,* forthcoming.

— "Book Banning and the New Right: Censorship in the Public Schools." *The Educational Forum,* forthcoming.

Ravitch, Diane. "There's a Lot Washington Can Do." *Washington Post* (June, 1983), p. C8.

Rumberger, Russell W. "The Rising Incidence of Overeducation in the U.S. Labor Market. *Economics of Education Review* (Summer, 1981), pp. 293–314.

Twentieth Century Fund Task Force on Federal Elementary and Secondary Education Policy. Excerpts from the report of the Twentieth Century Fund's Task Force. *The Chronicle of Higher Education* (May 11, 1983), pp. 5–8.

Will, George F. "Bad Report Card." *Washington Post* (June 1, 1983).

Wilson, James Q. "Response." *Harvard Educational Review* (November, 1982), pp. 415–418.

Tuition Tax Credits and the First Amendment

Martha M. McCarthy
Indiana University

Measures providing income tax credits or deductions for educational expenses are generating substantial political debate in legislative forums. Within the past year such provisions have been introduced in Congress and in 13 state legislatures. A central question in the tuition tax credit controversy is whether the measures violate the First Amendment to the Federal Constitution. Critics assert that tuition tax credits and deductions serve the special interests of parochial school patrons, resulting in unconstitutional governmental aid to sectarian schools. Proponents counter that tax relief measures are similar to tax deductions for individual donations to churches and constitute no subsidy to religious institutions. In this paper, these competing positions are discussed within the context of judicial interpretations of First Amendment religious guarantees.

It is not my intent to argue the related social and individual advantages or disadvantages of tuition tax relief measures. Rather, my purpose is to present the constitutional framework within which the legal status of tuition tax credits must be assessed. After a brief overview of the First Amendment from a historical perspective, the judicial criteria which have been developed to evaluate claims under the establishment clause are examined. The remainder of the article focuses on litigation in which courts have applied these criteria to various legislative efforts to aid sectarian schools and to provide tax relief for parents of nonpublic school pupils.

FIRST AMENDMENT RELIGIOUS LIBERTIES: HISTORICAL CONTEXT

The First Amendment to the United States Constitution stipulates in part that "Congress shall make no law respecting an establishment of religion or prohibiting the free exercise thereof." The sentiments expressed in these religious protections emerged from a heritage of centuries of religious persecution and strife in the western world. Many colonists fled to America seeking religious freedom, and the framers of the First Amendment were painfully aware of the religious inquisitions and wars associated with a union of church and state.[1]

Yet, the deeply ingrained tradition of a state-established religion also traveled across the Atlantic. The individual's right freely to exercise religious beliefs was far from an accepted notion during the colonial period.[2] Roger Williams and Anne Hutchinson were among settlers banned from their colonies for religious reasons. In New York, all settlers were required to support the Dutch Reformed Church, and Quakers and Baptists were subjected to persecution. In New England, for all practical purposes, the Calvinist Congregational Church was the established religion, and in Virginia, all ministers were required to perform canons of the Church of England.[3] Discrimination against minority faiths was typically political, resulting in the denial of voting privileges or the opportunity to hold public office. For example, in Pennsylvania, only

From *Issues in Education,* Volume 1, No. 2 & 3, 1983, pp. 88-105. Copyright ©1984 by the American Educational Research Association, Washington, DC 20036.

those who professed a belief in Jesus Christ could hold office, and civil servants in New Jersey were required to take an oath against the Pope. Moreover, in a majority of the colonies at the time of their independence, taxes were imposed to support sectarian institutions.[4]

The primary efforts to secure religious toleration and a separation of church and state in America came from colonial leaders in Virginia. Thomas Jefferson and James Madison denounced taxation to support religion and championed the removal of sectarian concerns from civil government. Both Madison and Jefferson relied heavily on the theory of church-state separation espoused by John Locke, who maintained that "the care of souls cannot belong to the civil magistrate."[5] Locke's philosophy provided a third alternative to the Erastian and theocratic theories on church-state relations which were in vogue in Europe in the latter eighteenth century. Those adhering to the Erastian theory, named after the German philosopher Erastus, claimed state superiority over the church, arguing that religion should be used to advance state interests. The theocratic theory was grounded in the opposing notion that the church is superordinate and the state should be used to further ecclesiastical interests.[6] Locke's theory eventually prevailed in the United States, but support for this philosophy was not universal at the time the federal Constitution was written.

When the convention met in Philadelphia in 1787 to revise the Articles of Confederation, it was soon apparent that a totally new Constitution would be drafted. The overriding focus of the convention delegates was on the powers of the national government rather than on individual rights. Not until the final sessions were there discussions of a preamble to the Constitution with a declaration of rights, the prevailing sentiment being that such a statement was unnecessary because the federal government had no authority to enact laws touching personal freedoms. The only mention of religion in the Constitution signed by the delegates on September 17, 1787, was the prohibition on religious tests for federal office-holders.

However, the inclusion of a Bill of Rights became a major issue during the struggle to secure ratification of the Constitution. Anti-federalists objected to the Constitution on a number of grounds, but the absence of a statement of individual rights had the most popular appeal. Federalists successfully secured endorsement of the Constitution in some state ratifying conventions only when they agreed to submit a list of proposed amendments, focusing primarily on civil liberties.

The majority of the members of the first Congress felt the details of the new system of government compelled more attention than constitutional amendments, but Madison argued convincingly that it was essential to garner support among those who had opposed the Constitution because it lacked a declaration of individual freedoms. Ultimately, 17 amendments were proposed by the House; 12 remained after Senate revisions; and 10 were ratified by sufficient numbers of states to become the Bill of Rights in 1791.

The religious guarantees contained in the First Amendment certainly represented a bold experiment and a radical departure from the norm of civil and sectarian entanglement among European nations. They also provided evidence that substantial enlightenment had taken place in America during the eighteenth century. Robert Rutland has aptly noted that "the Salem witchcraft trials and the adoption of the Federal Bill of Rights virtually opened and closed the eighteenth century; and these historical incidents indicate the tremendous intellectual advancement during that stirring span of time."[7]

Although all states ultimately followed the federal lead in guaranteeing religious liberty in their respective constitutions, it was assumed until the mid-twentieth century that the First Amendment did not obligate them to do so. In 1845 the United States Supreme Court declared:

> The Constitution makes no provision for protecting the citizens of the respective states in their religious liberties; this is left to the state constitutions and laws; nor is there any inhibition imposed by the Constitution of the United States in this respect on the states.[8]

Long after the federal Constitution was adopted, several states provided support for religious institutions, including sectarian schools, and had laws placing political restrictions on certain sects, typically Catholics and Jews.[9]

The growth of public schooling in most states was strongly influenced by sectarian concerns. Protestantism exerted a pervasive effect on the public school curriculum well into the twentieth century. William McGuffey, a Protestant minister, wrote readers and spellers that sold over a million copies between 1836 and 1920. Ellwood Cubberley estimated that about half of the American students during this period "drew their inspiration and formulated their codes of morals and conduct from this remarkable set of Readers."[10]

Historically, most church-state conflicts pertaining to schools were settled in local communities. Individuals atypically sought judicial intervention to redress their grievances. Religious controversies were viewed primarily in terms of majority rule rather than constitutional rights. The dominant sect determined basic community norms, including the place of sectarian instruction in the school curriculum.

As communities became more heterogeneous, local consensus regarding the values that schools should instill was no longer assured. Some historians contend that the gradual secularization of the public school curriculum evolved not because of a commitment to the separation of church and state, but to disputes among various religious sects as to which tenets would be emphasized in the curriculum.[11]

Fearing that traditional American (i.e., Protestant) values would be lost in a pluralistic society, some state legislatures began to codify their versions of "appropriate" beliefs. In the early 1900s, there were legislative efforts to mandate school attendance at *public* schools only, to limit curricular offerings in conformance with religious doctrine, and to authorize devotional activities in public schools. While legislation requiring all children to attend public schools was judicially struck down as impairing Fourteenth Amendment liberties,[12] state laws authorizing prayer in public education and prohibiting instruction conflicting with the Genesis account of creation were judicially sanctioned in some states until the 1960s.[13]

It was not until the mid-twentieth century that state practices impairing First Amendment religious freedoms started to come under close judicial scrutiny. During the past several decades the Supreme Court has interpreted the Fourteenth Amendment as prohibiting state encroachment on fundamental liberties protected by the Bill of Rights. It is now well established that the Fourteenth Amendment renders "the legislatures of the states as incompetent as Congress" to enact laws interfering with religious liberties.[14] While interpretation of First Amendment protections remains controversial, it is indisputable that this amendment applies to state as well as federal action.

INTERPRETING THE RELIGION CLAUSES: THE JUDICIAL ROLE

The United States Supreme Court is the final arbiter of the nature and limit of the federal Constitution. In 1803 Chief Justice Marshall declared that the Court's interpretation of this document is the supreme law in this nation.[15] Thus, the ultimate responsibility to determine the scope of religious liberties as well as our other federal constitutional rights resides with the collective judgment of the nine individuals on the Supreme Court. These justices attempt to rely on precedent and to maintain consistency in applying legal principles, but judgments must be made and new doctrines must be formulated. Since justices are human, subject to bias and social influence, the Court's interpretations of the First Amendment's religion clauses have not been immune to shifts in societal sentiments.

The term "separation of church and state," first introduced by Thomas Jefferson, does not appear in the First Amendment, but many citizens and justices have accepted Jefferson's metaphor as law of the land. Supreme Court Justice Rutledge stated in 1947 that the First Amendment was designed not merely to prohibit governmental imposition of a religion, but to create "a complete and permanent separation of the spheres of religious activity and civil authority . . ."[16] Others have echoed his sentiment, arguing that the best interests of both religion and government are served by keeping civil and sectarian affairs discrete.

Even so, the Supreme Court has recognized on several occasions that "total separation" between church and state "is not possible in an absolute sense."[17] In 1963, when the Supreme Court barred Bible reading from public schools, Justice Goldberg commented in a concurring opinion:

> Neither government nor this court can or should ignore the significance of the fact that a vast portion of our people believe in and worship God and that many of our legal, political, and personal values derive historically from religious teachings. Government must inevitably take cognizance of the existence of religion and, indeed, under certain circumstances the First Amendment may require that it do so.[18]

While the religion clauses of the First Amendment may appear to be straightforward, they have created problems for the judiciary for over two centuries. Part of the dilemma arises from an inherent tension embodied in the establishment and free exercise clauses. If, on the one hand, the state becomes too assertive in safeguarding establishment clause prohibitions, it might disavow religion, thus impairing free exercise rights. On the other hand, if the state becomes too accommodating, it might advance religion, in violation of the establishment clause. In reviewing challenged state action, courts have struggled to identify the appropriate governmental role exhibiting *neutrality* toward sectarian concerns—a task which has proven to be awesome.

The Supreme Court has tended to view the two religion clauses of the First Amendment as discrete mandates. Accordingly, it has developed separate criteria for assessing the legality of governmental action under the establishment and free exercise clauses. Because First Amendment challenges to tuition tax relief measures have been grounded in establishment clause considerations, the remainder of this paper focuses on judicial interpretations of restrictions imposed by this constitutional provision.

Traditionally the Supreme Court used two criteria to assess claims under the establishment clause. In 1963 the Court explained that for legislation ". . . to withstand the structures of the Establishment Clause, [there must be] a secular legislative purpose and a primary effect that neither advances nor inhibits religion."[19] In 1970 the Supreme Court introduced a third criterion in establishment clause cases: The challenged state action must not foster excessive governmental entanglement with religion.[20] In subsequent church-state litigation, the judiciary has applied this tripartite test in evaluating establishment clause claims, but the criteria have been easier to state than to apply. Judicial consensus has not been reached regarding what constitutes a secular purpose or what types of governmental action serve to advance religion or create excessive governmental entanglement with religion.

THE ESTABLISHMENT CLAUSE AND STATE AID TO NONPUBLIC SCHOOLS

With some regularity courts have been called upon to interpret establishment clause prohibitions in connection with educational practices. Among other things, these cases have involved challenges to (1) devotional activities in public schools,[21] and (2) state aid to parochial schools. Litigation in the latter category is particularly relevant to the tuition tax credit issue because tax relief measures have been challenged as providing unconstitutional governmental assistance to sectarian education. What follows is a brief review of litigation involving the use of public funds to assist parochial schools.

A variety of state laws providing financial benefits to nonpublic schools, their students, and parents of private school pupils have been challenged on the ground that they advance religion, since about 85 percent of all nonpublic schools in this nation are church-related.[22] While it might appear that any form of indirect public aid to sectarian schools would run afoul of the establishment clause, several types of assistance understood to benefit *students* rather than religious *institutions* have been judicially endorsed. The Supreme Court has not provided clear guidance in these cases; indeed, recent decisions have provided more questions than answers about the scope of permissible governmental aid to sectarian education.

In its initial decisions, the Supreme Court majority relied heavily on the "child benefit" doctrine in sanctioning state aid to provide transportation and secular textbooks for nonpublic school students.[23] Recognizing that the constitutional provisions of some states may prohibit the use of public funds for such purposes,[24] the Court majority found no First Amendment bar to these types of state aid for private, primarily sectarian, school pupils. In 1947 the Court acknowledged that transportation aid might encourage some parents to send their children to parochial school, but nonetheless reasoned that such legislation serves a public welfare purpose with only incidental benefits accruing to religious institutions.[25] Similarly, when the Court ruled in 1968 that the use of public funds to purchase secular textbooks for loan to nonpublic school students does not have the primary effect of advancing religion, the majority noted that parochial schools perform a valuable public function in providing secular education in addition to religious training.[26] While the majority conceded that textbooks are essential to the educational enterprise, this form of public aid was not considered an unconstitutional governmental subsidy to parochial schools. In subsequent cases, the Court also has endorsed the purchase of reusable workbooks or manuals for loan to nonpublic school students.[27]

However, from 1971 until 1976, the Supreme Court struck down various types of state aid to nonpublic schools, applying the "excessive entanglement" criterion. For example, the Court invalidated legislation calling for the use of public funds for salary supplements for nonpublic school teachers and direct aid as reimbursement for the costs of teachers' salaries, textbooks, and instructional materials in specified secular subjects.[28] The Court also struck down statutes providing grants for the maintenance and repair of private school facilities, tuition reimbursements to low-income parents of nonpublic school students, the loan of instructional materials and equipment to private schools, and auxiliary programs such as guidance counseling, health services, and remedial instruction provided by public school personnel on private school premises.[29]

Although it appeared in the early 1970s that the Supreme Court was embarking on a course of disallowing most types of proposed state aid to elementary and secondary sectarian schools, recent decisions may portend a reversal of this trend. Since 1977 the Court has condoned the use of state funds to provide private school pupils with the same standardized tests and scoring services as are available in public schools, diagnostic services at nonpublic school sites, and therapeutic services (e.g., speech classes, remedial instruction) conducted away from private school premises.[30] However, the Court has disallowed public aid for field trip transportation for nonpublic school students, reasoning that the monitoring necessary to ensure that such aid is used only for secular trips would entail excessive governmental entanglement with religion.[31]

These recent Supreme Court decisions, reflecting a severely divided Court, have not provided objective standards to use in distinguishing permissible from prohibited types of governmental aid to parochial schools and their patrons. Justice Stevens asserted in 1980 that the current Supreme Court has rendered "largely ad hoc decisions about what payments may or may not be constitutionally made to nonpublic schools," and he called for a resurrection of the "high and impregnable wall between church and state constructed by the Framers of the First Amendment."[32] In the absence of clear directives from the judiciary, state legislatures continue to enact measures providing various types of governmental aid to nonpublic education.

THE ESTABLISHMENT CLAUSE AND TUITION TAX RELIEF MEASURES

The constitutionality of providing tax relief for parents of nonpublic school students rests on a judicial assessment of whether the primary effect of such measures advances religion or entangles the government in sectarian affairs. Do tuition tax credits or deductions provide a governmental subsidy to religious institutions?

Or are they similar to tax deductions for charitable contributions and tax exemptions for religious property, which have been endorsed by the Supreme Court? Does it affect the legal status of such tax relief measures if parents of public as well as private school students are eligible for the benefits? To date, the judiciary has provided only partial answers to these questions.

In 1973 the Supreme Court struck down a New York tax relief measure for private school patrons in *Committee for Public Education and Religious Liberty* v. *Nyquist.*[33] Under the provision, parents could subtract from their adjusted gross income for state income tax purposes a designated amount for each dependent for whom they paid at least $50 in nonpublic school tuition. Only parents with an adjusted gross income of less than $25,000 were eligible. Noting that over 85 percent of New York's private schools were church-related, the Court concluded that the measure aided sectarian institutions. The Court reasoned that the program rewarded parents for sending their children to parochial schools and, therefore, had the primary effect of advancing religion.

In the same year the Supreme Court affirmed, without an opinion, a decision of an Ohio federal district court striking down state statutes providing tax credits for educational expenses in elementary and secondary schools.[34] The Ohio statutes allowed a maximum credit of $90 per child the first year, with provision for the credit to be increased in subsequent years (based on the percentage increase in statewide per-pupil expenditures) up to 25 percent of the prior year's credit. Parents owing less in state income tax than the amount of their credit would receive a refund as long as the credit did not exceed their total state tax liability from property, sales, excise, and income taxes. Although the credit was not restricted to private school patrons, the court recognized that the vast majority of those benefiting from the statutes would be parents of parochial school children. The court found that the class singled out for an economic advantage was "suspect because of a predominantly sectarian character," thus necessitating strict judicial scrutiny to ensure that the state's taxing powers were not used in contravention of the First Amendment.[35] Reasoning that the proposed credit would provide indirect aid to sectarian schools, the court declared that it would make a "mockery" of the establishment clause if it allowed such indirect aid while disallowing direct state grants to such schools.

More recently, a New Jersey income tax benefit program that provided state taxpayers a personal deduction of $1,000 against gross income for any dependent child attending a nonpublic elementary school fulltime was contested.[36] Finding that the primary beneficiaries of the deduction would be parents of parochial school students, the federal district court reasoned that there was no constitutional distinction between this income tax deduction and the tax relief program invalidated earlier by the Supreme Court in the *Nyquist* case. The court concluded that the New Jersey law would have the direct effect of aiding religion and would further enmesh the state in political strife, thereby creating excessive governmental entanglement with religion. On appeal, the Third Circuit Appellate Court agreed that the income tax deduction would have the primary effect of advancing religion in violation of the establishment clause, and thus did not find it necessary to address the excessive entanglement issue. The United States Supreme Court subsequently affirmed by summary action the appellate court's ruling.

The following year, the First Circuit Court of Appeals affirmed a lower court's decision, striking down a Rhode Island statute calling for state tax deductions from personal gross income for costs associated with tuition, textbooks, and transportation for children in public or private elementary and secondary schools.[37] The deduction was limited to $500 for each dependent in kindergarten through grade six and $700 for each dependent in grades seven through twelve. The deduction for textbooks was restricted to secular books and equipment. The federal district court reasoned that the plaintiffs did not have to prove that the deduction directly benefited religious schools; they needed only to establish that the law conferred a special benefit on parents sending their children to sectarian schools. Based on the uncontradicted evidence that a vast majority of the parents eligible for the deductions sent their children to church-related schools, the federal district court ruled that the statute violated the establishment clause.

Affirming this conclusion, the appellate court reasoned that the tuition deduction "would confer a tax benefit along nearly solid sectarian lines."[38] Regarding the textbook deduction provision, the court further noted:

> The difficulty with this provision is not that the secular nature of the textbooks and instructional material for which deductions might be taken could not be guaranteed; it is that the involvement of church and state necessary to guarantee that result would excessively entangle church and state.[39]

While both the district and appellate courts suggested that the transportation deduction alone might pass constitutional scrutiny, they ruled that this "minor part" of the challenged statute could not be severed from the unconstitutional portions of the law.

In opposition to the prevailing judicial posture, the Eighth Circuit Court of Appeals in 1982 affirmed a federal district court's conclusion that a Minnesota tax benefit program, almost identical to the Rhode Island plan, does not abridge the First Amendment.[40] The federal district court, and subsequently appellate court, reasoned in *Mueller* v. *Allen* that the state income tax deduction for educational expenses is akin to a tax exemption for religious property which has withstood constitutional challenge.

The courts relied heavily on *Walz* v. *Tax Commission* in which the Supreme Court upheld a New York property tax exemption for churches as part of a broad category of exemptions for religious, charitable, and educational institutions.[41] Noting the long established tradition of tax-exempt status for religious property, the Court in *Walz* reasoned that the exemption created only minimal and remote involvement between church and state because places of worship were part of a broader class of exempt properties owned by not-for-profit institutions. Furthermore, the Court concluded that the tax exemption required *less* governmental involvement with religion than would taxation, thereby reducing the threat of excessive entanglement. The Court reasoned that tax exemption "restricts the fiscal relationship between church and state, and tends to complement and reinforce the desired separation insulating each from the other."[42] The Court declared that a tax exemption cannot be considered sponsorship because the government does not transfer revenue to the church; it "simply abstains from demanding that the church support the state."[43]

Finding the *Walz* precedent controlling in *Mueller,* the federal district court concluded that a tax deduction for parents sending their children to sectarian schools does not advance religion any more than an exemption for religious property or deductions for donations to sectarian institutions. The court further noted that the tax deduction is available to all taxpayers who incur school-related expenses for their children and thus satisfies the constitutional test of governmental neutrality toward religion. Under the law, public school patrons can deduct bus fare, equipment rental, summer school tuition, and costs of special sports attire associated with public school attendance. Therefore, the court concluded that the widely distributed tax relief cannot be considered a measure to advance religion.[44]

Affirming the lower court's decision, the appellate court distinguished the Minnesota law from the impermissible New York tax credit program that bestowed benefits *only* on parents of private school students.[45] The court concluded that, unlike the New York measure, substantial benefits flow to the general public in the Minnesota program. However, the court could not distinguish the Minnesota law from the Rhode Island provision, and admittedly differed from the First Circuit Court of Appeals in interpreting the applicable legal principles.[46] The court acknowledged that these deductions fall in the "gray area" between permissible tax exemptions for religious institutions and impermissible income tax credits designed only for parents of private school students.

Faced with opposing appellate rulings on comparable state provisions, in October 1982, the United States Supreme Court agreed to review the *Mueller* case. Eight months later, the severely splintered Court rendered its decision, upholding the controversial Minnesota law. The *Mueller* majority found the Minnesota law to be "vitally different" from the measure invalidated in *Nyquist* which granted "thinly disguised 'tax benefits,' actually amounting to tuition grants, to parents of children attending private schools."[47] In contrast, Minnesota's "decision to defray the cost of educational expenses incurred by parents—regardless of the type of schools their children attend—evidences a purpose that is both secular and understandable."[48] The majority reasoned that a state's efforts to assist parents with the burden of rising educational expenses advances the public purpose of ensuring an educated citizenry.

Turning to the question of whether the Minnesota law has the primary effect of advancing religion, the court noted that the educational deduction is simply one among many deductions available to achieve an equitable distribution of the state's tax burden. Since all parents are eligible for the educational deduction, the majority reasoned that the program providing "state assistance to a broad spectrum of citizens is not readily subject to challenge under the Establishment Clause."[49] Recognizing that most recent decisions in which the Supreme Court has invalidated state aid for parochial schools have involved the *direct* transmission of public funds to such schools, the majority found the "form" of public assistance to be a crucial consideration:

> The historic purposes of the clause simply do not encompass the sort of attenuated financial benefit, ultimately controlled by the private choices of individual parents, that eventually flows to parochial schools from the neutrally available tax benefit at issue in this case.[50]

The majority declined to address the petitioners' statistical evidence substantiating the fact that the primary beneficiaries of the Minnesota law are parents of sectarian school children. Exhibiting great respect for the contributions of parochial schools in providing high quality education, the majority indicated that even if the tax deduction has an unequal effect, it can be viewed as a "rough return for the benefits . . . provided to the state and all taxpayers by parents sending their children to parochial schools."[51]

The majority quickly dispensed with the third prong of the tripartite test, concluding that the Minnesota law does not create excessive governmental entanglement with religion. The only possible threat of entanglement would be the state surveillance necessary to ensure that deductions are claimed only for secular books and materials. Such inquiries were not found to be substantially different from those approved in prior

Supreme Court decisions involving state aid to sectarian schools.

Justice Marshall, writing for the four dissenting judges, claimed that the Minnesota law clearly serves to advance religion in violation of the establishment clause. Finding no significant difference between the tax credit in *Nyquist* and the deduction in *Mueller,* Marshall noted that parents of parochial school students and ultimately sectarian schools are the primary beneficiaries in both instances. The small benefits available to public school parents cannot alter the fact that tuition is the single largest expense that may be deducted under the Minnesota program: "The statute is little more than a subsidy of tuition masquerading as a subsidy of general educational expenses."[52] Marshall contended that the Minnesota statute requires "taxpayers in general [to] pay for the cost of parochial education and extends a financial 'incentive to parents to send their children to sectarian schools.' "[53]

Reasoning that it is irrelevant whether tax relief is in the form of a credit or deduction, Marshall declared that "what is of controlling significance is not the form but the 'substantive impact' of the financial aid."[54] He argued that a tax deduction has the primary effect of advancing religion if it is provided to offset expenditures, such as tuition, which are not confined to the secular activities of parochial schools.[55] Asserting that the lines drawn in *Nyquist* were done so on a reasoned basis with appropriate regard for the establishment clause, the dissent claimed that the same cannot be said of the lines drawn by the majority in *Mueller:*

> For the first time, the Court has upheld financial support for religious schools without any reason at all to assume that the support will be restricted to the secular functions of those schools and will not be used to support religious instruction. This result is flatly at odds with the fundamental principle that a State may provide no financial support whatsoever to promote religion.[56]

THE UNCERTAIN FUTURE

It is too soon to realize the full impact of the *Mueller* decision, but it will undoubtedly encourage other states to enact similar laws. The decision also has implications for the proposed federal tuition tax credit program championed by the Reagan administration. Although the 1982 Reagan proposal (calling for a credit up to 50 percent of each child's tuition with a maximum of $100 in 1983 and rising to $500 in 1985) did not receive congressional endorsement, the Senate Finance Committee did approve a modified provision with a maximum credit of $300 and stronger anti-discrimination protections. In November 1983, the Senate defeated an attempt to add this measure to another piece of legislation, but congressional activity pertaining to tuition tax credits seems likely to continue.[57]

In light of the *Mueller* ruling, advocates of tuition tax credits believe that a federal measure could withstand constitutional scrutiny. However, eligibility may have to be broadened to include public as well as private school patrons, and expenses beyond tuition, both of which would make the program more costly for the federal government. Also, the form of the tax relief may have to shift from credits to deductions.

Taken together, the *Nyquist* and *Mueller* decisions suggest that tuition tax credits *only* to parents of private school students would not satisfy the establishment clause. Yet, recent Supreme Court action in establishment clause cases has been difficult to predict. The wall of separation between church and state which the Supreme Court referred to as "high and impregnable" in 1947 has, more recently, been called "a blurred, indistinct, and variable barrier" by the Court.[58] Recent decisions interpreting the reach of the establishment clause have been characterized by dissension among the justices, and the outcomes of many decisions, such as *Mueller,* have hinged on one vote. The current Court majority seems to have adopted a more lenient application of the establishment clause than was true a decade ago, favoring "benevolent" rather than "strict" governmental neutrality toward religion.[59]

Given that the composition of the Court has changed since 1973 when *Nyquist* was rendered, it is conceivable that laws permitting tuition tax credits *only* for private school patrons might be approved by a majority of the Supreme Court. Proponents of tuition tax credits find some support for this position in *Mueller* because the Court majority showed great respect for the important public service provided by parochial schools and indicated that such schools deserve governmental benefits in return.

Even if the Court does not condone tax credits earmarked for private school tuition, it has by a slim margin endorsed a general state income tax deduction available to all parents for educational expenses. If the *Mueller* dissenters had been able to persuade one more justice to endorse their position, it would have taken a federal constitutional amendment to legalize educational tax relief measures. Such a precedent would have severely impeded—and perhaps totally curtailed—efforts to secure state and federal legislation providing tax relief for parents of private school students.

But instead, the *Mueller* decision has fueled the political debate over the efficacy of tax deductions for educational expenses. The impact of such measures on public education, national equity goals, individual liberty, and freedom of choice are among the sensitive issues being debated at the state and federal levels. The *Mueller* decision may also stimulate state litigation because educational tax deductions, like state aid for private school transportation and secular textbooks, might be found in violation of state law even if it is permissible under the First Amendment.[60]

Moreover, *Mueller* and subsequent establishment clause opinions may have ramifications for other church-state controversies involving education. It appears from recent rulings that the current Supreme Court majority is only giving lip service to the tripartite test.[61] The Reagan administration has urged the court to reassess its precedents established in the mid-twentieth century when the Court took a strong stand on separation of church and state. And it seems that the current majority is complying. Indeed, the Court's recent establishment clause opinions may signal a reinterpretation of what constitutes appropriate governmental neutrality toward religion, with accommodation, rather than separation, becoming the governing principle.

NOTES

1. *See* Joseph Blau, *Cornerstones of Religious Freedom in America* (Boston: Beacon Press, 1949); M. Searles Bates, *Religious Liberty:* An Inquiry (New York: International Missionary Council, 1945); Henry Lee, *A History of the Inquisition in the Middle Ages* (New York: Harper and Brothers, 1888).

2. For a discussion of church-state relations during the colonial period, *see* Leo Pfeffer, *Church, State and Freedom* (Boston: Beacon Press, 1967), 71–90.

3. *See* Tudor v. Board of Educ., 100 A.2d 857, 861–862 (N.J. 1953).

4. Pfeffer, *Church, State and Freedom,* 141.

5. Mario Montuoti, *John Lock, A Letter Concerning Toleration* (The Hague: Martinue Nijhoff, 1963), 19.

6. *See* Kern Alexander, *School Law* (St. Paul: West Pub. Co., 1980), 170.

7. Robert Rutland, *The Birth of the Bill of Rights 1776–1791* (Chapel Hill: University of North Carolina Press, 1955), v.

8. Permoli v. First Municipality of New Orleans, 44 U.S. 589, 609 (1845).

9. Maryland permitted taxation for the support of religion and denied civil office to non-Christians until 1833. A provision of the North Carolina Constitution, disqualifying for public office any person denying a belief in God or the truth of the Christian religion, was finally eliminated in 1868. *See* Pfeffer, *Church, State and Freedom,* 141; Jesse Choper, "The Religion Clauses of the First Amendment: Reconciling the Conflict," *University of Pittsburgh Law Review* (1980): 676.

10. Ellwood Cubberley, *Public Education in the United States: A Study and Interpretation of American Educational History,* rev. ed. (Boston: Houghton-Mifflin Co., 1934), 294; David Mall, "The Kingdom of God and Common School;" Carl Kaestle, *Pillars of the Republic: Common Schools and American Society, 1780–1960* (New York: Hill and Wang, 1983).

11. *See* Walter Berns, *The First Amendment and the Future of American Democracy* (New York: Basic Books, Inc., 1976), 66–67; Pfeffer, *Church, State and Freedom,* 335–338.

12. Pierce v. Society of Sisters, 268 U.S. 510 (1925).

13. *See* Scopes v. State, 289 S. W. 363 (Tenn. 1927) (upholding anti-evolution statute); Lewis v. Board of Educ. of the City of New York, 285 N.Y.S. 164 (Sup. Ct. New York County, 1935); Hackett v. Brooksville Graded School Dist., 87 S. W. 792 (Ky. App. 1905) (upholding daily devotional activities in public schools).

14. Cantwell v. Connecticut, 310 U.S. 296, 303 (1940).

15. Marbury v. Madison, 5 U.S. (1 Cranch) 137 (1803).

16. Everson v. Board of Educ., 330 U.S. 1, 31–32 (1947) (Rutledge, J., dissenting). *See also* Walfred Peterson, *Thy Liberty in Law* (Nashville, TN: Broadman Press, 1978), 120; Leo Pfeffer, *Religious Freedom* (Skokie, Ill.: National Textbook Co., 1977), 172.

17. Lemon v. Kurtzman, 403 U.S. 602, 614 (1971). *See also* School Dist. of Abington Township c. Schempp, 374 U.S. 203 (1963); Engel v. Vitale, 370 U.S. 421, 434 (1962); Zorach v. Clauson, 343 U.S. 306, 312–313 (1952). In its most recent establishment clause decision the Court majority announced that the Constitution "does not require complete separation of church and state." Donnelly v. Lynch, 52 USLW 4317, 4318 (1984).

18. School Dist. of Abington Township v. Schempp, 374 U.S. 203, 306 (1963) (Goldberg, J., concurring).

19. Id., 222.

20. Walz v. Tax Commission of the City of New York, 397 U.S. 664, 670 (1970). The tripartite test was first applied in an education case in Lemon v. Kurtzman, 403 U.S. 602, 612, 613 (1971).

21. For a discussion of litigation involving challenges to devotional activities in public schools, *see* Martha McCarthy, *Church, State and the Schools: A Delicate Balance* (Bloomington, IN: Phi Delta Kappa, 1983), Chapter 2.

22. This figure is based on a survey conducted by the National Center for Educational Statistics in 1981. *See Education Daily,* 14 July 1982, 1.

23. *See* Board of Educ. v. Allen, 392 U.S. 236 (1968) (textbooks); Everson v. Board of Educ., 330 U.S. 1 (1947) (transportation).

24. *See* McCarthy, *Church, State and the Schools.*

25. Everson v. Board of Educ., 330 U.S. 1 (1947). A few state legislatures have enacted laws authorizing special transportation benefits for private school students, and some of these provisions have been upheld under the first amendment. *See* McKeesport Area School Dist. v. Pennsylvania Dept. of Educ., 392 A.2d 912 (Pa. 1978), *appeal dismissed,* 446 U.S. 970 (1980); School Dist. of Pittsburgh v. Dept. of Educ. of Pennsylvania, 443 U.S. 901 (1979); Hahner v. Board of Educ., 278 N.W.2d 474 (Wis. App. 1979).

26. Board of Educ. v. Allen, 392 U.S. 236 (1968).

27. *See* Wolman v. Walter, 433 U.S. 229 (1977); Meek v. Pittenger, 421 U.S. 349 (1975). However, in 1973 the Court ruled that a state could not loan textbooks to students attending racially exclusive private schools because such use of public funds would unconstitutionally aid racial discrimination; Norwood v. Harrison, 413 U.S. 445 (1973). More recently, the Court applied similar logic in denying federal tax exempt status to religious schools that operate under racially discriminatory policies; Bob Jones University v. United States, Goldsboro Christian Schools v. United States, 103 S. Ct. 2017 (1983). *See* note 47.

28. Lemon v. Kurtzman, 402 U.S. 602 (1971).

29. Meek v. Pittenger, 421 U.S. 349 (1975); Sloan v. Lemon, 413 U.S. 825 (1973); Committee for Public Educ. and Religious Liberty v. Nyquist, 413 U.S. 756 (1973). It should be noted that during this period the Supreme Court was less inclined to find an establishment clause violation in connection with state aid to private institutions of higher education. Several differences between college and elementary and secondary school students (e.g., age, maturity, and vulnerability to indoctrination) have been offered as partial justification for this double standard. Also, students are compelled by law in all states to attend elementary and at least part of secondary school, whereas post-secondary education is totally voluntary. The Supreme Court has been more willing to accept the assertion that the religious and secular functions can be separated in sectarian institutions of higher education (where an atmosphere of academic freedom is maintained) than in parochial elementary and secondary schools (where religious indoctrination permeates the instructional program). The double standard applied seems to be based primarily on the *character* of the institutions and their

clientele, rather than on the *form* of the aid. *See* Roemer v. Board of Public Works, 426 U.S. 736 (1976) (upholding annual non-categorical state grants to private colleges and universities); Hunt v. McNair, 413 U.S. 734 (1973) (upholding the issuance of state revenue bonds to finance construction in a church-related college); Tilton v. Richardson, 403 U.S. 672 (1971) (upholding federal grants for private college and university construction under the Higher Education Facilities Act). Possibly this double standard eventually will be eliminated as the current Supreme Court seems less inclined to find an establishment clause violation in connection with aid to parochial elementary and secondary schools than was true from 1971 to 1976.

30. Committee for Public Educ. and Religious Liberty v. Regan, 444 U.S. 646 (1980); Wolman v. Walter, 433 U.S. 229 (1977). While the Supreme Court has ruled that state-supported compensatory education programs provided for private school students must be conducted at public or neutral sites, it declined to review a First Amendment challenge to the use of *federal* funds to pay public school teachers to provide compensatory instruction in sectarian schools. *See* National Coalition for Public Educ. and Religious Liberty v. Harris, 489 F. Supp. 1248 (S.D.N.Y. 1980), *appeal dismissed sub nom.* National Coalition for Public Educ. and Religious Liberty v. Hufstedler, 449 U.S. 808 (1980).

31. Wolman v. Walter, 433 U.S. 229 (1977).

32. Committee for Public Educ. and Religious Liberty v. Regan, 444 U.S. 646, 671 (1980) (Steven, J. dissenting).

33. 413 U.S. 756 (1973).

34. Kosydar v. Wolman, 353 F. Supp. 744 (S.D. Ohio 1972), *aff'd sub nom.* Grit v. Wolman, 413 U.S. 901 (1973).

35. Id.

36. Public Funds for Public Schools v. Byrne, 590 F.2d 514 (3d Cir. 1979), *aff'd* 442 U.S. 907 (1979).

37. Rhode Island Federation of Teachers AFL/CIO v. Norberg, 479 F. Supp. 1364 (D.R.I. 1979), *aff'd* 630 F.2d 855 (1st Cir. 1980).

38. 630 F.2d 860.

39. Id., 862.

40. Mueller v. Allen, 514 F. Supp. 998 (D. Minn. 1981), *aff'd* 676 F.2d 1195 (8th Cir. 1982), *aff'd* 103 S. Ct. 3062 (1963). *See also* Minnesota Civil Liberties Union v. Roemer, 452 F. Supp. 1316 (D. Minn. 1978).

41. 397 U.S. 664 (1970).

42. Id., 676.

43. Id., 675.

44. Mueller v. Allen, 514 F. Supp. 998 (D. Minn. 1981).

45. 676 F.2d at 1199–1200, distinguishing Committee for Public Educ. and Religious Liberty v. Nyquist, 413 U.S. 756 (1973). *See* text with note 33.

46. Id., 1200–1201. *See* Rhode Island Federation of Teachers AFL/CIO v. Norberg, 630 F.2d 855 (1st Cir. 1980); text with note 37.

47. 103 S. Ct. 3062, 3066 (1983). In Bob Jones University v. United States, Goldsboro Christian Schools v. United States, 103 S. Ct. 2017 (1983), the Supreme Court denied federal tax exempt status to sectarian schools that discriminate on the basis of race and denied charitable deductions for contributions to such schools. The Court reasoned that a tax benefit cannot be granted to private schools that operate in violation of public policy prohibiting racial discrimination. Thus, it appears that deductions for educational expenses could not be claimed for children attending racially discriminatory private schools.

48. Id., 103 S. Ct. at 3066–67.

49. Id., 3069.

50. Id.

51. Id., 3070.

52. Id., 3074 (Marshall, J., dissenting).

53. Id., 3073, quoting Committee for Public Education and Religious Liberty v. Nyquist, 413 U.S. 756, 786 (1973).

54. Id.

55. Id., 3077.

56. Id., 3078.

57. The tabled amendment would have allowed tuition tax credits up to $300 a year by 1986 for taxpayers earning less than $50,000. *See* Education Daily, (November 17, 1983): 1.

58. *Compare* Everson v. Board of Educ., 330 U.S. 1, 18 (1947) *with* Wolman v. Walter, 433 U.S. 229, 236 (1977).

59. *See* Steve Gey, "Rebuilding the Wall: The Case for a Return to the Strict Interpretation of the Establishment Clause," *Columbia Law Review* 81 (1981): 1468.

60. Although the Supreme Court has interpreted the First Amendment as allowing states to provide transportation and textbook aid for nonpublic school students, the supreme courts of several states have ruled that public funds cannot be used for such purposes under state law. For a discussion of these cases, *see* McCarthy, *Church, State and the Schools,* Chapter 6.

61. *See* Donnelly v. Lynch, 52 USLW 4317 (1984) (upholding the use of municipal funds to erect a Christmas display including the Nativity Scene); March v. Chambers, 103 S. Ct. 3330 (1983) (upholding the use of public funds to support a chaplain to open state legislative sessions with a prayer); Widmar v. Vincent, 454 U.S. 263 (1981) (endorsing students' free speech rights to hold devotional meetings in state-supported university facilities).

Serving Special Needs and Individualizing Instruction

People have differing levels of abilities and needs in certain areas. Exceptionalities of certain kinds, whether they be physical or cognitive, require special intervention or treatment skills. The Education of All Handicapped Children Act of 1975 (PL 94-142) was passed by Congress to address the needs of handicapped learners, regardless of their diagnosed handicaps. However, exceptionality does not just refer to handicaps. Gifted persons are exceptional too, and their least restrictive learning environments can indeed call for special intervention strategies. Herein lies one of the dilemmas of special education as one of the professional sectors of teacher specialization. There are so many types of special and exceptional children, youth and adults, that each person needs a carefully worked out strategy for optimizing his or her chances for a quality education. In addition to

Unit 7

diagnosed exceptionalities, children sometimes develop special needs for carefully individualized attention from their teachers due to injuries or mistreatment. So vast is the range of special needs which the nation's schools are called upon to address that the schools are financially and professionally stretched to the limits of their instructional capacity in doing so.

It is in this context that this topic is considered. An unfinished national educational agenda remains in this area. There are so many students with legitimate special needs of so many varieties, schools are hard pressed to serve them all well. Helping children adjust to the demands of life in schools and to find their best opportunities for fulfilling their own unique learning potential is no easy matter. This task challenges the talents of any teacher. Mainstreaming is the educational policy response to the federal legislation passed in 1975 to aid handicapped learners by placing them in individually prescribed, least restrictive learning environments. There is a big gap between the initial hopes and expectations for mainstreaming and the policy realities of efforts to implement it. The effort to develop individualized diagnostic and teaching strategies that classroom teachers can use with their students is part of the national effort to respond constructively to the needs of exceptional children and youth. The tensions between the goals of equality and quality in education are real and raise new educational issues.

Some of these issues have to do with how to provide enriched learning experiences to gifted students while providing least restrictive learning environments for cognitively handicapped students. Other issues relate to the demands on teachers' time and the difficulties involved in the total effort at individualization of the instructional programming of students. There are shortages of resources for both diagnosis and treatment. School systems have been very hard pressed on this issue in the past ten years.

The articles in this unit all relate to some exceptional or extraordinary need which students bring to school, whether it is a need for compassion and emotional help as a result of personal abuse or tense home situations or the need to learn what one can in spite of a handicap. The first three articles address the issue of mainstreaming and give the reader a sense of the complexities it presents in the efforts to achieve educational justice for exceptional students. Prior to 1975 many handicapped students were segregated into separate classrooms or institutions, or, as in some states prior to 1975, not allowed to enroll in public schools at all. The rights of handicapped students were established under the same arguments for Fourteenth Amendment rights to equality before the law as the desegregation effort discussed in the previous unit. The articles on mainstreaming are followed by a comparison of Soviet and American approaches to special education. The sexual abuse of children, the emotional needs of these children, and how teachers may be able to help them overcome their fear, hurt, and anger concludes the unit. Psychologists and therapists have been reporting that the sexual abuse of children has been increasing since the mid 1970s. The two articles on this topic summarize the nature of child abuse, outline the symptoms a teacher may observe, and suggest what can be done to help the mistreated students.

The readings in this unit are very relevant to all areas of curriculum and instruction, particularly in discussions or readings on the social or community origins of problems in education. They are also related to discussions of methods of teaching, to teacher behavior in disciplining students, and to equality of opportunity in education.

Looking Ahead: Challenge Questions

What is mainstreaming? What are some important professional issues to be considered in the implementation of mainstreaming?

In your opinion, what are effective alternative policies to the placement of "special" students in "nonspecial" classrooms?

What are some specific differences in the manner in which the Soviets and the Americans conduct special education for exceptional students? What are your views on these differences? Which approaches focus more on individual handicaps and talents? Which approaches optimize learning social skills?

What types of behavioral symptoms may a child exhibit to indicate sexual abuse? What can teachers do?

Are the professional situations of elementary and secondary teachers different when it comes to individualizing instruction? If so, in what specific ways? If not, why not?

What is meant by individualization? How can it be done?

Mainstreaming: Expectations and Realities

Patricia Reed

Guest Editor

Prior to the passage of the 1975 Education for All Handicapped Children Act, teaching of the handicapped was generally considered to be the responsibility of special educators. Current regulations accompanying P.L. 94-142 place expectations relative to educating the handicapped upon all professional educators. All teachers are now expected to demonstrate competencies essential to assure that handicapped students' educational placements constitute the least restrictive environment. These regulations further require that attention be given at both the preservice and inservice levels to the training of general as well as special educators and support personnel.

Translation of these expectations into realities has engendered controversy among professional educators in all fields and at all levels, including colleges and universities. Some of this controversy is attributable to fundamental opposition to the intent of the legislation. Much is related to varying interpretations of the letter of the law. Even more is reflective of the complexities involved in arriving at consensus as to how educational practices can and should be modified to meet the educational needs of all students.

Nowhere are the expectations or their translations into realities more controversial and more difficult than where they relate to educational programming for secondary students. Traditional concepts of roles and responsibilities, organizational patterns, instructional modes, and even the purposes of secondary schools seem to pose almost insurmountable obstacles to "mainstreaming" being accepted and implemented as an educationally sound process.

Two years ago a group of Bowling Green State University faculty who teach professional education coursework required of prospective secondary teachers began to grapple with the controversies and difficulties of placing handicapped students in regular secondary classrooms. Their major goal was twofold: (1) to determine the knowledge, skills, attitudes and values regular teachers need to make mainstreaming "work," and (2) to design and implement a revised curriculum which would assure that beginning teachers have initial competencies in these areas.

Clearly the preparation of teachers is but one aspect of the complex problem of providing appropriate education for the handicapped. That fact itself made the task faculty had before them potentially impossible to achieve—at least on the basis of factors over which they might exercise direct control. Nonetheless they began.

As work progressed, they found their expanding knowledge only generated more questions, thus making it even more difficult to formulate conclusions which could be acted upon with a reasonable amount of assurance. However, after two years of work they arrived at what they believe to be warranted assumptions about what regular secondary teachers can be prepared to do to promote the educational progress of students who need specialized services but need not be restricted to specialized environments. As might have been anticipated, they also arrived at certain assumptions about what other members of the profession can do to make this possible.

The articles which comprise this special issue have been selected to be representative of predominant concerns which surfaced during the two years of work. They are presented as a stimulus for considered thought and action by teachers, administrators, and teacher educators.

More importantly, these articles are evidence that the expectations of P.L. 94-142 are being translated into realities which recognize that the preparation of all teachers affects the teaching of all students.

Presently there is a major movement to "deregulate" P.L. 94-142. If successful, this action will eliminate many expectations now associated with this legislation, including a number pertaining to the preparation of teachers. Perhaps certain expectations of P.L. 94-142 have created realities which are not acceptable or educationally sound. But is the recognition that the preparation of all teachers affects the teaching of all students an unacceptable or educationally unsound reality? Let us think carefully, lest we permit the proverbial baby to be tossed out with the bath water.

Reprinted from *American Secondary Education,* Special Issue, Vol. 12, 1982. Copyright 1982 Bowling Green State University. All rights reserved.

A Holistic View of Mainstreaming

Conrad Pritscher

Conrad Pritscher is a Professor in the department of Educational Foundations and Inquiry at Bowling Green State University in Bowling Green, Ohio.

Teachers who hold a holistic view of education have been doing voluntarily what is now required by Public Law 94-142. Holistic teachers turn the idea of "least restrictive" into the idea of "most enabling" environments for both students and teachers.

A holistic view of education holds that enhancement of students' learning how to learn is a major reason for acquiring various skills and knowledge. According to this view, there is an underlying process that seems to be more fundamental than what is frequently termed the "basics" (i.e., skills and knowledge of reading, writing, arithmetic, and fundamental skills, and knowledge within various disciplines).

Holistic teachers do not view handicapped students in their classes as a burden, since mainstreaming emphasizes the idea of "most enabling environment." Holistic educators have had this emphasis for centuries. However, it is an emphasis that has existed for all students, not only for those who fall into the group called handicapped.

Creating Most Enabling Environments Through Holistic Teaching

When defined as "most enabling environment," the mainstreaming notion of "least restrictive environment" is welcomed by holistic educators as a major step toward the fuller development of each student's free, responsible choice. Holistic educators believe that one cannot make free, responsible choices without basic skills and knowledge, yet they do not usually teach these skills and knowledge apart from active, open-ended student inquiry. Holistic educators further maintain that through this process of open-ended inquiry, basic skills and knowledge are developed.

However, many teachers believe that these basic skills and knowledge ought to be taught in isolation (partly because the curriculum "says" these basic skills and knowledge "must be taught"). Often without wondering or questioning the wisdom of teaching basic skills and knowledge in isolation, these teachers prevent open student inquiry because "the material must be covered" or because "that's the way things are."

The holistic educator has long held that "things are that way" largely because man has made them that way. Furthermore, the holistic educator believes that what man has made, man can change; therefore, more things, processes, and events can be what man wants them to be.

Another characteristic of the holistic notion of "most enabling environment" is that of personal responsibility for what one is and for what one becomes. The holistic educator holds that the teaching-learning relationship with regular and "special" students is partially paradoxical in that the primary emphasis is on the teacher's intervening (directing, guiding, coaxing) so that the students will need less outside intervention, or so that the students will have these interventions primarily when they choose them. The holistic teacher directs in order to enable the student to become more self-directing. Built into this holistic view of teaching is the notion that the teacher helps provide conditions whereby the student relies less and less on outside authority and, instead, more and more on his authority.

Some people say "I do not want to be my own authority." This is acceptable if they are aware of what they are doing, if they choose to do it, and if they are responsible for the consequences. They are then choosing consciously to have somebody else choose for them. This aware, free, responsible choice makes them their own authority regardless of what they say.

Reprinted from *American Secondary Education,* Special Issue, Vol. 12, 1982. Copyright 1982 Bowling Green State University. All rights reserved.

Assumptions Underlying Holistic Teaching

Holistic teachers base their decisions and actions upon the following assumptions:

1. Above all else, a holistic classroom is a learning environment where education is viewed as a life-long process in which the learner is guided to his outer limits. In this way, creative, free, responsible choice is maximized to enhance the learner's ability and desire to invent his present and future.
2. Learning is viewed as a process in which the primary emphasis is on learning how to learn, and the secondary emphasis is on acquiring a body of "correct" information.
3. The priority in this learning environment is on the learner's self-image, which is enhanced through fusing intellect and feeling. One's self-image generates most of the achievement.
4. Because the learning process has not yet been fully conceptualized (and may, indeed, be incapable of total conceptualization), this learning environment is a relatively flexible structure. Inherent in this belief is the notion that there are many ways to teach.
5. The learner's inner experience is viewed as a context for learning that is coordinated with the external world as a context for learning.
6. This learning environment promotes whole-brain education in which right-brain nonlinear, intuitive, holistic strategies augment left-brain linear, anlaytical rationality. The learner is viewed as transrational.
7. This learning environment stresses that the human relationships between teachers and learners are of primary importance and technology is seen as a tool to be used by man for the humanization man.
8. This learning environment views the learner as an open system who continuously reconstructs his experience so that he can better invent his present and his future. Inherent in this is the belief that prior to a major reconstructing of experience, a feeling of discontinuity emerges. This discontinuity may be viewed as a productive stress whose intensity ranges from wonder, puzzlement, uneasiness, excitement, creative tension, and confusion, to, at times, anxiety. This learning environment is safe enough to explore, and it encourages exploratory (experimental) effort within the framework of safe emergencies that teachers can help provide. It is assumed that dealing with disequilibrium can foster greater equilibrium.
9. Teaching in this responsive learning environment is primarily an activity that fosters openness to strange new possibilities in which the teacher is a midwife of ideas and a facilitator of learner left-brain/right-brain integration. The teacher believes not only that the learner "causes" the learning, but also that learning can be assisted by providing appropriate conditions.
10. A part of this responsive learning environment is a desire to increase degrees of trust in teacher/learner relations.
11. This responsive learning environment encourages each learner's uniqueness to be developed and cherished.
12. Teachers as well as learners need to deal with ambiguity, puzzlement, conflict, and paradox if noticeable reconstructing (transformation) of experience is to occur. Awareness is a major key in this transforming process. Awareness allows greater access to unconscious anxieties that may stand in the way of this process of reconstructing experience.

As they see more and broade patterns, teachers develop a commo (whole) sense which they can also hel develop within their students (if such i their primary goal). This sense relate to knowledge and skills that they nee to accommodate various handicappe students. Common sense, as the terr is being used here, is that which help teachers generate "on the spot" th various skills and knowledge that the need when faced with uniqu situations. Common sense generate inventive resourcefulness. The holisti educator has always believed that n only is each student unique, but so each day, hour, or minute. Th individualizing of instructior consequently, has been, and continu to be, prized by holistic educators.

Conclusions

Holistic teachers have long bee voluntarily doing what is now legall required in the relatively ne mainstreaming law (P. L. 94-14 which aims at providing the lea restrictive environment fo handicapped students. Holisti teachers view their primary function a that of making the classroom the mo enabling environment for all student

Mainstreaming: Is It Secondary At the Secondary Level?

Ellen Williams
Isabel Hansen
Barbara Jackson

Ellen Williams is Assistant Professor in the Department of Special Education at Bowling Green State University.

Isabel Hansen is Assistant to the Director of the Dean's Grant Project at Bowling Green.

Barbara Jackson is a Graduate Assistant assigned to the Dean's Project at Bowling Green.

Preparing secondary teachers to work effectively with handicapped students requires that regular teacher education faculty make a behavioral commitment to incorporating mainstreaming instruction within the pre-service curriculum. Such commitment can be brought about through involvement of faculty in in-service programs which combine knowledge expansion, direct contact with handicapped students, and self-assessment.

It has been postulated that teacher attitude is the critical variable in the successful integration of handicapped students into the regular classroom.[1] If we are intent on providing successful mainstreaming programs for handicapped students, we must address both at the pre-service and in-service levels the issue of teacher attitude toward the handicapped student. Effective mainstreaming competencies cannot be developed at the pre-service level merely through lip service concerning the acceptance of the handicapped. If educators want to promote a positive attitude toward the handicapped among the pre-service population, they must first embrace and demonstrate an attitude of acceptance toward the handicapped.

Avenues have been provided to help faculty examine their own attitudes and promote instructional and curricular change related to mainstreaming through Dean's Grant Projects. Bowling Green State University was awarded a Dean's Grant in 1980 and again in 1981. Its major thrust has been to effect curricular change within the secondary education program by providing in-service education on mainstreaming for those faculty responsible for teaching secondary methods and foundations classes. During its first year of implementation, some of the strategies the Dean's Grant employed for changing attitudes were: 1) knowledge-based experiences, 2) simulation activities, 3) enforced contact, and 4) self-evaluation assessments.

Expanding Faculty Knowledge

As part of the knowledge-based experiences, consultants, resource people, resource information, and bibliographic references were provided throughout the year. The in-service format included lecture, informal discussion and suggested readings of bibliographic material. The education program utilized these sources to explore various aspects of the following: 1) P.L. 94-142, 2) individualized education plans, 3) types of handicapping conditions, 4) mainstreaming the special needs student, 5) accommodating exceptional students in the regular classroom, and 6) support services available to the regular educator.

In addition, faculty were required to participate in such tasks as simulations, panel discussions, examination of course objectives, and field visitations. Following one meeting, for instance, which focused on individual differences and similarities between non-handicapped and handicapped populations, written reactions of the participants were reviewed. Participants' comments reflected uncertainty and frustration:

> My reaction to this session is mixed. I feel that we rehashed philosophical problems that have emerged each time we've met. For that reason, we strayed from the topic at hand. If someone were to ask about characteristics, needs, and behaviors of a mainstreamed student, I'd be hard-pressed to speak in anything but generalities and platitudes. 'Meeting needs' appears to be a dead horse. Let's stop beating it and wrestle with some specifics.

Reprinted from American Secondary Education, Special Issue, Vol. 12, 1982. Copyright 1982 Bowling Green State University. All rights reserved.

Although the intent of the guest speaker at this meeting was to promote the idea that all too often we look at the handicapped populations in terms of differences, and fail to see the similarities of the handicapped population with the normal population, a number of the participants left the in-service feeling as if there were *no* differences between the handicapped and non-handicapped populations. This reaction and similar comments may reflect the uncertainty and lack of understanding that often precede positive attitudinal change.[2]

When these reactions surface, Hiltenbrand suggests employing a different paradigm for attitudinal change: simulation. Simulation requires the target group members to act out the roles and real-life situations of a dissimilar population. Thus, the target group is applying a practical application of knowledge and developing empathy toward the attitudinal object. Dean's Grant members participated in two types of in-house simulations. In the first simulation professors assumed the role of the regular classroom teacher as they read a case study describing their newly mainstreamed student. The information given to the participants included a brief case study, the student's individualized education plan, and his class schedule. Participants divided into small groups to discuss possible strategies for 1) gaining an understanding of the I.E.P. and its application to the classroom, 2) dealing with the students' behavioral problems (i.e., talking out, tardiness, authority problems), and 3) accommodating for his learning disability (i.e., visual memory problems affecting his reading level).

Participants' reactions to this session were consistently positive, although various viewpoints emerged. One participant noted:

> The session today was stimulating. I enjoyed the interaction with my small group and having to focus on a real problem that could confront any of our students when they get their first teaching job. This was the first time I have ever seen an I.E.P., and found that in itself invaluable. My reaction to the mainstreamed student was that he appeared on paper to be very similar to the average ninth grade student I encounter in urban schools. The session was well designed.

Whereas another member stated:

> Although it was a great experience and some reality contact, teachers are not prepared to deal with a behavioral problem because they are not trained in therapy techniques and group dynamics. I have long advocated an experiential growth-group type experience be required for all teachers. This would pay off for their work with the average student *and* the special student.

The second simulation activity occurred at an established field base site, a local area high school. This simulation differed from the first in that the Dean's Grant faculty participants did not simulate the actual roles, but were asked instead to observe the case staffing as it was role-played by the actual faculty in the secondary school field site. The purpose of the simulation was to provide university faculty with insight into mainstreaming case staffings. The university faculty were given the opportunity to ask questions, comment on decisions, and provide additional comments which they felt were relevant to the mainstreaming case staffing. Most of the participants described the experience as a new, exciting presentation; however, a few had been actual participants in previous staffings and felt that they had gained little additional information on specific strategies for mainstreaming a learning-disabled student. One member exhibited skepticism as a result of this simulation, and commented:

> I found the conference interesting but wondered how often this actually occurs. The regular teacher appeared to be involved only when discussing the student's placement in his class. Shouldn't there be communication among the total professional staff prior to the I.E.P. conference? How is the determination made concerning the child's probability of success in the regular classroom?

Thus it would appear that the simulation activities acted as a catalyst in the attitudinal change process. Although the uneasiness and uncertainty which occurred were not totally removed through the use of simulation, participants did become more cognizant of the "realities" involved in the mainstreaming process. In spite of this, it is unwise to conclude that simulation activities in and of themselves were responsible for helping participants make a more positive transition in the attitude change process, for while they were involved in simulation activities, they were also involved with enforced contact experiences.

Direct Contact Experiences

Enforced contact unites the target person with outgroup members under conditions thought to be conducive to attitude change. Two activities involving enforced contact were provided for the Dean's Grant participants. The first activity was a panel discussion comprised of junior high and secondary educators from a nearby school district. In this experience, the panel members were asked to share with the university faculty their roles and perceptions of the mainstreaming program in their school. During the presentation, the panel pointed out that one of the major criteria for a successful mainstreaming program was the importance of open and consistent communication between special education faculty and regular education faculty. The practical suggestions from these teachers were supported by research studies that view support systems as essential to successful mainstreaming.

> The role of the special teacher should be expanded to become one of resource person: one who is capable of working with other teachers, making recommendations, prescribing materials to be used, and serving as a specialist in the content areas as well as dealing with the general problems of the special student. There is a corollary to this recommendation: that it is necessary that the regular teacher be trained to accept advice and assistance from another person who may be of similar rank in the organization.[3]

This recommendation was supporte[d] by the faculty participants following th[e] enforced contact experience betwee[n] themselves and the secondary pane[l].

Although the faculty participants fe[lt] that they had benefited from conta[ct] with secondary school personn[el] involved in mainstreaming, membe[rs] expressed a need for dire[ct] xperiences with the mainstreamed upil.

Structured field experiences were esigned to provide contact between e faculty participants and the ainstreamed students. Each niversity faculty member was assigned specific mainstreamed student at the eld-based site. The students' ndicapping conditions included earing-impaired, learning-disabled, hysically-handicapped, educable-entally retarded, and behavior-sordered. Prior to meeting with the signed student, each participant viewed his student's I.E.P. and terviewed the special and regular achers involved in educating the udent. After establishing a rapport th the mainstreamed pupil through a ersonal interview, the faculty member ranged to observe the student in his gular and special classes. Each niversity participant was asked to aintain a log which included a record actual experiences and evaluative omments related to this field-based bservation.

Insights gained as a result of this perience were shared among grant articipants at a subsequent in-service. ollowing the in-service, one partici-ant commented:

> This session was valuable in that each participant had the opportunity to meet a special student firsthand, and to hear what effects the mainstreaming situation had on the student. It was interesting to note that some students were not accommodated or particularly welcomed in some of their mainstreamed classes due to the negative attitude of the teacher...All my colleagues appeared to be enthusiastic about their field visits, indicating that their understanding of special kids in a regular setting had increased considerably.

second participant reported:

> It is apparent that there is severe human cost when students are misplaced, when teachers who mainstream are indifferent to their students, or when needed resources for support are absent, unknown, or neglected. It's also important to note that there are inspired and dedicated teachers who are doing all they can for their students.

hese evaluation comments reinforce e concept that the teacher's attitude ward the handicapped student is critical to the success of a mainstreaming program.[4] The majority of participants indicated that the enforced contact experience promoted a greater understanding of problems facing mainstreamed students.

Assessing Attitudes

Even though the participants' evaluative comments given at the end of each seminar or activity do not provide empirical evidence to show a change in the attitude toward the handicapped, they do, however, tend to support the literature which suggests that effective attitudinal change programs should include direct contact experiences, cognitive information, and experiential activities.[5] Attempts were made, nonetheless, to gather empirical data for determining attitude change among the participants. The Mandell Opinionaire (1976), which measures attitudes toward mainstreaming the mildly handicapped, was administered on a pre-level at the first in-service session, and the post-level at the last in-service session. Using a five-point Likert scale ranging from "strongly agree to strongly disagree," participants were asked to respond to twenty items related to their attitudes towards mainstreaming of the mildly handicapped. Results of the survey were inconclusive, as only 85% of the participants were involved in both pre- and post-tests.

Pre-test results reflected a realistic and positive attitude toward mainstreaming the handicapped student into the regular classroom. The results of the post-test showed no significant change in attitude, but rather a maintenance of that previously held positive attitude. While positive attitudes are critical to effective mainstreaming, it is even more essential that they be translated into behavioral commitment. As noted in a study by Noar and Milgrim on pre-service strategies for regular class teachers for mainstreaming, "Willingness to work with exceptional children is probably a more valid indication of positive attitude change than mere verbal endorsements of positive statements about them."[6] On a comparative note, teacher educators who verbally adopt a receptive attitude toward mainstreaming must also make a commitment to a behavioral intention.

Translating Attitudes in Action

The faculty participants in the Dean's Grant were asked to make such a commitment by selecting and incorporating mainstreaming competencies in their courses for pre-service secondary teachers. Each participant then developed a list of mainstreaming competencies and activities to be implemented in their pre-service teacher training course for the fall of 1981. Thus, faculty participants are attempting to move beyond a positive attitude and into the realm of commitment to behavioral intention. The purpose of the Dean's Grant during its second year of implementation is to provide continued support to the faculty participants as they integrate the mainstreaming competencies into their secondary education teacher program. If the Dean's Grant has been effective, then perhaps the title of the next article will not be entitled "Mainstreaming: Is It Secondary at the Secondary Level?" but rather "Mainstreaming: It Isn't Secondary at the Secondary Level."

Notes

1. D. Mitchel, "Teacher Attitudes Toward Handicapped Children and Regular Class Integration," *Journal of Special Education,* X (1976), 393-400.
2. D. Hiltenbrand, "Detours Towards Dead Ends," *Vocational Education,* LVI (1981), 41-43.
3. V. DuBasik and F.C. Fietler, "Attitudes of Regular Classroom Teachers Toward EMR Students," U.S., Educational Resources Information Center, ERIC Document ED 155 857, 1978.
4. A. Hiroshoren and T. Burton, "Willingness of Regular Teachers to Participate in Mainstreaming Handicapped Children," *Journal of Research and Development in Education,* XII (1979), 93-100.
5. H. Lombana, "Fostering Positive Attitudes Toward Handicapped Students: A Guidance Challenge," *School Counselor,* XXVII (1980), 176-182.
6. M. Noar and R.M. Milgram, "Two Preservice Strategies for Preparing Regular Class Teachers to Mainstream," *Exceptional Children,* XLVII (1980), 126-128.

A Comparison of Soviet and American Approaches to Special Education

Janice T. Gibson

JANICE T. GIBSON is a professor of educational psychology at the University of Pittsburgh. Over the past decade she has spent 12 months in the USSR studying day care and education. In 1977 she was appointed National Academy of Sciences Research Exchange Scholar at the Institute of General and Pedagogical Psychology in Moscow. In 1978, as a member of a delegation from the Council for International Exchange of Scholars to the Soviet Ministry of Education, she interviewed directors responsible for research on education of the handicapped.

Soviet and American views of education and special education differ considerably. The following conversation, recorded in a Moscow school by a member of a visiting delegation of American teachers, points clearly to differences of opinion:

American teacher (politely): The program you just showed us is very impressive. But the work looks so hard! It must be impossible for *all* the students to do it. What do you do with your "slow learners"?

Soviet teacher (puzzled): What is a "slow learner"?

American teacher: There are always a few children who can't keep up with the rest. We call them slow learners.

Soviet teacher: Oh? (Pause) In the Soviet Union, you see, we have no slow learners. Our programs are designed for *all* children to learn.

The American teacher stopped at this point, assuming that the Soviet teacher was spouting "party rhetoric." In fact, there are studies showing that the Soviet Union has approximately the same percentage of mentally handicapped and slow learners as America.[1] The Soviet teacher was not simply reporting the party line, however. Like the foreign tourists, business executives, and scholars who visit the USSR and even live there for extended periods of time, she probably never saw a handicapped child of any kind — on the streets or in school. The reason lies in the Soviet educational system and in the methods by which special children are screened and educated.

In regular Soviet schools it has always been the responsibility of the teacher to assist *all* children to learn. If some children are not learning, it is considered the teacher's, not the student's, problem. The Soviet teacher who was interviewed might not have been telling the entire truth — because admitting that some children don't learn some of the material might reveal a bad job of teaching.

Soviet teachers do, in fact, give very special care to children who have trouble with their lessons. Although schools operate officially six days per week from 8:30 a.m. till 12:30 or 2:30 p.m. (depending on the age of the children), teachers are expected to remain after school for the next several hours to give assistance where needed. They are aided at this task by other children — those who have no trouble with their lessons. It is considered the duty of Soviet children to help their peers. The task of helping society in general as well as other students in the group is one prerequisite for entrance later into Komsomol, the youth Communist league, and, finally, the Communist Party.

The identification of special children in the Soviet Union usually takes place well before it does for their American counterparts. The extensive *yasli* (nursery) and *detskii sad* (kindergarten) programs accept children on an all-day basis as young as three months of age and keep them through age 6. This long preschool period provides the opportunity for caretakers and specialists to screen these children long before first grade at age 7. Pediatricians in the programs identify physically handicapped children. In many cases such children are placed immediately in special preschools for the physically handicapped. Other specialists identify mentally retarded, emotionally disturbed, or learning disabled children, often before they enter first grade.

Children who have trouble learning the fundamentals of reading and writing are usually identified in the USSR before age 7; *detskii sad* programs begin these subjects at ages 5 and 6. This makes it possible for specialists to detect learning difficulties before regular school. Once special children have been identified during the preschool years, the Soviet government provides what it calls "differentiated care," so that these children almost never attend regular primary grades. They attend special schools. It is possible that the Soviet teacher who didn't know what a slow learner is had never had a mentally handicapped child in her classroom. Furthermore, she may not even have had any idea of what kind of education special children receive in their special schools. Even teacher training and program development for these schools are done under separate auspices.

The Soviet Union has been committed since 1919 to a direction quite opposite from that of the U.S. with respect to special children, especially since 1975, when Public Law 94-142 was passed. Rather than mainstream handicapped children together with their normal counterparts, the Soviets have developed an elaborate and specialized system of schools. In most cases, with the exception of some few schools in very large cities, they have used boarding schools for this purpose.

The Soviet System

In order to compare the Soviet system of educating special children with our own in any useful way, we must understand the political-ideological system that gave rise to Soviet beliefs about how all children, including the handicapped, learn. We must also examine ways that Soviets identify children who have special needs. Finally, we need to examine the effects of the programs on the children themselves.

Marxism and its effects on special education. Marxist dialectical philosophy suggests that higher-order mental processes develop through direct interaction with the environment. Soviet researchers, unlike their American counterparts, are not interested in *proving* the role that the social environment plays in learning. Instead, they begin with unquestioned acceptance of this role. Soviet research therefore involves demonstration of *how* the social environment affects learning and what manipulation of the environment produces maximal desired learning.

The work of two famous Soviet psy-

"A Comparison of Soviet and American Approaches to Special Education," Janice T. Gibson, *Phi Delta Kappan*, December 1980. Reprinted by permission.

chologists, A. S. Luria and L. S. Vygotsky, demonstrates this point. Luria's studies are designed to show how schooling affects the abilities to think and solve problems.[2] Vygotsky's research concludes that both language and thinking are social in origin, and, further, that complex thought processes develop early in childhood through manipulation of real objects and through direct interaction with adults.[3] These basic points are used today by Soviet educators. Schooling for all students, including special students, is much more important in Soviet society than in our own. According to the Marxist approach, children who seem to learn more slowly in regular settings require different manipulation of the environment and different interaction with adults. In 1919, in a decree signed by Lenin, the Council of People's Commissars first recognized officially the need for these very specialized environments for handicapped children. The council decided then to care for and educate the blind, deaf, and physically handicapped, and the children with nervous and mental disorders, differently and separately. In recent years research on programs for these children has been consolidated under the auspices of the Institute of Defectology of the Academy of Pedagogical Science. The direction of the schools has been consolidated under one ministry.

Identifying "special needs." Physically handicapped children in the Soviet Union are usually screened first by caretakers at the state-run *yaslis* and *detskii sads*, who send them to pediatricians for examination. When pediatricians think that special help is necessary, they send the children to *yaslis* or *detskii sads* with specialized programs. In the USSR, children whose handicaps are not so severe as to be noticeably crippling usually are picked up earlier for special help than they are in the U.S. (This is because our special screening is normally done privately with preschoolers, and therefore is more frequent among the middle and upper classes.) All Soviet children, by the time they reach age 6, are required to have complete physical examinations. Physically handicapped children who have not been previously screened out by *yaslis* or *detskii sads* are referred to special schools at this time.

Children with mental handicaps that result in learning difficulty are often screened out during the preschool years also. Children at *detskii sad* levels begin to learn the rudiments of reading and writing. By the last year of *detskii sad* (designated the year of preparation for the first grade), caretakers often request that children who exhibit learning problems be given special evaluation.

Methods used to select children with mental handicaps in the USSR differ considerably from those in the U.S. V. I. Lubovskii, head of the Laboratory of Higher Nervous Activity and Psychology of Abnormal Children at Moscow's Institute of Defectology, points out that intelligence, or the ability to think logically and to solve problems, is not a single entity. Thus it cannot be measured quantitatively by a single score such as an IQ.[4] Testing, according to Lubovskii, should not consist of one single administration. It should take place in real-life situations where children are likely to be learning rather than in the artificial, laboratory-like situations in which, Lubovskii points out, American IQ tests are usually administered. Tests designed in Lubovskii's laboratories do not measure the level of functioning until a child makes a mistake. Instead, they measure how much additional information needs to be provided before the child can solve a problem.

Lubovskii and his colleagues are currently comparing their clinical diagnostic procedures with scores obtained on measures similar, they say, to the Wechsler Scales of Intelligence. They report that their multiple diagnostic procedures provide much more useful information, particularly in predicting children's abilities to respond in day-to-day, real-life interactions.

In America we have heard many of the same complaints that Lubovskii and other Soviet researchers are voicing about IQ testing as a method of screening children according to ability. One of the primary reasons that P.L. 94-142 was passed in the U.S. was that parents complained that their children were being classified as handicapped on the basis of "grossly inadequate methods of testing."[5] Parents of minority children, in particular, filed legal suit against the schools because of their belief that their children were being labeled unfairly by culturally biased tests.

The Soviet system of employing "multifaceted clinical assessments" allows many personnel, including teachers, physicians, neuropsychologists, and whatever other experts might be needed, to pool their efforts and to arrive at a consensual diagnosis. Interestingly, the assessment requires much the same information that many American educators feel should be required to develop the individualized educational plans (IEPs) mandated by P.L. 94-142.

Once the recommendation has been made that a child be considered for evaluation, the Soviets collect very specific data. First, they obtain medical and psychological histories from the *yasli* records. They also require complete physical examinations. If specialists believe that a child has a mental or physical handicap, they may give neurological examinations; tests of sensory acuity; electrophysiological evaluations (these include electroencephalographic and rheoencephalographic tests); tests of what the Soviets term "higher nervous activity" (ability to respond in different ways to Pavlovian conditioning); psychological tests involving memory, perception, and cognitive skills; and, finally, extended observation of classroom learning.

What Soviet researchers term "temporarily retarded in psychological development" (TRPD) is a classification very similar to that of "learning disabled" in America. Soviet differential diagnosis of TRPD children frequently shows them to have prenatal medical histories that include mothers who were toxemic during pregnancy; there are no particular measurable neurological symptoms present. Electroencephalographic and rheoencephalographic recordings show electrical recordings from the brain and blood circulation to the brain that differ somewhat from normal children. Tests of higher nervous activity and tests of memory, perception, and cognitive skills show that TRPD children tend to be impulsive and make mistakes but, and this is important, they can profit by instruction. Psycho-educational assessment is used to determine to what extent these children can profit by instruction and what types of instruction are most helpful. A number of tasks are given to determine how effective specialized instruction is and to determine what Soviet researchers call the "zone of potential development." Soviet psychologists suggest that, for TRPD children, unlike mentally retarded children, further cognitive development is possible. The main problem is learning how to organize materials in meaningful ways. The best way for the teacher to help TRPD children, therefore, is to help them internalize appropriate organizational cues, and teach them gradually to do this by themselves.

Programming for "special needs." The goals of the special Soviet schools match those of their regular schools in many respects. The methods of instruction, however, differ considerably, as does the time it takes to meet these goals. As just one example, the program of instruction for the blind or visually handicapped is designed to take 12 years rather than the usual 10.

Using TRPD children as an example of cases in which differentiated care and programming are provided, the following basic components have been designed at the Institute of Defectology:[6]

1. *Integration of instruction with systematic observation.* Teachers have extensive and current daily information describing each child. Their observations include both general debilities and task-specific problems encountered in completing mastery of each skill.

2. *Design of materials and methods based on task analysis.* Soviets agree with American instructional psychologists that the best instruction is composed of tasks divided into logical and small steps, keeping in mind the total task at all times. They believe this to be especially important for TRPD students. Children also need to be taught self-control and specific methods to organize subject matter.

3. *Individualization of instruction.* This is particularly important to the Soviets, because TRPD children's levels of ability are likely to vary more than normal children's.

4. *General transition to independent performance.* TRPD children differ from retarded in that they can learn if the teacher provides the methods. TRPD children then need to be weaned from this type of learning situation to another in which they eventually learn to think independently.

5. *Coordination of theory and practice.* Interestingly, these components all are part of American special education and are today considered useful components of IEPs for many learning-disabled children here. No discussion of special education in the Soviet Union is complete, however, without a description of one last aspect of its special schools. Special education in the USSR is segregated education. It is segregated by design, beginning with the initial 1919 decree establishing special programs and schools. Today, some of the special programs meet goals similar to those of the regular schools, using different methods and different time periods. Children in the special schools for visually or hearing-impaired children, for example, may complete the regular 10-year program in 12 years. Other special schools have different goals. Children in some of the special schools for the retarded, for example, complete elementary and vocational training in eight years. Emphasis here is on development of working skills.

Comparing Methods

Researchers at the Institute of Defectology point out a number of advantages that their special system of schools has for the handicapped student and for the development of truly differentiated learning. First, they say, special schools have lower pupil/teacher ratios than regular schools. They have larger staffs, with counselors and physicians on the premises. They have close physician/teacher relationships. The fact that most of these schools are boarding schools provides an additional benefit: Student learning can be monitored for many more hours per day. Teachers on special school staffs may be better; Soviet publications report that they receive 25% higher pay.[7]

American educators tend to react negatively to the concept of special segregated schools, regardless of the similarity or quality of programming. To Americans committed to mainstreaming, Soviet segregation of handicapped children is of the worst sort: Handicapped children are segregated not only from children with no handicaps but from their families and also from children with handicaps different from their own. How can these children learn how to live in the normal world with other people if they are not exposed to it?

The Soviets respond to this question with some of their own: How can American teachers provide adequate differentiated care for children with different handicaps unless they *all* receive special training and learn to use the special teaching techniques that work most effectively with these children? How is there time for the regular teacher in the regular American classroom to do all of that and still keep up with new research and new methods? These are the same questions that American teachers are asking.

Soviet and American special educators and education programs differ in another significant respect. That is in the ease with which people can answer the very important question, Do the programs work? With some children? With most children? With all children? The Soviet special schools are sufficiently out of sight that it is difficult to measure just what is going on within their walls. The Soviet teacher who asked what a "slow learner" is probably doesn't know how much the TRPD child is learning in the special school nor even, probably, where the special school is. Theory and research, as outlined by the researchers of the Institute of Defectology, do not necessarily dictate the behavior of teachers in special schools, any more than research in graduate schools of education in the U.S. dictates policy within our public schools.

If the Soviet schools are effective in helping handicapped children, they must help these students return to the regular classroom. Lubovskii was somewhat vague in his answer to the question of how this is accomplished. He suggested that additional extensive screening takes place on the advice of teachers. With so little se of handicapped children, it is unclear ju what this means. One possibility is th they are "stuck" in the system.

In the U.S., unlike the USSR, speci children are being placed in the forefro of the news and are being taken "out the closet." Newspapers, magazines, ar television make daily issue of our pro lems, both for our regular and speci students. We have few, if any, hidd schools; our dirty linen (if it *is* dirty) han in full view for everyone to see. In o new mainstreamed classes, if teachers a not being provided sufficient assistance deal adequately with their new jobs; if t pains we now are feeling are not, as son suggest, just growing pains; if students a not learning; we shall all soon know There is no way now to hide mistake They will appear in nationally circulat journals. They will be aired on " Minutes." They will come in the repo of schoolchildren to their parents. Fro our mistakes we can develop better pr grams. This may be, after all, the prima advantage and result of Public La 94-142.

---

1. Robert Wozniak reports, in "Psychology a Education of the Learning-Disabled Child in USSR" [in William M. Cruikshank and Donald Hallihan, eds., *Research and Theory in Minimal Ce bral Dysfunction and Learning Disability* (Syracus N.Y.: Syracuse University Press, 1975), p. 22], th 10% to 11% of school-age children experience d ficulties in academic activities. Of these, the menta retarded account for 3.5%, while the remaining 7 can be grouped as TRPD (temporarily retarded in ps chological development), a category closely r sembling that of "learning disabled" in the U.S. contrast, Bill R. Gearhart and Harold Weishahn, *The Handicapped Child in the Regular Classroom* (S Louis: Mosby, 1976), report that approximately 5% 7% of American children fall into these categorie with between 2.5% and 3% mentally retarded (e cluding a tiny percentage of severely mentally retar ed), and with between 2% and 4% having learning di abilities.
2. A good example of Luria's thoughts on this iss appears in his article, "A Child's Speech Respons and the Social Environment," published in English *Soviet Psychology*, Fall 1974, pp. 7-39.
3. See Lev S. Vygotsky, *Thought and Languag* trans. by Eugenia Hanfmann and George Vak (Cambridge, Mass.: MIT Press, 1962).
4. Information obtained from Lubovskii came fro a personal interview conducted at the Institute of D fectology in Moscow in September 1978.
5. See, for example, Bill R. Gearhart and Harol Weishahn's descriptions of *Diana* v. *State of Ca fornia*, pp. 13 and 14 of their book, *The Handicapp Child in the Regular Classroom*, op. cit.
6. Wozniak, op. cit., pp. 106-12.
7. This statistic is reported in the pamphlet, "Educa tion in the USSR" (Moscow: Progress Publisher 1972), p. 68.

Child Sexual Abuse

The Educator's Role in Prevention, Detection, and Intervention

Sally Koblinsky and Nory Behana

Sally Koblinsky, Ph.D., is Associate Professor of Family Studies and Consumer Sciences, San Diego State University, San Diego, California.

Nory Behana, B.A., is an instructor at Grossmont College, El Cajon, California; a master's degree candidate at San Diego State University; and a former children's social worker.

"How can we protect children from sexual abuse without frightening them to death?"

"Preschool kids are too young to understand about molestation—and the subject is much too sensitive for classroom discussion."

"I'm scared that warning my girls will make them feel that all sex is perverted."

"Thank God I have a son and don't have to worry about it."

These responses are typical of those made by early childhood educators and parents in discussions about child sexual abuse. While the topic is highly distressing to most adults, the growing number of media reports on child molestation and the statistics concerning its prevalence emphasize the need for early childhood educators to take an active role in preventing the sexual victimization of children.

According to reported cases alone, girls born in the United States today have a one in four chance of being sexually assaulted before they reach their 18th birthdays (Gagnon 1965; Harborview Medical Center 1980; Kinsey et al. 1953). Cases involving boys are less likely to be reported (Finkelhor 1979), but recent research indicates that boys may be equally at risk (Kent 1979). Young children are among the targets of such abuse, with several studies reporting that children under six are involved in 15 to 25 percent of reported cases (Finkelhor 1979; Harborview Medical Center 1979). There seems little doubt that the secrecy and taboos surrounding this offense prevent the reporting of thousands of additional incidents, with the staggering possibility that almost 1 million children are sexually abused each year (National Committee for the Prevention of Child Abuse 1982).

Despite the growing estimates of sexual abuse cases, most children receive little information to protect themselves from this offense. Warnings about strangers do not alert them to the possibility that an abuser could be a person they know and trust. Children are rarely told that they have the right to control who touches them, and that they should say *no* to an inappropriate touch. Nor do many understand that they don't have to keep a promise of secrecy made to an adult. Children are in great need of realistic information about sexual abuse in order to avoid being tricked or misled into undesirable situations solely out of ignorance.

Reprinted by permission from *Young Children*, Vol. 39, No. 6 (September 1984), pp. 3-15. Copyright ©1984, National Association for the Education of Young Children, 1834 Connecticut Ave., N.W., Washington, DC 20009.

Early childhood educators can play a critical role in protecting young children from sexual abuse. In addition to providing prevention-oriented programs for parents and children, they can identify and report suspected cases that might otherwise go unnoticed. As coordinators of San Diego State University's Early Childhood Sexuality Education Project, we have been making presentations to educators and parents on child sexual abuse. While the topic was originally handled as one component of a general sexuality education program (Koblinsky 1983), the overwhelming concerns of our audience led us to deal exclusively with this topic.

Comprehensive approach

Because child sexual abuse is a highly emotional topic, it is important for educators to develop a comprehensive staff and parent education program before attempting to work with children. Trained staff can work to increase parents' awareness of the problem, and to supply them with concrete, nonthreatening prevention strategies which they can introduce to young children in their homes. Skills for coping with incidents of sexual assault may also be provided for parents and teachers who might later confront this situation. Finally, educators may elect to organize classroom programs that review ways in which children can avoid potentially abusive situations. The sequence of these initiatives is important in ensuring that both teachers and parents are able to handle children's concerns and to support their acquisition of prevention skills.

Programs for parents and teachers

Most parents and educators don't discuss sexual abuse with children until *after* it occurs. Their reluctance to present information about this topic stems from their own anxiety and discomfort, as well as their lack of knowledge about the prevalence of this offense (Kent 1979; Sanford 1982). Because they cannot envision young children as victims, many worry that they will frighten children needlessly or make them wary of affection from all adults.

We have found that adults are most comfortable dealing with child sexual abuse as a safety topic. We explain that information about what to do in an abusive situation is just as important to children's welfare as information about what to do when one gets lost, sees a fire, or finds a poisonous snake. The most effective presentations for adults include four components: (1) background information on child sexual abuse; (2) the severity of the problem; (3) effective prevention strategies; and (4) methods for detecting and handling sexual abuse cases (Didi Hirsch Community Mental Health Center 1982; Koblinsky 1983). Presentation of local statistics and cases involving sexual abuse, together with nationally published data, may emphasize the need for parents and teachers to become informed about this topic.

Definition of sexual abuse

The terms *child sexual abuse, child sexual assault,* and *child molestation* refer to the exploitation of a child for the sexual gratification of an adult. Such abuse should not be confused with the warm, affectionate, physical exchanges between an adult and a child which show respect for the child's feelings. Rather, sexual abuse involves coercing a child to engage in sexual activity through subtle deceit, bribes, or outright threats and force (Adams and Fay 1981; Summit and Kryso 1978). Incest refers to sexual contact between nonmarried family members, such as a father and daughter or a boy and his uncle (Justice and Justice 1979).

Most child sexual abuse involves genital handling, oral-genital contact, or sexual abuse of the breasts or anus, rather than sexual intercourse (Finkelhor 1979; Peters 1976). Some abuse situations involve no physical contact, but require the child to undress and/or look at the genitals of adults (May 1982). While violent acts may include injury and even murder, the sexual abuse of children typically involves less physical force and violence than adult rape (Peters 1976). Since children are small and often compliant, the authority and persuasive powers of abusers are generally sufficient to establish sexual contact.

Characteristics of offenders

One of the common myths is that abusers are likely to be strangers to the child. In fact, 70 to 90 percent of sexual abuse cases involve someone the child knows, such as a family member, a neighbor, or a babysitter (DeFrancis 1969; Finkelhor 1979). More than 40 percent of offenders in these cases are related in some way to the victim. Thus, it is not surprising to discover that child molestation most often occurs in the home of the victim or offender, rather than in automobiles, parks, or local school yards (DeFrancis 1969; Geiser 1979; Peters 1976).

Sexual offenders are not easily identified by their appearances. More than 97 percent are male, but contrary to the stereotype of the dirty old man, their age range spans from the early teen through elderly years (Groth 1978). In some cases, the offensive behavior is a continuation of the offender's own childhood abuse. Sexual offenders are unlikely to have prior criminal convictions (DeFrancis 1969), but this does not mean that they typically offend only one child. Indeed, the most extensive investigation to date indicates that the average molester of girls abuses 62 victims in his life, while the average molester of boys offends 31 victims (Sanford 1982).

Child sexual abusers typically exhibit low self-esteem, poor impulse control, and child-like emotional needs (Groth 1978; Summit and Kryso 1978). Many are married or have another sexual outlet, but continue to use children in an exploitive manner (DeFrancis 1969). Men who molest boys are rarely homosexual; they are men whose preference stems from the greater accessibility of boys or the fact that they were victimized as boys (Gebhard et al. 1965). The discovery that a significant proportion of convicted offenders report sexual abuse in their own families (Groth 1978) emphasizes the need to accelerate prevention efforts in order to halt this destructive cycle.

Characteristics of victims

Angela, age 5, is a typical victim of sexual abuse. When her mother needed to handle business downtown, she sometimes left Angela with her uncle. Angela enjoyed playing hide-and-seek and other games with Uncle Jim; but one day he asked her to play a *secret* game in which they both undressed and touched each other's bodies. Angela felt funny about this request, but she liked Uncle Jim and her parents had taught her to "do as adults tell you." She continued to comply with his requests for more than a year before the abuse was discovered.

Angela is similar to thousands of children from all ethnic backgrounds, religions, and social classes who are vulnerable to sexual victimization. Her lack of information about the problem and the steps she might take to prevent sexual abuse place her at greater risk than children who have been prepared to protect themselves. There are other factors which also appear to increase children's vulnerability. Specifically, children with low self-esteem or who are lonely or hungry for affection are often sought out by offenders (DeFrancis 1969; Weiss et al. 1955). Abusers may similarly gravitate toward children who have been taught to blindly obey adults (Sanford 1982). Parents who leave their children poorly supervised (DeFrancis 1969), or entrust their children to individuals who drink heavily also increase the risk of victimization. At least one-third of assaults involve the use of alcohol by the offender (Browning and Boatman 1977; Gebhard et al. 1965).

Severity of the offense

Child sexual abuse is a serious crime, regardless of the amount of coercion involved. Professionals agree that this offense is always the responsibility and fault of the adult. Children do not seduce adults; it is always the case of an adult taking advantage of a frightened or dependent child. Most sexual assaults of children follow a gradually escalating pattern in which the offender attempts to gain the child's trust before attempting sexual contact (DeFrancis 1969). Children may then be repeatedly victimized over a period of months or even years (Geiser 1979).

The impact of such incidents can be traumatic for both the child and the family involved. The degree of harm depends upon a variety of factors, including the relationship between the victim and offender, the age of the child, the nature and duration of the offense, and the manner in which it is handled by others (Sgroi 1978). While there are few studies involving the long-term effects of sexual abuse, researchers have found that some victims experience shame, guilt, depression, low self-esteem, and difficulty in establishing intimate, trusting relationships with others (Finkelhor 1979; Steele and Alexander 1981). Daughters involved in incestuous relationships may suffer anxiety, masochism, and a need for punishment, especially if the situation resulted in the break-up of the family (Kaufman, Peck, and Tagiuri 1954). Yet despite these pessimistic findings, there is evidence to suggest that detrimental effects can be modified or overcome by sensitive intervention efforts (Steele and Alexander 1981). Significant adults may help to reduce the probability of adverse reactions, and to prevent future occurrence of the abuse.

Prevention strategies

There are many ways in which parents and educators can prepare children to avoid potential abuse situations, and to prevent an initial approach from becoming a sexual assault. These prevention strategies can be presented in a realistic, nonthreatening manner, just as one might give children other safety advice. While adults may worry that children will be frightened by discussions of sexual abuse, it appears that children who know what to look for and who to tell will be less fearful than those with sketchy or exaggerated information. For example, one child whose parents had not discussed this issue believed "sex maniacs take off your clothes, murder you, and cut you up into about a hundred pieces."

Teach children that some parts of their bodies are private. It is important to provide children with correct terms for their genitals and the private areas of their bodies, just as they are given correct terms for other body parts. Such terms not only give them a vocabulary for discussing body functions, but also help them to recognize and report sexual abuse. Children should be informed that their breasts, buttocks, anus, and genitals (penis, vulva/vagina) are *private parts.* They may be helped to remember these areas by noting that they are parts of the body covered by their bathing suits. Point out that no one has the right to touch these private areas—even when one is wearing clothing—with the possible exception of a parent or teacher dressing a child or a health professional conducting an examination in a medical office. Children should also know that no one has the right to ask them to touch another person's private parts.

Help children identify different types of touching. Rather than teaching children to be wary of certain individuals, adults should help children to discriminate between different types of touching. Parents and teachers can provide examples of *good, confusing,* and *bad* touches (Kent 1979). *Good touches* make children feel positive about themselves and include the welcome hugs, kisses, and handshakes from relatives and friends. *Confusing touches* make the child feel a little uncomfortable, such as when a parent requests that a child kiss an unfamiliar relative or friend. *Bad touches* include hitting, prolonged or excessive tickling, or touches involving the private areas of the body.

Children should be given concrete examples of bad touches to ensure that they understand the concept. For example, adults might explain that, "It would be very bad for an adult to put her or his hand on a child's breasts, anus, vulva, or penis, or to ask the child to touch the adult's own vulva or penis. It would also be wrong for someone to take pictures of you without clothes on or to ask you to lie down in bed with her or him." Emphasize that adults may try to bribe, trick, or force children into *bad* types of touching.

Teach children to say* no *to unwanted touches. Children should be told of their right to control who touches them. Teaching them when and how to say *no* is important in preventing the onset of abuse. *No* should be used whenever the child encounters unwanted touches or is offered special treats in exchange for certain behaviors. Children can be coached to respond to these situations with statements such as "No, don't touch me there! That part of my body is private!" or "No, I'm not allowed to do that." Practicing such phrases may help children to respond assertively when approached by a potential offender.

Explain that bad touches could come from someone the child knows. Children often believe that an abuser is *weird, ugly, monster-looking,* or *wearing a dark coat* (Kent 1979). Therefore, it is important to point out that bad touches may not only come from unattractive strangers, but from friendly, attractive relatives or people the child knows. Children may be told that, "Although most teenagers and adults are nice, there are some who have a hard time making friends. They may ask you to do things that aren't right, such as getting undressed or putting your hands in their pants" (Sanford 1982). If children ask why an adult would do this, try to avoid saying "because she or he is mean or sick." These words have concrete meaning to the child and may not fit the situation the child encounters. For example, when one boy was told that abusers were "sick in the head," he looked for men with bandages on their heads (Sanford 1982). Adults can admit that they don't know why some people do these things, but they want to warn children about individuals who might try to touch them in uncomfortable ways.

Encourage open communication and discourage secrets. Sexual offenders often instruct children to keep abusive behaviors secret, and may frighten children by threatening that telling will bring harm to the child, the child's parents, or the offender ("If you tell, I'll go to jail"). Offenders may also attempt to convince children that their behavior is normal or a reflection of the offender's love for the victim (Adams and Fay 1981). Therefore, children should be encouraged to share all incidents that make them feel frightened or uncomfortable with a parent or a trusted adult. Children should be told that they never have to keep secrets from these significant adults, even if the abuser made them promise or threatened to hurt them in some way.

Adults should also inform children that they will not be angry or blame them if an abusive event occurs—even though they were warned about bad touching—but want children to come to them with the information. They can explain that everyone makes mistakes, and that the inappropriate touching was not the child's fault. Children should be helped to understand that reporting an assaultive attempt or actual incident involving themselves or one of their friends will protect others and make it possible for the offender to receive help.

Although most adults believe children's accounts of abusive incidents, children may be prepared for the possibility that someone (for example, a grandparent or caregiver) may doubt the truth of their story. After acknowledging how hurt or sad a child might feel if this occurred, adults should emphasize the importance of telling another person so that the problem can be eliminated. Children may be asked to name several adults they could tell if they were to encounter bad or confusing touches.

Teach children how to tell. Children may have difficulty informing adults about unwanted touches, especially if they involve a relative or family friend. Therefore, adults may help them to practice ways of reporting sexual abuse until they feel comfortable with the words. For example, if a child encountered unwanted touching, he might say, "Mr. Smith is touching my penis and the private parts of my body. I want him to stop."

Use games and stories to reinforce prevention concepts. Games such as "What if . . ." are effective in helping children to think for themselves and to formulate a plan for responding to possible abuse. Adults might ask a child, "What would you do if a neighbor asked you to look at some kittens in his bedroom?" or "What would you do if a cousin put his hand on a private part of your body at a family picnic?" Parents and teachers may also tell stories about other children who have successfully avoided difficult situations, providing children with positive role models. For example:

> Timmy, age 4, was being cared for by his favorite babysitter, 16-year-old John. When John put Timmy in the bath, he tried to rub his penis over and over—even though it wasn't dirty. Timmy remembered what his mother had told him about bad touching and firmly told John not to touch his penis or private parts. The next morning Timmy told his parents about his "touching problem."

Opportunities to talk about sexual assault and play prevention games arise frequently. For example, parents may initiate "what if" games on general safety during dinner, interspersing questions about sexual assault with other safety predicaments. Discussions may also be motivated by news articles or televised reports of sexual assault. Currently, most of the curriculum materials which address the problem of sexual abuse in children are in coloring book or workbook format. Parents and teachers can use these materials for background information, and adapt them for use with children in more creative ways. (See the Resources section at the end of the article for a listing of recommended resources for children, parents, and teachers.)

Continue to discuss safety rules concerning strangers. Although the majority of sexual assault cases involve adults familiar to the child, a significant number of offenses are perpetrated by strangers (DeFrancis 1969). Offers of candy, a ride in a car, or the chance to play with some puppies or kittens are common inducements used to obtain a child's company (Macdonald 1981). While most parents do warn their children about the dangers of accompanying strangers, our own research indicates that many children do not understand the definition of *stranger*. Adults might explain that, "A stranger is a person you don't know, even if the person says she or he knows your mom and dad. Strangers often look and act very nice, so you can't spot them by the way they look."

Children should be warned to say, "No, I'm not allowed to do (the stranger's request)," even if they feel that there is no harm intended. Permission should first be obtained from a parent or responsible caregiver. Parents, teachers, and crime prevention specialists may also convey specific safety tips about what a child should do and where a child should go (for example, to a neighbor's house or crime watch house) if bothered by a stranger.

Encourage children to trust their own instincts. Children cannot be protected from sexual assault by safety rules alone since specific rules may not apply to all potential abuse situations. Consequently, they should be encouraged to trust their own feelings and intuitions about people and places in order to protect themselves from possible harm. Adults can encourage children to rely on their *inner voice* which tells them that some requests from adults are unreasonable or inappropriate (Sanford 1982).

Nory Behana

The most effective classroom presentations on sexual abuse prevention for preschool and elementary children employ high interest, nonthreatening materials such as puppets.

Teach children about the positive aspects of sexuality. In teaching children about sexual abuse, it is important to communicate that sexuality is not bad or wrong. Rather it is the trickery, bribery, coercion, and taking advantage of another person that is harmful. To balance the information provided about exploitive touch, adults should make special efforts to point out the positive, nurturing, and joyful aspects of sexual interactions between loving persons. Adults who demonstrate warmth, affection, and support for others provide children with positive role models for later intimate relationships.

Prevention programs for children

Teachers may complement their staff and parent education efforts with classroom presentations on sexual abuse prevention and stranger awareness for young children. It is important, however, that parents be supportive of and informed about these classroom activities. Parent meetings on sexual abuse prevention provide an excellent opportunity for review of curriculum materials intended for classroom use.

The most effective curriculum units for preschoolers and elementary school children employ high interest, nonthreatening materials such as puppets, skits, and stories (see Resources). These units ensure that children learn: (1) the private areas of their bodies; (2) the difference between good and bad touches; (3) children's right to say *no* to touches they don't like; (4) the importance of telling a trusted adult about unwanted touch; and (5) that sexual assault is never the child's fault. Curriculum materials should include many examples of nonstranger sexual abuse.

The Coalition for Child Advocacy has developed one of the few week-long prevention programs designed specifically for preschool children (McFaddin 1982). Early sessions focus on helping children to identify different feelings. A general safety film, "Who Do You Tell?" (see Resources) gives children the chance to consider who they could inform if they had uncomfortable feelings about being touched by a specific adult. Later sessions ensure that children understand the private parts of their bodies, and allow them to rehearse ways of avoiding potential sexual abuse.

Programs for the kindergarten and elementary school children emphasize similar prevention concepts, with activities appropriate for the child's developmental level (Kent 1979). Role play activities are one means of helping elementary age children to think about how they might handle approaches from abusers. Incomplete stories, as exemplified below, are another technique which may familiarize teachers with children's understanding of the problem and may spark discussion about prevention strategies.

> One hot day Sara was invited to run through the sprinklers of the man who lived next door. After a little while the neighbor asked her to sit on his lap. As he began to tell Sara a story, he rubbed his hand between her legs. Sara didn't like it and wiggled free. She ran home without saying goodbye. Should Sara tell someone? Who?
> Had Sara done anything wrong? Why or why not?
> Had her neighbor done anything wrong? Why or why not?
> How do you think Sara felt?

Because adults rarely discuss child sexual abuse, it is important to help children feel comfortable with the topic. Should children begin to act silly, embarrassed, or restless in classroom activities, teachers may acknowledge their discomfort with a new topic, and encourage discussion about why they feel this way. A few children may appear especially agitated by a prevention program, avoiding eye contact with the teacher, withdrawing from the discussion, and/or asking to be excused. In such cases, teachers need to seriously evaluate the child's behavior for any sign of victimization. It is also possible that a child may display considerable interest in the topic, and relate incidents of current or past sexual assault. Should this occur during the program, teachers should calmly thank the child for bringing it up and explain that they will talk about it privately after the presentation.

Detecting child sexual abuse

Because educators are in close personal contact with young children, they are in a strategic position to detect sexual abuse. Any report suggesting its occurrence should be addressed immediately, since research indicates that it is extremely rare for a child to invent a story about being sexually molested (Kent 1979). Educators should be especially alert to behaviors that go beyond the normal sex play and curiosity of a young child. For example, one five-year-old boy demonstrated a game involving oral-genital contact to other little boys on the preschool playground. Another four-year-old girl told her friends that she liked to tickle her stepfather's "peepee." Any unusually precocious or seductive behavior, such as a child attempting to fondle an adult's breasts or genitals should be treated as highly suspect. Teachers may also be wary of artwork with a dominant sexual theme, such as paintings of men with very large penises or pictures of sexual encounters between children and adults.

A variety of physical symptoms are similarly indicative of victimization. These include unexplainable pain or injury in the genital area, sexually-transmitted disease, discomfort in walking or sitting, and unusual odors around the genitals.

Other indicators of sexual abuse may be more subtle. Although one symptom may not be positive evidence of an assault, it does suggest the need to explore further. Virtually any change in the child's normal behavior may stem from sexual victimization, including abnormal sleep patterns or nightmares, bedwetting, loss of appetite, sudden dependency, unusual shyness, running away, behavior problems, or difficulties in school. Personality changes may be accompanied by changes in social skills, with some abused children exhibiting low self-esteem and withdrawal from friends. Sudden fear of being alone with male teachers and reluctance to accompany a babysitter, parent, or stepparent home may also be considered as possible signs of a problem (Schultz 1973).

Although sexually abused children come from a variety of different family situations, certain family characteristics are more strongly associated with the offense. Some victimized children come from families in which there is a marked role reversal between the mother and daughter, with the father responding to the daughter in a flirtatious manner that is usually reserved for a spouse or girlfriend (Forward and Buck 1982). It is not uncommon for fathers or stepfathers who sexually abuse children to exhibit extreme dominance and overprotectiveness of the child, and to personally handle school transportation, parent conferences, and notes for illness (Justice and Justice 1979).

Family loyalty, fear, and confusion about how to tell prevent many children from reporting sexual abuse or make it likely that they will be misunderstood by others. Teachers, therefore, must be alert to statements suggestive of sexual relations between children and teenagers or adults. Examples of such comments include, "My father does things to me when mom's not there," "The babysitter fooled around with me yesterday," "He checked me inside my privates," and "Will you help me to live with my aunt?" (Adams and Fay 1981; National Committee for the Prevention of Child Abuse 1982).

Coping with child sexual abuse

Teachers who suspect sexual abuse of children should immediately discuss their suspicions with their administrator or head teacher. Dates and observations pertinent to the situation should be carefully noted for future use. If the decision is made to ask a child about a specific problem (for example, injury to the genital area), adults should remember that young children generally lack the cognitive maturity to remember exact details, such as times and places. Indeed, younger children may appear less traumatized by sexual abuse than their older peers who have a more sophisticated understanding of the offense (Summit and Kryso 1978). A child should never be asked to confront the accused offender because her or his denial will only make the event more upsetting.

The discovery of a sexually abusive situation can be a traumatic experience for both the teachers and parents involved. Anger, guilt, and the desire for swift revenge are normal reactions, especially if the offender is a relative or trusted adult. It is essential, however, that adults stay calm, sympathetic, and supportive for the child's sake. Professionals agree that handling the incident in a sensitive and direct manner may considerably lessen the likelihood that a child will suffer permanently from the offense (Summit and Kryso 1978).

A teacher who has learned of a sexual assault might say to the child: "I know how scared and hurt you must feel. I feel that way too. But I'm so proud of you for telling me. I'm sorry you had such a bad experience, but it wasn't your fault. Come to me, your parents, or another adult you trust if he or anyone else ever bothers you again."

Reporting offenses

Educators have both a moral and legal obligation to report any reasonable suspicion or known case of child sexual assault to the police, child protective services, or the appropriate social service agency. All states include sexual abuse in their criminal codes (National Committee for the Prevention of Child Abuse 1982). The laws state that teachers do not have to prove the existence of such abuse, nor do they have to know who did it. If further investigation indicates that there was no offense, teachers who reported in good faith are protected from any possible prosecution. On the other hand, teachers who had reasonable knowledge of an incident and did not report it can be prosecuted.

Reports are generally followed up by a visit from a child protective services worker or a representative of the reporting agency, often in the home or at the school site. Teachers should make efforts to prepare the child and the nonoffending parents for the visit, informing them that the child will be asked to discuss the situation in a sensitive manner. Teachers may volunteer to attend the interview for moral support, especially in cases where the suspected offender is a member of the child's family.

Teachers or parents should consult with the child protective services worker about the need for the child to receive a medical examination. If so, adults should carefully select medical personnel trained in handling sexual abuse cases. Such individuals can explain the reasons for the examination and can reassure children that their bodies haven't been changed by this experience. Some children may also benefit from the opportunity to discuss the event with a psychologist, psychiatrist, or family counselor. Parents may also need professional help, since they often bottle up a great deal of rage and emotion.

Continuing support for the victim

Teachers should show respect for the privacy of the child and family by only sharing the incident with others who must know (for example, parents whose children may be in contact with the suspected offender). Care should be taken to avoid projecting judgmental attitudes toward the family since this may only hinder the recovery process. The abused child should be helped to follow regular routines, rather than being treated in a special, overprotective manner.

Sexually abused children often have questions for a long time after the incident was discovered. Allowing them to talk about the experience with a trusted adult may be an important therapeutic step. It is especially important to reassure children that the abusive incidents were not their fault. The continuing support of nonoffending fathers and other male caregivers is especially important in reassuring children that most men are not like the offender.

If parents elect to pursue prosecution of the offender, it is the district attorney who has the major responsibility for deciding whether to go to trial (Adams and Fay 1981). Teachers may assist parents of victims by helping them to investigate local procedures that are followed in court cases involving sexual abuse. In many cities the district attorney allows children to use anatomically correct dolls to explain what happened, which increases the chance that children will be understood and that offenders will be convicted. In some areas, a rape crisis worker can assist the child during the proceedings, and an advocate can testify on behalf of the child.

Unfortunately, the majority of child sexual abuse cases are never reported. Many of the sexual offenders brought to trial are not convicted because these cases are difficult to prove (National Committee for the Prevention of Child Abuse 1982). However, failure to press charges increases the likelihood that sexual assault will continue. Most offenders go on victimizing children as long as there is no outside intervention from authorities (Finkelhor 1979).

Conclusion

Early childhood educators can play a critical role in prevention, detection, and intervention efforts related to child sexual abuse. To take effective action against this problem, they must be knowledgeable about sexual abuse, alert to its symptoms, and prepared to report and follow up on suspected cases. Staff and parent education programs should be organized to assist adults in communicating with young children about this sensitive issue. Teachers may cooperate with parents in planning classroom activities that attempt to protect children from sexual exploitation. Finally, support can be provided for legislative, treatment, and law enforcement programs aimed at combating this problem. Although there is currently no panacea for child sexual abuse, the efforts and skills of informed educators can make children's lives more safe and secure.

Recommended Resources for Children, Parents, and Teachers

Books for children

Suggested age levels are designated with overlapping age ranges as follows:

N—nursery, up to age 5
K—kindergarten, ages 4–6
P—primary, ages 5–9

Red Flag, Green Flag People (1980). Joy Williams. Rape and Abuse Crisis Center, P.O. Box 1655, Fargo, ND 58107. KP
Designed to be used with adult direction, this coloring book describes good, *green flag* touches and bad, *red flag* touches involving strangers or relatives. Includes suggestions about what children can do if they encounter bad touches.

Annie: Once I Was a Little Bit Frightened (1983). Becky Montgomery, Carol Grimm, and Peg Schwandt. Rape and Abuse Crisis Center, P.O. Box 1655, Fargo, ND 58107. NKP
A brief story about a young girl who is touched in a hurtful way by a familiar person. Annie learns that children can get help for a touching problem from a trusted adult.

My Very Own Book About Me! (1983). Jo Stowell and Mary Dietzel. Lutheran Social Services of Washington, 1226 N. Howard St., Spokane, WA 99201. KP
Emphasizing children's rights, this informative workbook helps children to respond assertively to avoid touches they don't like. Includes multicultural illustrations and comes with a guide for parents. Guides for teachers and therapists are also available.

Private Zones (1982). Frances Dayee. The Charles Franklin Press, 18409 90th Ave., W., Edmonds, WA 98020. NKP
A short, nonthreatening book that helps children understand the private areas of their bodies, who can touch their private zones, and what to do if they are threatened by sexual abuse. Includes guidelines for adults on prevention and coping with the problem.

What If I Say No! (1982). Jill Haddad and Lloyd Martin. M. H. Cap and Co., P.O. Box 3584, Bakersfield, CA 93385. KP
A clever workbook that defines strangers, friends, and relatives, and explains that any of these individuals could try to touch the private parts of children's bodies. Presents *what if* situations that allow children to practice saying *no.*

Something Happened to Me (1981). Phyllis Sweet. Mother Courage Press, 224 State St., Racine, WI 53403. NKP
Designed for victimized children to read with the loving guidance of a parent and/or therapist. A girl tells of her fear and confusion after an incident involving sexual abuse, but does not describe the incident. Her self-worth and confidence are restored after discussing her feelings with trusted adults.

Resources for parents and teachers

Come Tell Me Right Away (1982). Linda Sanford. Ed-U Press, P.O. Box 583, Fayetteville, NY 13066.
A concise, easy-to-read pamphlet presenting the most important strategies adults can use to prevent and cope with child sexual abuse.

He Told Me Not to Tell (1979). Jennifer Fay. King County Rape Relief, 305 S. 43rd, Renton, WA 98055.
Nonthreatening games and storytelling ideas in this pamphlet prepare children to say *no* to a potential abuser. Includes information for reporting child molestation.

The Silent Children: A Parent's Guide to the Prevention of Child Sexual Abuse (1982). Linda Sanford. New York: McGraw-Hill.
In addition to providing background on the problem of child sexual abuse, this straightforward book helps parents teach children to act assertively and confidently in troublesome situations. Includes advice on building children's self-esteem and chapters which address the special needs of single and minority parents.

No More Secrets: Protecting Your Child from Sexual Assault (1981). Caren Adams and Jennifer Fay. Impact Publishers, P.O. Box 1094, San Luis Obispo, CA 93406.
A practical, thorough book that defines sexual abuse, carefully describes preventive techniques, and discusses what parents should do if their child is assaulted.

The Touching Problem (1982). MTI Teleprograms, 3710 Commercial Ave., Northbrook, IL 60062.
An 18 minute film/docudrama that increases awareness of the emotional trauma experienced by a victimized child, while presenting techniques for teaching prevention skills to children. Suitable for staff and parent education programs.

Resources for curriculum development

Feelings and Your Body: A Prevention Curriculum for Preschoolers (1982). Shelly McFaddin. Coalition for Child Advocacy, P.O. Box 159, Bellingham, WA 98227.

Sexual Abuse Prevention: A Lesson Plan (1982). Sandra Kleven. Coalition for Child Advocacy, P.O. Box 159, Bellingham, WA 98227.
Simple, direct lesson plans for classroom presentations in the preschool or grades K–6. Units review different types of touching, private body zones, and what children should do if they encounter a touching problem.

Child Abuse Research and Education Kit (1982). Jan Sippel and Catharine Smailes. Harold Bishop Public School, 15670 104th Ave., Surrey, British Columbia, Canada Z3R 1P3.
A comprehensive teaching kit for use in the elementary grades which includes a puppet, child's book, visual aids, and parent and teacher's manual.

Child Sexual Abuse Prevention Project: An Educational Program for Children (1979). Cordelia Kent. Hennepin County Attorney's Office, C-2000 Government Center, Minneapolis, MN 55487.
A carefully developed and field-tested curriculum for elementary and secondary teachers on sexual abuse prevention. The touch continuum shown in the book is a major component of most recent prevention work.

Talking about Touching—A Personal Safety Curriculum (1981). Ruth Harms and Donna James. Committee for Children, P.O. Box 15190, Seattle, WA 98115.
A three to six week curriculum for K–6 students focusing upon decision making, assertiveness, touching, and available community support systems.

Who Do You Tell? (1978). MTI Teleprograms, 3710 Commercial Ave., Northbrook, IL 60062.
Aimed at children 5–11, this 11 minute film uses both animation and live action to show children who they should tell if there is a fire in their house, they are lost, or they encounter an uncomfortable touch. A good discussion starter.

References

Adams, C., and Fay, J. *No More Secrets*. San Luis Obispo, Calif.: Impact Publishers, 1981.

Browning, D., and Boatman, B. "Incest: Children at Risk." *American Journal of Psychiatry* 134 (1977): 69–72.

DeFrancis, V. *Protecting the Child Victim of Sex Crimes Committed by Adults*. Denver, Colo.: American Humane Association, 1969.

Didi Hirsh Community Mental Health Center. *Primary Prevention of Sexual Assault*. Culver City, Calif.: Southern California Rape Prevention Study Center, 1982.

Finkelhor, D. *Sexually Victimized Children*. New York: Free Press, 1979.

Forward, S., and Buck, C. *Betrayal of Innocence: Incest and Its Devastation*. Los Angeles: J. P. Tarcher, 1978.

Gagnon, J. "Female Child Victims of Sex Offenses." *Social Problems* 13 (1965): 176–192.

Gebhard, P.; Gagnon, J.; Pomeroy, W.; and Christenson, V. *Sex Offenders*. New York: Harper & Row, 1965.

Geiser, R. *Hidden Victims: Sexual Abuse of Children*. Boston: Beacon, 1979.

Groth, A. "Patterns of Sexual Assault Against Children and Adolescents." In *Sexual Assault of Children and Adolescents*, ed. A. Groth, L. Holstrom, and S. M. Sgroi. Lexington, Mass.: Lexington Books, 1978.

Harborview Medical Center. *Sexual Assault Center Client Characteristics, 1979*. Seattle, Wash.: Harborview Medical Center, 1980.

Justice, B., and Justice, J. *The Broken Taboo: Sex in the Family*. New York: Human Sciences Press, 1979.

Kaufman, I.; Peck, A. L.; and Tagiuri, C. K. "The Family Constellation and Overt Incestuous Relations Between Father and Daughter." *American Journal of Orthopsychiatry* 24 (1954): 266–277.

Kent, C. *Child Sexual Abuse Prevention Project: An Educational Program for Children*. Hennepin County, Minn.: Hennepin County Attorney's Office, 1979.

Kinsey, A.; Pomeroy, W.; Martin, C.; and Gebhard, P. *Sexual Behavior in the Human Female*. Philadelphia: Saunders, 1953.

Koblinsky, S. *Sexuality Education for Parents of Young Children*. Fayetteville, N. Y.: Ed-U Press, 1983.

May, G. *Understanding Sexual Child Abuse*. Chicago: National Committee for the Prevention of Child Abuse, 1982.

Macdonald, J. M. "Sexual Deviance: The Adult Offender." In *Sexually Abused Children and Their Families*, ed. P. Mrazek and C. Kempe. New York: Pergamon, 1981.

McFaddin, S. *Feelings and Your Body: A Prevention Curriculum for Preschoolers*. Bellingham, Wash.: Coalition for Child Advocacy, 1982.

National Committee for the Prevention of Child Abuse. *Basic Facts About Sexual Child Abuse*. Chicago: National Committee for the Prevention of Child Abuse, 1982.

Peters, J. "Children Who Are Victims of Sexual Assault and the Psychology of Offenders." *American Journal of Psychotherapy* 30, no. 3 (1976): 398–421.

Sanford, L. *The Silent Children*. New York: McGraw-Hill, 1982.

Schultz, L. "The Child Sex Victim: Social, Psychological and Legal Perspectives." *Child Welfare* 52, no. 3 (1973): 146–157.

Sgroi, S. M. "Child Sexual Assault: Some Guidelines for Intervention and Assessment." In *Sexual Assault of Children and Adolescents*, ed. A. Groth, L. Holstrom, and S. M. Sgroi. Lexington, Mass.: Lexington Books, 1978.

Steele, B. F., and Alexander, H. A. "Long-Term Effects of Sexual Abuse in Childhood." In *Sexually Abused Children and Their Families*, ed. P. Mrazek and C. Kempe. New York: Pergamon, 1981.

Summit, R., and Kryso, J. "Sexual Abuse of Children: A Clinical Spectrum." *American Journal of Orthopsychiatry* 48, no. 2 (1978): 237–251.

Weiss, J.; Rogers, E.; Darwin, M.; and Dutton, C. "A Study of Girl Sex Victims." *Psychiatric Quarterly* 29 (1955): 1–27.

You can help a Sexually Abused Child

Straightforward advice on what to do when a child confides in you

Janet Rosenzweig

Janet Rosenzweig is executive director of the Girls Club of Dallas, Texas, and a consultant to the Texas Department of Human Resources for sex abuse programs.

The sexual exploitation of children is a statistically startling fact of life. The National Center on Child Abuse and Neglect predicts that 20 out of every 100 children, both girls and boys, will be victimized in some manner before they reach their eighteenth birthday.

Statistics on sexual abuse are inexact, due in part to variations in the definition. Sexual abuse can include a wide range of behaviors, from fondling to rape, including juvenile prostitution and pornography. For practical purposes, and for explaining the issue to children, *sexual abuse can be described as being touched, looked at, or spoken to in ways that children feel is an invasion of their privacy.*

Profile of an abused child

How do you know that a child has been sexually abused? There is a myriad of signs and symptoms. While the appearance of any one symptom does not signify sexual abuse, the presence of several signs may indicate a possible victim.

The behavioral symptoms are similar to those associated with depression. Withdrawal or aggressive behavior may be noted. Self-destructive acts are often common among older children. These include substance abuse, self-mutilation, promiscuity, attempts to run away, and suicide threats or attempts. Younger children may exhibit a preoccupation with their own genitalia or those of other children. Many sexual abuse victims will refuse to dress for physical education classes, often fearing that there is something different or dirty about their bodies that others will notice.

Some sexual abuse victims may impose sex play on other children; however, the key word is *impose.* A mutual decision to engage in "you show me yours and I'll show you mine" is not necessarily problematic. However, should a child use force of any nature to secure the cooperation of another child, the act cannot be considered mutual and the instigator should be suspected of being a victim.

Children's art may also provide a clue. Drawings of adults displaying prominent genitalia and self-portraits indicating great isolation are two common signs.

Low self-esteem is typical in victims. They are implicitly taught that their value is for *what they do* (in this case, be a sex partner for an adult) as opposed to *who they are.* When they demonstrate such poor self-esteem, they may become the target for scapegoating by peers.

Sexual abuse victims have often been robbed of the chance to learn to make smart decisions concerning their own safety. For this reason, they may be revictimized in other circumstances.

When a victim confides in you

A child will often try to communicate that something is wrong. This is extremely difficult for younger and older children alike; our culture gives young people the message that sex is not something they talk about with adults. In addition, they most likely have been told by the abuser not to tell. And, if incest is the problem, they are often dreadfully afraid of what will happen to their family when people find out. But many children will test the water with a trusted adult, possibly seeking an opinion on hypothetical problems. If you are the one a child confides in, there are several do's and don'ts to keep in mind.

Do believe the victim. A child rarely lies about sexual abuse, and even if he or she does, a need for professional help is still indicated. Not believing someone adds to the problem—most likely other people the child may have tried to talk to have not believed the child either. A child may seriously begin to doubt his or her own sanity when repeatedly told that what he or she knows to be true is not.

Do emphasize that the victim is not at fault. Often a child has been led to believe that he or she provoked the attack. Under no circumstances is a child

Reprinted from *INSTRUCTOR*, April 1984, pp. 62-64. Copyright ©1984 by The Instructor Publications Inc. Used by permission.

victim ever considered at fault. Regardless of the child's appearance, manner of dress, or behavior, the adult must be responsible for his or her own behavior. Moreover, if a child is behaving in a precociously seductive fashion, someone must have encouraged and rewarded such behavior.

Do acknowledge the child's conflicts, which arise from several places. Primarily, the child is confused about the repercussions of the report, which will certainly cause a crisis for both victim and family, as the social and legal systems begin their intervention. A child may also have a conflict regarding feelings for the offender; in spite of the attack, there may be true affection for the offender. It is possible, and with male victims of female offenders often probable, that the victim experienced sexual arousal. Given that the sexual response system is a function of the autonomic nervous system and a reflect response to stimulus, the child may be terribly confused about something that in some way felt good, even though he or she is sure it was wrong. An analogy to laughing when tickled, or getting goose bumps when cold, can be understood by a child.

Do not ever make a promise to a child that you cannot keep. Victims have most likely been lied to by adults in the past. They need to learn to trust adults again. A common temptation is to let a child talk you into promising not to tell anyone. This explicitly removes your ability to take control of the situation. Relinquishing control to responsible adults is a vital step in the healing process of the victim. Of course, it is also illegal to fail to report child abuse of any type to local child protective services authorities. Explain to the child that you want to find a special person to help him or her, someone with the child's best interests at heart, someone who understands sexual abuse problems.

Do know the resources in your community. Every state has a Child Protective Service Unit, located within a larger state agency. Many Child Protective Service Units even have specially trained sexual abuse case workers. Local police and sheriff departments and some hospitals have either specialized child abuse or sex crime teams. Many family service agencies provide treatment for victims and their families, as may your local mental health agency. It would be good to call these agencies and learn who the specialists are before you need to contact them. An agency might also provide speakers at faculty meetings on identifying and helping victims.

Do not ever ask an incest victim why he or she let it go on so long. Data from different treatment programs indicate that the incest may have been going on from several months to several years before a report is made. By asking why a victim let it go on so long, you are implying that the child had the ability to stop it.

Do cooperate with Child Protective Service workers. They will often want to interview the child at school. Unless the first contact with the child is away from parents, he or she may defer and retract the allegations in their presence. Protect the child's confidentiality; have him or her called to the school nurse or counselor's office as if nothing is particularly out of the ordinary. If a child's protection will be best served by removal from home, make lessons and homework available. A child often loses ground in schoolwork while in protective custody.

Do be as supportive as you can be to a victim seeking help. It is truly difficult to take that first step. It is our job as caring adults to make that first step as rewarding as possible.

Programs and resources

Programs designed to help prevent sexual abuse generally incorporate many of the basic health education principles. The goals of prevention programs are to teach children that their bodies belong to them, that they need to learn to make good decisions about them, and that there are people who can help them do this. The American Cancer Society's "Early Start to Good Health" curriculum may be used to introduce these points to young children.

The Illusion Theater in Minneapolis has pioneered the idea of the touch continuum; there is good touch and bad touch and children can sense the difference. Learning that they do not have to accept the bad touching is important. Parents should let children make their own decisions about whom to touch, and should be discouraged from forcing a child to hug or kiss people if the child does not want to.

Staff from local sexual abuse programs will often be available to present special programs in the classroom or in special assemblies. Often after a sensitively done program on sexual abuse, victims will identify themselves to the speaker or their teacher. Be prepared for this. It is important to know in advance exactly how you need to proceed in your community.

Child sexual abuse is a serious and complex problem, requiring input from all community systems concerned with the welfare of children and their families. Schools can play a vital role by directing child victims to help, and by implementing prevention programs.

The following groups and centers will provide information or materials to help you develop your own prevention program.

Bubbylonian Encounter (film): National Committee for Prevention of Child Abuse—Kansas Chapter, Suite 301, 214 W. 6th St., Topeka, KS 66603. See INSTRUCTOR, January 1984, p.26.

Child Abuse and Neglect: A Teacher's Handbook for Detection, Reporting, and Classroom Management ($7.95 in paperback, $14.95 hardbound); NEA Professional Library, PO Box 509, West Haven, CT 06516. A companion leaflet, "What Parents Should Know about Child Sexual Abuse," is available in packages of 25 for $4.95 from the same address.

Child Sexual Abuse Prevention Project, a guidebook for developing a curriculum for children, created by Illusion Theater. For complete information, write: Sexual Assault Services, Hennepin County Attorney's Office, C-2000 Government Center, Minneapolis, MN 55487. Cost is $8 including postage. Other resources such as posters and study cards are also available.

Come Tell Me Right Away (booklet); Edupress, Inc., PO Box 583, Fayetteville, NY 13066. Cost: $2.50.

Dangerous Stranger, 11-minute videotape for elementary children. Available free except for small cost of dubbing the video on the videotape you provide. For information write: Charles F. Ash, Jr., Pennsylvania State Police, U.S. 422, Limerick, PA 19468.

Some Secrets Should Be Told, conversation with puppets on sexual abuse, geared to grades K-6. Developed by Massachusetts Society for the Prevention of Cruelty to Children. Can be purchased as a 10-minute film or as a filmstrip; a video version can be rented. For prices and further information, contact: Family Information Systems, 69 Clinton Rd., Brookline, MA 02146.

What Everyone Should Know about Sexual Abuse of Children (100 pamphlets for $39); Channing L. Bete Co., Inc., 200 State Rd., South Deerfield, MA 01373.

The Profession of Teaching Today

More and more the debate over improving the quality of education is becoming one concerning how to reform teacher education and the conditions of teaching in schools. The profession of teaching is being subjected to many critical reports on how and why teachers succeed or fail. One of the most intensive and extensive periods of reexamination and redesign of teacher education in the history of modern education is now under way. Difficult teaching conditions, induced to a large extent by phenomena such as mainstreaming and competency based education (CBE), are intensifying pressures on teachers, even though these movements have been in the schools for the past ten years. Teachers are being asked to do more and more while they receive less and less assistance in meeting the demands of nontraditional social and testing pressures in their classrooms.

Economic frustrations—caused by the fact that real wages and real purchasing power continue to decline after inflation is taken into account—continue to plague teachers. The President's Commission Report and others have called for higher pay for teachers and merit pay to attract more academically talented young people into the profession. But as yet there have been no specific moves in either the national or the state legislatures to fund such an effort, and most local communities are unable to do so.

How does a nation achieve qualitative advancement in the field of education if it is unwilling to pay for it? In order to improve the quality of education, it is necessary to fund more in-service education for teachers, revise the funding of education so that teachers can earn wages adequate to their level of professional preparation, and demonstrate teacher competency in order to win greater public confidence in the profession.

If conditions do not improve, a major teaching shortage may occur in the next few years. Some schools are already experiencing critical shortages in teachers of science, mathematics, and foreign languages (particularly Spanish). There is also a shortage of qualified bilingual teachers for the linguistic minorities.

Renewed efforts must be made to develop and support an academically talented national teacher force. Criticizing teachers and refusing to alter those social and economic conditions which affect the quality of their work will not solve the nation's educational problems, nor will it lead to excellence at the elementary or secondary school levels. To achieve quality schools, the conditions of work and the means of funding elementary and secondary schooling must be examined by national, state, and provincial legislatures with wisdom, foresight, and compassion.

All of the articles selected for this unit relate to an issue confronting teachers or to a topic concerning developments in the profession of teaching today. The first article reflects on two models of the "art" of teaching. Diane Ravitch comments on the issues involved in "scapegoating" the teachers. The article from *Newsweek* on "Why Teachers Fail" has caught some of the popular rhetoric with which teachers have to contend. Also, it reviews some of the major criticisms of practices in teacher education. Finally, the articles on merit pay and teacher burnout relate to very important issues in the lives of teachers.

The articles of this unit can be related to any sector of a course where qualifications for teaching and the social status or working conditions of the profession are discussed.

Looking Ahead: Challenge Questions

Is teaching an art? What dimensions of teaching make it an art? Why is teaching more of an art than a science?

Why do some teachers fail? What can be done to help more teachers succeed and remain in the profession?

Can merit pay work? How? What would have to be done to make it work? How could it be financed?

Why do some teachers experience teacher burnout? What should be done to help those teachers who experience this problem?

What are the best reasons for a person to choose a career in teaching?

What are the most pressing social pressures on teachers? Why are they scapegoated?

Unit 8

The Art of Teaching

Steven M. Cahn

Steven M. Cahn is director of the Division of General Programs at the National Endowment for the Humanities in Washington, D.C., and adjunct professor of philosophy at the University of Vermont.

Teaching is an art, and, as in the case of all arts, even its most gifted practitioners can improve their skills through review of fundamentals. But is it possible to explicate the essentials of good teaching? To meet that challenge I begin with the basic principle that a teacher is responsible to both students and subject matter. Sacrificing either one for the other amounts to failure.

Consider the simple case of teaching a friend how to play chess. You start by explaining the different possible moves of the various pieces, and soon your friend assures you that he has grasped these basic maneuvers. Suppose, then, after stressing the importance of strong openings, you proceed to demonstrate your favorite, the slashing King's Gambit. Knights, bishops, and pawns whiz back and forth over the board, accompanied by your running commentary on the strengths and weaknesses of the complicated variations. At last, you complete this detailed analysis and look up proudly, awaiting your friend's approval. He stares at the board, shakes his head, and finally remarks, "I guess I'll stick to checkers. I like it better when all the pieces move the same way."

King's Gambit may have been flawless, but while concentrating on the details of the subvariations, you have overlooked your friend's confusion as he tried to keep in mind such fundamentals as how pawns can move and where knights can jump. A good instructor anticipates such difficulties, realizing how tenuous a beginning student's claim to understanding may be. Lacking this insight, you might succeed as a chess analyst but not as a chess teacher.

Assume, however, that in an effort to sustain your friend's involvement, you do not warn him about the complexities of opening theory but merely advise that he attack quickly with his queen. You regale him with anecdotes of your triumphs over weak players who fell into such elementary traps as the Fool's Mate. Your friend supposes he has mastered a surefire strategy and, full of confidence and enthusiasm, marches to the nearest chess club. There he soon encounters some intermediate players who deftly parry his premature assaults and defeat him with ease.

What went wrong this time? Unless your friend eventually realizes the inadequacy of the preparation you provided and possesses the dedication to study the technical materials you suggested he bypass, he will again and again be beaten badly, quickly grow discouraged, and perhaps give up the game altogether. He may, nevertheless, have thoroughly enjoyed his lessons with you. If so, you succeeded as an entertainer but, again, not as a teacher.

Anyone who thinks teaching is easy has never stood in front of a class of thirty restless teenagers and tried to arouse and maintain their interest while simultaneously attempting to communicate a subject's complexities. In such circumstances, individuals quickly become aware that not everyone cares who they are or what they have to say.

Of course, the mechanics of sheer drill backed by the pressures of reward and punishment will normally result in some learning. But if the attention of students is engaged only by gold stars or raps on the knuckles, the removals of these reinforcements may well be accompanied by loss of interest. Students will thus have failed to acquire that most important of qualities, the desire to continue learning. Persons whose educations end when they leave school are doomed to spend much of their lives in ignorance. Good teaching, therefore, is not merely the transmission of information and skills, but the encouragement of zest for further study.

Sheer gusto, however, is not sufficient. If it were, teachers could succeed merely by going along with the whims of their students. If the students wanted to learn history but not economics, instructors could teach history and not economics. If students found most history boring but were fascinated by the history of the American cowboy, instructors could teach that

This article first appeared in the Fall 1982 issue of AMERICAN EDUCATOR, the quarterly professional journal of the American Federation of Teachers.

history and nothing else. If students wanted to see cowboy movies but not read any books about the West, instructors could turn their classrooms into movie houses. And if students wanted just to picnic in the park, instructors could make themselves useful cooking the hamburgers.

THE INTERESTS of students, however, may not match either their own needs or the needs of a democratic society whose welfare depends in great part on the understanding and capability of its citizens. Teachers, therefore, have the responsibility to lead their students to master appropriate subject matter without misrepresenting or diluting it yet at the same time arousing appreciation for it. How can they achieve this result?

Since teaching is a creative endeavor, there are no infallible guides to success. Good instruction, however, typically involves four elements: motivation, organization, clarification, and generalization.

As to motivation, I have found it useful to distinguish two types of teachers: those who pull the subject matter behind them and those who push the subject matter in front of them. The former use their own personalities to attract students and then try to transfer the students' interest from the instructor to the subject. The latter minimize their own personalities and seek to interest students directly in the material itself.

Those who pull the subject behind them usually have little difficulty in arousing enthusiasm, but their characteristic pitfall is the failure to redirect student interest away from themselves and toward the subject matter.

As Sidney Hook in *Education for Modern Man: A New Perspective* (Knopf) has noted, a teacher "...must be friendly without becoming a friend, although he may pave the way for later friendship, for friendship is a mark of preference and expresses itself in indulgence, favor, and distinctions that unconsciously find an invidious form....A teacher who becomes 'just one of the boys,' who courts popularity, who builds up personal loyalty in exchange for indulgent treatment, has missed his vocation. He should leave the classroom for professional politics."

But this is not to say that teachers who pull the subject behind them cannot be superb instructors. Indeed, if they succeed in involving students as much in the material as in the instructors' own manners, they can exert an enormously beneficial influence on an extraordinary number, for such teachers invariably attract many devoted admirers who will follow wherever such instructors lead.

On the other hand, those who push the subject in front of them need have no worry about misdirecting a student's interest. Their worry, rather, is whether such interest will be aroused at all. In many cases they must overcome the necessarily abstract quality of their subjects and make apparent the connections between the seemingly esoteric material and their students' own sphere of experience. Perhaps the most reliable tool for doing so, and one instructors need to master, is the use of well-chosen examples that relate to the purposes or passions of the students. The subject itself thus becomes their personal concern.

But whatever the particular approach of their instructors, students should be led to appreciate the subject not merely as a means but as an end, something of intrinsic worth to be enjoyed on its own account. Their lives will thereby be enriched and the material rendered more vivid and even more useful when serving some purpose beyond itself.

Teachers who fail to convey the significance of what they are discussing can see their own inadequacy reflected in the eyes of their apathetic students. Obtaining a sound education is difficult enough for a person interested in the work; for one who is bored, the process is intolerable.

A MOTIVATED student is ready to learn, but a teacher must be organized enough to take advantage of this situation. Admittedly, inflexibility can hinder an instructor from making the most of opportunities that arise spontaneously in the course of discussion, but a rambling presentation may well dissipate initial enthusiasm. What is too often forgotten is that lack of planning usually leads to stream-of-consciousness instruction, resulting in the sort of class that meanders idly from one topc to another, amounting to nothing more than an hour of aimless talk.

Each day before setting foot in the classroom, teachers should decide exactly what they intend to accomplish during a particular session and precisely what they expect their students to know by the time the period ends. In the words of Alfred North Whitehead in *The Aims of Education and Other Essays*, "a certain ruthless definiteness is essential in education." A teacher's obligation is to guide students, and to guide requires a sense of where one is headed. If the teacher does not know, then everyone is lost.

Careful organization, however, must be complemented by an equal concern for clarification. Otherwise, even the most highly structured course of study may prove incomprehensible to the uninitiated.

Since academic subjects tend toward complexity, classrooms are often rife with confusion. But good teachers foresee this problem and substantially reduce it by making every effort to be as clear as possible. They use concrete cases to exemplify abstract concepts, and, realizing that individuals differ in how they arrive at an understanding of particular ideas, good instructors take pains to explain fundamental principles in a variety of ways.

Of course, not every train of thought can be rendered in very simple terms. A book entitled *Kant Made Easy* is surely the work of a charlatan or a fool. Effective teachers, therefore, must be shrewd judges of both the difficulty of their materials and the ability of their students.

Why do some instructors seem to make so little effort to express themselves clearly? Many do not realize that good teachers direct their remarks not only at the best student, or at the top 10 percent of the class, or even at the majority; instead, good teachers speak so that virtually all their listeners can follow. These teachers realize that when more than one or two

When a student is exposed only to the objective facts and figures of any course of study, the relevance of these facts to the true texture of the discipline is often never made until the student's experience broadens to include college. Good teaching in elementary and secondary schools must make the topics of study a meaningful learning experience.

students complain they are lost, many others, whether they themselves realize it or not also need help.

Having now discussed motivation, organization, and clarification, I turn to the fourth element of good instruction: generalization. Because a thorough knowledge of any subject matter depends upon a firm grasp of its details, the tendency of many instructors is to emphasize analysis at the expense of synthesis. But to master a subject requires awareness of its connections to related areas of inquiry. Details are necessary to understanding, but they are not sufficient. Also required is perspective, and that can be achieved only by viewing specific information within a broad framework.

I still vividly recall my high school history teacher who insisted that we memorize the dates, locations, and names of the commanding generals for every major battle of the Civil War. Only in my college years when I heard a series of enthralling lectures on the causes, strategies, and results of that war did I come to understand and share my earlier teacher's fascination with the events of that period.

A student should not be allowed to become lost in minutiae. For although generalizations without details are hollow, details without generalizations are barren.

I HAVE thus far been considering the components of good teaching, but great teaching involves yet another element. Great teachers not only motivate their students, organize the class, clarify their material, and provide illuminating generalizations, they also project a vision of excellence.

Even after considerable study, it is not easy to distinguish what is adequate from what is excellent. How many of us, observing two physicians, would know which was merely competent and which superb? How many of us, reading a history of Europe, would realize whether the account was exceptional or just satisfactory? Recognizing such distinctions depends upon an awareness of critical subtleties, and each great teacher in inimitable ways leads students to acquire and prize such insight.

Excellence is not only of value to those who possess it. Equally important is its significance for those who have been taught to appreciate it, for by developing the acuity and sensitivity needed to comprehend the magnificent achievements of which human effort is capable, one's perceptions are rendered more vivid and one's experience enormously enriched.

The hallmark of superb instruction is not the applause of students but rather their informed and abiding commitment to recognize and respect quality. Achieving that goal is the ultimate challenge inherent in the noble profession of teaching.

Scapegoating the Teachers

Diane Ravitch

Diane Ravitch's latest book is *The Troubled Crusade* (Basic).

THE MOST common response to the current crisis in education has been to assail public school teachers. Not only are they incompetent, goes the charge, but good people have abandoned or are shunning the teaching profession. Teacher competency tests, which have spread during the past five years to some three dozen states, have produced embarrassing results in many districts; for example, when a third of Houston's teachers took a competency test, 62 percent failed the reading section and 46 percent failed the mathematics section (and the scores of hundreds of other teachers were ruled invalid because of teacher cheating). Those who major in education in college tend to have below-average grades in high school and lower scores on their SATs than the already depressed national average (in 1982, the national average on the SAT-verbal was 426, while the average for those planning to major in education was only 394).

This state of affairs has prompted a plethora of proposals. Some call for merit pay. Others call for increased salaries across the board. To some reformers, the answer lies with the designation of master teachers or with the promotion of more doctorate degrees in educational practice. Still others argue that the teacher problem would be ameliorated by abolishing schools of education.

THE PROBLEM of teacher competence is serious, since there is no chance that the schools will improve unless the teachers know more than the students do. Yet the rush to attack teachers and teacher education programs smacks more than a little of scapegoating. Teachers did not single-handedly cause the debasement of educational standards, and their preparation is better today than it was twenty years ago, when test scores began to fall. Though we now look back to 1962-63 as the golden age of student achievement, these years coincided with the publication of two major critiques of teacher education, James Koerner's *The Miseducation of American Teachers* and James B. Conant's *The Education of American Teachers*. Teachers, it seems, can't win: when scores go down, they are to blame; when scores are high, they get no credit.

It is comforting to blame teachers for the low state of education, because it relieves so many others of their own responsibility for many years of educational neglect.

—Why not blame the colleges and universities for lowering entrance requirements, thus undermining high school graduation requirements? Why not blame them for accepting hordes of semiliterate students and establishing massive remedial programs, instead of complaining to the high schools that gave diplomas to the uneducated?

—Why not blame businesses and employers, who set

Reprinted by permission of *THE NEW REPUBLIC*, ©1983, The New Republic, Inc.

up multimillion-dollar programs to teach basic skills to their work force instead of telling the public, the school boards, and the legislatures that the schools were sending them uneducated people? Why didn't representatives of major employers—like the telephone company and the banks—join forces to demand improved education?

—Why not blame state legislatures, which quietly diluted or abolished high school graduation requirements? Why were they willing to pile on new requirements for nonacademic courses (drug education, family life education, consumer education, etc.) while cutting the ground away from science, math, history, and foreign languages?

—Why not blame the press, which has been indifferent to educational issues, interested only in fads, and unaware of the steady deterioration of academic standards until a national commission captured its attention?

—Why not blame the federal government, which has toyed with the curriculum and introduced programs, regulations, and practices that narrowed the teacher's professional autonomy in the classroom?

—Why not blame the courts, which have whittled away the schools' ability to maintain safety and order? (Several weeks ago, the New Jersey Supreme Court invalidated evidence that students were selling drugs in junior high, because the drugs had been illegally seized in one student's purse and in another student's locker—the court's decision that the students' right to privacy outweighed the school's obligation to maintain order nullified the school's obligation to act in loco parentis.)

With so many guilty parties still at large, it should be clear why almost everyone seems eager to pin responsibility on the teachers for the bad news about the schools. The reality is that teachers should be seen not as perpetrators of the deleterious trends in the schools, but as victims of them. As teaching conditions worsen, it is teachers who suffer the consequences. When judges rule that disruptive youths cannot be suspended, it is teachers who must lock their classroom door and worry about being assaulted.

JUST AS SERIOUS as the problem of teacher competence is the state of the teaching profession. Some teachers insist bitterly that teaching is no longer a profession, but has been reduced to a civil service job. Other professionals are subject to entry tests and to supervision by senior professionals, but they usually retain a large measure of control over where they work and how they perform their duties; in teaching, governmental agencies and policymakers have bureaucratized hiring practices, curriculum development, student placement, and other areas that once engaged the experience and participation of teachers. The effort to make schools "teacher-proof" ends by making the teachers technical functionaries, implementing remotely designed policies. With so many laws and regulations and interest groups on the scene, wise teachers look for protection to the rulebook, their union, their lawyer, or to some job with more dignity. For the person who simply wants to teach history or literature, the school has not been a receptive workplace.

In response to declining enrollments and worsening working conditions, the number of people who want to be teachers has dropped sharply over the past decade. The number of undergraduate degrees awarded in education reached a peak of two hundred thousand in 1973, when they were 21 percent of all bachelor's degrees awarded in the nation, but have dropped to only one hundred and eight thousand in 1981, fewer than 12 percent of all bachelor's degrees awarded. The tight job market has meant not only a decline in the number preparing to teach, but a decline in the ability of those who want to teach. Apparently the brighter students were smart enough to pick another field, and the flight of academically talented women to other fields has particularly depressed the quality of the pool of would-be teachers. The low starting salary for teachers is undoubtedly a factor in shrinking the pool: a college graduate with a bachelor's degree in mathematics would get a starting salary in teaching of about $13,000, while the same person would receive about $17,000 as an accountant in private industry.

The outlook for a better pool in the future is not very promising. In the fall of 1970, 19 percent of college freshmen said that they wanted to teach in elementary or secondary school. A year ago, less than 5 percent of college freshmen expressed the same ambition. Less than 2 percent wanted to teach in high school, a choice that was doubtless informed by their own recent observation of the life of high school teachers.

Would reforms in teacher education help the situation? For years, critics of education have heaped scorn on schools of education and on the required education courses that prospective teachers must take. Thirty years ago, critics like Arthur Bestor and Mortimer Smith charged that entry to the teaching profession was controlled by an "interlocking directorate" made up of schools of education, bureaucrats in state education departments, and teacher associations, and that the hurdles these groups erected (such as "Mickey Mouse" courses in educational theory and methods) excluded talented people from the public schools. Since the early 1950s was a time of baby boom and teacher shortage, nothing much came of the grumbling, and the agencies of certification and accreditation are, if anything, even more powerful today.

YET SCHOOLS of education are not solely responsible for the intellectual inadequacies of those entering teaching. The important fact to bear in mind about students preparing to teach is that they take most of their courses outside of the undergraduate education department. Would-be high school teachers take only about 20 percent of their courses in education, and would-be elementary teachers take about 40 percent of their courses in education. If their academic preparation is deficient, the fault lies with the arts and sciences faculties.

Even though education majors take most of their courses outside the education department, it would be preferable if there were no education majors at the undergraduate level, if every would-be teacher majored in some subject or combination of subjects. As matters now stand, the one hundred and eight thousand bachelor's degrees in education awarded in 1981 were divided up among students preparing to be elementary teachers (35 percent), physical education teachers (17 percent), special education teachers (13 percent), and teachers of such specialized areas as home economics, vocational education, prekindergarten instruction, and health education. Less than 3 percent of the education degrees went to secondary teachers, which suggests (happily) that those who want to teach in high school take their Bachelor of Arts degrees in the subjects they want to teach and get their education credits on the side or in graduate school.

Elementary teachers need a wide preparation, since they will be teaching reading, writing, mathematics, science, social studies, art, and music. But they can take the courses in how to teach these subjects to young children while majoring in a discipline or combination of disciplines. The case for requiring physical education instructors to major in a subject area is even stronger, because a large number of them teach their minor subject (usually social studies) and end up as high school principals.

Since prospective secondary teachers rarely major in education in college, they do not get counted or measured by the researchers who examine the quality of the teaching pool. In most studies and government reports, statistics are gathered only for those who major in education in college. Thus the numbers that are tossed about refer *only* to those who are academically weakest. In fact, when we are warned about the onrushing tide of incompetent teachers, we are hearing only about the coaches, the school nurses, the elementary school teachers, and the shop teachers, but not the would-be teachers of history, the sciences, English, and mathematics. We should still be concerned, particularly about the low academic ability of those who are supposed to teach young children the basic skills and impart to them their attitudes toward learning, but we should recognize that the data are biased.

GRADUATE SCHOOLS of education have shown little interest in training teachers. Some professors and programs involve themselves with the public schools, but most of these institutions emphasize research and the training of educational administrators. Because they are parts of universities, their concept of status derives from the traditional academic model. They have low status within the university, which considers the graduate school of education little better than a vocational school.

Yet the graduate school has a useful role to play. In particular, it cares about education, which is one of the major social and economic activities in the nation. This sets it apart from the rest of the university, which tends to look down upon any interest in or involvement with the public schools. Just last summer, however, the presidents of Harvard and Stanford met with leading university presidents and their education deans to discuss how to help the schools and how to overcome the traditional snobbery that has kept the "ed" schools out of the academic mainstream. Whether this resolve is translated from rhetoric into programmatic commitments remains to be seen.

Perhaps a personal note at this point will explain my own bias. In 1972, when I had been out of college for a dozen years, I decided to get a Ph.D. in history while writing a political history of the New York City public schools. I approached a young history professor at Columbia, who told me that I was a bad bet for his department: "You have three strikes against you," he said. "First, you are a woman; second, you are more than ten years away from your B.A.; and third, you are interested in education." At Teachers College, the graduate school of education at Columbia, none of those characteristics was considered a handicap, and I pursued my studies there. This lack of interest in elementary and secondary schooling and in education as a profession and as a research field is typical of major research universities.

The present crisis in education and the depressed condition of the teaching profession offer an unusual opportunity to reassess our present arrangements for preparing teachers. As Gary Sykes, until recently the National Institute of Education's specialist on the teaching profession, has observed, the profession needs both "screens and magnets," ways to keep out incompetent teachers and ways to lure in the highly talented. The traditional screen—state certification—is almost entirely ineffective, since it guarantees only that a prospective teacher has taken required courses and received a degree. Recognizing that a college degree today certifies very little, a number of states have begun to adopt teacher examinations and to reassess their requirements for entry into the profession. If school boards and state legislatures were to raise their hiring standards—to insist that new teachers have an undergraduate major other than education, for instance, and to determine whether the education courses they require are valuable—the message of the marketplace would be heeded by institutions that prepare teachers.

Developing magnets to attract good people to teaching will be far more difficult. It must involve better pay, so that a life of teaching is not equivalent to an oath of penury. It may or may not involve some form of salary differentiation for teachers who win the respect and admiration of their peers, but some salary incentives should be available to keep gifted teachers in the classroom. It should involve generous public fellowships to underwrite the education of those willing to commit themselves to the classroom for several years. It should mean a readiness by school boards to provide teachers with opportunities for continuing intellectual and professional growth. It should mean a flexibility by teachers' unions to permit the employment of graduate students in science and mathematics, college-educated housewives, and professional writers to meet critical shortages on a temporary or part-time basis. It requires a willingness by education officials to defend the teacher's professional autonomy and to preserve a climate in the schools that honors teaching and learning.

Like every other educational problem, the difficulty of attracting top-flight people to teaching will not yield to simple solutions. Demography contributed to the problem; smart people looked for other jobs as enrollments declined. But demography may help ease the problem, as enrollments begin to grow again, increasing the demand for new teachers. The opening of other career opportunities has shrunk the talent pool, but teaching will continue to be an attractive occupation for those who wish to combine a career with family responsibilities.

As a mass, public profession, teaching will never offer salaries that compare favorably with law or medicine, but it does offer satisfactions that are unique to the job. In every generation, there are people born with a love of teaching. They want to open the minds of young people to literature, history, art, science, or something else that has seized their imagination. To recruit and hold onto such people, the nation's schools must not only reward them adequately but must provide the conditions in which good teaching can flourish. That will not come about through public incantations; it will demand realistic programs and imaginative solutions. But a nation that has led the world in popular education for more than a century owes it to itself to meet the challenge.

MERIT PAY the great debate

Marge Scherer

Marge Scherer is managing editor/editorial of INSTRUCTOR.

"If we're going to give schools only one improvement, let it not be merit pay."

"I do not know how anyone, especially a teacher, can be against the idea of merit pay."

"Merit pay could restructure the entire teaching profession by providing the career ladder we've been needing."

"Merit pay! In an underpaid profession, it's like putting icing on a cake that doesn't exist."

The voices in the debate on merit pay are discordant even when they are all addressing the same proposal, which isn't often the case. For, as newscasters, presidential candidates, and the general public join in the discussion raised by the National Commission on Excellence in Education, the deceptively simple issue of merit pay threatens to disrupt the education profession to the same degree as the allegation of mediocrity has. Complicating matters is the fact that the merit pay plans are as various as they are numerous.

The recent furor over an issue that is at least 75 years old has prompted the NEA to decide to monitor all merit pay and master teacher plans. At the same time, it is on record as opposing any compensation system based on "favoritism, subjective evaluation," or arbitrary standards, including those based on student achievement or grade and subject taught. The AFT, on the other hand, passed a resolution that said, "While merit pay is not AFT policy, under certain circumstances state federations may feel the need to negotiate" plans that would promote significant numbers of teachers to more highly paid master teacher positions.

Meanwhile, in circles in and outside of education, people on opposite political and ideological sides continue to endorse and attack concepts rather than specific plans. Some proponents who want schools to improve but who are convinced that the vast majority of teachers are mediocre, feel merit pay is the way to reward good teachers and avoid paying the rest. Other merit pay advocates feel some of the plans could provide teachers more recognition, more career latitude, more money, as well as attract and keep better teachers and help to increase student achievement.

Many educators who have not been enthusiastic about merit pay in the past now feel that taking advantage of the current national interest in education is the astute thing to do. If merit pay is the way to get higher salaries for teachers, they say "so be it," but they want teachers to speak out about what kinds of merit pay are adopted in their districts. Both critics and proponents of merit pay warn that the wrong merit plan, the wrong procedures, could increase competition among teachers, lower student and teacher morale, and, worst of all, by inaccurately defining what it means to be a good teacher, effectively cut off true educational reform.

What kinds of plans are being discussed?

Bonus pay based on student performance What some people are talking about when they say "merit pay" is

Reprinted from INSTRUCTOR, October 1983. Copyright ©1983 by The Instructor Publications, Inc. Used by permission.

a bonus given to teachers for what is considered to be superior teaching and not given to those who don't meet the criteria. For instance, in Seiling, Oklahoma, merit pay is a $500 bonus given to every teacher in the elementary school if all children in school average above the targeted increase in reading scores. In addition, each teacher may receive another $250 for each of his or her classes whose reading scores reach the target and another $250 if math scores meet the goal. The maximum merit pay an elementary teacher can earn is $1,000.

A committee of teachers headed by the superintendent sets the target, each year trying to increase the standard over the previous year. Scores from standardized, criterion-referenced, and teacher-made pre- and post-tests are keyed into a computer that is programmed to convert the scores to Normal Curve Equivalency points, and to figure the class average, school average, and amount of bonus each teacher will receive. So far, all participating teachers (38 out of 42 this year) have earned the $500 because the school each year has exceeded the target. About 85 percent of these teachers have earned additional bonus money above and beyond their salaries, which range from $15,000 to $21,000.

Gerald Daugherty, Seiling superintendent, says the system "rewards extraordinary teachers and encourages those who are teetering on the brink of mediocrity." The four-year-old plan, which is not used as a substitute for annual salary raises, has resulted in "a definite trend toward higher scores and greater teacher concentration on goals."

Teachers in Seiling mention drawbacks in the plan—a major one being that students are aware their scores control merit pay for teachers and that some deliberately score low on the tests of teachers they don't like. (The tests do not necessarily affect students' grades.) To protect against this problem, the top and bottom 10 scores are disregarded in figuring class averages. Other criticisms by teachers are that the tests don't accurately measure the full scope of what is being taught; that tests take valuable time; and that teachers must teach to the tests, although not exclusively.

Educators outside the system direct their criticism not at the Seiling plan but at the general principle of using student achievement as the basis of merit pay. Their major criticism is that reliance on such tests indicates a narrow notion of what teaching is. "Teachers are seen as review books, not educators," says Samuel Bacharach of Cornell University, who is currently reviewing all arguments for and against merit pay for the National Education Association. He says that any system based on student tests reflects a belief in the scientific objectivity of tests to a degree of predictability and accuracy we just don't have.

Thomas Good of the University of Missouri, author of *Looking in Classrooms* and *Teachers Make a Difference*, comes to the same conclusion: "If good teaching means high test scores, then teachers will mobilize all teaching to that purpose." Because it is easier to come up with valid measures in math and reading as opposed to social studies, art, or music, the latter subjects may be neglected. "Not only is the content of what is being taught narrowed, but teaching students abstract processes like problem-solving and self-evaluation are dropped in favor of teaching them what is measured on tests. . . .I would be very much interested in the attitudes of the students in such a system. Do they see classrooms as more answer oriented than learning oriented?"

Richard Murnane, an associate professor of economics at the Harvard Graduate School of Education, voices another concern about using student achievement tests for the purpose of merit pay. "It could put a premium on having the brightest students in the classroom and result in teachers lobbying for students who would respond well to instruction," he says. In other systems that are weighted in favor of average achievers, "teachers would allocate less time to both the gifted and low ability children, figuring the gifted would make a year's gain with very little teaching, and the lowest students, even with great effort, might not achieve the target." Despite the fact that seniority-based contracts may unfairly pay both the poor and the good teacher the same amount, Murnane thinks that the system is truer to the concept of equal opportunity for students than are many merit pay plans.

Increments based on teacher performance A completely different approach, an incentive increment plan, is taken in Ladue, Missouri, where teachers are observed and evaluated by principals three times a year. Teachers are awarded points in such categories as classroom performance, interaction with colleagues, effective communication with the community, contributions to the school district, and professional self-improvement. Each year the school board determines how much the points are worth. In the 1982-83 year a teacher could earn $300 per point, and teachers could earn up to $4,500 in merit pay. About 10 to 15 percent of teachers get the maximum amount, giving some teachers salaries in the $38,000 range. (The beginning salary is $14,500, and the average salary about $30,000.)

Carol Hampton, a Ladue teacher, says the system works because "when it started, the teachers and administrators had a family feeling that has filtered down through the years." The system has an appeal procedure that teachers can use, as well.

Charles McKenna, Ladue superintendent, says that when he came to Ladue 20 years ago, 10 years after the program started, he took a "look-and-see attitude." Now he's convinced: "There's no way to defend using college credits and years of experience as the only criteria for paying teachers. Everyone's willing to admit there is such a thing as a good teacher, yet few are willing to say how outstanding performance can be determined. Any kind of evaluation program requires time and effort and training for those who will conduct it. There's a margin of error in our system but less than if we had a strictly automatic seniority-based system."

Those who question the plan say that while it might work in Ladue, they have their doubts that such a system would work in a less wealthy or less closely knit group, mostly because the merit increments would not be enough to matter or because charges of favoritism would be overwhelming.

Glen Robinson of the Educational Research Service, a nonprofit corporation sponsored by eight national associations, found in a 1978 national study that many districts that had abandoned merit plans did so because evaluation procedures were unsatisfactory. Among problems reported were difficulties in determining who deserved extra pay, inconsistency among evaluations, poor evaluative instruments, too much record-keeping, and a belief of teachers that impartial ratings were impossible.

A major decision to make in such plans is which person or group will be responsible for the evaluation. Principals who do not often visit classrooms or know curricula are not the best evaluators, and problems may result with peer review as well. "I had a wonderful review one year," says New York teacher Valerie Bang-Jensen, who recently studied merit pay proposals for a graduate course. "But I felt my evaluators did not really understand what I was trying to do in the classroom. Some evaluators have philosophical blinders and may like what they see only if it coalesces with their own educational theories." Others may be impressed with the obvious—straightened blinds or a creative desk arrangement.

If evaluators come from outside the district, they may not understand the specific school situation. If they come from inside, the politics of the district may override their objectivity. Even if an evaluation is done with care and integrity, whether it really measures the quality of superior teaching or is at all related to student achievement are two more questions worth debating.

"It's so much easier to describe what is not working in a classroom than it is to describe the difference between an average classroom and a good one," Thomas Good says. "Too often we evaluate teachers as if they were actors on the stage," noting their movement, appearance, voice quality, and enthusiasm, but "part of the quality of teaching is continuity—building meaning over time.... Our rating systems usually are based on three or four observations; it all boils down to the question 'How spellbinding was she?' "

Evaluators also tend to assume that if something is good, more will be better, Good says. Thus if evaluators consider that homework leads to student achievement, the teacher who assigns a good deal of homework may be rated superior. Research doesn't bear that out though, he says. "A teacher can assign too much homework, ask too many questions, even allow too much time for response. What we should really consider is the effect on the student."

Educators also criticize using evaluations of teacher performance as a basis of merit pay because administrators often have to impose a quota system on the number of teachers eligible for merit pay. If a superintendent does not impose some limits, everyone will receive excellent ratings, and the merit pay will be spread too thin, says Joe Shedd, a doctoral candidate in industrial relations at Cornell University. "And if grade creep does occur, the school board will request extra documentation.... It will be such a headache to document a high or low rating, they might find it easier to give average ratings." And if quotas are imposed, the collegiality of the staff will suffer. "Effective school research shows that education is a group effort," Shedd says. "The very worst thing to do is to set up a compensation system that rewards only individual effort and discourages teachers from sharing ideas and advice with one another."

Another question often raised in the debate on merit pay is who is most motivated by it—the average teacher, the new teacher, the extremely good teacher, or the poor teacher? The average teacher who could be good but needs more money might well decide to moonlight at another job rather than put extra effort into teaching, Bang-Jensen says. And if money is the object for bright new teacher candidates, there are many other career options open.

Gerald Daugherty says in his experience, the average teachers benefit most. "Good teachers whose egos are wrapped up in their students and teaching will do yeoman's work no matter what you pay. And no amount will make a sorry teacher into a great one." But for the majority, "a little incentive causes them to be more concerned with the outcome of their work." Samuel Bacharach says the person who is *hurt* the most by a merit pay system is the one who aims for merit pay and doesn't get it. "The average worker thinks he is better than 80 percent of his coworkers. No person will be as frustrated as the one who is *almost* a good teacher."

Individualized Productivity Plan A third type of merit pay proposal attempts to combine the best features of other merit plans and to avoid their problems. Developed by the Educational Research Service, the plan is based on student achievement and on teacher performance, and if adequately financed, theoretically would be available to all who qualify. It has not yet been put into practice, according to Glen Robinson, ERS president, but a number of school districts are studying it.

Under this plan, a teacher could be awarded merit pay when he or she had met his or her own individual productivity goals and submitted an individualized performance plan for verification to an approved committee. In this plan a seventh-grade math teacher might suggest she could teach the same content in less time than she did previously while maintaining or improving test scores, and then would use the remaining time to teach a computer literacy course. If that teacher could satisfactorily prove she had met her own goal, she would receive the agreed upon bonus. Other personal productivity proposals might include ways of increasing student learning (including that of a special group of students with learning or behavior problems); improving student attitudes; teaching more students while maintaining achievement; and so on. The key to this plan is that the teacher is responsible for designing the proposal and objectively measuring whether it's been successful, says Robinson. It ideally would be used in conjunction with a conventional evaluation plan based on staff relations, classroom management, and techniques of instruction to help teachers improve performance. The productivity plan would not take teachers out of the classroom or establish a hierarchy of teachers, but would raise the morale of all, Robinson says.

Whether or not such a plan is practical depends greatly on what types of proposals are made and on the committee who accepts or rejects them. "I'd want to know who's on the committee, what role parents have, and how varied the plans could be," Richard Murnane says. "I'd also want to know who determines which students teachers get because many times the more difficult and harder to handle students would not be those who teachers feel increase their personal productivity." Yet the plan has potential, he says, and although he can't see it working in urban Philadelphia with 30,000 teachers negotiating proposals, he believes the program might work in smaller districts.

Thomas Good concurs with the idea of rewarding careful teaching and encouraging teachers to think instead of "trying to standardize what it means to be a good teacher." The quality of the proposals would have to be good, however. Individualized criteria could not be gratuitous or silly. "Any goal can be reached if set low enough." Another consideration is whether such a proposal could expect too much of teachers. "If teachers are expected to broaden their capabilities they would have to be very skillful indeed to do it without changing their classroom situations in any material way. They should have the option of requesting additional equipment, additional help, someone to help them grade papers, a team of teachers to work with. . . .We should think of adding more resources as well as altering compensatory systems if we are going to achieve excellence."

Differentiated staffing The differentiated staffing approach differs significantly from bonus or incentive plans to the extent that some persons who advocate them disavow the use of the term *merit pay*. Instead of giving extra pay for superior teaching, these plans assign higher salaries to positions considered to be more important, have more responsibility, or be in more demand.

David Rhone, president of National Management Associates in Shippensburg, Pennsylvania, proposes a plan that would pay teachers of "more difficult" subjects more; for instance, first-grade and math teachers would receive higher salaries, with middle school teachers' salaries falling in the middle range, and possibly driver education teachers' in the lowest. The idea behind the plan is to relate compensation to job and "to stop paying everyone the same rate based on years of time in the system. . . .Each district would have to determine which jobs to reward more, making it necessary for the community to think hard about what it values the most," Rhone says.

The Houston Second Mile Plan incorporates differentiated staffing as well as other ways teachers can earn stipends. Teachers in a school with many disadvantaged students; those who teach subjects where there are staff shortages (bilingual education and secondary mathematics, for instance); and those whose schools exceed predicted achievement on standardized tests all can apply for stipends ranging from $400 to $2,000. Teachers who miss five or fewer days in attendance are also eligible for stipends ranging from $50 to $500. The multiple provisions in the plan reflect specific needs of the district and are ways to respond to teacher shortages, staff absenteeism, and the need for improved standardized test scores. Criticism of the arbitrariness of some of the provisions aside, educators say the problem with differentiated staffing is in establishing the relative importance of different teaching jobs. NEA and AFT affiliates have both opposed the plan, and many teachers question the judgment of those who say math is more important than social studies.

The career ladder approach This approach differs from differentiated staffing in that it creates new career steps and promotes teachers to more highly paid teaching levels. Under such a plan, teachers at higher levels may be responsible for teaching and evaluating other teachers or developing the curriculum. Some may teach more hours and months, as well. Tennessee Governor Lamar Alexander's career path approach establishes four career levels: apprentice, professional, senior, and master teachers. Teachers advance to the next highest level based on the number of years at the previous level (at least three); performance evaluations by supervisors; competency or subject-area tests; and student performance. In addition, those who are advanced to the master teacher level would have to demonstrate the ability to work with and evaluate other teachers. State and local committees of evaluators would be formed to continuously reevaluate and recertify teachers.

Under the plan, professional teachers would receive $1,000 in incentive pay in addition to across-the-board raises; senior teachers (25 percent of Tennessee teachers would be eligible) would get $2,000 or $4,000 more, depending on whether they had a 10- or 12-month contract; and master teachers (another 15 percent) could earn from $3,000 to $5,000 more. Senior and master teachers would work in the summer with gifted or remedial students, or they would conduct inservice for teachers or develop curricula.

The advantage of the plan, says Chester Finn, professor of education and public policy at Vanderbilt University, is that it fulfills teachers' needs. "A good teacher is motivated by intrinsic rewards, a decent salary, and by being recognized by others in society," he says. "In the last few years the intrinsic rewards have been harder to achieve and material rewards have been less. This plan will keep good people in the system."

One major problem may be that apprentice teachers will want to achieve promotions at a faster rate. "For new teachers it will take 11 years before they become master teachers. If they're real hotshots, other careers could pay off sooner," Finn says.

Other unknowns about career ladder systems are how teachers who remain in the lower categories throughout their careers might be affected and how their students and students' parents will react to not having the "best teachers." (In the Tennessee plan, apprentice teachers must advance at least to the professional level in a certain period of time or lose their position.)

Most career path systems also establish an additional bureaucracy of evaluators, and require a great deal of record-keeping, and much time given to evaluating teachers. Most master teacher plans also take those judged to be the best teachers out of the classroom or require them to take on an additional work load. "The good teacher

Questions to ask

Eric Rhodes, the president of the consulting firm Educational Futures Research, suggests the following questions to ask before considering a merit pay plan.

1. What's your purpose? Is it to improve instruction, reward outstanding teachers, attract better teaching candidates, motivate teachers?
2. Will you evaluate teachers on the basis of their assignment and degree of responsibility? on students' standardized test results? on peer or administration observation of performance? or a combination of the above?
3. How will teachers' associations and unions participate in decisions about implementing merit pay? What will your appeal process be?
4. What is your time line? (A year of planning is realistic.)
5. What costs are you willing to bear? Rewards must be sufficiently attractive, at least 10 percent of average salary. A merit pay plan in a district of 500 teachers with an average salary of $20,000 could cost a minimum of one-third of a million dollars.

might want to spend the energy and effort in the classroom," Valerie Bang-Jensen suggests.

What else is there?

Many merit pay plans have a primary objective to attract or to keep good teachers and thereby to improve the quality of education for students. According to a great many educators, merit pay is surely not the only way of doing that. Almost all mention that a reasonable salary to begin with is most important. "If we want to attract excellent teachers, we won't do it just by dabbling with merit pay or master teachers programs," says Louis Fischer, a professor of education at the University of Massachusetts, Amherst. "One of my key concerns is that through endorsing merit pay for a few people, we provide a rationalization for not looking at greater salaries for all concerned."

Beyond that, educators offer their own ideas for what else besides money motivates good teachers. Harvard's Richard Murnane suggests that "trying to make the job of teaching more pleasant will go a longer way in improving education than merit pay will." To do this he suggests decreasing bureaucracy so that teachers with good ideas can put them into effect, and dividing large-school faculties into teams of teachers working with smaller groups of students. To attract new candidates to teaching, he thinks a dramatic salary boost in the second year ("if you're going to get good, you get good fast") coupled with on-the-job help from older teachers would improve the performance of young teachers more-so than would the possibility of having a career ladder in later years.

When Karen Zumwalt, associate professor, Teachers College, Columbia University, conducted a survey to determine why veteran teachers had positive feelings about their teaching jobs, she found that the teachers identified respect, recognition, and reinforcement as those things that had improved their teaching. Participating in research studies; being a member of a teaching team; earning grants for curriculum development; as well as being encouraged by principals, parents, colleagues, and students all motivated these teachers to keep striving for excellence. She believes, "It's a leap of faith to think merit pay will solve our problems. We'll need merit pay, plus a lot of other things."

Why Teachers Fail

With public attention focused on educational reform and a shortage of instructors ahead, new ways are being tried to improve the way we teach teachers.

Bill Rietmann's friends think he's crazy. Last spring, he graduated from the venerable University of California at Berkeley with highest honors in English, and he wants to be: *a schoolteacher*. "I debated what to do," he says. "I could have gone to law school. Most people reacted by pointing out that teaching is a dead-end career with no money in it." Most people may have been putting it mildly. If Rietmann completes the graduate teaching program at Berkeley and goes on to spread his love of literature to a high-school classroom, he will become part of the most scorned quasi-profession in America.

At the present time, it is also perhaps the most controversial. Last year's school-reform movement turned public attention on the quality of instruction, but not on the quality of the instructor's instruction. How well are teachers being taught? Two reports in the last month, by the Rand Corp. and the National Center for Education Information, suggest that may now be the main problem. "Without a doubt," says David Imig of the American Association of Colleges for Teacher Education, "teacher education is and ought to be the next focus of those trying to improve the schools."

Changes within the teacher corps both compound and reflect the problems in the nation's public education systems. "The current highly educated and experienced staff is dwindling as older teachers retire and many younger teachers leave for other occupations," declares the Rand report. It predicts that in just four years the supply of teachers will meet only 80 percent of the demand (chart, page 208). And the profession gets no respect from this generation: two years ago just 5 percent of entering college freshmen said they were interested in teaching, compared with 1970 when nearly one in five wanted to teach. The coming gap affects nearly every area of study, with math and science especially vulnerable. Last year 43 states reported shortages of the teachers, and 42 needed more physics teachers.

At the same time, teacher training is perhaps the biggest running joke in higher education. And nearly every public-school teacher in the country is a product of such training, because of certification requirements designed to bring "professionalism" to teaching. Unfortunately these programs do not attract enough top students. The combined Scholastic Aptitude Test score of college-bound high-school seniors intending to major in education is only 812 (1600 is a perfect score), compared with 987 for intended engineering majors and 893 for all seniors taking the test (chart, page 209). Worse, while prospective doctors and lawyers try to claw their way into medical and law schools, would-be teachers all too often waltz into schools of education as if they were signing up for intramural softball. Three-fourths of the schools polled by the National Center of Education Information for its report, "The Making of a Teacher," used nothing more than college grade-point-average as the admission criterion—with 2.29 the average requirement. "That's a little above a C to get into a teacher-ed program," notes center director Emily Feistritzer, the report's principal author. "Rarely does anyone who applies for admission to a teacher-education program get rejected." As many as half of these schools are little more than diploma mills, Feistritzer says, and should be shut down.

'Boring': While the course work may be easy, it is also too often irrelevant—a complaint voiced by the teachers themselves. "Most of the material is not intellectually challenging," says Robert Koff, dean of the school of education at the State University of New York at Albany. "The course work is unrelievedly boring." Union president Albert Shanker of the American Federation of Teachers is even harsher: "Education is the only professional field where after people graduate they say they could have been

From *Newsweek*, September 24, 1984, pp. 64-70. Copyright ©1984 by Newsweek, Inc. All rights reserved. Reprinted by permission.

better off without the training." In a survey of teacher attitudes conducted last summer by Louis Harris and Associates, Inc., for the Metropolitan Life Insurance Company, only 10 percent of teachers "strongly agreed" that their training does a good job preparing them for the classroom.

Critics blame the curricula, which emphasize teaching techniques and educational theory—called pedagogy—at the expense of academic subjects. The average elementary-education major, for example, is required to take 36 credit hours of pedagogy and 17 hours of fieldwork, leaving little more than half a course-load for preparation in academic subjects. Secondary-school teachers-in-training get 25 hours of education and 15 hours of student teaching. Education courses may be on subjects like "Using Media Materials" or "The Secondary School Student," focusing on practical skills without much intellectual content.

Rites of Passage: Graduation comes easy. Only 47 percent of the schools require graduates to pass any form of exit test; a paltry 5 percent of those tests are on academic subject matter, and only 11 percent gauge basic skills. "I really don't see any evidence that we're requiring very much of prospective teachers," says Feistritzer. "We do not have national criteria. There are no rites of passage. To a large extent anybody who wants to teach can find a place." She proposes a national proficiency test, similar to a bar exam, to stiffen the standards for teaching.

In the wake of the discovery that Mr. Johnny can't teach, a wide range of reform plans has emerged. Educators and legislators in every state are seeking what Diane Ravitch, a professor at Teachers College of Columbia University, calls "screens and magnets," devices to weed out undeserving candidates or teachers while attracting better students to the profession. Arkansas last fall became the first state to require all practicing teachers to pass a competency test or be fired. Eighteen states now require new teachers to take written tests, such as the Educational Testing Service's National Teacher Examination Core Battery Tests (box, page 210), for certification. Thirty more are planning such tests. Florida, Alabama and Georgia have promised to place schools of education on probation if a majority of their graduates cannot pass statewide proficiency tests.

Scholarships: As for magnets, the U.S. House of Representatives recently approved a four-year program to lure top high-school students into teaching with $5,000-a-year college scholarships. The 10,000 recipients would promise two years' teaching service for each year of aid. Though the bill is unlikely to win Senate adoption before the adjournment of this Congress, its easy House passage suggests favorable action next year.

Trinity University in San Antonio is offering **"forgiveness loans" to local high-school students who graduate in the top 10 percent of their class, attend the school of education and go on to teach for at least two years. Trinity's "Brackenridge scholars" get $5,000 each of their first two years and $6,000 their junior and senior years. Tuition at Trinity is $5,400. The program also promises to supplement the salary of graduates by $2,000 a year for two years once they start teaching. But the program, supported by the George W. Brackenridge Foundation, is a one-time demonstration project, and may not survive when the seed money is gone.**

Meanwhile, there is the bypass operation known as alternative certification. Two weeks ago, New Jersey approved a plan that would allow teachers to become certified without having taken any ed tion courses at all. "Our department significant numbers of applicants from eral arts colleges, adults who want change their careers and teachers in vate and parochial schools who have taken the required education cours says Leo Klagholz of the New Jersey partment of Education. "We have to them away. The way to get better peop by getting rid of artificial hurdles." new system allows candidates wit bachelor's degree to receive provisional tification if they pass a competency test in subjects they will teach. Then, after a ye training and supervision, the certification be made permanent. Other states are wa ing the experiment closely.

Open Admission: New York City, w needs 4,000 new teachers, is trying a pa bypass: the city has begun hiring people no teacher training but with bachel degrees and minimum college credit-hou certain education-related subjects. Those teachers will then have two years to comp 12 hours of education courses—if manage to survive the classroom. response to the new open-admissions po has been "staggering," says the Boar Education's Gerald Brooks, who reports ing received 3,000 inquiries in the mont July alone. Los Angeles has had a similar perience with alternative approaches. In 32 states are considering similar measu

Ernest Boyer of the Carnegie Founda for the Advancement of Teaching hails s alternative routes as "good strategy" breaking down rigid certification req ments that have kept inferior educa schools in business. But teachers' uni whose demands for compensation respect rest greatly on the faint aur professionalism conferred by educa

schools, are less than thrilled. The AFT's Shanker believes the New Jersey plan "is likely to weaken standards rather than strengthen them" because the training new teachers get is uncontrolled. Mary Futrell, who heads the National Education Association, thinks it "a little scary to say we are now going to open up the profession to people who have not been trained."

Sophists: Education schools will still dominate the profession, however, and without sweeping curricular change there, warns Carnegie's Boyer, teachers will become like the ancient Greek Sophists, "saying nothing well," possessing enviable blackboard skills but a dim understanding of algebra or history. He favors more concentrated doses of pedagogy *after* a student completes a full four-year liberal-arts curriculum.

One such program is already underway at the University of New Hampshire, which draws about 130 students each year—40 percent of them honor students—into a five-year commitment. After earning a liberal-arts degree, students go on to a program whose centerpiece is a full-year's unpaid teaching internship; they complete the required four graduate education courses during two summers. UNH also requires at least 65 hours of fieldwork before the internship, in a sophomore-year course that places them as teacher aides in a school. Their early exposure persuades about half the students who take the course to pursue a different field—and bolsters the resolve of the other half. Another unusual aspect of the program is its weekly seminar groups that provide advice on everything from handling a class to living on a teacher's paycheck. Graduate Lori Ferraro believes that kind of support is essential for teacher survival. "When you shut that classroom door and you're all alone with those children," she says, "it can get awfully lonely."

Some schools like the University of Miami and the University of Tulsa have attacked the problem of insufficient academic preparation by eliminating education as an undergraduate major. In both cases, enrollment had declined in the school of education, and their programs were criticized for not being academically rigorous. Now, students will still get the methodology, but they have to concentrate in a "real" subject. "We are still offering education courses," says Miami dean Lou Kleinman. "A teacher does have to understand children and how to motivate them. If we start doing away with requirements in teacher education, we're going to be sorry."

'Knowledge Base': While agreeing that teacher trainees need more straight academic preparation, Koff of SUNY-Albany makes a stronger case for what he calls the "knowledge base" undergirding good teaching. "We know a great deal in general about what improves student learning, but we're bad at transferring that to individual circumstances." He notes, for example, that teaching students learn general rules of child psychology but not how and when to apply certain techniques to certain children to achieve a given response. Simple things like knowing how to pick the right test or using videotape to gauge performance, he says, would aid teachers greatly but are not taught well in most schools of education.

Seeking a middle way, Illinois State University, which for more than a century has trained young people for "the grandest of enterprises," has undergone two major shifts in the last 15 years. In the early '70s, the secondary-education program was reorganized into a competency-based system called the Professional Education Sequence. PES was a self-paced, ungraded system wherein students had to master specific instructional skills one at a time. "They had to demonstrate that they could take a particular objective and develop a lesson around that objective," says Prof. Robert Fisher. "You just didn't get out until you could do it." Some students completed the eight-credit package in nine weeks, while others took several years. Student pressure forced a switch back to a more traditional approach, with grades and an emphasis on time spent in education classes. The problem now, says Fisher, is that "after a while you just have to let the C kids go on."

Real Kids: ISU's elementary-education program is even more traditional, requiring 52 hours of methodology courses. Students are admitted after passing a basic math- and language-skills test at the beginning of junior year; few fail to get in. Unlike the way at many schools of education, though, courses are taught by both education professors and colleagues from other departments. An art professor, for example, takes part in the art-teaching segment. Students must also spend 120 hours in classrooms with real kids before they begin student teaching.

Illinois State remains far from an avid reformer's dream; both the education course work and fieldwork still cut into undergraduate time that might be spent broadening academic horizons. But the university is committed to a balance. "The issue isn't to reduce the pedagogical and increase the [academic] content," says education dean William Dunifon. "It's to establish high expectations on both sides of the ledger." Indeed, ISU is considered well above the norm and is a Mecca for would-be teachers in Illinois: there are 57 teaching schools in the state, but one of every seven Illinois teachers has an ISU degree. School

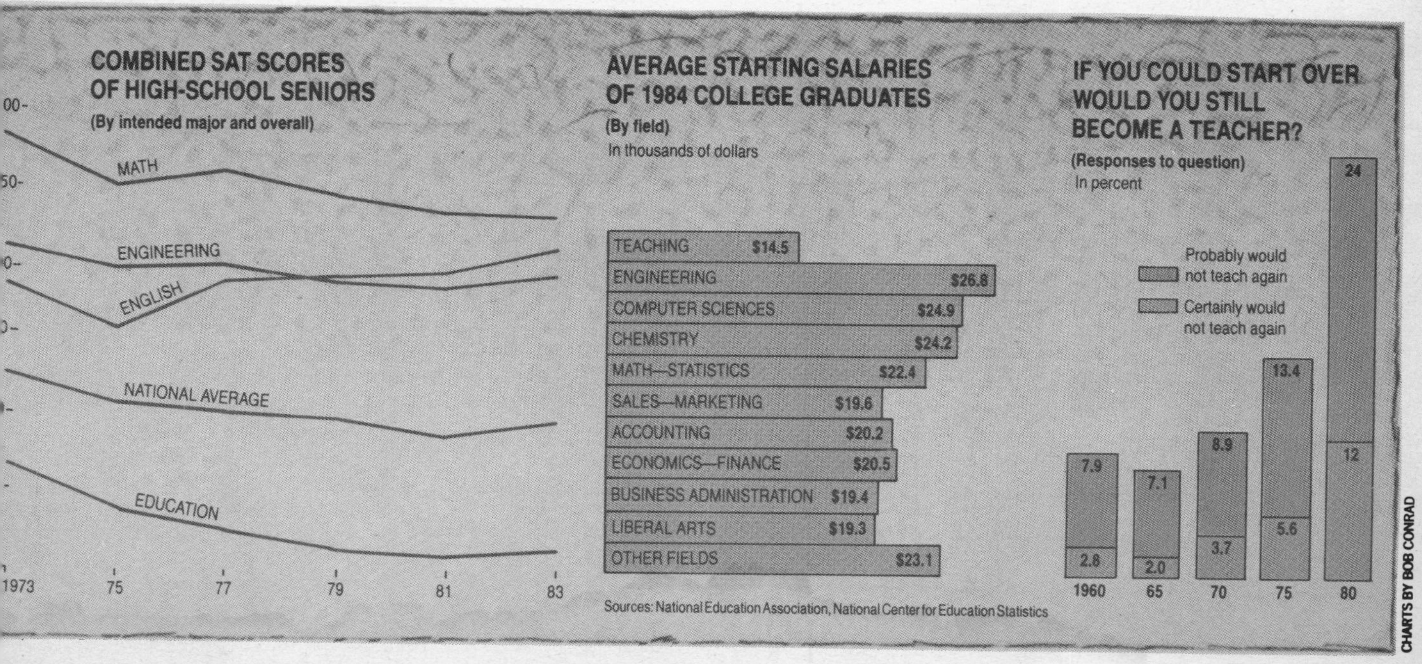

The Test: Untrivial Pursuit

Following is a sampler of questions from the NTE test for prospective teachers. It has four parts, two represented here: professional knowledge—awareness of classroom techniques—and general knowledge. Local districts set their own passing standards.

LANE SMITH

Professional Knowledge

1. Development of which of the following is likely to be furthered more in a classroom with a competitive atmosphere than in one with a cooperative atmosphere?
   (A) complex intellectual problem-solving
   (B) social problem-solving
   (C) interest in school and learning
   (D) affective development
   (E) drill- and speed-dependent skills

2. A policy of equal educational opportunity obligates the teacher in which of the following ways?
   (A) Every child must be taught the same things.
   (B) All children must be treated alike.
   (C) Instruction must exclude use of multicultural learning materials.
   (D) Every class must have a proportionate minority population.
   (E) Instructional strategies must be adapted to the individual.

3. A teacher with a grievance against the local school board would most likely obtain help and information about teacher rights and and the available grievance or arbitration procedures from the
   (A) United States Department of Education
   (B) state education agency or department
   (C) local law-enforcement agency
   (D) local parent-teachers organization
   (E) local teachers' organization

General Knowledge

4. The process by which all people learn the rules according to which they are expected to behave is called
   (A) adaptation
   (B) institutionalization
   (C) normalization
   (D) socialization
   (E) naturalization

5. Which of these is NOT a correct way to find 75% of 40?
   (A) 75.0 x 40
   (B) (75 x 40) ÷ 100
   (C) $^{75}/_{100}$ x 40
   (D) $^{3}/_{4}$ x 40
   (E) 0.75 x 40

6. The growth of which of the following was LEAST stimulated by the growth of United States railroad lines during the 19th century?
   (A) wheat production
   (B) insurance companies
   (C) steel production
   (D) iron mining
   (E) tobacco production

7. Which of the following changes on Earth has taken place most recently?
   (A) appearance of humans
   (B) development of the atmosphere
   (C) formation of the seas
   (D) formation of the first fossils
   (E) appearance of reptiles

8. "They embrace. But they do not know the secret in the poet's heart." The stage direction above ends a play; the second sentence is not a typical stage direction for which of the following reasons?
   (A) Poets do not often appear in plays.
   (B) Plays are not often built around secrets.
   (C) The direction does not summarize the plot of the play.
   (D) The direction does not list the names of all the characters.
   (E) The direction cannot be acted out for the audience to see.

Question Number	Correct Answer	Percent Answering Correctly
1	E	73
2	E	59
3	E	56
4	D	73
5	A	76
6	E	15
7	A	73
8	E	73

officials have also conducted studies sh ing that teacher-education graduates h higher admissions-test scores, grade-p averages and high-school class ranks t others in the university, and that they the same grades in academic courses.

Harvard, meanwhile, is reaching ou other fields for prospective teachers. T semester twenty students, among the former meteorologist and a missiles-sys designer, began a new one-year Midcar Math and Science program that leads t master's degree in education and certifi tion in 33 states. They will take eight edu tion courses and do a student-teaching s before transferring their real-world exp ence to the classroom. "Midcareer pro sionals can bring something special to classroom," says program director Kath ine Merseth. "They have used math a science in the private sector, out in the fi They can relate problems and theories to real world." The program, however, is for anyone with large outstanding bills. T students left jobs paying an average $35,000 a year to prepare for $13,000 job and must pay $8,000 Harvard tuition. people like Virginia Flook, a scientific p tographer, who at 27 is the youngest of MCMS class, it's worth it. "The future bright, there was money and travel, bu was not making me happy," she says. missed having personal involvement think I can get kids interested in scie who aren't expecting to be interested."

Consensus: The greater challenge is to more people interested in teaching and t train them well. Exactly what constitu good training, however, is the question one seems to be able to answer to anyo else's satisfaction. The American Ass ation of Colleges for Teacher Educatio taking a crack at it, with a national comm sion chaired by C. Peter Magrath, presid of the University of Minnesota, which ha highly regarded school of ed. Another eff is being carried on by "the Holmes grou a collection of 20 education deans who ta their name from the late dean of the H vard education school, Henry W. Holm By next year, both groups hope to ha reached some consensus about what it tak to make a good teacher. They are unlikely suggest abolition of education schools or methodology courses, but they may re fine teacher education. It's about time.

DENNIS A. WILLIAMS with LUCY HOWARI Washington, DIANNE H. McDONALD in New Y RENEE MICHAEL in Chicago and bureau rep

Teachers Get No Respect

If Rodney Dangerfield were an educator he might describe his affliction as "congenital prestige deprivation"—the academic world's windy term for the profound lack of respect for teachers that now bedevils American education. "For many of our students," says Anne Wheeler, who trains teachers at the University of Chicago, "Dad's a lawyer and Mom's a doctor and they both ask: 'You want to be a *teacher*? What do you want to do a thing like *that* for?'" Providing a convincing answer to that question may be the most pressing teacher-training challenge of all.

One reason for the disrespect, of course, is money. "An ambulance-chaser can make $200,000 a year and a teacher does more good than bandits in the law or in medicine, yet we celebrate . . . the ambulance-chasers," complains Bernard Gifford, dean of the School of Education at the University of California at Berkeley. Then, too, teachers are believed to be less smart, as a group, than other professionals. Perhaps most important, however, the discipline of education is held in low regard in its own world. Many top colleges do no training of teachers, and where graduate schools and departments of education do exist, they are far down the status totem pole—well below the sciences and only barely above library "science." It is a syndrome found even within the field: the most prestigious education schools are more interested in producing researchers than in training teachers.

Bias: So it was, for example, that the University of Chicago, renowned for its educational research, closed a teacher-training school in 1975 partly because it was too "practical" to conform to the university's definition of scholarship. (A small group of teacher-trainees remains within the department of education.) "People who train teachers are somewhat different," the department's academic secretary, William D. Pattison, ruefully explains. "Their knowledge is derivative, and it lies beyond the pale of strict intellectual pursuit." The bias in favor of research is so strong that instead of rating schools of education by their ability to turn out good teachers, the academic world considers "mean citation rates"—the number of footnotes in scholarly articles that mention a given school's professors.

Another reason for lack of interest in teacher training may be that few faculty at the best education schools have much public-school classroom experience themselves. Researchers who completed a recent study of the Stanford and Berkeley education programs say that 70 percent of the faculty have never taught in public schools—a perversity the California Assembly may legislate out of existence this year. And like teacher, like pupil: at Berkeley's School of Education, only 91 of the 370 students intend to teach. The rest will become administrators or scholars.

Hearts: But now the idea that new teachers are a more pressing need than new theories is beginning to sink in. "It's important not to give our teacher-trainees too much philosophy and theory too early," says Chicago's Wheeler. "Teachers come into this field because of something in their hearts."

Aside from training a new generation of teachers who deserve respect—and firing some of those who don't—educators agree that the best way to build the profession's reputation is to restore its sense of idealism. There is more talk nowadays of a need for nurturing "missionary zeal." Students must "recognize that most people will not understand their desire to teach," says Frances Bolin, a professor at Teachers College of Columbia University. "That's a given." By coming to view teaching as a calling—as something special that most of materialistic American society cannot appreciate—the lack of respect may be easier to live with.

Then again, American society may already be catching on. "Two years ago you didn't mention that you were a teacher when you went to a cocktail party," says Allen Black, a coordinator of a teachers program at Berkeley. "Now you're proud of it." Like Rodney Dangerfield, teaching may get respect after all.

JONATHAN ALTER with JOHN McCORMICK in Chicago and NADINE JOSEPH in Berkeley

Teacher Burnout and Professionalism

Mark C. Schug
University of Wisconsin-Milwaukee

The late 1970s and early 1980s have seen a dramatic increase in reports about professional burnout. Newspapers, popular magazines, as well as professional journals, are replete with articles and stories about job burnout among business executives, lawyers, physicians, dentists, social workers, child care workers, prison personnel, nurses, and teachers. More recently, nearly a dozen national reports on education have recognized problems associated with burnout among teachers such as limited opportunities for career development, low pay, and lack of rewards for high quality work. Yet there are few studies that tell us much about the extent of burnout in teaching, its characteristics, and how it can be reduced or prevented. The purpose of this article is to provide educational leaders with a brief look at some of the research findings related to teacher burnout. Specifically, this article analyzes studies about the job satisfaction of teachers, the characteristics of burnout in the helping professions, and empirical and interpretative studies of teacher burnout.

THE ECONOMICS OF TEACHER SATISFACTION

Education is a labor-intensive enterprise. Usually, about 85 percent of school district budgets involve teachers' salaries. Improving the quality and quantity of education in a school district is tied closely to the levels of satisfaction among the teaching staff. Improving productivity in education can be done only by reducing costs or increasing the level of "output" per student. A case can be made that school districts, in reducing costs in ways that severely diminish teacher satisfaction, are achieving a false, superficial economy, for as teacher dissatisfaction increases, both the quantity and the quality of education decline. The result is a net loss for individual students and teachers as well as for the society as a whole. When the level of teacher dissatisfaction reaches a high point, it can result in speeding the onset of the psychologically debilitating condition popularly referred to as teacher burnout. Burnout usually involves signs of physical and emotional exhaustion resulting in the feeling that one cannot go any further. In order to better understand teacher burnout, it is useful to first consider some of the more general research about the characteristics of teacher satisfaction and how it might be changing.

There is considerable evidence that teachers as a group receive greater satisfaction from intrinsic rather than extrinsic rewards. Lortie in interviews with 94 teachers found that most teachers receive considerable satisfaction from having good results with students or from influencing students. Lortie also reports the results of a survey he conducted with 5,818 teachers which found that over three-quarters of those surveyed emphasized psychological rewards, expressing satisfaction about "the times I have reached a student or a group of students and they learned."[1] It appears that fulfillment for most teachers comes from the immediate feedback they receive as a part of the instructional process.

More recent research, however, suggests that both the intrinsic and extrinsic rewards of teaching may be declining. This results in an increase in teacher dissatisfaction. The National Education Association reports that 37 percent of the public school teachers

From *Issues in Education,* Volume 1, No. 2 & 3, 1983, pp. 133-153. Copyright ©1983 by the American Educational Research Association, Washington, DC 20036.

whom it surveyed were dissatisfied with their jobs. Teachers in urban areas were more dissatisfied than teachers working in other areas. Less than half (44 percent) of the teachers planned to remain in teaching until retirement age and one out of ten teachers expressed a desire to leave teaching as soon as possible. Forty-five percent of the teachers surveyed reported that, if they had it to do over again, they would not have entered the teaching profession. Reasons given for this expressed dissatisfaction with teaching was stress on the job, low salaries, the amount of time spent on non-teaching duties, student misbehavior, and attacks on education in the media.[2]

Sweeney tried to explore teachers' career satisfaction by asking a sample of 1,295 Iowa teachers to distinguish between the actual and ideal characteristics of a teaching position. He also used comparative data from a study done with 1,593 Illinois teachers a decade earlier. The greatest reported need among the Iowa teachers was in the esteem category. Teachers seemed to feel that teaching did not provide an adequate level of prestige or status. When he compared attitudes between teachers in 1980 and 1970, the data revealed some dramatic shifts. The biggest change occurred in security, with apparently more teachers worried about their uncertain employment status in 1980. Increased teacher concerns were also noted in the areas of esteem and self-actualization. Sweeney concludes that schools are apparently not meeting the higher level needs of secondary school teachers and that the situation has been aggravated over several years.[3]

The findings of Sweeney are reinforced and extended by a 1982 study by Cooke and others. They compared the job satisfaction level of 200 Michigan teachers with a national sample of workers from 1977 and found that the general level of job satisfaction reported by Michigan teachers was significantly lower than that reported for other workers—even those workers who possessed college degrees. Over one-fourth of all the Michigan teachers believed that they were in danger of being laid off. The finding that 70 percent of the Michigan teachers, compared to 42 percent of the workers, believed that they would have difficulty finding another job suggests that teachers who continue on in education feel they are trapped. Cooke and others also found that teachers were more likely than other workers to report an unpleasant work environment, exposure to safety hazards, and related illness or injury. Furthermore, 60 percent of the teachers cited inconvenient or excessive hours compared to one-third of the workers.[4]

Work by Heath suggests that career dissatisfaction for teachers may not be as great as reported by Cooke and others. He surveyed 250 classroom teachers from across the United States, some of whom had attended teacher improvement workshops, and 106 other professionals including physicians, lawyers, social workers, accountants, ministers, musicians, and others. Heath found that members of each profession were "quite satisfied" with most attributes of their respective professions. In addition, he found that teachers did not differ from other professionals in the satisfaction they derive from their careers. However, Heath's data did reveal some important ways in which teachers differed from other professions. While teachers were more satisfied with their relations with other people on the job, they were far less satisfied than other professionals with their salaries, status of the teaching profession, and opportunities for reaching their full potential.[5] While the unrepresentative nature of the participants in this study may have resulted in an overly optimistic view of teacher satisfaction, it is worthwhile to note that salary, status, and limited opportunities for growth appear to be key variables in teacher satisfaction.

A National Education Association study, conducted in October 1982, stresses that the level of monetary rewards for teachers is compounding problems in education. This study, reported in the *Milwaukee Journal,* found that the average national starting salary for a teacher with a bachelor's degree was $12,769. Starting salaries for those with a bachelor's degree in selected other fields are the following: engineering, $22,368; accounting, $16,980; business administration, $16,200; and mathematics, $18,600. The level of first-year salaries for teachers may be contributing to the decline in the number of qualified people interested in going into education. The National Center for Educational Statistics found that 3.4 percent of males and 10.3 percent of female high school seniors planned to become teachers. A decade ago, comparable figures were 6 percent and 8 percent.[6]

The publication of numerous national reports on education in 1983 and 1984 substantiates the view that teacher salaries need to be improved. These reports usually discuss low teacher salaries within the context of the need to improve the prestige of the teaching profession. Calls for better teacher pay are made in *Action for Excellence: A Comprehensive Plan to Improve Our Nation's Schools* by the Task Force on Education for Economic Growth;[7] *High School: A Report on Secondary Education in America* by the Carnegie Foundation for the Advancement of Teaching;[8] *A Nation at Risk: The Imperative for Educational Reform* by the National Commission on Excellence in Education;[9] and a study of high schools cosponsored by the National Association of Secondary School Principals and the National Association of Independent Schools.[10]

As pointed out by Lortie, teachers do not perceive monetary rewards as their most important source of job satisfaction.[11] However, as noted in several of the national reports above, salaries are one symbol of the value placed by the society on the teaching profession and the importance of education. The level of salaries is a reflection of the prestige or status ascribed to teaching. The low level of teacher salaries compared to other professions reinforces the belief by many teachers that society discounts the value of education and thus contributes to teachers' doubts about their own ability to make worthwhile contributions to society. One result may be that the best and most capable teachers decide to leave the profession. Evidence from the work by Schlechty and Vance in their study of over 32,000 North Carolina teachers concluded that academically capable teachers are less likely to remain in teaching. They observe that the growth of the human service sector in the United States economy since World War II has increased the competition for academically capable individuals with jobs of higher salaries and more prestige than those offered by teaching.[12] These conclusions, combined with recent evidence of the declining academic ability of beginning teachers, suggest that our society may be facing a serious problem in the eventual deterioration of the quality of the public school teaching corps.

The above studies and reports suggest that the aggregate level of teacher career satisfaction has been declining and, in some cases, the degree of decline has been dramatic. Many variables have contributed to this decline, but the most important appear to be low teacher salaries, a low level of status ascribed to teaching, fear of physical injury on the job, and limited opportunities for individual growth. It is hard to imagine that individuals working under some or all of these conditions could be performing at their maximum potential. It appears that the existence of these problems is becoming more widely recognized as bright and capable young people increasingly choose occupations in business, computer science, and engineering over careers in education. There is also evidence that due, in part, to increased competition in the human service industry, the most academically capable teachers are those who choose to leave the profession. The decreased level of teacher satisfaction has the potential to damage the short-term and long-term quality and quantity of public education.

BURNOUT IN THE HELPING PROFESSIONS

Research on burnout among teachers is only a subset of studies conducted on individuals in the helping professions. Professional burnout among lawyers, business executives, physicians, dentists, social workers, clinical psychologists, and child care workers has been a frequent subject for investigation. A series of studies in the late 1970s by Maslach and her colleagues defined and clarified many of the characteristics of professional burnout.

Maslach points out that a key characteristic of professional burnout is the loss of concern for the people with whom one is working. This involves emotional exhaustion in which the professional's sympathy and positive understanding of the client is reduced. In addition, professional burnout is associated with other aspects of personal stress including physical exhaustion, illness, psychosomatic symptoms, and increased use of alcohol or other drugs. Not surprisingly, personal stress on the job is often carried home and can be a cause of marital and family conflicts.[13]

Why are professionals, especially persons in human service fields, susceptible to burnout? Freudenberger observes that people who work in the helping professions view themselves as dedicated and committed people who are exposed to several types of pressure which can help bring about burnout. First, there is internal pressure from trying to do the job one was trained to do. Through the process of self-selection, the human service professions tend to attract individuals who are highly motivated to be of service to others. Second, there is external pressure from the people one is trying to serve. Professionals are often exposed to highly emotional situations involving physical abuse, illness, drug problems, and marital difficulties. Constant exposure to these problems can be an emotional drain. Finally, Freudenberger notes that there are pressures from administrators who want their program to succeed and consequently place additional pressures on workers to avoid any appearance of failure.[14]

How do professionals deal with burnout? In their interviews, field observations, and surveys of social welfare workers, psychiatric nurses, poverty lawyers, prison personnel, and child care workers, Pines and Maslach found that the majority of their subjects had experienced some of the characteristics associated with burnout. These individuals displayed very similar changes in their attitudes toward clients. The following is a brief summary of some of these changes from a 1976 study by Maslach and a 1978 study by Pines and Maslach:[15]

Detached Concern: Professionals who are successful in avoiding high levels of stress have learned to maintain a balance between concern for their clients and an objective approach to their clients' problems.

Intellectualization: Professionals often try to recast emotional problems they encounter into more intellectual and less personal terms as a way of reducing the stress such problems may hold for the professional.

Compartmentalization: Another way of coping with job disenchantment is to make a clear separation between job and home life. Avoiding "shop talk" at home is one example of making distinctions between work experience and personal life.

Withdrawal: Stressful situations are sometimes dealt with by reducing all forms of direct contact. For example, professionals might spend less time with clients, avoid eye contact, or increase the distance between themselves and their clients.

Reliance on Staff: Sharing frustrations and seeking comfort and advice are other ways that professionals deal with stress. Talking about problems on the job with coworkers helps to diffuse responsibility and provide distance from the problem.

In interviews with mental health professionals, Pines and Maslach were able to identify significant organizational and personal variables which are related to job stress. The following were some key institutional variables:

- Large patient-to-staff ratios are related to fewer staff members who like their jobs.
- The higher the percentage of schizophrenics in the patient population, the less job satisfaction was reported by staff members.
- Staff members who could temporarily withdraw from patients to work on other activities showed more favorable attitudes toward patients.
- Longer hours were correlated to increased staff stress.
- Staff members who spent more time with other staff rather than patients were likely to feel a sense of failure on the job.

Some of the personal variables found in the Pines and Maslach study were the following:

- Lower ranking staff members who had more contact with patients had less dehumanizing attitudes toward patients than higher ranking staff who had less contact with patients.
- The longer staff members had worked in the mental health field, the less they liked working with patients and the less successful they felt.
- Staff members who believed they had a voice in shaping institution policies and felt free to express their views had a more positive view of themselves and of the patients.[16]

What do these findings mean for teachers? The general work by Maslach and her colleagues on burnout in the helping professions in general is suggestive of what one might expect to find specifically among teachers. First, one would predict that some evidence of burnout would be present among most teachers. Second, teachers would be expected to adopt a variety of techniques to detach themselves from intense emotional encounters in teaching. Intellectualizing problems ("He's a 'L.D.,' so what can you expect?"); spending less time in actual instruction of students; or participating in extended "bitch" sessions in the faculty lounge might be evidence of the use of detachment techniques. A third expectation would be that teachers with the most difficult teaching duties would be candidates for burnout. Stress in these cases might be induced by large classes and long hours spent correcting papers and preparing materials. Work with students who have low abilities or behavior problems might be an important contributor to teacher burnout. Finally, Maslach's work suggests that length of service and position may be variables in burnout. For example, one would expect that more experienced teachers, administrators, and school support personnel would have more negative views of students than less experienced classroom teachers.

RESEARCH ON TEACHER BURNOUT

While much has been written about teacher burnout in the educational literature, few empirical studies are actually reported. Much of the empirical work that exists has been designed to study topics related to but not identical with the concept of burnout. The limited number of empirical studies may be explained in different ways. Perhaps researchers have not had sufficient time to develop and apply the concept of professional burnout in education. Another explanation may be that researchers understand the concept of professional burnout as being vague and difficult to apply. A reasonable conclusion is that the notion of teacher burnout may be meaningfully thought of by researchers as related to broader professional concerns such as alienation, stress, and anxiety.

Coates and Thoreson conducted an extensive and thoughtful review of research on teacher anxiety. They observed that concerns about the emotional strain of teaching is not a phenomenon unique to this decade. They cited studies done earlier in this century which found 17 percent of teachers reporting being "unusually nervous" and 33 percent of teachers suffering from nervous symptoms.[17]

In an effort to clarify the sources of anxiety in classroom teachers, Coates and Thoreson reviewed 15 studies of beginning teachers and seven studies of experienced teachers. Data used in the studies were based largely on self-reports. Coates and Thoreson found that sources of anxiety for new teachers have to do with getting established as a professional in a school setting. Specifically, beginning teachers were concerned about maintaining classroom discipline, having students like them, having an adequate knowledge of the subject matter, making mistakes or running out of material, and building good relationships with other faculty and parents. Established teachers, on the other hand, expressed a somewhat different set of concerns. Chief sources of anxiety for experienced teachers include time demands, difficulties with students, large classes, budget difficulties, and lack of educational resources.

More recent research helps to further clarify the extent that teacher stress may be a problem and suggests some sources of stress. Based on a careful analysis of studies of occupational stress, Kyriacou and Sutcliffe developed a model which helps to define teacher stress. They observe that potential sources of stress for teachers can be psychological (poor relationships with colleagues or pressure to work harder), physical (running to class, noise in class), or a combination. Potential sources of stress become a problem when the teacher perceives that there is an actual threat to the teacher's self-esteem or well-being. At that point, the teacher reacts by taking steps to cope with the stressful situation. If the steps taken do not reduce the stress, the teacher may respond with anger or depression accompanied by evidence of dissatisfaction with teaching. High levels of stress can result in various serious physical and mental difficulties including heart disease, peptic ulcers, or mental illness.[18]

There is some evidence about the extent of stress among teachers and the factors which are related to it. Another study by Kyriacou and Sutcliffe, for example, reports on their study of 257 teachers in 16 British schools. They found that nearly 20 percent of the participants rated teaching as being very stressful or extremely stressful using a five-point scale. The questionnaire data revealed 51 sources of stress reflecting diverse aspects of the teacher's job. Factors which received relatively high mean stress ratings included pupils' poor attitudes toward work, efforts to uphold/maintain values and standards, poorly motivated pupils, the practice of teaching lessons for absent teachers, and too much work to do. Further analysis revealed four broad categories as important sources of stress for teachers. These were identified as pupil misbehavior, poor working conditions, time pressures, and poor school ethos.[19]

Moracco and others obtained questionnaires from 691 teachers in a large school district in a Middle Atlantic state. A factor analysis of the questionnaire data produced five major factors which differ somewhat from what Kyriacou and Sutcliffe as well as other researchers have found.[20] Moracco and others found the following categories to be meaningful sources of teacher stress: administrative support, work with students, financial security, relationships with teachers, and task overload. This list of factors is helpful because it takes into account sources of teacher stress beyond the classroom environment by including salary and relationships to school administration and other teachers.[21]

Schwab and Iwanicki conducted a systematic study of how organizational stress produced by role conflict and ambiguity may be related to aspects of teacher burnout. They analyzed questionnaires from 507 Massachusetts teachers and found that stress related to role conflict and ambiguity accounted for a statistically significant amount of variance in the emotional exhaustion dimension of teacher burnout. They concluded that role conflict and ambiguity are important variables in explaining teacher burnout. In addition, they made several suggestions for more clearly defining the teaching role and involving teachers in decision making within the school and school district.[22]

Empirical research in the area of teacher burnout currently has a number of limitations. There are few studies which focus directly on burnout itself. Farber and Miller note there has been no study which has "systematically investigated the process or dimensions of teacher burnout."[23] Those interested in knowing more about teacher burnout need to draw on related literature dealing with teacher stress and anxiety. In addition, most studies are limited to self-report devices for gathering data. Coates and Thoreson note that a more informative approach would be direct observation of teachers' performance in the classroom. They note that such an approach is needed to "pinpoint situations leading to teacher anxiety in other teacher and student behaviors, and to assess adequately interventions designed to reduce it."[24] Nonetheless, the research conducted thus far is helpful to improve our understanding of some factors related to teacher burnout. The following are some conclusions drawn from the studies reviewed above:

- Teachers, like other members of the helping professions, experience high levels of stress and anxiety.
- Anxiety is a concern for both beginning and experienced teachers, but the sources of anxiety may differ.
- Beginning teachers are more concerned with establishing themselves as professionals by maintaining discipline, avoiding mistakes, and establishing good relationships with students, other teachers, and parents. Sources of anxiety for experienced teachers are more concerned with demands on their time, large enrollments, and budget problems.
- Multiple aspects of a teacher's job are sources of stress including student misbehavior, poor working conditions, lack of administrative support, poor salaries, and task overload.

INTERPRETATIVE STUDIES

The most prevalent literature on teacher burnout is a series of essays which uses first-hand observations and professionally informed impressions as the basis for describing the causes of and ways for reducing or preventing teacher burnout. Table 1 presents a summary of some key points made in 10 such studies from 1978–1981. Most of the sources of teacher burnout in Table 1 can be described as fitting into the following three categories: organizational structure, students, and parents. Each of these is discussed in turn.

The claim is frequently made that the organizational structure of the school predisposes teachers to experience high levels of burnout. Key variables cited are the enormous amount of student contact time expected of teachers and the lack of contact with other colleagues. Lortie notes that even during the colonial period in the United States, teaching was a lonely, isolated enterprise.[25] Today, little has changed. Elementary teachers continue to teach several subjects to one group of students while secondary teachers teach the same subject to different groups throughout the day. There is little time in the teacher's school day for anything other than being with students. This is especially true for teachers at the elementary level where preparation time is particularly scarce. Evidence that a high level of direct client contact is related to professional burnout was reported by Pines and Maslach when they found that burnout was less for professionals who could temporarily withdraw from direct contact with clients in order to work on other activities.[26] The amount of student contact time for teachers is aggravated still further by overcrowding in many classrooms around the nation. The result is that teachers in many schools have little time left for better planning of lessons; constructive interaction with other faculty, administration, or parents; or participation in long-term planning for the school or school district.

There are several other organizational variables which contribute to teacher burnout. Low salaries and lack of public and administrative support contribute to the feeling of some teachers that they are being "used" by the society. Teachers have few opportunities to receive positive reinforcement for their efforts. In addition, there is difficulty in achieving career mobility in the public schools. A sixth grade teacher, for example, returns to a 20-year high school reunion to find many friends, who often have less formal education and ability, being promoted to higher and higher levels of responsibility in business while the teacher continues at the same level with little prospect for upward mobility unless he/she wishes to forego teaching as a career. Thus, it appears that the organizational structure of the public schools with its heavy demand for constant student contact, low salaries, and lack of upward mobility seems to contribute significantly to the problem of professional burnout.

A second frequently mentioned cause of teacher burnout is that students today have less desire to learn than did students in the past. While this charge is difficult to make, it is not without some support. For example, both teachers and parents frequently mention school discipline as a problem. Every year, thousands of teachers in the nation's public schools report being physically assaulted. Even more disturbing are comments such as the following by teachers who feel students just don't care.

> . . . no matter how brilliant the lessons I prepared, no matter how much I personally cared for learning, no matter how expressive the tools I brought to my classroom, little learning could occur when the students didn't care to learn. Unable to learn for them, unable to sit at my desk and ignore them, I found the only solution for me was to quit teaching.[37]

Related to the suspicion among some teachers that students today are somehow different is the belief that parents also care less about education today. There is some evidence of a decline in the highest grade given to the schools by the public from 1974–1982. However, the same Gallup report also shows evidence that support for public education may be starting to improve. For example, lack of proper financial support was listed by the public as the second most important problem confronting the public schools. Financial support was mentioned by 12 percent of those surveyed as a problem in 1981. This figure increased to 22 percent in 1982. Perhaps the public is beginning to sense that education is suffering from an inadequate level of local and national support. A related finding in the same study is that citizens rate their own local schools higher than they rate public schools nationally. It appears that parents who know most about the schools hold a better opinion of the school than those who lack firsthand knowledge. Gallup concludes that the public schools may be suffering from an image problem.[38]

What are some suggestions for dealing with teacher burnout? Numerous recommendations have been made on ways to reduce or prevent teacher burnout. The studies in Table 1 mention a variety of long-term and short-term approaches, many of which would require creative changes in school structure. The difficulty, of course, is that implementing many of the approaches requires careful planning and significant amounts of effort on the part of school leaders. The literature is not very helpful in recommending which types of changes are easiest to implement or which are most effective. Some of the suggestions listed in Table 1 are summarized below:

Restructure the job of teaching: Reduce and restructure teaching loads to provide for periodic breaks from students, planning time, team teaching, inservice programs, and flexibility in grade levels and subjects which are taught.

Planning: Encourage teachers to have clear educational goals and objectives to help them use their time better and note their achievements.

Training: Provide training programs so that teachers can recognize the causes and symptoms of stress in their own lives and steps which can be taken to reduce it.

Professional and personal growth: Provide incentives for teachers to attend courses and workshops; take short leaves of absence or sabbaticals for extended study; get proper rest, nutrition, and physical exercise; and learn ways to make life more enjoyable through such things as music, hobbies, and travel.

Participation in school planning: Give teachers the time and resources necessary to help plan for program improvements at the individual school and system level.

Community involvement: Involve parents and other representatives of the community in school planning and carrying out educational programs in schools.

Table 1

Informal Studies of Teacher Burnout

Study	Sources of Burnout	Recommendations for Prevention/Reduction
Gmelch, W. A.[27]	Too much time change in a short period of time; mobility and "keeping up with Jones';" the knowledge explosion, changing personal relationships.	Better time management; establish clear objectives; build short rest periods into the day; introduce stress training programs; know personal limits; establish and update life goals.
Youngs, B. B.[28]	Incompatible relationships between supervisors and teachers; poor organizational communication; increased responsibilities for teachers.	Assess interpersonal relationships in the school; build group support for teachers; develop teacher training programs which promote humaneness.
Bardo, P.[29]	Devaluation of education resulting in students who don't want to learn.	None presented.
Hendrickson, B.[30]	Demands of the institution and the immediate environment of teaching.	Recognize symptoms of burnout; assess if you are overloaded; keep a journal; create a school support system; arrange a retreat with colleagues; arrange an inservice program on a non-teaching subject; try some new teaching idea or borrow an idea from someone else; change grade level; take a support job in the school; team teach; focus on a theme for lessons; take up a new hobby; take personal leave days; when ill, stay home; take a semester leave; join a support group; decompress between leaving school and arriving at home; review educational ideas; lighten load outside of school.
Moe, D.[31]	None presented	Exercise; leave teaching at school; develop a hobby; get plenty of sleep; don't feel guilty if ideals are not all met; keep a diary of student comments; avoid worrying; say no; treat yourself well; always have something to look forward to; do something daring or unusual; continue to learn new ideas and skills; travel; don't structure all leisure time; set realistic goals; take a sabbatical or leave of absence.
Reed, S.[32]	Lack of professional mobility; less turnover on teaching staffs; fewer new teachers being hired; attacks on schools by the public and the media; budget constraints; inadequate professional training; poor organizational structures; burnt out supervisors; lack of teacher control over their job and in school decision-making; involuntary transfers; disruptive students; threat of personal injury; isolation of teachers from collegial contact.	Restructure jobs to provide greater variety; build self-esteem of teachers; involve teachers in decision-making; improve communications with all staff members; encourage professional growth; promote physical and mental health; offer released time; reduce or consolidate tasks assigned to teachers; involve parents in schooling; help supervisors avoid burnout.
Scrivens, R.[33]	Professional disillusionment related to mid-life crisis; feeling of being used as a result of low pay, self-centered students, and high ideals; inability to deal with today's young people; emotional drain of students' problems.	None presented.
Walsh, D.[34]	Administrative harassment; assaults by students; pressure from paper work; isolation.	Professional support groups.
Cacha, F. B.[35]	Disruptive children in the classroom; lack of administrative support; maintaining self-control when angry; large classes; disagreements with supervisors; dealing with community racial issues; verbal abuse by students; theft and destruction of teacher property; financial insecurity; lack of involvement in decision-making; limited job mobility; lack of encouragement to try new ideas.	Participation in stress management workshops; cites Moe's 16 points listed above; follow suggestions for maintaining a safe school such as having a visible and available principal and involving teachers in decision-making.

Study	Sources of Burnout	Recommendations for Prevention/Reduction
Farber, B.A. and Miller, J.[36]	Lack of a psychological sense of community in teaching; discipline problems; student apathy; overcrowded classrooms; involuntary transfers; excessive testing; lack of support from parents, public, and administration; psychological predisposition of some teachers.	Establishing an understandable philosophy which provides hope; changing the organizational structure to encourage collaboration; actively involving the community. Specific suggestions are: ongoing case conferences; team teaching; variation in teaching schedules; regular program planning and problem-solving contact between administration, teachers, and paraprofessionals; teacher center; after-hours use of school facilities by teachers; use of community volunteers, community and school coalitions.

SUMMARY AND CONCLUSIONS

This article has reviewed research which helps to provide a perspective on the extent, causes, and ways of reducing teacher burnout. There is evidence suggesting that the intrinsic and extrinsic rewards for public school teaching are diminishing, thus making teaching a less attractive career for capable inservice teachers as well as young people who might otherwise be attracted to teaching. Some variables that contribute to teacher dissatisfaction are low salaries in comparison to other professions, low prestige, and reduced job security. One would expect that in education, as in industry, high levels of dissatisfaction lead to reduced productivity.

The most systematic research on professional burnout are studies conducted on individuals in the helping professions. The work of Maslach and her colleagues has helped to clarify the physical and emotional symptoms of burnout; the techniques used by professionals to detach themselves from stressful situations; and some of the organizational and personal correlates of burnout including large patient-staff ratios, long work hours, and severity of the patients' problems. These findings are useful in suggesting some hypothetical variables involved in burnout among teachers.

While the empirical research on teacher burnout is limited, there are some studies on teacher anxiety and stress which suggest that teachers experience high levels of stress on the job stemming from several factors. These include student misbehavior, poor working conditions, lack of administrative support, low salaries, and overwork. Interpretative studies emphasized organizational variables such as the isolation of teachers from colleagues, heavy student contact, low salaries, and the lack of career growth as important causes of teacher burnout. Other factors mentioned as being important causes of burnout were the changing nature of students and the lack of public support. Several suggestions made to reduce or prevent teacher burnout included restructuring the job of teaching, encouraging better planning, providing stress management training programs, encouraging personal and professional growth, and involving teachers and the community in school planning.

The recent publication of numerous local, state, and national reports on the current status of education is helping to create a context in which public officials may be receptive to bold initiatives for improving the productivity of teachers by enhancing professional development. Experiments to enhance the teacher profession and diminish teacher burnout might include the following:

- Restructure the school day to enhance the autonomy and authority of teachers. Evidence of autonomy might include giving teachers greater control over their daily teaching schedules, increasing the amount of preparation time for elementary as well as secondary teachers, and examining certification requirements to allow qualified teachers to offer new or interdisciplinary courses.
- Provide a career path for teachers. Several states are beginning to experiment with the idea of establishing a series of stages in the professional life of a classroom teacher. Many have adapted the higher education model which has stages progressing from assistant professor to associate professor to full professor. Current proposals for the public schools call for career stages such as moving from associate teacher to professional teacher to teacher specialist. It is understood that progress to each new stage would depend upon a performance assessment and the accomplishment of a professional growth plan. It is also understood that movement to each new stage would include financial rewards.
- Develop incentive programs to encourage and reward excellence in teaching. Several states and local districts have begun work on establishing merit pay systems for local school districts. Steps are being taken to develop ways objectively to evaluate teaching performance

with the help of local teachers, administrators, and community representatives. In addition, steps need to be taken to insure that merit pay plans are voluntary for the participants, are based on actual teaching performance as observed directly by colleagues and administrators, and provide a significant amount of funds to make merit pay meaningful.

The research done to date on professional burnout has been helpful in communicating to educators and the public the nature and extent of a problem which is potentially very damaging to public education. Yet, the small number of empirical studies on teacher burnout suggests that there is much more that we do not know or understand about the subject. The following are some suggestions which researchers might wish to consider:

- Research on the subject of teacher burnout is limited. Most of the written accounts are impressionistic and personal. While valuable, these do not substitute for carefully designed and implemented empirical studies. A theoretical base for such studies might be drawn from the research done on organizational structure, burnout in the helping professions, and studies of teacher dissatisfaction, stress, and anxiety.

- There is a danger that researchers may conclude that burnout explains nearly every negative behavior displayed by teachers. The potential for exaggerating the importance of burnout contributes to the phenomenon being seen as a "trendy" topic in educational literature soon to be replaced by another fashionable topic. Researchers might be wise to more carefully delineate what are and what are not considered to be important characteristics of burnout in teaching.

- The research on teacher burnout tends to emphasize the causes of professional burnout and to give less attention to those variables which contribute to reducing professional burnout in education. It would be worthwhile to investigate school districts with low levels of staff burnout to identify why they are successful. Similarly, few studies include evidence that the recommendations made for reducing burnout are successful. Carefully designed and implemented studies would inform school district officials about the types of organizational and program changes which might be most beneficial for their teachers.

- It is important that researchers focus on long-term as well as short-term approaches to reducing teacher burnout. For example, while stress management training sessions may have short-term advantages in reducing teacher burnout, it is likely that important organizational changes are necessary to deal with the problem effectively. Some approaches which may have a long-term benefit for teachers involve restructuring teacher jobs to reduce isolation and increase contact with colleagues; improving the respect and appreciation of the local community for the teaching profession; and providing incentives to improve the professional growth of teachers.

NOTES

1. Dan C. Lortie, *Schoolteacher: A Sociological Study* (Chicago: The University of Chicago Press, 1975).
2. National Education Association, "Teacher Opinion Poll: Job Satisfaction," *Today's Education* 70 (September-October 1981): 65.
3. Jim Sweeney, "Teacher Dissatisfaction on the Rise: Higher Level Needs Unfulfilled," *Education* 102 (Winter 1981): 203–207.
4. Robert Cooke, Hy Kornbluh, and David J. Abrams, "Michigan Teachers vs. A National Sample of Workers on Quality of Worklife," *Phi Delta Kappan* 63 (May 1982): 636–637.
5. Douglas Heath, *Faculty Burnout, Morale, and Vocational Adaption* (Boston: National Association of Independent Schools, 1981).
6. "Economics Hits Teaching Field," *Milwaukee Journal,* January 1983.
7. Task Force on Education for Economic Growth, *Action for Excellence: A Comprehensive Plan to Improve Our Nation's Schools* (Denver: Education Commission of the States, 1983).
8. Carnegie Foundation for the Advancement of Teaching, *High School: A Report on Secondary Education in America* (New York: Harper and Row Publishers, Inc., 1983).
9. National Commission on Excellence in Education, *A Nation At Risk: The Imperative for Educational Reform* (Washington, DC: U.S. Government Printing Office, 1983).
10. Theodore R. Sizer, *Horace's Compromise: The Dilemma of the American High School* (Boston: Houghton-Mifflin Co., 1984).
11. Lortie, *Schoolteacher.*
12. Phillip C. Schlechty and Victor S. Vance, "Do Academically Able Teachers Leave Education? The North Carolina Case," *Phi Delta Kappan* 63 (October 1981): 106–112.
13. Christina Maslach, "The Client Role in Staff Burn-out," *Journal of Social Issues* 34 (1978): 111–124.
14. Herbert J. Freudenberger, "The Staff Burn-out Syndrome in Alternative Institutions," *Psychotherapy: Theory, Research and Practice* 12 (Spring 1975): 73–82.
15. Ayala Pines and Christina Maslach, "Characterization of Staff Burnout in Mental Health Settings," *Hospital and Community Psychiatry* 29 (April 1978): 233–237; Christina Maslach, "Burn-out," *Human Behavior* 5 (September 1976): 16–22.
16. Pines and Maslach, "Characterization of Staff Burnout."
17. Thomas J. Coates and Carl E. Thoreson, "Teacher Anxiety: A Review with Recommendations," *Review of Educational Research* 465 (Spring 1976): 159–184.
18. Chris Kyriacou and John Sutcliffe, "A Model of Teacher Stress," *Educational Psychology* 4 (March 1978): 1–6.
19. Chris Kyriacou and John Sutcliffe, "Teacher Stress: Prevalence, Sources, and Symptoms," *British Journal of Educational Psychology* 48 (1968): 159–167.
20. Kyriacou and Sutcliffe, "A Model of Teacher Stress."

21. John Moracco, Deborah Danford, and Raymond V. D'Arienzo, "The Factorial Validity of the Teacher Occupational Stress Factor Questionnaire," *Educational and Psychological Measurement* 42 (Spring 1982): 275–283.

22. Richard L. Schwab and Edward F. Iwanicki, "Perceived Role Conflict, Role Ambiguity, and Teacher Burnout," *Educational Administration Quarterly* 18 (Winter 1982): 60–74.

23. Barry A. Farber and Julie Miller, "Teacher Burnout: A Psychoeducational Perspective," *Teachers College Record* 83 (Winter 1981): 235–243.

24. Coates and Thoreson, 159–184.

25. Lortie, *Schoolteacher.*

26. Pines and Maslach, "Characterization of Staff Burnout."

27. Walter H. Gmelch, "The Principal's Next Challenge: The Twentieth Century Art of Managing Stress," *NASSP Bulletin* 62 (February 1978): 5–12.

28. Bettie B. Youngs, "Anxiety and Stress—How They Affect Teacher, Teaching," *NASSP Bulletin* 62 (November 1978): 78–83.

29. Pamela Bardo, "The Pain of Teacher Burnout: A Case History," *Phi Delta Kappan* 61 (December 1979): 252–254.

30. Barbara Hendrickson, "Teacher Burnout: How to Recognize It; What to Do About It," *Learning* 7 (January 1979): 37–39.

31. Dorothy Moe, "A Prescription," *Today's Education* 68 (November/December 1979): 35–36.

32. Sally Reed, "What You Can Do to Prevent Teacher Burnout," *The National Elementary Principal* 58 (March 1979): 67–70.

33. Robert Scriven, "The Big Click," *Today's Education* 68 (November/December 1979): 34–35.

34. Debbie Walsh, "Classroom Stress and Teacher Burnout," *Phi Delta Kappan* 61 (December 1979): 253.

35. Frances B. Cacha, "Teacher Burnout: Causes and Solutions," *Phi Delta Pi Record* 18 (Fall 1981): 26–27.

36. Farber and Miller, 235–243.

37. Bardo, 252–254.

38. George H. Gallup, "The 14th Annual Gallup Poll of the Public's Attitudes Toward the Public Schools," *Phi Delta Kappan* 64 (September 1982): 37–50.

The author wishes to thank C. Jean Birkey, who worked as the graduate assistant on this study.

A Look to the Future

Unit 9

The future of American education will be determined by responses to current criticisms of American educational institutions and practices. We must learn from the past and the present what our best attainable possibilities may be. The reshaping of curriculum at the elementary and secondary school levels, as well as the reshaping of teacher education curricula, will reflect certain socioeconomic trends in society. The drive for greater excellence and achievement in schooling will direct effort toward a reconstruction of American values with reference to both the ends and the means of schooling. Will the revised unified conception of national educational ends (goals) and means (methods of goal attainment) be defined from conservative, centrist, or leftist perspectives? That is the issue implicitly imbedded in the many different conceptions of national educational values being debated in the nation today.

The struggle to define the educational future is a microcosm of the present national struggle to define the educational ethos. Educational values have been and will continue to be under close reexamination as we begin to make long-range decisions regarding the many recommendations for change and continuity now before us. Many of the educational goals which were established in the 1960s and 1970s have not been fully attained. Yet many of them can be attained.

Trends in national economic and political life have great effects on future achievements in national educational development. Those trends which will shape the future of American education are the same ones which will shape the social, political, and economic life of the nation. Educational systems are not autonomously independent of the social structures which produce them. The public schools in particular exist in all nations to serve the people in terms of those social values which prevail in the national, social, political, and economic life.

The three articles in this unit provide perspectives on what can occur in American education. United States Senator Richard Lugar describes his vision of future excellence in American education and the possibility of a new moral synthesis of cherished American values. Michael Apple focuses on the content and organization of curriculum and on those social forces which affect its development. David Breneman explores enrollment projections in different regions of the United States.

This unit can serve as a valuable "summation" to any course in education. The selections can also be used in any areas of a course where values and educational policy issues are discussed.

Looking Ahead: Challenge Questions

What will be the conditions for the achievement of excellence in education?

Is a future national consensus on educational values possible?

Can an integrated future national strategy for excellence in education be achieved?

What are the most important external pressures on school curricula?

How can curriculum development today prepare students to work in a future that cannot be fully anticipated? What skills ought to be emphasized?

How will future enrollment trends and general demographic trends affect educational development in your area?

How can the information we have now about population trends affect educational planning?

Forging a New Ethos for Education in America

Until education achievement becomes as important as athletic glory in our society, the Nation will be faced with redistributing the benefits of a diminishing economy.

Richard G. Lugar

Senator Lugar of Indiana, a former Rhodes Scholar, chairs the National Republican Senatorial Committee and the European Affairs Subcommittee of the Senate Foreign Relations Committee. A former school board member, he addressed the Session on Roles and Responsibilities at the Forum.

The National Commission on Excellence in Education recently reported that "the educational foundations of our society are presently being eroded by a rising tide of mediocrity that threatens our very future as a Nation and a people. What was unimaginable a generation ago has begun to occur—others are matching and surpassing our educational attainments." The Commission report concludes the next paragraph with the dismal finding that "We have, in effect, been committing an act of unthinking, unilateral educational disarmament." Thus the stage is set for another national discussion of educational reform and the roles and responsibilities which levels of government and other actors in the education drama should assume if we accept the reality of the crisis and are determined to address it. Some skeptics may experience a sense of *déjà vu* in the demands for urgent reforms. But I will argue that the current criticisms are compelling in their emphasis on international interdependency and the underlying premise that the United States will suffer a severe decline in employment, in the standard of living for most citizens, and perhaps even in an eroding defense capability if we are insufficiently bright and competitive as a people.

The truth of our predicament has not sunk in for most Americans. The extent of our peril is not well understood. For many years, the federal government of the United States has entertained no hope of paying the bills which we have accumulated in our democracy for services and supports which we have demanded and promised to one another.

Paying our bills

At the national level, we have established a social security system and supplemented that program with Medicare, Medicaid, and other extensive income supplement, health, and nutrition programs. Over half of the federal budget, or over $400 billion, is spent on social programs and supplementary income payments to individuals. Only about half that much is spent on defense. Mo than $100 billion a year is requir to pay interest on a national debt roughly a trillion and a half d lars. In the last fiscal year, we f short of paying our bills by $1 billion. A few educators will su gest that the federal governm should cut defense spending a raise taxes in order to narrow intolerable deficit. I have no do that defense expenditures will scrutinized even more carefully years to come and our fervent tempts to reach arms control cords with the Soviet Union will pursued vigorously. But the maj ity of dollars in the defense bud go to pay and support directly million Americans employed in volunteer armed service. As a n tion, we have opposed the draft. a nation, we have committed ou selves to pensions and health ca for those who have served o country in the past.

We are also committed to ke ing the peace through continu development of credible det rence to attack on our count Credibility implies an invulnera deterrent capability and that quires scientific genius and mon I have found few persons at edu tion reform meetings who advoc substantial cuts in social securi

Reprinted with permission from *American Education* Magazine, March 1984, pp. 10-16. U.S. Department of Education.

Medicare, Medicaid or food stamp payments. I have found equally few who support cutting veterans benefits or reinstituting the draft and paying active duty personnel lower wages to save money.

The difficult truth is that we have made fundamental decisions in our democracy and have committed long and sizable streams of income to tens of millions of our fellow citizens who claim legal entitlement to these funds now and in the future.

Other citizens have suggested that raising taxes on individuals and businesses will generate revenues necessary for a variety of worthy programs. Each such suggestion assumes that further taxes will have no harmful impact on economic growth, and that modernization and job creation can proceed effectively with smaller returns on capital investment.

The jury may still be out on the question of whether lower taxes stimulate individuals and firms to produce more, to invest more, and to risk more—factors which will surely be required for maintaining our standard of living. But we have embarked on this course because our economic growth in recent years had come to a virtual halt and because we saw no better alternative. No growth means no prospect for ever paying the bills we have now, to say nothing of the downstream consequences of our promises of income and health care to all who are legally entitled.

Examining American education

Now into this general predicament comes a national inquiry into education. At almost the same time that our country has been staggered by the realization that firms in other nations may be producing cars and various steel products at less cost than we are, and that many Americans judge the quality of foreign products as superior to some American entries, we note that American high school students are compiling achievement scores which rank well behind students in other nations. They rank behind those nations whose populations are currently producing goods and services which threaten to overwhelm many American firms and to eliminate jobs for millions of American wage earners. What, then, does the future hold?

Of course, many Americans do not see a crisis in industry or in education. The America which they choose to see is our country at a time when exports and imports were less than 5 percent of the Gross National Product. When informed of our extraordinary interdependence with the rest of the world, they wish to go back. Some Americans demand simply that we build tariff walls and other protectionist devices to save American industry, American jobs, American prices and, unfortunately, American economic stagflation. This is a policy of no growth, and it will not pay our bills.

If schools are not succeeding fully, it is fair to say that parents, churches, and other institutions are not either.

I believe that a majority of Americans know that our country will thrive only to the extent that we are successful in the competition of ideas and ideals and to the extent that we maximize freedom of trade and the laws of comparative advantage. In our domestic economic policies, we are now undertaking substantial deregulation of transportation, financial institutions, and energy resources because we believe that a majority of Americans will receive better services and better values from this stimulation of competition.

But expanded trade internationally and deregulation at home have created enormous and often wrenching adjustments for millions of Americans. Many Americans are demanding protectionism and regulation by the federal government in order to restore economic advantages which were enjoyed by some groups before the new rigors of competition were felt so keenly.

My own suggestions for what we ought to do carry the burden of certain experiences which have emboldened me to speak up. I attended the public schools in the City of Indianapolis, manufactured capital machinery for world competition with a brother who was an engineering genius, served for three years on the Indianapolis School Board from 1964–1967, a time of ferment in civil rights activity and compensatory education ideas in our city, served as Mayor of Indianapolis for eight years, and have served as United States Senator for the last seven years. As one who has survived this sequence of public and private careers, I say with conviction that compassion, intelligence, and successful political action can be combined and will be combined to meet our educational challenges.

A local and state responsibility

My first suggestion is that public education should be clearly understood as a responsibility of local school districts and state governments. For many years, educational reformers have fixed their eyes on the federal government and federal revenues. That fixation is bound to be futile, because the federal government will be hard pressed within the foreseeable future to meet the safety net and defense needs of the country and to maintain sufficient credibility to borrow hundreds of billions of dollars to meet those obligations.

Federal legislators have authorized educational expenditures in the past. The G.I. bill in 1944, science and mathematics instruction in the National Defense Education Act of 1958, emphasis on disadvantaged students in 1965, and subsidized and guaranteed student loans in the 1970's were important national programs. In 1981–82, the federal government supplied 10 percent of school dollars. But substantial new monies will not be forthcoming. Dynamic national economic growth will be required even to meet the obligations we have already undertaken.

The role of state governments will increase both from an organizational and financial standpoint.

Our constitutional system gives states the ability to reorganize school districts and to help equalize the flow of expenditures per child. States also have the opportunity to reorganize the civil governments of urban areas and to maximize the efficiency with which the governments, special and general, work together. Such political reorganization is hard and politically dangerous work. Raising revenues to pay for more services is equally dangerous. Without economic growth, many state governments will face strong taxpayer resistance and most states will not be able to afford large increases in educational funding. Each request for funds will be weighed carefully against demands for road and bridge repair, prison reform, and environmental reform, important objectives which have well-organized constituencies.

Competition among public agencies

Local school systems will compete for funds with local governments with priorities similar to state governments, plus the imperatives of better police and fire protection and more efficient waste collection.

Capital is scarce throughout the world. It will be difficult to borrow money at any level of government, and the interest costs will be high even in recovery periods such as the present one. These are realities.

In my judgment, the Administration will not request substantial new funds for education, the Congress will not appropriate $7 billion or $11 billion, or $21 billion of new money, and teacher salaries will not be increased by 25 percent across the board. These things will not happen because the federal government will be deep in deficits which have arisen in connection with other public policy objectives. I would predict, too, that taxpayers at the state and local levels will not wish to pay every teacher, regardless of talent or merit, more money just for the sake of it. Given skepticism about the ways in which educational time is spent, the idea of extending the school day or the school year will most likely be debated case by case.

Having said all that, I predict that citizens will decide to spend more money on education and I believe it is important to note that record of support in recent years.

National expenditures for education

The *National Journal* of July 9, 1983, sets forth the following report:

For whatever the current complaints about the schools, the problems cannot plausibly be laid to neglect. Precisely the opposite is true. Since the end of World War II, Americans have lavished money and attention on education. Consider:

Public education in the United States is the world's most successful system of mass education yet devised.

- Between 1945 and 1975, the share of the nation's output (gross national product, or GNP) spent on all schools, including colleges and universities, rose from two to eight percent. Although it declined to 6.8 percent in 1981, much of the slide reflects a shrinkage of the traditional school-age population—an aging of the "baby boom" generation— rather than a fall-off in per capita spending.
- More students than ever have remained in school—and gone on further. Between 1940 and the 1970's, the proportion of students graduating from high school rose from 42 to about 75 percent. About half of all high school graduates (or about three-eighths of all young Americans) now attend college, in contrast with a fourth (or an eighth of young Americai in 1940.
- The teaching resourc committed to students public schools have risen si nificantly. Between 1959 a 1980, student-teacher rati declined 27 percent. Accor ing to the National Cent for Education Statistics, p pupil spending—adjust for inflation and express in 1979–80 dollars—ro from $395 in 1929–30 $2,275 in 1979–80 befo slipping to $2,228 1980–81. The growth spending reflects mo teachers, higher salari more remedial courses and growing proportion of hi school students, who a more expensive to educat On paper, teachers are bett qualified than ever; near half of primary and secon ary schoolteachers hold ma ters' degrees, compared wi less than a fourth in 1960.
- School buildings are gene ally more elaborate a better-equipped than th once were. As recently 1940, more than half the n tion's public elementa schools were small, on teacher schools. Now, on room schools make up le than 1 percent of the total.
- Compared with all but a fe advanced industrial cou tries—Canada, the Nethe lands, Sweden—the Unit States spends more on ed cation. For most countri the gap is significant. Whi public spending on educ tion in the United States w 5.7 percent of GNP schools in 1979, Franc spending was 5.3 perce and Germany's 4.6 percer Japan's, on the other han was about the same as for t United States.

Are we asking too much of ou schools?

My second suggestion is that w should go a little easier on predi tions that the sky is falling on pu lic educational achievement in th country. In saying this, I do not wish to define the crisis in achievement out of existence. To the contrary, the drop in Standard Achievement Test (SAT) scores is real and the secular decline has been dismal. It is apparent that many students in other nations are learning faster and learning more.

In part the decline in achievement scores has come because we have asked the schools to widen responsibilities for instruction and opportunity to all Americans. It is not enough now that schools teach reading, writing, and arithmetic. They are also asked to teach children how to drive, how to cook, what to feel about emerging sexuality, how to respond to pressures regarding alcohol, tobacco, and drugs, and what to think about the prospects for nuclear war. This is a tall order for all institutions, and if schools are not succeeding fully, it is fair to say that parents, churches, and other institutions are not either. The other—and more profound—problem associated with declining test scores and declining capabilities to perform simple intellectual tasks, is exemplified by the "greening of America" period through which our country has passed. I believe that most of us survived this period, but it is apparent that not everyone has.

The question for many young people has not been preparation for a life of competitive work, family support, or the sophisticated enjoyment of pleasure such as music, art, world literature, or civic involvement. Instead, many young and not-so-young people accepted as permanently given the affluent status of the nation and prepared to enjoy leisure alternatives which did not include serious academic discipline or achievement.

Until recently, many Americans had lost or never gained the desire to compete successfully in intellectual pursuits. A common assumption was that our large and wealthy economy would provide employment for those who wished to work and would accept them in the work force at any level of preparation they offered. Those who did not wish to work could enjoy other self-chosen pursuits with an ever-widening safety net to support them.

In fact, many Americans have never been enamored with academic work for themselves or for others. The notion that one could get by without learning to spell, read, or write very well had wide appeal. In such an atmosphere, many Americans also saw no need to serve the nation by volunteering for the armed services, or teaching school children, or entering into even modest public service. Now all of this is changing because we are a nation at risk. We are locked in a struggle with the Soviet Union which will continue for many years and in which we must keep the peace through a credible deterrent. Our ability to keep the peace will be directly proportional to our talents as scientists, physicists, and broad-gauged diplomats with strong preparation in the liberal arts, languages, Soviet and other studies. We will put bread on the tables of this country if our engineering, machining, and quality control is superior and if we innovate and modernize rapidly and continuously. We shall make wise decisions at all levels of government only if we learn to read and write again at all ages and to entertain serious subjects with better recognition of how scarce resources should be allocated and examine continuously the promises we have made to each other in public policy.

Only those who themselves know why learning is important can possibly teach important lessons to others.

Athletics vs. academics

Achievement scores will improve when and if students really want to learn. As parents and sports fans, we stand on our heads to stimulate athletic achievement and our children achieve in a spectacular fashion. Underpaid or even unpaid coaches bask in community esteem. But when it comes to academic achievement, we have still not caught the spirit. That is the crisis of American education. We are able to appreciate the need for endless calisthenics, weight training, wind sprints, and any other preparation needed to outrun or outplay an opponent at a Friday night high school game, the NFL, or the Olympic games. But as a nation we have not grasped the significance of the sheer drudgery, the repetition, the discipline to read, to speak, and to write in clear sentences, to master foreign languages, to analyze economic and social relationships, and to master higher mathematical skills.

The plaudits of each of us in this nation had better be directed toward academic achievement and to the successful competitors on the intellectual playing fields. Great moments in sport will come and go, but the academic achievers are those who will keep international peace, provide jobs for the American people, and enrich the cultural life of this country. And we are talking about millions of achievers. It is the strength and breadth of participation in our democracy which will be of the essence.

There is a national interest in this. Young Americans ought to be concerned about it, because it is their future which is at stake. But so ought older Americans. If we cannot produce steel and automobiles and other products efficiently, who is going to pay the bills for social security? If we cannot create new products and attain new advances in productivity, who will pay for the ever-increasing demands for better and fuller health care? If we cannot remain at the cutting edge of technological developments, who will insure our security against nations which threaten us? Our national leadership has every reason to be concerned about the quality of American education. Our cultural life, our commercial life, our health, and our very survival depend on it. If there are dangers of elitism in the encouragement of excellence, there is surely a far greater elitism in *pretending* that standards make no difference—when we all know that they do. Is it fair to a poor, unemployed youth to pretend that his inability to command the English language is of no hindrance to him? This pretense is really the province of those who have already "made it," and it is as far from the hungry desire for learning that characterizes people who are striving to better themselves as anything could be.

Those who cannot do well, those who are weak or infirm, depend the most upon a system which encourages success and creativity. Our compassion for the weak and the poor and the handicapped will be empty if we are not able to provide real help to them.

Teachers: of critical importance

If we capture this vision for the future of American education, will highly motivated, heavily supported students achieve as much as they should with the present group of American teachers?

Obviously, teachers had better feel the warmth of our esteem, too. To recruit and to keep the best teachers for our children, we will need to pay those teachers more money and we will want to do so.

The embattled outlook of teacher organizations is understandable. The role of a protective organization in a field of declining numbers and demand might be to circle the wagons, protect all members, demand the same for all so as not to threaten unity, and to use political action to try to negate marketplace supply-and-demand equations. The United Auto Workers, The United Steelworkers, and a host of other embattled unions are attempting similar tactics. With full appreciation for the strength of teacher organizations, I pray that they will come to favor higher compensation for superior teachers and will cooperate with those who wish to remove the barriers to entry for many intelligent citizens in many walks of life to teach our children.

And while in an attitude of prayer, I will blurt out two additional pleas. Surely a nation at risk can support fast track, accelerated learning opportunities for very bright and capable students. And surely a nation at risk can encourage examination of school policies which restrict the ability of a teacher to expel troublemaking students from a classroom of students who want to learn and listen and which restrict administrators from expelling from schools various students who vent their antipathy to school attendance by disrupting the general atmosphere of the school. It will not do to point to a crisis in American education and sidetrack the whole thrust of the discussion by asserting that current arrangements are beyond challenge.

There are some hopeful signs. Many parents are demanding more homework and are pledging to spend more time encouraging study for their children. Courageous school superintendents at the local and state levels are demanding competency testing. Some students haven't been doing much reading and writing for a while, but in coming years they will, because diplomas will rest on passing a reasonable test. Bold Governors and State Legislators are spelling out concrete steps which will take planning, adjustment, and money, and they are seeking support for all three with good chances for success. Private citizens donated approximately $2 billion to public education last year, a small contribution when measured against the $116 billion of public monies. But this is a harbinger of good deeds and additional resources. There must be no prohibition or discouragement of endowing public education at every level with private means.

When it comes to academic achievement, we have still not caught the spirit. That is the crisis of American education.

We have been a nation at risk because we have not cared enough about learning. But this is changing, because it has dawı on many Americans that the wo does not owe us obeisance and c gratulations. It is now dawning many Americans that we must co pete in the world today. Once up a time, many American firms co rest content with a broad natio market in the United States. T is no longer possible. Americ businesses are confronted by f eign firms which are eager to s ceed. Societies which do not e cate their children will confr even more difficult challenges the world. We need to foster th people who will dream what is n who will take risks, and who succeed.

Merely "getting by" is no pro standard at all, and those who a no higher should not be surpri to see themselves eclipsed by oth who aim at a higher goal.

In Germany, recently, a lead political figure mentioned to that he believed that we had tered into an era in which nothi much new was happening, would happen. The automob had been invented, he said; all t remained was the question of h to squeeze out marginal impro ments in mileage. The teleph had been invented, he said; all t remained was to make telepho in different colors and shapes. A so forth.

I find this way of thinking to simply incredible. We are on verge of some of the most fun mental changes in years. The tr sition from an industrial society one marked more by informati the implications of all this for centralization (or centralizatio the need for new products; the velopment of new generations computers; genetic engineeri space exploration and travel— world is as large as on imagination.

Which vision for the future?

But the thought is sobering, it reminds us that there are two ferent visions for the future bef us. The one, represented by political figure I have mention is tired and seeks to withdraw. I uncertain of itself and of its al ties and of its right to play a role in the world; it is one of resignation, where the chief task of politics, economics, and education is to distribute and re-distribute a limited number of goods and services.

The other view is, I think, more in tune with the spirit of the American people. It holds that it *does* matter whether one does well or ill, and that one can tell the difference between the two. It holds that it is better to know than not to know, to strive than to accept, to make something well rather than poorly, to create rather than to take.

Our task is not just to distribute and to re-distribute; our task is to help to forge a new ethos in which learning is important. We need to say at the national level, at the state level, and at the local level in no uncertain terms: Scholarship is important. Learning is important. Education is important.

We may take hope from the spirit of young people who can be motivated in many different ways. Students, after all, often survive even anti-intellectual parents, mediocre teaching, and haphazard educational administration if somewhere there is one family member, one teacher or dean, one employer or coach, or even one public servant who cares deeply and lights sparks with regularity.

The nation will not be at risk if our children are determined to succeed as family members, career makers, citizens, and sensitive individuals who are in awe of nature and the best works of man. Only those who themselves know why learning is important can possibly teach important lessons to others. Our job is to light the sparks.

CURRICULUM IN THE YEAR 2000: TENSIONS AND POSSIBILITIES

Michael W. Apple

MICHAEL W. APPLE is professor of curriculum and instruction and educational policy studies at the University of Wisconsin, Madison. He has written extensively on the relationship between curriculum and society. Among his books are Ideology and Curriculum *(1979) and* Education and Power *(1982). He thanks Shigeru Asanuma, Esteban De La Torre, David Hursh, Ki Seok Kim, Dan Liston, Yolanda Rojas, and Leslie Rothaus for their important contributions to this article.*

Predictions of the future, even in the best of times, are hazardous. So many unforeseen variables and unexpected circumstances can influence outcomes. If this is so in the best of times, it will be even more the case in the next few decades, for these are certainly not the best of times. Thus all of my claims in this article should be preceded by a single word: *if.*

Much of what I am predicting about U.S. education in general and the curriculum in particular depends on political and economic factors. For example, I am not very optimistic about the future for urban school districts. I see the curriculum in urban schools becoming more dated and less flexible in the next 10 to 20 years. I arrive at this prediction from a sense — backed by a decent amount of evidence — that our economy will continue to sputter, if not to stall, in the foreseeable future, thereby creating a serious dilemma for the hard-working teachers and administrators in numerous school districts across the U.S.[1] However, there are also hopeful signs, especially in attempts — even in the face of serious financial difficulties — to keep necessary programs alive and to make curricular content more representative and honestly reflective of a significant portion of the U.S. population.

Basically, though, I see the next two decades as a time of increasing conflict in curriculum. School programs will reflect the splintering of common interests and the polarization of the larger society, trends largely caused by pressures and conflicts over which the schools have little control. A significant amount of the blame will also lie in curricular decisions made as long ago as the early Sixties or as recently as today.

Before going further, I must review some important social and economic facts. It is unfortunate but true that 80% of the benefits of current social policies go to the top 20% of the population. Moreover, the gap between the haves and the have-nots is widening, due in part to the severe economic problems that the U.S. is now experiencing.[2] To their credit, most Americans feel uncomfortable about this situation. But this general discomfort will not prevent many interest groups from arguing that it is not "our" responsibility to alter economic disparities. Nor will it prevent economic inequities from creating serious tensions in U.S. education. If anything, the state of the economy and contradictory attitudes toward it will exacerbate the problems that educators now face. In the next two decades, the curriculum will reflect many of these tensions in the larger society. This should not surprise us. Only rarely has curricular content *not* reflected what is happening outside the school.[3]

I will focus here on three interrelated areas: the content of the curriculum, its form (or how it is organized), and the process of decision making that shapes it. Only by considering all three factors can we understand the forces, building today, that will set limits on and create possibilities for the curriculum in the year 2000.

One major issue that is brewing now and will continue to grow is the debate about "basics." This is not a simple problem. There are many competing conceptions of what everyone should be taught, of what knowledge will be the most valuable to students and to the society. The current controversy over bilingual programs in elementary schools and contemporary proposals to "upgrade" content and to reduce electives in the secondary schools are cases in point. Defining the basics will prove to be one of the most difficult issues that the schools will face, because schools will serve as arenas in which various groups will do battle for their differing conceptions of what the society should value.

It is clear, for instance, that the content of the curriculum has become a major political issue. The activism of conservative and extremist groups has increased measurably. This activism will continue to grow, feeding on past successes that result in increased funding. Mel and Norma Gabler of Longview, Texas, are prime examples; they speak for a larger movement that spends considerable time denouncing textbooks that are "unpatriotic," that reject "absolute values" and "free enterprise," that emphasize too strongly the contributions of minority groups, and so on. Armed with the notion that God is on their side, they are likely to scrutinize an ever-broader swath of curricular content, intent on purging it of any taint of "un-Americanism" and "secular humanism." The increase in book banning and the evolution/creation controversy document the growing willingness of such groups to enter into debates over what should be taught in the schools. Thus educators will have to give more attention to justifying *why* they teach what they do. And this task will be increasingly difficult, because

Reprinted from Phi Delta Kappan, January 1983. ©1983, Phi Delta Kappan, Inc.

teacher-training institutions are moving toward greater stress on *how* to teach, not on providing justifications for and skills in arguing about *why* educators teach particular information, skills, and attitudes. Unless this trend is reversed, teachers and administrators will be hard pressed to defend curricular decisions against well-organized and well-funded attacks.

Tension between business and organized labor will also manifest itself in conflict over curricular content. On the one hand, we are currently witnessing the emergence of industry as a powerful pressure group that seeks to influence education. Businesses across the U.S. have established departments whose goals are to distribute curricular materials to schools, to convince textbook publishers to tout the benefits of free enterprise, to lobby state legislators, and to provide summer internships for teachers that will help them develop a more positive perspective on business. I see no sign that this type of pressure will abate.[4] On the other hand, labor unions have begun to stress the importance of labor education. A movement is growing to teach labor history and to encourage students to examine critically the problems of the U.S. economy and the imbalance in economic planning. These conflicting goals — to teach content that will produce citizens who will meet the needs of industry and simultaneously to examine critically industrial models and power and the putative lack of concern of big business with the needs of workers — will create a good deal of friction over what should be taught.

This friction will be heightened by the growing cooperation between state departments of education and the business community. In times of economic difficulty, when tax revenues are lower and jobs are hard to find, it is not unusual for school programs to become more closely aligned to the needs of business. We can expect to see more emphasis on teaching job-related skills and on disciplining students according to the norms that guide the workplace. This shift will be difficult to accomplish, because the U.S. job market is clearly changing. New skills rapidly become obsolete, and new jobs are not being created quickly enough.[5] Furthermore, many individuals will object to this closer relationship between the schools and industry, arguing that business generally has its own profits, not the common good, at heart. Thus one more conflict over curriculum will arise.

These two "political" issues — defining the basics and determining the proper relationship of the school to business and to labor — will not be the only ones to surface. The basics will also be expanded to include academic areas that now seem to receive less attention than they deserve. Clearly, there will be attempts, largely positive, to strengthen the teaching of mathematics and science. Several states are already preparing to mandate more science and mathematics courses for high school graduation and the retraining of teachers at state expense, in an effort to reverse the current shortage of qualified math and science teachers. This increased emphasis on mathematics and science will be accompanied by a greater focus on computers in all areas of the curriculum, but especially in math and science. We must be exceptionally cautious and avoid jumping on yet another technological bandwagon. There is no quick fix for the difficult problems we face. Without higher salaries and greater prestige to attract and keep well-trained teachers in these curricular areas, the prospects for success are mixed.

An unfortunate trend will accompany this increased emphasis on mathematics, science, and technology: increased differentiation of the curriculum. Schools will try to identify "gifted" students much earlier. We will see a return to tracking systems and more ability grouping than is currently in evidence. When large amounts of financial, material, and human resources are available, such differentiation may make it easier for teachers and support personnel to meet individual needs by working intensively with students, taking each to the limit of his or her capabilities. But in a time of fiscal crisis, such resources will not be readily available; in such a time, the reinstitution of differentiated curricula and tracking systems will often have the opposite effect: to ratify the low socioeconomic position of many children.[6]

The fiscal crisis will have other profound effects. Since less money will mean fewer teachers and support services, we will see an accompanying steady decline in curricular alternatives as well. There will simply be fewer programs and options.

Moreover, fiscal constraints will hinder the replacement of existing instructional materials (which provide the foundation for nearly all curricula); the average age of textbooks used in the schools will increase and perhaps even double. This trend will be most evident in large urban areas, because they will suffer disproportionate declines in tax revenues and in state and federal support. As a result, the gap in the quality of curricular offerings and instructional materials will broaden between cities and their more affluent suburbs. Thus curricular content will differ by race and social class.

As I have already noted, we must consider curricular content, form, and the process of decision making simultaneously. There is no guarantee that President Reagan's New Federalism will go beyond rhetoric, but evidence suggests that decision making will shift to the state level. Oddly, this shift — though aimed at increasing the responsiveness of state authorities to local districts — will actually decrease curricular diversity. As decision-making power coalesces at the state level, publishers will tailor their textbooks increasingly to the values of those states that encourage statewide textbook adoptions — generally through reimbursements to local school districts for some portion of the cost if they select their instructional materials from an approved list. For publishers, getting materials placed on such lists is quite important, since it nearly guarantees high sales and profits. Given this economic fact, states such as Texas and California, which have state textbook adoption policies, will have disproportionate power to determine which textbooks and resources will be available throughout the U.S. Hence we will see even greater standardization of the curriculum. The curriculum will become "safer," less controversial, less likely to alienate any powerful interest group.

I have argued that curricular content will become both a political football and more homogenized (due to economic pressures on publishers and political and economic pressures on local and state education authorities). A third trend will also become apparent: The form or organization of the curriculum will become increasingly technical and management-oriented. And this will have a serious impact on teachers.

A fundamental change in the curriculum of the American school began in the early 1960s, especially at the elementary level. Sputnik inspired fear that the teaching of mathematics and science lacked sufficient rigor and that the academic disciplines were not central enough in the curriculum; in response, the U.S. government funded a large number of projects that focused on producing new curricular materials. A significant proportion of these materials turned out to be "teacher-proof." They specified everything that a teacher had to know, say, and do. Often, they even specified acceptable student responses. This approach — to specify *everything* and leave nothing to chance — was tacitly sexist, since it seemed to assume that elementary school teachers (most of whom were women) could not cope on their own with sophisticated mathematics and science.[7] To insure that these materials would be purchased and used, the government reimbursed school systems for the bulk of their costs.

Although many of these new materials were not used in the ways that their developers had envisioned,[8] they did signal an important modification in the curriculum — one that we will be living with for years to come. The curriculum became less a locally planned program and more a series of commercial "systems" (in reading, mathematics, and so on). These systems integrated diagnostic and achievement tests, teacher and student activities, and teaching materials. Such integration has its strengths, of course. It does make possible more efficient planning, for example. But its weaknesses may prove to outweigh its strengths.

What we have actually seen is the *deskilling* of our teaching force. Since so much of the curriculum is now conceived outside the schools, teachers often are asked to do little more than to execute someone else's goals and plans and to carry out someone else's suggested activities. A trend that has had a long history in industry — the separation of conception from execution — is now apparent as well in U.S. classrooms.[9]

This trend will have important consequences. When individuals cease to plan and control their own work, the skills essential to these tasks atrophy and are forgotten. Skills that teachers have built up over decades of hard work — setting curricular goals, establishing content, designing lessons and instructional strategies, individualizing instruction from an intimate knowledge of each student's desires and needs, and so on — are lost. In the process, the very things that make teaching a professional activity — the control of one's expertise and time — are also dissipated. There is no better formula for alienation and burnout than the loss of control of the job. Hence, the tendency of the curriculum to become totally standardized and systematized, totally focused on competencies measured by tests, and largely dependent on predesigned commercial materials may have consequences that are exactly the opposite of what we intend. Instead of professional teachers who care about what they do and why they do it, we may have only alienated executors of someone else's plans. Given the kinds of materials that now dominate many classrooms in such curricular areas as mathematics and reading, this danger seems likely to increase over time.

The economics of this process of deskilling is worth noting. In essence, we have established a capital-intensive curriculum in our classrooms. Simply to keep the program going, a large amount of money must be set aside for the ongoing purchase of consumable materials. School districts may soon find themselves burdened with expensive "white elephants," as school budgets are reduced and money is no longer available to purchase the requisite workbooks, tests, worksheets, revised editions of "modules," and so forth. School districts will then have to turn to their own staffs to create materials that are less expensive and more responsive to their students' needs — only to find that the necessary skills for doing this have been lost. This will be a very real predicament.

At the same time that teachers are being de-skilled, however, they are gaining greater control over which curricular materials and textbooks will be purchased for use in their classrooms. Curricular decision making is becoming more formally democratic; less power now resides in central curriculum offices or with select groups of administrators. Both teachers and parents are becoming more involved. Meanwhile, an increasing concern for accountability and for measurable achievement outcomes in a few "basic" areas will also bring a movement toward more standardized testing, more objectives, more focus on competencies, more centralized curricular control, and more teaching to the tests.

As this movement gains momentum, a vicious circle will develop. Publishers will further standardize content, basing it on competency tests and routinizing it as much as possible, so that their materials will produce measurable outcomes with little variability that will fit cost/control models.

Thus far, I have not been very optimistic about what will happen in the areas of curricular content, form, and decision making. I do not intend simply to be a nay-sayer. It is critically important to be realistic about the very difficult times that we educators will confront in the not-too-distant future. Only then can we begin to plan how to cope with what may happen. I would be remiss, however, if I did not point out some of the very beneficial tendencies that will become more visible by the year 2000.

Certain content areas — quite positive ones, in my opinion — will receive more emphasis than they do at present. Just as greater attention will be focused on mathematics and science (which, I hope, will be taught *not* as mere technical skills, but as creative and powerful ways of constructing meaning[10]), so, too, will teachers devote more time to the topics of ecology and peace. People from all walks of life, representing a variety of political persuasions, will coalesce around the topic of peace and urge that it be given more attention in the curriculum.

However, positive outcomes from additions to the curriculum will not be the dominant trend in a period of fiscal constraints. In fact, many school districts will be forced to save money by eliminating necessary programs. But this may prove beneficial, as well — especially in generating closer and more cooperative bonds between school personnel and the communities they serve. Teachers and parents will form coalitions to save programs that they see as essential. Difficult decisions will cause closer relationships to develop between community groups and the educators who must make those decisions. In a period of declining revenues and with the projected rise in enrollments, few outcomes will be more important. Funds will be needed to hire new teachers, to maintain and expand curricular offerings, to deal with students with special needs, and to carry on other essential tasks. Such funds can be generated only through greater cooperation with and increased support from the public. Even the scrutiny of the curriculum by conservative groups, to which I alluded earlier, should not be seen as merely a threat. The fact that parents — of whatever political persuasion — take a serious interest in their children's education suggests possible avenues for cooperation and fruitful discussion.

If we were freed from some of the tensions, conflicts, and pressures that will probably affect us as we strive to build or preserve a high-quality educational program for the children entrusted to us, what might we do about content, form, and decision making? Here I must be honest. A portion of what I will say has been recognized for years by knowledgeable educators. But such educators have seldom had the time, the resources, the support, or the freedom from contradictory pressures to act on this knowledge.

Let us look first at content. As attempts accelerate to redefine and to drastically limit what is taught to children, we should *broaden* our definitions of literacy and of the basics to include not only reading and writing — which are very important and must not be neglected — but also social, political, aesthetic, and technological literacy. Community action projects that provide curricular links between students and their local communities can help youngsters develop social and political responsibility and learn the necessary skills for active participation in the society.[11] At the same time, we should expose all students to beauty and form, aesthetics, and various ways of creating personal meanings — including research, poetry, dance, the visual arts, and film making. In other words, we should give equal weight to both "discursive" and "nondiscursive" subjects, so that each student has an opportunity to discover his or her talents and to develop the wide range of tools with which individuals control their own lives and their futures.[12] Thus we must define the "basics" very broadly.

Given the important role of technology in the future, *all* students — not just a select few who are "gifted and talented" — should be literate both in using computers and microcomputers *and* in analyzing their social implications. For example, computers and video-display equipment increase efficiency, but they may also cause untold thousands of workers (primarily women) to lose their jobs, become de-skilled, or work under stressful conditions. "Literacy" means the ability to analyze and deal with the social as well as the technical implications of this new technology.

In a recent column in the *New York Times*, Fred Hechinger noted that, if we approach computer literacy as a narrow vocational issue, we are bound merely to add one more relatively ineffective career education program to the many that already exist. As he put it:

> The visions of brave new electronic worlds of microchips and robots raise simultaneous demands for a schooling that looks to the future by learning from the past. Yes, the computer must be mastered by all, regardless of race, sex, or economic condition. But at the same time . . . the computer must be mastered by young people who are secure in a broad understanding of what used to be called general education — including language, history, economics, mathematics, science, the arts; in short, the human condition.[13]

To focus on a broad and general education requires that we be sensitive to the fact that the curriculum must represent us all. A "selective tradition" has operated in curriculum to date. This tradition may be more visible in some subjects than in others, but it is quite clear that the knowledge of some groups is not represented adequately in the curriculum.[14] For instance, we tend to teach military history or the history of U.S. Presidents; we teach less rigorously the history of the U.S. working class. Obviously, we have made advances here, just as we have made advances in teaching the real histories, contributions, and cultures of ethnic minorities and of women. Our progress in eliminating sexism and racism and in recapturing the lost past of U.S. labor is too important to allow these advances to slip away in the next decade or two. We must continue to pursue curricular balance. The content that we teach cannot be determined solely by the needs of any one group, even in times of severe economic difficulty. That would be short-sighted.

The curriculum must simultaneously be both conservative and critical. It must preserve the ideals that have guided discourse in the U.S. for centuries: a faith in the American people, a commitment to expanding equality, and a commitment to diversity and liberty. Yet it must also empower individuals to question the ethics of their institutions and to criticize them when they fail to meet these ideals. Curricular content should give people the ability to interpret social change and to reflect critically on what is happening in their daily lives. This is not a formula for an "easy" curriculum. It requires hard work and discipline on the part of both teachers and students.

Moreover, participation in such a curriculum is not merely an individual act; it is a profoundly social act as well. In an interdependent society, the curriculum should encourage cooperation and the testing of each individual's ideas against those of others. This requires countering — at least to some degree — the individualized instructional models now widely practiced in schools. All too many children sit isolated from one another in the elementary grades, completing worksheet after worksheet with little or no opportunity for serious discussion, deliberation, debate, or cooperation. Individualization is important; however, to be truly meaningful, it must be balanced by a sense of social responsibility.

The issue of time looms large here. Educators must have time to consider the curriculum carefully. Too many curricular decisions today focus on *how* to teach, not on *what* to teach. Teachers and other educators must have opportunities to discuss in detail what they want to do and why they want to do it. Creative scheduling is essential, in order to make time available for frequent, in-depth discussions of curricular content among local educators.

Obviously, teachers are not the only ones who are affected by what is taught. As much as possible, all individuals who are affected by a curricular decision should be involved in making it.[15] This includes parents, concerned citizens, organized labor and other interest groups, and, when possible, the students themselves. I recognize that such broad participation can lead to political conflict and to interminable meetings, but it can also lead to a greater sense of trust and cooperation on the part of all those involved. Indeed, broad participation may be one way to bolster flagging community (and financial) support of public education.

Educators who act on this suggestion must be willing to take risks and to work hard. School officials must aggressively present their curricular proposals and programs to the community — especially to the most disenfranchised groups. They must show their publics what they offer and communicate the justifications for these offerings. They must take criticisms seriously and respond to them honestly.

I have good reasons for making these suggestions. Available evidence suggests that, unless participation in curricular planning is widely shared among teachers, principals, central office staff members, students, and parents, the amount of support for any program is significantly reduced.[16]

In addition, direct parental involvement in the classroom tends to foster both more and longer-lasting changes in the daily activities of teachers. And evidence suggests that *how* a program is carried out is just as important as the specific content of a program.[17] The prospect of a continued decline in educational funding will give impetus to broad participation in the classroom. Parents will have to become more deeply involved, since schools will be hard pressed to afford many of the programs essential to high-quality education. As parents (and the elderly, I hope) volunteer to serve as tutors, as resource people, as counselors, and in other capacities, they will become more knowledgeable and more skillful at dealing with curricular issues. This is an important step toward a genuinely cooperative effort to guarantee high-quality programs for children.

If parental participation in decision making is important, teacher participation is even more important. There tends to be a very high correlation between the involvement of teachers in decisions related to changes in the curriculum and "effective implementation and continuation" of such changes.[18] When we consider going from what *is* to what *should be*, there are few things we know for certain. However, we do have some guidelines for strategies that seem to foster more effective and lasting changes in the curriculum, in what teachers do, and in what students learn. The findings of several studies have suggested that "what should be" will be enhanced to the extent that there is: 1) concrete, extended, and teacher-specific training related to the curricular change; 2) continuing classroom assistance from the district; 3) opportunities for teachers to observe similar projects in other classrooms, schools, or districts; 4) frequent meetings among the people involved that focus on practical problems; 5) local development of materials, insofar as this is possible; and 6) emphasis on teacher participation in curricular decision making.[19] As the financial crunch worsens, these guidelines will become even more important, especially in larger school districts.

So far, I have suggested certain attitudes and activities that should guide our policies on curriculum content, form, and decision making. However, this article would be both incomplete and deceptively simplistic if I did not add that, just as many of the tensions and conflicts over the curriculum arise outside the school, so too do many solutions to these problems require changes in the larger society. The issues of raising students' achievement levels and preventing dropouts are cases in point; solving these problems will require coordinated efforts by the larger society.

Educators have given a good deal of attention to reforming the secondary school curriculum to prevent dropouts. These reforms have had mixed results, in part because focusing solely on internal curricular changes is too limited a strategy. As Christopher Jencks has recently shown, the economic benefits for students who complete secondary school are still *twice* as great for whites as for blacks.[20] Moreover, completing secondary school provides relatively few benefits to students from economically disadvantaged backgrounds. Jencks and his colleagues have summarized their findings thus: "Apparently, high school graduation pays off primarily for men from advantaged backgrounds. Men from disadvantaged backgrounds must attend college to reap large occupational benefits from their education."[21] Clearly, those minority and economically disadvantaged students who stay in secondary school longer receive few economic rewards for their efforts — regardless of what common sense tells us about the benefits of increased schooling.

The future context of education must broaden the student's educational experience. Literacy should be defined to include social, political, aesthetic, and technological literacy.

I am *not* arguing against making the curriculum more responsive to the needs of such youngsters. Rather, I am saying that, without a societal commitment to altering the structure of the economic marketplace so that these more responsive programs pay off for participants, such efforts may be doomed to failure. Why should such students wish to take part even in well-designed programs, if the statistical probability that these programs will improve their lives is very low? We *do* need better secondary programs, but these programs will be successful only to the extent that students feel that the school has something to offer — both now and for the future.

Improving the achievement of students poses similar problems. We have spent many years and huge sums of money attempting to raise achievement — especially scores on reading tests — through better instructional materials and curricula, more intensive teaching strategies, and so on. Yet these efforts, too, have had mixed results. We may have to take seriously the evidence that suggests a marked relationship between socioeconomic status and achievement in schools. The answers to many of the curriculum questions we face now and will certainly face in the next two decades — such as how best to increase the achievement of minority and poor students — may be found as much in social policies as in better teaching and curricula. As I mentioned earlier, doing well in elementary and secondary school does not guarantee economic success in later life.

The implications of this fact are striking. If we are really serious about increasing student mastery of content, especially among economically disadvantaged groups, then we might consider embarking on a serious analysis of the prevailing patterns of educational financing, of the possibility of redistributing income, and of ways to create jobs that would make possible a decent standard of living for the many families who will suffer the most if the economy continues its downturn. However, such analysis must not serve as an excuse for failing to do the important work of revising the curriculum and teaching practices. My point is that we must take seriously the complications that hinder the schools from reaching their goals. If we are to reach these goals by the year 2000, we will have to consider how our ability to do so is linked to the existing distribution of resources in our society.

If our aim is a society in which all people are more equal in their opportunities to experience success and to exercise control over their own destinies, not a society in which the chasms between groups grow larger every day, then we must deal now with these larger social issues. Otherwise, the public will continue to blame the school and its curriculum, its teachers, and its administrators for something over which they have much less control than do other social agencies.

If I am correct that the success of the schools is very much tied to conditions in the larger society, then the training of curriculum specialists, teachers, and administrators for the year 2000 cannot be limited to such things as techniques of teaching, management approaches, and methods of financial planning. We must focus more rigorously — starting now — on the skills of democratic deliberation about such questions as social goals, the proper direction for schools to take, and what we should teach and why.[22] We will never have a curriculum free of tensions and conflicts. And it would probably not be good if we did, since such conflicts demonstrate the vitality of democracy. We must learn to work creatively with conflicts, seeing them not as hindrances but as possibilities for cooperative improvement of education.

The results of the decisions we make today about curriculum policies and classroom practices will be with us in the year 2000, which is just around the corner. It is crucial that we debate now the questions of what we should teach, how it should be organized, who should make the decisions, and what we as educators should and can do about (and in) a society marked by large and growing disparities in wealth and power. I hope that I have stimulated such debate, because that is the necessary first step to taking seriously the question of what the curriculum should be in the year 2000.

NOTES

1. I have discussed this in much greater detail in Michael W. Apple, *Education and Power* (Boston: Routledge and Kegan Paul, 1982). See also Manuel Castells, *The Economic Crisis and American Society* (Princeton, N.J.: Princeton University Press, 1980); and Lester Thurow, *The Zero-Sum Society* (New York: Basic Books, 1980).
2. For a detailed analysis, see Martin Carnoy and Derek Shearer, *Economic Democracy* (White Plains, N.Y.: M.E. Sharpe, 1980).
3. See Michael W. Apple, *Ideology and Curriculum* (Boston: Routledge and Kegan Paul, 1979).
4. See, for example, Sheila Harty, *Hucksters in the Classroom* (Washington, D.C.: Center for Responsive Law, 1979); and Apple, *Education and Power*, esp. Ch. 5.
5. Castells, pp. 161-85.
6. For a review of the literature on tracking and differentiation, see Caroline H. Persell, *Education and Inequality* (New York: Free Press, 1977); and Thomas Good and Jere Brophy, *Looking in Classrooms* (New York: Harper and Row, 1978).
7. Michael W. Apple, "Work, Gender, and Teaching," *Teachers College Record*, in press.
8. See, for example, Seymour Sarason, *The Culture of the School and the Problem of Change* (Boston: Allyn & Bacon, 1971).
9. For an empirical analysis of what is happening to some teachers in elementary schools because of this separation, see Andrew Gitlin, "School Structure and Teachers' Work," in Michael W. Apple and Lois Weis, eds., *Ideology and Practice in Schooling* (Philadelphia: Temple University Press, forthcoming). See also Apple, *Education and Power*.
10. For an interesting discussion of various forms of meaning and "representation," see Elliot Eisner, *Cognition and Curriculum: A Basis for Deciding What to Teach* (New York: Longman, 1982).
11. Fred Newmann, Thomas Bertocci, and Ruthanne Landsness, *Skills in Citizen Action* (Skokie, Ill.: National Textbook Co., 1977). See also Fred Newmann, "Reducing Student Alienation in High Schools," *Harvard Educational Review*, Winter 1981, pp. 546-64.
12. Elliot Eisner, *The Educational Imagination* (New York: Macmillan, 1979).
13. 10 August 1982, Sec. 3, p. 7.
14. Apple, *Ideology and Curriculum*, pp. 6-7.
15. Joseph Schwab, "The Practical: A Language for Curriculum," in Arno Bellack and Herbert Kliebard, eds., *Curriculum and Evaluation* (Berkeley, Calif.: McCutchan, 1977), pp. 26-44.
16. Paul Berman and Milbrey W. McLaughlin, *Federal Programs Supporting Educational Change, Vol. VIII: Implementing and Sustaining Innovations* (Santa Monica, Calif.: Rand Corporation, May 1978), p. 14.
17. Ibid., p. 24.
18. Ibid., p. 29.
19. Ibid., p. 34.
20. Christopher Jencks et al., *Who Gets Ahead?* (New York: Basic Books, 1979), pp. 174-75.
21. Ibid., p. 175. It is unfortunate that most of this research has dealt only with men.
22. Kenneth Zeichner is doing some of the best work on helping teachers to develop the skills of deliberation and reflection. See his "Reflective Teaching and Field-Based Experience in Teacher Education," *Interchange*, vol. 12, no. 4, 1981, pp. 1-22.

The Coming Enrollment Crisis

Focusing on the Figures

David W. Breneman

David W. Breneman is a senior fellow at the Brookings Institution in Washington, D.C. He serves as executive editor of Change *and president of Kalamazoo College. This article is excerpted with permission from the monograph "The Coming Enrollment Crisis: What Every Trustee Must Know" published by the Association of Governing Boards, Washington, D.C. Copyright 1982, Association of Governing Boards.*

Those concerned with the well-being of higher education may have noted a curious—and troublesome—paradox. On the one hand, most people are aware that the "baby-boom" generation has passed through the nation's colleges, and that for the next fifteen years colleges and universities in most states will face the much smaller "birth-dearth" generation.

Many people also know that the traditional college-age population will decline in number between now and the mid-1990s by roughly 25 percent. On the other hand, a recent national survey of college and university presidents reported that only 16 percent of the presidents expected their institutions to lose enrollments, while 42 percent expect their enrollments to increase! The remainder see their enrollments as holding steady. This paradox suggests that most presidents are either incurable optimists or they know something that the rest of us do not. A more troubling possibility is that most presidents are unwilling to admit—or do not believe—that enrollment decline will hit their colleges, although they fully expect other institutions to have trouble.

The purpose of this report is to provide college and university trustees with information about enrollm prospects, and to suggest questi that trustees might ask in order probe the adequacy, compreh siveness, and realism of t institution's long-range planni Although the report does not adva its own enrollment projection, it d accept the rather widespread view t between now and the mid-199 enrollments will decline nationally about 15 percent.

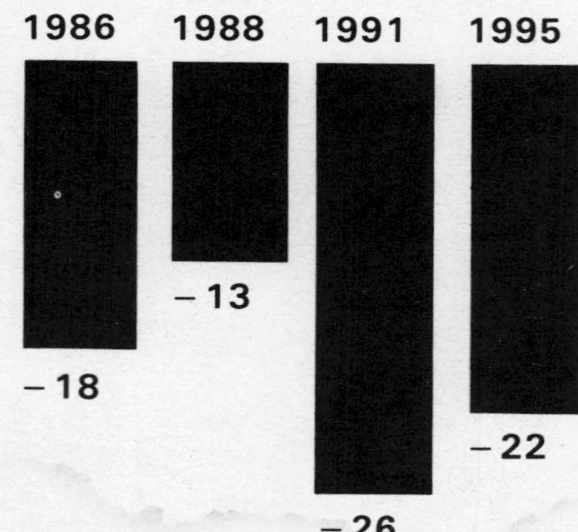

Percentage of change in the number of 18-year-olds calculated on the base year of 1979. Projections by the Western Interstate Commission for Higher Education.

One of the main reasons that Association of Governing Boards co missioned this report was the conc that far too many colleges and univ sities were entering this difficult peri without sound long-range plans management techniques suited to era of retrenchment. There was pa ticular concern that many trustees not fully aware of the challeng ahead, and could benefit from a br discussion of what is known—and n known—about enrollment projectio and the economic environment which higher education will be fun tioning.

Enrollment Projections

In looking ahead, the one solid pie of information that we have is t future age distribution of the popul

From *Change,* March 1983. Reprinted with the permission of the Association of Governing Boards of Universities and Colleges in Washington, D.C. The full publication on which this article is based is available from AGB.

tion, including the number of 18-year-olds for each of the next eighteen years. These are counts of people already born, and thus are hard data, not forecasts. The size of this age group from 1950 through 2000 reveals three important points.

First, the number of 18-year-olds roughly doubled between 1950 and 1980, with the most rapid growth occurring in the 1960s (45 percent increase) and a considerably slower rate of growth in the 1970s (13 percent increase). These data help to explain why the 1960s witnessed such explosive growth in higher education enrollment, while the 1970s witnessed continued growth, but at a slower rate.

Second, the figure shows the sharp drop in this age group that will occur between 1979 (the peak year) and 1994 (the trough). The population drops from 4.3 million to 3.2 million, a 26 percent decline, which helps to explain why the years between now and the mid-to-late 1990s are of great concern to higher education.

Finally, the population of 18-year-olds begins to climb again in the last years of the 1990s, reflecting an "echo" baby boom—the children of the earlier baby-boom generation. This final point is important because it shows that enrollment decline is not forever. The nation's colleges and universities must weather a difficult fifteen years, but they can expect enrollments to climb again in the late 1990s. The fact that the downturn is not permament must be factored into each college's long-range plan, and state officials must weigh the financial benefits of closing programs or campuses now against the costs of rebuilding them when once again enrollments surge.

While research findings on college enrollments are useful both to institutional and governmental planners and policymakers, many imponderables influence the college-going decision, complicating efforts to forecast future student behavior. Furthermore, the next ten to fifteen years will be very different from the last two decades, making extrapolation of past patterns of behavior a dubious activity. The biggest change will be the shift from a seller's to a buyer's market, and no one understands fully the implications of that change. One can say with certainty, however, that the competition among colleges will get much stiffer, and that a poorly prepared and poorly directed institution will be highly vulnerable to institutional decline, even closure.

Northcentral Region

1986	1988	1994	1995
−23	−20	−32	−28

When we move beyond birth statistics to enrollment projections, considerable uncertainty is introduced. Consider the factors that have to be included in making an enrollment projection:

- High school graduation rates;
- College entry rates;
- College retention rates;
- Enrollment rates for older age groups;
- Enrollments of foreign students;
- Enrollments of graduate and professional students;
- Full-time vs. part-time attendance (in order to measure full-time equivalence).

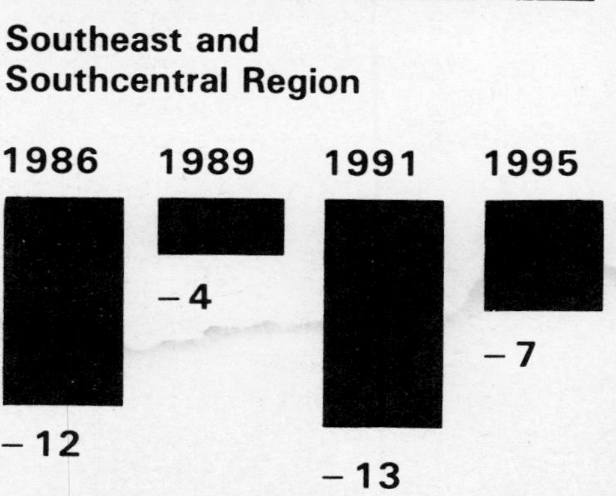

Projections of high school graduates are of particular importance because recent graduates still comprise the bulk of full-time enrollments. William R. McConnell of the Western Interstate Commission for Higher Education (WICHE) recently made such projections for each of the fifty states by year to 1995. McConnell's projections take into account differences in birth rates by state as well as migration patterns among the states. The Northeast and Northcentral regions will be the hardest hit, with projected declines from the 1979 level of 40 and 32 percent, respectively. By contrast, the Western and Southeast-Southcentral regions are projected to decline by only 16 and 13 percent. Because many colleges and universities draw their enrollments from the state or region in which they are located, it is clear that the pattern of enrollment decline will not be distributed evenly among institutions.

The projections for individual states are even more sobering. Several states, such as New York, Massachusetts, Connecticut, Rhode Island, and Delaware, are projected to have declines in excess of 40 percent, while others, such as Pennsylvania, New Jersey, Maryland, Michigan, Illinois, Minnesota, Ohio, Wisconsin, and Iowa, have projected declines of between 34 and 40 percent. Most of these states have large numbers of public and private colleges and universities, making the adjustment to greater-than-average enrollment decline particularly severe.

Possible Offsets

Faced with falling numbers of traditional college-age students, many colleges and universities have sought increased enrollments elsewhere. A report written by Carol Frances and published by the American Council on Education in 1980 received widespread attention. (See *Change*, July–August 1980.) Titled *College Enrollment Trends: Testing the Conventional Wisdom Against the Facts*, it discussed several strategies for increasing enrollments in the years ahead. These were:

- Increased high school graduation rates of students who would otherwise drop out;
- Increased credentialing by testing of high school dropouts;
- Increased enrollment of low- and middle-income students;
- Increased enrollment of minority youths;
- Increased enrollment of traditional college-age students;
- Increased retention of current students;
- Increased enrollment of adults;
- Increased enrollment of women aged 20 to 34;
- Increased enrollment of men aged 35 to 64;
- Increased enrollment of graduate students;
- Increased enrollment of persons currently being served by industry;
- Increased enrollment of foreign students.

The report presented estimates of the potential enrollment gains nationally that could be made between 1980 and 1990 with each of these strategies. It also provided an illustrative example in which the combined effect of three strategies—enrolling more lower- and middle-income young people, more adults over age 25, and more foreign students—could by 1990 result in a 3.5 percent increase over 1980 enrollments.

Leaders in higher education are concerned that institutions are not preparing adequately for enrollment decline, and view the optimistic interpretations of the Frances report as both unrealistic and counterproductive—the future seen through rose-colored glasses. They worry that the report might mislead presidents and trustees, or be used by some presidents as a justification for putting off difficult decisions that would have to be made if a substantial drop in enrollments were the accepted forecast.

In retrospect, it seems clear that the controversy surrounding the report need not have occurred. At the level of the individual institution, there is no inherent conflict between a careful effort to assess possible sources of new students, and an equally careful effort to make realistic enrollment projections for the institution. A residential liberal arts college of 1,200 students in a rural town of 8,000 people, for example, simply does not have the same possibilities for enrolling older part-time students that an urban university has.

It would be irresponsible, however, to approach those strategies for increased enrollments on the assumption that each college will find some combination of nontraditional students to offset the loss of the traditional college-age population. Several of the strategies outlined are not within the power of colleges and universities to determine. Actions of others will be required if high school graduation rates for majority and minority youths are to increase, or if greater numbers of dropouts are to earn high school certificates through equivalency tests.

The fact that black and Hispanic youngsters will make up a growing percentage of the 18-year-old population between now and the late 1990s must also be considered, for these minority students have substantially lower rates of high school completion than majority youngsters. In 1977, the high school graduation rate for whites 18 to 24 years old was 83.9 percent, for blacks 69.8 percent, and for Hispanics 55.5 percent. In the absence of concerted action to raise the completion rates of blacks and Hispanics, their increasing numbers in the age group will cause the high school graduation rate to fall—not rise—over the next fifteen years.

Perhaps the most promising strategy for boosting enrollment of younger people is to increase retention rates of those already enrolled. Presumably, students who drop out of the university were fit for admission, suggesting a need to look within the institution for possible reforms. While attrition c[illegible] never be eliminated, most colleges c[illegible] probably do a better job of keepi[illegible] more of their current students enrolle[illegible] This strategy is hardly new, howev[illegible] and many colleges may have reduc[illegible] attrition about as far as possible.

Older students constitute the gro[illegible] most commonly looked to as an off[illegible] to the declining population 18 to [illegible] years old. Indeed, between 1970 a[illegible] 1978, the number of students 25 to [illegible] years of age did increase significant[illegible] with enrollment of women experien[illegible] ing a particularly sharp 187 percent i[illegible] crease.

Community colleges accounted f[illegible] much of this enrollment growth, wi[illegible] over 27 percent of their students in t[illegible] 25 to 34 age group in 1978, compar[illegible] to 14 percent in the four-year colleg[illegible] Projecting enrollments for the popu[illegible] tion over age 25 is subject to gre[illegible] uncertainty, but those who have e[illegible] amined the matter closely do not e[illegible] pect enrollment rates to continue risi[illegible] as rapidly as they did in the 1970s. O[illegible] reason is an assumption that the sha[illegible] increase of female enrollments is a on[illegible] time "catching-up" phenomenon th[illegible] will not repeat itself. In recent yea[illegible] younger women have enrolled in co[illegible] lege in roughly the same proportion [illegible] men, whereas those in the generati[illegible] preceding them did not. Women fro[illegible] this older generation enrolled in lar[illegible] numbers during the 1970s, making [illegible] for educational opportunities miss[illegible] earlier. A second reason that ad[illegible] enrollments may grow less rapidly [illegible] the 1980s is the expiration of GI B[illegible] benefits for Vietnam veterans. Old[illegible] students drawing these benefits co[illegible] tributed substantially to enrollme[illegible] growth during the 1970s.

The vast majority of students ov[illegible] age 25 enroll part time, usually in eve[illegible] ing courses offered at a convenie[illegible] location near the student's home. [illegible] must be remembered that several pa[illegible] time students are required to genera[illegible] the equivalent workload and revenu[illegible] of one full-time student, so head-cou[illegible] projections must be discounted to fu[illegible] time equivalence.

A similar caution concerns increas[illegible] enrollment of foreign students.

1980–81, some 312,000 non-immigrant foreign students were enrolled at 2,734 U.S. colleges and universities, making up a little more than 2.5 percent of total enrollments. This figure represents more than a doubling of such enrollments since 1970–71, when 1,748 institutions enrolled 145,000 foreign students. Over 43 percent of the foreign students in 1980–81 were enrolled in engineering or business management programs, areas currently crowded with U.S. students.

Few foreign students enroll in humanities or education programs, where excess capacity currently exists on many campuses. Given this pattern of foreign student enrollments, it is far from certain that the nation's colleges could absorb a further doubling in the number of such students during this decade.

How best to evaluate the potential net effect of these several strategies for combating enrollment decline? Each suggests a wide range of possible forecasts that could be made, depending upon the assumption adopted. Several analysts have independently arrived at an estimated enrollment decline of about 15 percent. This figure incorporates a view that various recruitment strategies will offset about 40 percent of the 25 percent decline that would follow from demographic factors alone. As mentioned earlier, even if this rough national estimate turns out to be accurate, considerable variation will occur among regions and institutions.

Other Factors that Influence Enrollments

In addition to the demographic considerations discussed above, a number of other factors will affect enrollment patterns during the 1980s and beyond. Among these are the state of the economy, both nationally and locally; trends in federal and state student aid; the rate of increase in college prices relative to the general rate of inflation and to the growth in family incomes; employment prospects for new graduates; and the relative attractiveness of alternatives to college, such as military service or the labor market.

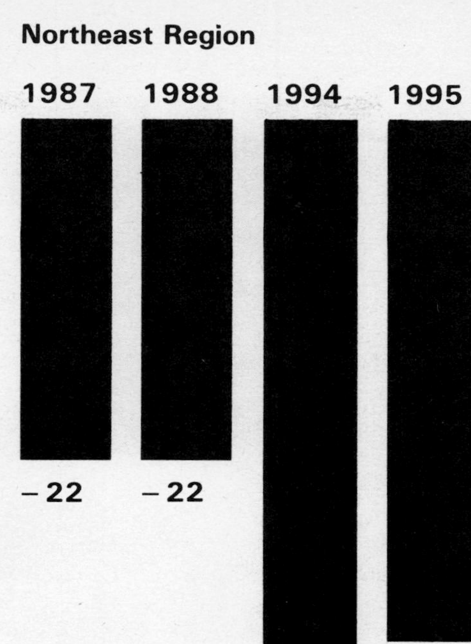

Factors such as quality and diversity of programs, location, prestige, price relative to competitors, and recruitment policies will largely determine how students distribute themselves among the various campuses.

For the foreseeable future, it would be prudent to assume that federal student aid will be less plentiful and a less reliable source of support. Although additional student and family resources may be forthcoming, it also seems likely that a bumping process will occur, in which some students shift from high- to low-priced institutions, some from full- to part-time status, and some from resident to commuter status, while others withdraw from college altogether. Clearly, the overall effect will be both to reduce and redistribute enrollments.

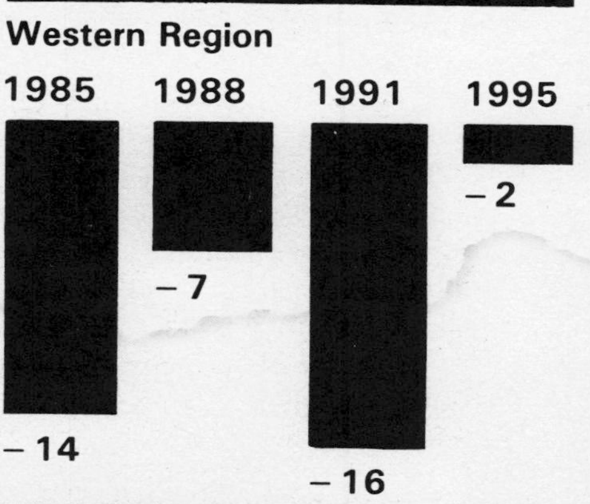

One bright spot that may help to shore up enrollments later in this decade is a likely upturn in the labor market for college graduates. The flip side of declining enrollments is a reduced labor supply of new graduates. All else being equal, a reduced supply of college graduates should lead to a stronger market for their services, an effect that should be visible by the mid-1980s. An improved market, in turn, may help to restore student interest in those liberal arts fields that have suffered in recent years from the emphasis on vocationally focused majors.

In general, one can expect the relative scarcity of young people over the next fifteen years to enhance the opportunities available to them, not just in college but in the labor market and in the military as well. Competition for their services will increase, and colleges will find themselves competing not only with each other but also with the all-volunteer military and with employers.

Prospects for the Sectors of Higher Education

How will the different types of institutions be affected by the prospect of enrollment decline? Are there any generalizations that might be helpful to trustees?

A fairly broad consensus exists that two groups of colleges and universities are particularly at risk—nonselective private liberal arts colleges and public state colleges and universities, many of them former state teachers colleges. Private junior colleges are also highly vulnerable to enrollment decline.

By contrast, state university systems, and particularly the flagship campuses, should experience limited loss of enrollments because in most states these institutions have an excess of applicants and can largely determine the size of entering classes. Similarly, the high-prestige private colleges and universities will fare well in the competition for enrollments because they draw on national pools of applicants. Public community colleges are also favorably positioned by their relatively low prices, their ability to serve the adult part-time population, and their flexibility in shifting program offerings rapidly in response to changing demands. In general, institutions located in urban settings will have more opportunities to offset enrollment decline than will those located in rural areas.

But even the more favored institutions will face dilemmas that require hard thinking, sound planning, and dedicated effort. Research universities, public and private, can expect difficulties in financing graduate programs and maintaining their strength as research institutions. Prestigious private colleges will have to struggle to maintain diverse student bodies rather than becoming enclaves for the very rich and a limited number of the very poor. Community colleges will face stiff competition from four-year institutions and universities for the traditional college-age students who enroll in transfer programs, and will have difficulty financing the large number of part-time students who enroll in noncredit courses.

No group of institutions, in short, will escape the need to plan for—and adapt to—the difficult circumstances in which higher education will find itself over the next fifteen years. Well-informed trustees who raise thoughtful and timely questions for college administrators and for themselves will be of extraordinary value to their institutions.

The following questions are illustrative of those that should be raised. A caution is in order, however: Some of these questions are more easily answered than others, and some must be addressed first by the board as matters of policy.

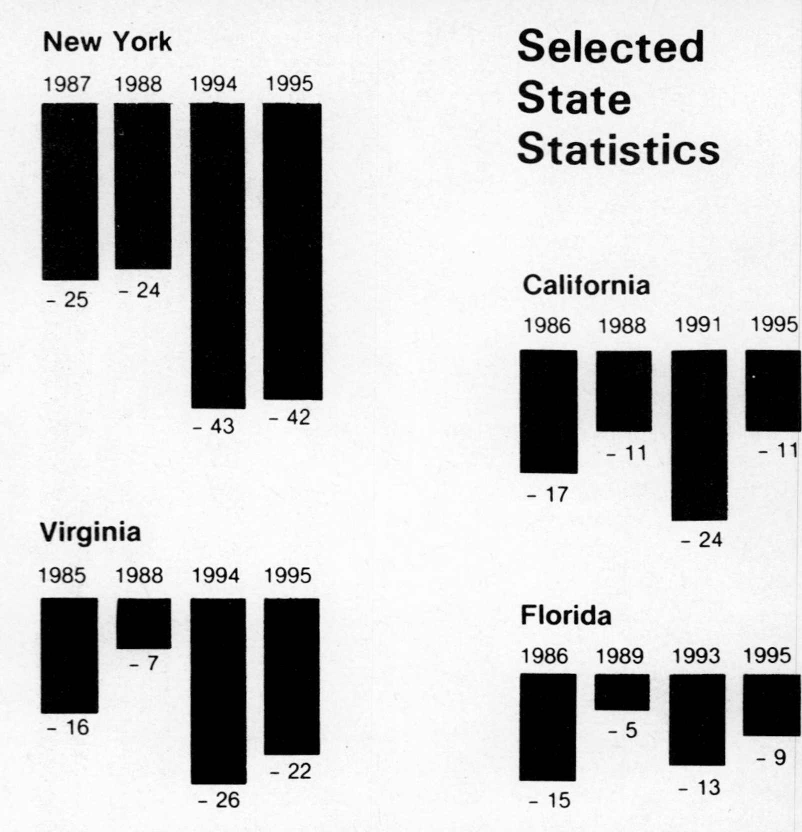

General Questions

- Is the college's present planning process adequate for the years ahead? How realistic are institutional enrollment projections? How accurate have past projections been, and are current projections congruent with state and regional figures? If not, why not?
- What have been the relationships between enrollment levels, costs, and revenues in recent years? What approximate effect would a 10 or 15 percent decline in enrollments over the next five years have on costs and revenues?
- What is the student attrition rate from the various degree programs, and how has it changed over time? Has the institution taken any steps to try to reduce it?
- Average costs per student are not useful for the type of analysis that focuses on changes in costs as enrollments rise or fall. Instead, colleges should have estimates of marginal (incremental) costs or estimates of fixed and variable costs. Can such data be estimated for the college for use in planning and financial analysis?
- In light of possible enrollment decline and the accompanying loss of revenues, should the college take a fresh look at its pricing policies? Is there a case for charging different tuition rates by program or level of study to reflect cost differences more a curately? Should the college match, e ceed, or lag behind price increases its competitors? Have fee structur been examined recently to align the more closely with current costs?
- Should the college seek to attra new clientele groups to mainta enrollments? If so, what will be the i pact on the institution's tradition m sion? Will a change in educational e phasis help or harm the college's tractiveness to its traditional client groups?
- Given current staffing patterr how flexible is the college in shifti program direction? Would new pr grams require a net increase in facult or will retirements and normal attriti offset the addition of new faculty? faculty development and redirection realistic possibility? At what poir under what circumstances, and wi what procedures might it be necessa to dismiss tenured faculty?
- Are there alternative uses for ca pus buildings (including dormitori that are rendered superfluous for

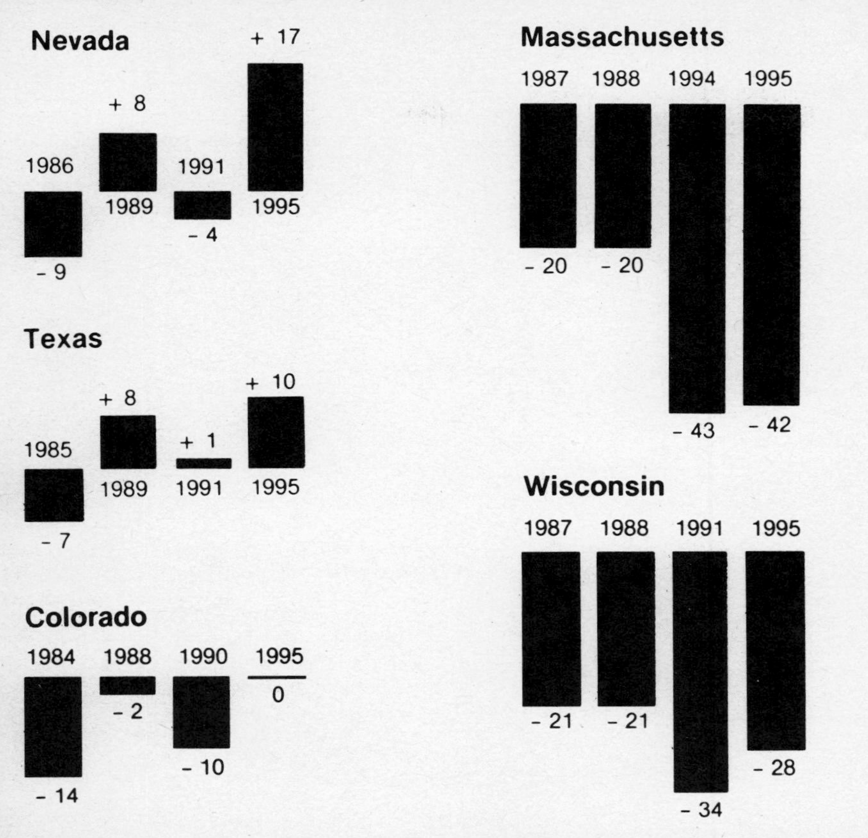

decade or more by enrollment declines? Can these surplus physical assets be converted into revenue producers? What can be done to avoid defaulting on long-term loans covering such properties?

- At what point will continued deferred maintenance and aging equipment adversely affect enrollments?
- How dependent has the college become on federal and state student aid? Is it possible to estimate the proportion of the student body that would withdraw if significant cuts were made in grant and loan programs? Can the college realistically plan to replace government aid by support or credit commitments from new sources?
- How much of the institution's own money is being spent on student aid? What percentage of the educational and general operating budget is being used for such aid, and how has that percentage changed over time? How much is drawn from restricted and unrestricted funds?
- How have the college's annual costs of attendance changed relative to the consumer price index and family income over the last decade? Has the college's competitive pricing position changed relative to the institutions with which it competes for enrollments?

Next Steps

After reading this candid report on enrollment prospects and problems facing the nation's colleges and universities, there is a danger that trustees may be overwhelmed by the difficulties ahead, and not know how to proceed. Stunning trustees into inaction, however, is not the purpose of the Association of Governing Boards in publishing this paper. Instead, the intent is to disabuse trustees of the notion—should some still hold it—that the position they occupy is not demanding and is largely ceremonial.

As the report makes clear, the next ten to fifteen years will be utterly unlike those of recent decades, when the challenge facing colleges and universities was to meet the demands of growth. The challenge now is not just to survive, but to do so while enhancing the quality of instruction, research, and public service rendered by the institution during a time of general retrenchment.

Those who serve and those who attend the nation's colleges and universities must rely on the support and informed guidance of trustees to a degree not required before. This report will have served its purpose if the discussion that it generates on campus leads to improved decision making and stronger institutions for the years ahead.

Index

Credits/ Acknowledgments

Cover design by Charles Vitelli

1. Perceptions of Education
Facing overview—United Nations/Y. Nagata. 24—Courtesy of The National Catholic Education Association.

2. Continuity and Change
Facing overview—IBM. 44-47—Arlene Gottfried.

3. The Struggle for Excellence
Facing overview—EPA Documerica. 88—©Ronald Chironna, 1985.

4. Morality and Values
Facing overview—United Nations/W.A. Graham.

5. Discipline Problems
Facing overview—Courtesy of Traver Steiner/Barbie Heid. 132, 134—Catherine Kanner.

6. Equality and Opportunity
Facing overview—UN photo by L. Solmssen.

7. Serving Special Needs
Facing overview—United Nations/photo by S. Dimartini.

8. The Profession of Teaching Today
Facing overview—United Nations/photo by L. Solmssen. 196—University of Texas at Austin.

9. A Look to the Future
Facing overview—United Nations photo. 234—Mattel Toys.

We Want Your Advice

Annual Editions revisions depend on two major opinion sources: one is our Advisory Board, listed in the front of this volume, which works with us in scanning the thousands of articles published in the public press each year; the other is you—the person actually using the book. Please help us and the users of the next edition by completing the prepaid article rating form on this page and returning it to us. Thank you.

ANNUAL EDITIONS: EDUCATION 85/86

Article Rating Form

Here is an opportunity for you to have direct input into the next revision of this volume. We would like you to rate each of the 48 articles listed below, using the following scale:

1. **Excellent: should definitely be retained**
2. **Above average: should probably be retained**
3. **Below average: should probably be deleted**
4. **Poor: should definitely be deleted**

Your ratings will play a vital part in the next revision. So please mail this prepaid form to us just as soon as you complete it.
Thanks for your help!

Rating	Article
	1. Is This Any Way to Build a Better School?
	2. Education Moves to Center Stage: An Overview of Recent Studies
	3. The Good News About American Education
	4. The Educational Pendulum
	5. How to Save the Public Schools
	6. The 16th Annual Gallup Poll of the Public's Attitudes Toward the Public Schools
	7. Who Are These Educational "Experts" and What Are They Really Up To?
	8. Vocational Education That Works
	9. Education and the Sony War
	10. Computers and a New World Order
	11. Bilingual/Bicultural Education: Its Legacy and Its Future
	12. The New Pioneers of the Home Schooling Movement
	13. The Continuing Crisis: Fashions in Education
	14. A Nation at Risk: The Report of the National Commission on Excellence in Education
	15. A Nation at Risk: How's That Again?
	16. Improving Educational Standards in American Schools
	17. What Do the SATs Mean? SATs Are Getting in the Way of Education
	18. Just Among Us Teachers
	19. Making Schools Work Again
	20. Latest Educational "Reforms" Ring a 19th Century Bell
	21. Ethics Without Virtue: Moral Education in America
	22. The Obligations of American Citizenship: A Historical Perspective
	23. The Effect Upon Minorities of the Civic Education of Teachers

Rating	Article
	24. Schools and Democratic Values
	25. Good, Old-Fashioned Discipline: The Politics of Punitiveness
	26. Disciplinary Strategies
	27. Class Struggle: Should Schools Permit Searching of Students for Weapons, Drugs?
	28. Coercion in the Classroom Won't Work
	29. There's Only One True Technique for Good Discipline
	30. Achieving Quality Integrated Education—With or Without Federal Help
	31. Magnet Schools Used as Tool for Equality
	32. The State of Education for Black Americans
	33. From Equity to Excellence: The Rebirth of Educational Conservatism
	34. Tuition Tax Credits and the First Amendment
	35. Mainstreaming: Expectations and Realities
	36. A Holistic View of Mainstreaming
	37. Mainstreaming: Is It Secondary at the Secondary Level?
	38. A Comparison of Soviet and American Approaches to Special Education
	39. Child Sexual Abuse
	40. You Can Help a Sexually Abused Child
	41. The Art of Teaching
	42. Scapegoating the Teachers
	43. Merit Pay: The Great Debate
	44. Why Teachers Fail
	45. Teacher Burnout and Professionalism
	46. Forging a New Ethos for Education in America
	47. Curriculum in the Year 2000
	48. The Coming Enrollment Crisis

(cont. on next page)

ABOUT YOU

Name ______________________ Date ________
Are you a teacher? ☐ Or student? ☐
Your School Name ______________________
Department ______________________
Address ______________________
City ______________ State ______ Zip ______
School Telephone # ____________

YOUR COMMENTS ARE IMPORTANT TO US!

Please fill in the following information:

For which course did you use this book? ______________________
Did you use a text with this Annual Edition? ☐ yes ☐ no
The title of the text: ______________________
What are your general reactions to the Annual Editions concept?

Have you read any particular articles recently that you think should be included in the next edition?

Are there any articles you feel should be replaced in the next edition? Why?

Are there other areas that you feel would utilize an Annual Edition?

May we contact you for editorial input?

May we quote you from above?

EDUCATION 85/86

BUSINESS REPLY MAIL

First Class Permit No. 84 Guilford, CT

Postage will be paid by addressee

The Dushkin Publishing Group, Inc.
Sluice Dock
Guilford, Connecticut 06437